DESCRIPTIVE ETHNOLOGY

OF

BENGAL

DESCRIPTIVE ETHNOLOGY

OF

BENGAL.

BY

EDWARD TUITE DALTON, C. S. I.

GYAN

Published by

GYAN

Gyan Publishing House
5, Ansari Road
Daryaganj, New Delhi-110002
Phone: 011-47034999, 9811692060
E-mail: books@gyanbooks.com

Distribution Network
gyanbooks.com
India, USA, Canada, UK, Australia

ISBN: 978-81-212-7079-3 (PB)
First Published, 1872

2nd Impression 2024

Printed at: Gyan Press, Delhi.

DESCRIPTIVE ETHNOLOGY OF BENGAL
Author: EDWARD TUITE DALTON

DESCRIPTIVE ETHNOLOGY

OF

BENGAL.

BY

EDWARD TUITE DALTON, C.S.I.,

COLONEL, BENGAL STAFF CORPS; COMMISSIONER OF CHUTIA NAGPUR; MEMBER OF THE ASIATIC SOCIETY OF BENGAL, ETC.

Illustrated by Lithograph Portraits copied from Photographs.

PRINTED FOR THE GOVERNMENT OF BENGAL, UNDER THE DIRECTION OF THE COUNCIL OF THE ASIATIC SOCIETY OF BENGAL.

CALCUTTA:
OFFICE OF THE SUPERINTENDENT OF GOVERNMENT PRINTING.
1872.

PREFACE.

EARLY in the year 1866, Dr. J. Fayrer, C. S. I., submitted to the Asiatic Society of Bengal a proposal for a great Ethnological Congress in Calcutta, which was to bring together in one exhibition typical examples of the races of the Old World, to be made the subject of scientific study when so collected.*

The Council of the Society were unanimous in regarding the proposition as one highly calculated to advance the science of ethnology, and in submitting it to the Government of India warmly advocated its adoption, suggesting that it would form an appropriate adjunct to the general industrial exhibition which it was then intended to hold in 1869-70.

The scheme was a grand one, and there is no capital in the world possessing greater facilities for its successful accomplishment than Calcutta.

But difficulties presented themselves. It was of importance that the wild tribes of India should be fully represented. Yet it is sometimes no easy matter to induce those strange shy creatures to visit even the stations nearest to them, and to induce them to proceed to a remote and unknown country for a purpose they could not be made to comprehend, would in many cases have been utterly impracticable. It was also pointed out that such people were liable to suffer in health from change of climate. The Commissioner of Asám stated his conviction that twenty typical specimens of the hill tribes of his province could not be conveyed to Calcutta and back at any time of the year without casualties that the greatest enthusiast for anthropological research would shrink from encountering; and he added—"if specimens of the more independent tribes fell sick and died in Calcutta or on the journey, it might lead to inconvenient political complications."

For these and other reasons the scheme was allowed to drop. But in the meantime the Government of Bengal and the Supreme Government had, in compliance with the request of the Society, called on all local authorities to furnish complete and accurate lists of various races found within their respective jurisdictions; and

* Proceedings of the Asiatic Society of Bengal for April, 1866.

under the impulse thus given, some valuable papers from different parts of India were received.

Before the design of a Congress was abandoned, I had been asked to edit the ethnological information submitted in compliance with this requisition by the Commissioners of Divisions and Provinces under the Bengal Government; and in undertaking the duty, my intention was to draw up a descriptive catalogue which might prove a useful guide to the ethnological exhibition; for had the scheme been carried out, the compilation of a more elaborate descriptive work on the subject would have been best left to the scientific visitors of the Congress. However, on examining the papers made over to me, I found no material sufficient even for a catalogue: in truth, there was nothing to edit.

It was then suggested that I should draw up an account of the tribes in Bengal from all available sources of information, and this proposition I have endeavoured to carry out. It is right, however, to state in apology for the selection made of a compiler, and for my acceptance of such a duty, that I am conscious I was applied to solely because it was known that I had spent the greater portion of a long service in Asám and Chútiá Nágpúr, the most interesting fields of ethnological research in all Bengal; and though without any pretension to scientific knowledge of the subject, without practice as an author, or experience as a compiler, I have probably had more opportunities of observing various races and tribes, especially those usually called Aborigines, than have been conceded to any other officer now in the service.

The Asiatic Society of Bengal did me the honor to approve of the proposal, and kindly offered to give me all the assistance in their power. On the 3rd October, 1866, the Council tendered their services to Government to superintend the printing of the work, and the Government in reply thankfully accepted the offer.

The first step was to bring together all the materials available; and in this I was cordially aided by Dr. J. Anderson, then Honorary Secretary of the Asiatic Society, and subsequently by Dr. F. Stoliczka, who succeeded him in that office. Any publications on the subject in the library of the Bengal Secretariat were also placed at my disposal by the Honorable Ashley Eden, who was the first to propose my being employed on the work, and who interested himself generally in the undertaking.

When the project of a collection of the tribes in Calcutta had been reluctantly abandoned, it occurred to all who were interested in the matter that any descriptive work of the kind proposed should be abundantly illustrated.

For this purpose a few of a series of photographs taken for the London Exhibition of 1862 were available; and Dr. B. Simpson, who had contributed them, received a commission to the valley of the Bráhmaputra to add to the collection from that most prolific of ethnological fields. The majority of the illustrations which are now given have been copied from the beautiful photographs taken by Dr. Simpson, one of the most successful of Indian photographers, and he has kindly added much to their value by contributing also the measurement of the individuals photographed, all of which were carefully taken by himself. The photographic skill of Dr. Brown, Political Agent at Manipúr, was also utilized for illustrations of the Manipúrís and neighbouring tribes; others were sought elsewhere, and quite recently, after the work had approached completion, the Chútiá Nágpúr collection was enriched by the artistic labors of Messrs. T. F. and Tosco Peppé. The latter gentleman, at my request, proceeded into wild parts of Singbhúm and Keonjhur, and brought his camera to bear on some of the most primitive of human beings, the Juángs, never previously subjected to the process.

It will be observed that the plates are not referred to in the body of the work; this was unavoidable, as, while putting together my notes, I did not know what illustrations I could have, and the manuscripts of the different chapters or sometimes of sections, were sent to Calcutta as completed. Explanatory notes and references to the pages of the work in which the tribes illustrated are described have, therefore, been given with the plates.

The cost of publication of a work which had thus advanced from the modest project of a catalogue to a copiously-illustrated quarto volume of considerable dimensions, became matter for serious consideration; but on application to the Government of Bengal a grant of Rs. 10,000 was accorded. Steps were now taken for an immediate commencement, and in May, 1870, I received the gratifying intelligence that Dr. Thomas Oldham, Superintendent of the Geological Survey of India, and Mr. H. Blochmann, of the Madrasah College and Secretary of the Asiatic Society, had kindly undertaken to superintend the printing of the Ethnology on the part of the Council of that Society; and to those gentlemen, both so well-known to the scientific world, I am deeply indebted for most valuable advice, and for the unremitting care and attention they have been so good as to devote to the work in the midst of other arduous and important duties. Dr. Oldham specially took charge of the illustrations, and I am informed by him that the success of the plates is due to the artistic skill of Dr. George Wallich, London, who, as a gifted artist and one of the first photographers of the day, was specially qualified to undertake the duty of seeing to their execution, and without whose guiding hand a result so satisfactory could not have been attained. At considerable inconvenience, he at once, on being applied to, undertook the revision of the lithographs. Messrs. Hanhart have also ably carried out his suggestions.

It will be found that I am myself responsible for the accuracy of a large proportion of the descriptions given. During my Asám career, I was employed in various expeditions amongst the hill tribes, and always kept journals of such trips. Some of these had appeared in print in different publications, and I knew where to look for them, but the manuscripts of the remainder were lost to me during the mutinies; and from this circumstance, and the want of other material, my notices of some of the Asám tribes are not so full as I should like to have made them. But I did not confine myself to my own reminiscences. I availed myself of various other sources of information, gleaning from all published works that I could find bearing on the subject, and freely using valuable original notes drawn up at my solicitation by friends in different parts of the country, for whose contributions I now wish to make my grateful acknowledgments.

I am especially indebted to Mr. T. E. Ravenshaw, C. S., Commissioner of the Province of Orissa; to Captain W. L. Samuells, Boundary Commissioner, Bengal and Rewa; to Babús Rakhaldas Haldar and Kalidas Palit, and Mr. L. R. Forbes, all Assistants to the Commissioner of Chútiá Nágpúr; to Mr. J. F. K. Hewitt, Settlement Officer, Central Provinces; Captain J. Johnstone, Assistant to Superintendent, Katak Tributary Maháls; Dr. W. H. Hayes, Deputy Commissioner of Singbhúm; Mr. W. Atkinson, of Rájmahál; Mr. W. Ritchie, District Superintendent of Police, Singbhúm; Mr. V. Ball, of the Geological Survey of India; and Dr. J. M. Coates, Superintendent of Jails, Hazáríbágh. All the above gentlemen I have to thank for supplying information which they will find embodied in the following pages.

TABLE OF CONTENTS.

INTRODUCTION.

I COMMENCE with the North-Eastern Frontier, the basin of the mighty Brahmaputra, where the population, like the conglomerate-boulders shining as mosaics in the beds of the great river and its upper affluents, is formed of materials found *in situ* in the hills to the north and south. There is doubtless an intimate connection between the Indo-Chinese population of Asam, and some of the people that formed nations in the Gangetic provinces before the Aryans appeared in them. We can trace the path of many hordes from the North-Eastern Frontier to remote regions of India and Burma; and we find in Asam colonies formed as it were of the stragglers of the parties that had passed through. With the northern regions, from whence these hordes came, I have now no concern, but I take these tribes up first as the most archaic form we possess of the materials out of which the ancient population was formed.

I do not introduce the Asam hill and border tribes as the aborigines of that province, but have rather endeavoured to show that its colonization, as a branch of the Aryan family, dates from a very remote period. It is probable that the hill people of Lower Asam, now known as Garos and Kasias, were earlier settlers, for we find them holding an isolated position, as if the Aryan invasion pushing in like a wedge had cut them off from communication with the parent northern nations,* but otherwise the plains of Asam appear to have been unoccupied, and to the Aryans may be ascribed the honor of first peopling them.

Their colonies gradually expanded into what was eventually known as the kingdom of Kámarúpa or Kámrúp; they occupied all the country that is now embraced within the confines of the British Empire in that direction, and they had fortified cities in advance of the existing British outposts, but their dynasty was overthrown by barbarians from the north, the hordes that gave birth to the Kacharies or Bodos, the Chutia, Lahong, and Mech whose chiefs became rulers of the country, but adopted the language and civilization which they found there. After seven hundred years of their rule, the country was invaded by a dark-skinned people, from the west and south-west, who overthrew the Kachari or Chutia dynasty in Lower Kámrúp and established there the authority of their own chiefs. This dark-skinned people are the Ko'cch, who have hitherto, erroneously I think, been classed as belonging to the Lohitic or Indo-Chinese race. I believe the Ko'cch to be a branch of the great Bhuiya or Bhuniya family, whom I class as Dravidian.

* And it is very remarkable that it is through them, especially through the Kasias, that the connection between the Lohitic tribes and the aborigines of the Gangetic provinces is most clearly traced.

The Chutia or Kachari dynasty continued to hold southern Upper Asam and Sadiya and part of Naugáon (Nowgong), where they built a fortified city called Dimapur; but about the middle of the thirteenth century of the Christian era they were subjugated by hordes of Shans from the south, who, after establishing themselves in Upper Asam, pursued their career of conquest in a westerly direction, and forced the eastern portion of the Ko'cch-Hindu kingdom to submit, whilst the lower or south-west part of Kamrup fell under the sway of the Muhammadan rulers of Bengal.

I have noticed the Asam tribes in order corresponding with their geographical position. Massed and connected as they are, this appeared the most convenient arrangement, but in treating of the aboriginal or non-Aryan tribes of Bengal proper, Bihar, and Orissa, I have endeavoured to group them according to their most obvious affinities. I believe they might all be comprised in two great divisions, the Dravidian, or those who speak a language allied to the Tamil or Telugu, and the Kolarian, or those whose linguistic affinities are with the Santal, Munda, and their cognates. Of the remote north-eastern origin of the latter people, there cannot, I think, be a doubt, but there is a most important section of the population, comprising several millions of people, who are certainly non-Aryan, but whom (from their having lost their own language, mystified their early history, and adopted much that is Hindu in their customs and religion) it is not at first sight easy to class. I have described all these under a third denomination as Hinduised Aborigines.

The remainder of the fixed population I treat as Aryan, or mixed. In the former class I include the masses of Kurmis and Goalas or Gwallas and other Sudras whom many are inclined to regard as mixed, or as a distinct people subjugated by the Brahmans: but in this subjugation I do not believe; and consider there would be far more reason in treating the upper ten thousand in England as a distinct race from the remainder of the population than in so regarding among the Hindus the "twice born" and the Sudras.

I have not deemed it necessary to describe the ceremonial law, the doctrines and rules of life promulgated for the guidance of Brahmans, but I have been at some pains to collate accounts of rules and ceremonies practised by Hindus that are not enjoined by the sacred writings. And symbolical as they generally are, they cannot, I think, fail to be of interest to the historian and ethnologist.

The population of Bengal includes a vast multitude who profess the Muhammadan religion; but this multitude, if analyzed, would be found for the most part to be composed of elements that are separately treated of in the following pages; masses of the aborigines as well as of the Hindus having under Muhammadan rulers been forced or induced to embrace Islam. It would no doubt be interesting to note the effect, morally and locially, of the conversion;—to ascertain if the different races operated upon come down to us most amiable as Muhammadans or as Pagans, but for this I have at present no material, and there is nothing else that I can think of entitling them to separate notices.

I have endeavoured in my chapter on the Hinduised Aborigines, when I found any basis for doing so, to indicate the great division, Dravidian or Kolarian, to which each belongs; thus I have given reasons for affiliating the Chèros and Kharwars on the Kolarian family, and the Ko'cch, Bhuniya and others on the Dravidian; but it is quite possible that further research may show that I am not always correct in my classification, and the subject is far from exhausted.

In treating of the Chota Nagpur tribes, I have gone more fully into their past history and described their progress and present condition more in detail than in other cases, because I have been so long among them, and there is so little in print about them. The brief historical narratives given may not be very attractive, but it cannot but be of moment to Indian statesmen and administrators to have, when dealing with such people, a clear understanding of the nature of our relations with them, since they and the officers of the British Government first met; to possess an account sufficiently in detail of the circumstances under which they have been found so frequently in an attitude of hostility to a Government that certainly has no prejudices against them, but on the contrary is inclined to treat them with favor bordering on partiality. Yet it often happens that we fail to conciliate them, and that sometimes, when lulled into the belief that we have quite succeeded in doing so, we are rudely awakened from our dream by some unmistakable demonstration of hostility.

It has certainly sometimes happened, owing perhaps to the difficulties of applying the complicated machinery of civilized laws to a wild and rough people, that real grievances have remained unredressed till they were resented. And instances have occurred of insurrection having been traced to official acts or omissions that were subsequently considered impolitic and were atoned for; and it is surely of importance that all such features in the exciting causes of disturbances should be kept well in sight. The same law for all is a very high-sounding and popular cry, and it is one that has been much favored in the legislature of recent years; but I think in this craving for homogeneity, the heterogeneous character of the component parts of the population of India should always be borne in mind.

Juangs dancing

ERRATA.

Page 1, line 14,	*for* as a branch,	*read* by a branch.
„ 1, line 25,	„ Lahong,	„ Lalong.
„ 18, line 13,	„ Maintze,	„ Miautze.
„ 18, line 15, et passim,	„ Chalikata,	„ Chúlikátá.
„ 18, line 31,	„ the prowling,	„ their prowling.
„ 21, line 5,	„ villanous,	„ villainous.
„ 21, last line,	„ Miaoutes,	„ Miautze.
„ 29, line 12,	„ ornament,	„ ornamental.
„ 37, line 9,	„ Arkas,	„ Ankas.
„ 39, line 37,	„ Paidwarias,	„ Panidwarias.
„ 45, line 11,	„ H. S.,	„ H. J.
„ 62, line 5, from below,	„ mild,	„ wild.
„ 79, line 6, „	*dele* and.	
„ 81, line 9, „	*for* Bhara Bhuya,	„ Barah Bhuiya.
„ 85, second foot note,	„ Khunds,	„ Kands.
„ 89, „ „	„ then,	„ there.
„ 91, line 16, from below,	„ regimé,	„ regime.
„ 92, foot note,	„ 1847,	„ 1857.
„ 113, line 11,	„ Lamgam,	„ Lhungum.
„ 117, in three places,	„ Sgan,	„ Sgau.
„ 119, line 4, from below,	„ Tonguin,	„ Tonquin.
„ 139, line 26,	„ Máhals,	„ Maháls.
„ 188, line 16,	„ Jhár,	„ Jáhir.
„ 209, line 27,	„ Mann,	„ Man.
„ 228, line 4,	„ accompanies,	„ accompanied.
„ 249, line 17,	„ 2′ 5″,	„ 5 ft. 2 in.
„ 317, in the heading, et passim,	„ Agareah,	„ Aghareah.

DESCRIPTIVE ETHNOLOGY OF BENGAL.

GROUP I.

HILL TRIBES OF THE NORTH-EASTERN FRONTIER.

SECTION 1.—THE KHAMTIS.

THE Shan or Tai or Thai race have exercised a powerful influence over the fortunes of Asam. The Siamese are now the most important branch of this family. They are called by the Burmese Shangyai, or eldest branch of the Shans; but there was once a great nation of this people occupying a tract known to the historians of Manipur as the kingdom of Pong, which touched Tipperah, Yunan and Siam, and of which the city called Mogong by the Burmese, and Mongmarong by the Shans, was the capital.

In the reign of Sukempha,* the thirteenth sovereign of the empire of Pong (who succeeded his father A. D. 777), his brother Samlonpha, who was the general of his forces, having subjugated Cachar, Tipperah and Manipur, pushed across the hills to the valley of the Brahmaputra, and commenced there a series of conquests by which these Shans gradually reduced the whole country, from Sadiya to Kamrup, to subjection. It is probable that this was effected by several inroads extending over several centuries, as the Asam annals give the year, corresponding with A. D. 1228, as that of the commencement of the reign of Chukupha,† who is said to have been the first to assume for himself and people the name Ahom the 'peerless,' and to have given this name, now softened to Asam, to the country. His successor Chatamla in A. D. 1554 adopted the Hindu religion and changed his name to Jaiyadhaja Singh, and from his time the Asam Kings always took Hindu names and favored Brahmins, and the Ahom Shans, adopting the language and customs as well as the religion of the conquered people, grew to be regarded as a new division or caste of the Hindu Asamese population, rather than as intruders of an alien race.

The kingdom of Pong was finally broken up by the Burmese King Alompra about the middle of the last century, and on its dismemberment other branches of the Shan race migrated to and settled in Asam.

The Phakis or Phakials on the Dihing river, the Kamjangs of Sadiya, and the numerous settlements of Khamtis are all colonies of this race, retaining the costume, customs, and religion they brought with them into the valley. It will be sufficient to describe the latter, who are the most numerous and important.

---

* Pemberton, R. B., Report on the Eastern Frontier of British India, 1835.

† Robinson,—Asam, Descriptive Account of, 1841.

B

Whatever may have been the original seat of this people, they emigrated to Asam, within the last hundred years, from the country known to us as Bor-Khamti near the sources of the Irrawaddy, which was visited by Wilcox in 1826, and according to their own annals they had occupied that country for many centuries. Captain Wilcox found them a divided people. Two great clans had been at feud for fifty years, and it was partly owing to these dissensions that horde after horde continued to flow into Asam.

The Khamtis.

Their first settlements in the valley were, by permission of the Asam Rajahs, on the river called the Tenga-pani, but during the civil wars in Rajah Gaurinath Singh's time (A. D 1780 to 1790) they pushed on to Sadiya, ousted the Asam Governor of the Province, called the 'Sadiya Kowa Gohain,' and gave that title to their leader; and the people of the country acquieseing in the arrangement, the Asam Government was too weak to disturb it. The Khamti chief was acknowledged by the Asam, and subsequently by the British, Government as Sadiya Kowa Gohain. But in A. D. 1839 the Khamtis rebelled against the latter Government, and, having been expelled from Sadiya in consequence, they for some years lived the life of the hunted, scattered on the frontier, but were eventually allowed to settle somewhere in the vicinage of their old villages.

Early settlement.

The Khamtis are very far in advance of all the north-eastern frontier tribes in knowledge, arts, and civilization.. They are Buddhists and have regular establishments of priests well versed in the recondite mysteries of their religion, and a large proportion of the laity can read and write in their own language.

Religion.

The houses built by the leading Khamtis in Asam are precisely similar to those that Wilcox saw in Bor-Khamti.* For the residence of a chief and his family two large houses are built, framed of strong timber with raised floors and thatched roofs, contiguous to each other, a trough of wood being fixed under the junction of the two roofs to carry off the water. As each roof covers a breadth of 18 to 20 feet, and is 80 or 100 feet in length, great space for the family and retainers is thus obtained. The interior is divided into chambers, private and for reception, and the whole terminates in a railed open balcony, a prolongation of the raised floor beyond the eaves affording a convenient airy place for the family to sit and work or lounge in. The roof of the houses comes down so low that externally there is no appearance of wall. The people of the common order have similar houses, but single instead of double.

Houses, &c.

The temple and priests' quarters are also of timber and thatched, but the temples are elaborately carved, and great neatness and taste are evinced in the arrangement of the internal fittings. The priests have shaven heads and amber-colored garments and rosaries. The office is not hereditary: any person may enter upon it after the necessary novitiate and instruction in the bapuchang, as the priests' quarters are called, but they must, so long as they wear the sacerdotal habit, renounce the world and devote themselves to a life of celibacy.

* Asiatic Researches, Vol. XVII, page 436.
Pemberton, R. B.—Report on the Eastern Frontier of British India, 1835.
Robinson—A Descriptive Account of Asam, &c., 2 vols., 1841.
Hannay, Col. S. F.—Note on the Shans, published by Government in 1846.

Every morning the priests move quickly through the villages preceded by a boy with a little bell, each holding a lacquered box in which he receives the offerings of the people, generally presented by the women, who stand waiting at the door with a portion of their ready cooked food.*

The priests in their hours of relaxation amuse themselves by carving in wood, bone or ivory, at which they are very expert. In making ivory handles of weapons they evince great skill, taste, and fecundity of invention, carving in high relief twisted snakes, dragons, and other monsters with a creditable unity and gracefulness of design.

Arts, &c.

It is customary for the chiefs also to employ themselves in useful and ornamental arts. They work in gold, silver, and iron, forge their own weapons and make their wives' jewels. They also manufacture embossed shields of buffalo or rhinoceros hide, gilding and lacquering them with skill and taste.

The women are skilled in embroidery; they make elaborately worked bags for their husbands and for sale, embroidered bands for the hair and other pretty things, and are not the less capable of bearing a very severe share of the out-door farm work.

Features; origin, &c.

The Khamtis are not a handsome race. They are of rather darker complexion than the other Shans, and of coarser feature; the Mongolian peculiarities being more strongly developed in them than in their reputed brethren.† It may be on this account that Mr. Klaproth supposes them to be of Tartar origin; but, as observed by Wilcox, if it be so, the period of their migration to the Shan provinces must be very remote, since all traces of their original language have been lost. He (Captain Wilcox) nevertheless found them in Bor-Khamti as an isolated people, a very extensive district inhabited by Singpho tribes intervening between them and the other place where the Shan language is spoken. Moreover, the country they occupied was not peopled solely by Khamtis, but also by Muluks, Khalongs, Kumongs and others, cognates of the Singpho, and the mass of the laboring population were Khapoks, whose dialect is closely allied to the Singpho. These lower tribes were apparently the remains of the earlier population who had been subjugated by the Khamtis.

After settling in Asam the Khamti chiefs frequently took to themselves Asamese wives, and in some families the effect of this mingling is very marked in softening and improving the features of the generations that follow it.

New settlement.

In 1850 a large colony of fresh settlers from Bor-Khamti—between three and four hundred individuals—under a chief, a scion of one of their best families, migrated to Asam in a body. He was a young man of remarkably good address and unusually fair and good looking. He had two wives, one a pure Khamti, the other half Asamese, both good looking girls. They settled a few miles above the old outpost of Saikwah on the left bank of the Brahmaputra not far from the Nao Dihing, and when I first visited them about six months after their arrival, I was surprised to see how rapidly and admirably they had after their own fashion established themselves.

---

* Asiatic Researches, Vol. XVII.

† A recent visitor, Sir R. H. Schomburgh, talks in raptures of the long glossy hair of intense black, and the exquisitely formed mouth of the Laos Shan girls. See Journal Asiatic Society Bengal, No. 4, 1863.

The chief's first wife had frequently visited me at Dibrughar, and transacted business with me on behalf of her husband and his people, for which she showed great aptitude. As I entered the village I saw her at the head of the women returning from their farm labor; each woman bore an axe and a faggot of wood, but that borne by the chief's wife was a tiny little ornamented implement, and her faggot a miniature bundle of little sticks neatly cut and tied together, evidently emblematic rather than useful. She received me smilingly, and leading the way to her house did the honors with grace and dignity.

I was lodged in a part of the newly raised priests' quarters, and in the evening was entertained by a very creditable display of fireworks and fire balloons, all of their own making.

Religious festivals.

The Khamtis have two great religious festivals in the year,—one to celebrate the birth, the other to mourn the death, of Gautama. At these ceremonies boys dressed up as girls go through posture dances, for which, I believe, Burmese women are celebrated, and at the anniversary of the saint's death the postures are supposed to be expressive of frantic grief; but as a more distinct commemoration of the birth, a lively representation of an accouchement is acted. One of the boy girls is put to bed and waited on by the others. Presently something like infantile cries are heard, and from beneath the dress of the invalid a young puppy dog is produced squeaking, and carried away and bathed, and treated as a new-born babe.

Treatment of wives.

It will be seen by what I have stated above that Khamtis are not restricted to one wife. I do not, however, recollect having met with more than two to one husband, and though the second wife may be the favorite companion of her lord, the supremacy of the first wife is always maintained. The Shan tribes have no idea of a 'purdah,' *i. e.* of secluding their females; they all go to market and pay visits in a very independent manner, and the Khamti women have not suffered in character from the freedom allowed to them. The ladies of the Ahom families in Asam are equally unrestricted; indeed, till the occupation of the country by aliens of our introduction, the seclusion of even well-born Hindu maidens was not enforced, and to the present day, I believe, the ladies of the ex-royal family are in the habit of visiting the officials when they have an opportunity of doing so.

Costume.

The dress of the Khamti is simple and neat: the men commonly wear tight-fitting jackets of cotton cloth, dyed blue, a white muslin turban so twisted as to leave exposed the top knot into which their long hair is twisted, projecting somewhat over the forehead. The nether garment is of colored cotton of a checquered pattern or of silk, more or less ample according to the rank of the wearer. The upper classes wear the Burmese 'patso,' a piece of parti-colored silk.

Weapons.

They are seldom seen without the useful weapon the 'dao' hanging in its sheath, plain or ornamented according to the condition of the wearer, by a sling made of split rattan. It is worn somewhat in front, so that the hilt is readily grasped in the right hand; this and the defensive round shield of buffalo hide are sufficient for a Khamti to take the field with, but many of them now carry muskets or fowling-pieces.

When they rebelled in 1839, their combinations for attacks were well planned, but they lacked the courage to carry them out. They are, however, wonderfully useful auxiliaries in mountain warfare, capable of enduring great fatigue, of subsisting on any kind of food, and full of resources. They will start on an expedition, each man carrying his own provisions for ten days and all necessaries. These generally include a small cooking vessel; but a Khamti can cook his rice in a fresh-cut joint of a bamboo. If it be a dash at a particular point, and they are to return by the same road, they lighten their burden by making a 'cache' of food for one day at each halting place. If they come to an unfordable river, they construct rafts in a very short space of time, solely of bamboo. They will navigate rock-broken rivers on these rafts, skilfully shooting the rapids, and often thus pleasantly breaking a journey.

Women's costume.

The costume of the women is like that of the men, plain but neat. They wear their hair drawn up from the back and sides in one massive roll, which rises four or five inches, so much in front as to form a continuation of the frontal bone. This gives an appearance of height to figures that require an artificial addition. The roll is encircled by an embroidered band, the fringed and tasseled ends of which hang down behind; the lower garment, generally of dark-colored cotton cloth, is folded over the breasts under the arms, and reaches to the feet. This style of wearing the principal garment, common to the Shans and Manipuris, appears to have been introduced into Asam by the former, as the Asamese women of the lower classes have all adopted it; but the Khamti women wear in addition a colored silk scarf round the waist, and a long sleeved jacket. The chief ornaments are cylindrically shaped pieces of bright amber inserted in the lobes of the ears, and coral and other bead necklaces.

Burial grounds.

The burial ground of the Khamtis is generally a tidily kept spot apart from the village. The graves are surmounted by conically shaped tumuli which, when first constructed (to the best of my recollection) diminish from the base to the apex in a series of steps; the earth being kept in position by bamboo matting round each step. The Ahoms, notwithstanding their conversion to the Hindu faith, retained this method of sepulture to a recent date. The tumuli constructed over the graves of the Asam (Ahom) sovereigns are very extensive, and when opened the remains of the dead have been found in coffins of massive timber with gold and silver ornaments, and outside the coffin various utensils, arms, and implements of agriculture.

SECTION 2.—THE SINGPHOS.

The Singphos or Kakhens, the Cacobee of the ancient maps.

The Singphos, like the Khamtis, have settled in Asam within the memory of man. They are said to have first made their appearance in the valley during the rebellion of the Muttuck or Mahamaria sect against the Rajah Gaurinath Singh, about A. D. 1793.

Early settlements.

Their first settlements were on the Tenga-pani, east of Sadiya,* and on the Bori-Dihing river in the tract called Namrup, and they not only met with no opposition from the scattered and harassed Asamese population of that tract, but were well received as an element of strength to assist the inhabitants to hold their own. By degrees the Singphos formed large villages under

* Sketch of the Singphos, by Colonel S. F. Hannay, published by Government in 1847.

C

their chiefs, the Dapha, the Bisa, the Latora, and other Gâms (the head of a family is so called, the second branch assuming the affix 'La,' and the third 'Thu' or 'Du'), and not only maintained themselves in a state almost independent of the Asam government, but absorbed into their own communities the few Asamese left in that part of the country.

The Singphos are of the race called by the Burmese Ka-Khyen or Kaku, whose original settlements were on the great eastern branches of the Irrawaddy river; they are there in contact with the Kunungs, with whom they are closely allied in language and origin. They extended east to the confines of Yunan, and west to the valley of the Kyendwyen; but it was only on spreading into the valley of Asam that they assumed the name of Singpho, which in their own language means 'man.'

When Upper Asam came under the rule of the British Government, it was not till after several engagements with our troops that the Singpho settlements were brought into some sort of subjection. It was then found that their villages contained great numbers of Asamese slaves, who, whenever they got the opportunity, left their masters no more to return, and the action of the authorities in refusing to restore them and giving them every possible facility of escaping was a constant grievance to the Singphos,—a wound to their pride which more than once rankled into open insurrection.* No fewer than 5,000 are reported to have been released by one officer, the late Captain Neufville.

Duániahs.

From the intercourse of the Singphos with their Asamese female slaves, a mongrel race has sprung up, well known in Upper Asam under the denomination Duániahs. They have been found very useful auxiliaries in frontier wars from their knowledge of the Singpho language and tactics, and from their fidelity to the Government that relieved them from the Singpho yoke.

Villages.

The Singphos on the frontiers of Asam occupy large villages often in somewhat unassailable positions, consisting of sixty or more large houses, each from eighty to a hundred feet long and about twenty in breadth, with raised floors throughout and open balcony at one end, where the ladies of the family sit and spin, weave and embroider. The house is divided into different apartments on both sides of a long passage open from end to end.† There are generally several hearths round which the family sleep, and over the fireplace are large bamboo racks hanging from the roof, on which are placed meat or fish requiring to be smoked.

Size; costume.

They are generally a fine athletic race, above the ordinary standard in height, and capable of enduring great fatigue; but their energies are greatly impaired by the use of opium and spirits, in which they freely indulge. The men tie the hair in a large knot on the crown of the head, and wear a jacket of colored cotton and checquered under-garment of the same material or of silk, or the Burmese 'patso.' The respectable chiefs assume the Shan or Burmese style of dress, and occasionally short smart jackets of China velvet, with gilt or amber buttons. They also wrap themselves in plaids of thick cotton much in the fashion of Scotch Highlanders.

* Robinson's Assam. † Hannay, loc. cit.

The features are of the Mongolian type, very oblique eyes and eyebrows, mouths wide, cheek bones high, and heavy square jawbones. Their complexion, never ruddy, varies from a tawny yellow or olive to a dark brown. Hard labor tells on the personal appearance of the females,* rendering them coarse in feature and awkward in gait, but in the families of the chiefs light complexions and pleasing features are sometimes seen. Their dress consists of one piece of colored cotton cloth, often in large broad horizontal bands of red and blue fastened round the waist, a jacket and a scarf. The married women wear their hair, which is abundant, in a large broad knot on the crown of the head, fastened with silver bodkins with chains and tassels. Maidens wear their hair gathered in a roll resting on the back of the neck and similarly secured. They are fond of a particular enamelled bead called deo-mani, and all wear as ornaments bright pieces of amber inserted in the holes in the lobe of the ear. The men tattoo their limbs slightly, and all married women are tattooed on both legs from the ankle to the knee in broad parallel bands.

Physiognomy.

The national weapons of this tribe are the heavy short sword called Dao or Dhá, so well known in Asam, admirably adapted for close quarters in war, and for clearing jungle and preparing the ground in peace,—the frontier tribes can dispense with the trouble of converting their swords into plough-shares, they use them as they are:—a spear with a short shaft used for thrusting, and a strong cross-bow with bamboo arrows: but they affect the use of the musket whenever they can get one, and are sometimes seen with China matchlocks.

Arms; warfare.

They use shields of buffalo hide, four feet long, and helmets sometimes of that material, sometimes of thick plaited rattan work, varnished black, decorated with boars' tusks, &c.

In warfare their attacks are confined to night surprises, which are speedily abandoned if they meet with steady opposition. They are skilled in fortifying naturally difficult positions, using freely the 'panja,' a bamboo stake of different lengths sharpened at both ends and stuck in the ground, with which the sides of the hills and all approaches to their position are rendered difficult and dangerous. If they use muskets on these occasions, the weapons are generally fixed in loopholes of breast-works, ready loaded, and the trigger is pulled when the enemy reaches the point of the road (previously ascertained) covered by them. If they fail by such means to beat off the attacks at once, they abandon the position for another behind it.

In travelling the Singphos carry a haversac, of very neat appearance, cleverly adapted to the head and shoulders. It is made of very finely plaited fibre on a frame of wood covered with the skin of the large grey monkey. They are also provided with handsome bags, woven and embroidered by their wives, in which they carry their pipes and tobacco, opium, &c.

The Singphos understand the smelting of iron, and their blacksmiths with no implements but a lump of stone as an anvil, and a rude hammer, forge weapons,—especially daos,—which are highly prized all over the frontier for their temper and durability.

Arts, &c.

* Hannay, loc. cit.

The Singphos manufacture their own wearing apparel.* The thread is dyed previous to being woven, and thus are produced the checks and colored garments of which they are so fond. They use as dyes a kind of indigo called 'Rom,' 'Seing Lung,' or 'Asso Khat,' and the bright yellow root of a creeper called 'Khai Khiew.'

The Singphos repudiate all affinity with the Shans, and are not considered by ethnologists to be connected with them except very remotely. Their language is entirely different, approximating more to the Karen, Manipuri, Burmese, Kukī, Naga and Abor dialects, and their religion is a rude paganism, whilst the Shans are most of them Buddhists.

Deities.

The Singphos have a confused notion of a Supreme Being, but they propitiate only malignant spirits called Nhats, of which there are three,—the *Mu* Nhat or spirit above, the *Ga* Nhat or spirit below, and the household Nhat or *penate*. They sacrifice fowls, pigs, and dogs to the Nhats, and when about to proceed on important expeditions a buffalo is offered, and acceptance of the flesh of the animal, when cut up and distributed amongst the friends of the chief, is considered as a pledge that binds them to his service on this particular occasion. There is no regular priesthood amongst the Singphos, but they pay great deference to the Pungyes or priests of the Buddhist Shans. Some of them are, however, supposed to possess powers of divination, and Colonel Hannay mentions having witnessed the process. The diviner was seated by himself at some distance from the crowd, and had beside him a small fire and a bundle of common '*nul*' grass, which grows to a large size in swamps. Taking a piece of 'nul' containing several joints he held it over the flame, until by the heat one of the joints burst with a sharp report, the fracture on each side threw out a number of minute hair-like fibres which were carefully examined and put aside. Another piece was then put in the fire and similarly treated. This continued for at least an hour, when the result was disclosed, namely, that a certain chief, whose arrival was awaited, would make his appearance in three or four days, and so it happened.

Marriages, &c.

Polygamy prevails amongst the Singphos, and chiefs especially rejoice in a plurality of wives. The girl is bought with a price, and a feast completes the ceremony. As a maiden she is allowed considerable liberty. I have been informed by Duániahs† that the girls of some villages occupy a house appropriated to their use in which, under charge of an old woman, they receive visits from young men, but I have never seen such an institution, and if it exists it is not shown to strangers.

Burial.

They bury their dead, but in the case of a man of note the body is kept for two or more years in order that the scattered relations of the deceased may have time to attend his funeral: ‡ the body being removed to some distance during the process of decomposition, after which it is placed in a coffin and brought back to the house, where it remains in state, decked out with all the insignia of rank used during life. The body of the Gâm of Gakhind was thus found by Captain Neufville in a Singpho stockade.

---

* Colonel Hannay's sketch of the Singphos, published by Government, 1847.

† Duániahs, mongrels previously referred to, children of Singphos and Asamese slave girls.

‡ Selections, Bengal Government, No. XXIII, page 10.

If deceased met his death by violence, they sacrifice a buffalo, the head of which is fastened as a memorial in the centre of a cross of wood of the St. Andrew's form. This ceremony is omitted if the deceased dies a natural death. The gods took him at their own good time and do not need propitiation. When finally committed to the earth a mound is raised to mark the spot, sometimes of considerable dimensions. This custom they appear to have taken from their neighbours the Khamtis.

Tradition of origin.

According to Bisa, one of the most influential and intelligent of the Singpho Gâms that settled in Asam, the Singphos believe* 'they were originally created and established on a plateau called Májai-Singra-Bhum, situated at a distance of two months' journey from Sadiya, washed by a river flowing in a southerly direction to the Irrawaddy. During their sojourn there they were immortal and held celestial intercourse with the planets and all heavenly intelligences, following the pure worship of one Supreme Being.' Why they left this Eden is not stated in connection with this tradition; but they have another, in which the fall is assigned to an act of disobedience on their part in bathing in interdicted water. On descending to the plains they became mortal, and having imbrued their hands in the blood of men and animals in self-defence and for subsistence, they soon adopted the idolatries and superstitions of the nations around them.

Right of property.

In succession to patrimonial property the Singphos have a peculiar custom. The eldest takes the landed estate with the titles, the youngest the personalties, the intermediate brethren, when any exist, are excluded from all participation, and remain in attendance on the chief or head of the family as during the lifetime of their father.

SECTION 3.—THE MISHMIS.

Mishmi settlements have been found by Wilcox as far south as the Nemlang river, an affluent of the Irrawaddy; their colonies sweep round to the east of the great mountain called the Dapha Bhum, and then up the valley of the Brahmaputra proper to the confines of Tibet. They extend west to the Digaru river (96°—97° 30′ east longitude, 27° 40′—28° 40′ north latitude).

The Mishmis situated to the west of the Du river, an affluent of the Brahmaputra above the Brahmakund, trade with the British possessions, and are in habit of constant intercourse with us; the tribes to the north-east of that river trade only with Tibet.

The people of the tribes that we have intercourse with are quiet and inoffensive, but very keen traders.† Those beyond them have shown themselves at all times hostile to the visits of British officers. Wilcox was permitted to enter their country and to proceed as far as the village of a chief called Jingsha situated at the point where the Brahmaputra in its hill course, after flowing nearly due south from Tibet, suddenly changes its direction and continues its course in a western direction, but from that point he was forced to return.

* Selections, Bengal Government, pages 7 and 14. Notes by Captain Neufville.

† Selections, Bengal Government, No. 23, page 77; also Asiatic Researches, Vol. XVII. *Ibid.* page 14. Compare with Karen traditions.

D

Captain Wilcox's expedition was in the year 1827. In 1836 the friendly villages as far as the Dilli were visited by Dr. Griffiths.* Lieutenant, now Colonel, E. A. Rowlatt in 1845 penetrated to the Du, and up that river in a northerly direction to the village of Tuppang, where he met some Lamas, as all Tibetans in this locality are called. In 1851 the French Missionary Monsr. Krick accompanied by a Khamti chief from the neighbourhood of Sadiya, the well known Chokeng Gohain, started on his mission to Tibet. After passing through the friendly villages he appears to have been so guided as to avoid the hostile clans, including that of the formidable Jingsha, but in passing near that chief's residence, a young girl significantly pointed out to him the spot where two pilgrims from India had not long before been massacred, and intimated that a like fate awaited him if he were caught. However he reached in safety the Tibetan village of Oualong, where he was well received. Proceeding onward from that village he found himself in a country presenting a strong contrast to the rugged, grand, but uncultured tracts he had recently been struggling through. The valley of the Brahmaputra expanded, presenting a succession of well cultivated fields. The inhabitants, their houses, and the general appearance of the country assumed a more cheerful aspect. Pine forests covered the hills most luxuriant on their crests. The alluvial soil below, watered by numerous small streams, is described as producing groves of bamboos, orange trees, citron, peach trees, and laurel. Two marches through such scenery brought him to Sommeu.

Mr. Krick's visits.

This village is composed of about a dozen houses irregularly grouped on a hill in the midst of evergreen trees, half a mile from the banks of the Brahmaputra. As far as the eye could see, the view up the valley gave a succession of cultivated fields, herds of oxen, horses, asses and mules, and three miles to the north Rima Castle, the residence of a governor, was discovered. Unfortunately, Monsr. Krick's resources were exhausted in making his way through the Mishmi country, and finding the people, when the novelty was over, disinclined to support him gratuitously, he was under the necessity of returning. On his way back he stopped at Jingsha's village and was very roughly received, but having medically treated a sick member of the family, who fortunately for the Abbé recovered, he was allowed to depart in peace and pursue his journey to the plains unmolested, and he reached the frontier post of Saikwah† on the 28th March, 1852.

In 1854, the Reverend Monsr. Krick with a colleague, the Reverend Monsr. Bourri, escorted by the friendly Mishmi chief Krosha, again proceeded to Tibet, and by a different route marched in safety to the Tibetan villages he had visited in 1852, but unfortunately in his journey across the mountains he gave dire offence to an independent Mishmi chief, called Kaisa, refusing to submit to his extortionate demands and making a circuit to avoid passing through his territory. The incensed savage armed, followed the party to Sommeu, and in utter disregard of the authority at Rima attacked and murdered the two priests, carried off all their property as plunder, and their servant Singpho as a slave.

The next expedition to the Mishmi hills was by order of the late Marquis Dalhousie to avenge their fate. In 1855, Lieutenant Frederick Grey Eden at the head of a small party of picked men of the 1st Asam

Eden's expedition.

* Griffiths' Journal, pages 26, 59. Rowlatt's Notes of an Expedition, Journal Asiatic Society Bengal, 1845.

† Saikwah, south bank of Brahmaputra, three miles below Sadiya.

Light Infantry, a band of carefully selected Khamtis, and a few hill men as carriers, after a series of forced marches, suddenly crossed the Du, surprised Kaisa's stronghold on the other side, captured that chief and many members of his family and followers, recovered the greater portion of the plundered property and released the servant Singpho.

Villages.

The Mishmi villages to the south of the Brahmaputra are scattered and mixed up with Khamti and Singpho settlements. The north bank as far as the Digaru river and both banks of the river from Jingsha's country to the Tibetan frontier, they have all to themselves. A more rugged, a more difficult, but a more beautiful country it would be difficult to find, and the exertion necessary to travel in it is powerfully illustrated in the fine development of calves and muscles of the thighs by which the Mishmi lads and lasses are invariably distinguished. Steady nerves are as necessary as strong limbs, or unhappy is the traveller who has to cross a swollen torrent roaring hundreds of feet beneath him by a Mishmi suspension bridge, thus described by Monsr. Krick:—The point selected for the construction of these aërial bridges is where the river is most narrowly confined by rocks; across this a rope made of three or four rattans is flung, the extremity fastened to rocks or trees, and the rope tightened as much as possible. On this chain or rope a moveable ring of the same material is bound. The person who has to cross places his body in the ring, and, if necessary, his head in a small loop formed for the purpose, and then, with his face turned upwards, he allows the ring to move. It slides down rapidly to the middle, and the remaining portion of the distance the passenger accomplishes by grasping the suspender and working his way up with hands and feet.

Settlements.

The Mishmi settlements consist of few houses, sometimes of only one, but each house is capable of holding all the members of a family and numerous slaves and retainers. Dr. Griffiths describes the house of Gallom Gâm, one of the chiefs he visited, as of great length (Wilcox gives the dimensions 130 feet by 11), built of bamboos raised high from the ground, divided into twelve compartments and containing one hundred men, women and children. The house of Krosha, another chief, is described as considerably larger. It is divided into twenty compartments. On the right hand side of the passage were ranged the skulls of the cattle the chief had killed, including mithuns (*Bos frontalis*), deer and pigs. On the other side are the domestic utensils. It is considered shabby for a chief to retain in his show-room the skulls of animals killed by his predecessors. Each compartment contains a fireplace, over which hangs a tray for the meat that they wish to smoke. This one manor house is the head quarters of the settlement. The store-houses for grain are at some distance and out of sight.

Sources of wealth.

The Mishmis are constantly on the move in their trading expeditions, and attend less to cultivation than their neighbours, but they are rich in flocks and herds. They purchase cattle every year in Asam, and have besides large herds of the fine hill ox, the mithun; they call it 'cha.' The possession of these animals is, next to the number of their wives, the chief indication of their wealth. They do not use them for agricultural purposes or for their milk, but on great occasions one is slaughtered and eaten, and they are given in exchange for brides. They are allowed to remain almost in a wild state, roving through the forests as they please, but they are fed with salt by their master, and when he calls they know his voice and respond.

Resources.

The chief sources of wealth to the Mishmis are the poisonous root '*Aconitum ferox*,' which grows in their hills at high elevations, the valuable medicinal plant '*Coptis teeta*' or Mishmi teeta, and the musk bags of the musk deer, also a native of these hills in the higher ranges. With these and a few articles of hardware and woollen goods obtained from Tibet, they carry on extensive trade with the people of Asam and the neighbouring hill tribes. Everything that a Mishmi trader carries about him, to his last garment, is purchasable.

Marriages.

They are extensive polygamists. Each man may have as many wives as he can afford to purchase, the price ranging from a pig to a bonus of twenty oxen. One chief well known in Upper Asam, Matchisong, made his appearance in the plains almost every year with a new, young, and generally pretty wife. On his death all that survived him became the property of his heir with the exception of the mother of the heir,—should she be amongst them,—who would go to the next of kin amongst the males. This custom obtains also amongst the Subanshiri Abors.

When a woman's confinement is near at hand, a small shed is erected for her in the jungle near the house, and there she must remain till delivered,* and till the days of her purification—ten days for a boy, and eight for a girl—are completed.

Religion.

The religion of the Mishmis is confined to the propitiation of demons whenever illness or misfortune visits them. On these occasions the sprig of a plant is placed at the door to intimate to strangers that the house is for the time under *tabu*. They appear to have no notion of a supreme and benevolent deity. They worship 'Mujidagrah' as the god of destruction, 'Damipaon' as the god of the chase and of knowledge, and 'Tabla' as the god of wealth and disease, and a great many others without name. It appears both from Lieutenant Rowlatt and the Abbé Krick's notes that the Mishmis have priests, but they are few in number and have to be brought from a distance when required. Monsr. Krick describes one that he saw at a funeral ceremony.

Burials.

This took place over the remains of the wife of a chief who had been dead and buried three months. The tomb was near the house covered with a roof, under which were suspended the deceased's clothes and her drinking cup. For several days previous to the arrival of the priest, an attendant was employed singing a mournful devotional chant to the accompaniment of a small bell. There was also a preliminary sacrifice of a red cock and hen, the blood of which was received in a vessel containing some other fluid, and the mixture carefully examined, as it is supposed to indicate if the result will be fortunate or otherwise. At last the priest arrived, dressed like an ordinary chief, but he wore a rosary of shells and, attached to the front of his head-dress, two appendages like horns.

For two days, at intervals, the priest and his son employed themselves in singing chants, marking the time by waving a fan and ringing a bell; on the third day he put off his chief's Tibetan robe and assumed what may be regarded as his pontifical dress,—a tight-fitting coat of colored cotton, a small apron, a deer skin as a mantle; from his

* Rowlatt's Notes of an Expedition, Asiatic Society's Journal, 1845, page 48.

right shoulder descended a fringe of long goat's hair dyed bright red, and over his left shoulder he wore a broad belt embossed with four rows of tiger's teeth and having attached to it fourteen small bells. On his head he placed a bandeau ornamented with shells and, round the knob of hair at the top of his head, a moveable plume which turned like a weathercock.

This was followed by a wild demoniacal dance, but whether a *pas seul* by the priest, or one in which the people generally joined, we are not informed. The object was, however, to make as much noise as possible to frighten the devils.* After this, lights were all extinguished, and the party remained in darkness, till a man suspended from the roof obtained a fresh light from a flint. He was to be careful not to touch the ground as he produced it, as the light thus obtained was supposed to be fresh from heaven.

When the burial is of a person of note, animals are slain, and the skulls arranged round the tomb; and under the shed built over the grave, raw and cooked flesh with grain and spirits are placed (the share of the dead), and all the arms, clothes and implements he was in the habit of using when living. The poor, it is said, burn the dead without much ceremony, or throw the bodies into the river.

Costume.

The dress of a Mishmi is, first a strip of cloth bound round the loins and passing between the legs and fastened in front; a coat without sleeves, like a herald's tabard, reaching from the neck to the knee,—this is made of one piece of blue and red or brown striped cloth doubled in the middle, the two sides sewn together like a sack, leaving space for the exit of the arms, and a slit in the middle, formed in the weaving, for the passage of the head;—two pouches covered with fur attached to leather shoulder-belts, with large brass plates before and behind, like cymbals; a knapsack ingeniously contrived to fit the back, covered with the long black fibres of the great sago palm of these hills, and further decorated with the tail of a Tibetan cow; a long straight Tibetan sword; several knives and daggers, and a very neat light spear,—head of well-tempered, finely wrought iron attached to a long thin polished shaft.

The head-dress is sometimes a fur cap, sometimes a wicker helmet.

The women wear a colored cloth fastened loosely round the waist, which reaches to the knees, and a very scanty bodice which supports without entirely covering the breasts. They wear a profusion of beads, not only of common glass but of cornelian agate and some of porcelain. On their heads they wear a bandeau of a very thin silver plate, broad over the forehead and tapering to about half an inch in breadth over the ears, thence continued round the back of the head by a chain of small shells. Both men and women wear the hair long, turned up all round and gathered in a knot on the brow secured by a bodkin. They are thus distinguished from their neighbours, the Chalikatas or crop-haired Mishmis.

Small girls go naked about the villages, but wear a little billet of wood suspended from a string round the loins, which hangs in front and serves as a sort of covering, especially when they are seated in their favorite position in the porch on the edge of the raised floor of the house. They look as if they were ticketted for sale.

* Compare with the ceremonies of the Kukis.

E

The Mishmi men and women are inveterate smokers. They commence at the earliest possible age, and when they are not sleeping or eating they are certain to be smoking; they use brass pipes, many of them of Chinese manufacture.

Physical appearance.

The Mishmis are a short sturdy race of fair complexion for Asiatics, well-knit figures and active as monkeys; they vary much in feature, generally exhibiting a rather softened phase of the Mongolian type, but sometimes with regular, almost Aryan, features, the nose higher and nostrils longer than is usually seen in the Indo-Chinese races. They have themselves a legend to account for this. I forget the particulars, but I know it connects them in some way with Hindu pilgrims to the Brahmakand.

The Mishmis I am describing are divided into many clans, those best known in the plains are the *Tain;* the *Maro* are to the south of the Brahmaputra. The most eastern that we know are the *Mizha;* perhaps they are connected with the *Maintze*, the aborigines of Yunan and other provinces of China.

SECTION 4.—THE CHALIKATA (CROP-HAIRED) MISHMIS.

Geographical position.

The hill country bordering on Asam, between the Digaru and Dibong, and on both banks of the hill course of the latter river, is occupied by a tribe nearly allied to the people last described as Mishmis, called Chalikata Mishmis by the Asamese in consequence of their habit of cropping the front hair on the forehead. Their country lies to the north of Sadiya, and their villages extend across the Sub-Himalayan range to the borders of Tibet. The hills being loftier, it is more rugged and difficult of access even than the country of the Tain Mishmis. So difficult indeed, that though we have had aggravation enough, an expedition into the interior of their country has never been attempted. I have been informed by the Khamtis that one route to the plains traversed by the Chalikatas is along the cliffs of the Dibong river. The path is generally a narrow ledge winding round a precipice, but in one place there is no ledge! *only holes in the face of the rock for the hands and feet.* The proper name for the Chalikata clan is, if I recollect right, Midhi. They are greatly detested and mistrusted by their neighbours, the Abors and Tain, and they are much dreaded by the Sadiya population in consequence of the prowling expeditions to kidnap women and children. They are full of deceit. They come down in innocent looking parties of men and women to the plains, apparently groaning under the weight of the baskets of merchandise they are importing for barter. They proceed thus till they find an unprotected village, then throwing aside their fictitious loads, they pounce on the women and children, and carry them off to the hills. They thus attack villages of Tains and Digáru Mishmis, as well as Asamese villages, but they are afraid of the Abors, who are always on the alert.

The Midhi have some villages situated in low hills, about 16 miles to the west of the Dibong gorge, which are accessible, and which I have visited. I much regret that I have lost my journal of this expedition undertaken in company with Captain Comber in 1856, as we have no published account of the Midhi, and I have now nothing but my memory to trust to.

The inhabitants of the villages I visited were, in those days, in habits of intercourse with the plains, and frequented the Saikwah market. Wilcox tells us that they opposed

Captain Bedford in his attempt to ascend the Dibong river in 1826. The attempt to visit their villages had been made by that officer, but the people came down in large numbers to the river, and showed themselves so unfriendly, that Captain Bedford deemed it expedient to retire.

The villages belonging to the people then so hostile are those we visited, and we found them very friendly. I recollect being much struck with a considerate act of delicate attention on the part of the women of the first village we came to, Anandia I think. The march from the river to this village was a long one, and there was no source of water on the road. When we got rather more than half way, and our people were suffering greatly from thirst, we came upon a group of girls with delicious spring water in new vessels made of the great hollow bamboo, called the 'káku bans,' who had come thus far to meet, welcome, and refresh us.

Houses.

The villages contained from 10 to 30 houses, each very lightly framed; they were long and narrow, about 60 feet by 12. One side was a narrow passage from end to end, the remainder was divided into small apartments in some of which were seats,—a sign of civilization not often met with in Indian huts.

The Gâms rejoice in very sonorous names as Alundi, Alunga. They are hereditary chiefs, and have considerable influence over their clansmen, but no power over their persons or property, and no authority to punish crime or even to take notice of it. The notions of the Midhi on this subject are truly savage. If an injury is inflicted on one of them by a member of another tribe, it is incumbent on the tribe of the injured party to avenge it; if one of his own tribe offend, it is the business of the person offended only. He has no law except that which he can take in his own hands, and between people in the same village feuds are thus perpetuated for ages.

I was told of some very large villages in the interior, and I have heard from released captives of chiefs of great wealth in cattle and slaves. One or two of these great men occasionally visited us, but generally there was cause of quarrel between us that kept them in their hills. The number of wives a man possesses is with them, as with the Tain, an indication of wealth, some chiefs having as many as sixteen. Marriage ceremony there is, I believe, none; it is simply an affair of purchase, and the women thus obtained, if they can be called wives, are not much bound by the tie. The husbands do not expect them to be chaste; they take no cognizance of their temporary *liaisons* so long as they are not deprived of their services. If a man is dispossessed of one of his wives, he has a private injury to avenge, and takes the earliest opportunity of retaliating, but he cannot see that the woman is a bit the worse for a little incontinency.

Marriage tie.

The Midhi, like the Mishmis previously described, are a trading people. Large parties are continually on the move trading with Tibet. On such occasions, men send their wives if they cannot go themselves, and to any one who has seen how the men and women promiscuously *bivouac* at night, the exceeding complaisance of the husband will not appear wonderful.

The color of the Midhi varies from dark brown to the fairness equalling that of a European brunette. Some amongst them have rich red lips and ruddy complexions, and I have seen Midhi girls that were decidedly good looking, but their beauty is terribly marred by their peculiar method of cropping the hair. The front hair is combed down on the brow, then cut straight across from ear to ear, giving them foreheads 'villanous low,' and they are generally begrimed with dirt. The back hair is collected in a knot behind, and secured with long bodkins of bone or porcupine quills. The men wear wicker helmets that come down in front right to the eyebrow, and unlike modern bonnets are large enough to cover the *chignon* behind. This gives them the appearance of having very large heads (they have not got small ones) and very scowling countenances. Their features are in fact of a coarse Mongolian type. The faces flat and broad, the nostrils wide and round, and the eyes small and oblique, but these characteristics, though stronger in the Midhi than in the Tain Mishmi, are less marked in the former than they are in the faces of their neighbours—the Abors. It has always struck me that the Midhi women are comparatively taller and finer creatures than the men.

Physical appearance.

Notwithstanding the bad character that I have given them (and I would not venture to have done so on any authority but their own), they are the most ingenious of the family; they have learnt to utilize for clothing many of the fibrous plants that grow wild in their hills, as well as cotton and wool.

They were probably the first people on this side of the Himalayas to discover the valuable properties of the *Rhea nivea*, and many others of the nettle tribe; with the fibre of one of these nettles they weave a cloth so strong and stiff that, made into jackets, it is used by themselves and by the Abors as a sort of armour. They supply themselves and the Abors with clothing, and their textile fabrics of all kinds always sold well at the Saikwah market. It was very interesting to watch the barter that took place there between these suspicious, excitable savages and the cool, wily traders of the plains. The former took salt chiefly in exchange for the commodities they brought down, and they would not submit to its being measured or weighed to them by any known process. Seated in front of the trader's stall, they cautiously take from a well-guarded basket one of the articles they wish to exchange. Of this they still retain a hold with their toe or their knee as they plunge two dirty paws into the bright white salt. They make an attempt to transfer all they can grasp to their own basket, but the trader, with a sweep of his hand, knocks off half the quantity, and then there is a fiery altercation, which is generally terminated by a concession on the part of the trader of a few additional pinches. In addition to the cloths, the Chalikatas bring to market large quantities of bees-wax, ginger, and chillies.

Arts, &c.

The costume, with the exception of the head-dress, is very similar to that of the Tains, but the jackets worn by the women are larger and are sometimes tastefully embroidered. This garment is generally worn open, exposing an ample bust heaving under a ponderous weight of agate and glass beads. Their favorite weapons are straight Tibetan swords, daggers, bows and cross-bows, and they are the only tribe who always carry poisoned arrows. They have neatly-made oblong shields of buffalo hide, attached to which, inside, is a quiver full of finely-made poisoned 'pangis;' with these they invariably garnish the path by which they retreat with their prey.

Costume.

By an exchange of weapons, warriors become sworn comrades, and if one falls, it is the duty of the other to avenge his fate and recover his skull.

For the entertainment of their guests, the people of one village that we visited got up a very characteristic dramatical entertainment. The first scene represented a peaceful villager with his children hoeing the ground, and singing and conversing with them as if utterly unconscious of danger. A villanous-looking crop-head glides in like a snake scarce seen in the long grass, takes note of the group, and glides away again. Presently armed savages are seen in the distance. They come gradually and stealthily on, till within a convenient distance they stop and watch their prey like so many cats, then there is a rush in, the man is supposed to be killed, and the children carried screeching away.

Amusements.

This was followed by a dance. The Gâm dressed himself in robes similar to those worn by the Mishmi priests, described by Monsr. Krick, and danced a stately measure with a young woman also similarly robed. I recollect being much struck with the imposing appearance of the dresses worn on this occasion, but I am unable to describe them accurately.

The robe of the female was ampler than usual, and had a fringe of more than a foot in breadth. She bore aloft, as she moved, a small drum which gave forth its sound at every motion. The male performer had a head-dress with horns, a broad belt round his waist with an enormous brass buckle, according with the popular notion of a bandit's girdle, and across the body was worn the singular embroidered shoulder-belt with its peal of small bells. This was a religious dance, used at funerals and other ceremonies. They bury their dead in the wood away from the village: a place is cleared in the forest in which the grave is made, and the remains of the deceased and his arms and clothes are deposited in it. They then dance over it.

Burials.

I have met with no people so entirely devoid of religious feeling as are the Chalikatas. I had long conversations on the subject with several of the chiefs, and they utterly rejected all notions of a future state, or of immortality of any kind. The spirits they propitiated were, they declared, mortal like themselves, and though they admitted there must have been a creator, they flatly denied that the being who called into existence their hills, rocks, rivers, forests, and ancestors could still be alive. Men die and worms eat them, is their creed, but when I suggested that their custom of placing in the grave, with the dead, weapons, food, and clothes must have originated in some idea that the spirit would regain such things, they said, it was nothing of the kind; it was done as a mark of affection to their departed relative,—a feeling that indisposed them from using what he had used, and thus benefiting by his death.

Religion.

SECTION 5.—THE ABOR GROUP: (1)—THE PÁDAM AND OTHER ABORS.

The next tribe in geographical order are the Abors, or as they call themselves the Pádam. It has been said that the Abors, Mishmi, and Midhi are of common origin, but there appears to be very little, if any, affinity in their languages, and in custom, habits, religion, and notions of government, no two people could be more dissimilar. Now as the Midhi and Pádam cultivation is only separated by a small river, it is inconceivable that kindred people should for ages be thus contiguous and yet show no trace of the common origin assigned to them. I think it will be found that the Mishmi, including the Midhi, are of nearer kin to the Miaoutes, the supposed aborigines of Yunan

&c., than to the tribes south and west of them, whilst the Pádam and their cognates are of nearer affinity to the Tibetan.

Geographical position.

Commencing with the Pádam on the banks of the Dibong river, we have, in the northern barrier of the valley of the Brahmaputra, a chain of tribes occupying the whole of the hill country between Asam and Tibet (between the 95° 40′ and 92° parallels of east longitude), to the north of the Luckimpur and Durrung districts, which all evidence, physical, psychical, and philological, prove to be one people, though they are known to us under the different names Abors, Hill Miris, Daplas or Dophlas and Akas. The Nagas occupy a somewhat similar area of the hill country between Asam and Burmah on the opposite side of the valley.

Proceeding, as I am now taking my narrative, down the valley, the first Abor or Pádam village that we come to is Bomjir on the Dibong. This must have been established within the last 40 years, as it was not there when Captains Bedford and Wilcox explored the river. It is a compact village of some twenty or thirty houses on a high bank overlooking a western branch of the river, strongly stockaded, and was evidently placed here as an outpost of the confederate Pádam states to resist the encroachments and prevent the marauding expeditions of the Chalikatas.

The term 'Abor,' signifying barbarous and independent, is, by the Asamese, applied very indefinitely to all the independent hill tribes on both sides of the valley, but it is more especially the appellation of the great section we are about to treat of. The word in Asamese is opposed to *Bori*, which means dependent. It has the same signification as *Malwa* and *Be-malwa* applied to the Garos.

The Abors on or near the Dibong river and between that river and the Dirjmo, due north of the station of Dibrugarh, call themselves Pádam. It has been assumed that they are in some measure dependent on the kindred clans occupying the loftier ranges behind them, but I believe that the villages of the Pádam, bordering on Asam, are larger, and in all respects more flourishing than those in the interior, and I am inclined to think that they consider themselves as independent of their northern as of their southern neighbours. Sometimes great councils of the different settlements are convened, and then, if they agree, they act together as confederate states, but each community in its internal affairs is governed by its own laws devised and administered on purely democratical principles.

Membu is the largest of these neighbouring Pádam settlements, and is reported to be the most influential in the confederate councils. It was visited by Wilcox in 1825, and by the late Lieutenant Frederick Grey Eden, Doctor R. Moir, and myself in 1855, and I cannot better describe the people and the Pádam generally than by giving extracts from the journal in which my impressions on seeing them were at the time recorded.

The village is built on a range of hills rising from a small stream called the Shiku, about four miles from the confluence of that stream with the Dibong. It occupies some 20 acres of rocky, craggy ground at different elevations, varying about 200 feet. It is sheltered by lofty peaked hills that, as you look towards the north, embrace it on three sides. To the south from the elevated sites, a fine view of the plains of Asam is obtained. The course of the Dibong river from the hills to its junction with the Brahmaputra and many miles of the combined river are discernible.

Houses.

The houses are nearly all of the same size, about 50 feet in length by 20 in breadth, with a verandah or porch, one hearth and no inner enclosure. They are apparently not intended for the accommodation of more than one married couple. Girls till they are married occupy at night the same house as their fathers and mothers; boys and young men are not permitted to do so, and when a man marries, he and his bride leave the paternal roof and set up a house for themselves. In building this they are assisted by the community, and all the component parts having been previously collected, prepared, and arranged, the house is framed, floored, thatched and ready for their reception in four and twenty hours.

I had an opportunity of seeing a house thus commenced, and of watching its progress. Next day it was completed and occupied by the young couple.

In trimming and fitting the frame-work of timber, some art is displayed; the flooring of bamboos is four feet from the ground; the walls and the doors are of planks, and the thatching, which comes down on all sides as low as the flooring to keep off the high winds, is of grass, or more commonly of dried leaves of the wild plantain.

Village.

As we could only see a portion of the village at one view, it was difficult to estimate the number of houses, and from the inhabitants, whose notions of arithmetic are limited to the enumeration of their fingers and toes, I could get no information. From one crag I counted one hundred and fifty, the lower and most compact part of the town. There are probably as many more on the outskirts. All round, bamboos and jack trees are planted and carefully fenced; one of the most influential men has near his house a grove of beautiful palms surrounded by a loose stone wall.

Water-supplies.

The inhabitants are well supplied with water; there are several elevated springs, and the discharges from these are collected and carried to different parts of the villages in aqueducts or pipes of bamboos, from which a bright, pure stream continually flows. Notwithstanding these privileges, water is seldom used for ablutionary purposes. The Abors consider dirt an antidote to cold, and positively cherish it.

The Town-hall.

In a conspicuous part of the village is the Morang or town-hall. This is in the same style of architecture as the private houses, but it is 200 feet in length and has 16 or 17 fireplaces. The assemblage that met me there consisted of about 300 adult males, and an infinite number of small boys, who took up observing positions on the rafters.

The Council.

The head-men, elders or Gâms, congregated round the central fireplace. No one is permitted to arrogate the position of the chief, but here sat Bokpáng, a short, stout, jolly looking individual, who, from the influence he exercised generally in the assembly, especially when a call to order was necessary, and from his manner of opening the debate, I was inclined to consider as the chairman or president, and in charge of the foreign relations of the state. Then came Loitem, the Nestor of the republic, the first of their orators, the great repository of traditional lore, who expatiated with spirit and strong enthusiasm on the renown, virtue and valour of the Pádam race. Next came Julong, the war minister, a young man of stalwart frame, tall and well built, with a fine open countenance, the most trusty friend or dangerous foe of all the Membu notables. Then there was a factious demagogue called Jaluk, who appeared to be the leader of the opposition.

The notables meet daily in the Morang for the discussion of affairs of state, and are kept amply supplied with liquor all the time they are so employed at the public expense. The most important and the most trivial matters are there discussed. Apparently nothing is done without a consultation, and an order of the citizens in Morang assembled is issued daily regulating the day's work. The result is rapidly promulgated by the shrill voices of boys who run through the village giving out the order in a clear monotone like a street cry. I heard it thus proclaimed, that in honor of our arrival the next day was to be a holiday, and that the women and children might all go and see the queer-looking strangers.

Criminal Code.

I found that no presents were openly received by the Gâms or notables for themselves. Everything given on public grounds is lodged in the common treasury for the benefit of the whole body corporate. Belonging to the Morang are public pigs, poultry and other possessions to be used as occasion requires. Fines, forfeitures, and escheats are similarly appropriated. In regard to persons accused of crime, the system is just the reverse of that described as in force amongst the Chalikatas. The crime of an individual is treated as a public disgrace to be expiated by a public sacrifice. The culprit has eventually to bear the expense of this; it may therefore be regarded as a fine, but the process of realization is most singular. Suppose it to be decreed that a pig is to be sacrificed. The 'Raj,' that is the community, appropriate the first animal of the kind in good condition and private property that comes to hand. The owner is at liberty then to fix his own value upon it and recover it as best he can from the culprit. It may be said it would have been simpler to have proceeded in the first instance against the property of the offender; but when all are judges who will condescend to act as sheriff's officer? The system adopted provides an executive without any trouble to the Raj or expense to the estate.

There is no power vested in the community to take life or inflict corporal punishment on a free-born citizen, but slaves may be put to death, and I heard of one that had been so condemned by the Raj for having seduced a free-born girl.

The Morang is occupied every night by all the bachelors in the village, both freemen and slaves, and with them a certain proportion of the married men are nightly on duty, so as to constitute together a sufficient available force for any contingency of attack, fire or other public emergency.

I witnessed an instance that forcibly impressed me with the practical utility of this institution, and of the ready alacrity and good feeling and discipline of the body that constituted it.

A woman, a widow with two children, one an infant at the breast, the other a boy of three or four years old, had gone to the farm early in the morning, and on reaching it she tied the small child on the back of the boy, and set to work at her field. When she gave over work for the day and was preparing to return, the children were missing; she searched till evening without success, but was not much alarmed as she hoped they had gone home, but when at night she reached her home and found no children, then she made her cries heard through the village, and soon they reached the Morang.

There sat the village youth and men on duty round the blazing hearths carousing, but at this poor widow's sorrowing cry at once they rise and go forth prepared to pass the night in searching for the lost children. There was no discussion; no mandate was sent forth, no apathy was shown, no excuses were made. The widow's appeal was at once responded to by benevolent action. There was no delay except to prepare torches, and in a very few minutes a band of not less than 100 young men, armed and equipped, followed the woman to the scene of the disaster. They had not returned when we left the village in the morning, and I never heard the result of the expedition.

Losses of children in the manner described are said to be of frequent occurrence. They are most probably kidnapped by the Chalikatas, but this the Pádam will not admit. They assert that the spirits of the woods hide them, and they retaliate on the spirits by cutting down trees till they find them.

This causes a great commotion amongst the spirits: 'What's the row now?' says one; 'Oh,' replies another, 'the Pádam have lost a child.' 'Then whoever has got it give it up quick, or the rascals wont leave us a tree.' Then the child is found in the fork of a tree or some other out-of-the-way place.

Religion.

The religion of the Abors consists in a belief in these sylvan deities, to each of whom some particular department in the destiny of man is assigned. They have no medicine for the sick: for every disease there is a spirit, and a sacrifice to that spirit is the only treatment attempted. A mountain called Rigam is the favorite abode of the spirits, and is held in great awe. No one can return from its summit, consequently its mysteries are undisclosed.

They acknowledge and adore one supreme being as the great father of all and believe in a future state, the condition of which will in some measure depend on the life led here below; but on this question their ideas are undefined, and it is probable that some of them are derived from the Hindu. I have heard them speak of a judge of the dead; but as they gave his name as 'Jam,' they were no doubt thinking of the 'Yama' of Hindus.

They have no hereditary priesthood, but there are persons called Deodars who acquire the position of augurs or soothsayers from their superior knowledge of omens and how to observe them. The examination of the entrails of birds and of a pig's liver appears to be the most usual method of divination. On visiting Bomjir, a pig's liver was brought to me on a tray, and I was asked what I thought of it. I said it was good, healthy looking liver; they replied, 'But what does it reveal in regard to your intentions in visiting us?' I suggested they should find that out from my words and looks. They rejoined that the words and faces of men were ever fallacious, but that pig's liver never deceived them!

In regard to their sacrifices one trait is particularly worth noticing. In cases of sickness or death, when a mithun or a pig is offered no one is allowed to share the feast with the gods but the old and infirm, who, as poor and superannuated, may be regarded as on the parish, and who live in the Morang at the public expense.

They are said to hold as inviolate any engagement cemented by an interchange of meat as food; this is called sengmung. Each party to the engagement must give to the other some animal to be killed and eaten; it is not necessary that they should eat together, or that the feast be held at the same time. They presented me with a fine bull mithun, and I purchased and gave them a similar animal.*

* I was informed not long ago that, although since my visit to Membu we have had several brushes with the Abors, the confederacy of which the above is the head-quarters have remained perfectly friendly and loyal to their engagement with me.

G

The Deodar gave me the following legend of the origin of the race:—

Tradition of origin.

The human family are all descended from one common mother. She had two sons, the eldest was a bold hunter, the younger was a cunning craftsman; the latter was the mother's favorite. With him she migrated to the west, taking with her all the household utensils, arms, implements of agriculture and instruments of all sorts, so that the art of making most of them was lost in the land she deserted; but before quitting the old country she taught her first-born how to forge daos, to make musical instruments from the gourd, and she left him in possession of a great store of blue and white beads.* These beads and the simple arts known to him he transmitted to his posterity the Pádam, and from him they received the injunction to mark themselves on the forehead with a cross.

The western nations, including the English, are descended from the younger brother, and inherited from him and the continued instructions of the mother their knowledge of science and art.

Art; agriculture.

Absolutely the Pádam have no knowledge of arts, except what they thus account for. Their implements of husbandry are their long straight swords, or daos, crooked bamboos to scrape the earth, and pointed sticks to make holes, into which they dexterously shoot the seed. Nevertheless they have a wide area and great variety of cultivation and get good crops. Industry and the richness of the soil make up for all deficiencies, and seasons of scarcity are rare with them. They cultivate rice, cotton, tobacco, maize, ginger, red pepper, sugarcane, a great variety of esculent roots and pumpkins, and opium. Their cultivation is almost all in the plains, and they have gradually extended it to a distance of about seven miles from their village. Against unnecessarily breaking up new lands they have a wholesome prejudice; when the land they cultivate appears exhausted they revert to that which has been longest fallow. Under this system the whole space from their villages to the most distant point of their cultivation has been cleared and appropriated, and the forests beyond it are spared. The boundaries of each man's clearing are denoted by upright stones, and property in cultivated and fallow land is recognised.

Property in land.

The cultivation commences from the Shiku river, and along the banks of that stream there is strong palisading to keep the village cattle from trespassing. The importance of having at all times the means of crossing the river to their cultivation, has led to the construction over it of a suspension bridge of cane. The canes forming the main support are thrown across beams supported partly on triangles of strong timbers and partly on growing trees. These trees have stays to counteract their flexibility, and these and all the suspending canes are made fast to the stumps of other large trees, or to piers of loose stones. The roadway is also made of cane interlaced, supported by elliptical girders of the same material passing round the main suspenders. This bridge is carefully repaired every year, and I am informed that in about four years every part of it is renewed.

Physical appearance.

The Abors are a much taller race than the Mishmis, but clumsy-looking and sluggish; they have strongly marked Mongolian features, and are of rather a uniform olive complexion. They have very deep voices and speak with a peculiar sonorous cadence, never hurriedly. The dress

* The blue beads above referred to are very handsome. They are an exact imitation of turquoise, and vary in size from the dimensions of a pea to that of a large cherry. I believe they are made in China.

of the men consists primarily of a loin cloth made of the bark of the Udal* tree. It answers the double purpose of a carpet to sit upon and of a covering. It is tied round the loins, and hangs down behind in loose strips about fifteen inches long, like a white bushy tail. It serves also as a pillow by night. The garment thus described by Wilcox is seldom now seen in the plains, but is still worn by the Abors of the interior. When full dressed the modern Abor is an imposing figure. Colored coats without sleeves, of their own manufacture, or of the manufacture of their neighbours, the Chalikatas, are commonly worn. Some wear long Tibetan cloaks, and they weave a cloth from their own cotton with a long fleecy nap like that of a carpet, which they make into warm jackets. On state occasions they wear helmets of a very striking appearance. The foundation is a strong skull-cap of cane; it is adorned with pieces of bear skin, yak tails dyed red, boars' tusks, and, above all, the huge beak of the buceros.

Costume.

For arms they have cross-bows and common bows with arrows, the latter used with and without poison, very long spears, daggers, and long straight-cutting swords. By their own account it is on the latter weapon they chiefly rely in warfare, and they are fond of exhibiting their skill in using it.

Arms.

The hair of both males and females is close cropped; this is done by lifting it on the blade of a knife and chopping it with a stick all round. The practice of tattooing is resorted to by both sexes. The men all wear a cross on the forehead between the eyebrows. The women have a small cross in the hollow of the upper lip immediately under the nose, and on both sides of it above and below the mouth are stripes, generally, but not always, seven in number.

The dress of the females as ordinarily seen consists of two cloths, blue and red in broad stripes. One round the loins forms a petticoat just reaching to the knees; it is retained in its position by a girdle of cane-work: the other is folded round the bosom, but this is often dispensed with, and the exposure of the person above the waist is evidently considered no indelicacy. Their necks are profusely decorated with strings of beads reaching to the waist, and the lobes of the ears are, as usual with the hill races, enormously distended for decorative purposes. Round the ankles, so as to set off to the best advantage the fine swell of the bare leg, broad bands of very finely plaited cane-work are tightly laced, and some of the belles, most particular about their personal appearance, wear these anklets of a light blue tinge. But the most singular article of their attire remains to be described. All females with pretensions to youth wear suspended in front from a string round the loins a row of from three to a dozen shell-shaped embossed plates of bell-metal from about six to three inches in diameter, the largest in the middle, the others gradually diminishing in size as they approach the hips. These plates rattle and chink as they move, like prisoners' chains. Very young girls, except for warmth, wear nothing but these appendages, but the smallest of the sex is never seen without them, and even adult females are often seen with no other covering. At Bomjir I witnessed a dance in which they divested themselves of everything else, and behaved in a very indecorous manner.

Female costume.

Brass petticoats.

* Wilcox, Asiatic Researches, Vol. VII.

In feature and complexion the Abor women are a coarse type of the Chinese. They are not so ruddy nor so good looking as the Mishmis. Many of them are disfigured with goitre, and their antipathy to the use of water and their very unbecoming coiffure take greatly away from their personal appearance.

They are hard worked, but the whole burden of field labor is not thrown upon them, as is the custom amongst most of the hill tribes. Wives are treated by their husbands with a consideration that strikes one as singular in so rude a race; but I have seen other races as rude who in this respect are an example to more civilized people. It is because with these rude people the inclination of the persons most interested in the marriage is consulted, and polygamy is not practised; I do not say it is the rule, but it is certainly the prevailing practice of the Pádam to have only one wife. They spoke with contempt of those who had a plurality, and I was assured both by the Membu and Siluk Abors that the Pádam generally repudiated the custom, as leading to jars and dissensions. I was informed that in the Membu village there was only one individual with more than one wife.

Marriages.

Marriages are sometimes settled by the parents, but generally the young people arrange these affairs for themselves, and from all I could learn a feast is the only ceremony required to ratify and declare the happy event; but it is customary for a lover to show his inclinations whilst courting by presenting his sweetheart and her parents with such delicacies as field mice and squirrels. In a society where all, except slaves, are equal in rank, and where the productive industry of a man and his wife is sufficient to maintain them in all the necessaries and luxuries enjoyed by their neighbours, where moreover the community assist the young couple at starting by building a house for them, fathers and mothers have little occasion to "manœuvre" matches. It is a fact that amongst the Pádam they seldom interfere: and to barter their child's happiness for money would be regarded as an indelible disgrace.

The Abors, however, view with abhorrence the idea of their girls marrying out of their own clan, and I was gravely assured that when one of the daughters of Pádam so demeans herself, the sun and the moon refuse to shine, and there is such a strife in the elements that all labor is necessarily suspended, till by sacrifice and oblation the stain is washed away.

We are certain that the settlements of the Midhi and Mishmis extend right across the hills from Asam to Tibet, and that even those living nearest to the British territories are in habits of constant intercourse with the Tibetans. We can see that the Pádam have, directly or indirectly, trade with Tibet, as they wear coats, and possess pipes of metal, vessels, swords, and beads, of Tibetan or of Chinese manufacture: but for some reason they throw a veil of mystery over their intercourse, and always repudiating direct trade with Tibetans, tell you of the existence of barbarous tribes on the high snowy ranges behind them: and you meet with no one of the clan who will acknowledge to have passed this barrier of savages.

SECTION 5. (2)—THE MIRIS AND HILL MIRIS.

Proceeding still down the valley, after crossing the hill course of the Dirjmo, we come on tribes nearly allied to the Pádam or Abors who are known in Asam as the Parbatia or Hill Miris; but before we enter their domains it may be as well to explain who the Miris of the plains are.

Miris of the valley.

The Miris of the plains are off-shoots from the Abors and claimed by that people as runaway slaves, but there are various clans of them differing in external appearance, and some of these clans have been settled in Asam for ages. They, however, keep much to themselves, leading rather a nomadic life, living in houses on stilts built on the precarious banks of the Brahmaputra and its estuaries or affluents, and cultivating the alluvial flats of that river. With exception to the clan called Chutia Miris, the traditions of all of them take them back to the valley of the Dihong. It is probable they had advanced from the north, made settlements in the country now occupied by the Abors, and the latter people, of the same race but more powerful, following on their footsteps pushed them on into the plains. There are clans, the Saiengya and Aiengya, who crop their hair like the Abors, and having done so the young women attach to the cropped ends an ornament fringe of cowries and brass, which gives them the appearance of being wigged in a very fantastic manner. Other clans clothe themselves and dress their hair more after the fashion of the Asamese, but they keep their blood pure and have lost none of the physical characteristics of the tribe. They are of the yellow Mongolian type, tall, and powerfully framed, but with a slouching gait and sluggish habits. They have the deep-toned voice and slow method of speaking that I have noticed as characteristics of the Abors.

For a long period under the Asam Government, the Miris managed to keep to themselves the entire trade between Asam and the Abors; and as being thus the only medium of communication between the two peoples, they obtained this name Miri, which means mediator or go-between, and is the same word as '**miria**' or '**milia**' used with the same signification in Orissa. Perhaps the **meriah** applied to the sacrifice of the Khunds is a cognate word, the meriah being the messenger or mediator between man and the deity.

The Miris in the plains have generally abandoned the vague religious notions of their ancestors, and adopted ideas put into their heads by the Asamese Gosains or Brahminical priests, that each of them chose to adopt as their Guru or spiritual instructor: but all efforts on the part of the Hindus to wean them from their impure mode of living have utterly failed. They eat pig, fowl and beef, and drink spirits and beer, and have no caste notions about the preparation of food.

Dances, &c.

They keep the Asam feasts, and during the great Bihu festival groups of Miris are to be found amongst the gayest of the revellers. The Miri girls dance the somewhat sensual Bihu dance with great spirit, and they have a dance of their own which is quite free from this sensuality somewhat resembling the Naga movement. They have also a festival that few of the uninitiated ever hear of. At one season of the year the adult unmarried males and females of a village spend several days and nights together in one large building, and if couples manage thus to suit each other, they pair off and marry.

Houses.

The Miri houses are what are called in Asam **chang-garh**, *i. e.*, houses with raised floors, and space underneath for the pigs, poultry, &c. The houses are generally in a line on the banks of the river, and they have no gardens or enclosures. The cultivation is with them, as with their brethren in the hills, apart from the village, and their granaries are in their cultivated fields, often left quite unprotected. They trust to the isolated position for protection from alien thieves, and have perfect confidence in the honesty of their fellow villagers.

H

Hill Miris.

Returning to the hills we find, west of the Dirjmo and to the north of the Sisi and Damáji mauzas of the Luckimpur district, the Ghy-ghási Miris; the Sárák north of Bordoloni, and on both banks of the hill course of the Súbanshiri river. Then the Panibotia Miris, so called because in their journeys to the plains they travel part of the way in canoes on that river, and Tarbatia whose journey is wholly by land, whence Tár. These tribes having, under the Asam Government, obtained a sort of prescriptive right to levy black-mail on the Luckimpur villages skirting their hills, now receive annually from our Government an equivalent in the form of a money payment.

They tell a singular story in detailing the circumstances under which black-mail was formerly guaranteed to them by the Asam Government. They had plundered some Asamese villages, and that Government sent an army against them which was ignominiously defeated by the hill people and fled, leaving in the hands of the victors their camp equipage and magazine. The Hill Miris not knowing to what use to apply the muskets, matchlocks, guns, and powder, determined to make a grand bonfire of their spoils, and their astonishment and dread may be conceived when they found that the guns left loaded went off of themselves and killed several of their number, and when the grand explosion of the magazine took place which killed many more. They thought that a Raja whose weapons, unhandled, had the power of inflicting such injury on his enemies must be worth knowing, and they sent a deputation to him, offering to abstain in future from plundering if they were allowed certain privileges of collecting from the ryots. All they asked was readily accorded, and thus originated the black-mail.

Though in language and in many of their customs they resemble and are no doubt of common stock with the Abors, they differ from them greatly in form of government, and in many social observances and customs.

Policy.

They live in small communities under hereditary chiefs, and in some instances one family has obtained sufficient influence to be acknowledged as chief over clusters of communities. They have no Morang, or town-hall, in which the elders meet and consult during the day, nor do the youths, armed for the protection of the village, keep watch by night. They have no regulation for the safety of the commonwealth like the Abors, nor does each settlement consist of only one family as amongst the Tain Mishmis. The villages consist of ten or a dozen houses of as many families, built pretty closely together, in some position rather difficult of access, and it is left to the chief to look after its safety as best he can.

The Ghy-ghásis are a poor, meanly clad, badly fed, ill-looking clan of stunted growth compared with the Abors; their villages extend back as far as the eastern branch of the Súbanshiri.

Female costume.

The women of this clan, in lieu of the brass plates of the Abor lasses, wear a small petticoat made of filaments of cane woven together. It is about a foot in breadth, and fastened so tight round the loins that it restrains the free use of the thighs, and causes the women to move with a short mincing motion chiefly from the knee. The women are often seen with nothing on but this singular garment. They wear their hair long, but the appearance of this tribe is altogether unprepossessing, and I will pass to those on the opposite side of the Súbanshiri, with whom I am better acquainted. I believe I am the only officer that ever penetrated into their country. Wilcox made the attempt, but meeting with no encouragement from the chiefs, he returned from the first rapids of the Súbanshiri above the Asamese gold-washers' village of Patalipam. He describes the river as scarcely inferior to the Ganges at Allahabad, with a discharge in the month of November of 10,000 cubic feet per second. Its course through the plains is not interesting, as the banks are low, liable to inundation, and covered with jungle, but nothing can possibly exceed the loveliness of its hill course.

For eight or ten miles the river flows without a ripple in graceful sweeps round the bases of rocks that rise precipitously hundreds of feet from the clear mirror which reflects them, and blend into lofty forest-clad hills. Throughout this glen the average depth of water cannot be less than sixty feet. Above it the stream is broken by boulders into roaring rapids, presenting a wild contrast to its peaceful current through the glen.

The chief who befriended me in my excursion to the Hill Miri villages was Tema, the head of the Panibotia Miris. After a journey of three days and a half from Patalipam in canoes up the river, I met him and his people at the point called Siplumukh, and thence proceeded by land. Two long marches over a most difficult road, impracticable for any quadruped except a goat, and infeasible by a biped who had not the free use of his hands as well as his feet, brought us to the settlement. My baggage was nearly all carried on the heads of sturdy-limbed hill lasses who merrily bounded like roes from one slippery rock to another, laughing at my slow progress.

I found the villages situated on hills to the north of the great range seen from the Luckimpur station, which I had crossed. They were small, consisting each of not more than ten or a dozen houses two or three miles apart. Every village had its Gâm or chief, but my friend Tema was looked upon as head of the clan.

On the arrival of the first British officer ever seen in the hills, fowls were killed in every village by augurs with the view of ascertaining, from the appearance of the entrails, if the visit boded them good or ill. Fortunately the omens were all pronounced favorable, and the people vied with each other in treating me and my party with kindness and hospitality.

Chief's house.

A description of Tema's house will suffice for all, and show how they live. It is 70 feet long; the flooring is of split bamboos on a very substantial framework of timber raised several feet from the ground; the roof has gable ends, and is thatched with leaves; under the gable a cross sloping roof covers an open balcony, one at each end. The interior consists of one long apartment 60 feet by 16, from which a passage at one side, extending the entire length, is partitioned off in the large apartment down the centre; four fires burn on hearths of earth. On one side neatly ranged were the arms, pouches, marching equipments, and another portion of the hall was decorated with trophies of the chase; in the centre, between the fires, frames of bamboo suspended from the roof served as tables on which various domestic utensils were deposited.

In the passage partitioned off there was nothing but a row of conical baskets lined with plantain leaves, in which the grain was undergoing its process of fermentation for the production of their favorite beverage. The liquor slowly percolated into earthen vessels placed underneath, and was removed for use as they filled.

In the large apartment the whole family eat, drink, and sleep; Tema and his two wives at the upper end or first fire, his sons and daughters round the next, and servants and retainers round the third and fourth. Fearful of being pillaged by the Abors they do not venture to display much property in their houses. Their stores of grain are kept in houses apart from the village, and their valuables buried. The latter consist chiefly of large dishes and cooking vessels of metal, and of great collections of Tibetan metal bells called deogantas, which appear to be prized as holy things, and are sometimes used as money. Miris pretend that they cannot now obtain these bells, and that those they possess are heirlooms. They are valued at from four annas to twelve rupees each, according to shape, size and ornaments. Those with inscriptions inside and out are most highly prized. Those without inscriptions are little valued, and as these inscriptions are nothing more than repetitions of the Shibboleth, "Om Máni pedmi Om" of the Tibetans, it is easy to see that the Miris must have been inspired by that people to treat them with such veneration. The superstition regarding them should be compared with the veneration of the Garos for the vessels called Diokoras; also, it is believed, of Tibetan manufacture.

Costume.

The costume of the ladies of this clan is elaborate and peculiar. A short petticoat extending from the loins to the knees is secured to a broad belt of leather, which is ornamented with brass bosses. Outside this they wear the singular crinoline of cane-work, which I have described as often the sole garment of the neighbouring clan. The upper garment consists of a band of plaited cane-work girding the body close under the arms, and from this in front a fragment of cloth depends and covers the breasts. This is their travelling and working dress, but at other times they wrap themselves in a large cloth of *éri* silk of Asamese manufacture, doubled over the shoulders and pinned in front like a shawl.

They have bracelets of silver or copper, and anklets of finely plaited cane or bamboo. Their hair is adjusted with neatness, parted in the centre and hanging down their backs in two carefully plaited tails. In their ears they wear most fantastic ornaments of silver, which it would be difficult to describe. A simple spiral screw of this metal, winding snake-like round the extended lobe of the ear, is not uncommon amongst unmarried girls, but this is only an adjunct of the complicated ear ornaments worn by married ladies. They wear round their necks an enormous quantity of large turquoise-like beads made apparently of fine porcelain, and beads of agate, cornelian, and onyx, as well as ordinary glass beads of all colors.

Physical aspect.

The men of this clan have fine muscular figures, many of them tall, at least over five feet eight inches, and in feature generally resembling the Abor, but they have admitted Asamese into their fraternity, and the expression of some is softened by this admixture of race. They gather the hair to the front, where it protrudes out from the forehead in a large knob secured by a bodkin. Round the head a band of small brass or copper knobs linked together is tightly bound. Chiefs wear ornaments in their ears of silver, shaped like a wine-glass, and quite as large. A cap of cane or bamboo-work with a peak behind is worn when travelling, and over this a piece cut out of a tiger or leopard skin, including the tail, which has a droll appearance, hanging down the backs. Their nether garment is a scarf between their legs fastened to a girdle of cane-work, and their upper robe, a cloth wrapped round the body and pinned so as to resemble the Abors' sleeveless coat. As a cloak and covering for their knapsack, they wear over the shoulders a half cape, made of the black hairy fibres of a palm-tree, which at a distance looks like a bear skin. Their arms are the bow and arrow and long straight sword, and the arrows are generally poisoned. They also make shafts from a bamboo, which is said to be poisonous without any addition to render it so.

Occupation.

The time of the men is chiefly occupied in journeys to the plains with loads of (munjista) munjit or other produce, or in hunting. They have various methods for entrapping animals of all kinds, from an elephant to a mouse, and all is fish that comes to their net. The flesh of a tiger is prized as food for men; it gives them strength and courage. It is not suited for women; it would make them too strong-minded.

Marriages.

Polygamy is practised to a great extent by the chiefs; there is no limit, but his means of purchase, to the number of wives a man may possess, and (as amongst the Mishmis) when he dies, his son or heir will become the husband of all the women, excepting his mother. As amongst the Hos of Singbhum, a woman is valued more on account of her family than her good looks, but the chiefs' daughters are generally the belles of the clan, and there is great competition for a pretty girl. The belle of Tema's village, when I was there, was a niece of his, named Yáday, and I was assured that several chiefs had made proposals for her. The price put on this beauty amounted to two or three mithuns, twenty or thirty pigs, and a quantity of fowls.

Occasional polyandry.

With the poorer classes a man has to work hard to earn the means of buying a wife, and from this results in a few instances the practice of polyandry. I never heard of any cases of this practice amongst Tema's tribe; but occasional instances of it are met in the tribes to the east and west of them. Two brothers will unite, and from the proceeds of their joint labor buy a wife between them. When the stipulated price is paid, the parents of the bride invite the suitor and his friends to a feast, and at the close of it he carries off his bride, who is accompanied by all her relations and friends, and a return feast is given by the bridegroom or his father.

The Miri women make faithful and obedient wives. I have often heard them express their astonishment at the unbridled license of an Asamese woman's tongue, even in addressing her husband. They are trained never to complain or give an angry answer, and cheerfully do they appear to bear the hard burden imposed on them, which includes nearly the whole of the field labor, and an equal share of the carrying work of their journeys to the plains. They seldom possess any implement solely adapted for cultivation, have never taken to the plough, or even to a hoe. They use their long straight daos, or swords, to clear, cut, and dig with.

Cultivation.

Each village has a certain extent of ground to which their cultivation is limited, but not more than one-fifth of this is under cultivation each season. They cultivate each patch two successive years, then suffer it to lie fallow for four or five, taking up again the ground that has been longest fallow in lieu. They have, like the Abors, a superstition which deters them from breaking up fresh ground so long as their available fallow is sufficient,—a dread of offending the spirits of woods by unnecessarily cutting down trees. Their crops are the *aoos* rice, millets, Indian corn, yams, sweet potatoes, tobacco, and red pepper; but they barely rear sufficient for their own consumption, and would often be very hard pressed for food, if it were not for the large stock of dried meat they take care to have always on hand.

Not less than two-thirds of the population spend several months of the year in the plains, and their main occupation whilst there is to procure meat and fish, dry it, and carry it back to their hills. A Miri encampment, whilst this process is going on, may be sniffed from afar, and the unpleasant odour clings most disagreeably to the people, rendering it desirable to keep to the windward of all you meet.

Cattle.

The only cattle of the ox kind kept by the Hill Miri are the mithun, and they are only useful as food, as their masters never touch milk. They have pigs and poultry in plenty, and a few goats.

Arts.

I suppose there are no people on the face of the earth more ignorant of arts and manufactures than the tribe I am treating of. They are decently clad, because they can exchange the wild produce of their hills for clothes, and they purchase cloths with the money received from Government as black mail commutation; but they cannot make for themselves any article of clothing, unless the cane bands and bamboo crinolines can be so called. The most distant tribes, their cognates, manufacture coarse cotton cloths; but though the Miris are in constant communication with them as well as with the people of the plains, they have not the remotest idea of weaving. They cannot journey two or three days from their village without having to cross a considerable river. If it be not fordable, a rough raft of káku bamboos (*Bambusa gigantea*) is hastily constructed, butthough constantly requiring them and annually using them in their journeys to the plains, they have never yet attempted to construct a canoe. This is the more strange as the Abors of the Dihong river make them for use and for sale.

Religion.

The religious observances of the Miris are confined to the slaughter of animals in the name of the sylvan spirits, and vaticination by the examination of the entrails of birds when the deities have been invoked after such sacrifices. They profess a belief in a future state, and have an indefinite idea of a God who presides in the region of departed souls; but, as they call this god Jam Raja, I believe it to be the Hindu Yama. They, however, bury their dead as if they were sending them on a long journey, fully clothed and equipped with arms, travelling-pouch and caps, in a deep grave surrounded by strong timbers to prevent the earth from pressing on them; nor do they omit to supply the departed with food for his journey, cooking utensils, and ornaments, according to the position he enjoyed in life, in order that Jam Raja may know whom he has to deal with. They attach great importance to their dead being thus disposed of and buried near the graves of their ancestors. If a man of rank and influence die in the plains, his body is immediately conveyed to the hills to be so interred, should the disease of which he died not be deemed contagious.

Disposal of the dead.

Traditions.

Of migrations or their own origin the Hill Miri can only say that they were made for the hills and appointed to dwell there, and that they were originally much further north, but discovered Asam by following the flights of birds, and found it to their advantage to settle on its borders.

Tribes to their north.

There can be no doubt that the Hill Miris do their utmost to deter the people of the wild clans to their north from visiting the plains, but the northmen occasionally creep down bearing heavy loads of munjista,*

* The Indian Madder. They chiefly depend on this export to provide them the means of purchasing all they import from the plains.

and, beyond looking more savage and unkempt, they are undistinguishable from the poorer class of Miris. They are described, however, as living in detached houses, as, whenever they have attempted to form into a society, fierce feuds and summary vengeance, or the dread of it, soon break up the community. Thrown on their own resources, they have acquired the art of forging their own daos, which the Miris know not, and their women weave coarse narrow cloths.

Anka Miris.

To the north-west of the Hill Miri country we hear of a tribe called 'Anka Miris' by the Asamese, who never visit the plains, but who, from the accounts we have received of them, must be very superior to the tribes of this family that we are acquainted with, resembling the Padam in their polity and customs. Surrounded by lofty hills, the country which they inhabit is an extensive valley, represented as being quite level and watered by a branch, or perhaps the principal stream, of the Sundri river, and richly cultivated.

Their position.

They have fifteen large villages in this valley, and broad sheets of cultivation. They irrigate the land from the river, and it gives them in return rich corps, chiefly of rice. The women wear blue or black petticoats and white cotton jackets, all of their own making. Their faces are tattooed, whence the name 'Anka', given to them by the Asamese. They call themselves 'Tenae.'

Costume.

The males have an article of dress made of cane hanging down behind in a bushy tail, apparently like the under-garment worn by the Padam, made of the bark of the Udal tree. There are other points in which, differing from the Hill Miris, they resemble the Abors of the Dihong. The Miris, however extensive the family and the number of married couples it includes, all occupy one house. The young men of the Tenae tribes, when they marry, have to leave their father's house and set up for themselves.

Mode of war.

The Tenae are peaceably disposed, but they occasionally have to take up arms to punish marauders, and they are said to do the business at once effectually and honourably. Whilst the Abors and the Miris confine their warfare to nocturnal and secret attacks, and if successful in effecting a surprise, indiscriminately massacre men, women, and children, the Tenae declare hostilities, march openly to attack their enemy, and make war only on men, inflicting no injury whatever on non-combatants. If this be true, the Tenae may claim a hearing as the most humane of belligerents at the next International Congress.

SECTION 5. (3)—THE DOPHLAS.

We next come to the country of the Dophlas, of which we know very little, but the people so called are so nearly allied to the Hill Miris we have been describing, that it will not be necessary to give a very detailed notice of them. I am ignorant of the signification of the name 'Dophla',* but Robinson tells us it is not recognised by the people to whom it is applied except in their intercourse with the inhabitants of the plains. 'Bangni', the term in their own language to signify a man, is the only designation they give themselves.

Two hundred and thirty-eight Gâms of this clan are in receipt of compensation for black mail from Government, dividing amongst them a sum of Rs. 2,543.

* Journal Asiatic Society, Bengal, No. II, for 1851.

The number of Gâms does not necessarily indicate the number of villages. The Dophlas affect an oligarchical form of Government, and acknowledge the authority of from two or three to as many as thirty or forty chiefs in each clan. Their villages are larger than those of the Hill Miris. They are richer in flocks and herds, but they are inferior physically, being I think the shortest in stature of this division of the hill tribes.

Physiognomy.

They have normally the same Mongolian type of physiognomy, but from their intercourse with the people of the plains and the number of Asamese slaves, which they have by fair means or foul acquired, it is much modified and softened, and I have sometimes seen Dophla girls with pleasing and regular features. Their complexion varies much from olive with a ruddy tinge to dark brown.

Religion.

I never heard of Dophla priests, but Robinson says they have priests who pretend to a knowledge of divination, and by inspection of chickens' entrails and eggs, declare the nature of the sacrifice that is to be offered by the sufferer and the spirit to whom it is to be offered. The office, however, is not hereditary, and is taken up and laid aside at pleasure, so it resolves itself into this, that every man can, when occasion requires it, become a priest. Their religion consists of invocations to the spirits for protection of themselves, their cattle, and their crops, and sacrifice and thank-offerings of hogs and fowls. They acknowledge, but do not worship, one Supreme Being which, I conceive, means that they have been told of such a being, but know nothing about him.

Polyandry.

Marriages and marital rights are the same with Dophlas as with the Hill Miris. Those who can afford it are polygamists, but polyandry is far more common amongst the Dophlas than amongst the eastern tribes

A very pretty Dophla girl once came into the station of Luckimpur, threw herself at my feet and in most poetical language asked me to give her protection. She was the daughter of a chief and was sought in marriage and promised to a peer of her father who had many other wives. She would not submit to be one of many, and besides she loved and she eloped with her beloved. This was interesting and romantic. She was at the time in a very coarse travelling dress, but assured of protection she took fresh apparel and ornaments from her basket and proceeded to array herself, and very pretty she looked as she combed and plaited her long hair and completed her toilette. In the meantime I had sent for 'the beloved' who had kept in in the background, and alas! how the romance was dispelled when a *dual* appeared! She had eloped with two young men!!

Costume.

The costume of the Dophlas is very similar to that of the Hill Miris last described, except that I do not think the Dophla women wear the crinoline of cane work.

I have no particulars as to their mode of burial, but it is probably the same as that of the Hill Miris.

Extent of country.

The Dophla country extends from the hill course of the Sundri river to the Bhoroli river, comprising the hills to the north of Chedwar in the Luckimpur and of Naodwar in the Tezpur District. They are in communication with the Tibetans as they possess many articles of Tibetan or Chinese manufacture, but like the Dihong Abors and Hill Miris, they tell wild stories of the savages between them and Tibet. It is said of these savages that they go absolutely naked, and have, or assert that they have, an abhorrence of the *smell* of clothes.

Arts.

The Dophlas are a trifle more ingenious than the Hill Miris. The women spin and weave and are spared much of the labour of the fields that the Miri women are subjected to; but they are still very backward in the commonest arts. I do not think they have any pottery; and they import from Tibet or Asam nearly all their weapons and implements.

SECTION 5. (4)—THE AKAS, OR HRUSSO.

The Akas or Arkas are the only occupants of the remaining segment of the hill-country lying between the Dophla territory and Butan.* They are divided into two clans—the Hazarikowas, 'Eaters of a thousand hearths,' and the 'Kupa-chor,' 'the thieves that lurk in the cotton fields.' These are all Asamese nicknames. We are informed by the Revd. C. H. Heselmeyer that they call themselves Hrusso.†

The direct road to their settlement is reported to be exceedingly difficult, up water-courses including the bed of the Bhoroli river which divides the Aka from the Dophla country, or clambering with the aid of cane ropes the almost perpendicular faces of rocks; but there is a more circuitous, but easier, approach through a part of the Butan territory by which the journey may be made in six days.

The Migi.

To the north of the Akas are the Migi with whom the Akas intermarry. So they may be regarded as kindred clans. The former are the more powerful, numbering from three to four hundred households, but they rarely visit the plains unless it be to support the Akas in mischief. The trade of these tribes with Asam is thus monopolized by the Akas, who have no wish to forego the advantages that this gives them.

The Akas only number about 230 families, but they were nevertheless for many years the terror of the inhabitants of Chardwar, in the district of Durrung, and were notorious as the most daring marauders of the frontier.

Relations to the Government.

The Hazarikowas had obtained fromthe Asam Government a right to levy black mail which they rigidly enforced. Hence probably their name of the 'Eaters of a thousand hearths.' The Kupa-chors exercised the right without having so obtained it, and under a chief, called the Tági Rája, insatiably plundered the people that it pleased them to prey upon; but in 1829, this formidable free-booter was captured, and for four years kept close in the Gowhatty jail. Whilst there he attached himself to a Hindu spiritual guide, who perhaps had something to say to his obtaining his freedom, as the Guru offered to be surety for the good behaviour of his proselyte, and in 1832 the Governor General's Agent released him; but when he once more set foot on his native earth, he forgot the Guru, and his first action was to put to death all that had been in any way concerned in his capture. He then attacked and cut up a British outpost established at the head of the pass leading to his country, massacring men, women, and children; and for seven years after this, though vigorously hunted, he not only evaded capture, but continued to make

* Memorandum on the North-Eastern Frontier Tribes, by A. Mackenzie, Esq., C. S., 1869.

† Journal, Asiatic Society, Bengal, Vol. XXXVII, page 194.

K

raids on the plains. At length weary of this life, he with all his subordinate chiefs surrendered, and on their taking a solemn oath to maintain the peace on their frontier in future they were amnestied. Small pensions were granted to them, amounting in the aggregate to Rs. 360 per annum, and they have since kept inviolate their engagements. In administering the oath, the chiefs were made to kill a fowl, to take in their hands a tiger, and then a bear, skin and finally some elephant's dung.

The Tági Rája after his return from his first forced visit to Asam, became somewhat reformed, and introduced his people to the worship of Hari. Mr. Heselmeyer thus describes the previous religious notions of the Akas:—

Religion.

"The Aka though uncivilized is not devoid of religious ideas; he has no written shastras or religious books of any kind it is true, but the Aka fears the high mountains which tower aloft over his dwelling and form the snow-clad sides, off which leaps the thundering avalanche, he fears the roaring torrents of the deep glen which interposes between him and his friends beyond, and he fears the dark and dense jungle in which his cattle lose their way."

"These dark and threatening powers of nature he invests with supernatural attributes. They are his gods, and he names them, **Fúxo** the god of jungle and water, **Firan** and **Siman** the gods of war, and **Satu** the god of house and field."

The Akas have a priest, called **Deori**, for every hamlet, who performs daily worship at the shrines of these gods, small huts in which are images, their representatives. The **Deoris** also attend at marriages to tie the nuptial knot. This, the only ceremony of marriage, was probably introduced from the plains by the reformed Tági.

Offerings to the gods are made at the different cultivating seasons, and also in token of gratitude when children are born. If a Hrusso falls sick, fowls or other animals are offered to **Fúxo**, and the patient is mesmerised.

Houses.

The houses of the Akas are like those of the Hill Miris, but more carefully and substantially built. The flooring is of well smoothed and close fitting planks. All the household utensils are of metal. Large copper vases for water vessels are obtained from Tibet or Butan, and brass pots and brass plates for cooking in and eating off, obtained from Asam.

They eat the flesh of mithuns and common cows, and have large herds, but they do not touch the milk. They breed pigs and rear fowls and pigeons in great numbers, but ducks and geese are forbidden to them by their gods. Their new god **Hari** has not been very severe on them. He only objects to and curbs their predilection for the flesh of dogs and other animals not ordinarily eaten by civilized beings.

The burial arrangements are the same as those of the Hill Miris.

SECTION 6.—THE NAGAS OF UPPER ASAM.

Having now reached the Butan boundary, let us cross the valley of the Brahmaputra and glance at the tribes occupying positions *vis-à-vis* to the Abor-Miri-Dophla-people in the opposite hills.

The learned leave us to take our choice as to whether the term **Naga**, the name applied by the Hindus to the inhabitants of the hills we are about to explore, is from the Sanskrit root, meaning 'naked,' or the Sanscrit '**nag**,' snake. Whichever derivation we take, it must be admitted that the word is aptly applied, as the Nagas love to decorate, rather than to clothe, their persons, and are decidely snake-like in their habits.

Extent of country.

We ascend the valley again and go back to the Singphos on the Bori Dihing river and valley of the Kyendwen, where the Nagas appear so much mixed up with the Singphos that the Burmese have the same name for both—'Kakhyens*.' In the basin of the Brahmaputra they are found only on the left bank of the Bori Dihing river, and the people called Nagas extend from that river to the Kopili of the Nowgong District and to the great southern bend of the Barak river and the eastern frontier of Tipperah, between the 83rd and 97th degrees of east longitude; but we cannot, simply from their having this common appellation, predicate that all the tribes in that great area are one people. There seems to be a very broad distinction between the Nagas to the east, and the Nagas to the west, of the Dhunsiri river. From the Dihing to that river the dialects spoken, though greatly differing, have indubitable indication of a common origin, but there appears to be no such obvious affinity between those dialects and the language of the Angami bordering on North Kachar, and there appears to be likewise very wide divergence in their polity, religion, and customs.

Villages.

The Nagas east of the Doyang river† are divided into great clans under hereditary chiefs, who appear to exercise great influence over their people. They live in large villages, some of not less than 300 houses. The villages occupy commanding and secure positions on the peaks or ridges of hills, the spurs or approaches to which are fortified, and the steep places made as inaccessible as possible.

Houses.

The houses of the chiefs are of great size; that of the Sangnoi Chief was found to be 250 to 300 feet in length, a well constructed building occupying the centre and highest position in the village as the manor house. The houses of the common people are very much smaller, but still considerable and substantial buildings. I find no written description of any of these houses, and so many years have elapsed since I saw one, that I cannot altogether trust to my memory.

In front of the Chief's house, as well as inside it, are numerous trophies of the chase and memorials of feasts, and in a separate house, dedicated to the collection, memorials of ferocity and vengeance,—human skulls arranged in shelves like books, the records of recent achievements, and baskets full of fragments of skulls, the memorials of the bloody deeds of their forefathers.

On our assuming the government of Upper Asam, attention was soon directed to the cold blooded murders committed by the Nagas on British subjects, and several expeditions to their hills were undertaken with the view of putting a stop to the practice. We thus became acquainted with various tribes of Abor Nagas‡ as the Mithun, Tablong, Changnoi, Mulong, and Joboka. The Namsangyas, Bordwarias and Paidwarias, Soto, and others, had been previously in habits of peaceful intercourse with the people of the plains.

Tattooing.

It was the custom of these clans to allow matrimony to those only who made themselves as hideous as possible by having their faces elaborately tattooed. The process of disfiguration is carried to such a length, that it gives them an unnatural darkness of complexion and that fearful look which results when a white man blackens his face.

* On the authority of Mr. Robinson in his book on "Assam," but I am not sure of it.
† The eastern affluent of the Dhunsiri (Long. 94° E., Lat. 26° N.)
‡ Abor, in Asamese, means 'independent'.

To this rite of disfiguration they are not admitted till they have taken a human scalp or a skull, or shared in some expedition in which scalps or skulls were taken. It is by no means essential that the skulls or scalps should be trophies of honorable warfare, or that they should even be taken from the bodies of declared enemies. A skull may be acquired by the blackest treachery, but so long as the victim was not a member of the clan, it is accepted as a chivalrous offering of a true knight to his lady.

The various tribes were gradually induced to enter into engagements to give up the horrible custom; but how, in refraining from it, they satisfied the cravings of the young women for this singular marriage present I know not.

Communication and Cultivation.

The communications between friendly villages in the interior of the Naga Hills are admirably kept up. The paths are of course steep and difficult, but considerable engineering skill is sometimes shown in zig-zagging and bridging them. Much of the cultivation in the villages is of a permanent character, terraced and irrigated, but the glorious forests are very wantonly destroyed for the dry crops. They appear to have no superstitious dread of the sylvan deities like the Abors to restrain them. The trees are not cut down, but they are tortured by the ringing process till they are leafless and dry, then set fire to, and the cleared ground, scraped and sown, yields sufficient crops for a year or two.

Burials.

The approaches to the village are often carefully planted with mangoe and jack trees and bamboos, and under the shade of these groves are miniature houses which contain or cover the bones of their dead. At least it was the custom of the Nagas of the interior between the Deko and Dihing rivers, thus finally to dispose of them.

The bodies are first placed in wooden coffins like boats, and exposed suspended to trees outside the village till complely desiccated; then the obsequies take place. If the deceased was a person of consideration, two buffaloes, several pigs, and a great number of fowls are killed. The friends from all the neighbouring villages, equipped in their war dress, arrive, and bearing gongs and drums proceed to the place where the remains are laid. Each man carries a shield, a spear, and a dao or battle axe.

They then sing and dance, the burden of the song is a defiance of the demon of death that has taken their friend; they address him as if he were an enemy who, in their own fashion, had treacherously made away with their clansman, the chorus brandishing their weapons and repeating yes! yes! at the end of each denunciation. Music, dancing, and feasting, are continued all night and all next day. Then a large company of young women come and completely cover the remains with leaves and flowers, after which they are disposed of according to the custom of the tribe.

The above is taken from a description by an American Missionary of a funeral he witnessed in Namsang*, or some other of the eastern border villages: and at the close of the ceremony the bones were burnt. In the more remote villages the bones are preserved in the little houses I have alluded to above, or buried.

Religion.

I have no knowledge of the religious ceremonies of the Nagas east of the Dhunsiri. They have no temples and no priests, and I never heard of any form of worship amongst them, but I do not doubt that they sacrifice and observe omens like other tribes.

* See Robinson's Assam, quoting Baptist Missionary Magazine.

According to Robinson they have 'confused and faint ideas' of a divine power, which I understand to mean none at all, and they believe in a future state which, however, they consider must be just such an existence as the present one, showing great want of imagination on their part.

Marriages.

Marriages are contracted comparatively late in life. This was the necessary consequence of the condition that it must not take place till the candidate for a bride could present her with a gory token of his love; but there is also a price on the young lady, and the youth unable to pay often serves like Jacob for his wife, and at the end of his servitude is in like manner provided and set up by his father-in-law. The Nagas confine themselves to one wife, who has to work hard, but is otherwise well treated. They participate with their husbands in all festivities and social amusements.

War dance.

The Naga war dances commence with a review or sham fight. I witnessed one at Sangnoi, in which vast numbers were engaged. The warriors are armed with a spear used as a javelin, a battle axe or dao, and a shield of buffaloe hide or of bamboo work covered with tiger or other skin, large enough to cover the whole person.

They advance in extended order, making admirable light infantry practice, for nothing can be seen but the black shields creeping along the ground. They are thus impervious to arrows, but their cover is no protection against a bullet. When sufficiently near to their imaginary enemy, they spring up and fling the spear; this is supposed to take effect; a tuft of grass represents the head of the dead foe; they seize it with the left hand, cut it out with the battle axe, and retreat with the clod hanging by the grass over their shoulder as the skull or scalp. A sort of triumphant song and dance in which the women join follows this.

Costume.

Many of the Naga chiefs, as the Namsangya Raja or Kúmbo, dress respectably as Hindus when they visit the plains, like highlanders putting on the trews, but at home they wear the national dress of a Naga chief or warrior, which is very fantastic but very picturesque.

They wear singular coronals made of pieces cut out of large shells, and on the crown of the head a little periwinkle-shaped basket-work cap, black with a scarlet border with peacocks' feathers and goats' hair dyed scarlet. Necklaces, bracelets, armlets of beads, shells, brass, and of cane-work, are worn in profusion, but no drapery to speak of. The girdle is of polished plates of brass with a kind of double stomacher above and below. A very small apron of black cloth decorated with small shells is seen below this in most of the tribes, but I have seen tribes who wore nothing of the kind. The legs are also ornamented with bands of cane colored red. The arms are a gleaming pole-axe with a short black handle, decorated with a tuft of red goats' hair; a broad headed barbed spear, the shaft of which is covered with colored hair like a brush, and a shield of buffaloe hide from four to five feet long.

The women's costume is simpler, consisting of necklaces and an apron, or sometimes *without the apron.*

The great chiefs have chairs or rather stools of state on which they and their sons sit; the ruler's stool being the highest, that of the heir apparent a step lower, and the other members of the family lower still. On one occasion we had been for some time waiting for the attendance in camp of the Chief of Sangnoi, and the officers had left the camp

I.

to view some part of the adjoining country. On our return, we found within the beat of our sentries, a scaffolding of bamboos twenty or thirty feet high, on the top of which was seated the Sangnoi Chief's son prepared to receive our homage! He was made to descend very rapidly and accommodated with a stool.

Guard houses.

In all these Naga villages of the interior there is, at each of the fortified entrances, a large building well raised as a look-out or watch-house in which a band of young men keep guard at night. They have huge drums composed of trees hollowed out, which are sounded to give the alarm, and they have also fire signals.

Physical traits.

The young chiefs are sometimes fine looking men, and it is not an uncommon occurrence to find the chief himself a very portly personage; but the physique of the Nagas generally is very inferior to that of the northern tribes. They are smaller boned and have much less muscular development, and are of darker complexion.

Their faces are very lozenge-shaped, features flat and eyes small. They have amongst them many Asamese who have taken to the Naga costume. They are at once recognizable by the difference of feature: nothing can make them look like Nagas. Of the Naga females my recollections are, they are short, ugly, and waistless; too hard worked perhaps to be beautiful.

SECTION 7.—THE LOWER NAGA GROUP: (1)—THE NAGAS WEST OF THE DOYANG RIVER.

Of the Naga tribes beween the Doyang and Kopili Rivers, we have a comprehensive account in Major Steward's very interesting Notes on Kachar, published in the *Journal Asiatic Society, Bengal*, No. VII, for 1855. It appears from it that their polity is very different from that of the Naga tribes East of the Doyang. West of that river they acknowledge no chiefs. They appoint, as spokesman of the village, some elder who has the reputation of superior wisdom, or, perhaps, more frequently, the influence of wealth, but they give him no real power, and are not bound by anything he says. The office is not hereditary, nor always held for life. A council of elders sometimes sits to decide disputes, but no one is bound to attend to their award. Disputes between people of the same clan become feuds and lead to intestine wars, but the very great misery that this entails on the community acts as a deterrent. Passions are repressed by fear of the consequences of giving them vent, and order is thus generally maintained from the very absence of any rule or legitimate power to enforce it. It is, however, found necessary to give the fighting propensities of the people full vent once or twice in the year. A meeting is appointed at a convenient time and place, and a general *melée* takes place, every one fighting but using no weapons, except those with which nature has provided him.

Government.

Gods; sacrifices.

These Nagas sacrifice to several spirits to whom different attributes are ascribed, but these are creatures, and they do not profess to have any knowledge of a Creator. They appear in their polity and psychology very much to resemble the Chúlikata Mishmis, but they have names for the gods or spirits they adore. The first is 'Semes,' the god of riches, to whom large animals, buffaloes, mithuns, and cows, are offered, and 'Kuchimpai,' the god of harvests, who has to put up with goats, fowls, and eggs.

Among the malignant deities 'Rapiaba' is first. He is appeased by sacrifices of dogs and pigs. His assistant is the spirit 'Kangniba,' very fierce but blind, and as he cannot distinguish between costly and trifling offerings, the poorest things are given to him.

When omens have to be consulted in behalf of the community, the village is placed in a condition of *tabu*, called Genna. No one is permitted to enter or to leave it, and all labor is suspended for two days. If the Genna is established in consequence of the villagers being about to cultivate new ground, all the fires in the village are extinguished, and fresh fire for the purpose having been obtained by the friction of sticks, a buffaloe is roasted, and after the offering and feast, they proceed with torches ignited from the fresh fire to burn the felled jungle*.

Houses.

The houses are built with one of the gables elevated, whilst the other, that to the rear, slants down almost to the earth. The floors are not raised on platforms. The houses contain two rooms, one reserved as a sleeping apartment, the other appropriated to pigs, fowls, and general purposes. Each family has a separate house, but the bachelors have a house to themselves, where are hung up the trophies of the chase and the implements of war, and which forms at the same time the Caravanserai or inn.

Dances.

These Nagas are fond of dancing. The men have a war dance, in which, as previously described, a representation of a battle is enacted, a dance in which the men and women unite, and one in which the women dance alone; the latter is the most lively.

Ornaments and Dress.

They are very fond of ornaments: one peculiar to this tribe is a coil of brass wire twisted round the arm above the elbow. They greatly affect cylindrical beads of a yellowish, almost greenish looking opaque substance, but few are rich enough to have a complete necklace of these valuable jewels: as clothes, a fragment of cloth is all that is worn by the males; the women are covered from the navel to the knees. The married women wear their hair long and plaited behind. The unmarried cut the front hair square across the forehead, and wear it brushed down nearly to the eyebrows. This is also the custom of the Manipuri virgins.

Marriages.

The marriages are arranged by payment to the parents of the bride of her estimated value in cows, pigs, fowls, or drink. A feast is given, and those who are invited to it help to build a house for the young couple. The maidens are prized for their physical strength more than for their beauty or family. The women have to work incessantly, whilst the men bask in the sun.

Burial.

These Nagas bury their dead close to their houses in a coffin formed of the hollow of a tree. A large stone marks the spot, and the antiquity of the village may be estimated by the number and appearance of the cenotaphs found in them. They evince great tenacity to their village sites, and Major Steward attributes this mainly to their reverence for the dead.

Food, &c.

In regard to food they are truly omnivorous—frogs, lizards, snakes, rats, dogs monkeys, cats, &c., are all delicacies, and an animal that has died a natural death is as acceptable to them as the best butcher's meat They drink daily quantities of rice beer, which is made of such consistency that it serves them for breakfast. Their use of tobacco is unique. They collect

* Compare this with the Mishmi custom, page 15.

the tobacco oil that is precipitated in the bowl of the pipe, and drink it mixed with water.

The Angami or Kachu Nagas.

The Angami and Kachu Nagas occupying the tract of land immediately to the east of northern Kachar are computed at about 125,000 individuals. The several clans are frequently at war with each other, and it is noticeable that in these intestine wars the women of the contending parties visit each other at their different villages without fear of molestation. But when at war with other tribes, their attacks are treacherous, and they spare neither sex nor age.

Weapons

The Angamis have of late years taken to fire-arms, and have succeeded in supplying themselves with a considerable number. Their national weapons are the spear and the dao. They use *panjies* to protect their villages and the positions they take up and to cover their retreat, and they carry shield five or six feet in length, made of mat work covered with tiger or bear skins, and decorated at the sides and top with dyed goats' hair and feathers.

The other Nagas described by Major Steward are the Arúng tribe, numbering about 7,500 souls.

On the whole the Nagas to the *west* of the Doyang appear to have affinity with the Manipuri or the Cathay Shans; and the Kukis and the Nagas to the *east* of the same river are of distinct race allied to the Singpho and other pagan tribes further east.

If there be any virtue in philological similitude, the comparatively refined Manipuri and the dog-eating, dirty, Kuki savage, are very nearly allied. Moreover they can be traced by their own written history to a Kuki origin (Steward, page 618). A more detailed notice of the connection thus traced would be interesting.

SECTION 7. (2)—THE KUKIS.

Steward gives us accounts of two clans of Kukis now settled in Kachar, the old and the new; but they are obviously the same race, and the points of divergence arising from their having settled at different periods in that district are not so great as to necessitate here a separate notice. The Kukis are now found as neighbours of the Nagas in Asam and in contiguity with the Mugs of Arracan. The hill country occupied by them extends from the valley of the Koladyne, where they touch on the Khumis, to Northern Kachar and Manipur, a distance of about 300 miles.

Early notices.

The first notice of this tribe appeared in the "*Asiatic Researches*," Volume VII, in a paper from the pen of Surgeon McCrea, dated 24th January 1799. They are described as a nation of hunters and warriors, ruled as a nation by their principal hereditary chiefs or rajahs, but divided into clans, each under its own chief, whose office was not hereditary but elective, with a preference for particular families. They are said to be traditionally of the same origin as the Mugs, to live in villages called khuahs, having from 500 to 2,000 inhabitants, built on most inaccessible hills, and in houses with floors raised 6 feet, underneath which are kept the domestic animals. When engaged in hostile expeditions, they sleep at night in hammocks swung in trees, which gave rise to the fiction revived, if I mistake not, in a notice by Doctor McCosh, that they lived in trees. They were constantly at war with the Banjugis, a neighbouring tribe, and when successful in their attack, spared none except children, of whom they made captives and afterwards adopted.

The accomplishment most esteemed amongst them was dexterity in thieving. The most contemptible person is a thief caught in the act.

Polygamy was not practised amongst them, but a man might have concubines in addition to his own wife.

They have an idea of a future state, and he who in this life commits most murders obtains the greatest happiness in the next. The term for the Supreme Being is "Khogem *Putiang*,"* and they also worship Shem Sank, represented by a wooden figure of human form, before whom the heads of the slain are presented.

Physiognomy.

There appears to be considerable variety in the Kukis of the Chittagong jungles. Some are represented as very dark, but a recent visitor to some of the tribes called Tipperahs, Mr. H. S. Reynolds,† was struck with the fair complexion of those he saw, who were not darker than a swarthy European. He says they were like the Manipuris in physiognomy, but the greater part bore more resemblance to the *Kasias*, having strongly marked Mongolian features with flat faces and thick lips.

Settlement.

The Kukis first made their appearance in the hill country south of Kachar, 50 or 60 years ago‡. They came in a state of nudity, but were induced by the rulers of the country to adopt clothing, and they grew to be considered together with the Mikirs the best subjects in Northern Kachar.

More recently four large tribes of Kukis (Thadan, Shingson, Changsen, and Lhungum) defeated in a war with the Lushais, fled into Kachar, were allowed to settle there by the British Government, and from amongst the fugitives a body of two hundred men were selected and equipped and disciplined under their own chiefs as a border force.

Government.

Each of the tribes has a raja, whose dignity they consider themselves bound in honor and duty to maintain. The rajas are all supposed to be descended from one divine stock. Their persons are therefore sacred, and they are regarded by their people with almost superstitious veneration. They are entitled to receive annually from each subject one basket of rice, containing about two maunds; one out of each brood of pigs and fowls reared; one quarter of every animal killed in the chase, and four days' labor. The raja is assisted by a council called Thuspois or Mantris (Hindi) and sits with them to administer justice. Under their own criminal law, treason alone was punishable with death. The ordinary murderer and all his family became slaves of the raja. In cases of theft, the criminal only loses his freedom. In cases of adultery or seduction, the punishment is left to the aggrieved husband or father, but all the women of the village, married or single, are at the pleasure of the raja.

Deities.

The Kukis recognise a Supreme God and Creator whom they call *Puthen.* He is regarded as a benevolent deity, but he is the omniscient judge of man's actions, and awards punishments both in this world and in the world to come to those who deserve it. His wife *Nongjar* is adored in consequence of her own power to remove or inflict disease, and is also appealed to as an intercessor. They have a son *Thila*, a harsh and vindictive god with a vixen of a wife, called *Ghummoo.* But the spirit of evil is *Ghumoishee*, who is represented as an illegitimate son of *Puthen's*! He has a wife *Khuchoan*, as malignant as himself;

* Asiatic Researches, Vol. VII. No doubt the modern Puthen.

† Journal Asiatic, Cachar.

‡ Steward's Note on Cachar.

prayers are never offered to them, but sacrifices are made to appease their wrath. Their daughter *Hilo* possesses the mischievous power of making food unwholesome when eaten by those who offend her. The household god is called *Khomoungno.* Then there are forest gods and river gods, and gods of the mountains and rocks, and a god for each kind of metal.

Diseases and cures.

As with nearly all the aboriginal tribes, diseases are attributed to the malevolence of some deity, and the only cure thought of is a sacrifice to propitiate him. Some diseases from their nature indicate the deity who gives them; a pain in the stomach for instance at once suggests 'Hilo,' but in other cases it is necessary to consult one of a class of priests called Thimpu, who take the place of Sokhas and Ojhas of other tribes. Steward says the office is not much coveted, and the rajas have found it necesary occasionally to coerce some of their people to become Thimpu, and so keep up the order; but the duties do not appear to be difficult or onerous.

The Thimpu, however, goes to work scientifically; he feels his patient's pulse, looks sapient, asks a few questions, and determines from the replies who has to be appeased, and how. If a fowl is deemed sufficient, the Thimpu kills, roasts, and *eats* it on the spot pointed out by the invalid as the place where he was first taken ill, throws what he cannot eat as an offering to the jungle, and goes home. If the animal selected is a pig or a dog as he cannot eat all himself, he invites some friends to assist him, and if it be a buffaloe, he gives a grand dinner party.

Idea of future state.

The paradise of a Kuki is a place situated in some northern region, exclusively devoted to Kuki shades, where rice grows spontaneously and game abounds—the happy hunting fields. All the enemies he has killed will be in attendance on him as slaves, and the animals of all kinds that he has eaten with his friends will live again as his farm stock. This system has the peculiar merit of encouraging unbounded hospitality.

Nomadic habits.

The Kukis are very nomadic but gregarious, seldom occupying a village site more than three years, but migrating and re-settling in large bodies, sometimes sufficient for 1,000 houses. On a change of site becoming necessary, a new one is selected by the raja, and the first work executed is a dwelling-house for himself.

Villages.

The village generally takes the form of a street with several rows of houses on each side. The houses have raised floors, and their size is regulated by the number of inmates. The Raja's house is, however, of exceptionable size, sometimes 150 feet long by 50 in breadth. When the dwelling places are all completed, they first stockade the Raja's house, then fortify the village, barricading all the approaches. Guard-houses are built at the barricades, where the young men watch and sleep at night. In their own country, as above mentioned, they love to build on the tops of hills as an additional defence; since their migration to Kachar they prefer to be nearer to their cultivation. In Upper Asam it is found that new settlers from the hills form large villages on first arriving, but afterwards take up, as permanent dwellings, detached farm-houses constructed in their cultivation.

The Kukis are great tobacco smokers, and have the same eccentric fancy for the oil of tobacco, that is a distinguishing feature of the Angami Nagas.

They have a peculiar custom after parturition. Three days after the birth of a girl, and five after the birth of a boy, a feast is given, of which the child partakes. The mother gives rice to the child from her own mouth as birds feed their young, and this is occasionally continued till the child is weaned. At 12 or 13, a boy is excluded from the family mansion at night and compelled to take rest or share of the vigil with the young men in the watch-houses.

Birthday feasts.

A bride must be bought with a price which may be Rs. 30, or served for by a bondage of two years. This settled, there is a meeting of mutual friends and a feast at the house of the bride's father. Next morning the young couple are led before the Thimpu, who presents them with a stoup of liquor which they both drink, and then two threads of cotton are tied round the neck of the man. These strings are not taken off, but when they rot away are not renewed. Lastly, the Thimpu presents each with a small comb and his blessing.

Combs, perhaps these particular combs are very sacred things. It is very unlucky to lose them, and man and wife only may use the same comb. When a man dies, his comb is buried with him, and his near relations break their combs and must roam with dishevelled hair for a few days before they renew them.

Combs.

The national dress of the Kuki appears to be about as light and airy as that of the Naga. They wear a turban, which the more wealthy decorate with the 'red downy feathers of the *hattee pakee* bird, and red ribbons of dyed goat's hair.' The rajas for a distinction wear plumes of the long tail feather of the king-crow. The shoulder pouch and dao belts are of leather ornamented with (*cowrie*) shells in rows. The dao is described as a triangular weapon. Garters of a singular kind are worn, a goat's beard with band cut from the skin of the neck. The only other weapons used are javelins; but they trust chiefly to their daos and defensive armour of rhinoceros hide, a piece of which, suspended from the shoulders, is worn round the body. They also carry shields of buffaloe hide of peculiar shape described as trapezoid, and they use the *panji* very freely in all warlike operations.

Costume.

The Kukis wear pebble beads, and calling them heirlooms, attach to them an extravagant value. To a stone called toino, which is not described, a value equal to Rs. 3,000 in cash has been ascribed.

The Kukis have songs in an old dialect of their language now obsolete, which, from the specimen given by Major Steward, are not without a trace of poetic imagery. They have an instrument called the 'ghosen,' consisting of bamboo pipes with stops inserted into a gourd, which produces different tones at the will of the performer when the gourd is blown into by a mouth-piece. They use chimes of gongs when they want more noise.

Songs.

The Kukis bury their dead; but even amongst the poor the bodies are first allowed to lie in state for several days. The bodies of great men are placed before slow fires till the flesh is effectually smoke dried, and then laid out dressed and equipped for a month or two, during which time open house is kept amidst great feasting. Eventually the body is buried with food and drink, and with the skulls of the animals slaughtered for the funeral feast a fence is made round the grave. It was at one time considered essential that a fresh skull of a human

Disposal of the dead.

victim killed for the occasion, should adorn the grave of a raja, but the Kukis settled in British territory have found it convenient to abandon this observance.

It is not uninteresting to observe that the exhaustive notice of the Kukis in Kachar by Major Steward, of which the details I have given are an imperfect abstract, shows that notwithstanding their repeated emigrations they have not in their most salient characteristics swerved from the customs of their forefathers, as depicted by the author in the Researches quoted above, who wrote about them sixty years ago.

SECTION 7. (3)—THE MANIPURIS AND THEIR NEIGHBOURS.

I have alluded to the Manipuris as a comparatively refined race, my personal knowledge of them having been confined to settlers in Asam and men belonging to the Asam Light Infantry, who certainly, when compared with the hill savages, their cognates, might be classed as a civilized and polite people. The Manipuri native officers were remarkable for their courteous manners and good address. They were people of some education and well versed in such portions of the Hindu mythology as they professed to believe.

The Manipur soldiers, living with their families in the lines, formed there a little colony, the members of which were distinguished for cleanliness and neatness in their persons, habiliments, and dwellings. They, as Hindus, affected the necessary amount of abstinence in food, and conformed to the Hindu ritual of daily life, but then they were all living under the observing eyes of brother soldiers, Hindus of caste, recruited in the Gangetic provinces.

Mythical age.

In their own country they appear to oscillate between the wild paganism, unsophisticated manners, and savage customs of their hill cousins, and a desire to be esteemed worthy of the beautiful visionary history which the Indian epics have been so kind as to assign to them. Manipur was one of the most favored of the regions visited by the Pandava Arjun during his self-imposed punishment of twelve years wandering in exile. He remained some time in the beautiful valley, and espoused the daughter of the king and another maiden; and again in the wake of the sacrificial horse, he re-entered Manipur and found it flourishing wonderfully under the dominion of his son by the Manipuri princess. It is described as a country abounding in gold and silver, precious stones, lovely women, valorous men, beautiful flowers, luscious fruits, and exquisite perfumes. The only traceable resemblance between this valley of romance and the valley of our time is, that both adjoin the country of the Nagas, but the Nagas of the romance were fascinating creatures of the serpent race, gorgeously apparelled and abounding in wealth, and the Nagas of our day are very unamiable and unsavoury naked savages.

Affinities.

The linguistic affinities and physical characteristics of the Manipuris clearly connect the present race with the Nagas and the Kukis. The valley* was at first occupied by several tribes, the principal of which were named Kumul, Luang, Moirang, and Meithei. By degrees the Meithie became dominant, and that name was applied to the entire colony, and now that they have

* Account of the Valley of Munipore, by Major McCulloch, Political Agent, in Selections from Records of the Government of India, No. XXVII.

adopted the Hindu faith, they claim to be of Hindu descent. It is highly probable that these hordes overran a country that had been previously occupied by people of Aryan blood known in Western India and to the bards. The present population of Manipur includes a tribe called Meiung* who speak a language of Sanskrit derivation. They are now in a servile condition performing the duties of grass-cutters to their conquerors.

Origin.

It is traditionally asserted that the Moirang tribe came from the south, the direction of the Kukis ; the Kumul from the east, the direction of the Murrings, and the Meithei and Luang from the north-west, the direction of the Koupúis. The languages of all these tribes and the Meithei or Manipuri bear a strong resemblance to each other, and each tribe has the tradition that the Manipuris are off-shoots from them. The Manipuris though more refined in feature still resemble the Nagas, and on ceremonial occasions, when it appears that civilized and uncivilized nations love to revive the customs of their progenitors, the rulers proclaim their origin by appearing as Nagas. Colonel McCulloch tells us that the ceremony called '**phumbankaba**,' or ascending the throne, is performed by the king and queen in full Naga costume (so that the cost of the coronation robes is not a heavy item in the civil list), and the '**yinchan**' or great house, the official residence of the Meithei chief, is always constructed on the most approved principles of Naga architecture.

History.

The historical annals of the Court commence with the 30th year of the Christian era, and they record the achievements of 47 rulers† who appear to have been little known beyond the precincts of the valley till the country was visited by Samlong, the general and brother of the sovereign of the Shan State of Pong, about the year A. D. 777, who, it is said, first induced the people to wear clothes. In A. D. 1475, the King of Pong sought a Meithei or Manipuri princess in marriage. This led to his visiting the country and to his giving his father-in-law lessons in house building, and it is a fact that the Manipuri houses, as described by Colonel McCulloch, are precisely similar to those now constructed by the Khamtis, a Shan people in Upper Asam.

At the commencement of the present century, the royal family of Manipur appear to have aspired to a more costly style of building, as the erection of a gilded palace, by Raja Marjet Singh, was one of the causes that brought upon them the wrath and the armies of the Burmese, and they were only saved from annihilation by the Burmese war and the protection of the British Government.

Colonel McCulloch fixes the date of the adoption of Hinduism by the Manipuris as somewhat anterior to the accession of Gharíb Nawáz, *alias* Sambeiba, who, it is said, was a Naga boy adopted by Raja Churai Rombu, who shot his adopted father and seized on the throne in the year of Christ 1714.

It was apparently about this time that Brahmins were introduced. They appear to have brought with them no females of their caste, and they were provided with Manipur wives from the Kei class. The modern Manipuri Brahmins are of this mixed race, and they show it in their physiognomies. The oldest family of Brahmins is called Hungoibun, from 'hungoi' a frog, assigned as a nickname to the first Brahmin, because he astonished the Manipuris by the frequency of his ablutions.

---

* See Vocabulary.

† McCulloch.—Pemberton's Eastern Frontier.

N

The principal Hindu festival kept up is the "Dussera," in Manipuri 'Kwaktalba.' The custom of old Hindu families is adopted. The vassals attend, make offerings, and do homage to their chiefs, receiving honorary dresses or trifling presents in return.

Ancient priesthood.

There is another order of priesthood of more ancient standing than the Brahmins. The Maibees are priestesses of an order said to have been instituted many hundreds of years ago by one of the royal princesses. Any woman who chooses to declare herself inspired, and can give evidence of the afflatus by going into fits, may enter upon her noviciate as a priestess, and on her admission may practise on the credulity of the people by divination. They dress in white, and some making a good thing of their trade, have lands and slaves.

Love of horses.

For their enthusiastic love of horses and skill in equitation the Manipuris are distinguished amongst all the neighbouring tribes. Their breed of small horses is celebrated; but it is said they are fast dying out. The great national game of the Manipuri, hockey on pony back, has been adopted as one of the manly amusements of the English in India.

Festivals.

The principal national festivals are the Hiyang, the Lumchail, and the Hanchong, at which the national games of hockey, with boat racing and foot racing, are the chief attractions. It is not stated that these festivals are of a religious character; but as it is said the sports conclude with a feast at which the hill people are regaled with the flesh cured of all the cows, buffaloes, dogs, and cats, that had died in the valley during the year preceding the festival, they could never have been founded by the propagators of the Hindu doctrines, and must belong to the old faith.

The Manipuri women are no *purdah* (screened) ladies. They have the entire management of the household in their hands, and do most of the outdoor as well as the indoor work, including all the marketing. Colonel McCulloch notices a game called 'Kangsanaba,' which is played indoors by young women and girls with a *sprinkling of men on both sides.* The Kei women must have exercised considerable influence over their priestly husbands to have reconciled them to such Frankish indiscretion: though the game appears innocent enough, throwing with an ivory disc at the seed of a creeper called kong, stuck up in the floor of the house.

The Manipuri women are pretty when young, but hard work soon dissipates the bloom of youth and makes havoc with their beauty. They are generally of a tawny complexion (29 to 30 of Brosac), with a very softened and pleasing modification of the Mongolian type of feature.

Costume.

The dress of the women is somewhat peculiar. The chief garment of an adult female is folded over the bosom and under the arms, so as to press somewhat injuriously on the contour of the bust, whence it flows to the feet, and is generally of gay colours with a neat border. Young girls are more becomingly clad in spencers or bodices, and the lower garment is folded round the waist. Whilst in a condition to wear these spencers, that is, so long as they are growing maidens, the girl's front hair is worn cut straight across the forehead level with the eyebrows to the temple, thence, on each side, it is left for a space somewhat longer so as to cover the ear; behind the ear the hair is allowed to grow and flow loose over the shoulders; when the girl is full grown, it is all tied up in a knot. There is nothing peculiar in the costume of the males. They wear the hair long, tied up in a knot behind, and have plenty of it on the head, black and straight, very little on the face.

Laws and custom.

The Manipuris are said to be without written law, but they possess many customs having the force of law, some of which appear to have been wisely and kindly conceived. Thus, slavery is an institution amongst them; but if a slave flies from one master and selects for himself another, it is presumed that he has been badly treated by the first, who cannot therefore reclaim the fugitive. Ordinarily the slaves are treated as members of the family with kindness and consideration. A man may put away his wife, but if he does so without fault on her part, she takes all his personal property, except one drinking cup and the cloth round his loins. The severest punishment which can be inflicted on a woman is her exposure with shaved head; on a Brahmin, banishment. The reigning prince is an autocrat, and treason against him is the most heinous of crimes.

SECTION 7. (4)—THE KOUPÚIS.

The hills surrounding the valley are sparsely inhabited by tribes more or less the cognates of the Manipuris and subject to them; all are either Kukis or Nagas, and, therefore, as classes previously described. I cannot, however, resist the temptation of transcribing from Colonel McCulloch's very interesting account of the Koupúis, who occupy the country between Kachar and Manipur. They live in permanent villages to which they are much attached, not liking to leave sites sacred and endeared to them as containing the graves of their ancestors.

Villages.

The villages are perched on the summits of hills, and are difficult of approach. The houses are substantially built. They are gable-ended, the ridge pole is not in a horizontal position, but declining to the rear, where the house is very much lower than in front, and the thatch on both sides comes down to the ground. The granaries, where all the valuable property as well as the grain is stowed, are grouped together at some distance from the village in sheltered positions. They are left quite unprotected, but even in times of scarcity a theft from a granary is an unknown crime. These granaries are replenished by the cultivation called *jhum*. The jungle on the land selected is cut, and when perfectly dry, burned; and the earth, hoed up with an inch or two of the ashes, is fit for the reception of the seed. The crop harvested, that land is left unmolested for ten years.

Colonel McCulloch's account, &c.

"In the grey of the morning the females of the family are astir, and the village resounds with the blows of the long pestle in the wooden mortar beating out the rice from the husk; this finished, the breakfast is cooked, both for the family and the pigs: for the latter the husk mixed with other refuse serves the purpose. Breakfast over, which it usually is about sunrise, the women proceed for water, which they fill into bamboo tubes and bring on their backs in baskets. Then they go for fire-wood, and this brought, they set about the internal economy of the house, that is, to see that there is sufficient of the good home-brew ready for the master, to their spinning or weaving, to everything but cleaning up. They have unfortunately no great taste for that necessary labor. They rather glory in a dirty house, in having the front room half covered with rice husk, in which pigs are lying fast asleep or grunting about, and fowls are busy seeking for food. The family, except the boys, from the time they begin to wear a cloth round their waist, sleep in the rear room of the house, and in it they also cook their meals. In the front part, there is a fire-place, and along the two sides are boards or platforms of bamboos, which may be used as seats or beds by any one that comes. Some of these boards are as much as 24 feet long by 4 feet broad. They are made with dáos and little axes, a whole tree being used to make one. If not employed in the labours of the field or in the chase, the men do little more than loll about the houses during the day, drinking their peculiar drink, a harmless one, consisting of pounded rice mixed with boiling-water, brought into fermentation by the addition of germinated paddy. In the morning and evening they will generally be found sitting in groups in front of their houses* on large flat stones which cover the graves of their deceased relatives. They then appear to be enjoying themselves greatly, they are exceedingly loquacious, and speak always in a loud tone. Pipes containing green tobacco are then smoked; at such a rate do they pull, that they appear to be smoking for a wager."

Peculiar smokers.

"I believe the pleasure of smoking is nothing to them compared to that of holding in the mouth a sip of the water of the bowl of the pipe whichhas been well impregnated with the fumes of smoke passing through it, and it is only for the purpose of obtaining this that they so laboriously pull at their pipes morning and evening."

It has been observed that the young men do not sleep in the family houses. "According as the village is large or small they assemble in one or several houses which for the time become their homes. These clubs are ruled over despotically by the seniors amongst them, who exact from their juniors, with unsparing hand, service of all kinds. The young women also have their separate places of resort, and between them and the young men intercourse is quite unrestricted, without leading to immorality." The resemblance between the Koupúis and Oraons of Chota Nagpur in this distribution of the youths and maidens is most striking.

Festivals.

Throughout the year the Koupúis have various festivals which they are very particular in observing. "These are first the Enghan, which happens in December. During the five days of its continuance all the inhabitants of the village, dressed in their best attire, keep up the dance and song, interrupted only by short intervals of repose and breaks dedicated to feasting. Next is the Reingnai in or about January, which lasts for three days. In one day during this festival the men and women fetch separately the water that each may require. The men having killed pigs take a portion for themselves and give a portion to the women; they cook and eat separately, the men in the house of the head of the family, the women each in her own house. An effigy of a man made of a plantain is hung on a tree, and at it they throw pointed bamboos or sticks. At this festival the graves of the ancestors are sprinkled with the national drink, and on its termination omens are sought for the selection of land for cultivation and general welfare in the ensuing year. In February there is a festival of three days' continuance, at which all the children born since the last festival of the kind have their ears bored. This is followed by the clearing of the jungle on the land they intend to sow, and when that is done, they drink the

* See Account of the Mundas of Chota Nagpur.

juice of ginger at a festival called from that circumstance Udoe yung. In July there is a festival which is followed by the clearing of all the village paths. Their dancing is described as very lively. Drums are the only instruments, but there is always the accompaniment of songs."

There are so many customs common to these Koupúis and the Nagas previously described, living west of the Doyang River, that it would probably be found that all the traits above described as characteristics of the Koupúis are also common to the Nagas to their north. There is one more mentioned by Colonel McCulloch which I have not met with in other accounts of Naga tribes.

Peculiar custom.

On the death of a man's wife the singular practice exists of recovering from the bereaved husband the price of her bones by her father or next of kin. This is called múndú; no múndú is demandable when the death is by the hand of an enemy, by wild beasts, by cholera or small-pox, or from any swelling.

The strange custom of placing villages or people under *taboo*, noticed as obtaining amongst the Kukis, is practised by the Koupúis, they call it 'neina.'

Adjoining the Koupúis are the Songbu and Poirons who resemble them in manners, in customs and appearance, and next to these are the Quoireings with a language differing, but having a great similarity in other respects to the tribe last described.

The tribes to the south and south-east of Manipur are varieties of Khongjais or Kukis, a race already noticed.

The Luhupas.

In the east the tribes are rather Naga than Kuki, and of these the most important are the Luhupa, a very powerful and pugnacious clan who are always fighting with each other if they are not fighting with their neighbours. Their weapons for close quarters are very long spears and shields, but they also use bows and poisoned arrows. As ornaments to their head-dress they wear the tresses, not alas! of the women they have loved, but of the women they have slaughtered! When the eldest son of a Luhupa marries, the parents and the rest of the family move out of the house to make way for him. They have again to remove on the marriage of the second son. The working dress of a Luhupa consists of an ivory ring, through which the preputium is lightly drawn!

The Mow and Muram tribes.

West of the Luhupas are the Mow and Muram tribes, who, though of common stock and closely allied by intermarriages, are at deadly feud.

For the security of the community the Muram married men sleep in the bachelors' hall, probably by batches, as amongst the Abors north of Asam. The Mow occupy twelve villages; the Muram live in one large village of 900 houses under two chiefs. To the north of the Mow tribe are the Angami or Guami Nagas, already noticed amongst the Asam tribes.

SECTION 8.—THE MIKIRS.

Adjoining the Kukis on the Kopili River, and occupying all the hilly portion of the Nowgong District almost to the Brahmaputra,* we next meet with the Mikir tribe, who hold etymologically a very isolated position. According to their own legend, they

* Steward's North Cachar. Robinson's Assam.

were driven by the Kacháris from what is called Tolaram's country between Nowgong and Kachár, and sought refuge in Jyntia, but not being satisfied with their reception, they placed themselves under the Rajas of Asam, and have ever since peaceably occupied the hill country in which they are now settled. It is said they were disarmed or made to forswear the use of arms by the Asam Government, and this is assigned as the cause of their unwarlike disposition, which makes them good subjects, but exposes them to the attacks of their more warlike neighbours.

Dress, Houses, &c.

The Mikirs dress like the Kasias and are in other respects very like them. The dress is peculiar, consisting of two pieces of cotton cloth, made with red stripes, fringed at both ends, sewn together like a bag and worn like a shirt, apertures being left for the head and arms. They are very like the Kasias in countenance, but inferior to them in physique. They live like the Miris all huddled together in one large house with raised floor, a notched stick serving as ladder or stair-case; sometimes as many as thirty married couples with their children occupy one house, which is not divided into rooms. They will eat of almost any animal food except the cow, which they affect to reverence, though they have a dislike to milk. Marriages are not contracted till the parties are adult. There is no ceremony, but a feast is given in honor of the event; also when a child is born. Polygamy is discountenanced, and widows are allowed to re-marry.

They appear to have very few original notions on the subject of religion, but worship a Supreme Being whom they call Hempatim.

The tribe is supposed to number about 25,000 souls.

SECTION 9.—JYNTIAS AND KASIAS.

Crossing the Kopili brings us to Jyntia and the Kasia tribes. The inhabitants of the hill tracts in the former district are always called Kasia by the people of the plains, and are no doubt the same as the people of the Kasia Hills, but they call themselves Khyi.* "They are a handsome, muscular race of men, of an active disposition, and fond of martial exercises. They always go armed, in general with bows and arrows and a long naked sword and shield, which latter is very large, and occasionally serves them as a defence against rain."

Law of succession.

The Raja of Jyntia, deposed for his misdeeds by our Government, was not altogether an uncivilized potentate, and had amassed considerable wealth, as his personalties were found to be worth a lac of rupees, which was made over to him on his retiring into exile. The immediate and remote descendants of the Raja conformed to the customs of the Hindus, and were treated by the Brahmins as orthodox Sudras; but under the peculiar laws of succession that characterize the people of this race, the purity of the Kasia blood in the person of the chief was inviolably maintained. The sceptre descended not in his line, but went on his demise to the son of his sister, who was called the Kunwari (princess), and her husband was selected from certain noble Hill Kasia families by a general assembly of the chief people. Thus the line of Rajas was constantly renovated by fresh dips into the best Kasia blood, and under this system there could be no alienation from the original

* Report by David Scott, quoted in Pemberton's Eastern Frontier, page 219.

stock by the mixture of the foreign element. The Kasias have maintained their physical characteristics better than any other race that I know of.

The attempt to open direct communication between Asam and Silhet in 1826, first brought our officers into contact with the Kasias.* The Kasia Raja of Nanklao, Tirut Singh, having expressed a wish to recover some lands that had been held by his ancestors in Asam, his request was granted, on condition of his using his influence with other Kasia chiefs to obtain for all British subjects an unrestricted passage through the Kasia territory. This was agreed to, and most cordial relations were established, which lasted about two years. Then, without any apparent reason for the change, came the treacherous murder of Lieutenant Bedingfield, and the sudden attack on, and ruthless slaughter of, Lieutenant Burton and his native followers and attendants, between 50 and 60 native British subjects, on the 4th April 1829. The result was the complete subjugation of the Kasia Hills after a tedious war, brought to a close on the surrender of Tirut Singh in January 1833.

The Kasia Hills were found to be divided into several states under hereditary chiefs forming a confederacy. Nanklao, Kyrim, Cherra, Nartang, Naspang and others having each from 20 to 70 villages. The nation (says Mr. Robertson), or horde, presents the appearance of a congregation of little oligarchical republics, subject to no common superior, yet of which each member is amenable in some degree to the control of his confederates. It was this that led to the Nanklao massacre. One of the chiefs, Tirut Singh, had taken too much on himself.† The whole tract of the hill country occupied by these confederates embraces an area of about 3,500 square miles, between Kasia, Silhet, Asam and the country of the Garos. Some of the hills attain a height of 6,000 feet, but the country includes belts of arable soil about 2,000 feet above the plains, on which grow, in great luxuriance, oranges, limes, pine-apples, the jack fruit and mangoes, betel nut and plantains, with the wild raspberry and strawberry.

Remarkable monolithic monuments.

To the peculiar aspect of the Kasia Hills from physical conformation and natural features must be added the various remarkable monumental stones that give a marked character to the scenery.‡ These are of several kinds, but most of them, says Colonel Yule, recall strongly those mysterious solitary or clustered monuments of unknown origin, so long the puzzle and delight of antiquaries, which abound in our native country, and are seen here and there in all parts of Europe and Western Asia.

It is probable that the stones, compared to Stonehenge found in the Nilghiries, were set up by a people who honored their dead as do the Kasias, and that the similitude of custom in this respect points to some connection between the Kasias and the Hos of Singhbhúm, and the Munda race, generally, of the Chota Nagpur Province. The sketch given by Colonel Yule shows that the monuments consist of large, flat, circular slabs, supported on very short pillars, as if they were intended for stools to sit on, and long, upright, rough pillars of irregular shape; the same forms are found in and about every Ho village. The collections of large flat slabs in the village, supported on little stones are often used as seats when the old people meet to gossip over the graves in which the ashes of

* Pemberton's Eastern Frontier.

† He made arrangements with the British Government without consulting the other chiefs of the confederacy.

‡ Colonel Yule's Note on Kasia Hills and People, Asiatic Society's Journal, No. 152, for 1844.

the dead have been reverentially deposited, whilst fantastically formed oblong stones are set up on the way side outside the village as an additional commemoration of the deceased.

Kasia funeral.

The details given of the ceremonies observed at a Kasia funeral, and those I have noticed at a Ho funeral, have just that coincidence with divergence in the order of the events, which one might expect to find in the practice of two peoples long separated, deriving their ceremonies from a common source, but having only tradition to guide them in their observance.

Yule says, the round flat stones resting on the heads of so many flat pillars are sarcophagi or cineraries, sometimes in clusters so close together, that you can step from one to the other. This is precisely as they are found in an old Ho village and on deserted sites of Mundári villages. The upright pillars are merely, he says, cenotaphs, and if you ask a Kasia why their ancestors went to the trouble of erecting them, the answer is 'to preserve their names.' The Ho gives precisely the same answer when asked the object of the pillars set up by the village way-side.

I will give at once an account of the Kasia funeral ceremonies taken from *Robinson's Assam.*

"The corpse is kept in the house four or five days, and in some cases for as many months; in such instances the body is put into the hollow trunk of a tree and fumigated. When all preparations are completed, the remains are burnt. The body is borne on a bier by four men, with great solemnity, to the place where the cremation is to take place. During the procession, a funeral dirge is played on bamboo flutes, accompanied by the groans and shrieks of the bereaved friends. Arrived at the appointed place, the body is taken from the bier, carefully concealed from view, and placed in a wooden box standing on four legs, under which the fuel is placed. Sometimes the body is conveyed from the house in this box. While the body is being burnt, sacrifices are offered, and offerings of betel nut (areca nut), fruit, &c., are made to the spirit of the deceased. Arrows are occasionally discharged towards the four points of the compass. When the body is burnt, the ashes are carefully collected, put into an earthen vessel, carried home, and kept until, by divination, a favorable day is fixed for finally disposing of them. There is then great feasting and dancing, in the midst of which the ashes are removed to the burial place, and finally deposited in a grave and covered by one of the circular slabs above mentioned. On these occasions the people are dressed in their best richly embroidered outer shirts of broadcloth, silk turbans and *dhotis,* large bangles, heavy silver chains, gold necklaces, plumes of down or peacock feathers, and ornamented quivers. In the dances the maidens in the centre of the group, in lines of two or three, set to each other with eyes demurely cast on the earth. They too, are in their best array, having on their heads circlets of silver, with a tall spearhead-like ornament rising behind. They are swaddled in long petticoats, with an upper garment passing lightly under the right arm and tied in a knot on the right shoulder."

The ashes of a tribe are deposited under one vault or in one burial ground. The remains of man and wife are never mingled, because they belong to different tribes. A husband is therefore in death separated from his wife and children, as the latter belong to the tribe of the mother, and their ashes are deposited with hers.

As it is through the mother that children inherit, and that the transmission of the pure blood of a tribe is secured, it is not surprising to find that this connection between the mother and her offspring is maintained after death.

This system is also the cause of disunion between the living. Marriages are made without ceremony. If the proposal of a youth is accepted by the young lady and her parents, he enters the household of the latter, or sometimes only visits his wife there occasionally, and the union thus loosely made is easily broken. Separations are frequent, and when they mutually agree to part, they publicly intimate their wish by throwing away a few shells taken from each other, the children remain with the mother.

Muscular development.

The Kasias are remarkable for great muscular development, especially of leg, both men and women rejoicing in limbs that would vex the shade of a chairman, and make 'Jeames' bilious with envy. They have rather fair, often ruddy complexions, and the good humoured expression of the young people is always very pleasing; but with such flat round faces and oblique eyes beauty must be rare, and they greatly disfigure their countenances by the constant and untidy chewing of the pan leaf, the stains from which they care not to remove. Their ordinary attire, though originally of gay colors, is generally dingy with dirt, and their persons are equally innocent of ablution.

Character, Arts.

Colonel Yule gives them a very good character for honesty and fidelity as servants. They are, however, rather lazy, and have made very small progress in the arts. They are unacquainted with weaving, and although affecting a peculiar style of dress, it is all made for them by other tribes.

Food.

Rice, millet, maize and the *kachu* and other roots are the commonest articles of food, but they partake of nearly all kinds of flesh and dried fish. Yule says, some individuals have a superstitious objection to particular kinds of food, and will not allow such to be brought to their houses. Is not this superstition connected with their tribal divisions as amongst the Oraons of Chota Nagpur and the Béchuánas of Africa, who must not eat the animal after which their tribe is called?

Religious ideas.

The Kasias do not appear to be strong in theology. Yule says, they have a name for the Supreme Being, which he does not give, but they pay more devotion to inferior spirits who reside on hills, or in rocky dales, or in groves. They have no temples or idols connected with their ancient faith. Like all the tribes we have yet touched on, they are much addicted to consulting auspices, especially from the appearance of eggs on being broken. As they go on breaking eggs, till they find the signs they want, fate must generally appear in their favor. They offer a libation to the deity before they drink spirits, by dipping the finger three times into the vessel and filliping a drop successively over each shoulder and down by their right and left sides.

Punishments, Ordeals.

In the courts of the Raja, fining was the general punishment; but occasionally, as with the Kukis, the entire property and personal liberty were confiscated, and the convict and his family become slaves of the Raja. The water ordeal was sometimes used. The opponents had to plunge their heads under water on opposite sides of a holy pool, and the decree was given to him who longest kept submerged. Yule says that the parties could undergo this ordeal by attorney, so that long-winded lawyers were as much in request in the Kasia Hills as elsewhere.

P

The English might be characterized by Asiatics as a people that whistle, so little is that expression of a satisfied mind an Eastern accomplishment, but the Kasias are also great whistlers,* and the boys have amongst their amusements peg tops and greased poles.

Amusements.

Major Fisher, in his Memoir of Silhet, Kachár and adjacent countries, tells us that the Kasias or Khyee are called Miki by the Kacháris, and he supposes they may be connected with the Meoh, though he does not consider them connected with the Kacháris.

SECTION 10.—THE GAROS.

The Garo tribes are generally supposed to commence with the Nunyas, who are the clan immediately to the west of the Kasias; but the Nunyas are more Kasia than Garo. Their position, occupying the extreme north-western portion of the mountainous tract that extends from Cape Negrais to the Brahmaputra, is well known. By the writers of the days of Buchanan Hamilton, the Garos, Kasias, and Jyntias are spoken of as one people. Buchanan says, "the Raja of Jyntia is by birth a Garo." Several of the petty Rajas of Kamrup, whose estates skirt the Kasia and Garo Hills, are Hinduized Garos, who have maintained their footing in the valley during several changes of dynasty. It is supposed that during the Koch and Mughul government the Garos of Mechpara, Habra-ghat, and other places had equally valuable possessions in the plains from which they were subsequently dispossessed by Mech and Koch zemindars. It is, however, the uncivilized, unconverted, Garo that I wish to describe, not the Hinduized animal of the name, and they merit a careful notice, as they are, I believe, the primitive type of the great Mech Kachari, or Bodo, nation, and have a variety of customs that are singular and interesting.

The observant Buchanan has a short article on the Garos, from which we learn that about two-fifths of the whole population of the Garo Hills are slaves. This is a feature that at once strikes the visitor to a large Garo village. They are called "Nokol" in contradistinction to "Nokoba," the freemen, and the distinction is jealously preserved: a freeman must not marry a slave girl or even keep her as a concubine. The slaves are well fed and cared for, they are generally the best looking people in the village. It is from the possession of a large number of them that a man obtains influence amongst his tribe. Each great chief can go to war each with a body-guard of 60 such followers entirely devoted to him.

Slaves.

The following account of the Garos is taken from notes of a tour made amongst them by me in 1846:—

Their territory lies between the 25th and 26th degrees of northern latitude. To the north and west, they have the perganahs of Habra-ghat, Mechpárá Kalumalupárá, and Karibari, all of the district of Gowalpara lying between them and the Brahmaputra, to the south, Sherpur and Susung of the Midnapore District, and to the east, the Kasia Hills.

A great portion of the interior is quite unexplored. It is said to contain lofty mountains with great masses of naked rock and large spaces destitute of vegetation. My own observations lead me to suppose that these mountains have few inhabitants, the

* Yule's Notes loc. cit.

Garos generally preferring, as sites for their villages, hills of the second order, which rise from 100 to 300 feet above the adjacent valleys. Thus, the highest of these mountains that was ever visited by a European, that called Tura, estimated at 4,000 feet, the skirts and valleys of which are cultivated by the Garos of Witurgiri, has no vestige of human habitations on its south-western slopes, and its other faces are said to be equally destitute of inhabitants. The Garos are divided by the Bengali into Malawa and Bemalawa, which, like the 'Bori' and 'Abor' of Upper Asam, means dependent and independent Garo: 'Garo' like 'Naga' is a term applied to this people by the Hindus. They consider themselves as forming three or four nationalities with different names. Of those subject to the Gowalpara jurisdiction, or having communications with it, the most eastern bordering on the Kasias, are called the Nunya; the central tribe are the Lyntea,* and the remainder are the Abengya. Buchanan says that the independent Garos of the interior rejoice in the grand sounding name of Kochna-sindeya, but it appears that each tribe has its dependent and independent branches. The Nunyas are the fairest of these tribes resembling the Kasias in feature and complexion and in language. The language of the Western Garos is unintelligible to the Nunyas.

Malawa, Bemalawa.

The Garos have no tradition regarding migration; they imagine themselves to be autocthonous, and the only people with whom they claim alliance are the Bûts and the English!

Robinson is of opinion, from the construction of their language, that they are allied with the Bûts. Hodgson doubts this, and truly the connection, if it ever had any existence, must be very remote, for the specimens of the language that we possess give no analogues, and they have not a custom in common. Their linguistic affinities are decidedly with the Bodo, the Mech, and the Chutia.

As they have no written language, nothing but memory to trust to for the preservation of their traditional myths, it is probable that these have been altered according to circumstances so materially as to afford us but little clue to their early history. We see this in their having assigned a place in their system to the mother of all the 'Feringis', a race with whom they have not been acquainted a century.

The most salient points in their religious belief I find thus noticed:—

Rishi Salgong is supreme amongst the gods; he lives in heaven (Rang). Apongma, his wife (or Manim according to Buchanan, which appears to be the same as Mainon, the wife of the supreme deity Batho of the Kacharis) left her heavenly parent to elope with him. They became residents of this world and lived for a time on Tura, where they had two children, a son named Kengra Barsa, who is the father of fire and of all the heavenly luminaries, and a daughter named Mining Mija, who married the son of Donjongma, the mother of mankind. Mining Mija and her daughter Ret Rebong lost their husbands, and resided as widows on the summit of Tura; but Rishi Salgong and Apongma have returned to heaven.

Deities, mythology.

Nustoo sprang from a self-begotten egg and created the world; previous to that time she had existed on a *padam*, water-lily (Garo—*monglal*), but finding her position uncomfortable she sent to Hiraman, the king of the lower regions, for earth, with which she formed a seat for herself and progeny, and commenced filling it with the

* Lyntea is from *langta*, naked, a name given by the Bengalis.

animal and vegetable creation. First streams of water issued from her womb, and were the origin of all the rivers, then a reptile Magar* was produced from a similar source. The first of the vegetable world that appeared were the grasses and reeds (*kosi chai rikal bolan*). The first animal was the matchidobo, an elk, the "deochagal" of the Asamese, which is seldom seen, and the man who beholds it dies. Then came fish of all kinds, frogs (*cumna*), snakes (*mempo*), trees, buffaloes, geese, a priest (!), and the catalogue ends with a daughter, who perhaps married the priest. At all events she had children, a son married to Rishi Salgong's grand-daughter as before stated, and three daughters for whom it may be presumed husbands of divine origin were provided, as those daughters are the mothers of three races of mankind. The eldest Mishali is the mother of the Bûtias, who are the first of mankind, the second daughter is the mother of the Gáros, who consequently rank second. Midili, the third daughter, is the mother of the 'Feringis.' The Bengalis are of unknown origin!!

Donjongma founded Rangsiram, which is situated in the heart of the Garo country. She still lives there, and is exceedingly hospitable. The inhabitants of Rangsiram are to all appearance Garos, but have not been heard to speak. It is believed that the Garos who die may occasionally be re-born there, but the place usually assigned for their re-appearance is Naphak, said to be situated in the interior amongst the higher ranges.

It must not be supposed that the mythology of the Garos is all comprised in the above. They have marvellous legends of wonderful animals, and the feats of the immortals who fought and destroyed them, of unnatural alliances between goddesses and beasts, and the equally unnatural offspring of such amours, which are recited and sung by the priests at funerals and on other solemn occasions.

Buchanan says that salgong or saljang is the firmament or visible heaven. The heavenly bodies, moon and stars, and spirits who preside over hills, woods, and rivers, are the agents employed to manage the affairs of the world. White cocks are offered to the heavenly bodies, and fermented liquors, rice and flowers to superior deities. There are no temples or images, but before each house a dry bamboo with its branches adhering is fixed in the ground, to this the Garos tie tufts of cotton threads and flowers, and before it make their offerings.

Priests.

The priests in their own language are called kamál. "†They marry, cultivate the ground, go to war like their neighbours, and the office is not hereditary, any man who has committed to memory the requisite forms of prayer" (myths?) "may assume the office."

Like the priests or elders of all the other pagan tribes we have been considering, they pretend to foretell events by the examination of the entrails of animals, especially of the liver. They are therefore called 'ojhas' by the Bengalis. Hodgson says, the priests of the Bodo are also called 'ojha,' so are the priests of the Kols; but it is a Hindi word, and means an examiner of entrails, from the root 'ojh,' entrails.

Having witnessed a sacrifice I may state that the full canonicals of a priest are peacock's feathers stuck in his hair, and wooden sandals on his feet. He is consulted in sicknesses, names the deity to whom the illness is to be ascribed or who

* Hindí for a crocodile or alligator, a saurian.

† Buchanan Hamilton, loc. cit.

has the power to remove it. He seats himself below the bamboo altar, and addresses it in a long monotonous chant. Another person meantime leads the kid, or whatever the sacrifice is to be, round and round the shrine. It is occasionally taken away and washed, and on being brought back again petted and fed with salt by the priest, and after several repetitions of this ceremony, the animal's head is chopped off with one cut, and the altar is smeared with the blood. All the time the sick person for whom the offering is made lies beside the priest.

Watch.

On approaching a Garo village, the first objects that strike the stranger are the picturesque spectre-like edifices they construct as watch-houses for their crops. These airy structures consist of a low hut 20 or 30 feet long, about two-thirds of which is enclosed, and the remainder open at the sides and front, built entirely of bamboos on a platform of the same material. Of this one end is supported by the stem and branches of a tree lopped 30 or 40 feet from the ground, and the remainder rests on uprights of bamboos of the same length.

Villages.

The ordinary villages nearest the plains contain about 20 houses, often built on the slope of a hill. The length of the houses runs out from the hill, the inner supports of the flooring near the hill being short and the outer supports long to preserve its level. The houses average about 80 feet in length. The interior is very cleanly kept; rather more than half the house is open from end to end forming one long apartment for general use, in which are the earthen hearths for cooking; on the right side are enclosures, little chambers screened off in which the married members of the family and females sleep. The young men of the village are obliged to follow the custom I have so often noticed, and are not allowed to occupy any portion of the family residence. They club together in a separate house, called very generally in the Asam Valley the *dekachang*. This is an Asamese term. This building is lofty and most substantially built: one-half of it forms an open hall in which the village conferences are held, and the chief "Laskar" holds his court. The remainder is enclosed as the dormitory for the young men. The posts and beams are fantastically carved.

In the interior are villages of a hundred and fifty and more houses. Such is Rupagiri, an Abengya settlement. The houses are spread over a considerable tract of undulating ground, a plateau in a circular valley sheltered by hills, the streams from which are artificially brought into the village by aqueducts of bamboos. Each considerable householder has his own aqueduct spouting out a liberal supply of water clear as crystal close to his door: vessels are instantly filled, and you have only to squat under the pipes to obtain a delightfully refreshing shower bath—both males and females may be frequently seen so enjoying themselves in a state of nature. As they squat, they remove the sole garment and cleverly resume it as they rise from the bath.

Houses.

The family residence of the Chief, Sambal, successor to the illustrious Tokal Laskar of Dulungiri, the most noted chief in Mr. D. Scott's* days, may be taken as a good specimen of their best style of house. It is a large gloomy mansion about 260 feet in length by 40 in breadth, raised on piles varying in height according to the inequalities of the ground, and supported by substantial posts of sâl timbers rudely carved with grotesque figures and placed with

* The first Commissioner of Asam.

the broad ends uppermost as more convenient to support the beams. There is an open balcony at one end of the house, and a portion of the opposite end is reserved unfloored for stalling the bulls kept for fighting and for carousals. The more private portion of the residence forms a wing at right angles with the main building, raised on piles like the rest, and with a separate balcony in which the ladies of the family sit.

The interior of the great house chiefly consisted of one large apartment, only a small portion of it at the end opposite the entrance being partitioned off into sleeping chambers. All down the side, however, were benches of bamboo used as beds by attendants or guests. The porch in front was ornamented by quite a *chevaux-de-frise* of wooden images intended as representations of deceased friends and relations. Conspicuous amongst them was the monument to Tokul, which was evidently regarded as a triumph of art. It was a full length wooden figure of a male, decorated with all kinds of finery, and had an old silk umbrella supported over it. In front of the house, there was an open space for games, dances, village conferences, and the like, round which the houses of the slaves were circled; and very numerous they appeared to be. All the finest looking young men and women of the village were amongst the slaves of this family, but they do not appear to repine at their lot in life.

In the open space before the Laskar's house I witnessed a very curious spectacle. A great feast was given in honor of the investiture of the Chief with a dress of honor which I had brought for him, and of which he was so proud that, to my knowledge, he kept it on for a whole week day and night.

Festivals.

The food prepared was a savoury mess of minced pork, rice, and vegetables. The guests, about 200 in number, were seated in a huge ring round the flesh pots. The cooks took from the pots as much of the mess as they could conveniently carry on a platter of large leaves, and went round one after the other thrusting into the open mouths of the sitters great handfuls of the greasy food. Other attendants followed with gourd bottles full of the favourite home-brew, which in the same way was poured down the throats of the guests who had nothing to do but to sit still and open their mouths when the cooks came round, as young birds in a nest open their mouths when the old birds return from foraging for them. This was followed by a bull fight, a spectacle of which they appear to be as fond as are the Spaniards.

Food.

The Garos are not much restricted in regard to food. They rear for the purpose, kine, goats, swine, dogs, cats, fowls, and ducks. They eat dried fish and tortoises which they buy in the plains, and their hills supply them with deer, wild-hogs, frogs, and snakes, all of which they eat. In fact they have no aversion to any food, except milk, which they abominate, and they have no objection to eat in company, nor to eat what has been prepared by aliens.

Some Garo chiefs appeared to me to live entirely on beer. I believe when they take it to this extent it is thickened with flour of millet, which makes it more nourishing, and though it keeps them in a perpetual state of 'mild but sweet ebriety,' they get fat on it.

In settling political differences the mode of feasting described above must be resorted to as a final ratification of the arrangement. The tribes at variance must be brought together by a third party on neutral ground, and if the arbitrators be successful in effecting peace, the parties swear to observe it by biting their swords, and, as a sign that friendly relations are restored, the representatives of both clans must put food into each other's mouth and pour beer down each other's throats, which seals the compact.

Inheritance, marriage, &c.

The Garo laws of inheritance and intermarriage are singular and intricate, and it was after many enquiries in different quarters and testing the information, received in various ways that I recorded the following note on the subject:—

The clans are divided into different houses called *mahâris* (Buchanan calls them *chatsibak*), which may be translated *motherhoods*. A man cannot take to wife a girl of his own *mahâri*, but must select from one of the *mahâris* with whom his family have from time immemorial exclusively allied themselves. In some of the now noblest families there is but one *mahâri* with which, as a rule, they can intermarry. This however is not irrefragable, and should maidens of that particular house be wanting, the young men may choose, or more correctly speaking, be chosen by a daughter of some other. If it be not on this account necessary to look elsewhere, a man's sister should marry a son of the house of which his wife is daughter, his son may marry a daughter of that sister, and his daughter may marry his sister's son who, in such case, comes to reside with his father-in-law and succeeds to the property in right of his wife and her mother. Inherent in males there is no right to succeed to property of any description, and this is all to secure a transmission of pure blood; but though a son cannot inherit his father's property, his mother cannot be ejected from the position she enjoyed conjointly with her husband. The successor must recognize in her the mistress of the house not only as his mother-in-law, should she stand in that relation to him, but also as his wife, though the marital rights be shared with her own daughter. It is consequently not uncommon to see a young Garo introducing as his wife a woman who, as regards age, might be his mother, and in fact is his mother-in-law and his aunt.

Indications exist of this custom having once obtained amongst the aboriginal tribes of Central India. At the ceremonies of some of the lowest agricultural tribes of Bihar supposed to be descended from aborigines, probably Kols, the sister's son (bhanjá) of the person who is married or mourns performs the ceremony.

It appears, the custom is not unknown to the African tribes. Messrs. D. & C. Livingston tell us, speaking of the Kebrabasa people on the Zambési, a sister's son has much more chance of succeeding to a chieftainship than the chief's own offspring, it being unquestionable that the sister's child has the family blood.*

Children, as with the Kasias, belong to the *mahâri* of the mother. From the paternal parent they derive nothing, and it would certainly appear from the social customs of the Garos that their great lawgiver must have been a female. The men do much of the heavy work and all the fighting, and are so far not deprived of their natural obligations as the stronger animal, but in other respects they are dependent on the females.

When there is an object to serve by it, such as the acquisition of, or the disposal of, a reversionary interest in property, marriages are sometimes made when the parties are infants, and sometimes for similar reasons very young girls are united to very much

* Livingston, The Zambési, &c., page 162.

older men, in such cases the inclination of the infant is not of course consulted. The preliminaries of the marriage are settled by the two *mahàris* concerned in it, and when all is arranged it takes place with the usual feastings and rejoicings.

As, however, all young ladies are not heiresses, many of them attain a ripe age in single blessedness and continue in that state till inclination, which is not in any way coerced or interfered with so long as there is no infringement of the *mahàri* system, induces them to select a partner from amongst the spruce lads of the dekachang, or bachelors' hall. As there is no restriction on innocent intercourse, the boys and girls freely mixing together in the labors of the field and other pursuits, an amorous young lady has ample opportunity of declaring her partiality, and it is her privilege and duty to speak first. I do not know if, in such a state of society, the party proposing is ever rejected, but I should think the proposal comes in too tempting a shape to be so received.

Husbands selected by the wives.

The maiden coyly tells the youth to whom she is about to surrender herself that she has prepared a spot in some quiet and secluded valley to which she invites him; she gives him sufficient clue to discover the retreat, and goes there herself, taking with her supplies for two or three days. The favoured youth, after communicating his good fortune to the most intimate of his associates in the bachelors' hall, quickly joins his mistress in her retreat, into which it would be impertinent to follow them. In two or three days they return to the village and their union is then publicly proclaimed and solemnized.

Any infringement of the rule which declares that the initiative shall in such cases rest with the girl is summarily and severely punished. If a male makes advances to a girl, and the latter rejecting them, chooses also to tell her friends that such tenders of affection have been made to her, it is looked on as an insult to the whole *mahàri* to which the girl belongs, a stain only to be obliterated by the blood of pigs and liberal libations of beer at the expense of the *mahàri* to which the man belongs.

The marriage ceremony chiefly consists of dancing, singing, and feasting. The bride is taken down to the nearest stream and bathed, and the party next proceed to the house of the bridegroom, who pretends to be unwilling and runs away, but is caught and subjected to a similar ablution, and then taken in spite of the resistance, and the counterfeited grief and lamentation of his parents, to the bride's house.

Marriage ceremonies.

The presence of a priest is now necessary to invoke the gods to bless the union and consult the omens regarding it. For this purpose the heads and necks of a couple of fowls, cock and hen, are fairly laid together, and simultaneously struck by the priest a sharp blow with a stick. If they fall dead side by side it is symbolical of the faithful attachment and long continued happiness of the young couple. If only one be killed and the other flies off, or if they separate before dying, the union is not expected to be a happy one.

A Laskar amongst the Garos is generally chief over a group of villages. Buchanan considers this a Bengali expression, and says that their own word for chief is nokma, but we now find that lokma (which I suppose is the same word) is the head of the village, subordinate to the Laskar.*

* See Account of Expedition by Captain Reynolds in the Asiatic Society's Journal for January 1849, page 57.

The Garo implements of husbandry are a hoe, a dao, and a battle-axe called lumbiri, with which they make a tooth-pick, or fell a tree, skin a mouse, or decapitate a human being. No male Garo is ever seen in his hills without this weapon carried naked in his hand, or a spear.

Husbandry.

With such rude implements the Garo and his wife manage to cultivate every year from three to four bighas of land.* This must include about one-third of newly cleared land, as they take but three crops in rotation—one of *aous dhan* (autumn rice), one of cotton, with which millet is sown, then *aous dhan* again. After this, the land must remain fallow, until it is completely overgrown with bush and tree jungle, which takes seven to eight years.

The chief productions of the hills are cotton, Indian-corn, *aous* or *asu dhan*, millet, chillies, and yams. It is on cotton that they chiefly depend for the necessaries of life their hills do not produce. Buchanan estimated the quantity they could export at 60,000 maunds.

Products of the hills.

The Garo hâts, or markets, at which the cotton is sold or bartered are very interesting scenes. That at Putimári, frequented by the Abengya Garos, is the largest. It is held in a grove of pípal trees on the banks of a small river, the Kalú. On the evening preceding the market day, the channel of the Kalú, in which scarce a boat is at other times seen, becomes crowded with all kinds of small craft; at the same time long lines of Garos are seen winding their way to the grove from various directions, bending under their bulky loads of cotton packed in baskets seven or eight feet high. The man is altogether lost in the vastness of his burden, and you behold hundreds of these elongated baskets apparently furnished with legs and walking on them briskly to market. The market is supplied with everything that can possibly be required either by the Garos or by the lowlanders. Provisions of all kinds, pigs, poultry, sheep, oxen, goats, rice, millet, pulses, vegetables, clothing of every description worn by the people, ornaments, agricultural implements, spinning wheels, salt, tobacco, and a great deal more; all of which articles and thousands of maunds of cotton brought in by the Garos change owners in a primitive way without any employment of the current coin of the realm!

Markets.

The Garos arriving on the preceding day bivouac in groups sheltered by the long cotton baskets. In the morning a still greater influx takes place. About noon the market drum beats, and the scene, which till then had been a quiet one, changes into one of the utmost bustle, confusion, and noise. The Garos are all in motion, rushing about with bundles of cotton weighing two pounds, the small change with which they provide their wants; but it is difficult to follow their evolutions in such a crowd, and in a short time a great part of the cotton appears to have changed hands without your knowing why or how. By degrees as the commerce becomes slacker, you may note an isolated transaction. A Garo has fixed his eye on that fine white chanticleer. He wildly rushes up to the owner, into whose hands he thrusts a bundle of cotton and seizes the bird; but the poulterer turns coldly away as if he and his cock had only come as spectators, and were not inclined to do business at all. The poor Garo, as excited as a gambler, doubles his bid; at last the bargain is effected, the hillman joins his com-

* Reynolds. Asiatic Society's Journal, January, 1849.

R

panions exulting in the possession of the cock, and the Bengali methodically proceeds to weigh the cotton and calculate how much he has made by the transaction.

Physical traits.

Buchanan says, "the Garos are short, stout-limbed, active people, with strongly marked Chinese countenances, as is the case with all the aboriginal tribes from the Brahmaputra to Cape Negrais. In general, the features of the Garos are harsh, but their chiefs are rather handsome." The beauty of the aristocracy did not strike me. I consider on the contrary they had, in comparison with the lower classes and the slaves, degenerated in physique, a result perhaps of close inter-breeding; but Buchanan may not have seen much of the Garos of the interior, who are generally fairer and better looking than those who live in villages bordering on the plains. The women are, on the whole, the most unlovely of the sex, but I was struck with the pretty, plump, nude figures, the merry musical voices and good humoured countenances, of the Garo girls. Their sole garment is a piece of cloth less than a foot in breadth that just meets round the loins, and in order that it may not restrain the limbs, it is only fastened where it meets under the hip at the upper corners. The girls are thus greatly restricted in the positions they may modestly assume, but decorum is, in their opinion, sufficiently preserved if they only keep their legs well together when they sit or kneel. They wear brass rings in their ears, and a few strings of beads of cornelian round their necks, as well as occasionally brass chains; amongst the Lyntea Garos many may be seen unadorned, and that clan never carry their decoration to such an extravagant length as do the Abengya Garo females. The latter wear huge curtain rings in their ears. The head gear is arbitrary; some appear with turbans, some without, and some wear round their heads a simple band of colored cotton.

Costume.

The Garo males, on the whole, become their nudity better than the females. Their sole garment is a long and narrow strip of cloth which is worn as a girdle round the waist, and passing from behind between the legs is brought up again to the waist, from which the end, as a flap, about six inches in breadth and often highly ornamented, hangs down in front. Their faces are round and short. The forehead is not receding, but projects very little beyond the eye, which is small, on a level with the face, very dark and obliquely set. The want of prominence in the nose is remarkable. The whole face has the appearance of being flattened, the mouth sharing in the compressed appearance and not at all prognathous. Amongst the youthful there are intelligent, mirth-loving faces not devoid of interest; but the beauty of both sexes is ephemeral. The women soon grow into hags: and the features and countenance of the males become after maturity, from hard work, constant exposure, free indulgence of passions, and the use of intoxicating drinks to which all are devoted, bloated, coarse, fierce, and sensual.

Features.

From the life scene of the markets we must come at last to the grave. Buchanan says, the funeral of the Achhiks (the name he gives to the Lynteas) are inconvenient and expensive. When a person dies, the relations are summoned to attend, and ten or twelve days are allowed for their convenience; as they assemble they are feasted till the number is complete. In the mean time the body falls into a dreadful state of corruption, but no attention is paid to that. The head of a stake is then formed into an image supposed to resemble the deceased,

Funeral ceremonies.

and the point of the stake is driven into the ground. The body is then burnt, the bones are collected in an earthen pot, and the relations retire. After some months, when the family has recovered from the former expense, and has laid in a stock of food and liquor, the relations are again assembled and feasted for three days. The bones are then thrown into a river.

The several clans may have different customs, or customs may change. Dr. Latham, quoting Mr. Elliot,* says,—"The dead are kept for four days, then burnt: the ashes are buried in a hole on the place where the fire was. A small thatched building is next raised over them, which is afterwards railed in. For a month, or more, a lamp is lit every night in this building. The clothes of the deceased hang on poles one at each corner of the railing. When the pile is set fire to, there is great feasting and drunkenness."

The following is an account of what took place under my own observation in an Abengya village:—

The daughter of the Sirdar had died previous to my arrival; the body had been burnt the preceding night, and the people were about to dispose of the ashes when I entered the village. This portion of the ceremony I had consequently an opportunity of observing. The funeral pile had been ignited within three or four paces of the house. This is the orthodox practice, and notwithstanding the proximity of the fire, no accident ever occurs, the house being at such times under the special protection of the gods. The village carpenter was preparing one of the posts that are on such occasions always erected under the porch, or just outside it. He had completed the carving and was painting it with the blood of the bullocks that had been slaughtered for the feast. It had further to be decorated with the beads and earrings of the departed and the skulls of the bulls that had been killed in her honor. In front of the house, an oblong frame of bamboo work was constructed, about two feet high, three feet broad, and six feet long, four carved poles diagonally placed protruded from the four corners, and a lid of open lattice work was lying ready prepared to be put over it. Inside the frame a small round hole was made, in which the remains of the young girl, collected from amongst the ashes of the funeral pile, were reverentially deposited by her nearest female relatives—her mother and her aunts. When this was done and the hole filled up with earth, the same individuals proceeded to fill the frame above it with various offerings, of which I noted the following:—Three baskets of raw cotton, four baskets of unthrashed rice in husk, two grilled fowls, a few dozen shrimps, boiled rice, eggs, red pepper, turmeric, pulses, salt, gourds full of rice-beer, and, lastly, earthen vessels, all of which were broken as they were thrown in. They said, the spirit of the girl would not benefit by them if they were given unbroken, but for her the fragments would unite again. The lid was then put on, and over it, as a canopy, a silk cloth supported on hoops was extended.

Whilst this was going on, the lads of the village were beating drums, striking gongs, and blowing horns. A bull fight was exhibited which attracted crowds of spectators, and but for the solemn demeanour and sad face of the old mother, as she slowly and quietly put one offering after another into the tomb of her child, all bore the appearance of a merry meeting, an occasion rather of rejoicing and carousal than one the cause of which was death. The deceased had only numbered ten years. The veneration paid

* Asiatic Researches, Vol. III.

to their dead is irrespective of sex or age. The frame I have been describing with its contents is allowed to remain a twelve month, after which it is burned, and the event is made the occasion of fresh rejoicings and feastings. The carved posts of the Garos take the place of the stones set up as cenotaphs by their neighbours, the Kasias, by the remote Hos and other tribes.

It was formerly the practice amongst the Garos, whenever the death of a great man amongst them occurred, to send out a party of assassins to murder and bring back the head of the first Bengali they met. The victims so immolated would, it was supposed, be acceptable to their gods, and the clans preserved the skulls as the proudest trophies they could adorn their halls with. Such bloody and inhuman trophies have, it is believed, disappeared from all the Garo villages in connection with the British Government, and amongst them the immolation of human victims in honor of the dead has been discontinued, and they even profess a proud horror of the practice.

National temperament.

Turning from this dark spot in their character, we find in it many good points. They are lively, good natured, hospitable, frank and honest in their dealings, till contaminated by their intercourse with Bengalis, and they possess that pearl of great price so rare amongst Eastern nations—a love of truth. They will not hastily make engagements, because when they do make them, they intend to keep them. They are affectionate fathers and kind husbands, and their conduct generally towards the weaker sex is marked by consideration and respect. Notwithstanding the lavish exposure of their persons, the women are chaste and make good steady wives.

VOCABULARIES

VOCABULARIES OF THE TRIBES DESCRIBED IN GROUP I.

1.—THE SHAN GROUP. *

ENGLISH.	AHOM.	KHAMTI.	LAOS.	SIAMESE.
One	ling	nung	nung	nung.
Two	sang	song	song	song.
Three	sam	sám	sám	sám.
Four	sí	sí	sí	sí.
Five	há	há	há	há.
Six	ruk	hok	hok	hok.
Seven	chit	tset	tset	chet.
Eight	pet	pet	pet	pet.
Nine	kau	kau	kau	kau.
Ten	sip	sip	sip	sip.
Twenty	sau	sau	san nung	ye sip.
Fifty	há sip	há sip	há sip	há sip.
Hundred	pak	pák	hoi	roi.
I	kau	kau	ku, ong	khá.
We	rau	hau	hau	rau.
Thou	mo	maü	toa	tua, mung.
You	khau	mau su	......	su.
He	heu	man	man, tan	khon, man.
They	khreu	man khau	......	khau ar ai.
Of me	......	......	......	......
Of us	......	......	......	......
Of thee	......	......	......	......
Of you	......	......	......	......
Of him	......	......	......	......
Of them	......	......	......	......
Mine	au, kau	kau	......	khonkha.
Our	rau	hau	......	khonkha-tsoung.
Thine	mo	mau	......	khoung-aeng.
Your	khau	mau-su	......	khrong-tsoung-aen.
His	heu	man	......	khoung-troung.
Their	khreu	man-khau	......	khonkha-tsoung-aen.
Hand	khá	mu	mu	mu.
Foot	tin	tin	tín	tin.
Nose	......	......	......	......
Eye	tá	tá	tá	tá.
Mouth	sup	sop	pák	pák.
Tooth	khiu	khiu	khiau	fan, khiau.
Ear	pik	hú	hú	hú.
Hair	phrum	phom	phom	phom
Head	rú	ho	ho	hoa.
Tongue	......	......	......	......
Belly	......	......	......	......
Back	......	......	......	......
Iron	lik	lek	lek	lek.
Gold	......	......	......	......
Silver	......	......	......	......
Go	ká	ká	pai, men	pai.
Eat	kin	kin	kin	kin.

* Journal, Asiatic Society, Bengal, No. IV, of 1850, page 313.

ENGLISH.	AHOM.	KHAMTI.	LAOS.	SIAMESE.
Sit ...	nang ...	nang ...	nang ...	nang.
Father ...	po ...	po ...	po ...	po.
Mother ...	me ...	me ...	me ...	me.
Brother ...	......	......	......	......
Sister ...	......	......	......	......
Man ...	kun ...	kun ...	khon ...	khon.
Woman ...	......	......	......	......
Wife ...	......	......	......	......
Child ...	......	......	......	......
Son ...	......	......	......	......
Daughter ...	......	......	......	......
Slave ...	......	......	......	......
Cultivator ...	......	......	......	......
Shepherd ...	......	......	......	......
God ...	......	......	......	......
Devil ...	......	......	......	......
Come ...	má ...	má ...	má ...	má.
Beat ...	......	......	......	......
Stand ...	tí ...	sau ...	song ...	yun.
Sun ...	bán ...	wan ...	kangwan ...	tawan.
Moon ...	den ..	lun ...	deun ...	tawan.
Star ...	dau ...	nau ...	lau ...	dau.
Fire ...	fai ...	fai ...	ai ...	fai.
Water ...	nam ...	nam ...	nam ...	nam.
House ...	ren ...	hun ...	heun ...	reuan.
Horse ...	má ...	má ...	má ...	má.
Cow ...	hu ...	ngo ...	ngoa ...	woa, ngoa.
Dog ...	má ...	má ...	má ...	má.
Cat ...	men ...	miau ...	meau ...	meau.
Cock ...	......	......	......	......
Duck ...	......	......	......	......
Ass ...	......	......	......	......
Camel ...	......	......	......	......
Bird ...	nuktú ...	nok ...	nok ...	nok.
Die ...	......	......	......	......
Give ...	heu ...	hau ...	hu ...	hai.
Run ...	paikhan ...	len ...	len pai ...	wing pi.
Up ...	......	......	......	......
Near ...	klai ...	kau ...	kai ...	klai.
Who ...	phreu ...	phau ...	khai, phai ...	khrai, sung.
And ...	......	......	le ...	le, kap, tak.
Yes ...	khewo ...	tsau ...	tsai, men ...	khá.
Down ...	......	......	......	......
Far ...	jau, sai ...	kai ...	kaí ...	kli.
What ...	re ...	sang ...	sang ...	arai.
But ...	......	......	......	......
No ...	bukhewo ...	ma tsau ...	bo-tsai ...	míchi.
Before ...	......	......	......	......
Behind ...	......	......	......	......
Why ...	wá ...	......	......	phrá, aurai.
If ...	......	......	......	......
Alas ...	......	......	......	......

2.—SINGPHO, AND EASTERN AND ANGAMI NAGAS, AND KAREN.

ENGLISH.	SINGPHO.*	MITHAN NAGA.†	TABLUNG NAGA.†	KHARI NAGA.†	WHITE KAREN.‡	RED KAREN.‡	ANGAMI NAGA.§
One	aimá	áttá	chá	akhet	ta	ta	po.
Two	nkhong	ányí	íh	anne	khie	ne	kana.
Three	masúm	ázam	lem	asam	theu	theu	se.
Four	melí	álí	pilí	phalí	lwie	lwie	da.
Five	mangá	ágá	ngá	phangá	yay	nya	pengoo.
Six	krú	árok	vok	tarok	khu	theutho	shúroo.
Seven	sinit	ánath	nith	tani	nwie	theuthota	thena.
Eight	matsat	áchet	thath	sachet	kho	lwietho	theta.
Nine	tsekhú	aku	thu	teku	khwie	lwiethota	the koo.
Ten	sí	ban	pan	tarah	tahsie	tashe	kerr.
Twenty	khún	chá	......	makhi	khiehsie	neshe	mekoo.
Fifty	mangásí	......	......	tanam	yay hsie	nya shie	lhi pengoo.
Hundred	latsá	pugá	......	rukrá	takaya	tayay	kra.
I	ngai	ku	tau	ní	ya, yeu	va	a.
We	í	......	......	akau	peu, pa	pay	úko.
Thou	náng, ní	nang	nang	nang	na, neu	na	no.
You	nítheng	......	......	nikhala	thu	thie	neko.
He	khí	mih	taupá	pau	a *or* way	a	loo.
They	khíní	......	......	tungkhala	a *or* way	a	lúko.
Of me	......	......	......	......	ya, yeu	va	......
Of us	......	......	......	......	peu, pa	pay	......
Of thee	......	......	......	......	na, neu	na	......
Of you	......	......	......	......	thu	thie	......
Of him	......	......	......	......	a	a	......
Of them	......	......	......	......	a	a	......
Mine	ngená	kukuhe,	tesei	ní	......	......	ave.
Our	......	......	......	......	......	......	ukove.
Thine	náná	......	......	nang	......	......	nove.
Your	......	......	......	......	......	......	nekove.
His	khíná	......	......	......	......	......	lúve.
Their	......	......	......	......	......	......	lukove.
Hand	lettá	chak	yak	takhet	su	su	u bijú.
Foot	lagong	tchyá	yah-lan	tachang	khau	kha	uphi ju.
Nose	......	......	......	......	......	......	únheu.
Eye	mi	mik	mik	tenik	may	may	umhí.
Mouth	ninggup	tun	chusim	tabaun	......	......	ume.
Tooth	wá	vá	phá	taphá	may	kho-khe	uhoo
Ear	ná	ná	ná	tenhaun	na	kha-lay	uneu.
Hair	kará	kho	min su	kwá	kho-thoo	kho-lya	uchitha.
Head	bong	kháng	sang	telim	kho	hoo-krau	úchú.
Tongue	......	......	......	......	......	......	......
Belly	......	......	......	......	......	......	ûva.
Back	......	......	......	......	......	......	uche.
Iron	mpri	jián	yan	ayin	hta	hto-htay	thejirr.
Gold	......	......	......	......	......	......	......
Silver	......	......	......	......	......	......	rakahurr.
Go	wán	tong	angsi	wá	lay	syeu	phiche.
Eat	sháu	sá há	háchi	tsaung	au	e	chiche.
Sit	dúngu	ngo dau	um chi	manio	hse-nau	o-nya	bá le.

* Journal, Asiatic Society, Bengal, September, 1[illegible], p. 969.
† Ditto, No. IV of 1850, p. 313.
‡ Ditto, No. IV of 1866, Pt. II., p. 239.
§ Ditto, No. VII of 1856. p. 658.

NOTE.—The Red Karen is placed here because Red Karen and Singpho languages have been compared. But the examples given do not substantiate the supposed connection.
The Angami Nága has been introduced to show how distinct it is from the language of the Eastern Nágas.

ENGLISH.	SINGPHO.	MITHAN NAGA.	TABLUNG NAGA.	KHARI NAGA.	WHITE KAREN.	RED KAREN.	ANGAMI NAGA.
Father	wá	apá	opáh	tabá	pa	phay	apú.
Mother	nú	ánnu	onu	tu	mo	meu	azo.
Brother	......	......	......	......	......	......	shajou.
Sister	......	......	......	......	......	......	lúpú.
Man	singpho	mí	sauniak	ami	pgha-knyau	pray-ka-ya	ma.
Woman	......	......	......	......	......	......	thenúma.
Wife	......	......	......	......	......	......	......
Child	......	......	......	......	......	......	......
Son	......	......	......	......	......	......	no.
Daughter	......	......	......	......	......	......	ponoiye.
Slave	......	......	......	......	......	......	......
Cultivator	......	......	......	......	......	......	......
Shepherd	......	......	......	......	......	......	......
God	......	......	......	......	......	......	durhoma.
Devil	......	......	......	......	......	......	......
Come	sáu	ráhai	ongkoi	hinnerang	hay	ray, ha	wáng lao.
Beat	......	......	......	......	......	......	......
Stand	tsapu rotu	ajong	yong chi	hun ligili	hseu-hteu	se-htau	se le.
Sun	ján	rang hán	wang hí	suhih	mu	lamoo	naki.
Moon	sitá	letnu	le	leta	la	lay	thirr.
Star	sigan	lethi	cháhá	peti	hsa	shay	themu.
Fire	wan	van	áh	matsu	me-oo	me	mí.
Water	ntsiu	ti	riang	atsu	htie	htye	zu.
House	ntá	ham	nok	aki	hie	híe	kí.
Horse	gumrang	man	kowai	kungri	ka-the	ta-the	kirr.
Cow	kansú	máhu	máhu	masu	klau, po	po, pu	mithoo.
Dog	guí	hí	kui	ai	htwie	htwie	thafú.
Cat	ningyau	miáh	ami	mochi	tha-mie-yeu	htoo	leno.
Cock	......	......	......	......	......	......	......
Duck	......	......	......	......	......	......	......
Ass	......	......	......	......	......	......	......
Camel	......	......	......	......	......	......	......
Bird	wu	o	ouhá	ozah	hto	htu	pura.
Die	......	......	......	......	......	......	satale.
Give	yáu	láhai	yakhu	khiugo	he	dye	chú le.
Run	gagátu	rikle	phal chi	semekwa	sie	kywa	ta-le.
Up	......	......	......	......	......	......	......
Near	ní	hole	otike	anhagu	boo	phoo	jeu.
Who	gadaimá	oveh	owai	sui	matataghalay	......	s opo gh.
And	......	......	......	......	dau	vau	di.
Yes	raia	vai	aiya	hau	eu, me yeu	eu, ma hau	úwe.
Down	......	......	......	......	......	......	......
Far	tsán	atai	kátike	uragu	yie	ye	cha cha.
What	phakaimá	tem	toi nan	chabau	......	......	kajibo.
But	......	......	......	......	......	......	sá.
No	galai	mantai	mang cha	nongo	ta-me-bá	to	mowe.
Before	......	......	......	......	......	......	lookí.
Behind	......	......	......	......	......	......	ussa.
Why	fári	......	......	chibatsawi	bamanulay	baytiete	kele.
If	......	......	......	......	......	......	nole.
Alas	......	......	......	......	......	......	......

3.—Abor, Miri, Dophla, and Angka Vocabulary.

English.	Abor.*	Miri.*	Dophla.†	Angka or Hrusso.‡	Angka (second column)
One	áko	áko	áken	......	á.
Two	áni	ániko	áni	......	'kse.
Three	angom	áumko	á-ám	......	'tse.
Four	ápi	ápiko	áplí	......	pferi.
Five	pilángo	angoko	ángo	......	pfúmu.
Six	ákye	ákengko	ákple	......	ri.
Seven	konange	kinit ko	kánag	......	'mue.
Eight	pini	piníko	plag-nag	......	khi or ksi.
Nine	kinide	konángk	káyo	......	stho.
Ten	linge	uyingko	ráng	......	erh.
Twenty	......	i-ling-ko	ráng chách	......	b'shá.
Fifty	......	......	......	......	serre.
Hundred	......	......	......	......	púrrúá.
I	ngo	ngo	ngo	......	'nyo.
We	......	ngoluke or ngolu	ngo-lu	......	ni.
Thou	......	no	no	......	bá.
You	......	no-lu	no-lu	......	jö, jöe.
He	bu	bu	ma	......	phö.
They	......	bu-lu	má-lu	......	b'goúná.
Of me	......	ngog	ngog	......	náthi or nad ki.
Of us	......	ngolug	ngo-lug	......	nithi.
Of thee	......	nog	nog	......	báthi.
Of you	......	no-lug	no-lug	......	báthi.
Of him	......	bug	mág	......	öthi.
Of them	......	bu-lug	má-lug	......	b'góunáthi.
Mine	......	......	......	......	...
Our	......	......	......	......	...
Thine	......	......	......	......	...
Your	......	......	......	......	...
His	......	......	......	......	...
Their	......	......	......	......	...
Hand	elág	elág	lák	lák	gsi.
Foot	ale	leppa	lágá	lágá	'ssi.
Nose	nobung	nye wung	nyopom	......	nusu.
Eye	áming	ámidá	nyúk	nyek	ni.
Mouth	nepáng	náppáng	gám	gám	'nsú.
Tooth	áye	áye	fig	phi	thú.
Ear	narung	jerung	niorong	nyárung	phú.
Hair	dumid	dumid	dumuk	demuk	kechu.
Head	dumpong, tupko	tupko, mito-oko	dompo	dumpa	khfe.
Tongue	aiyo	joper	ro	......	jáblá.
Belly	áki	áki	kopo	......	negúju.
Back	lámku	lámku	gárpo	......	súbúe.
Iron	yogir	yogir	rokdor	kakdhar	'ssa.
Gold	ángin	áiná	aen	......	shu.
Silver	ámel	ámel, rup	tángku	......	lumma.
Go	gikángku	gikánka, gitoká	ángne	......	khábúe.
Eat	dolá	dolá	do	......	tsánúe or cháúe.
Sit	dulá	du toká	dong-to	......	roúeorriúe.

* Journal, Asiatic Society, Bengal, March, 1849, p. 226.
† Ditto, No. 2, 1851, p. 135.
‡ The first column of Angka or Hrusso words is taken from Robinson's Asam, p. 339, A. D. 1841; the second column from Revd. C. H. Hesselmeyer's paper in Journal, Asiatic Society, Bengal, Vol. XXXVII, Pt. II, 1868, p. 202.

ENGLISH.	ÁBOR.	MIRI.	DOPHLA.	ANGKA OR HRUSSO.	
Father	bábá	bábá	ábo	abba	áu.
Mother	náne	náná	áne	ane	áni.
Brother	ani, ábing	ani, payá	(a) tette (b) boro	......	'nyu.
Sister	búrne	átungá	(a) ámá (b) burmá	......	numi.
Man	ámie	ámie	bángni	bangne	nuná.
Woman	menge	mimmo	niemá	......	pfumi.
Wife	meng	miyeng	mige, niofáng	......	gsi.
Child	ko	ko	ángá	......	ángásá.
Son	o	áue	káo	......	sáú.
Daughter	ome	ammah	niomeká	......	sámi.
Slave	......	......	......	......	khlá.
Cultivator	......	......	......	......	víddóu.
Shepherd	......	......	......	......	fudsúsúen.
God	......	doinitálenge?	oyuk	......	shemúzu.
Devil	......	......	......	......	......
Come	ápolá	kápe	angkubo	......	ágekhaue.
Beat	dídúng	demtoká	mo-to	......	gugá.
Stand	dág	dág toká	dok-to	......	gudzulúe.
Sun	árung	dainyá, arung	dani	dahani	dsú.
Moon	polo	polo	polo	pala	khúbie.
Star	tekár	tákár	tákar	takar	lítsie.
Fire	eme	ummá	ame	ummah	mí.
Water	ásí	áchye	esi	issi	khú.
House	ekum	ekum	ou	ú	'nie.
Horse	gure	gore	gorá	ghurá	fúgrá.
Cow	sou	goru (Asam)	su	shye	fúlúkhú.
Dog	ekki	ekkye	ek-ki	eki	sulo.
Cat	kedári	mendári	áche	ásá	áshásá.
Cock	......	......	......	......	dámrou.
Duck	pezák	pezáb	háns	......	ossá.
Ass	......	......	......	......	fúbábá.
Camel	......	......	......	......	......
Bird	pettáng	pettáng	páttá	putáh	duo.
Die	sikkai	si-káng	sig-to	......	budzíbi.
Give	bi	bi-toká	ke-bikto	......	jíbá.
Run	dup to ká	duptoká	fár-to	......	godzue.
Up	......	......	......	......	ráfú.
Near	mong-yo	ánindág	berá	......	enísá.
Who	......	......	he	......	ánínáshe.
And	......	......	......	......	hámso.
Yes	árwe	hu, awe, eggidá	u	......	o.
Down	......	......	......	......	rámge.
Far	mordo	mordo	ádopá	......	ánierá.
What	......	......	hogo	......	hándo.
But	......	......	......	......	hámso.
No	má	má	má	......	ma.
Before	......	......	......	......	ávvá.
Behind	......	......	......	......	fúmú.
Why	......	......	hogo-áráng	......	hándo.
If	......	......	......	......	soio.
Alas	......	......	......	......	áh! kíníá! duniá.

(a) elder.
(b) younger.

4.—KUKI GROUP.*

ENGLISH.	MANIPURI.	KUKI.	ARUNG NAGA.	ANGAMI NAGA.	OLD KUKI.	MIKIR.
One	amá	khut	kut	po	khat	hisí.
Two	ani	ni	kaná	kana	nik	hiní.
Three	ahoom	thúm	kachúm	se	thúm	kithom.
Four	mari	lí	madai	da	li	phi li.
Five	manga	nga	mingou	pengoo	ranga	phanga.
Six	tarúk	goop	sherúk	shúroo	irook	therok.
Seven	taret	suggi	siná	thena	surri	theroksi.
Eight	nipál	get	tisat	theta	riet	nir kep.
Nine	mápal	ko	sikooi	the koo	ikok	sir kep.
Ten	tará	som	kerou	kerr	som	kep.
Twenty	kool	som ni	ng kai	mekoo	som nik	ing koi.
Fifty	yáng khai	som nga	rengeo	lhi pengoo	som rangá	phongo kep.
Hundred	chámá	za khut	hai	kra	rizá	pháro sí.
I	ei	kei	í	......	kei	nge.
We	ei khoi	keiho	anui	úko	kei ma ni	nge túm.
Thou	nung	nung	nung	no	nung	nung.
You	nung khoi	nung ho	nung nui	neko	nung mani	nung túm.
He	ma	hi khú	wi	loo	khú	náng.
They	ma khoi	hi ho	wi nui	lúko	khú mani	náng túm.
Of me	......	......	......	......	......	......
Of us	......	......	......	......	......	......
Of thee	......	......	......	......	......	......
Of you	......	......	......	......	......	......
Of him	......	......	......	......	......	......
Of them	......	......	......	......	......	......
Mine	ei gi	kei ma	agoo	ave	keimarhung	nge li.
Our	ei khoi gi	kei ho a	anui goo	ukove	keimanirhung	nge túm li.
Thine	nunggi	nung ma	nung goo	nove	nungmarhung	nung li.
Your	nung khoi gi	nung ho a	nung mugoo	nekove	nungmanir-hung	nung túm li.
His	magi	hima	wi goo	lúve	khúmarhung	náng li.
Their	ma khoi gi	hi ho a	wi niu goo	lukove	khúmanirhung	nang túm li.
Hand	khút pák	khut páng	miba	u bijú	khút ja	ri pa.
Foot	khúng pa	keng pang	mi pi pa	uphi jú	phei ja	keng pak.
Nose	na tol	ná	mi neo	únheu	nár	ino kan.
Eye	mit	mit	mi mík	umhí	mit	mek.
Mouth	chil	kum	mi mooi	ume	bai	ingho.
Tooth	yá	há	mi geo	uhoo	ha	isso.
Ear	na	bil	mi kon	uneu	kúr	ino.
Hair	shum	shum	mi tám	uchitha	shum	choo.
Head	moko	loo	mi pei	úchú	loo	iphoo.
Tongue	......	......	......	......	......	......
Belly	púk	of	mi búng	úva	phoom	ipok.
Back	nungul	tong tum	mi ching	uche	búk	inoong.
Iron	yot	thík	hegei	thejirr	cheng chí	inchin.
Gold	suna	lángkecha	kuchák	......	ráugke chuk	hon er.
Silver	loopa	danka	gofoo	rakahurr	shúm cheng	hon lok.
Go	......	......	......	......	......	......
Eat	cháo	nen	jeo lao	chiche	neng	cholo.
Sit	phumo	touvin	intao lao	bá le	i thúng rou	kang ni.

* Journal Asiatic Society, Bengal, No. VII of 1856, p. 658.

ENGLISH.	MANIPURI.	KUKI.	ARUNG NAGA.	ANGAMI NAGA.	OLD KUKI.	MIKIR.
Father	ipá	pa	apeo	apú	pa	po.
Mother	imá	noo	apúi	azo	noo	ipei.
Brother	nao	náo	así	shajou	nai	ík.
Sister	ichem, ichul	naonoo	así púi	lúpú	oonai	ingyirpi.
Man	mi-nipa	mi	jai mana	ma	mí	ar leng.
Woman	núpi	númei	mi púi	thenumá	núpung	ar loso.
Wife	......	......	......	......	......	......
Child	......	......	......	......	......	......
Son	ichá	pashul	aná	no	rothur	neso po.
Daughter	ichánúpi	pashulnoo	aná púí	ponoiye	dongma	niso pi.
Slave	......	......	......	......	......	......
Cultivator	......	......	......	......	......	......
Shepherd	......	......	......	......	......	......
God	lai	puthen	hurá	durhoma	putbín	arnam.
Devil	shuroi	hilo	ghumpeo	medovi	khori	hi í.
Come	láo	húng in	phir che	wáng loa	húngro	wáng.
Beat	......	......	......	......	......	......
Stand	lebo	ding in	sáb lao	se le	iding	kurjáp.
Sun	númit	ni	tingnaimek	naki	iní	arní.
Moon	thá	lha	hekeu	thirr	ithlha	cheklo.
Star	tho mucha	ashi	higgí	themú	arshi	cheklo longsho
Fire	mei	mei	mí	mí	mei	me.
Water	ishing	tui	doi	zú	tui	lang.
House	yim	in	kí	kí	in	hem.
Horse	sagol	sakol	hokon	kirr	sakor	losai.
Cow	sul	silát	kútom	mithoo	sirát	cháinong.
Dog	hwí	wicha	settei	thafú	wíte	mathán.
Cat	houdong	mengcha	miyou na	leno	imeng	meng.
Cock	......	......	......	......	......	......
Duck	......	......	......	......	......	......
Ass	......	......	......	......	......	......
Camel	......	......	......	......	......	......
Bird	úchek	vacha	hin-rooi	pura	ivá	vo.
Die	shíro	thí in	chei lao	satale	thíro	thi not.
Give	pi o	pen	pe lao	chú le	pero	pi not.
Run	che lo	tájin	págh lao	tale	herai	kikát.
Up	......	......	......	......	......	......
Near	nugle	nai cha	ná da	jeu	kho nai	ti bo kher.
Who	kunáno	koi	chow lo	sopo gha	tú pei	mád lo.
And	súng	chile	chaine	di	khun chu	kúlapoo.
Yes	hoi	henge	eoo	úwe	anit	hoi tema.
Down	......	......	......	......	......	......
Far	arápa	ghum cheng	deoda	cha cha	rum mohl	hi lo ving.
What	kuri	í	indai	kajibo	ím	pí.
But	adoga	chú in	chaine	sá	......	polo.
No	nate	......	eh	mowe	ni muk	kali.
Before	mangda	amusa	rei lou	lookí	amása	ako.
Behind	tungda	núnga	na lou	ussa	núng ita	aphi.
Why	karigi tumuk	í dínga	dai lou	kele	irhungime	kopi lo.
If	bacli	ma	indamei	nole	ait nága	molo.
Alas	......	......	......	......	......	......

GROUP II.

POPULATION OF THE ASAM VALLEY.

SECTION 1.—GENERAL VIEW.

We have been hitherto surveying the people occupying the upper tiers of the amphitheatre of Asam. As we must now take up a new group, tribes who are rather in the plains than in the hills, it may be convenient, before we go further, to descend into the arena and to take note of the performers we find there.

I have already stated that the Shan people, calling themselves Ahoms, who effected the conquest of all the tribes in the valley and founded the kingdom of Asam, became proselytes to Hinduism at an early period, and, adopting the language and customs of Hindus, have now nothing but feature to mark them as of different origin. From the very softened type of Indo-Chinese features which they exhibit, it is probable that the blending of the races was not confined to an adoption of religion, language, and custom. Indeed, it is stated that the Shans brought no women with them into the country, and found the daughters of the land so fair, that they deemed it quite unnecessary to send for the girls they had left behind them. This sufficiently accounts for their improvement in looks and deterioration in other respects. I have seen very handsome faces amongst the Ahom nobility. The ladies of the ex-royal family were noted for their beauty, with oval faces, features not very prominent but sufficiently raised and regular, large eyes, and long, silky, hair.

The Hindu population of Asam, including mongrels and proselytes, now consists of Brahmans, Ganaks,* Káists, all of comparatively modern importation, Kolitas, who appear to be the only remnant we have of the early Aryan colonists, Keots, who are partly of Hindu extraction and partly proselytes raised to that position, Doms, who form the class of boatmen and fishermen, and Haris, low caste immigrants, and converted Ahoms, Chutias, Lalongs, Kocchis, Mechis, and Kacharis.

The Chutias were the dominant race in Upper Asam when the Ahoms swarmed into the valley. Their kingdom was overturned by the Ahom chief Chutupha about A. D. 1350, and great numbers of the nation were deported and forced to settle in other parts of Asam, as in Chutia of the Durrung District; but still a great many of the Sadya and Upper Asam population are Chutias. The tribe called Bihiya are of the

---

* Who also have pretensions to be Brahmans. Several of this class obtained high appointments under the Asam Government, and their superior intelligence has secured to them the same positions under our Government. They are employed at funeral obsequies.

U

same family, and as a tribe of Lalongs in Upper Asam claim to be of Chutia descent, it is not unlikely that all the Lalongs are Chutias.

The Chutias, long before the appearance of the Ahoms, had adopted Hindu customs, and placed themselves under the tutelage of Brahmanical priests; they are now therefore less distinguishable from the Hindus of pure extraction than are the Ahoms, and I find from a note to an article on the antiquities of Upper Asam, by the late Colonel Hannay, that he classed them with the Kolitas as a remnant of the old Kshettrya race of Kamrup.

The Chutias are of a light olive complexion, with rather regular features; but there is generally amongst them a flatness of face and a want of sharpness in the features, which militates against the theory of their Aryan origin; moreover, they rank low as a Hindu caste in Asam, and they call themselves 'Hindu Chutia,' to show that they are no longer 'Mlechchas.' It was long before anything was discovered of their language; but an isolated colony on the river Dikrung in Luckimpur, calling themselves 'Deori Chutia,' were found, who had a peculiar language which they called Chutia, and they were styled Deoris, because they had been attached as priests to a certain temple, formerly of great celebrity, above Sadya, called the Tamasuri Mai, where human sacrifices were yearly offered. Another colony of the same tribe was found by Colonel Hannay occupying a very remote position in Upper Asam, and still performing the priestly duties of a certain shrine dedicated to Kali. If the dialect spoken by these Deoris be truly the language of the Chutias, it proves the linguistic affinities of the tribe to be with the Garo and Bodo. In the number of the Asiatic Society's Journal for May 1849 will be found the Deori Chutia vocabulary, which does not appear at all at home amongst the Naga and Shan languages with which it is placed; but if it be compared with the Garo and Bodo vocabularies in the Journal No. 4 for 1850, its relationship with those languages will be very apparent. I find more than 20 analogues in 64 words, and when it is added that the Deori Chutias were found hundreds of miles from the Garos, or people speaking the Bodo tongue, such a proportion, of nearly a third, must be sufficient to establish a pretty close connection.

I once met with an old Asamese 'Burinji' (chronicle), purporting to be a history of the Chutias. According to this they entered Upper Asam from the northern hills; it is noticed that they crossed the Subanshiri, (though no mention is made of the Dihong), and proceeding east established themselves at Sadya, and, in conjunction with a Brahmanical race already settled there, founded a kingdom of sufficient importance to receive an embassy and to interchange presents with the king of Gaur. The legend has it that the Hindu ruler of Sadya, who was a descendant of the father of Rukmuni, offered his daughter to be competed for at a great archery meeting, and she was won by a Chutia youth, who married her and was adopted by her father, and afterwards on succeeding to the *gaddi* took the name of Sisopal. This story was in all probability invented by Brahmans to disguise the fact that the ancient Hindu Pal dynasty, who had for many generations ruled over Kamarupa and Namarup, *i. e.*, Lower Asam, with part of Eastern Bengal and Upper Asam, were overthrown by a barbarian horde. Captain Rowlatt found the remains of a fort ascribed to this monarch, Sisopal, and other relics of Chutia rajahs, on the banks of the Dholla river to the east of Sadya, not far from the copper temple or Tamasuri Mai above mentioned. That temple was visited by

Colonel Hannay in 1848 and found dismantled and deserted.* The Burmese have the credit of having put a stop to the human sacrifices annually offered there. The victims were provided by a particular tribe who, in consideration of this unpleasant duty, were exempted from other service and taxes, and called 'sar,' free.

The Kolitas are to be found in every district of Asam, and as no one appears to know how they got there or where they came from, we may infer that they are the remnant of the earliest colonists of the valley. Hodgson, in his paper on the Bodos, speaks of the Kolitas as Bodo priests. It is true that many of the Bodos adopted their religion and priesthood. But no one who has studied their physical characteristics can for a moment suppose them to be relations of the Bodo, or doubt their distinct Aryan origin.

They are not only themselves a good-looking race, but they are the people to whom the Asamese population generally owe the softening of feature which has so improved those of Mongolian descent. The Kolitas exhibit a greater variety of complexion, and, on the whole, are not so fair as the Ahoms and Chutias or as the people of the hills, but they have oval faces, well-shaped heads, high noses, large eyes, well-developed eye-lids and eye-lashes, and the light, supple frame of the pure Hindu. Colonel Hannay observes in the note above alluded to, that many Kolitas have the grey eye so frequently found amongst the Rajputs of Western India. The Kolitas are in great request in Asam as servants in respectable Hindu families. They are, I think, the only Sudra caste in the valley from whose hands the higher castes will take water.† I do not know of any castes corresponding to them in the western districts; but I find Buchanan-Hamilton says that the Kolitas once had great sway in Rungpur, and many of those remaining there have assumed the title of Káists. As Rungpur was once part of the kingdom of Kamrup, we might expect to find Kolitas there, but a Hindu tribe in every way resembling them and bearing the same name, Kolita, is to be found in the Sambalpur districts and some of the Cuttack and Chota Nagpur Tributary Mehals.‡

These Southern Kolitas are noted for their industry as an agricultural class like the Kurmis, and are a cleanly, well clothed, and good-looking race. There are other circumstances connected with the ethnology of these southern tracts that lead me to infer a very near affinity between their inhabitants and the Hindus of Asam.

I believe we have good grounds for supposing that Asam or Kamarupa was amongst the earliest established of the Eastern Aryan settlements,—Bhagadatta, king of Kamrup, is mentioned as a warrior in the Mahabharata and in the antiquities and traditions of the country,§ and we have proof of its having passed through several phases of faith,—Budhism, Adi Budhism, Sivism, and Vishnuism,—and indications of many fierce struggles for ascendancy by the different sects.

Sivite shrines built on the ruins of a different type of temples, || apparently Budhist, abound in Kamrup, and to many of them the test of antiquity by which the age of the deposits in Egypt were calculated might be applied, as they are found in places far below the surface.

* *See* Journal, Asiatic Society, Bengal, June, 1848.

† In the days of slavery, a Kolita was valued at double the price of a Koech.—*See* Buchanan on Asam, M. Martin's edition, vol. III, page 681.

‡ *See* Journal, Asiatic Society, Bengal, No. 1, for 1855, page 5.

§ *See* article on Chronicles of Tripura, by the Reverend J. Long in Journal, Asiatic Society, Bengal, No. 7, for 1850.

|| *See* note on Temple Ruins in Asam, Journal, Asiatic Society, Bengal, No. 1, for 1855.

The Kalika Purana gives long descriptions of rivers and mountains in Kamrup,—the country rendered holy by the celebrated temple of Durga called Kamakhya, (or as some have it 'Kamichcha')—the region of love according to the Hindus, near the ancient city of Pragjyotisha, the modern Gowhatty.

Wilson observes in the preface to his Vishnu Purana:—" It is a singular and as yet uninvestigated circumstance that Asam or at least the north-east of Bengal (*i. e.*, Kamrup) seems to have been in a great degree the source from which the Tantrica and Sakta corruptions of the religion of the Vedas and Purans proceeded."

These remarks on a topic, the following out of which would lead me away from my subject, are given to shew the great antiquity of the Hindu race in Asam. It is by no means improbable that they occupied the fairest portion of it, " the lovely Paphian region" from Dubri to Bishnath, before it was discovered by the Mongolian or Turanian tribes. It is very difficult indeed to account for, and time, the various dynasties that have at different epochs obtained historical importance in the valley of the Brahmaputra, but they fall best into place by supposing, not that the Bodo and such tribes were the aborigines, but that branches of the Lunar and Solar races were the first to appreciate its beauty and resources. We find no tradition or other indication of their having had to struggle with savage tribes on their first discovery of the valley, but we have, in the places of refuge constructed by them in the hills on both sides, ample proof that they were forced to defend themselves against attacks from the plains. An examination of the hill forts shews them to have been constructed for this purpose and not to repel irruptions of the hill tribes, and thus it is that we find the hordes of Chutias, Kacharis, Kocchis and Ahoms, who successively invaded the country, though prevailing by their rude arms and brute force, succumbing to the influence of the civilization which they found, and sinking into the effeminacy and luxury, that rendered them in their turn an easy prey to the next spoiler.

It appears from the earliest notices of Kamrup that the Aryans who first occupied it were subsequently regarded as infidels by their western brethren, that is, in all probability they were Budhists, and some of the oldest temples are of Budhist origin. The great temple of Haju on the north banks of the river contains still a large image of 'Budha' or 'Mahamuni,' as the principal object of worship, attracting yearly to its shrine thousands of worshippers from Butan and Tibet, but it is now also a place of pilgrimage for Hindus from all parts of India, the object of worship being styled by them 'Madhob.'

Notwithstanding the apostacy of the early settlers, there was a sacred halo about the holy river and its lofty banks that endeared it to the Hindus of all sects, and it is stated in the *Jogini Tantro* that King Norok, though an 'Asúr' infidel, was nevertheless in such favor with the gods, that they made him guardian of the temple* of Kamikhya.

" The Magh and Baisakh Bihus are the two national festivals of the Asamese. The observances connected with these festivals have nothing to do with the Hindu religion, and their origin is involved in some obscurity. They belong not to the present but to the ancient religion of the country, and what this was may be inferred from the fact

* Situated on a hill rising about 700 feet from the river Brahmaputra just below Pragjyotisha or Gowhatty. It is said that the number of young girls attached to this temple was in early times 5,000. There are still some hundreds.

that the Budhist, Shans, and Burmese on the borders of Asam, at the same time of the year or nearly so, have their two great festivals (Pocham and Pochi) in honor of Budha."*

The Baisakh Bihu festival is a very peculiar one, unlike anything of the kind practised by Hindus elsewhere. It is as gay as a carnival, and whilst it lasts, the women, especially the maidens, enjoy unusual liberty. For many days before the actual festival, the young people in the villages may be seen moving about in groups gaily dressed or forming circles, in the midst of which the prettiest girls dance with their long hair loose on their shoulders. The first day of the festival is devoted to interchanges of visits, the next to the bathing and worshipping of all the cattle, and on the third day the inhabitants of several groups of villages, old and young, meet at some appointed place and give themselves up to thorough enjoyment. The girls on these occasions do not like to dance before the men of their own village.

The existing religious establishments in Asam are monasteries on a large scale. The votaries are now Vishnavis, but they resemble more the Budhist monasteries than any Hindu institutions elsewhere. We learn from Hwan Thsung, the Chinese traveller in India in the seventh century, that they existed in Asam in his day and were then considered Budhistical, though unorthodox. The existing heads of these monastic establishments are Brahmans, but this has not been always the case; in some the Brâhmans have supplanted Sudra head priests within the memory of man. The older head priests were probably Kolitas, who called themselves Káists. It appears certain that there were no Brahmans with the earlier Aryan colonists.

Thus, the glimpses of history that we possess tell us that the valley of the Brahmaputra was first colonized by Aryans, that at a very early period the religion of the country was Budhist, and it was probably what was called Adi Budhist when the old type of temples were overthrown, and in their place rose structures dedicated to the worship of Siva and Kali; but great struggles took place between the various Hindu sects for ascendancy, and eventually Vishnuism became the religion of a majority of the people. About the eighth century of our era the Hindu dynasty was overthrown by the Chutia or Kachari hordes; but though the old settlers succumbed to the physical strength of their invaders, they maintained their mental superiority and imparted their religion and civilization to their conquerors, and so Hinduized had the Kacharis become, that it is said that the Kocchis about the twelfth century availed themselves of their religious prejudices to effect their conquest, advancing to the attack preceded by Brahmans riding cows whom the Kacharis would not assault. The Kocchis then gave a line of princes to Kamrup; at this time a part of Upper Asam was under a mysterious dynasty called the Bhara Bhuya, of which no one has ever been able to make anything, but it is in all probability connected with the following tradition which Buchanan gives in his account of Dinajpur:—"On a certain occasion twelve persons of very high distinction and mostly of the Pal family came from the west country to perform a religious ceremony on the Korotya river (the boundary between the ancient divisions Matsya and Kamrup), but arrived too late, and as the next season for performing the ceremony was twelve years distant, they in the interval took up their abode there, built palaces and temples, dug tanks, and performed many other great works. They are said to have belonged to the tribe called Bhungyas to which the Rajah

* *See* Journal, As. Soc., Beng., No. 1, for 1855, page 17, article, Temple Ruins in Asam, by the author.

of Kasi (Benares) and Bhettiah also belong." According to Wilford, Bhupal of the Pal dynasty was alive in 1017 A. D., when his country was disturbed by the invasion of Sultan Muhammad, and he retired into a remote part of the country with his family and chief officers. All the works still existing in the deserted forests on the northern bank of the Brahmaputra are attributed by the people to the Bhara Bhungyas or Bhuyas. They were probably connected with the great Bhuya tribe, who will come under notice when we enter the Chota Nagpur and Orissa provinces.

When the Ahoms entered the country, the Chutias defeated by the Kocchis in Lower Asam still held out in Sadya, and Southern, Upper, and Central Asam; they submitted to the Ahoms about the middle of the thirteenth century; the Bhara Bhuyas were next subjugated by that power which two hundred years later overthrew the remnant of the Kocchi kingdom of Kamarupa, the Muhammadans having about the same time extended their sway over the part of that kingdom nearest to Bengal: the Ahoms then ruled from the Brahmakundh to Gowalparah, having foiled an invasion of the Muhammadans under Mír Jumlah and maintained their sway till A. D. 1810, when, weakened and maddened by intestine wars, the leader of one of the parties appealed for assistance to the Burmese, and the usual result followed. Within ten years, the Burmese were in possession of the country; but it brought them into collision with the British: the Burmese war followed, and Asam became a British Province.

SECTION 2.—THE KACHARIS OR BODO, MECH, AND DHIMAL TRIBES.

Locality.

The Kacharis are one of the most numerous and widely spread of the tribes on the Eastern Frontier. They are seldom found at high elevations, preferring to live amongst low hills on the skirts of the higher ranges or on alluvial flats. Though many of them are completely fused into the mass forming the Hindu-Asamese population living like the Hindus under the shade of ancestral fruit trees and pursuing the same system of permanent cultivation, the majority cling to their nomadic habits, dwelling always amidst new clearings and supporting themselves chiefly by the hoe and hand cultivation of virgin soil. They are, in comparison with the average run of the people of the plains, their neighbours, a fine athletic race, industrious and thriving, of light olive complexion and rather strongly marked Mongolian features. The hair of the head, black and plentiful, is always worn long by both sexes. They have very little hair on other parts of their bodies; no beards or whiskers to speak of.

Extent of their conversion to Hinduism.

The Kacharis are found in small distinct settlements all over Upper Asam. The majority call themselves 'Soronia,' that is, purified Kacharis, to indicate that they have adopted the customs of the Hindus and abstain from forbidden food. The Soronias keep fowls, but not pigs, and will not eat beef; they are cleanly in their habits. They listen to the occasional exhortations of their 'Guru,' and pay him his dues, and this is all that is required of them, and as they are exempted from the necessity of sacrificing to the malignant spirits, and released from the spells of witchcraft, they do not make a bad bargain.

They are of cheerful disposition, fond of merry village meetings and dancing, and with these amusements their Hindu Gurus do not interfere, nor do they attempt to alter their customs, such as that of marriage not taking place till both parties are of ripe years. I consider this to be one cause of the superior physique of the Kacharis as compared with the Hindu-Asamese.

The work of proselytism is carried on by the Hindu-Asamese priests amongst the Kacharis and cognate tribe by one simple but very powerful adjuration. You are unclean, be ye clean! It is the outward and visible sign of cleansing alone that is demanded, but it must be admitted that when the terms are accepted, the improvement in their appearance is great. They do not renounce the devil and all his works, but they promise to abstain from *pig* and live cleanly.

Kachar.

Reasoning from all analogy, the country called Kachar takes its name from this tribe. I recollect meeting an old Asam Brahmanical Burinji in which an account was given of their first settlement there, and some old Brahmanical fables about Jaintia, (and 'Jyunthi,' the goddess, from whom the name was taken). I have lost my notes of this book, and can call to mind no more than that it was an attempt to connect some portion of the race with the Hindu celestials. Pemberton tells* us that the population of Central Kachar in the days of one of its last Rajahs, Kishn Chandra, amounted to about 14,000 souls, of whom 6,000 were Kacharis, 7,500 Kocchis, and the remainder Lalongs.

The proportion of Kacharis in the population of Southern Kachar we are not told, but they are spoken of as the dominant race.† In Northern Kachar they are divided into Hazai and Parbatia, low land and high land Kacharis. The former are said to have been forced north from Lower Kachar by propulsion from the south. They are more Hinduized, civilised, and sophisticated than their brethren of the hills, the educated amongst them emulating, it is said, the Bengali in chicanery, and rivalling him in intrigue. They are physically much the inferior of the Parbatia Kachari, who are described in the same paper as a hardy and courageous race, very industrious, though rather inclined to be quarrelsome and turbulent.

Tularam's country.

North of Kachar we have the tract long known as Tularam Sinapati's territory, a Kachari country with a Kachari chief, and, on the western verge of this tract in latitude 30°N. on the banks of the river Dhunsiri, the remains of an ancient city, called Dhimapur,‡ said to have been for many generations the capital of the Kachari Rajahs, but after the conquest of the place by the Ahoms, it was abandoned, and from having been one of the best cultivated became one of the wildest parts of Asam.

The chief, Tularam, is descended from one of the Dhimapur Rajahs. Grange tells us, they have a tradition that they founded Dhimapur after having been driven from Girgaon by the Ahoms.

Affinity with the Chutia.

Girgaon is in the part of Upper Asam said to have been under the rule of the Chutias when the Ahoms invaded that country. I have already pointed out the remarkable linguistic affinities between the Chutia and Bodo or Kachari, and this tradition of their having been driven from Upper Asam by the Ahoms is confirmatory of the common origin of the two races, and the expulsion alluded to must mean the conquest of the Chutia.

* Pemberton's Eastern Frontier, pp. 197-199.
† Stewart's notes on Northern Kachar, Journal, As. Soc., Bengal. No. 7, of 1855.
‡ *See* Account of Grange's Expedition, in the Journal, As. Soc., Bengal, No. 106, for November, 1840.

Eastern Duars.

The Kacharis of the newly annexed Eastern Duars describe themselves as coming from a district which they call Rung-Shar, on the south side of the Upper Asam valley.* They call themselves 'Shargiah' after that country.

Whilst the Kacharis in Asam are becoming Hinduized, those under Tibetan or Bút influence are said to be adopting Lamaism, and on conversion call themselves Shargiah Butias. We shall thus soon lose all trace of the customs of the old Kacharis. Major Fisher in his *Memoir of Sylhet, Kachar, &c.*, says:—"According to records preserved among the family of the last princes of Kachar (which, however, are but traditions reduced to writing) the Kacharis conquered the kingdom of Kamrup, and gave to it a succession of Rajahs from whom the late royal family of Kachar of the line of Ha Tsungtsa derive their descent. The term 'Kachari' is of modern date; the proper name by which that people call themselves, *viz.*, Rangtsa,† and the country from which they trace their origin, is situated in the north-east of Asam."

People of Tiparah of the same origin.

The people of Tiparah are, he says, of the same origin as the Kacharis, and the similarity of their religion, customs, and appearance makes this probable. Their tradition is, that they conquered Kamrup more than 1,000 years ago, and they were turned out of it by the Kocch princes, who were in possession till dispossessed by the Muhammadans on one side and by the Ahoms on the other.

There is a certain mystery over the origin of the successors of the last truly Aryan dynasty that reigned in Kamarupa, which in connection with these traditions of the Kachari conquest of that kingdom renders it very probable that those successors were Mlechchas and Kacharis. The Brahmans who first appeared in Kamarupa after the destruction of the Pal dynasty, will not tell us how that dynasty was overthrown, but the next sovereign was admittedly a person of obscure origin, declared by the Brahmans from the traces on his feet to be of noble birth.

Thus we find the Kacharis in scattered communities more or less Hinduized all over the valley of Asam, and massed in Kachar, Durrung, the Asam Northern Duars, and the Duars newly annexed from Butan. As placed by Hodgson, they extend from Tiparah in the south-east to Morang and the country of the Kichaks in the north-west direction. He gives them from 25° to 27° of north latitude, and from 88° to 93½° east longitude, (and no doubt the longitudinal parallels might be put much farther apart,) and estimates their numbers at 200,000, which I believe they greatly exceed.

Having, when at the zenith of their power, adopted the religion and, to a great extent, the habits of the people they supplanted, we do not now find amongst this scattered tribe any very salient peculiarities to distinguish them from, or affiliate them with, other races. Hodgson only tells us of the desultory nature of their cultivation and their generally nomadic habits. Thus, they nowhere acquire any property in, or have much affection for, the soil they cultivate, but are content to take the land on the terms that the Government or proprietors may be pleased to demand from them.

---

* Letter from J. C. Geddes, Esq., to Commissioner, Butan Duars, dated 24th April, 1866.

† This in the Garo language, and I suppose in the Boro or Kachari language, means *heavenly*. The Asamese called their royal race 'Swargia,' heavenly. The other name, Shargiah, is probably a corruption of this, and a translation into Asamese of their old name Rungtsa or Rungshar.

The Kacharis, who still cling to their ancient religion, appear to have much the same notions on the subject as the Garos, under different names. They worship the "starry host" and the most striking of the "terrene elements,"* but the simplicity of their ideas on religion may be inferred from their having in their own language no words for sin, for piety, for prayer, for repentance. Hodgson adds heaven and hell, but I think words indicating a belief in both may be found in the language of the Kachari or some of their cognates. Hodgson gives a long list of their gods; the chief god Batho is singularly enough represented by the Sij plant *(Euphorbia)* which may be found greatly cared for, much in the fashion of the Tulsi by Hindus, in the enclosure before the house of every Kachari. Why they should so venerate this plant I do not know, but a veneration for particular plants is a very ancient and universal superstition. The worship of the Sij is not confined to the Kacharis; we shall meet with it again amongst some of the tribes in Orissa and Chota Nagpur. Its milky juice is used by natives medicinally, but the tribes of the family have in their pristine state such a horror of milk, that we can hardly fancy their predilection for the plant to proceed from the appearance of what it exudes.

Religion.

The priesthood amongst the Bodo is not an hereditary office; any person possessing the necessary knowledge of the ritual and divinities, may take on himself the functions, and the elders of the people may perform all sacred offices without troubling the priests, who are called Deoshis. This is not unlike the name of the primitive priests of the Chutias, the 'Deoris,' and, I think, I have heard the Kachari priests called Deoris. "The priests or the elders superintend the administration of oaths and ordeals; the priests alone direct and conduct those high festivals which thrice a year are celebrated in honor of the elemental gods, and once a year in honor of the household divinities, as likewise those occasional acts of worship which originate with more or less diffused, or individual, calamity."

Priesthood.

"Diseases are considered to arise entirely from preternatural agency, and hence there are no medical men, but a regular class of exorcists, who are a branch of the priesthood. They are called 'Ojhas,' and are the sole physicians." The above is as applicable to the Kols of Chota Nagpur as to the Kacharis, even to the number of festivals, and the name given to the exorcist; but *Ojha* is a Hindi word meaning an examiner of '*ojh*,' entrails.

Exorcism.

The *modus operandi* is thus described by Hodgson. Thirteen leaves, each with a few grains of rice on it, are placed by the exorcist in the segment of a circle before him, and represent the deities.† The Ojha squatting on his hams before the leaves, causes a pendulum attached to his thumb by a string to vibrate before them, repeating invocations the while. The god who has possessed the sick man is indicated by the exclusive vibration of the pendulum to his particular leaf, which is then taken apart, and the god in question is asked what sacrifice he requires. How the reply is given is not stated; but the Ojha declares it, and the animal named is then promised, but only paid when the sick man recovers! This is a great improvement on the system adopted by the Chota Nagpur tribes. With them the animal is sacrificed immediately, and if the sickness still

* Hodgson, Journal, Asiatic Society, July, 1849.

† Compare this with the custom of the Khunds.

W

continue, vaticination is again resorted to, and slaughter goes on till the patient dies or there is nothing left to kill.

Festivals.

The three great festivals to the elemental gods are celebrated on some spot out of the village, generally on the banks of the river, and the attendance on them is therefore called 'going forth to worship.' The worship of the household gods is celebrated at home. One festival, called the Bamboo festival, recalls the bamboo shrines before every Garo's door. On this occasion thirteen men carry as many lofty bamboo poles decorated with clothing, and having a yak's tail at the head. It is very strange that the low Musalmans of Chota Nagpur called Jholahs, &c., have a festival which they celebrate in Chaith, the most singular part of which is the exhibition of long bamboo poles decorated in a precisely similar manner.

The priest 'Deoshi,' and the person who is to become inspired, and to reply to the priest, the 'Deoda,' are with the party, and the latter is occasionally sprinkled with water by an attendant. The Deoda dances with the rest, striking the bedizened poles till he goes off in a fit.

At the yearly domestic festival, the 'Deoshi' sacrifices a cock, and offers prayers to the 'Sij,' as representative of Batho, whose emblem is outside the house; but his wife, the goddess Mainon, is more especially the household divinity, and she is represented in the interior of each house by a bamboo post, three feet high, fixed in the ground, and surmounted by a small earthen-cup full of rice. At this shrine a hog is sacrificed yearly, but before it monthly offerings of eggs are made by the females of the family.

Witchcraft.

It often happens that sickness or other misfortune is ascribed to the spells of witchcraft rather than to the wrath of the deity, and then three Ojhas are summoned, "with whose aid, and that of a cane freely applied, the elders endeavour to extort from the witch a confession of the fact and her motives," and if condemned, she is expelled the district. A natural desire to get rid of troublesome and ugly old women was perhaps the origin of this custom.

Marriage.

The marriage ceremony is said to consist of an interchange of the *pan*-leaf; at least this ceremony is performed by the Dhimals, who appear to be of the same family and are located with the Bodo. Now, this interchange of the pan-leaf is either borrowed from the Hindus, as another part of the ceremony, the anointing the bride and bridegroom with oil and turmeric undoubtedly is, or else the Kacharis, on ceasing to be a dominant race in Upper Asam, bequeathed it to the population there, as it is, amongst all the agricultural classes who do not care to follow strictly the Brahmanical ritual, the symbol of marriage, and the tearing of a pan-leaf by husband and wife a dissolution of the tie.

Mr. Geddes, the Assistant Commissioner of the Eastern Duars, in the letter previously quoted, says, the marriage ceremony of the Mech and Kacharis still preserves the most primitive form, forcible abduction. "The bridegroom proceeds with a posse of his friends to the residence of his intended. Her friends are assembled and endeavour to retain her; a mock combat ensues between the two parties in which the bridegroom is successful. Afterwards he gives a feast to the bride's friends, conciliates with a money present, usually about Rs. 60, the father who is supposed to be incensed, and the rite is completed."

This fiction of a pretence to win a bride by force of arms is common to many of the Turanian races. Perhaps the Hindu *Barát* has a similar origin. There is another curious custom which seems to point to days gone by practised by some tribes. The bride and bridegroom are carried home on a platform which is called a *ship*.

Burials.

The Bodo bury the dead immediately after decease, and erect no monuments to their memories. In this they act differently from most of their cognates, but with such erratic propensities a reverence for the spot where the remains of their ancestors repose would be inconvenient.

Interdicted food.

The following animals are interdicted as food to the Bodo,—oxen, dogs, cats, monkeys, bears, and tigers. I imagine this is under Brahmanical influence, and that their ancestors were as free in this respect as are the Garos.

Deities.

From the list of Bodo or Kachari divinities given by Hodgson,* it would appear that they are not very faithful to their ancestral faith, but go gallivanting after strange gods wherever they can find them. Thus, we find included Hindu deities, names of rivers and hills, and in some, perhaps as "Hajo," the names of deified heroes of their own.

It was probably the Kachari dynasty that gave names to many of the rivers in Upper Asam. The affix Di to so many of them is the Kachari word for water or river. We have the Di-hong, Di-bong, Di-hing, Di-garo, &c. The Brahmaputra is called Doima, the River mother.

Hodgson describes the Bodo and Dhimal tribes as of the same race, and there appears no reason for separating them in a work of this nature, as their customs, religion, &c., appear nearly identical. It must be observed, however, that the comparison of language does not support so close a connection, and the names of deities are different. "The Dhimals,† whose numbers do not now exceed 15,000 souls, are at present confined to that portion of the Saul forest lying between the Konki and the Dhorla or Torsha, mixed with the Bodo, but in separate villages and without intermarriage."

The Rabhas and Hajongs of the Gowalparah District are also branches of the Kachari race, and connected with the Garos. Buchanan estimated the former at 2,000 families. They were then as now divided into two tribes, the Rongdaniya and the Páti. The former have shown themselves more conservative of race, purity, and ancient customs than the latter, who have adopted the language, and many of the customs, of Bengalis.

The true Rabha customs, with the exception of their laws of inheritance and marriage, resemble those of the Garos already described, or those of the Pani Kocch to whom we are coming. Rishi is their chief or most powerful deity.‡ Have they and their cognates taken this title from the Aryans, or is it one of their own importation?

Religion.

The Saints called Rishis (the constellation of the Great Bear) occupy a conspicuous place in the Hindu books, and the word is applied as an affix to the name of the Garo deity Saljong. The Rishi of the Rabhas is considered very old (*rish*, a beard), and has a wife called Charipak. Every Rabha

* See Journal for July, 1849, page 723.

† Hodgson's Aborigines of India, page 151.

‡ Buchanan.

who has the means should once a year offer a hog to Rishi and a goat to his wife. This Rishi and his wife are the gods that are worshipped throughout Asam as the 'Bura Buri,' though, under Brahmanical influence, in most places the 'Bura Buri' are now worshipped as if they were Siva and Durga. Rishi and his wife live in heaven (Rongkorong). One of the terrestrial deities, Dhormong, who presides over Chorihachu, a very lofty mountain terminating the Garo Hills, is a deity common to Garos and Rabhas. In times of drought the people offer a black goat on the rocky top of this hill for rain.

Costume.

The costume of the Rongdaniya Rabha females is peculiar; they are at once distinguished in the markets by their dress, and by the fact of their carrying their loads hill fashion in a little square basket resting on their back and slung from the forehead. The dress is a turban of dark brown cloth worn very much off the head, and as a scarf a cloth of the same color and material folded round the bosom. The petticoat, like that of the Garo woman, encircles the body below the hips, instead of round the waist, but it flows decently to the feet, whilst the Garo apology for a robe does not reach half down the thigh. The males of the race are not in costume distinguished from the Bengalis, but they are more powerfully framed and very unlike them in face; nevertheless the anti-Aryan characteristics are less strongly marked in the Rabha than in the Garo, and less in the Pati than in the Rongdaniya, showing how the races become mixed as they approach the plains.

The Hajong appear to be identical with the Hazai Kacharis of North Kachar noticed above (page 83).

SECTION 3.—THE MECH.

Locality.

All the authorities agree in considering the Mech and Kachari as the same people, or at least of common origin. Buchanan calls them a tribe of Kamrup, who appeared to have been at one time more numerous than he found them to be, and to have undergone great changes. The large tract of country called Mechpara in the Gowalparah District no doubt took its name from them, and the proprietor is a Mech; but he and most of his people repudiate this origin and call themselves *Rajbangsis*. The Mech are to be found in the recently annexed Butan Duars.* They extend from thence in a westerly direction into the Nepal Terai as far as the Konki river, subject, respectively, to the Nepalese, Sikim, Butan, and British Governments, and their habits and customs are found much modified by the people with whom they come in contact, *viz.*, the Pani Kocchis, Rajbangsis, Dhimals, Thawas, and Garos on one side, and the Limbus, Kerantis, Lepchas, Murmis, and Butias on the other. They are fairer than the Kocchis, and have more markedly the Mongolian characteristics, but accompanied by a softness of outline which distinguishes them readily from the more marked features of the same order, as exhibited in the Lepchas, Limbus, and Butias. They are said also to resemble the Mugs and Burmese, and to be like them, and like the Kásias (with whom Fisher compares them) greatly addicted to drinking spirits, smoking, and pan chewing.

It is said that when living beyond the pale of Hindu influence, they are as omnivorous a race as any in the world, but they will not eat the flesh of the elephant.

* Campbell, Journal, Asiatic Society, Bengal, August, 1839.

Habits.

They are very nomadic in their habits, seldom settling down in permanent villages, but continually shifting their cultivation and abodes, that they may have the full benefit of the virgin forests to which they cling. It is their love for such forests that retains them under Nepalese or Bután rule. Their constitutions have become so much accustomed to the malarious influences of the Terai, that apparently they cannot live without the poisonous gases they imbibe there, and in the purer atmosphere of the plains, or in breathing the more invigorating air of the higher ranges, they pine and die.

I find no further information regarding the Mechs that assigns to them noteworthy peculiarities. They worship the Sij *(Euphorbia)* as the emblem of the supreme deity like the Kacharis, and they call themselves, and no doubt are, Bodo or Boro, which means a great people, and Rangta, a heavenly, and all other designations in which the Kacharis rejoice.

SECTION 4.—THE KOCH OR KOCCH.

Locality.

There can be no doubt that the Kocch is one of the most ancient of the peoples in India. Of their origin we know nothing; their linguistic affinities were supposed to be with the Mech Kachari, but this rests on an uncertainty, and they are distinguished from those tribes by the darkness of their complexion. Kocch Behár must be regarded as the present nucleus of the race, but they are still numerous in the old Kamarupa and the ancient Matsiya-desh, that is, in Rungpur and Lower Asam and Purniah, extending west as far as the 87°45′ of E. longitude, or to the boundary of ancient Mithila, and east to 93° E. longitude. Hodgson has estimated their numbers at upwards of a million.

Conquests.

They were a recognized power to the north of Eastern Bengal, coeval with the Hindu kingdom of Kamarupa, and spread east till their chiefs became lords of the marches between Kamarupa and Bután. It was, I think, from the opposite direction that Kamarupa was invaded, and the eastern part of it subjugated by the Kacharis some centuries previous to this extension. It appears to be about the year 1550 A. D. that the two powers came into collision, when the Kocch under their great leader Haju expelled the Kacharis and established a dynasty which lasted two hundred years. These Kocch princes were driven from power in Western Kamrup, Rungpur, and Gowalparah by the Muhammadans, and from Eastern Kamrup by the Ahoms; but "the descendants of Haju still exercise *jura regalia* in that portion of the ancient possession of his family which is called Kocch Behár."

The grandson of Haju, Vishu Sinh, with all the people of condition, apostatized to Hinduism, and took the name of *Rajbangsis*;* those who declined, finding they were treated as vile, adopted Islam. Thus the mass of the Kocch people became Muhammadans and the higher grades Hindus; the latter now reject and contemn the very name of Kocch, and it is bad manners at the court of the descendant of Haju to speak of the country as Kocch Behár;† strange that rather than declare himself the representative of a line of heroes, who so long maintained their position against the haughty invaders, claiming to be of the Solar or Lunar race, he should accept the myth which, by a

* Buchanan—Rungpur, Vol III, page 419. Hodgson, Journal, Asiatic Society, Bengal, XXXI, July, 1849.

† It is then called Nij Vihar.

reflection on the chastity of the daughters of Haju, gives him for ancestor the god Siva.

Kamrup temples.

A large vaulted vestibule, measuring 40 feet by 20 feet, in front of the old temple of Haju in Kamrup,* was built by Noro Narain, Haju's great grandson, in 1550 A. D. He found the temple entirely deserted and almost lost in impenetrable jungle. He not only repaired it, but endowed it with lands, priests, musicians, and dancing girls; but the vaulted brick addition of Noro Narain replaced a dismantled edifice of stone, which he had not the skill to restore. The temple is situated on a hill about 300 feet high, whence probably it takes its name, as *haju* means 'hill' in the Bodo and cognate languages, and from the fragments of the old vestibule a rude flight of steps have been constructed from the tank below to the ancient fane on the hill, in which, as I have stated before, the object of worship is in fact an image of Budha. Noro Narain also rebuilt the temple of Kamakhya, which had been destroyed by Kálápahár, the great renegade and iconoclast.

A few more words anent the upper ten thousand of the Kocchis. The Rajbangsi are all very dark; and as their cognates, the Kacharis, Mechs, Garos, are yellow or light-brown, and their northern, eastern, and western neighbours are as fair or fairer, it must be from contact with the people of the south that they got their black skins.

Here is a description of the Kocch *in situ* by a medical officer now on the spot.†

Physical traits.

"Face flat, giving rather an appearance of squareness; eyes black and oblique; hair black and straight, in some curling; nose flat and short; cheek bones prominent; beard and whisker *rather* deficient" (mark the rather; in the Kachari, &c., these adjuncts are *very* deficient); "color of skin in *most instances* black; side of head rather flattened; forehead retreating."

Dr. Campbell, in writing of the Mechs, says, they are fairer than the Kocch, and have more markedly the Mongolian features. Yet in the Mechs those features are, he says, much modified and softened. He speaks of the Kocch in another place as having more of a Hindu physiognomy.

On referring to notes of my own, written in 1847, I find the following:—"It is remarkable that whilst the facial line of the Garos is nearly vertical, in some of the Kocch tribes I have observed it exceedingly angular, though with as little prominence of nose as in the Garo tribes. The upper line along the forehead continuing in the Kocch tribes in one direction to the extremity of the upper lip, then suddenly receding to the bottom of the jawbone in the most unintellectual form imaginable."

I remarked of the Garos that their mouths, like their noses, were compressed, whilst the Kocch displayed the thick protuberant lips and maxillaries of the negro.

Of the Muhammadan Kocch of Purniah, the Magistrate, Mr. Beames, gives the following description:—"The peculiar dialect, the stunted figure, sharp wizened features, high cheek-bones, tufted beard, &c., mark them as a peculiar race."

Mr. G. Campbell would decidedly place the Kocch amongst his negritos, and I think we must allow that color and physical characteristics clearly separate them from the Bodo group, though the people called Páni-Kocch doubtless belong to that family.

* Notes on Asam Temple Ruins, Journal, Asiatic Society, Bengal, for 1855, page 9.

† In a letter from H. Beveridge, Esq., Deputy Commissioner of Kocch Behár, to Colonel Agnew.

The Páni-Kocch.

The villages of the Páni-Kocch lie along the skirts of the Garo Hills. They are much mixed up with that people and with the Rabhas,* and in their religion, language, and customs appear to lean sometimes to one, sometimes to the other. The dress of the women is put on like that of the Rabha women, but is scantier and of different color. Their clothes are of cotton, blue with red borders, made by themselves.

They greatly reverence the Garos for having retained their freedom in regard to food which they, the Páni-Kocch, in a weak moment, were induced to resign. It is strange that they should have adhered to an abstinence for which they had no respect, but they must not eat beef, and they reject dogs, cats, frogs, and snakes, which the Garos eat. They use tobacco and strong liquors, but refuse opium and hemp. They eat no tame animal without having first given one of their gods the refusal of it.

Marriage and inheritance.

In regard to marriage and inheritance, they show a leaning to the gallantry of the Garos, but do not follow strictly the rules of the female Solon who must have been the law-giver to that people. The Páni-Kocch leave to the women the cares of property, "who in return are exceedingly industrious, spin, weave, plant, sow, brew, in short, do every work which is not above their strength, such as felling trees and the like.† When a woman dies, the family property is divided amongst her daughters; and when a man marries, he goes to live with his wife's mother, and obeys her orders and those of his wife. Marriages are usually settled by the mothers when the parties are young, but not without consulting their inclinations. A girl not thus disposed of, when she grows up, selects a husband for herself, and, if he die, may take another. The husband or father appears to have nothing whatever to do with the arrangement. The expense of marriage is heaviest on the mother of the girl, who pays Rs. 10, while the boy's mother only gives Rs. 5. Girls who are frail can always procure their lover for a husband." Under such a regimé, a man is not of course permitted to have more than one wife, nor are concubines tolerated. If a man is known to commit adultery, he is fined about Rs. 60, and if his mother does not pay this, he is sold as a slave! Widows left with property generally manage to select young men as second husbands.

Marriage customs.

Burials.

"The dead are kept two days, during which time the family laments, and the kindred and neighbours assemble, eat, drink, dance, sing, and make merry. The body is then carried to the side of a river and buried."

Like the Rabhas they call their supreme deity Rishi, but his wife is Jágo. Every year at the end of the rainy season, a grand sacrifice is made to these deities by the whole tribe, and occasional sacrifices are offered in cases of distress. They also sacrifice to the sun, moon, and stars, and to the gods of the woods, hills, and rivers, and every year when they collect their first crops, they offer some of the first fruits to their ancestors, calling to them by name and clapping their hands, as they have no artificial method of making such a noise, as most Pagan nations, and even Hindus, consider necessary to rouse or please their gods.

Sacrifices.

---

* Buchanan.

† Buchanan's Rungpur, Vol. III.

The priests who officiate on these occasions are called 'Deoshis,' or Brahmans, or Lamas, from which we may assume that they have no national name for such a functionary.

What are these Páni-Kocch? They have been hitherto treated as the primitive type of the Kocch nation; but we have no evidence of the fact except the name. Buchanan says, they *assumed* the name of Páni-Kocch to distinguish themselves from their hill neighbours, the Garos, with whom they were often confounded in consequence of the similarity of their manners and customs; but their religion and language resemble rather those of the Rabha than the Garo. Hodgson gives a copious vocabulary* of the language spoken by the Kocch; it is all Bengali or Hindi or Asamese, not a word or grammatical construction that would affiliate them with any of the North-Eastern tribes. In religion and customs they have long been Hindu, and their princes all now claim to be the offspring of the amours of Hindu divinities. Latham in his descriptive Ethnology gives 15 words as Kocch. Three of these are Asamese, two Bengali, and the others are words used in all those three languages. The first word on Latham's list is remarkable. For man he gives 'beta-choa.' I never heard this expression in Asam or Bengal, but it is very common in Chota Nagpur; 'beta-choa,' a boy; 'beti-choa,' a girl; and it is used by the Uriya and by the Gonds.

Affinities of the Páni-Kocch.

Hodgson says that the Rabha is but a branch of the great Mech family. The Páni-Kocch are undoubtedly of the same lineage, and also closely connected with the Garo; but it is, I think, a mistake to regard them as the primitive type of the people called Kocch. They probably took the name of Páni-Kocch, when the real Kocch were dominant to conciliate the ruling power, without having any claim to be members of the family.

Physical characteristics are after all the most indelible indications of race. Even where blood is mixed, the source of the different streams may be often traced, one or other fitfully predominating in different generations. I have seen the descendants of Hindu-Asamese who had been for several generations in the Naga or Abor Hills, tricked out as Nagas or Abors, but nevertheless distinguishable at a glance from the people they imitated, and looking quite out of their element. The Kocch appear to me equally out of their element amongst the Lohitic tribes, and from all I have been able to glean regarding them, it seems more likely that they originally belonged to the dark people whom they resemble, who were driven out of the Gangetic provinces when the kingdoms of Mithila and Magadha were established by the lunar and solar races, rather than to the northern Turanian or Indo-Chinese family, to whom they are so unlike; in short, I consider they belong to the Dravidian stock, and are probably a branch of the great Bhuiya family, and we thus obtain a clue to the tradition of the Bhara Bhuiyas, to whose period of rule so many great works in Asam are ascribed.

Affinities of the Kocch.

But before taking up the thread put into our hands by this hypothesis, we must go back to the eastward, and notice briefly the tribes immediately to the north of those that we have been recently describing.

* Aborigines of India, Essay 1st, 1847.

VOCABULARY TO GROUP II.

English.	Chutia.*	Bodo or Kachari.†	Garo.‡	Dhimal.†	Mech.	Pani-Kocch or Kocch.	
One	dugsha	man-ché	sá	é-long	munché	gasak.	
Two	dukum	man-gné	gini	gne-long	munye	dui.	
Three	dúgdá	man tham	githam	súm-long	muntum	tin.	
Four	duguchi	man-bré	bri	día-long	munbre	char.	
Five	dugumna	man-bá	bañá	ná-long	munbha	panch.	
Six	duguchu	man-dó	dok	tú-long	mundho	choy.	
Seven	duguchi	man-sini	chhinni	nhü-long	munchini	sát.	
Eight	duguché	......	chet	yé-long	munjo kum	át.	Hindi.
Nine	duguchuba	......	sikú	kúhá-long	......	nau.	
Ten	duguchibá	......	chikiñ	té-long	......	dus.	
Twenty	......	chokai-bá thai-khon bisha-ché	khol	e-long bisha	......	korí.	
Fifty	......	......	kolchan gnnichhi	gné-long bisha	......	panchas.	
Hundred	......	bisha-bá	richesá	ná-long bisha	......	ek sau.	
I	an	ang	áña	ká	......	an.	
We	jarurau	jong (chur)	chiñá	kyél			
Thou	noáni	naug	ná	ná			
You	jákuroni	naugchur	......	nyé			
He	bareni	bi	bi	wa	......	uá.	
They	bario	bichur	bisáñ	ubal	......	ujarañ.	
Of me	......	ang ni	añni	kangko	......	ani.	
Of us	......	jong ni	chiñni	kuigko	......	nuñni.	
Of thee	......	nangni	naní	nangko	......	nini.	
Of you	......	nang churni	nashani	ningko	......	niruni.	
Of him	......	bini	bini	oko	......	úání.	
Of them	......	bichur ni	bíshoñni	ubalko	......	újurñui.	
Mine	ango	angni	ani	kang	......	auni.	
Our	......	jongni	chinni	king	......	nuni.	
Thine	nigo	nangni	nañni	nang	......	nini.	
Your	......	nangshúrni	naoñni	ning	......	niruñui.	
His	bigo	bini	biní	óko, wang	......	uani.	
Their	......	bichúrni	bishoñni	ubalko	......	uaruñni.	
Hand	otun	akhai or nakhai	jak	khur	......	chak.	
Foot	yapasu	yapha	jáchok	khokoi	yappa	jaten.	
Nose	......	gúnthúng	gúngthúng, giñ	nhápú	koontoong	nakun.	
Eye	mukuti	mogon	mukrun	mi	múkún	múkún.	
Mouth	dunga	khongá	khushik	núi	koogha	kakham.	
Tooth	hati	háthai	wá	sitong	hattye	pha.	
Ear	yoku	khomá	náchil	náhàthong	kumun	nákál.	
Hair	kin	khomon	khinni	poshom	kummá	khan.	
Head	guliong	khóró	skhú	púrin	koroh	dhakam.	
Tongue	......	chálai	sri	détong	chulai	thelái.	
Belly	......	údoi	búkmá	hémáng	udihi	ok.	
Back	......	bikhúng	jánil	gándi	......	kañju.	
Iron	sung	shúrr	sil	chir	shor	loa.	
Gold	......	sóna	soná	sona	......	sona.	
Silver	......	rúpá	rúpá	rúpá	tais	rúpá.	
Go	tupa	thángno	riañ	hadéli	......	lei.	
Eat	akená	jáno	chha	cháli	......	sa.	
Sit	harini	chóöno	ásun	yongli	jhopú	mosúñ.	

* Journal, Asiatic Society, Bengal, 1850, page 311.
† Hodgson's Aborigines of India, Essay 1st.
‡ Journal, Asiatic Society, Bengal, March, 1849, and Vol. XXXVIII, page 14 (Vocabulary by Lieutenant Williamson.)

Y

ENGLISH.	CHUTIA.	BODO OR KACHARI.	GARO.	DHIMAL.	MECH.	PANI-KOCCH OR KOCCH.
Father ...	tsipa ...	aphá ...	ájá ...	ábá ...	appa ...	awa.
Mother ...	tsima ...	áyá ...	ámá, ai ...	amma ...	áie ...	áme.
Brother ...	......	bida ...	áda ...	yolla ...	koi ...	bhái.
Sister ...	......	bina, now ...	áno ...	rima ...	......	jánn.
Man ...	mosi ...	hiwa, manshi ...	mándi ...	wával ...	manchi ...	márok.
Woman ...	mishigo ...	hinjou ...	mechiksa ...	bevál ...	hinjan ...	mágju.
Wife ...	......	bihi ...	jik ...	be ...	bihi ...	jugju.
Child ...	......	bisha ...	písá ...	cháu ...	katan ...	sasa.
Son ...	......	bisha ...	dephanthe ...	cháu ...	beesha	
Daughter ...	......	bishú ...	deníchikpísá ...	chamdi ...	beeshu hindow	magju sasa.
Slave ...	......	......	nokhol ...	......	......	ghulam.
Cultivator ...	......	porja ...	gáninimáude ...	......	......	grihastimurg.
Shepherd ...	......	......	mendá rákwál ...	berang ...	......	bhera rakwal.
God ...	......	batho (the sij-plant)	sáljoň ...	wáráng-béráng	modaie ...	iswar.
Devil ...	......	......	muttí ...	letang ...	......	why.
Come ...	nang kwa ...	phoino ...	riba ...	dhidhi ...	puki ...	phay.
Best ...	......	......	námbáttá ...	danghali ...	shibiknul ...	sabse penim.
Stand ...	takrini ...	gochongno ...	chadenlo ...	......	jhickat do ...	kharatún.
Sun ...	sanh ...	shán ...	sál ...	bélá ...	krandoong ...	ráshán.
Moon ...	yah ...	nokhábir ...	jájún ...	táli ...	nokabur ...	nárék.
Star ...	yetti ...	háthotki ...	jashki ...	......	hatoorki ...	
Fire ...	nye ...	wát ...	wál ...	máŭ ...	wad ...	wár.
Water ...	ji ...	dói ...	chhi ...	chi ...	diee ...	ti.
House ...	nya ...	......	nák ...	sá ...	nan ...	nok.
Horse ...	gori ...	gorai thángan ...	ghorá ...	ónyhá ...	ghorye ...	ghora.
Cow ...	masu ...	mushojo ...	machu ...	mahanipia ...	mashujuh ...	machu.
Dog ...	shi ...	choimá ...	áchák ...	khia ...	cheema ...	kwai.
Cat ...	midige ...	mouji jólá ...	meŭnŭ ...	dankha menkon	......	meyan.
Cock ...	......	dou jola ...	dho ...	dhángái kia	......	thak.
Duck ...	......	hangs ...	dhorájá ...	hangs ...	......	hansak.
Ass ...	......	gádhá ...	......	gadha ...		
Camel	......	......	......	......	......	......
Bird ...	duá ...	doucheu ...	dho ...	jihá ...	tansee	
To die ...	......	thoino ...	siná ...	sili ...	......	thina.
To give ...	sarini ...	......	roná ...	......	......	lakham.
Run ...	jouanini ...	khonto ...	théŭri ...	dhápli ...	......	thalak.
Up ...	......	......	sákhá ...	......	......	kara.
Near ...	butugun ...	......	shéfáŭ ...	chengso ...	......	dakan.
Who ...	basani ...	chur ...	sa ...	jeti siti ...	......	chan.
And ...	......	bi, ré bó ...	ara ...	édóng ...	......	árá.
Yes ...	hoi ...	ongo ...	hoe ...	hé ...	......	hán.
Down ...	......	......	khámá ...	......	......	kámá.
Far ...	asain ...	......	chela ...	......	......	jáñan.
What ...	dam ...	má ...	ínhau ...	hai ...	......	átáwá.
But ...	......	kintú ...	......	kintu ná		
No ...	hoya ...	ongá ...	dúŭja ...	ahé ...	......	era.
Before ...	......	......	skuŭ ...	......	......	áge.
Behind ...	......	ja ...	jámán ...	......	......	pásé.
Why ...	dainno ...	mánó ...	mauna ...	haipáli ...	......	átáni.
If ...	......	jélá ...	bá ...	......	......	jadi.
Alas! ...	......	há báp ...	áchai ...	hai ...	......	hai.

GROUP III.

THE NORTHERN BORDERERS.

Section 1.—The Butias.

In describing the tribes occupying the northern barrier of Asam, I left off with the Akas on the borders of Butan. Crossing that boundary we find ourselves amongst the Butias or Bhots; and this name opens to us a very extensive field comprising the Little Tibetans, the natives of Ladak, the Tibetans of Tibet Proper, and the people of Butan.

The learned tell us that the latter word is properly Bútant, the end of Bút,* and that Bút is the Bult in Bultistan, the Bet in Tibet, as well as the Bút in Bútan; but to trace out all that are included in this appellation would take me quite out of my jurisdiction. My concern is only with the fringe of this nation on the skirts of the Himalayas. Recent wars and blue books have made us familiar with the Buts, and I need only refer to the compilation and full report on the country by our late envoy the Honorable A. Eden for the best account of the people that we have got.

Their history, though they have written annals, is involved in some mystery. Mr. Eden says, the Butias have apparently not possessed Butan for more than two centuries; but how can we reconcile this with the passage quoted by Pemberton from the account of the voyage of Ralph Fitch in A. D. 1583, from which it would appear that the Government of Butan and the intercourse between Butan, Tibet, and Bengal, was very much in that day what it is now. The story, that 200 years ago some Kampa (that is, Tibetan) troops entered the country, and drove into the plains the old inhabitants called Tèphè, supposed to be the inhabitants of Kocch Behar, cannot be sustained, as we must have had in Asam the history of the clearing out of the Tèphè had it occurred within that time, and the Kocch are the least likely of all the tribes to come from that quarter. It is probable enough that an event of the kind did take place; we might believe, for instance, that the Garos or the Kacharis had been driven out of Butan by an invasion of Tibetans; but to make this agree with other well authenticated events, we must add at least 1,000 years to the 200 of the Bútan myth.

Their history.

Pemberton says, there is a tradition current in Butan that the country was once ruled by Tibetan Officers resident in it, and that all the palaces and castles now occupied by the Deb, the Dhurma, Pillos, and Zumpens, were originally constructed for

* Latham's Descriptive Ethnology, Volume 1, page 5.

the accommodation of the provincial Governors, but after holding the country for some time and finding it unprofitable, the officers were withdrawn and the colonists left to form a Government of their own. This is likely enough, and it is also probable that under the circumstances they would at once set about the establishment of a Government on the model of that of the parent state.

There were, no doubt, conflicts between the Kocch and the Butias about three hundred or four hundred years ago; but these were struggles for supremacy in the Duars, which ended in many of the Kocch leaders, as the Sidli, Bijni, and other chiefs, submitting to the Butias.

Government.

The Government finally established by the Butias included the Dhurma or Dhurm Rajah, (a perpetual 'avatar', or incarnation of an eternal spiritual ruler, disappearing at intervals, but immediately appearing again as an infant, who proves his identity by recognising and claiming all the personalities of the last 'avatar';) and the Deva, or Deb Rajah, who is in theory elected by Council.

The Council has seven ordinary members, the Chief Ministers of the Deb and Dhurm, and the Governors of the royal castles, and three extraordinary members, the Lieutenant-Governors of the provinces, called Penlos or Pillos. Under the latter are numerous district officers.

Theoretically the Government is well organized, but its constitution is violated at every succession to office. Captain Pemberton and Mr. Eden* agree in ascribing to the upper classes, especially the highest officers of state, the very worst of characters, 'shameless beggars,' 'bullies,' 'sycophants;' but the lower classes are described as very superior to them, "intelligent, tolerably honest, and, all things considered, not very untruthful."

Physical traits and dress.

"Physically the Butias are a very fine people: there are some really tall men amongst them, but though very robust as compared with the people of the plains, they are not nearly such a stalwart race as the Sikhimese and Tibetans, which is possibly to be attributed to their immorality and drunken habits." Their dress is a loose woollen coat reaching to the knees, bound round the waist by a thick fold of cotton cloth. The full front of the coat is used as a pocket, and into this opossum-like pouch, food cooked and uncooked is often thrust, including putrid fish and meat, and as one side of it is the naked skin of the owner, the nastiness of the arrangement may be conceived. The pouch always contains a store of betel-nut and prepared lime for the manufacture of the 'pan', which they are everlastingly chewing. The women's dress is a long cloak with loose sleeves.

They have all broad flat faces of the true Mongolian type, small oblique eyes, large mouths, noses short and low, not, on the whole, the most attractive combination of features; but many of the young women have fine plump rosy cheeks, healthy and pleasant to look upon, though their complexions, a light olive, have nothing in common with the lily. They appear rather careless about their personal appearance. Their tresses are generally left to float as nature pleases, though some of the more tidy and respectable bind theirs with a handsome bandeau of flat silver chains having a large jewelled ornament in front. Many women appear with shorn heads. These are the nuns who are

* Eden's Report, page 129.

said to have taken vows of celibacy, but they look as if they had pretty well exhausted their powers of enjoyment before they did so. As a rule, all are dirty in their persons, wearing their clothes till they rot off, and seldom indulge in ablutions.

On one occasion, several Butias, men, women, and children, who had settled in Kamrup, came to me for some kind of written certificate that they were British subjects. I said they were far too dirty, and unless they agreed to adopt habits of general cleanliness, including daily ablutions, I could not think of acknowledging them. They looked very grave at this, and requested time to deliberate over these hard conditions, which was granted. After several meetings and consultations with their friends, they all came washed with clean clothes, looking wonderfully the better for the process, and declaring their readiness to accept even such conditions.

Priesthood.

The Ghylongs, Lamas, or priests, form a very large proportion of the population. Admission to the priesthood is obtained by permission of the Deb, on payment of a fee. In addition to their religious duties, the Lamas are charged with the medical care of the people; but as exorcism is the only system of treatment attempted, assurance in the practitioner, and faith in the patient, are all that is needed. The Lamas have been estimated at 1,500 to 2,000. They live in monasteries, the chief of which is at the head quarters of the Government. In knowledge of the mysteries of the Budhist religion, and in the literature of their country, they are very inferior to the Khamti Bapus or Phungis.

The village Lamas, and the people generally, confine their religious exercises to telling their beads with the constant dreary repetition of the six-syllablic sentence 'Om-Mani-Padmi-Om.' Their preparation for a future state seems to consist in the personal or vicarious performance of this rite; hence the praying machines, by which countless repetitions of the sentence are produced. The priests all wear dresses of a garnet color, a woollen garment thrown loosely over the left shoulder, leaving the right arm bare. These priests will all tell you that the soul of religion is mental abstraction, the withdrawal of the mind from all mundane considerations, in order that the thoughts may be absolutely concentrated on the attributes and perfection of Budha; but the most devout of them may be seen listening to and smiling at the conversation of others whilst they pass the beads through their hand and mutter the everlasting 'Om-Mani-Padmi-Om.'

The conversion of the Butias to Budhism has not altogether eradicated their Paganism.* The common people believe in an innumerable host of spirits, and make offerings to them of flowers and bits of rags.

Marriage.

It is very singular that of the many intelligent observers who have visited and written on Butan, not one has been able to tell us that they have such an institution as a marriage ceremony. It is known that the tie of connubial union is a very loose one, and that chastity is not a virtue that is practised or appreciated. From my own observation, I believe the Butias to be utterly indifferent on the subject of the honor of their women, and the women themselves devoid of delicacy and modesty. They cover their persons most carefully, but it is to keep out the cold; of covering from feelings of modesty, they have no notions. A Butia Eve would have eaten a bushel of forbidden fruit without thinking of fig leaves.

---

* Griffiths.

Polyandry.

Polyandry is a recognized institution amongst them, but it prevails far more extensively in the northern and central portions of Butan than in the southern. Its origin is clearly traceable to Tibet, and Pemberton adds, that "political ambition is the main cause of so revolting a practice, as all aspirants for office are compelled to renounce the happiness of domestic life." Mr. Eden says, that even the restriction implied in the term polyandry, which once existed in northern Butan, is not adhered to in the present day, as the intercourse between the sexes is practically promiscuous. The law of inheritance is what we might expect it to be under such circumstances. Captain Pemberton tells us that on the death of any head of a family, however numerous his children, and whether male or female, the whole of the property becomes escheated to the Deb or Dhurma !

Houses.

In the construction of their houses, the Butias are rather in advance of their neighbours of the plains.* They are compared to small farm houses in England and to Swiss cottages, built generally of rubble stone and clay, of two, three, and sometimes of four, stories; all the floors are neatly boarded with deal, and on two sides are well constructed verandahs ornamented with carved and painted woodwork. One of these is sometimes enclosed for the women, the front opening by sliding panels when they wish to peep. The workmanship displays considerable skill in joinery, the panelling being very good of its kind. The interiors are preserved in a better state of cleanliness than from the general habits of the Butias we should have been led to expect.

The roofs are made of shingles of pine, five or six feet in length, laid over a framework of wood, and kept in their places with stone. Immediately under the roof is a store room for dried turnips, grain, &c., and the floor of this apartment, which is made of concrete clay, forms a second roof to the remainder of the house. The great desideratum is a chimney. The smoke has to find its way out as it can, and the consequence is, that the inmates emerging in the winter look as if they had come out of a coal mine.

Bridges.

It is not in houses alone that the Butias display their architectural and constructive skill.† Their embankments of rivers are represented as creditable works. Some of the stone embankments of the river at Paro, especially the revetments of the bridge, are described as admirably executed. "The bridge itself is a handsome structure made of large pine beams built into either bank, and projecting one over the other till a sufficiently narrow space is obtained for a platform." The approaches to the bridge are paved with large slabs of stone; "at each end is a large, strongly built tower of stone in which a guard remains at night under the warder of the bridge. The bridge is very neatly boarded with deal planks and the roadway is protected by a roof supported on arches at intervals of fifteen yards. The gates are lined with iron plates and studded with nails."

The following is a description of a temple near Dewangiri, which the writer visited in 1849 :—

Temple of Dewangiri.

"It is a square stone building with gable ends and a thatched projecting roof under the gable facing the north; there is a projecting balcony in front of a large bay window which lights a recess at the opposite

* Honorable A. Eden's Report of Mission, page 121.

† Mr. Eden's Report, pages 89-91.

end of the temple containing three large Budhist images, all seated in the usual crosslegged attitude of absorbed contemplation. They appeared to be formed of clay, and were exceedingly well executed and resplendent with gilding. The apartment, about 20 feet square, is boarded, and the walls are entirely covered with paintings of figures in similar penitential and devotional attitudes, but differently dressed. It was said, they were all the work of a native artist, the colors were particularly brilliant and well chosen and the drawing tolerably correct; gilding was introduced to heighten the effect. A priest's house also of stone stands near the temple; it is two storied, and with its projecting roof and balconies has a picturesque effect." This temple has, I fear, ceased to exist.

Manufactures.

It is only the coarser description of cloths worn by the Butias that are woven in the country; their silken dresses and finer woollen fabrics are obtained from Tibet and China. The women weave seated on the ground; the web passes round three rollers of wood forming a triangle, one of these being attached by a leather belt to the woman, another supported on the posts in front of her, and the third pinned to the ground further off. The woman by her position keeps the web stretched to the necessary tightness. The shuttle is a small hollow bamboo containing a roller for the thread; this she passes through the inclined web before her, working upwards and passing the woven part round below until the whole piece completed thus comes round; when done she shuts up her work and the loom disappears. The Tibetan, or Kampa, women on their journey to the plains all carry looms of this kind, and very shortly after their arrival on the encamping ground they may all be seen at work.

Another art that the Butias have acquired is paper-making from the bark of a tree called 'diah,' and in addition to the fermented liquor that they make from wheat, rice, and millet, like all the hill tribes, they have acquired a knowledge of distillation, and indulge very freely in alcoholic drinks.

The following description of the races seen by Mr. Eden at Paro is well worth extracting:—

Horse-racing.

"These had very little in common with horse-racing according to the English notion. A long string of ponies was brought out, each being ornamented with ribbons and colored streamers, mounted by men with very little clothing on except a long colored scarf hanging from the head. In front of the riders was the 'Tahpen,' master of the horse. It is curious that this functionary who is a high officer of the Court, should have a title so precisely similar to one of our own court officials, but 'Master of the horse' is a literal translation of his title (*Tah*, a horse, and *pen*, Master)."

"On arriving at the starting post all the riders dismounted. Sepoys armed with long whips rushed amongst the crowd and cleared a road with great brutality and insolence. At a given signal, the ponies were all one by one flogged by a number of men with whips into a gallop. The riders had to run holding on by the mane until the pony was well off, and then had to vault into their seats. Many shewed considerable dexterity in vaulting backwards and forwards over the ponies' backs. No saddles or pads of any kind were used. The ponies were started one after the other, and there was no attempt at testing their speed. The skill of the riders alone was on trial. After going a certain distance they all halted and were started again in the same manner. Some six different starts must have been made before the course was completed. At the end of the course the riders were all entertained at the expense of the Penlo, and they then went back to the palace in the same manner."

"The Tahpen was lifted on and off his horse with a great parade; for it is contrary to Butia notions of dignity for a man to mount or dismount from his horse himself."

Disposal of the dead.

In the disposal of the dead the Butias follow the practice of the Hindus. They burn the body and throw the ashes into the nearest stream.

SECTION 2.—THE LEPCHAS.

I have no personal acquaintance with the Lepchas, or the country they inhabit. The information I have to give regarding them is derived from Dr. A. Campbell's note in the Journal, Asiatic Society, Bengal, for 1840.

Geographical position.

The Lepchas are found in Western Butan, Eastern Nepal, and in the small territory between both called Sikhim. I find no estimate of their numbers. They are well known to the frequenters of the favorite Hill Station Darjiling, and are supposed to be the aborigines of the mountain forests surrounding that pleasant retreat of Bengal officials, and it is probable that they regard Sikhim as their father land.

They divide themselves into two tribes, **Rong**, the true Lepcha, and **Khamba**. The latter comprises the family of the ruler and his clansmen.

It is narrated that two centuries ago the people of Sikhim, consisting of Lepchas and Butias, tired of the intestine commotions that had long disturbed the little state, consulted their Lamas from beyond the snow as to the best means of obtaining good government and repose, and were advised to seek in that region for a ruler who would suit them.

Accordingly a deputation of their Lamas was sent to the North, and proceeding to the province of Kham in the Celestial Empire, they there found a youth whose horoscope presented the necessary indication of his fitness for the throne, which was offered to him and accepted, and accompanied by a body of his clansmen he returned with the Lamas, and was proclaimed Rajah of Dingong, as the Lepchas call Sikhim.

All the Tibetans who penetrate through Butan into Asam are called **Khampas**, or **Kampas**, and the name is, I suppose, of the same origin as that assumed by the Sikhim rulers.

Physical traits.

The Lepchas are described by all who have written about them as physically of the true Mongolian type. They are short of stature, averaging about five feet. Five feet six is considered tall, and four feet eight is a common stature amongst the men. The women bear towards them the usual proportion. The face is broad and flat, nose depressed, eye oblique, no beard, but a very little moustache, complexion olive, and boys and girls in health have generally a ruddy tinge which adds greatly to their good looks. The total absence of beard, and the fashion of parting the hair along the crown of the head, gives to the males a somewhat effeminate appearance, and the robes of the sexes being cut somewhat alike, it is not always easy to distinguish them. They are proud of their hair and careful in its arrangement, the women wearing theirs behind braided in two tails tied with silken cords and tassels. Their garments are ample, often of the coarse, flossy cloth of the silk that is spun by the castor-oil plant worm, the 'Eri' of Asam, and they wear over all a small, sleeveless, woollen cloak, covered with crosses, fastened by a girdle of silver chains.

Character.

Dr. Campbell says, they are amiable and cheerful in disposition, and of an intelligent and inquiring turn of mind, which renders them attractive to a European. Colonel Walter Sherwill calls them "the free, happy, laughing, and playful, no-caste, Lepchas, the children of the mountain, modest, social, and joyous in disposition." They are fond of racing, playing at hop-step and jump, quoits, wrestling, and jumping, and are great practical* jokers, but they are indolent and deficient in energy and particularly averse to serving for hire.

Agriculture.

They are poor agriculturists. Nomadic in their habits, they form no permanent villages, and cultivate barely sufficient for their subsistence. When their stock of grain and pulse falls short, they subsist themselves on wild roots, mountain spinach, fern-tops, fungi, and other natural products, and the produce of the chase. They seldom remain more than three years in one spot. This is indeed the usual time in which all similar nomads consider the freshness of the virgin forest soil on which they rely to wear out. They have no ploughs, and the implements they employ do no more than scrape and soften for the reception of seed the upper layer of vegetable mould.

The Lepchas are not a warlike race. They carry weapons, a long knife, bow and arrows, but are fonder of using them against the wild beasts than against their fellow creatures.

Food.

They eat all kinds of animal food.† Pork is their favorite dish, next to that beef, goat, and mutton. Those who live in Nepal are obliged to conform to Hindu practices and abstain from forbidden meats. It is the great delight of these unwilling abstinents to cross into Sikhim, Darjiling, and have a thoroughly good feed on beef.

They are fond of fermented and spirituous liquors, but are not much given to excess. They make themselves a beer from a fermented infusion of Indian corn and Murwa, which is acidulous and refreshing. The art of distillation they have not yet acquired.

Priesthood.

Dr. Campbell says, the Lepchas are Budhists and have priests, some of their own tribe educated at home, a few of the same race who go for their education to the great monastic establishments beyond the snow, and some Tibetan priests. The latter two classes adhere to the monastic discipline, and are supposed to be devoted to celibacy. The country-born and country-educated priest is permitted to marry.

Dr. Latham‡ tells us that the Lepcha is no Budhist, and that the priests, though they carry about the Budhist prayer machines, wear Budhist rosaries, and profess monkish mendicancy, are also the medicine men, the exorcists, and the directors of the feasts, ceremonies, and sacrifices in honor of evil spirits; but notwithstanding all

* Journal, Asiatic Society, Bengal, 1853, page 638.

† Major Sherwill found that they would not feed from the carcases of sheep killed because diseased, though they ate snakes, frogs, and other extraordinary food.

‡ Latham's Descriptive Ethnology, Vol. II, page 88.

this they may be just as good Budhists as the Butias, who whilst flirting with the mysteries of that religion retain much of their original Paganism or Shamanism.

In morality the Lepchas appear much superior to the Butias. Polyandry is not mentioned as one of their institutions, and a marriage ceremony is acknowledged.

Marriages.

They do not marry young, as they often find it difficult to make up the necessary sum demanded by the parents of the girl; but the marriage is sometimes allowed to take place on credit, the girl remaining in her father's house and her husband living with her there till he can pay or has earned the money which entitles him to take her home.

Chastity in adult girls previous to marriage is not very rigidly insisted on.

The Lepchas bury their dead as is the custom generally of the Budhists.

SECTION 3.—THE LIMBUS AND KIRANTIS.

The next tribe in geographical order, proceeding west from the confines of Butan, are the Limbus. They are a branch of the people called 'Kiranti' or 'Kirati,' and for the earliest notice of them we must refer to the Purans.

The Kiratis, it is said, occupied the country to the east of 'Bharata,'* and in the list of peoples further on we find them alongside the 'Barbaras,' and are told in the note that these latter are considered by all the authorities as borderers and foreigners and nations not Hindu. The Kirantis are still numerous in Dinajpur, which was part of the ancient Matsyadesh, all the inhabitants of which were considered as foreigners and borderers. They are as Limbus an important segment of the population of Sikhim, and as Kirantis of Nepal, but the people indicated do not themselves affect either of these designations, preferring, according to Mr. Hodgson†, the names Khwombo, or Khombo, and Kirawa. Dr. Campbell‡ says that the correct denomination of the people is 'ekthúmba'; but the term Limbu is generally used to indicate the whole population of the country between the Dudkusi and the Mechi. Mr. Hodgson defines the Kirant country thus:—

1. Sunkosi to Likhu 2. Likhu to Arun	Khwombuan.
3. Arun to Mechi, Singilela ridge ...	Limbuan.

Tribal affinities.

In regard to the affinity of the tribes thus conjoined, he observes that they are, at all events, closely allied races, having essential community of customs and manners, and they all intermarry. Dr. Campbell also says that in the generic term Limbu are included the Kiratis, the Eakas (Hodgson, *Yakhas*,) and Rais, and that in appearance and habits they are all very much alike, and they intermarry, which amongst the Hill Tribes, as well as the people of the plains in India, is the great test of national connection.

The Kirantis are divided into Wallo Kirant, or Hither Kirant, Mángh or Middle Kirant, and Pallo or Further Kirant. The Wallo include the Limbus and Yakhas. Their numbers, Mr. Hodgson thinks, do not now exceed a quarter of a million, but they

* Wilson's Translation of the Vishnu Purana.

† Journal, Asiatic Society, Bengal, 1858, page 448.

‡ Journal, Asiatic Society, Bengal, 1840, page 595.

have a tradition that they once numbered two and a half millions. The above appear to be geographical divisions; they are also divided into several tribes. Dr. Campbell says, they are ranged under two great divisions, called Hung and Rai; these are sub-divided into various tribes, each bearing the family name of Hung or Rai, according to which of the great divisions they belong, as Phedahung and Kembang Rai.

Physical traits.

In describing the physical character of the Limbus, Dr. Campbell* starts by an opinion that they belong to the great Mongolian family, but though they are much mixed up with the Lepchas, he evidently considers them as less Mongolian than that tribe. "The Limbu is a little taller than the Lepcha, somewhat less fleshy, and more wiry in the limbs, as fair in complexion, and as beardless. He is scarcely ever ruddy as the Lepchas are, his eyes are if any thing smaller, and placed more to the front than those of the Lepchas, and his nose, though somewhat smaller, is somewhat higher in the bridge than that of the Lepchas. He wears his hair long, but does not plait it into a tail, has no fancy for bead necklaces, wears a 'kukri'† instead of the 'ban', and wide trowsers and a jacket instead of the robe and long jacket of the Lepchas.

Mr. Hodgson has given a very minute description of three individuals of the tribe selected by him as typical; the traits as described are not Mongolian, and he sums up thus:—"All these men have a depth of color and defect of bone and muscle assimilating them to the low land Turanians generally, and differencing them from the Highlanders, but especially from the Palasen, the Gurung, the Sunwar, the Murmi, the Magar, and the Lepcha; and Bontawa" (one of them) "has a head and a face carrying on the resemblance with the low land Turanians, which I believe to be so frequent amongst the Kirantis as to deserve to be called the rule, not the exception."

Linguistic affinities.

In regard to their language which he has carefully analyzed and described he says—"The complex pronominalization of the Kiranti verb points to a special connection with the Munda (*i. e.*, Kolarian) sub-division." He also notes analogies of formation between the Kiranti and Dravirian languages.

Traditions.

The Kirantis have a tradition that they had rulers five centuries ago, who were called Hang or Hwang. They have none now but village headmen, who are called 'Pasung', who collect the taxes and settle disputes.

Proprietary rights.

The Kirantis, like the Mundas of Chota Nagpur, tenaciously cling to the lands reclaimed by their ancestors. They appear to have in Nepal full proprietary rights in these tenures, called Walikha. Each proprietor 'Thang-pung-hangpa' pays 4 Rupees per annum as land tax, and 1 Rupee in commutation for the corvèe.

Arts and agriculture.

They have ploughs, but from the nature of their cultivation on the slopes of hills seldom use them. "Their general, almost exclusive‡, status is, however, agriculturists, their produce maize, buckwheat, millet, dry rice, and cotton. They have no craftsmen." In this, too, they resemble the Kols, who, even when most civilized, are dependent on other races for the commonest articles of domestic use for raiment and utensils. The Kirantis, however, spin, weave, and dye cloths for their own use, and make fermented and distilled liquors.

* Journal, Asiatic Society, Bengal, 1840, page 596

† Curved knife, *Ban!* probably the long straight sword of Tibet, Butan, &c.

‡ Hodgson.

Religion.

The Limbus or Kirantis, though subjected to the sneers and frowns of a Brahmanical priesthood on one side and the more indulgent exhortations of Budhist monks on the other, have, like the Kols, obstinately adhered to their primitive paganism. Mr. Hodgson found the Kirantis had no name for God, and no recognised order of priests. The Limbus, says Dr. Campbell, believe in the existence of a Supreme God, who is called Sham Mungh, the God of the universe, and worship other deities named Mhang Mo, Takpaka, Hem-sung-mung, the destroyer, Teba-sum, the God of wisdom, Mungol Mo, the preserver, and Hem-sung, the household God. They do not build temples or make images of their gods, but propitiate them by sacrifices of animals, *i. e.*, killing an animal in the name of the God they wish to propitiate and eating it themselves, giving, as they observe, "the life to the God and the flesh to themselves." The places set apart for sacrifices are marked by the erection of bamboo poles with rags attached. On these occasions, the persons employed as priests are either Bijowas, or Phedangkos; the former are mendicant friars, apparently of no particular race, who wander about in the garb of Budhist priests, who by cunning and charlatanism inspire their votaries with considerable awe, but who are ready for a consideration to sing or dance for those in health, prescribe for those who are sick, and cast the devil out of those who are vexed. One doctrine most important to themselves they have succeeded in propagating, *i. e.*, that ill betides the man who sends a Bijowa dissatisfied from his door.

The Phedangko is more exclusively the Limbu priest, and the office is sometimes hereditary, but in a large family one of the sons is generally told off for it, and he is declared to be specially called to the work of propitiation. The Kiranti priest is called Nakchong. It is his duty to propitiate the penate and the manes of the ancestors of each family in his care by an annual worship constituting two festivals in the year, the first celebrated after the harvest; and he attends at marriages and deaths.

They believe in all kinds of sorcery and witch craft, and have exorcists.

Births.

Amongst the Kirantis* births are not attended by any religious observances, but the Limbus† call in the Phedangko, who examines the infant carefully, sacrifices a fowl or kid, and invokes for the young stranger the blessings of the Gods. The parents name the infant on the third day.

Marriages.

The Limbus and Kirantis have to buy their wives; those who are too poor to pay in cash serve like Jacob in the father's house till they have given an equivalent in labor. The men select for themselves. They employ friends to arrange price and preliminaries, sending by them an offering to the parents of two or three rupees to gain their consent. On the day fixed for the ceremony, the bride and bridegroom are seated side by side and the priest admonishes them, then he gives a hen into the hands of the bride and a cock to the man, and cuts off the cock's head first and next the hen's; their blood is allowed to mingle together and auguries as to the prospects of the happy pair drawn from the form it assumes as it flows.

Burials.

The funeral ceremonies of the Kirantis are like those of the Mundas and Kasias. They burn their dead, selecting the summits of mountains for the purpose, and afterwards collect and bury the ashes, over which they raise a square tomb of stone, about four feet high, placing an upright stone on its summit.

* Hodgson. † Campbell.

On the upright stone is engraved a record of the quantity of largess distributed at the funeral of the deceased. This inscription is either in the Devanagari or Lepcha character, according to the comparative facility of procuring an engraver in either of these characters.

Language.

They have no written character of their own. Their language is described generally as pleasing to the ear, being labial and palatal rather than nasal and guttural.

SECTION 4.—THE MURMIS.

The Murmis appear to be a nomadic and pastoral branch of the Butias. They are Mongolian in appearance, Budhist in religion, and speak a language which appears to me to be a dialect of Butia. They live in houses built of stone on mountain tops at an elevation of from 4 to 6,000 feet. They are found in all parts of Nepal from the Gunduk river to the Mechi, and in smaller numbers in the Sikhim country. They are divided into several families or clans. The Murmis like the Butias burn their dead.

SECTION 5.—THE HAIOOS (CAMPBELL), OR HAYAS, OR VAYAS.

I do not know that any members of this tribe are at present located in any part of Bengal, but as there appear to be good grounds for affiliating them with one or other of the families of the aborigines of the Gangetic provinces, I will close with them my account of the northern races.

Geographical position.

The Hayas* appear in Nepal as the fragment of a tribe of great antiquity with peculiar traditions, language, and appearance; all tending to isolate them from the people amongst whom they dwell, and to direct our attention to swarthy southerners for their affinities.

They are now found "tenanting the basin of the river Kosi between the confines of the great valley of Nepal Proper, and that point where the Kosi turns southwards to issue to the plains"—a single people distinct from all their neighbours, they appear to be rapidly diminishing in numbers. As they are represented as only forming a population of a few thousands, they will probably ere many years elapse cease to exist as a separate tribe.

Traditions.

Mr. Hodgson tells us that they have a tradition of a very remote time when they were a numerous and powerful people. Doctor Campbell† gives as their tradition that they originally came from Lanka (Ceylon), having left that country after the defeat of their king Rawan by Ram Chandra, but the Raksha king Rawan is still their hero and God, they have no other; they remained a long time in the Dakhin, "whence they journeyed on to Semrounghur in the days of its glory, and that, lastly, but a long time ago, they reached the hills, their present abode."

I have suggested that the ancestors of the Bhuyas were the people who formed the army of the ape general Hanuman, the ally of Ram Chandra, in his famous operations against Rawan.‡ It is interesting to find a remnant of the host that opposed him, and

* There is a tribe in Ceylon called Vaidas.

† Journal, Asiatic Society, Bengal, 1858, pages 443-456.

‡ Journal, Asiatic Society, Bengal, Vol. IX, for 1840.

1 B

however far-fetched this tradition may appear, there is much to support the theory of their southern origin.

Language.

I have no Haya vocabulary to refer to, but Mr. Hodgson in analyzing the construction of the language, has noted many peculiarities common to it and the Sonthal, or Kol language, and this connection takes them as far south as Ceylon, if not to Ceylon.

Physical traits.

In regard to their physical characteristics, he deduces from the specimens he examined, that they are darker and of a less Mongolic caste of countenance than the Lepchas. The sample that he considered most typical of the race was 5 feet 4½ inches in height, moderately fleshy, and dark brown; vertical view of the head oblate, wider, and flat behind; greatest breadth between the ears, rising pyramidically from the zygomata to the crown of the head; facial angle not bad, the forehead retiring, and narrowing only slightly; the mouth not being porrect, nor the chin retiring but pointed; eyes remote but small, and the upper lids flaccid and somewhat down, curved at the inner canthus; nose pyramidal, not levelled between the eyes, nor the extremity much thickened, but the nares large and round; mouth large but well formed, with neatly shaped lips and vertical fine teeth.

The above, as I understand it, would answer well for a description of an ordinary Singhbum Ho, but on the whole the Ho would probably be handsomer.

We have very little information regarding the customs of the Hayas, but Doctor Campbell made good use of an opportunity he met with to witness their national dance, and thus he describes it—

Peculiar dance.

"The nautch was indeed a singular one and novel. About 30 males and as many females were drawn up in line as closely packed as possible, the first a man, the next a woman, and so on alternately, not standing side by side, but back to belly, and all holding on to each other by throwing forward the hands and grasping the arms of the persons in front. The column thus formed, and preceded by half-a-dozen men beating drums and cymbals, and shouting in a barbarous dialect what was said to be a metrical lament, moved slowly in a circle nodding and keeping time to the music. In this pastime and so closely packed that the circle of sixty individuals had the appearance of a machine with a row of heads and feet set in motion, did they revolve and mourn for an hour." The mourning being for the death of their hero Rawan.

Resemblances with the Hos.

I should like very much to have seen this dance. It may possess features peculiarly its own, but judging from the description given, I am confident that wherever these Hayas came from, they were taught dancing at the same school as the Hos, and there may be something in the similarity of the names. I do not indeed think that the Ho youths and maidens mourn as they dance, and they know nothing of Rawan or Lanka; but many an hour have I seen them revolve just as described by Doctor Campbell locking up as no soldiers ever locked up, keeping admirable time both in the movements of the feet and undulations of the head to the monotonous beat of the drums. It is the dance of Hos and Sonthals, not of the Mundas, though they too have something resembling it, and it can be made to assume a mournful cadence, as the same step and drum-beat is used at their funeral dances.

VOCABULARY TO GROUP III.*

ENGLISH.	BUTIA.	LEPCHA.	LIMBU.	KIRANTI.	MURMI.
One ...	chi ...	kát ...	thit ...	ektai ...	ghrik.
Two ...	nyi ...	nyet ...	nyetsh ...	hasat ...	gni.
Three ...	súm ...	sam ...	syúm sh ...	súmyá ...	sóm.
Four ...	zhi ...	pha li ...	lí sh ...	layá ...	blí.
Five ...	gná ...	pha gnon ...	gná sh ...	gnáyá ...	gná.
Six ...	dhú ...	tarok ...	túk sh ...	túkyá ...	dhú.
Seven ...	dún ...	ka kyok ...	nú sh ..	bhágyá ...	nis.
Eight ...	gyé ...	kakeu ...	yet sh ...	réyá ...	pré.
Nine ...	gu ...	ka kyot ...	pháng sh ...	phángyá ...	kúh.
Ten ...	cha tham ...	katí ...	thi bong ...	kip ...	chíwai.
Twenty ...	khéchik nyi sho,	khakát ...	ní bong ...	......	nhi shú.
Fifty ...	khéphédángsúm	kha-nyet sa ka tí	gná gip ...	......	bokal-ni-shú-chú.
Hundred ...	khé gná ...	khá phá gnon ...	thi bong gip ...	......	bokal gná.
I ...	gná ...	go ...	ingá ...	ánka ...	gná.
We ..	gná chá ...	kayú ká ..	anigé ...	ankan ...	gnáni.
Thou ...	chhú ...	hau ...	khené ...	khaná ...	ai.
You ...	khá chá ...	háyú ...	khenih' ...	khananin ...	aini.
He ...	khó ...	heu ...	khúné ...	moko ...	thé.
They ...	khong ...	hóyú ...	khúnchi ...	moko chi ...	théni.
Of me ...	......	......	......	......	......
Of thee ...	......	......	......	......	......
Of you ...	......	......	......	......	......
Of him ...	......	......	......	......	......
Of them ...	......	......	......	......	......
Mine ...	gné gi ...	kaseusa ...	ingá in ...	ang ko ...	gná lá.
Our ...	gná chégi ...	kayú pongsa ...	anigen in ...	aín ko ...	in ná.
Thine ...	chhé gi ...	hadosa ...	khene in ...	am ko ...	ai lá.
Your ...	kheu chégi ...	hayú pongsa ...	khenih' in ...	ámno ...	an ná.
His ...	kheu gi ...	heusa ..	khune in ...	mósó ...	thé lá.
Their ...	khong gi ...	hoyú pongsa ...	khúnchi in ...	myaucho, moyo so	thenná.
Hand ...	láppa ...	kaliok ...	húktáphé ...	chúkúphémá ...	yá.
Foot ...	kanglep ...	diángliok ...	Lángdapphé ..	úkhúro ...	balé.
Nose ...	......	......	......	......	......
Eye ...	mido ...	amik ...	mik ...	mak ...	mí.
Mouth ...	khá ...	abóng ...	múrá ...	dóh ...	súng.
Tooth ...	soh ...	aphó ...	hébo ...	kang ...	swá.
Ear ...	navo ...	anyor ...	nekho ...	nábá ...	nápé
Hair ...	kyá ...	achom ...	thágí ..	moá ...	krá
Head ...	gútoh ...	athiak ...	thagék ...	táng ...	thóbó
Tongue ...	......	......	......	......	......
Belly ...	......	......	......	......	......
Back ...	......	......	......	......	......
Iron ...	chyá ...	panjing ...	phenjé ...	phalám ...	phai.
Gold ...	......	......	......	......	......
Silver ...	......	......	......	......	......
Go ...	sóng ...	nón ...	bégé ...	khárá ...	nyú, syé go.
Eat ...	sah ...	zó, thá ...	ché ...	cho ...	chou.
Sit ...	deu ...	gnán ...	yúng ne ...	yúngá ...	tyú.
Father ...	appá ...	abó ...	amba ...	bá ...	ápá.

* From Hodgson's and Campbell's Vocabularies, Journal, Asiatic Society of Bengal, Vol. XVI, and Vol. XXXV, part II, special No. pp.

ENGLISH.	BUTIA.	LEPCHA.	LIMBU.	KIRANTI.	MURMI.
Mother	ai	amo	amma	má	amma.
Brother	......	......	......	......	......
Sister	......	......	......	......	......
Man	mi	maro, tagri	yapmi, yembecha	maná	mí.
Woman	......	......	......	......	......
Wife	......	......	......	......	......
Child	......	......	......	......	......
Son	......	......	......	......	......
Daughter	......	......	......	......	......
Slave	......	......	......	......	......
Cultivator	......	......	......	......	......
Shepherd	......	......	......	......	......
God	......	......	......	......	......
Devil	......	......	......	......	......
Come	syó	di	phéré	háná	khou. jyangou.
Beat	......	......	......	......	......
Stand	lóng	lúk, ding	pógé	yéwá lántá	ráb.
Sun	nyim	sachak	nam	nam	dini.
Moon	dau	lavó	láva	lá díma	lhá ni.
Star	kám	sahór	khéséva	sangyen	karchin.
Fire	mi	mí	mé	mí	mé.
Water	chhú	ong	chúá	cháwá	kwi.
House	khyim	lí	him	khím	dhim.
Horse	táh	ón	ón	ghora	tá.
Cow	gnó (*pr.* cattle)	bik	bit	pit	mhé.
Dog	khi	kazen	khíá	kochú	nángi.
Cat	pilli	aleu	myóng	myong	táwar.
Cock	......	......	......	......	......
Duck	......	......	......	......	......
Ass	......	......	......	......	......
Camel	......	......	......	......	......
Bird	bhyá	phó	bú	chongwá	námy
Die	......	......	......	......	......
Give	náng	bó	piráng-né	pai	pin.
Run	pán kyap	deung	lóktó	lóyá	yár.
Up	......	......	......	......	......
Near	thá ni	athol	neng dáng	nektá	jyat na.
Who	......	......	......	......	......
And	dá	lá	ang	ning	yen, den.
Yes	túp, in	ak, euk	ók	angá	ninná, yá.
Down	......	......	......	......	......
Far	thá ring	maram	mánkhó	mángsá	tháring.
What	káng chi, kan	shú	thé	dí, dé	tigi.
But	......	......	......	......	......
No	me túp, men	má né	men, ná	máng	ánin.
Before	......	......	......	......	......
Behind	......	......	......	......	......
If	......	......	......	......	......
Why	kám bé	shú mat	thé áng thé jokma thé yambókle	kháinsé	tik.
Alas	......	......	......	......	......

GROUP IV.

TIPPERAH AND CHITTAGONG TRIBES.

When I commenced writing this paper, I did so with the intention of confining myself to facts, leaving to others to deduce from them such evidence regarding the origin and affiliation of races as they might assist in establishing. I am doing my best, however, to throw my tribes into groups when relationship appears obvious, and I cannot refrain from recording the conjectures in regard to more distant connections that occur to me, or that I meet in the writings of others as I go on.

I have described the Gáros as occupying the most western portion of the long range of hills which extend from Cape Negrais to the Brahmaputra. In connecting them with the Bodo or Kachári, I link them with all the tribes who form a chain of settlements in that range of hills, and I think it will be best to take up those links as well as we can and so finish with the Eastern Frontier.

Major Fisher in his 'Memoir of Sylhet, Kachár, &c.,' tells us that the people of Tipperah, or Tripura, are said to have the same origin as the Kacháris, and the similarity of religion, customs, and appearance, makes this probable. It may be added that the Rajas of both countries, Tipperah and Kachár, have formally acknowledged the connection. The Tipperah family are described as a younger branch of the ancient royal family, who, on the expulsion of the latter from Kámrúp, established themselves independently in the country which they formerly held as a province.

The Kacháris of the Brahmaputra valley had emerged from barbarism when they gave way in Kámrúp, and had in a great measure dropped their paganism; but doubtless the outlying members of the family retained most of their primitive customs.

Fisher observes that among the superstitions common to both is the practice of performing sacrifice before a bamboo planted in the ground. We have noticed something like this as a Kachári practice, and it has been prominently brought forward as a solemn observance of the Gáros.

The Brahmans have of course favored the family with a different origin. The Ráj-Mála, an analysis of which is given by the Revd. J. Long in the Journal of the Asiatic Society of Bengal for 1850, tells us that the ancient name of Tripura was Kirat, from a person of that name, meaning 'the hunter' of the lunar race, the brother of Puru. He was succeeded by his son Tripura, who so worried his subjects, that they fled in a body to Hirumba (Kachár); they returned votaries of Shiva who promised them

2 c

a ruler by the *widow* of Trilochun. The promised prince was born in due course. He married the daughter of the Hirumba Rájá, who is also called 'Hirumba', Rájá of Kámrúp. Thus even the Brahmans support the theory of the connection between the Kacháris and Tipperahs.

In a Survey Report by Mr. H. J. Reynolds, the following description is given of the Tripuras. He had previously, following a common practice, spoken of them as Kúkis; but he found them to be different in many respects from the Kúkis of the Chittagong jungles, and says that the name by which they are commonly known is Tipperahs. In physiognomy some of them are like the Munipúris, but the greater part bear more resemblance to the Kásias, having strongly marked Mongolian features with flat faces and thick lips. They are not shorter in stature than Bengalis and are far more muscular and strongly made. Many of them have fair complexions "scarcely darker than a swarthy European."

The following note on Tripura is extracted from the General Report of the Tipperah District, by J. F. Browne, Esquire, Civil Service, recently printed :—

"The Tipperahs, or inhabitants of the Tipperah hill ranges, are said by some to be colonists from Munipúr, from which place they were driven by a Burmese invasion. But there can be little doubt that the opinion of those who assert them to have inhabited this part of the country from time immemorial, is equally well founded. Nothing is known about the ancient history of these people, but tradition names as their first king Asango, who is said to be the ancestor of Trilochun mentioned in the Máhabhárat as king of Tripura.

"The religion now prevailing is a form of Hindu idolatry, but it is said that before the accession of Trilochun, they worshipped no idols but objects of nature, *e. g.*, trees, stones, animals. A trace of their old faith is to be found in their present practice of sticking a bamboo in the ground during one of their religious festivals and worshipping it."

It is probable that the worship of the bamboo by the Tipperahs, Kacháris, Gáros, has its origin in a feeling or sentiment kindred to that which induces the Kols to worship the Sál tree. The Sál tree had to be dispossessed in the one case, and the bamboo in the other, before the new settlers could derive any benefit from the soil.

"The tribes of the Tipperahs are four in number,—the Rájbangsis, Nowatyahs, Jomalias, and Reyangas. The first is looked upon as highly respectable, whilst the last is held in very low estimation." (? by Hindus and proselytes).

"The priests of the first three tribes are called Tojaees, but the Reyangas have priests of their own; celibacy is not practised by them.

"No religious ceremony is necessary for a marriage, but only the consent of the parents. If the bridegroom can give a dower, the marriage takes place at once; but if he cannot, he must serve one year in his father-in-law's house. Early marriages are not prevalent, and polygamy, though not objected to, is very rare."

"Tipperahs eat flesh of every description except beef, and, after the decease of a relation, abstain from flesh for a week. Both men and women are very fond of dancing. They are, as a rule, truthful and simple-minded. No man is looked on as a person of any importance till he is married.

"Their mode of cultivation is of the same desultory kind as we find practised by the Kacháris, &c."

This is a very brief account of the Tipperahs, but considering their proximity to the Kúkis, and the fact that the Kúkis who migrated into Kachár came from the Tipperah hills, we may infer that a more detailed account of the customs of the primitive Tipperahs would be a repetition of the information which Major Stewart has given us regarding the Kúkis.

That the Kúkis were known of old in Tripura is apparent from the Ráj Mála, as it represents Shiva falling in love with a Kúki girl who was in consequence put to death by his shrew of a wife. In another place the Kúkis are represented as allies of the Rájá of Udaipur who invaded Tripura, but was defeated, and Udaipur became the capital of Tripura. Again, the Kúkis are brought forward as accusing the Tripura general Raja Chachag of a design to make Tamul which he had subjugated in the name of his master, an independent state. This general flourished in A. D. 1512.

The Tipperahs as worshippers of Shiva appear to have practised human sacrifice very extensively. It is said that till the reign of Sri Dharma, the complement was one thousand victims a year. Sri Dharma ruled that human sacrifices should only be offered triennially, and at one time.* It can, I think, be demonstrated that the tribes most addicted to human sacrifices throughout Bengal were aborigines who had substituted a debased Hindu idolatry for the purer paganism of their ancestors.

It is remarkable that in the Tripura District and in Hill Tripura there are very few families of pure Aryan descent. There is a tradition† that the sons of Pandu travelling to the East sent Bhima, one of the brothers, across the Megna to view the land, but he found the inhabitants so barbarous, that all thoughts of a settlement there were abandoned.

Mugs.

To the east and south-east of the open country of the Chittagong District there is a tract of hill and forest about 140 miles from north to south, and about on an average 50 miles in breadth, known to the revenue authorities‡ as the 'kapás' or Cotton Mehal.

When we took possession of Chittagong, we found two Mug chieftains located in this tract who paid their revenue in cotton. The tribes subject to these chiefs are called Jumeas, or Jumea Mugs.

They are in fact Mugs who are called Jumeas from their affecting the peculiar mode of cultivation called jhúm, from a word, which, in the language of these people, means 'to burn.' The jungle is cut and when dried burned, and the ashes are spread over and dug into the ground as manure.

We thus come to the Mugs who form the bulk of the population of Arakan, and are the aboriginal inhabitants of that province.

The tradition of the Kúkis respecting their origin is, that they and the Mugs are the offspring of the same progenitor,§ who had two sons by different mothers, and the Mugs have the honor to be descended from the first born. This tradition of their common origin receives much support from the similarity of the Mug and Kúki languages, "many words of which are the same, and their general resemblance is such that a Mug and Kúki can make themselves understood by each other."

* I do not know if he was the first monarch so to regulate them, but at a comparatively recent period they were thus limited in many parts of Bengal.

† General Report on Tripura by J. F. Browne, Esquire, C. S.

‡ Mr. Ricket's Report on Wild Tribes of the Chittagong Frontier, 10th August 1847.

§ Asiatic Researches, Volume VII, page 184.

The population of Arakan was estimated in 1851 at 321,000, and about half the number are Mugs.

The term 'Mug' is exclusively a foreign epithet unknown to the Arakanese themselves; the Arakanese and Burmese are of the same race, and have the common national name of Myam-ma, which is however a comparatively modern appellation for the several tribes which conjointly form the nation. The difference between the languages spoken by the Burmese and Arakanese is mainly in pronunciation. The written languages of both countries are for the most part alike.

The Kúkis remain Pagans, their elder brethren have become Budhists; but the connection between the two being established, we may expect to find amongst the Mugs vestiges of customs that will help us in affiliating them.

Physical traits and costume.

"In personal appearance* the Mugs resemble the Chinese; the cheek bone is high and broad, the nose flat and the eyes oblique. They are of a mulatto colour. Though short, they are a well-made people, hardy, muscular, and athletic." The hair both of men and women is generally very beautiful and of a glossy black; both sexes pride themselves on its fine quality. The females wear it parted in the middle and tied in a knot at the back of the head. The men wear a kind of turban of fine white cloth, which they entwine with their hair. They wear no ornaments except in the ears, the lobe being largely perforated for their reception, but the half smoked cigar is often carried in one of the holes. The dress of the women consists of a cloth tightly bound round the bosom and flowing to the feet, and a large outer dress thrown over the whole person and reaching to the knees. The unmarried women wear a jacket, which is assumed by girls when marriageable, and abandoned when they become wives; it is again adopted upon widowhood. The dress of the men is composed of a cloth round the middle, and one thrown over the shoulders. The bachelors amongst them live in a part of the village separate from the rest.

Dwellings.

The hut in which the Mugs reside is constructed of bamboo and is raised on piles several feet from the ground. The dwellings are easily and expeditiously erected, and assistance is always given by the neighbours to the person engaged in the construction of one. The space between the earth and the floor is occupied by pigs and poultry.

Food.

In regard to animal food, there is nothing, from the rat to the elephant, which does not suit the palate of the Mug. Boiled rice and fish is, however, their ordinary aliment. Both sexes smoke tobacco and chew tobacco and pán. There is in most villages what is called a travellers' home, where a stranger is sure to meet with every care and attention. Is not this the bachelors' hall? It is generally so amongst the tribes that have this institution, and they appear to be legion.

Manly exercises.

Although somewhat slothful in disposition, they are very fond of hunting, and delight in manly exercises, such as wrestling and boxing, and a game peculiar to the country, called kilome, which is somewhat similar to battle-dore and shuttlecock, only instead of the hands the feet are employed. They are very partial to boat-racing.

* From Thornton's Gazetteer, article Arakan. Dr. Guerson, Translation of Medical and Physical Science, Volume II., Journal, Asiatic Society, Bengal, for 1841. Ditto, for 1835.

Education. Education is not neglected amongst them, and there are few persons to be found who cannot read. The instruction of the children is part of the duty of the priest who devotes several hours each day to the functions of a school master, and receives the children of all, rich and poor alike.

Lushais. A high range of hills called Modu-ting, Mranidong, and Yomdong, forms a natural boundary between Chittagong and Arakan.* To the eastward of this boundary range, the Koladine river flows at a distance of 10 to 16 miles, and here are a few villages, but for 60 miles higher up no other villages are met, the intermediate country being totally uninhabited. To the west of the boundary range reside the Lushai Kúkis, the Lushais, I suppose, of Stewart, the tribe that drove into Kachár the four clans of Kúkis—Thadon, Shingson, Changsen, and Lamgam, noticed above.

The country to the east of the Koladine river from the mouth of the Sulla Kheony northwards is occupied by the independent Shendus. Of the latter, Sir A. Bogle, writing in 1847, states "they are very powerful, and reside so far back as to be almost inaccessible."†

The Koladine (inner) circle includes within its limits 2,652 square miles. The population consists of Kheongthas, Mrons, Kumis, and Shendus. The Kheongthas live in 9 villages intermixed with the Kumis. They number 713 souls. The Mrons occupy 12 villages. They number 839 souls. Both Kheongthas and Mrons are quiet, inoffensive people similar to the Jumea Mugs. Latham says, the Mrons are also called Rukheng, *i. e.*, Rukhaing,‡ but that is the name of the country, whence Arakan.

Both 'Mru' and 'Kheong' are used by the Arakanese as generic terms for hill tribes. The people who called themselves Mru are now a small tribe, numbering altogether in Arakan about 2,800 souls,§ who have been gradually driven from the Koladine by the Kumis, and occupy the hills between Arakan and Chittagong. The Arakanese annals mention this tribe as already in the country when the Myan-ma race entered it; and in the fourteenth century one of them was chosen King of Arakan, and they allude to the Mrons as of the same lineage as the Myan-ma, though the connection is now repudiated by the Arakanese, who call them 'Toung Mru,' wild men.

Tulukmi is a Keongtha village of 30 houses.‖ During the day the people live on land, but at night they occupy large substantial floating huts moved into the middle of the stream, being afraid of the secret and sudden attacks made by their wild neighbours. These villages appear to be all within the British pale and are preyed upon. From the variety of names given they are probably seceders from the more savage and independent tribes who prey upon them. Beyond them the Kumis, the largest and most important of the hill tribes in Arakan, occupy the country on both banks of the Koladine. They do not acknowledge the authority of any Raja or paramount chief, but they have their own village chiefs, and these chiefs form a confederacy, to the orders of which as a body all are to some extent subservient. They are divided into 27 clans, and the estimated number of the people is about 12,000. Of this tribe there are

* Notes on Tribes of the Eastern Frontier, by J. H. O'Donel, Esq., Revenue Surveyor of Arakan. Journal, Asiatic Society Bengal, of 1863.

† Selections, Records of the Bengal Government, No. XI, page 95.

‡ *Vide* Colonel Phayre's note on the History of the Burmah race. Journal Asiatic Society, Bengal, for 1864.

§ Journal, Asiatic Society, Bengal, No. I of 1853. Notes by Colonel Phayre and Mr. Hodgson.

‖ Notes by J. H. O'Donel, Esq.

two divisions, called by themselves Kami and Kúmi, and by the Arakanese Awa Kúmi and Aphya Kúmi; they are not considered the aborigines of the country they occupy. They have driven before them the Mrus, and are themselves pressed forward in a westerly and southerly direction by Khyengs and other powerful tribes.*

The more remote clans are called Shendus; they reside in the higher ranges distant from the river, and pay no revenue. It would appear, then, that the names Kumi and Shendu are sometimes applied to the same tribe, the more inaccessible and independent being called Shendus. They are called 'Poehs' by the Munipúris, and in some maps are noted as wild Khyens: they call themselves Heuma. Altogether the nomenclature of these tribes is very puzzling. We have Mrus and Mru Khyens, Khyens, Keoks, wild Khengs, and very little information to enable us to assign to each its proper ethnological position. The probability is they are all but different clans or tribes of the same race, like the Ábors, Nágás, &c.

The plundering expeditions of the tribes† of the interior are chiefly to obtain slaves. The village attacked is surrounded at night and generally set on fire, or a volley of muskets is fired into it. The inhabitants are seized as they attempt to escape from the burning houses. The males are put to death, and the women and children carried away into slavery. In the distribution of the slaves and plunder, the leader receives a double share. For the release of a captive thus taken, a ransom of Rs. 200 is generally demanded.

The Khyens occupy both banks of the Semru river from the Wah Kheong to the Khee Kheong; the low hills west of the Jagarudony range, the valley of the Taroi Kheong, and the low hills and plains within the Tandan Guachrain, Prwanrhay and Dainboong circles. They are a quiet, inoffensive people, and number 3,304 souls. These are within the pale, and pay revenue to the British Government. The males go almost naked. The females wear a dark blue‡ cotton gown fastened at the neck and descending to the knees. Their faces are tattooed to a most disfiguring extent, and they have a tradition that the practice was resorted to in order to conceal the natural beauty for which they were so renowned, that their maidens were carried off by the dominant race in lieu of tribute. Figures of animals are sometimes imprinted on their flesh as ornaments. The operation is so painful, that the young girls are tied down when subjected to it, and their faces remain swollen for a fortnight from its effects.

The more remote Khyens are erratic in their habits, rarely remaining in the same place for more than two or three years. They move in large bodies, and when they have fixed on a suitable site for a new settlement, they build houses like those of the Mugs. In their nomadic habits and migrations they thus resemble the Kúkis.

The Khyens of the higher ranges are independent: they declare that they at one time lived under a monarchical government in the plains of Pegu and Ava§, but their king was deposed by invaders, and retreating into the hills they formed a confederacy of separate colonies, each under its own chief. They retained an hereditary priesthood, called passin, who officiate at weddings and funerals, are conservators of traditions, and exorcists in cases of sickness or seizure by devils or witches.

---

* Note by Colonel Phayre, Journal, Asiatic Society, Bengal, No. 1, 1853, page 16.

† Notes on Tribes of the Eastern Frontier by J. H. O'Donel, Esq., Revenue Surveyor, Arakan

‡ Other writers say black.

§ Latham, Descriptive Ethnology, Vol. I., pp. 157-159.

One of the objects of worship with the Khyens is a thick bushy tree bearing a small berry called subri. At certain seasons they hold festivals in honor of this tree, meeting under its branches and sacrificing to it, or eating in its name pigs and fowls.

When a tree is struck by lightning, they search for the missile or thunder-bolt, and any likely stone is accepted as such, made over to the Passin, and held sacred and sacrificed to as something given from heaven.

They bury their dead—the poor where most convenient; the bones of the wealthy must rest in a burial place on one of two holy mountains, Keyungnatin* or Zehantoung. A hut is constructed near the tombs in which people stay to drive away malignant spirits. The spot is marked by a log or post carved to represent the deceased, as with the Gáros.

All crimes against the community are punished by fine. Life must not be taken even for life. The penalty of not paying the fine is slavery.

The Mru Khyens are within the pale on the Semru river. They number 4,020 souls, and pay revenue which they raise by rafting down bamboos for sale.† One of their villages, Anungrua, is a refuge for deformed, maimed, and all sick persons, labouring under palsy, leprosy, or other incurable disease.‡ They are not allowed to beg, and would on no account receive shelter in any other village.

The Koos.

Near the sources of the Semru river another wild tribe is met with, called by Mr. O'Donel Koo.§ They number, at 5 per house, 14,485 souls. They have intercourse with the neighbouring Kumis of the Koladine circle, from whom they differ but little in their habits. On occasions of rejoicing they amuse themselves by dancing round a bull or Gayal tied down to a stake, and as the dance continues, the animal is slowly dispatched by numberless spear wounds aimed at every part of his body. The blood is caught in bamboo cups, and men, women, and children drink it. The Koos have the reputation of torturing|| human victims in a similar manner; but on this point Mr. O'Donel could obtain no satisfactory information. They appear to be the most savage of these eastern tribes. No carriers or interpreters could be found amongst the adjacent tribes who would proceed to their villages. Their chief food is Indian corn, and they are unacquainted with the use of salt.

The Karens.

In the same ranges of hills to the south of the Khyens, we come on the better known Karens. Latham thinks that word for word Khyen is Karen, and this is probable. Mr. Mason tells us, it is a Burmese word signifying 'aboriginal'. We are told that the Karens are sometimes called Ka-Khyens which is a name applied to the Singphos, and the Karen language has noticeable Singpho affinities. This must be accepted as my reason for noticing a tribe quite out of Bengal.

It may be recollected that the Singphos had a tradition of a form of worship purer than the paganism they adopted when driven out of their paradise. So with

* Probably Mayeng-Matong.

† Notes on Eastern Frontier Tribes by J. H. O'Donel, Esq.

‡ Here those who cannot work are assisted by their relatives.

§ Notes by J. H. O'Donel, Esquire. This is probably the tribe alluded to by Colonel Phayre as Kha. Mr. Hodgson considers all these terms,—as Khye for the Kásias, Kho or Kejo for Kambojian tribes, Khyen, Kakhyen for the Karens, and this Khas, Kho, or Ko, of the Koladine,—to be closely allied. So also the Ka Khyen, or Kakoo, applied to the Singphos. (See notes on the Indo-Chinese Borderers. Journal, Asiatic Society, Bengal, for 1853, p. 14-17, note.)

(And see ante, Chapter on the Singphos.)

|| This resembles a sacrificial ceremony called the 'Bhinda Purub' till recently practised in Dholbhum, in which the Santals and Bhumiz are said to take especial delight.

the untutored Karen we find a solid foundation of religious belief under an incongruous rubble structure of very foolish paganism, which Christian Missionaries found it easy to remove and on the original plinth to raise a structure of pure religion. Divested of the paganism their old doctrine is too identical with that of the Mosaical books to be of spontaneous growth. They believe that they once possessed books or received their religion from books, and the book must have been the Old Testament.

Of their having received instruction from the New Testament before the advent of the American Baptist Missionaries about 1830 A. D., there is not a trace in any of their traditions. Indeed their notions of the flood are rather indistinct, and the identity of their traditions and the Mosaical narrative ends at the dispersion of mankind and confusion of tongues: the first they represent as having arisen from a want of love to each other and a lack of faith in God; the latter as a natural result of the first. If their traditions had carried them further on in Bible history we might have regarded them as one of the 'lost tribes.'

Traditions.

It is suggested that as there have been Jews in China from time immemorial, the traditions of the Karens may have been received from them.* This is corroborated by the fact that the Karens speak of the books from which they received instruction, as having been made of skin or parchment, and not many years ago some Missionaries in China obtained from a few Jewish families at Khai-fung-fu several copies of the Pentateuch, the only part of the Bible they possessed, beautifully written without points or marks for divisions, on white sheep skins.

We can thus understand their calling the Supreme Being Ywah (Jehovah), and their having preserved even the names of our first parents in the words E-u and Tha-nai. Tha-nai, or Tennai, is one of the words for mankind amongst the Hill Miris and Dophlas. They are represented as having transgressed the commands of God at the instigation of the dragon and eaten of the white fruit which the dragon beguilingly told them was the sweetest of all, but enviously kept from them, as eating it would make them divine.

We can imagine their having thus acquired and preserved such fragments of oral instruction from the inspired writings, but I am sceptical on the point of their having, as is alleged, also retained a line of inspired prophets, and surely inspiration alone could have predicted to a race supposed to have come from Central Asia, before they had yet seen the sea, that white men would come to them in ships who would restore to them the book with the words of the eternal God. I have the same faith in the genuineness of this as a prediction that I have in the genuineness of the Gáro and Abor tradition of the origin of the English†.

The following notice of the Karen polity and paganism I take from Dr. Latham who quotes Mr. Crosse.

Their government‡ is patriarchal, but besides the elders, two classes of men exercise considerable influence, the **Bukho** and the **Wi**. The former is a priest, an adept at the conduct of ceremonials, somewhat of a

Government; Priests.

* Notes of the Karen language by Revd. F. Mason.

† The scriptural traditions are found chiefly amongst the Sgan Karens. All the tribes have traditions of God having once dwelt amongst them; but in regard to creation many have wandered away from the old tradition into childish myths, some evidently tinted with Hinduism, and some that appear to have been originated since they came in contact with the white men; *vide* Journal, Asiatic Society, Bengal, Volume 34, pages 176-196, &c.

‡ Latham's Desc. Ethnology, Vol. I.

magician and a little of a physician. The latter is a prophet or oracle, but he only predicts when the spirit throws him into epilepsy or into a state of quasi involuntary writhing and foaming. We have seen this before in the Kachári Ojha, and shall see it again. On recovering from the fit he delivers his prophecy.

The local, personal, and individual, genii of the Karens are called **Kelah**, or **La**, or **Lai**, or **Yo**.* Every object has its Kelah; if the rice crop is unpromising, its Kelah has to be invoked. Every man has his Kelah or La; it existed before him, comes with him into the world, and lives with him till his death, but the Kelah does not die with him. Some Las thus separated from the body which they have inhabited, remain on earth and become mischievous spirits. Some go to hades, some (thence ?) to hell, some to heaven. But besides this *alter ego* that each man possesses, bad passions, reckless folly, and madness, have each their Kelah, and a man ails, or appears according to the La of the kind that seizes him. The moral principle or soul is called '**Thah**'; when we do good, or when we do evil, it is the Thah that does it.

Genii.

The head is the abode of a deity called Tso (conscience ?); so long as he keeps his seat, no Kelah (evil propensity ?) can do any mischief.

Religion.

The God **Phi-pho** presides in a sort of purgatory, called **cootay**. Those who die ordinarily go to him. If the shades are good, and please him, they are passed on to heaven; if they fail to give satisfaction, they are sent to 'Lerah', hell.

But some mortals, as the Burmese generally, are so wicked, that they do not go to Phi. They become goblins, 'Kephoo', &c., and wander about feeding on the Kelahs (evil propensities ?) of men.†

In the **Mukhas** the parents and ancestors of the Karens are worshipped with offerings. They are regarded as the creators of the present generation, and they preside over marriages and births.‡

The '**Wi**' has the power of reviving the dead or dying, but he must first catch the spirit of some person alive and divert it to the dead one. The person thus robbed sinks into death, but he is revived by a similar process, and so the Wi may continue the operation *ad infinitum*.

One very benevolent deity, called **Phibi-Ya**, sits on a lonely stump and watches the corn-fields, and it is due to her kind care that the corn ripens and the granaries are filled.

Under the denomination Karen are included several tribes speaking different dialects of the same language. The **Sgans** are the most numerous; they are found from Mergui in latitude 12°N. to Prome and Toungoo in nearly latitude 19°.§ Beyond the Toungoo southern boundary, they call themselves **Man-ne-pgha**, and on crossing Mitnam creek **Paki**.

Other Tribes.

The **Pwos** are found scattered in the same region as the Sgans to a short distance above Sitang. They have generally adopted Budhism. The Sgans call this clan **Pwos**, but they call themselves **Sho**, and they are distinguished by wearing embroidered tunics.

---

* Revd. J. Mason, Journal, Asiatic Society, Bengal, Vol. 34, p. 200. † Latham. ‡ Mason.

§ Notes on the Karen language, &c., by the Revd. F. Mason, Journal, Asiatic Society, Bengal, 1858, p. 131.

2 E

Distinction by dress is common to other Karen tribes. The Red Karens are not, as one would suppose, so called from the color of their skins; they owe the appellation to the color of their breeches. The wild Karens have red radiating lines on the seats of the same garment, but this appears to be a compromise on the orthodox custom, which is to have the radiating lines tattooed on their backs.

The Bghai Karens are found in Pegu, south of Toungoo. Their eastern boundary is the Salween. They are greater savages than the other Karens, robbers and kidnappers by profession.

The Sgans, Pwos, and Bghais are the principal Karen tribes, but there are two or three smaller ones, the Mopgha, the Toungthus (which signifies 'southern mountaineers,' they call themselves Pa-an), and a tribe called Tari, who shave their heads leaving a tuft of hair on each temple.

I have no description of the personal appearance of the Karens. It would appear from incidental references that their features are more regular or more Caucasian than those of the tribes around them; but the best authority, Colonel Phayre, upholds that their national physiognomy is essentially Indo-Chinese, and their speech connects them with the same family.

Their tradition regarding their migrations is thus given by the Revd. Mr. Mason :—

Traditions of migrations.

" These cities of our jungles were in ruins when we came here. This country is not our own. We came from the north, where we were independent of the Burmese, the Siamese, and the Talaings, who now rule over us. There we had a city and a country of our own called Toungoo. All the Karens of Siam, Burmah, and Pegu, came originally from that region: their traditions carry them back far beyond Toungoo. There they had settled, but their ancestors had crossed the river of running sand in coming there. That was a fearful trackless region where the sands rolled before the winds like the waves of the sea, but they were supernaturally led through it."

Mr. Mason adds,—" To what this river or waters of running sand referred was quite an enigma to me for several years, till I met with the journal of the Chinese Budhist pilgrim, Fa Hian, who came from China to India in the early part of the fifth century of the Christian era. He thus designates the great desert between China and Tibet. The governor of the town of sands, he says, furnished his party with the necessary means of crossing the river of sand. There are evil spirits in this river of sand, he continues, and such scorching winds, that who encountereth them dies and none escape; neither birds are seen in the air, nor quadrupeds on the ground. On every side, as far as the eye can reach, if you seek for the proper place to cross, there is no other marks to distinguish it than the skeletons of those who have perished there; these alone seem to indicate the route."

Of these traditional migrations, Colonel Phayre says, " Such tribes, as the Burmese, the Karens, and the Mon (Talaings), would readily find their way from Central Asia by the course of the rivers Salween and Meenam towards the south; some would be led westerly, and so gain the valley of the Irawaddy in the upper course of that river. This the Talaings and Burmese probably did at an early period, whilst the Karens kept for ages to the mountain bordering east and west of the Salween and Meenam rivers, and only lately came into the Irawaddy valley and along the mountains bordering on the seacoast, as far as 12° northern latitude.

I have introduced the Karens into this work, though they are not in Bengal, in consequence of their evident connection with some of the Asám races. I must notice one more tribe for a similar reason. A people of no small importance, the Talaings, or Mon, of Pegu, who, we are informed, speak a language quite distinct from the Indo-Chinese tongues of the adjoining tribes, but which strongly resembles the Múnda or Ho language of Singhbhúm and Chútiá Nágpúr. Mr. J. R. Logan, quoted by Colonel Phayre, in his paper on the history of the Burmah race,* considers "the radical identity of the relative pronouns, definitives, and numerals of the Kol with those of the Mon-Anam group as established. Both groups in their glossarial basis are branches of one formation, much more akin to Tibetan Burman than to Dravidian.

The Talaings.

There appear to be good grounds for inferring that the ancestors of the Talaings or Mon people were amongst the earliest settlers in the Burmese Provinces, and they may be regarded as the aborigines of Pegu; but whether they came from the north or the south, is still, I think, an open question.

Following the rivers that had been their guides from the snows they may have pressed on to the seaboard, other hordes coming after them and filling up the most advantageous positions in their rear. They could extend only by crossing the sea to India; but Mr. Logan† considers it more probable that they followed the course of the Brahmaputra, as "the relation of the Mon-Anam to the Vindhyan dialects shows that the Dravidian traits of the former were wholly or chiefly acquired in Bengal."

The Asamese to this day call the Burmese Mon or Mán, and the country Mán-desh. The Chinese call them Mien.

Is there any connection between this word Mon and the Múnda,‡ as the Chútiá Nágpúr branch of the Kols call themselves? We generally find that the name used by one of these primitive tribes to indicate themselves is their word for 'man'. In the specimen of languages of Southern Africa given in Pritchard's Natural History of Man, we find the following:—

Frequent occurrence of the name *Mun*.

Delagoa Bay.	Mozambique.	Suali.	Niko.	Kamba.	Pokomo.	Nian.	Kongo.
Monhi.	*Mantu.*	*Mtu.*	*Mutu.*	*Múndu*	*Múntu.*	*Múndu.*	*Moontau.*

In the language of the Fiji islanders the word for sun is identical with the word used by the Múndas, *viz.*, 'singa.'

Mr. Logan notices that in the dialect of the Binnua and Simang people in Province Wellesley and Prince of Wales Island, the pronouns used have the peculiar forms that were current amongst the Himalaia people which predominated in the Gangetic basin and its confines before the Arians advanced. The pronouns and many other common vocables are still used by the Kols or Santál tribes on the Ganges, the Kgi or Kásia on the Brahmaputra basin, the Palaong, and the Mon, or Peguans, on the Irawaddy, the Kambojans on the Mekong, and the Anamese on the Tonguin. That a *Mon* colony flourished on the *Múnda* down to a period long subsequent to the intrusion of the Arians into India, is evidenced by rocky inscriptions in characters similar to the ancient Mon which are found in Province Wellesley and on Bukit Mariam.§

* Journal, Asiatic Society, Bengal, No. 1, for 1864, page 28, note.

† Journal, Indian Archipelago, paragraphs 157 and 159. See note, para. 24, to Phayre, on the History of the Burmah Race.

‡ Munda is generally said to be derived from the Sanskrit word signifying 'a head.'

§ Note on Races in Prince of Wales Island and Province Wellesley by Mr. Logan, forwarded to the Government of the Straits Settlements, in a letter from Colonel W. Man, dated October 12th, 1866.

VOCABULARY TO GROUP IV.*

ENGLISH.	BURMESE, MUG OR MYAMMÁ.*	KHYENG OR SHOU.	KAMI.	KÚMI.	MRÚ.	RED KAREN.
One	tit	nhát	há	há	loung	ta.
Two	nhit	pan-nhí	ní	nhú	pré	ne.
Three	t*h*on	thúm	ka-tún	túm	shún	theu.
Four	lé	lhi	ma-lí	pa-lú	ta-lí	lwie.
Five	ngá	nghau	páng-ngá	pán	ta-ngá	nya.
Six	khyouk	sauk	ta-ú	ta-rú	ta-rú	theutho.
Seven	khun-nhit	s'hé	sarí	sa-rú	ra-nhít	theuthota.
Eight	shyit	sát	kayá	ta-yá	rí yát	lwietho.
Nine	ko	ko	ta-ko	ta-kau	ta-kú	lwiethota.
Ten	s'hai	há	ha-suh	hau	há	tashe.
Twenty	nhit-s'hai	kúr	kúsuh	a-pum-ré	pí-ra-mí	neshe.
Fifty	ngáz hai	nghau-gíp	kú-i-páng-ngá	wí-pá-rí	......	nya-shie.
Hundred	tayá	klá-át	ta-rá	chúm wá-ri	......	tayay.
I	ngá	kyi	ká-í	ká-i	......	va.
We	ngá-do	kin-ní	ka-chí	ká-i-no	......	pay.
Thou	men or nen	náng	nán	nang	......	na.
You	mendo	náng-ní	nán-chi	náng chí no	......	thie.
He	t*h*ú	ni	ha-ná-i	hú	......	a.
They	thúdo	ni-di or ni-li	hùn-na or ha-ni-chi	......	......	......
Of me	......	......	......	......	......	......
Of us	......	......	......	......	......	......
Of ye	......	......	......	......	......	......
Of him	......	......	......	......	......	......
Mine	ngái	ki-ko	ká-í-un	......	......	va.
Our	ngádoi	ki-ni-ko	ká-chi-un	......	......	pay.
Thine	meni	náng-ko	nán-un	......	......	na.
Your	mendoi	náng ni ko	nán-chi-un	......	......	thie.
His	t*h*úi	ni-ko	ha-ná-i-un	......	......	a.
Their	t*h*ú doi	ní-dí-ko	ha-ni-chi-un	......	......	a.
Hand	let	kúth	a-kú	ka	rút	su.
Foot	khyé	ka-ko	a-kho	khou	khouk	kha.
Nose	*na kaung*	......	......	......	......	......
Eye	myetsi	mí-ú-i	a-mi	mé	min	may.
Mouth	nhup	hak-kau	a-ma-ká	li-boung	naur	......
Tooth	t*h*wá	ka-hau	a-fhá	ho	yún	kho-khe.
Ear	ná	ka-nhau	a-ga-ná	ka-no	pa-rám	kha-lay.
Hair	s'haben	lu-sám	a-s'hám	s'hám	s'hám	kho-lya.
Head	ghoung	lú	a-lú	a-lú	lú	hoo-krau.
Tongue	......	......	......	......	......	......
Belly	*woon*	......	......	......	......	......
Back	*kyo*	......	......	......	......	......
Iron	t*h*án	thí	s'hein	ta-mhú	loung-há	hto-htay
Gold	*shwé*	......	......	......	......	......
Silver	*ngwé*	......	......	......	......	......
Go	t*h*wá	tsit	la	lá	......	syeu.
Eat	sá	é	tsá	tsá	......	e.

* The Red Karen words are taken from Journal, Asiatic Society, Bengal, Part II, 1866, p. 239; the Burmese, Khyeng, Kami, Kúmi, Mrú, from ditto, for 1853, p. 8; the Burmese words in Italics are taken from the Selections, Records of Government of India, Foreign Department, No. 27, appendix.

English.	Burmese, Mug or Myammá.*	Khyeng or Shou.	Kami.	Kúmi.	Mrú.	Red Karen.
Sit	tháing	ngúnge	ka-nú	tat	......	o-nya.
Father	phá-é	pau	pá-ei	am-po	pá	phay.
Mother	a-mi	nú	na-ú-i	am-nú	a-ú	meu.
Brother	*ako ngee*	......	......	......	......	......
Sister	*uma numa*	......	......	......	......	......
Man	lú	kláng	ka-mí	ku-mi	mrú	pray-ka-ya.
Woman	*meingma*	......	......	......	......	......
Wife	......	......	......	......	......	......
Child	......	......	......	......	......	......
Son	*chagau kya*	......	......	......	......	......
Daughter	*chum wee*	......	......	......	......	......
Slave	......	......	......	......	......	......
Cultivator	......	......	......	......	......	......
Shepherd	......	......	......	......	......	......
God	*phura*	......	......	......	......	......
Devil	*nat pik ta*	......	......	......	......	......
Come	lá, youk	lo	va	you	......	ray, Ha.
Beat (strike)	yáik, pok	mo-lé	ma-lé	pu-khou-orathum	......	mu.
Stand	thá, mát	tún-e	ka-do	áng-thou	......	se-htau.
Sun	né	ko-nhi	ka-ní	ka-ni	ta-nin	lä-moo.
Moon	lá	khlau	lá	hlo	pú-lá	lay.
Star	kyai	áá-shé	á-s'hí	ka-sí	ki-rek	shay.
Fire	mí	mí	má-í	mhá-í	má-í	me.
Water	yé	tú-í	tú-í	tú-í	tú-í	htye.
House	eing	ím	ín	úm	kín	hie.
Horse	myin	s'hé	ta-phú	koung-ngú	ko-ra-ngá	ta-the.
Cow	nuá	sharh	kha-bo-i	si-rá	tsi-yá	popu.
Cock	......	......	......	......	......	......
Duck	......	......	......	......	......	......
Ass	......	......	......	......	......	......
Camel	......	......	......	......	......	......
Bird	nghet	hau	ka-vá or ta-vá	ta-wú	ta-wá	htu.
To die	*tse do*	......	......	......	......	......
To give	pé	pe-ge	na-pú	pei	......	dye.
Run	pyé	cho-né	a-whi	lei	......	kywa.
Up (above)	apomhá	ada-ma-ka	a-koung-bé	i-klún	......	klau-khoo.
Near	ní	a-shyo-ro-yan	nei	ki-sá	......	phoo.
Who	bhé *thú*	ú-lí am	a-pá-i-mé	......	......	......
And	ligoung	......	......	......	......	vau.
Yes	hokhé	a-hi	ta-ko-ká	nán	......	eu, ma-han.
Down (below)	ouk mhá	dé-kan	ting-bé	i-klot	......	klau-lay.
Far	wé	tsu-á a-lhau a-me	khán-lá	pi-lú-pá-i	......	ye.
What	bhá	í-ní-hám	......	......	......	......
But	......	......	......	......	......	......
No	mahok	hí-a	na-u-ká	na-o	......	to.
Before	......	......	......	......	......	......
Behind	......	......	......	......	......	......
Why	bhé pyulo	í-na-to-ám	ta-u-sá-ne	......	......	Bay-tie-te.
If	......	......	......	......	......	......
Alas	......	......	......	......	......	......

GROUP V.

HINDUISED ABORIGINES AND BROKEN TRIBES.

SECTION 1.—PRELIMINARY REMARKS.

We are told in the Purans that the inhabitants of the Vindhya mountains are the descendants of 'Nishâda,' sprung or born from the thigh of King Vena.* They are described as being of the colour of charcoal or as black as a crow, and having flattened faces; and they are innately and hopelessly vicious, because Nishâda was so organized, or his birth was so arranged, that he bore away from the body of Vena all the sins for which that monarch had previously been notorious, and bequeathed them to his offspring, leaving his majesty free from all taint and ready for heaven.

We have in this and many similar legends indications that in the most remote times there was in Central India an intensely dark race, and though the classification might be deemed unscientific and indefinite, I do not think we should be wrong in fact, if we were still to speak of their descendants as the swarthy aborigines, in contradistinction to the people of Mongolian origin, who still retain their brown or tawny hues.

I do not wish to ignore the fact that a tropical sun and noxious climate have a powerful influence on the colour of the skin; but it is also true that under similar circumstances of climate and situation certain races of the early settlers retain a comparatively fair complexion, whilst others in the same position are almost black. When we find, as we often do, in particular tribes a great variety of complexion, it is generally under circumstances that on other accounts lead us to infer a mixture of races; but when we find one people nearly always yellow or tawny who have lived for ages in the same climate with another people who are nearly always black, we cannot suppose that climate is the only influence at work. Affiliating the blacks on Nishâda if it pleases us to do so, we look to some other origin for the tawnies.

In ascribing fanciful origins to the aborigines, the Aryans to a certain extent admitted them into their own families as bastard relatives of their own and of their gods. There is, says Menu, no fifth class from which impure tribes could have been born.

* Vena was an incorrigible heretic, perhaps some great potentate amongst the aborigines who would not be converted, but he is represented as ignoring all the heavenly host and ordering that he alone was to be adored. The sages and Rishis gaining nothing by their expostulations, slew him. The country was without a ruler, as he had left no progeny. The Munis rubbed the thigh of the dead king, and from it there sprung "a man like a charred log with flattened face, and very short. They said to him "nishâda," sit down; so he was called Nishâda, and from him are descended the Nishâdas of the Vindhyan Mountains, notorious for their wicked deeds. By this means the sin of King Vena was expelled. They then rubbed his right hand and his glorious immaculate son Prithu was produced, and Vena, delivered from hell, ascended to heaven.

Vishnu Purana, Book I, Chapter XIII. Wilson's translation, new edition, page 181.

According to the theory of the origin of the castes given in the Santi Parva of the Máhábhárat,* Brahmans were born white, Kshetryas red, Vaisyas yellow, and Sudras black. Brahmans, however, lost their colour by irregularities; those who became black were addicted to lying and covetousness! The impure races according to this theory are caused by admixture of castes. The same authority says, "the Nishádas are the offspring of a Sudra woman by a Brahman; a Chandala, 'lowest of men,' from a Sudra father and a Vaisya female, or a Kshetrya and a Brahmani. They became Mlechchas by abandonment of proper rites." In all probability, when Menu wrote, great masses of the aborigines had become, as we still find them, converts to Hinduism; but as the Brahmanical doctrines required that a man should be born in the faith, it became necessary to give the proselytes new pedigrees.

The Sudras are not, as a rule, a swarthy race. The dark Hindus may have become dark from climate or from admixture with the swarthy aborigines, or both; but, as a rule, all Hindus properly classed as Sudras show both in feature and colour an unquestionable Aryan descent, though from exposure and the rougher nature of their avocations they may generally appear to be darker and coarser than the so-called twice born classes. When we find them, as in the Jungle Maháls, in juxtaposition with the dark aborigines, the difference is distinguishable at a glance.

But the allusions to the Mlechchas and Dasyus in the early Sanskrit literature, denote that whilst there were amongst the earlier colonists people who had made some advance in civilization and were sufficiently powerful to be respected and conciliated, there were others who were despised and reviled as little above the level of the brute creation. They had then as now tawny aborigines and black aborigines. The Vindhyan range, which probably included all the hilly parts of Chútiá Nágpúr, are especially indicated as the locality of the latter, the black, ill-favored, people; and there we still find specimens of the lowest type of humanity; creatures who might justly be regarded as the unimproved descendants of the manufacturers of the stone implements found in the Damúdar coal-fields.† These are the true aborigines, the 'Asuras,' from whom a considerable proportion of the black pigment is derived that has darkened the skins of a large section of the population and given us the lowest type of feature.

The pre-Aryan inhabitants of the Gangetic provinces may have included the people described by Mr. Hodgson as the broken tribes of Nepal, who are dark, though in a climate favorable to fair and ruddy complexions:—the Kocch, who are the most eastern of the dark primitive races, the Cheros, the Kharwárs, the Kolarian tribes, and some others to be presently noticed. If we except the Dravidian dialect spoken by the Oraons and Rájmaháli hill tribes, who appear to be of comparatively recent introduction, the Kolarian or Múnda language is the only pre-Aryan tongue now spoken in Bihár and Bengal proper. It has been wonderfully preserved by different tribes, some massed together as the Múnda, Santál, and Bhúmij; some quite isolated and far apart, who have had no communication with those named or with each other for ages. The tribes I am about to describe in this chapter speak no language but a dialect of Hindi; but their physical

* Muir's Sanskrit texts, vol. I, page 38.

† Discovered by Mr. Ball of the Geological Survey. See Memoir, Jherria coal-field, page 265. It would be singular if these stone implements found on the banks of the Damúdar—*Da* in the Múnda language meaning water—and the great veneration of the Santáls for that river, were connected.

characteristics, some of their customs, the remnants they have preserved of their primitive paganism, and, in some cases their traditions, lead to the conclusion that they are the remnants of a people who, together with the Kolarian races, occupied Bihár and great part of Bengal proper prior to the appearance of the first Aryan invaders. And as the Múnda or Kol language is common to so many of the tribes who may be thus linked together, and as those who do not speak it can only converse in the tongue of the conquerors, it is highly probable that the Múnda was at one time the spoken language of all Bihár and Bengal.

The priests of Ceylon, according to Captain Mahoney, allege that in Madhyadesa (Gya), when Gautama was born, the art of writing was not known. The language spoken, says Buchanan Hamilton,* was no doubt that of the Cheros and Kols. The former are spoken of as a dominant, the latter as a subject race. It is said the Cheros accepted the doctrines of Gautama, the Kols rejected them. Buchanan thinks, they were originally the same people, but the Cheros adopting first Budhism subsequently obtained and maintained a position as purely born Hindus, whilst the Kols rejecting all change adhered to their impurity of life, and gradually isolating themselves, or driven from the society of those who affected to despise them, preserved their unlettered language and primitive customs to the present day.

That the proselytes should have gradually lost all recollection of their mother tongue, is not surprising. The process of absorption of the ruder forms of speech is rapidly progressing under our very eyes or in our hearing. I went this year (1868) to Jashpúr expecting to obtain there ready means of noting down the peculiarities of the language of the Korwás. A number of most uncouth-looking savages of the tribe attended on my summons. But they were 'Dihi Korwás,' that is, men who had abandoned their nomadic hill life and made settlements in the plains; and not one of them would acknowledge that he could speak a word of Korwá.

I may mention another instance. There are many Oraon villages in Chútiá Nágpúr in which the Oraon language is quite lost, but the inhabitants nevertheless speak two tongues—Múnda and Hindi. It is highly probable that other tribes speaking the Múnda language, have acquired it, losing their own. There is so much difference in character, physical traits, and customs between the Santál and the Singbhúm Ho, that I should not be surprised to find they were of distinct origin, though speaking the same language and having a common faith. It is an interesting fact that the language appears to have followed the religion. All the tribes that have become Hindu in faith, have lost their old language and speak a rude dialect of Hindi. The Oraons in Chútiá Nágpúr follow the Múnda paganism and adopt the Múnda language. The Múnda, Ho, Santál, and other Kolarian tribes, who adhere to their ancient faith, have preserved their old language, or at all events a pre-Aryan language.

SECTION 2.—THE CHEROS AND KHARWÁRS.

I have already observed that the Gangetic provinces were in all probability once occupied by a people speaking the Múnda or Kolarian language, and of these the latest dominant tribe were the Cheros.

* See Buchanan on Bihár, Martin's edition, page 26.

In the districts of Bihár are numerous monuments attributed, according to Buchanan, (and this is fully confirmed by all the enquiries I have been able to make,) to the Kols and Cheros. As these include temples dedicated to the worship of idols, it is not likely that the people now known as Kols were concerned in their construction, because, if there be a distinctive feature in the pagan worship of that people, it is the absence of all ideas of artificially lodging their deities or attempting to represent them. The Kols spoken of were in all probability Kharwárs, who have been for ages mixed up with the Cheros and subject to them. They claim affinity with each other, and have some customs in common.

They may have both originally formed one nation with the Kols; but the Kharwárs, like the Cheros, became proselytes to Hinduism, and established for themselves bastard connectionship with the Hindus. The temple ruins attributed to them were most likely built after they had undergone some process of conversion.

The distinctive physical traits of the Cheros have been considerably softened by the alliances with pure Hindu families, which their ancient power and large possessions enabled them to secure; but they appear to me still to exhibit an unmistakeable Mongolian physiognomy. They vary in colour, but are usually of a light brown. They have, as a rule, high cheek bones, small eyes obliquely set, and eyebrows to correspond, low broad noses, and large mouths with protuberant lips.

It appears from Buchanan that the old Cheros, like the dominant Kolarian family of Chútiá Nágpúr, claimed to be Nágbangsis, and had the same tradition regarding their origin from the great 'Nág' or dragon that has been adopted by the Chútiá Nágpúr family. The latter were, it seems, even in Gorakhpúr and Bihár, allowed to be the heads of the Nágbangsi family, and Buchanan considered them to be Cheros; but they are, no doubt, originally of the same race as their Kol subjects, though frequent alliances with Rájpút families have obliterated the aboriginal lineaments.

The western part of 'Kosala,' that is Gorakhpúr, continued sometime under the Cheros after other portions of that territory had fallen into the hands of the people called G o r k h a (hence Gorkhapúr, Gorakhpúr ?), who were in their turn expelled by the Thárus also from the north.* The Thárus have left numerous monuments in Gorakhpúr, and a few of them still remain in the district and in Mithila. They claim to be of the family of the sun, *i. e.*, the Aryan, but are said to have strongly marked Mongolian features. One of the Rajas of this dynasty had for his chief priest a man named Rásu, of the impure tribe of Músahar.*

In Sháhábád also the most numerous of the ancient monuments are ascribed to the Cheros, and it is traditionally asserted that the whole country belonged to them in sovereignty. Buchanan† suggests, they were princes of the Sunaka family, who flourished in the time of Gautama about the sixth or seventh century before the Christian era. An inscription at Budh Gya mentions one Phudi Chandra, who is traditionally said to have been a Chero. The Cheros were expelled from Sháhábád, some say, by the Savaras or Suars, some say by a tribe called Hariha; and the date of their expulsion is conjectured to be between the fifth and sixth centuries of the Christian era. Both Cheros and Savaras were considered by the Brahmans of Sháhábád as impure or Mlechchas, but the Harihas are reputed good Kshetryas.

* Buchanan, Martin's edition, Vol. II., page 342.

† Idem, Vol. I. page 405.

The overthrow of the Cheros in Mithila and Magadha seems to have been complete.

History.

Once lords of the Gangetic provinces, they are now found in the Sháhábád and Bihár districts, only holding the meanest offices, or concealing themselves in the woods skirting the hills occupied by their cousins the Kharwárs, but in Palámau they retained till a recent period the position they had lost elsewhere. A Chero family maintained almost an independent rule in that Pargana till the accession of the British Government; they even attempted to hold their castles and strong places against that power, but were speedily subjugated, forced to pay revenue and submit to the laws. They were, however, allowed to retain their estates; and though the rights of the last Raja of the race were purchased by Government in 1813, in consequence of his falling into arrears, the collateral branches of the family have extensive estates there still. According to their own traditions (they have no trustworthy annals), they have not been many generations in Palámau. They invaded that country from Rohtás, and with the aid of Rájpút chiefs, the ancestors of the Thákurais of Ranka and Chainpur, drove out and supplanted a Rájpút Raja of the Rakshail family, who retreated into Sirgúja and established himself there. It is said that the Palámau population then consisted of Kharwárs, Gonds, Márs, Korwás, Parheya, and Kisáns. Of these the Kharwárs were the people of most consideration, the Cheros conciliated them, and allowed them to remain in peaceful possession of the hill tracts bordering on Sirgúja; all the Cheros of note who assisted in the expedition obtained military service grants of land which they still retain. It is popularly asserted that at the commencement of the Chero rule in Palámau, they numbered twelve thousand families, and the Kharwárs eighteen thousand, and if an individual of one or the other is asked to what tribe he belongs, he will say, not that he is a Chero or a Kharwár, but that he belongs to the twelve thousand or to the eighteen thousand, as the case may be.

The Palámau Cheros now live strictly as Rájpúts and wear the 'poita', or caste thread. They do not, however, intermarry with really good Rájpút families. I do not think they cling to this method of elevating themselves in the social scale so tenaciously as do the Kharwárs. But intermarriages between Chero and Kharwár families have taken place. A relative of the Palámau Raja married a sister of Manináth Sing, Raja of Rámgarh, and this is amongst themselves an admission of identity of origin; as both claiming to be Rájpúts they could not intermarry till it was proved to the satisfaction of the family priests that the parties belonged to the same class. But the Palámau Cheros, and I suppose all Cheros, claim to be descendants of Choin Muni, one of the Rishis, a monk of Kumáon; some say the Rishi took to wife the daughter of a Raja, and that the Cheros are the offspring of their union; others, that the Cheros are sprung in a mysterious manner from the *Áshan*, or seat, of Choin Muni. They have also a tradition that they came from the Morung.

The Kharwárs have different legends. They declare their original seat to have been Rohtás, so called from its having been the chosen abode of Rohitaswa, son of King Harischandra of the family of the sun, and they, considering themselves to be entitled as subjects of his paternal Government to claim to be of the same family as their father and chief, call themselves Súrja-bangsas, and wear the 'poita', or caste string, as good Kshetryas; others say they are a mixed race originated during the reign of Raja Ben, by whose order all men were allowed to mate themselves with women of any caste or country, and the Kharwárs are the offspring of a marriage between a Kshetrya male and 'Bharni' female (*i. e.*, a woman of the aboriginal races) thus contracted. From the extreme ugliness of their physiognomies, I am inclined to believe that the mass of Kharwárs are of pure Turanian descent, and it is not improbable that they are allied to the Kiratis, who, we are informed by Mr. Hodgson,* call themselves by a nearly similar name, *viz.*, 'Kirawa,' and have like the Kharwárs one clan or division of the tribe called Mánjhi. The Kiratis are included amongst the descendants of Nishádas in the Bhagavat, and are described "as of black complexion," as "black as crows," with projecting chins, broad flat noses, red eyes, and tawny hair.† The tawny hair alludes, I imagine, to the rusty appearance it assumes when allowed to grow in a massed unkempt state. I have seen Korwás to whom the above description is very applicable.

There is in the seventh volume of the Asiatic Researches, a notice of the Kharwárs of the Kaimúr hills in the Mirzapúr District to the north of the Son River by Captain J. T. Blunt, who, in his journey from Chunár to Ellora in the year 1794 A. D., met with them and describes them as a very primitive tribe. He visited one of their villages consisting of half-a-dozen poor huts, and though proceeding with the utmost caution, unattended, to prevent alarm, the inhabitants fled at his approach. The women were seen, assisted by the men, carrying off their children and moving with speed to hide themselves in the woods. It was observed that they were nearly naked, and the only articles of domestic use found in the deserted huts were a few gourds for water vessels, some bows and arrows, and some fowls as wild as their masters. With great difficulty, by the employment of Kols as mediators, some of the men were induced to return. They were nearly naked, but armed with bows and arrows and a hatchet. Captain Blunt was under the impression that these mountaineers spoke a peculiar language, and collected a few specimens, but nearly half the words given are Hindi :—

English.		*Kharwár.*
Food	...	Gopuckney.
To sit down	...	Goburro.
Salt	...	Minka.
A goat	...	Chargur, H.
Fire	...	Ugundewta, Hindi, Fire god.
A tiger	...	Kerona.
A hut	...	Mujjarh.
The Moon	...	Chandurma, Chandhurma, H.
The Sun	...	Surjun dewta, Sun god, H.

Speaking of the Kharwárs of Sháhábád, Buchanan says that great confusion prevailed concerning them, because in different places they have in very different degrees adopted the rules of Hindu purity in very different situations of life. Some are found amongst the labouring classes bearing burdens and carrying palanqueens, some have attained positions as landowners, lording it over Brahmans and Rájpúts, their ryots, whilst others occupy the table-land unmixed with any other tribe, and there is little reason to doubt that they are its original inhabitants. These, he observes, have retained the features by which the aboriginal tribes of the Vindhyan mountains are distinguished, but no one has

* See Journal, Asiatic Society, Bengal, for 1858, page 448.

† See Wilson's Vishnu Purana, new edition, vol. I., p. 183.

met with any of the tribe who retain a trace of their original language. If the conjecture of affinity between Kiratis and Kharwárs be correct, the structure of the original language would connect them with the Múnda or Kolarian races. Mr. Hodgson has given a full account of the Kirant or Kirati languages in the journal quoted, and says that the complex pronominalization of the Kiranti verb points to a special connection with the Munda. In the fragments of an ancient religion preserved by the Kharwárs notwithstanding their Hinduism, there is much that supports the theory of their having been at one time in some way associated, if not connected, with the Kolarians.

Priesthood and Deities.

The Cheros and Kharwárs both observe like the Kols triennial sacrifices. Every three years a buffalo and other animals are offered in the sacred grove 'Sarna,' or on a rock near the village. They also have like some of the Kols a priest for each village called Páhn. He is always one of the impure tribes, a Bhúiya, or Kharwár, or a Parheya, and is also called Byga, and he only can offer this great sacrifice. No Brahmanical priests are allowed on these occasions to interfere. The Deity honored is the tutelary god of the village, sometimes called Duár Pahár, sometimes Dharti, sometimes Purgahaili, or Daknai, a female, or Dura, a Sylvan god, the same perhaps as the Darhá of the Kols. I found that the above were all worshipped in the village of Munka in Palámau, which belongs to a good typical Chero, Kunwar Bhikári Sing.

Buchanan estimated the Kharwárs of Sháhábád at about 150,000. They are still more numerous in the districts of Chútiá Nágpúr, especially in the Palámau and Rámgarh estates, and a large proportion of the landed gentry are Kharwárs.

Intermarriages.

The Rajas of Rámgarh and Jashpúr are members of this family who have nearly succeeded in obliterating their Turanian traits by successive intermarriages with Aryan families. The Jashpúr Raja is wedded to a lady of pure Rájpút blood, and, by liberal dowries, has succeeded in obtaining a similar union for three of his daughters. It is a costly ambition, but there is no doubt that the infusion of fresh blood greatly improves the Kharwár physique. The late Maharaja Sambhunáth Singh of Rámgarh, was a remarkably handsome man, sufficiently so to support his pretensions to be a true child of the sun; but according to the traditions and annals of his own family, his ancestors must have been very low in the social scale when they first came to Rámgarh. They are descended from the younger of two brothers, who, generations ago, came as adventurers, and took service under the Maharaja of Chútiá Nágpúr. The elder obtained Rámgarh as a fief on his doing homage to the Maharaja and receiving the 'tilak,' or mark of investiture, from that great potentate's toe!

Almost all the men of ancient standing with proprietary rights in the Rámgarh estate are Kharwárs. The Thákurs of Húsir Sáram and Babu Dalgovind of Khoyra, of Rájpút lineage, have become Kharwárs by marrying into the Raja's family.

The Kharwárs are divided into four tribes or families,—Bhogtas, Mánjhís, Ráúts, and Mahatos.

Sub-divisions.

The Bhogtas are found in the hills of Palámau skirting Sirgúja, in Tori and Bhanwar Pahár of Chútiá Nágpúr and other places. They have always had an indifferent reputation. The head of the clan in Palámau was a notorious freebooter, who, after having been outlawed, and successfully evading every attempt to capture him, obtained a jágír on his surrendering and promising to

2 H

keep the peace. He kept to his engagement, and died in fair repute; but his two sons could not resist the opportunity afforded by the disturbances of 1857-58. After giving much trouble, they were captured,—one was hanged, the other transported for life, and the estate was confiscated.

Physical traits.

The low Kharwárs in feature strongly resemble the Santáls. They are very dark, with pyramidal shaped low noses, thick protuberant lips, and cheek bones or zygomata that project so as to make the temples hollow. In their worship of the manes of their ancestors and their triennial, or sometimes biennial, sacrifices to the tutelary pagan gods, they follow the custom of the Kolarian tribes; but here, so far as I know, the similarity ends. The Kharwárs are of a lazy, sullen disposition, and have no festive meetings like the Santáls and their brethren. In adopting Hinduism, it is the bloody Káli as Chándi that they most delight to honor, and if they are not maligned, many a human victim suffers on the altars erected by them in her name. It is a fact that some of our people who fell into their hands in 1857 and 1858, were so dealt with.

Priesthood and Deities.

In a village* recently visited by the writer in Palámau on the borders of Sirgúja, I found all the inhabitants Kharwárs except one family,—that of the village pagan priest, who was a Korwá. I have often remarked this peculiarity of the borderers to take as priest the greatest barbarian they could find in the neighbourhood. They argue that the hill people, being the oldest inhabitants, are best acquainted with the habits and peculiarities of the local spirits, and are in least peril from them; besides, they are wholly pagan, whilst the people in whose behalf they make offerings having Hindu and Brahmanical tendencies, could only offer a divided allegiance to the sylvan gods which it might not be safe to tender. The chosen priest was called the **Byga**. He told me that he offered sacrifices in the name of the village every second year to Chindol, a male spirit, Chanda, a female spirit, and to Parvin. Buffalo, sheep, and goats are offered to all these promiscuously. They do not associate Chanda with Káli, and make no prayers to any of the Hindu gods; but when they are in great affliction, they appeal to the sun. They have no particular name for the luminary, calling it 'súraj,' and any open place on which he shines may be the altar. The other gods have shady retreats. These villagers honored their ancestors by a yearly offering of a wether goat; this is strictly a family affair. The animal is killed and eaten at home.

Dancing.

The Kharwárs do not indulge in dancing as an amusement after the fashion of the Kolarian and Oraons, but they have dancing festivals in which the women join. They dance apart from the male performers, and are so modest about it, that not only is each girl's head covered by her own dress, but a light cloth is thrown in addition over the heads of the whole group. The Korwás of this part of Palámau have adopted this mode of double veiling. It appeared strange to see Kolarian girls disporting themselves in so prudish a fashion, and I am satisfied that their cousins of Singbhúm, Mánbhúm, and Santália, would soon laugh them out of such *mauvaise honte*.

Marriages and burials.

In the above practices the Kharwárs appear to have retained their primitive or at least non-Aryan customs, but they generally follow the Hindu observances in marriages and in their disposal of the dead.

* Noka.

Parents arrange for the marriages of their children, whilst they are yet too young to choose for themselves, and a Brahman priest attends to direct the ceremonial and read the passages from the sacred books.

The dead are burned, and the ashes thrown into some river or stream with as little delay as possible.

It is worthy of notice that the Rájmahál hill tribes in their traditions accounting for the creation of various races of man,* make mention of the Kharwárs as a people, who, driven across the Ganges, lived in tents, having no settled abode.

SECTION 3.—THE PARHEYAS.

The people in Palámau so called appear to be the mere remnant of a tribe who, according to their own traditions and the traditions of other races in this district, once formed an important section of the population. I have little to say about them. They are one of the numerous tribes, or perhaps, it might be more correctly stated, one of the branches of the great tribe who, with Turanian features and many corresponding customs, have adopted Hindi as a language to the obliteration of all their primitive forms of speech, and who, though affecting Hindu customs, retain practices that are in the eyes of Hindus impure and abhorrent. Their marriages and funeral ceremonies are Hindu. In the former, the red powder called 'sindúr' is used, the bridegroom sealing the compact by touching and marking with it the forehead of his bride. The Kolarian races who have adopted the custom, show their superior appreciation of female dignity by requiring an interchange of the process, the bride respectfully returning the compliment by similarly marking her husband. The Hinduised tribes do not allow of her taking so active a part in the ceremony. The Palámau Parheyas have retained the adoration of sylvan deities, Dharti, whose name we shall frequently meet, and Gohet. These gods dwell in the hills and delight in the blood of goats.†

I have noticed considerable variety of features amongst the Parheyas. Of four I had before me at Rámkúnda in Palámau, two might have been classed as Negro, two as Mongolian. The two former were dark and prognathous; the latter bright copper colored with flat, broad faces and slightly oblique eyes.

SECTION 4.—THE KISÁNS OR NÁGESAR TRIBE.

As the word 'kisán', like 'chása', merely means a cultivator of the soil, the tribe so called has probably acquired the name from their devoting themselves peculiarly to that occupation. In some parts of the country they are called Nágesar; but they do not in consequence claim to be cousins or clansmen of the Rajas of Chútiá Nágpúr—the head of the Nágbangsis or Nágs. Much has been written on the origin of the Nágas, who figure in the Máhábhárat as antagonists of the Pándavas, and no doubt Mr. Talboys Wheeler is right in his conjecture that they were prior occupants of the forests whom the Pándavas sought to eject. Our Nágesars, still denizens of the jungles, or cultivating the skirts of the forests, may be a remnant of this ancient race.

*Asiatic Researches, Vol. IV., page 46.

† The Parheyas have a tradition that their tribe formerly held sheep and deer sacred, and used the dung of those animals to smear floors with, as they now use cowdung.

The Kisáns are found in Sirgúja, Jashpúr, Palámau, and a few in the Lohardagga District. My first introduction to them was at Moheri in Sirgúja. I found in this part of Sirgúja a great variety of aborigines of the type now under consideration. Here were the Márs, a mixed race, wild Korwás, Bhúiyas, Bhúihers, and Kisáns. The Kisáns in appearance resemble the Kol, but not the best type of Kol, more Santál than Ho. They showed to great advantage besides the Bhúihers, but were inferior in good looks to the Bhúiyas. Their resemblance to the Kol is not in looks alone.

Worship.

As with the Santáls, their chief object of worship is the tiger, the 'ban rájá,' lord of the jungles. They will not kill that ferocious enemy to man, and are disposed to think that the tiger in return for their devotion would spare a Kisán. They adore their ancestors, and a spirit called the 'Shikária deota,' offering goats to the latter. They also worship the sun, and when a sacrifice is necessary, offer a white cock to that luminary. All this is Kolarian, especially Santál, shamanism; and they dance somewhat in Kolarian fashion, but less lively in step. They have the 'jádúr', 'júmhir', and 'karm' dances as the Kols, but without so much variety of step, melody, and figure. They have introduced another dance for the Hindu Húli, and call it by that name. They speak no language but Hindi, and follow the Hindu custom in the disposal of their dead.

The Kisáns or Nágesars of Jashpúr are less civilized in appearance than those of Moheri. They live more isolated, and closely follow the practice of the Múndas in religious ceremonies. They do not worship the tiger, though they all swear by him; their principal deity is called Moihidhúnia, to whom they sacrifice fowls and small animals every year, and once in every three years a buffalo. Each village has two or more groves or 'sa,' one is sacred to Moihidhúnia, the other to Mahádeo, a Hindu appellation they have applied to some old pagan friend who is specially invoked at the festival of the harvest home, when his votaries are in their merriest mood. The 'khúnt', or tutelary god, of the villages is Darhá, as with the Kols, and there are various 'páts' or holy heights dedicated to divinities, as the Bamonipát and the Andaripát. They keep the ceremony of the 'sarhúl,' as the Kols, and have the Kol dances jádúr, júmhir, and karm, but not the 'kharria,' which they say is peculiar to the Oraons.

Marriages.

The Kisáns confine themselves to one wife and have no concubines. Girls are not married or betrothed till they are mature, but the old people nevertheless settle the matches, and there is no instance on record of a youth or maiden objecting to the arrangement made for them. Two baskets of rice and a rupee in cash constitute the compensatory offering given to the parents of the girl. The anointing of the bride and groom with oil takes the place of the usual sindúr ceremony. Notwithstanding the resemblance of this tribe to the Kols, they repudiate all connection with that race, and would scorn to eat with them. One outward mark of difference is carefully preserved, and was pointed out to me as quite sufficient to settle the question. The Kol and Oraon women are all marked distinctively with 'Godna'. The Kisán females have no such mark. If a female of the tribe indulges in the vanity of having herself tattooed, she is at once turned adrift as having degraded herself.

The Kisáns that appeared before me in the Jashpúr highlands were singularly ill-favored. The forehead receding, narrow and low, projecting as a ridge at the brow beyond the nose, which is short, broad at the base, and has there a truncated appearance, exposing the lateral development of the nostrils. This exposure is caused by the projection of the front teeth and jaws which tilt up the lip and end of the nose, and make the mouth decidedly prognathous. All were short of stature, and dark, deep brown to black. They are people of slovenly appearance, and are considered by their neighbours lazy and indifferent cultivators.*

Physical traits.

It is singular that the songs they sing as accompaniments to their dancing are fragments of old Hindu ballads, now so mutilated as to be unintelligible. Here is a morsel *verbatim* from the lips of the prima donna: "Sri Bindabun men Kusa Kanderio Jahan lotol Raor Kaia, Sundur lo Surbel nirdaia." The songsters had not the slightest notion of the meaning of the above, but it is apparently the lament of one of the Brindabun maidens at her desertion by the sportive and amorous but fickle Krishna.

Songs.

SECTION 5.—THE BHÚIHERS.

Another very primitive tribe met with in Palámau and Jashpúr are the Bhúihers, who must not be confounded either with the Bhúiyas or the Boyárs. I am not quite certain if I give the right spelling of the names, but I spell them as they are pronounced by the owners. The Bhúihers are about the lowest type of human beings that I have come across in my wanderings, and I have had more opportunities than most people of seeing varieties of race. They are very dark (41, about the average); faces, or rather heads, altogether round as bullets, projecting jaws and lips, scarcely any prominence of nose, pig's eyes, large bodies, and small limbs, no muscular development, very short of stature, not one of them more than five feet, very filthy in their persons, with diseased skins and sore eyes. One creature, an adult male of a group which appeared before me at Moheri in Sirgúja, looked to me like a disgustingly superannuated black baby. Baby-like his round head rolled about his shoulders on a very short and unnaturally weak neck. You could imagine his proper place to be bundled up in a cloth slung from the shoulders of his black mother, his head helplessly rolling about after the manner of native infants thus supported. They speak Hindí plainly enough, but appear as devoid of ideas as they are of beauty. They adore the sun and their ancestors, but they have no notion that the latter are now spirits, or that there are spirits or ghosts or a future state or any thing. They have no veneration for a tiger, but regard him as a dangerous enemy whom it is their interest to slay whenever they have the opportunity. They were asked to dance and did so; but it was a singularly feeble, motiveless performance. Men and women were scantily clothed, and appeared to take no thought for their personal appearance. The hair uncared for was matted and rusty coloured. The Bhúihers in Palámau are said to be good cultivators, but I believe this means, they are very docile farm labourers and beasts of burden. They appear to have no independence of character, and are for the most part in servitude or bondage, and content so to remain. If we have now in existence the descendants of human beings of the stone age, here I would say are specimens. They reminded me much of the representations I have seen of the Andamanese.

* The Raja of Jashpúr informed me that these were the general physical characteristics of the Kisáns or Nágesars in his territory, and he of his own accord mentioned that many of them had short crisp spiral or curly hair.

2 I

The Bhúihers constitute a small tribe of not more than a few hundred families, and they will probably disappear altogether in the course of a few more years.

SECTION 6.—THE BOYÁRS.

The similarity of names and in some cases in the condition of the tribes I am describing may lead to the inference that I am fancifully disconnecting them; but the people under these different, though nearly similar, denominations vehemently repudiate all connection with each other, and do not intermarry or eat together. The Boyárs are numerous and widely diffused. They are found in Palámau, Sirgúja, Singrauli, Korea, Bhakhár, Rewa, and other places in somewhat different phases of civilization, but always affecting the hills. They live much like the Korwás, cultivating millet and pulses on the virgin soil of newly cleared forests, but are much more peaceably disposed. I never heard of them as murderers or plunderers, and they do not carry arms with the same pertinacity as the Korwás, though they accustom themselves to the use of the bow and arrow as a protection against wild beasts.

Geographical distribution.

They live in small hamlets or detached houses, as a glance at a map of the country they are found in clearly indicates. The occurrence at intervals of the words, 'Boyárs,' 'hut,' in tracts otherwise devoid of inhabitants, shows their love of solitude and independence.

The first I saw were some Boyárs of the Korea hills, who at my desire were caught like wild animals and brought into camp trembling with fear. I was told, they spoke a distinct language, but I found it was only a peculiar dialect of Hindi: this first batch were too frightened to give me any information. I was subsequently introduced to some families living near Jilmilli in Sirgúja, who were more civilised and were induced to confide in me.

Language.

They gave **Jarbund** and **Bakeswar** as the names of their principal deities, who, they said, were adored as existing under Kúsum trees. The household god they called **Dúlhadeo**, and some Boyárs from Chánd Bhakhár, upwards of 150 miles to the west of Jilmilli, informed me that Dúlhadeo was their sole object of worship. The word is apparently Hindí, but I never heard of this god before.* To him fowls are offered on the last day of Phálgun, and at marriages a goat. In their languages I could not detect any words that were not Hindí, though I tried many radicals, but they have adopted no Hindu custom except perhaps their early marriages and the use of the *sindúr* at those ceremonies. A girl of 11 years was shown to me as a married woman. Her husband was present. He said, he had brought her from her parents in Singrauli, saw and fancied her for himself, and the matter was arranged for five Rupees and beer. This is the orthodox or standard price of a bride, the only ceremony a feast, dancing, and marking the girl's brow with red lead, *sindúr*.

Religion.

Marriages.

They bury their dead depositing with each body of a male, an axe, a knife, and a bow and arrow, the only implements they use in war or in peace.

Disposal of the dead.

The young men have no separate domicile, their societies are not sufficiently large to have suggested such an institution. They sleep in small sheds attached to the family

* He is one of the Gond divinities, as will subsequently appear.

houses, but though living thus isolated, or in very small communities, they have their periodical festivals and at each a merry gathering of the tribe.

Dances.

They have three dances—the '**dawa**,' the '**terriah**', and the universal '**karm**.' In each of these the position of the dancers is the same. The men beating drums dance facing the women and singing. The women joining hands dance facing the men, but with downcast eyes, respond to the singing, and bow their heads. The only change is in the song and the step. The women were all decently clad after the ordinary fashion of the Hindu agricultural classes of this part of the country. Their persons enveloped in one large country-made cloth, fastened or folded first round the waist, then crossing the bosom, and lastly veiling the head. They did not use the extra cloth or canopy that I have noticed as in vogue with the bashful maidens of Palámau.

Physical traits.

In complexion I found the Boyárs generally of a dark brown color, fairly proportioned, and averaging upwards of five feet in height. The features were characterised by great breadth across the cheek bones, very narrow forehead, nose broad, nostrils wide apart, but the nasal bone more prominent than in the types previously described; the mouth so wide as nearly to equal the space occupied by both eyes, lips protuberant, chin receding, but not so the brow. There was more appearance of hair on the face than is generally found amongst the tribes of this class.

The Santhas.

Very closely resembling the Boyárs are the Santhas,* a small tribe occupying a dozen villages on the Mainpát, a lofty table land in Sirgúja, and found also amongst the inhabitants of the villages skirting it. They do not number more than a hundred families, but they consider themselves a separate tribe, though they have no traditions that give any clue to their origin. They know nothing of the Santáls, but might very well be a detached fragment of that extensive tribe.

SECTION 7.—THE NÁGBANGSIS.

Between the rivers Maini and Eeb in the Jashpúr country, there is a valley so secured on all sides by precipitous hills and rocks, that it was regarded and used as a natural citadel by the ruling family in the Mahratta days—a place where the royal ladies of the family and the treasure were secreted, when a visit from those marauding rulers was impending. Here was space sufficient for several villages, and here I found a remarkable colony of the aboriginal type calling themselves Nágbangsis. They have occupied this nest for about ten generations, and their only tradition is that they came here from Nágpúr (*i. e.*, Chota, or Chútiá, Nágpúr), and that they are kinsmen of the Chútiá Nágpúr Raja. They are to be found in Udaipúr and Sirgúja as well as in Jashpúr, and may be estimated at about 300 families. Those in Jashpúr have recently become disciples of Gosains or Bairágis, but some that I met in other districts have no Brahmanical proclivities. They have, however, their own Byga, village priest, or exorcist, who conciliates the local deities, especially one to whom a huge rock forming the most prominent feature in the configuration of the valley is assigned as an abode, called the 'Bura-deo.' To him they every third year sacrifice a buffalo, clinging thus to the triennial sacrifice of their primitive faith like the Cheros and

* I have given further information about this tribe in the Section on the Korwás.

Kharwárs, and the claim of those tribes to be Nágas or Nágbangsis has been adverted to. They employ no Brahmans or other priests at their domestic ceremonies, and in regard to the disposal of the dead they follow the practice of the Kaurs. Those who have so forgotten their duty to society as to die unmarried are flung into graves any how. Those who have fulfilled their duties as husbands and fathers are rewarded by a funeral pyre.

Physical traits.

The Nágbangsis carry on their faces a most exaggerated type of the Turanian nose. It is low, scarcely rising at all between the eyes, very broad across the nostrils, and looks as if it had been there sliced off, so as to display prominently that they are not round orifices but elongated in the wrong direction. The lips are very full and prominent, and the chin receding. Their faces generally present a Chinese flatness of surface. Eyes on a level with the cheeks and frontal bones, but straight; complexion tawny to brown.

I made some remarks on the general fairness of their complexion, and was told that the people of the well shaded villages of the Jashpúr lowlands are fairer than those of the uplands. This is especially observable in the Oraons, Kharwárs, and others who are very dark on the tableland above the ghats, but a shade or two fairer below, the difference in elevation being about 1,000 feet. The Raja, himself a Kharwár and dark, told me that if he or any of his people usually living in the highlands made any long sojourn below, they all became for a time a shade fairer, but both color and feature indicate that the progenitors of the Nágbangsis belonged to the tawny, not to the swarthy, Turanians.

SECTION 8.—THE KAURS OR KAURAVAS.

It is solely from their physical traits that I include the Kaurs in the class of which I am now treating. Captain Blunt, in his narrative of a journey made in 1794, A. D., through a part of the country they occupy, published in Vol. VII of the Asiatic Researches, mentions them as "another hill tribe called Cowhirs," but he gives us no further particulars regarding them. In a paper entitled "Notes of a tour in the Tributary Máhals," published in the Journal, Asiatic Society, Bengal, I introduced them as a dark, coarse featured, broad nosed, wide mouthed, and thick lipped race, and it was natural to conclude from this that they were one of the aboriginal tribes. I cannot say that my opinions regarding their looks have undergone any change from the specimens that have since come before me. They are decidedly ugly, but are taller and better set up than most of the people described in this chapter.

Traditions.

The Kaurs form a considerable proportion of the population of Jashpúr, Udaipúr, Sirgúja, Korea, Chánd Bhakár, and Korba of Chattisgarh, and though they are much scattered, and the various divisions of the tribe hold little communication with each other, they all tenaciously cling to one tradition of their origin, that they are the descendants of the survivors of the sons of Kuru, called Kauravas in the Puráns, who, when defeated by the Pándavas at the great battle of Kuru Kshetrya, and driven from Hastinápúr, took refuge in the hill country of Central India.

They not only relate this of themselves, but it is firmly believed by the people of all castes of Hindus, their neighbours, who, notwithstanding their dark complexions and general resemblance to the offspring of Nisháda and some anti-hindu practices, do not scruple to regard them as brethren.

I met some very respectable intelligent-looking Kaurs in Jashpúr this year [1869,] whom I questioned regarding this anomaly. I was informed that the Kaurs were divided into four tribes—*1st*, the Dúdh Kaurs, we may call them not *milk* Kaurs, but the cream of the Kaurs. They are found in Chattisgarh and live very purely according to Hindu doctrines and have Brahman priests. *2nd*, Paikera, also orthodox, but a shade below the Dúdh. *3rd*, Rettiah Kaurs. The Kaurs of Udaipúr described by me in the paper above quoted belong to this class. They rear and eat fowls, and have no veneration for Brahmans. The village barber is their priest, and officiates as such at marriages and other ceremonies. At births, marriages, and deaths, the males affected by the casualty and all connected with them of the same sex, are clean-shaven all round. Some villages maintain, besides, a Byga priest, or exorcist for the Dryads, Naiads, and witches. The Paikera Kaurs therefore, who are, I think, the most numerous, cannot be regarded as Hindu in faith, though "they adore Shiva under the denomination of Mahádeva, and Párbatti as Gauri, and they have a festival for each every year, at which they dance and sing, men and women." *4th*, the Cherwa Kaurs, a scattered and impure tribe.

Tribal divisions.

The Dúdh Kaurs alone preserve the true blood of the Kuru race. The others admit that they have greatly degenerated in appearance since they took to the jungles and mixed with the Mlechchas or barbarians. There is no doubt that they must have brought into these wilds civilized ideas that were previously unknown to the older settlers. I have always found them a well-to-do, clean, industrious, people, living in comfortable, carefully-constructed and healthily-kept houses, and well dressed. The houses are built like bungalows with verandahs: and there is one to each married member of the family, and they are placed so as to form a court-yard of family apartments, which is kept scrupulously clean. In Udaipúr, Sirgúja, Jashpúr, they are not found in possession of proprietary rights, except such as long settled cultivators in this part of India always have in the lands they cultivate: the villages are all held in farm by one of the leading men of the clan on short leases. They have none of them, in the tracts mentioned, attained to the dignity of landlord either as zamíndár, or jágírdár. I am told, however, that the zamíndár of Korba in Chattisgarh is a Kaur.

All this makes me inclined to separate them from the aboriginal tribes of Central India, and to think that there is some foundation for their tradition; but as I cannot efface their Turanian traits, and from all I have seen of them must regard those traits as the predominating and original characteristics of the tribe, I find myself in the dilemma of having to come forward as the propounder of a new theory, and in opposition to the Mahábhárat to suggest that the war of the Pándavas and Kauravas was not a family quarrel but a struggle for supremacy between an Aryan and a Turanian nation! It is corroborative of this view that the Kauravas are spoken of in the Puráns* as forming with the 'Pánchálas' the principal nations of the middle districts of Bhárata, and they are classed with others as 'Jangalas,' dwellers in the thicket, in the topographical chapters of the Mahábhárat. It may be, however, that the Kauravas of the day are descendants of subjugated aborigines, who formed the bulk of the armies of Hastinápúr.

This last theory would account for their Hindu proclivities, which, notwithstanding the substitution for Brahmans of persons of impure caste as priests, are very strong.

* See Vishnu Pur., Wilson's Translation, Chapter III, 1st edition, page 176.

2 K

I found that the Kaurs of Sirgúja at one time encouraged widows to become Satis, and greatly venerated those who did so. Sati shrines are not uncommon in the Tributary Máhals. Between Partabpúr and Jilmilli in Sirgúja, I encamped in a grove sacred to a Kauraini Sati. Several generations have elapsed since the self-sacrifice that led to her canonization, but she is now the principal object of worship in the village and neighbourhood, and I was informed that every year a *fowl* was sacrificed to her, and every third year a black goat. The Hindus with me were intensely amused at the idea of offering fowls to a Sati. At Jilmilli there are Sati shrines appertaining to the Rájpút family that own the place, but the offerings are strictly confined to fruit and flowers.

There are no doubt amongst the present generation of Hindu females, ladies of high church sentiments who deplore their inability to attain this spiritual elevation, and envy the honors paid to their ancestresses, and I fear the Hindu dowagers in some high families make themselves so disagreeable, that the male descendants of the sainted ladies too often bewail that their grandmothers had not the opportunity of canonization enjoyed by their predecessors.

SECTION 9.—THE MÁRS.

Amongst the broken tribes in Palámau and Sirgúja are to be found a few families of the people called Már. They say that they came from Málwa, and are probably derived from the people called Málavas in the Purúnas and Mahábhárata, also assigned by Wilson to Málwa. Wilford considered Mála to be the Málabhúm of Medníprúr (Midnapore). One section of the Bengal Báori tribe are called Málya from that place.

The Márs I have fallen in with, like many other tribes, declare they were formerly Kshetryas, but disliking the trammels of caste, they gave up the distinctive brahmanical cord and took to the plough. They have Brahmans for priests, worship the host of Hindu gods, and, like the Kaurs especially, adore those amongst their ancestresses who became Satis, though in their present degraded state they allow of widow marriage, and a man always takes to wife, by the custom called *sagai*, his elder brother's widow.

The Márs live comfortably in good houses, and are careful cultivators. They exhibit a great variety of features and complexion. Some that I saw in Sirgúja were of yellow or tawny complexion, with handsome features, eyes well protected by prominent brow and nose, with good teeth and well-formed mouths, and they were of average height. Some had the same light complexions, with very flat features, and some were very dark. On the whole, it appeared to me that they were more Aryan than anything else, with a dash of aboriginal blood. The Sirgúja Márs say that they were expelled from Palámau; in the latter district there is a tradition that they were a very wealthy people when established there, and left much treasure when they were driven out of it, and it is said that Márs have been frequently seen hovering about the sites of their ancient settlements, seeking for the treasures that their ancestors left buried there.

Már or Mála is a very uncertain name applied to or assumed by different people in different parts of India; but it may be that there is some affinity between all the tribes who bear it. It is the name assumed by the Rájmahál hill-men, who from their language are one of the Southern Dravidian nations. In Sirgúja, Márs are probably sprung from an Aryan colony who settled amongst and intermarried with people of the Dravidian stock.

GROUP VI.

BHÚNIYA OR BHÚIYA.

SECTION I.—THE BHÚIYAS.

I now proceed to notice a tribe which is perhaps the most interesting and widely-diffused of the class we are considering—I mean the Bhúiyas. Buchanan Hamilton found them in Bhágalpúr, Bihár and Dinájpúr; he calls them Bhungiyas, and considers them to be the remains of the armies of Jorasandhu. He notes that whilst some of this tribe are thoroughly Hinduized, living pure according to Hindu tenets and having Brahmans for priests, others are regarded as amongst the dregs of impurity, eating beef, pork, camels, horses, asses, rats, cats, fowls, lizards,—everything that Hindus abhor, and worshipping chiefly the Víras or spirits of their deified heroes or ancestors.

Mr. G. Campbell, in his Ethnology of India, suggests that they are connected with the 'Buis' of Madras and Central Provinces. This is probable. The Bhúiya feature is, on the whole, of a Tamulian cast, and it is in the southern frontier of Bengal that we find them in greatest strength and greatest purity. They belong, I dare say, to the southern rather than to the northern races,—the Dravidian rather than the Kolarian.

In a preceding chapter on the population of Asám, I have noticed that a dynasty called the Bárah Bhúiya once ruled in that province, and that the country to the north of the Brahmaputra, from one end of the valley to the other, is full of great works ascribed to this people, and the origin of their dynasty is probably alluded to in the tradition given by Buchanan Hamilton in his account of Dinájpúr, where it is narrated that twelve distinguished persons of the Bhungiya race came to the Koladyne river, the boundary between Kámrúp and the ancient Matsyadesh, took up their abode there, extended their sway, and executed great works. In Northern and Eastern Bengal and Chútiá Nágpúr, the persons now included in the tribe are in the humblest positions of life, performing offices the most degrading, few of them attaining to the dignity of farmers or cultivators of their own fields; but there are grounds for supposing that some of the noblest families in Bengal are sprung from this race, and they still hold high positions in the Jungle and Tributary Máhals. The proprietors of the estates surrounding the Parisnáth hill in the Mánbhúm and Hazáríbágh districts, though pretending to be Kṣhetryas, are Bhúiyas, and they have not been able to efface the characteristic physical traits of their origin. They are swarthy, almost black (41), and have coarse, Negro-like, features.

Traditions.

They form an important section of the population of Singbhúm. Tradition says, they were once dominant in the western and southern parts of that country, but were subjugated by the 'Hos' (Kols). In the tributary estates of Gángpúr, Bonai, Keonjhur, and Bámra, they are almost the only class possessing proprietary rights under the chiefs. They are the barons from whom those chiefs originally derived their authority, and are either the support or the sap of that authority, according to the side they take in the politics of the state. They have, in all these little governments, that useful institution—an opposition.

Mr. Stirling, in his account of Orissa, classes them amongst the Kols; but there are no grounds that I know of for so connecting them. As I have said above, they appear to me to be linked with the Dravidian rather than with the Kolarian tribes. They were the veritable monkeys that aided Ráma in his invasion of Lanka. All the country now occupied by the Bhúiyas is full of traditions of that great hero. He is the favorite god of the Hinduized Bhúiyas. The most awe-inspiring of their stupendous rocks are his fanes; the most lovely of their pools are sacred in virtue of the tradition of his having bathed in them. Hanumán, the general of the ape army, was Pawan-ka-pút, 'the son of the wind;' and the Bhúiyas to the south of Singbhúm call themselves Pawanbans, the children of the wind, to this day. That they are the apes of the Rámáyana, there can therefore be no doubt.

Physical traits.

But though I have seen some individuals of the tribe of a very low type, they are not particularly simian in appearance. They are a dark-brown, well-proportioned race, with black, straight hair plentiful on the head, but scant on the face; of middle height, figures well knit and capable of enduring great fatigue, but light framed like the Hindu, rather than presenting the usual muscular development of a hill-man. The features are very much of the same cast throughout. The cheek and jaw-bones are projecting, so as to give a breadth and squareness to the face. The nose is but slightly elevated, still neither so depressed nor so broad at the root as the generality of Turanian noses and rather of a retroussé type; mouths and teeth well formed, and the facial angle generally good. The eyes well shaped and straight, but never very large or deep set.

Khandáits.

In costume and general external appearance there is nothing but feature to distinguish the upper classes amongst them from Hindus, and they like to be considered 'Súdras.' They sometimes call themselves Khandáits and claim to be of the same family as the Or-Khandáits or Paiks of Orissa, and assume the Brahmanical cord. Those who do so of course act up to their profession and abstain from forbidden meats, but in the countries bordering on the Ganges, where they occupy a very low position, they are classed with 'músahars,' rat-eaters.

They are the earliest known settlers in parts of Singbhúm, Gángpúr, Bonai, Keonjhur, and Bámra. The chiefs of these estates now call themselves Rájpúts; if they be so they are strangely isolated families of Rájpúts. The country for the most part belongs to the Bhúiya sub-proprietors. They are a privileged class, holding as hereditaments the principal offices of the state, and are organized as a body of militia. The chiefs have no right to exercise any authority till they have received the 'tilak,' or token of investiture, from their powerful Bhúiya vassals. Their position altogether renders their claim to be considered Rájpúts extremely doubtful, and the stories told to account for their acquisition of the dignity are palpable fables. They were no doubt all Bhúiyas originally; they certainly do not look like Rájpúts.

It is singular that these Hinduized Bhúiyas retain in their own hands the priestly duties of certain old shrines to the exclusion of Brahmans. This custom has no doubt descended in Bhúiya families from the time when Brahmans were not, or had obtained no footing, amongst them, and when the religion of the land, and the temples, were not Hindu. They are now indeed dedicated to Hindu deities, but there are evidences of the temples having been originally occupied by other images. At some of these shrines, human sacrifices were offered every third year, and this continued till the country came under British rule.

According to their own traditions, they were once united as a nation in Eastern India, and had a king of their own, but they were broken up and dispersed by invasion from the west. They have all lost the language that they spoke in those days, whatever it may have been, and now speak Hindí, Bengali, or Uriyá, according to their locality.

It may be said that I have not yet shown sufficient cause for treating them otherwise than as a section of the great Hindu people. I consider they bear the Turanian type of feature too markedly to be so classed, and I have yet to describe the more primitive type of the race.

In my notes on the Tributary Máhals named, published in the Journal of the Asiatic Society of Bengal, part II, No. 1, for 1865, I introduced the Bhúiyas, and mentioned that there was a hill section of the tribe which I had not seen, but who were, I was informed, a very primitive and unsophisticated people. In 1865, I made the acquaintance of the hill Bhúiyas in Bonai.* I had heard a very good character of them from their Rajá. He described them as singularly truth-loving, simple and amenable, and from all I saw of them, I am inclined to endorse this favorable opinion. I was accompanied on this occasion by Mr. T. E. Ravenshaw, the Superintendent of the Katak Tributary Máhals. We crossed a range of hills in which the Paharí Bhúiyas resided, and one of the first things that struck us was the care they had bestowed on the ordinary duty of clearing and smoothing our way. The road was not only repaired, it was carefully swept, and equal pains had been bestowed by them to get up a halting place which had been prepared for us in the midst of a forest. I found myself amongst a new undescribed people, and proceeded to note their peculiarities.

Bonai Bhúiyas.

In costume there is nothing peculiar, except that the men and women all wear dresses of brown cotton or dyed a light brown. They have their own priests called deoris,† and their sacred groves called 'Deota Sara,' dedicated to four deities, Dásum Pát, Bámoni Pát, Koisar Pát, and Borám. The three first are brethren, but there was some difference of opinion as to whether Bámoni was male or female. Borám is the sun, also worshipped under the name of Dharm Deota, as with the Oraons. The three minor deities are represented by stones in the Sara, but Borám has no representation. Borám, as the first and greatest of gods and as the creator, is invoked at the sowing season with the offering of a white cock. In cases of sickness, goats are offered to Dásum Pát and his brethren. On such occasions the goat is given by the owner of the house in which the sick person resides. On other occasions the victim is provided by the

Religion.

* One of the Tributary Máhals under the Commissioner of Chútiá Nágpúr, south of Singbhúm.

† The priests of the primitive tribes in Asám were also called 'deoris', *vide ante* page 85.

community. The sacrifices are all offered at the foot of trees in the Sara; only men partake of the meat. The deori gets the head.

They have no traditions regarding the order of creation, their own migrations, or any defined ideas of a future state. They burn their dead near a stream, and throw the ashes into the water, thus following the custom of the Santáls, Hindus, and others. Eleven days after the cremation all shave, put on fresh clothes, and have a feast.

Births, marriages.

The mother of a child remains unclean after its birth for seven days; the child's head is then shaved, and it is named, and the ceremony of naming it is precisely the same as that followed by the Múndas and Hos. The name of the grandfather is given to the eldest son (except where in consequence of the failure of the test it is found necessary to change it), the great grand father's to the second son, and then the names of collateral branches are given according to seniority. There are no religious ceremonies after this till marriage, which cannot take place till the parties are adult, and the parents have very little to do with the selection of partners. I was told by people who knew the tribes well, but did not belong to them, that the proposal of marriage came in the first place from the girl, as with the Gáros. This was not confirmed by the Bhúiyas themselves; they, however, may have had a delicacy in speaking of a custom which they could not fail to see astonished and amused all the natives in our camp. At the marriage there is much dancing and singing, and that is all I could find out concerning it, but they have a marvellous pretty and romantic fashion of bringing such matches about.

In each village there is, as with the Oraons, an open space for a dancing ground called by the Bhúiyas the 'Darbár,' and near it the 'bachelor's hall,' a separate house, for the young men, which is called the 'Dhángar bássa' or 'Mandarghar,' as here the young men, 'Dhángar,' must all sleep at night, and here the drums, 'mandar,' are kept. Some villages have a 'Dhángarin bássa,' or house for maidens, which, strange to say, they are allowed to occupy without any one to look after them. They appear to have very great liberty, and slips of morality, so long as they are confined to the tribe, are not much heeded. Whenever the young men of the village go to the darbár and beat the drums, the young girls join them there, and they spend their evenings dancing and enjoying themselves without any interference on the part of the elders. The Bhúiya dances have their peculiar features, but compared with the lively and graceful movements of the Kols, they are very tame performances.

Dances.

The men have each a rude kind of tambourine. They march round in a circle, beating these and singing a very simple melody in a minor key on four notes. The women dance opposite to them with their heads covered and bodies much inclined, touching each other like soldiers in line, but not holding hands or wreathing arms like the Kols. The dances when confined to the people of the village are regarded as mere rehearsals. The more exciting and exhilarating occasions are when the young men of one village proceed to visit the maidens of another village, or when the maidens return the call. The young men provide themselves with presents for the girls, generally consisting of combs for the hair and sweets, and going straight to the darbár of the village they visit, they proclaim their arrival loudly by beating their drums or tambourines. The girls of that village immediately join them. Their male relations and neighbours must keep entirely out of view, leaving the field clear for the guests. The offerings of the visitors are now gallantly presented and graciously accepted, and the girls at once set to work to prepare dinner for their beaux, and after the meal they dance and sing and flirt all night together, and the morning dawns on more than one pair of pledged lovers. Then the girls, if the young men have conducted themselves to their satisfaction, make ready the morning meal for themselves and their guests; after which the latter rise to depart, and still dancing and playing on the drums, move out of the village followed by the girls, who escort them to the boundary. This is generally a rockbroken stream with wooded banks; here they halt, the girls on one side, the lads on the other, and to the accompaniment of the babbling brook sing to each other in true bucolic style.

The song on these occasions is to a certain extent improvised, and is a pleasant mixture of raillery and love-making. There is a leader on each side who starts with some word or name or phrase introduced chiefly for the sake of the rhyme, but generally apposite to the idea that follows, somewhat in the style of that classical fragment of didactic poetry—

Blankets and pins! blankets and pins!
When a man marries his sorrow begins.

There is no doubt an intentional connection between the first and the second line. Blankets are suggestive of warmth and comfort which may be associated with fortunate matrimony, but blankets with pins in them are horribly expressive of the misery of ill-assorted unions.

I endeavoured to note down the song that was sung in our presence as a specimen, and I give a close imitation of a part of it.

BOYS.

A kanchan flower bring to us,
We'll listen whilst you sing to us.

GIRLS.

We'll gather greens for dinner, dear!
But cannot think of singing here.

BOYS.

As Radha's pretty little bird,
You sweetly sing and must be heard.

GIRLS.

You silken meshes o'er us fling,
But truly, love! we cannot sing.

BOYS.

A handful that of chaff and straw,
Us boys you surely beat at jaw!

GIRLS (pouting).

Ah! birds that chirp and fly away!
With us you care not then to stay?

BOYS (amorous).

Yes, yes, we've caught some pretty fish,
To part, dear girls, is not our wish.

GIRLS (pleased).

The clouds disperse, the day looks fair,
Come back then lads our homes to share.

BOYS.

No! by the bar tree blossom! but
You come with us and share our hut.

GIRLS.

The birds sing merrily, we agree
To leave pa ma and go with thee.

The song ended, the girls go down on their knees, and bowing to the ground, respectfully salute the young men, who gravely and formally return the compliment, and they part.

The visit is soon returned by the girls. They are received by the young men in their darbár and entertained, and the girls of the receiving village must not be seen.

I have faithfully rendered the beginning and end of the song, but have omitted more than half of the intermediate stages, and this makes the *denouement* more abrupt than it appeared in the original. When I asked one of the girls at the conclusion if there was no more, she archly replied, "What more would you have?" They have certainly more wit, more romance, and more poetry in their composition than is usually found amongst the country folk in India.

SECTION 2.—BHÚIYAS OR BHÚNIYAS OF KEONJHUR.

Keonjhur, a Katak Tributary Máhal, has long been one of the chief seats of the Bhúiyas. There we find them as an aboriginal race still dominant; for, if not the most numerous, they are certainly the most influential section of the population. The Bhúiyas of the plains, including the Sáonts, a thoroughly Hinduized portion of the clan, are the organized militia of the state. They all hold their lands on conditions of service, and maintain themselves in a state of preparation for taking the field at a moment's notice to oppose their Raja or fight for him, according to their humour. Some clans of the hill Bhúiyas are similarly organized, but the most powerful body amongst them, the Pawri (for Pahária), the true hill Bhúiyas, are on a different footing. They are not bound to fight for the Raja, though they occasionally take up arms against him. Their duty is to attend on him and carry his loads when he travels about, and so long as they are satisfied with his person and his rule, no more willing servitors or devoted subjects could be found. They are then in Keonjhur, as in Bonai, a race whom you cannot help liking and taking an interest in from the primitive simplicity of their customs, their amenability, and their anxiety to oblige; but unsophisticated as they are, they wield an extraordinary power in Keonjhur, and when they take it into their heads to use that power, the country may be said to be governed by an oligarchy composed of the sixty chiefs of the Pawri Desh, the Bhúiya Highlands. A knotted string passed from village to village in the name of the sixty chiefs throws the entire country into commotion, and the order which is verbally communicated in connection with it, is as implicitly obeyed as if it emanated from the most potent despot. It is not because they are stronger, braver, or better armed, that they exercise this supremacy; it arises from two causes, prestige and position. The Pawris dispute with the Juángs the claim to be the first settlers in Keonjhur, and boldly aver that the country belongs to them. They assert that the Raja is of their creation, and that the prerogative of installing every new Raja on his accession is theirs and theirs alone. The Hindu population of Keonjhur is in excess of the Bhúiya, and it comprises Gonds and Kols, but the claim of the Pawris to the dominion they arrogate, is admitted by all; even Brahmans and Rájpúts respectfully acknowledge it, and the former, by the addition of Brahmanical rites to the wild ceremonies of the Bhúiyas, affirm and sanctify their installation.

The 'gánthi' or knotted string of the sixty chiefs has been during the recent disturbances in Keonjhur in active operation. The last one I heard of was a forgery. An adherent of the Raja captured by the Pawris ingeniously fabricated a 'gánthi,' and having effected his escape from his guard, it passed him unquestioned through the remainder of the Bhúiya country to our camp.

Settlements.

The settlements of the Hill Bhúiyas are in valleys, some long and winding, some circular; each village or cluster of two or three villages snugly screened and protected by its own lofty barrier of hills, and accessible only by steep tortuous passes, or by paths winding in ravines. Thus secured, the Pawris are beyond the reach of retaliation when they choose to make a stoop on the lowlands, and are therefore as formidable to the people of the plains as were the Highlanders to the Lowlanders in Scotland a century ago. Some of the settlements are permanent, but many villages have within the boundaries allotted to them two or more sites, on one of which alternately they form a new village every ten years. The houses are nevertheless tolerably substantial and comfortable. Every village has its 'Darbár,' the town hall, resting place for travellers, and sleeping place for the young men, with dancing place in front for the recreations of the maidens and youths after their day's toil.

The hills rise to a height of 3,200 feet above the sea level, and amongst them are the sources of the Baiturni river. The valleys are fertile, irrigated by numerous streams and sundry rills, the waters of which may, with facility, be economized, and the inhabitants of this hill tract rarely suffer from drought.

Tribal divisions.

The Bhúiyas in Keonjhur are divided into four clans, the Mál or Desh Bhúiyas (they call themselves, and are called, the Desh-lok, or the people of the country), the Dandsena, the Khatti, and the Rájkúli Bhúiyas. The latter, as connected with the royal line, I should have placed first, but I give them in the order assigned to them by my informants. The Bhúiyas, it is said, twenty-seven generations ago, stole a child of the Mohurbhauj Raja's family, brought it up amongst them, and made it their Raja. He was freely admitted to intercourse with Bhúiya girls, and the children of this intimacy are the progenitors of the Rájkúli. But they are not considered first among Bhúiyas, because they are not of pure Bhúiya descent.

Having witnessed the installation of a Raja of Keonjhur by the Bhúiyas, I proceed to describe the ceremony.

Installation of a Raja.

A large shed attached to the Raja's palace and ordinarily used as lumber room, was cleared out, swept and garnished, spread with carpets, and otherwise prepared for the occasion. A number of Brahmans were in attendance in sacerdotal costume, seated amidst the sacred vessels and implements, and articles for offerings used in the consecration of Rajas, according to the ceremonies prescribed in the Veds.

Beyond the circle of the brahmanical preparations a group of the principal Bhúiyas were seated, cleanly robed for the occasion and garlanded.

2 M

When the company were all seated and these arrangements complete, the young Raja Dhananjai Bhanj entered and distributed pân, confections, spices, and garlands, and retired. Then after a pause there was heard a great crash of the discordant but wild and deep-toned wind instruments and drums of the Bhúiyas and other tribes, and the Raja entered mounted on the back of a strongly-built Bhúiya chief, who plunged and pawed and snorted under him like a fiery steed. Moving to the opposite side of the brahmanical sacred circle, followed by a host of the tribe, one of them placed himself on a low platform covered with red cloth, and with his body and limbs formed the back and arms of the throne on which the Raja, dismounting from his biped steed, was placed. Then the attendant Bhúiyas each received from the Raja's usual servants extemporised imitations of the insignia of royalty,—banners, standards, pankhas, chaurs, chhatrs, canopies,—and thirty-six of the tribe as hereditary office-bearers, each with his symbol, ranged themselves round their chief.

There was a temporary hitch in consequence of the unexpected absence of the hereditary sword, bearer, but after a slight delay a deputy was found and the ceremony proceeded, not, however, until the Bhúiyas had protested against such an irregularity being admitted as a precedent. Then one of the principal Bhúiya chiefs, taking a light flexible jungle creeper of considerable length, binds it round the Raja's turban as the 'siropá', or honorary head dress, conferred by them. The bands strike up whilst this is done. Bards chant hymns of praise, and Brahmans recite from the Shama Veda, and a leading chief of the clan, Bámdeo Ranha, dipping his finger into the saucer of sandalwood essence, makes on the forehead of the Raja the mark called 'tíká.' The Brahman priest, the prime minister or bewurtha, and others then repeat the ceremony of giving the tíká, so that a considerable amount of such sealing is required to constitute a Raja of Keonjhur. The brahmanical ceremony of consecration had been duly solemnized on a previous occasion by the Brahmans, but a portion of this ceremony, omitting the anointing with clarified butter, &c., was now again performed by the priests, ratifying and rendering sacred the act of the Bhúiyas.

Then the sword, a very rusty old weapon, is placed in the Raja's hands, and one of the Bhúiyas, named Anand Kopát, comes before him and kneeling sideways, the Raja touches him on the neck with the weapon as if about to strike off his head, and it is said that in former days there was no fiction in this part of the ceremony. The family of the Kopát hold their lands on the condition that the victim when required shall be produced. Anand, however, hurriedly arose after the accolade and disappeared. He must not be seen for three days; then he presents himself again to the Raja as miraculously restored to life.

The Bhúiya chiefs next make offerings to the Raja, rice, pulse, pots of ghee, milk, honey, and other things,—each article being touched by all the sirdars before it is presented. The chief sirdars now solemnly address him, and telling him they have, under the authority exercised by them and their ancestors from time immemorial, made over to him the realm and the people therein, enjoin him to rule with justice and mercy. It was a long speech, of which I could catch but little. The ceremony was then concluded with a salute of guns. The Raja arose and again mounted on his curvetting and frisky biped steed, left the assembly surrounded and followed by all the Bhúiya office-bearers with their insignia, and was thus escorted to his own apartment in the palace.

Soon after—it may be on a subsequent date—the Bhúiyas do homage to the Raja elect. They come in a body bringing in as gifts, produce, gourds, fruits, Indian corn, and laying them at the Raja's feet, they ask after his health, his establishment, his horses and his elephants, and in return the Raja inquires after their crops, cows, fowls, and children. This over, each sirdar prostrates himself, and taking the Raja's foot in his hand places the royal toe first on his right and then on his left ear, and then on his forehead.

Physical traits.

The Keonjhur Hill Bhúiyas are rather of an exaggerated Turanian type; very large mouths, thick and somewhat projecting lips, foreheads narrow and low, but not receding, eyes dark, but well-shaped, hair plentiful on the head, though rather frizzly and generally scanty on face, but to this there are notable exceptions. Short of stature, averaging about five feet two inches, round shouldered, and many of them with the lump that is produced by the displacement of the muscles in carrying loads banghy fashion. The color of the skin varies from a deep chocolate, the predominating tint, to tawny, embracing the shades 42, 43, and 44 of the test plate.

Religion.

The religion appears to be much the same as that of the Bonai Bhúiyas. They worship the sun as Dharam, and pay great attention to Borám, who is also called 'Bír,' that is Víra or Mahábír Hanumán; but their private and most frequent devotions are paid to a blood-thirsty tutelary goddess called Thákuráni something, generally 'Thákuráni Maie,' in all probability the origin of the Hindu Káli, for I firmly believe, that goddess with her bloody sacrifices, especially human sacrifices, was borrowed by the Hindus from the aboriginals. I have noticed that in three of the Bhúiya Tributary Máhals, Bámra, Bonai, and Gángpúr, human sacrifices were in former times offered at certain shrines to Káli every third year, and that the priests of these shrines are Bhúiyas, not Brahmans. That the same custom prevailed in Keonjhur is likely enough, and that the Pawris, if left to themselves, would take to it again is probable, as they recently* carried off and murdered the Raja's prime minister; and on his head being taken to the leader of the insurrection, it was treated as a sacrificial offering to the Thákuráni.

I have been favored by Mr. A. F. K. Hewit, C. S., Settlement Officer of Ráipúr, in the Central Provinces, with the following account of clans of the same tribe in that territory:—

The Búniyas.

"The Búniyas are, I think, evidently the same as the Bhúiyas of the Garhját estates; they have the same broad faces, with a considerable projection of the lower jaw, and they say they came into this part of the country from the east and south of the district; but if my information is correct, there are considerable differences in the customs observed by the Búniyas in these two quarters. Those south worship Bhawáni and a deity called Bhím,† those in the east call their god Karo Byro. Their marriage ceremonies also show points of difference. In both cases it is performed in the house of the bride's father, but the Búniyas in the

* 1st May 1868.

† Bhíma, the Achilles of the Pándús, the dread of the Asuras. When a divine origin was ascribed to him, he was reported to be the son of Vayu or Pawan, the wind, therefore, brother of Hanumán and of the same descent as that adopted by the Bhúiyas themselves.

south commence the wedding by the bride and bridegroom each taking seven handfuls of rice and throwing them at one another; then the bridegroom accompanied by the brides-maids' or rather their female relations, performs the 'bhánwar',* or circuit, seven times round a stake placed in the centre of a shed erected in the court-yard. After this the bridegroom acknowledges his wife and threatens any man who attempts to take her away from him. The Byga ties† their clothes together when the stars appear, and they are then left to themselves till morning. In the morning they are escorted to the tank and bathe together, the Byga untying the knot as they go into the water.

Marriages.

They then return to the house and are made to stand in the court-yard with pitchers of water on their heads, and after being kept a weary time in this position, the contents of the pitcher are refreshingly poured over them, and the ceremony is completed by a great feast.

"In the east, the Búniyas commence the ceremony by grinding *úrid dál,* and mixing it with warm water, after which the relations of the bride wash the bodies of both with the mixture. They are then anointed with oil, and the relations of the bride-groom touch his feet, knees, breast, and head, with mango leaves. Then the bride and bridegroom take branches of the mahua tree (*Bassia latifolia*) in their hands, and holding them go down to a tank or stream, and after steeping the branches in the water bathe together. Returning they perform the 'bhánwar' round a branch of mahua set up by the Byga, and the ceremony is concluded by a feast.

"These tribes after disposing of their dead, perform a ceremony which is supposed to bring back into the house the spirit of the deceased, thence an object of household worship. A vessel filled with rice and flour is placed for a time on the tomb, and when brought back, a mark of a fowl's foot is found at the bottom of the vessel, and this indicates that the spirit of the deceased has returned."

Buijwars and Bygas.

Mr. Hewit mentions another tribe called Buijwars and the Bygas of the Mundla District, who are nearly connected with them. They speak a dialect of Hindí, and generally observe Hindu customs, their marriage ceremonies being very similar to those of the Hindus, but the manes of their forefathers appear to be the chief object of their worship, and they live in a very wild state, subsisting chiefly by hunting. I have seen an account of the same tribe by Mr. E. Egerton, who says they are also called Bhúmias. Mr. Hewit considers they belong to the eastern aborigines, from the reverence they pay their dead, which, as he observes, is a characteristic of those races, distinguishing them from the Gonds and western tribes. Mr. Egerton says they worship the earth as Mái Dharti, mother earth. This appears to connect them with the Parheyas of Palámau, whose chief object of worship is 'Dharti.' They appear to lead the same kind of life as the Boyárs described above, and are probably a kindred people. The Kharwárs also worship Dharti.

---

* The ceremony of the 'bhánwar,' or circuit of the pole or branch, is noticed by Mr. Hislop as a characteristic feature in Gond marriages. It is, however, a ceremony observed in most Hindu marriages, though not one of the observances enjoined in the Puráns. Its origin is curious. As a Hindu bridegroom of the upper classes has no opportunity of trotting out his intended previous to marriage, and she is equally in the dark regarding the paces of her lord, the two are made to walk round the post a certain number of times to prove that they are sound in limb. There are many observances in marriages and other ceremonies common to Hindus and Aborigines, and when customs are practised by the former, which are not enjoined by the Shástars, it is highly probable that they have been adopted from the latter.

† This is done by a Brahman in Hindu marriages.

SECTION 3.—THE BENDKARS OF KEONJHUR, OR SAVARAS.

Distribution.

Scattered throughout the southern Tributary Maháls we find colonies of a people of the aboriginal type, bearing a name often met in the Hindu classics, the Suari of Pliny,* the Sabaræ of Ptolemy, the Savaras, commonly corrupted into Sauras, or Saurs. The Bendkars of Keonjhur, who have already excited some curiosity from a brief notice regarding them published in the Journal, Asiatic Society, Bengal, are a somewhat isolated fragment of the Savaras. I am informed that the Savaras are numerous in Lehera, in Bámra, and elsewhere in the tributary estates, but I have not fallen in with any large communities of the race. Those I have seen are broken up into parties of two or three families, living as menials or farm laborers in large Hindu villages; but a few of them are still found forming isolated colonies, cultivating lands, which they consider their own in out of the way places; and their most striking characteristic is that they till the land with a small hand plough and have no other agricultural implements.

The largest settlement of independent Bendkars that I have heard of is a village called Dulukri under the Thákurain hill, in the northern part of Keonjhur, called Chamakpúr. It consists of eleven houses, three of Kols, the rest Bendkars.

I have questioned the inhabitants of this village and several Bendkars living as dependants in other villages, and from the answers I have received and customs I have observed, it is difficult to regard them otherwise than as members of the great Bhúiya family, and thus connecting them we link the Bhúiyas and Savaras, and give support to the conjecture that the former are Dravidian.

The Savaras, occupying the country between the Kandh Maliahs or hill tracts and the Godavery, retain a primitive form of speech, but the Bendkar Savaras that I have fallen in with have no language of their own and no tradition that they ever possessed one. The form of speech used is Uriyá, and those living in mixed villages conform to many customs of Hindu Uriyás of inferior castes. The points of difference are, however, very noticeable; for on those points they follow exactly the customs of the Hill Bhúiyas, and the independent Bendkar communities have all the Bhúiya characteristics.

Religion.

They worship a female divinity, whom they call Bansuri and Thákuráini, no doubt the same as the blood-thirsty she-devil revered by the Bhúiyas, the prototype of the Hindu Káli. Every year, offerings are made to her of goats and fowls, but every ten years each community of Bendkars offers a buffalo, a boar, a sheep, and twelve fowls.

The Bendkars provide the necessary victims with difficulty, for it is not their custom to keep cattle of any kind. They buy what they require for sacrifice. It is not stated that there is any prohibition against their breeding such animals, nor are they restricted to the use of their hand plough, but they seldom till lands on which a bullock plough could be used. When they obtain such lands, they borrow ploughs from their neighbours, the Kols.

Festivals.

It is in their feasts, festivals, amusements, and methods of bringing about marriage that the points of resemblance between them and the Bhúiyas are most marked. I saw a dance by Bendkar boys and girls. The

* See Ancient Geography of India, by Major General Cunningham, vol. 1, p. 509.

2 x

girls dance with their heads covered, bodies much inclined, and faces looking to the ground or to their feet, which have to perform a somewhat intricate step, the right hand holds down at arms length the portion of the dress that is thrown over the head. The men playing on tambourines or half drums, sing as they dance. The girls appear too intent on their steps to respond to them, but their peculiar attitude in the dance, the steps, and *the melody*, are the same for all Bhúiyas, and are unmistakable characteristics of the race from the Ganges to the Mahánaddí. The Kolarian dances are quite different.

Marriages.

The marriage ceremonies are very simple. The formal preliminaries are arranged by mutual friends, but this generally follows a private understanding which the parties most interested have come to without intervention. After the bridegroom has made his election, the following gifts are bestowed in his behalf:—to the girl's father, a bullock; to the maternal uncle, a bullock; to the mother, 1 Rupee and a cloth.

The girl is then brought by her friends to the bridegroom's house. The young couple are required to make two and a half turns round a pot of water, in which are mango leaves. They are then bathed together, and their hands tied together, and the ceremony is at an end.

Agriculture.

When first I saw the Bendkar hand plough, it was of wood, only a branch cut with a large piece of the stem, from which it sprung, attached, and that shaped so as to give it the appearance of a miniature native plough, but they have improved on this, and now insert a piece of iron as a share in further imitation of the native plough. The implement answers well enough in preparing for seed the light vegetable mould of the forest to which they confine their cultivation; but in a stiff clay it would be inoperative.

The Hill Bendkars cultivate kangní,* kheri, khodo† or murowa, gangoi makai‡ or maize, a species of coxcomb, the seeds of which they eat, a cereal called 'siko', and a large bean which is intoxicating or acts as an emetic, if eaten raw, but is pleasant and wholesome when well cooked; also úrid. They have ordinarily no rice cultivation. They know well and use all the spontaneous edible productions of the forests, and showed me some wild yams which they largely consume: they take an immensity of cooking.

Disposal of the dead.

The Bendkars burn the dead, following the practice of the Hindus in regard to the position of the body on the pyre, that is, with the head to the north. In this they vary from the Kols, who affect the south, and the Hill Bhúiyas, who honor the quarter of the setting sun as most appropriate; but the Hill Bhúiyas are poetical.

---

* *Panicum italicum.* † *Eleusine coracana.* ‡ *Zea mays.*

GROUP VII.

THE KOLARIANS.

Preliminary Remarks.

In a preceding chapter I noticed certain traditions connecting the Kols with the Cheros, who prior to the Aryan occupation of the Gangetic Provinces were the dominant race in Gorakhpúr, Bihár, and Sháhábád, and ventured on the surmise that the now despised Kol was in those days the language of that part of India. I find this opinion has the strong support of Mr. Logan, who in a note which has been placed at my disposal, speaking of the Simang dialects of the Eastern Archipelago, says—

"The pronouns have the peculiar forms that were current in the dialects of that branch of the Himalayan people which predominated in the Gangetic basin and its confines before the Aryans advanced into it, and which spread its language and civilization eastward till they prevailed from Guzerat to Tonquin. These pronouns and many other common vocables are still used by the Kols or Santál tribes on the Ganges, the Kgi or Kasia in the Bráhmaputra basin, the Palaung and the Mon or Peguans on the Irawaddy, the Kambojans on the Mekong, and the Anamese on the Tonquin."

Mr. Hodgson thought he could trace an affinity with Múnda or Kol in the pronominalization of some of the languages of the broken tribes of Nepál analyzed by him, and some resemblance in physical traits and customs have been pointed out. Mr. Logan has noticed a linguistic affinity between the Kasias of Asám and the Kols, and I have in a previous chapter drawn attention to a very remarkable coincidence in the funeral ceremonies of the Hos (the Kols of Singbhúm) and Kasias. The language of the Santáls, the Múndas, and Kharriás of Chútiá Nágpúr, the Bhúmij of Mánbhúm, the Hos of Singbhúm is Kolarian, and though there are some slight dialectic differences, these tribes have no difficulty in understanding each other. The savage Korwá of Sirgúja speaks a language less readily comprehended by the Múnda or Ho, yet, when we examine it critically, we find that it evidently belongs to the same family. The Kúrs* or Muásí of the Central Provinces carry the same tongue across the Mahádeva hills and westward through the forests of the Taptí and Narbadá until it mingles with that of the Bhíls, and it is found† to extend to the Gávílgarh range of hills near Elichpúr. There is a tradition that the race speaking the Kolarian languages were once dominant in Talingána.

* Papers by Revd. G. Hislop, published by Sir R. Temple.

† Journal, Asiatic Society, Bengal, vol. XIII, for 1844, page 19.

Thus the vast area through which we find the Kol language permeating, disappearing at times like a river whose course is occasionally subterranean to appear again in distant regions as a stream from the same source, makes the study of the Kolarian people one of the most interesting that an Ethnologist can take up; but the interest is intensified when we find that, vast as the area is, it is insignificant in comparison with the numerous phases in the condition of the human race that varieties of existing Kolarians may be considered as exemplifying. They are living illustrations of the progress of mankind almost from the stone age to the confines of modern civilization.

The special Ethnographical number of the Journal of the Asiatic Society published in 1866 contains a paper by me entitled the Kols of Chútiá Nágpúr. Under this appellation, according to the ordinary acceptation of the term, are included the Oráons as well as the Múndas and their cognates, but I will now adopt the classification suggested by Mr. George Campbell in his Work on Indian Ethnology, and treating as Kolarians those only whose language is Múnda or Kol, exclude the Oráons who as a Dravidian race must be disposed of in a separate chapter.

In proceeding to describe the Kolarians of Bengal, I will commence with those who appear lowest in the scale of civilization and introduce my readers to the leaf clad mountaineers of Orissa.

SECTION 1.—THE JUÁNGS.

I class the Juángs with Kolarians chiefly in consequence of the linguistic affinity which apparently links them with that family.

Linguistic affinities.

It is by no means certain, however, that they may not at one time have spoken a different language. It will be found on reference to the list of words annexed to this chapter that a great many of the terms used by the Juángs for the most familiar objects are common or nearly so to them and to the Hos and Santáls, and the pronouns and first of the numerals are identical; but as they have lived for ages among people speaking the language of Utkála or Orissa, many Uriyá words have been adopted by them in supercession of the terms previously used, and they have besides a number of vocables that I cannot connect with any Aryan, Kolarian, or Dravidian language. I find some words employed both by the Juángs and the Kharriás that have dropped out of the other Kol dialects, as 'goné,' tooth, and 'lerang,' moon, for which the Hos and Santáls have adopted terms of Sanscrit derivation, and, on the whole, the Juáng language approaches more closely to the Kharriá than to the other Kol tongues.

Geographical distribution.

The Juángs are found only in two of the Katak tributary estates, Dhekanál and Keonjhur, and they are most numerous in the latter. I am informed there are thirty-two settlements of the tribe in Keonjhur occupying the hill country to the south of the Keonjhurgarh as far as Hundah, or between 21° 20′ and 21° 40′ of north latitude and 85° 30′ and 85° 45′ of east longitude. They have not got all this tract to themselves, the Hill Bhúiya villages and many colonies of Goálás occupying a superior portion of it. It is probable that they have been ousted by the Bhúiyas from the fertile valleys, and are thus compelled to restrict their cultivation to the steep sides of hills. We may give twenty as the average number of houses in each settlement, and estimate the Juáng population in Keonjhur at about three thousand people. They have no traditions which affiliate them with any other race, and notwithstanding the similarity in their languages (but of which they knew nothing till I pointed it out to them), they repudiate all connectionship with Hos or Santáls. They aver very positively that they are autochthones in Keonjhur, the direct descendants of the first human beings that appeared or were produced in that country or indeed in the world. For they assert a claim to be the first produced of the human race, though they make no pretensions to be the fathers of mankind.

The head quarters of the tribe or cradle of the race they consider to have been the Gonasika in north latitude 21° 30′ and east longitude 85° 37′, where issues from two holes in a rock, supposed to bear resemblance to the nostrils of a cow, a stream which is the source of the Baitarní.* They assert that the Baitarní on whose banks they were created, is older than the Ganges, and the present Juáng inhabitants of the village of Gonasika and other villages in the vicinity occupy the very soil from which the parents of their race were produced. They have no traditions to record, except that very long ago, nine hundred Juángs left the country of their birth and went to Dhekanál, and then the Bhúiyas came, and took up the lands of the brethren who had left them; but it is more probable, that they were driven out by the Bhúiyas who are now in those hills the dominant race. The Bhúiyas however deny this, asserting that they are the true autochthones and that the Juángs are interlopers. There is a tradition of a Bora Raja (probably some allusion to the Vará avatár of Vishnu) having had a fort in the heart of the country now occupied by Juángs, the remains of which are still in existence, and it is said that the Juángs are the remnant of his people.

Traditions.

The Juángs are in habits and customs the most primitive people I have met with or read of. They occupy a hill country in which stone implements, the earliest specimens of human ingenuity that we possess, are occasionally found, and though they have now abandoned the use of such implements and have lost the art of making them, it is not improbable that they are the direct descendants of those ancient stone cutters, and that we have in the Juángs representatives of the stone age *in situ*.

Until foreigners† came amongst them, they must have used such weapons or none; for they had no knowledge whatever of metals. They have no iron smiths, nor smelters of iron. They have no word in their own language for iron or other metals. They neither spin nor weave, nor have they ever attained to the simplest knowledge of pottery.

In the hills of Keonjhur they are still semi-nomadic in their habits, living together in villages during a portion of the year, but often changing the sites, and occupying isolated huts in the midst of their patches of cultivation, whilst the crops are on the ground.

Gonasika, one of the largest of their villages, I found to contain twenty-five houses of Juángs. The huts are amongst the smallest that human beings ever deliberately constructed as dwellings. They measure about six feet by eight, and are very low, with doors so small as to preclude the idea of a corpulent householder. Scanty as are the above dimensions for a family dwelling,

Dwellings.

* Vaitarani, the Hindu Styx.

† This was written before I had seen Mr. Ball's paper, who has a similar remark regarding the Kharriás, another Kolarian tribe noticed by him in Mánbhúm.

the interior is divided into two compartments, one of which is the store room, the other used for all domestic arrangements. The 'Paterfamilias' and all his belongings of the female sex huddle together in this one stall not much larger than a dog kennel; for the boys there is a separate dormitory.

This latter is a building of some pretensions at the entrance of the village. It is constructed with a solid plinth of earth raised about four feet, and has two apartments, one inner and closed, in which the musical instruments of the village are kept and most of the boys sleep. The other is open on three sides, that is, it has no walls but the eaves spread far beyond the plinth, and the inmates are effectually protected. This is where all guests are lodged, and it makes a convenient traveller's rest.

Cultivation.

The Juángs cultivate in the rudest way, destroying the forest trees by the deadly process of girdling them, burning all they can of the timber when it dries and sowing in the ashes. They thus raise a little early rice, Indian corn, pulses, pumpkins, sweet potatoes, ginger, and red pepper, seed all thrown into the ground at once to come up as it can.

Food.

They declare they subsist every year more on wild roots and fruits than on what they rear, but I doubt if they are so badly off as they pretend to be. The area of their cultivation appeared proportionate to their numbers. They pay no rent, being under obligation to serve the Raja, repair his house, and carry his burdens when required to do so in lieu of money payment, and they spend no money in clothes; it is difficult to under stand therefore their not having a sufficiency of wholesome food, unless it be that they spend all their substance in drink. They are no doubt addicted to ardent spirits, and they are obliged to buy what they consume, as they have not acquired the art of distilling or even of brewing rice beer which every Kol understands.

In regard to food they are not in the least particular, eating all kinds of flesh, including mice, rats, monkeys, tigers, bears, snakes, frogs, and even offal, and for them the jungles abound in spontaneously produced vegetables. In the quest of such food they possess all the instinct of the animal, discerning at a glance what is nutritive, and never mistaking a noxious for an edible fungus or root.

Weapons.

The Juángs do not look a war-like people, but when urged to it by the Bhúiyas whose lead they invariably follow, they are sometimes troublesome. They use the bow and arrow, but their favorite weapon is the primitive sling made entirely of cord. They take "pebbles from the brook," or stones as they find them. They have no idea of fashioning them to produce more efficient projectiles.

My first introduction to the Juángs was in 1866, whilst with the Superintendent of the Katak Tributary Mahâls engaged in settling a boundary dispute between Keonjhur and Bonai. We were far away from any Juáng village, but Mr. Ravenshaw sent for some specimens of this interesting people, and a well selected party, consisting of a matron, half a dozen comely maidens, and about as many men, responded to the call.

In the Journal of the Asiatic Society, Bengal, vol. XXV, for 1856, page 295, there is a brief notice of the Juángs accompanying some very clever but very grotesque sketches that give a correct idea of the singular costume of the women, but convey an impression of malformation and hideousness, which, judging from the figures of our visitors on the above occasion, grossly calumniates the race.

The females of the group had not amongst them a particle of clothing, their sole covering for purposes of decency consisted in a girdle composed of several strings of beads from which depended before and behind small curtains of leaves. Adam and Eve sewed fig leaves together and made themselves aprons. The Juángs are not so far advanced; they take young shoots of the Ásan *(Terminalia tomentosa)* or any tree with long soft leaves, and arranging them so as to form a flat and scale like surface of the required size, the sprigs are simply stuck in the girdle fore and aft and the toilet is complete. The girls were well developed and finely formed specimens of the race, and as the light leafy costume left the outlines of the figure entirely nude, they would have made good studies for a sculptor.

Dress.

The beads that form the girdle are small tubes of burnt earthen ware made by the wearers. They also wore a profusion of necklaces of glass beads, and brass ornaments in their ears and on their wrists, and it was not till they saw that I had a considerable stock of such articles to dispose of, that they got over their shyness and ventured to approach us.

They made their first appearance at night and danced by torch light; it was a wild weird-like sight. The men sang as they danced, accompanying themselves on deep-sounding tambourines; the girls holding together and circling round them in a solemnly grotesque manner. There was a want of spirit in the performance, for they were shy and timid creatures, and the dancing by torch light before so many strange spectators was evidently no pleasure to them. They executed the movements under the orders of the men with an unimpassioned obedience, as if they were so many dancing dogs or monkeys. The disarrangement of their leaves in the movements of the dance was a source of great anxiety to them, compelling them frequently to fall out of their places and retreat into the darkness to adjust their plumage. It had been the intention of the party to flit by night as they had appeared; but, moved by an exhibition and liberal distribution of bright glass beads, they were induced to stay that night and give us a performance by day light.

Dances.

Next day they came to my tent at noon, and whilst I conversed with the males on their customs, language, and religion, the girls sat nestled together in a corner, for a long time silent and motionless as statues, but after an hour or two had elapsed the crouching nymphs showed signs of life and symptoms of uneasiness, and more attentively regarding them, I found that great tears were dropping from the downcast eyes like dew drops on the green leaves. On my tenderly seeking the cause of their distress, I was told that the leaves were becoming dry, stiff, and uncomfortable, and if they were not allowed to go to the woods for a change, the consequences would be serious, and they certainly could not dance. It was a bright dry day, and the crisp rustling as they rose to depart confirmed the statement.

When they returned arrayed in fresh leaves, we induced them to give us not only the solemn measure of the evening before, but to perform a variety of sportive dances, some quite dramatic in effect, and it was altogether a most interesting "ballet." In one figure, the girls moved round in single file keeping the right hand on the right shoulder of the girl in front, in another with bodies inclined, they wreathed their arms and advanced and retreated in line. In this movement, the performance bore a strong resemblance to one of the Kol dances. Then we had the bear dance. The girls acting independently advance with bodies so much inclined, that their hands touch the ground; thus they move not unlike bears, and by a motion from the knees the bodies wriggle violently, and the broad tails of green leaves flap up and down in a most ludicrous manner.

The pigeon dance followed: the action of a love-making pigeon when he struts, pouts, sticks out his breast, and scrapes the ground with his wings was well imitated, the hands of the girls doing duty as wings. Then came a pig and tortoise dance, in which the motions of those animals were less felicitously rendered, and the quail dance in which they squatted and pecked at the ground after the fashion of those birds. They concluded with the vulture dance, a highly dramatic finale. One of the men was made to lie on the ground and represent a dead body. The girls in approaching it imitated the hopping, sidling advance of the bird of prey, and using their hands as beaks, nipped and pinched the pseudo-corpse in a manner that made him occasionally forget his character and yell with pain. This caused great amusement to his tormentors.

I had heard of a "ballet" called 'the Cocks and Hens,' but this they could not be induced to exhibit. It was admitted that it was impossible to keep the leaves in proper position whilst they danced it. It was too much of a romp, especially for a day performance.

The 'corps de ballet' were very favorable specimens of the Juáng race. They were belles who had taken evident pains in the arrangement of the simple elements of their toilet. Their hair was carefully put up and the leaves disposed of in the most becoming fashion. At Gonasika, I saw them in their more normal state, when they returned from their work in the evening with dishevelled hair, dusty bodies and disordered attire, *i. e.*, somewhat withered leaves, and it was truly like a dream of the stone age; but each lady had brought back with her fresh material for her evening dress.

The males of the community have abandoned the leaves and use in lieu the smallest quantity of cotton cloth that can be made to serve the purposes of decency. The women, it is said, are deterred by superstition from following their example, but the tradition or traditions to account for it are apparently of Bráhmanical concoction. There are several; the simplest and prettiest is connected with the origin of the Baitarní. The river goddess emerging for the first time from the Gonasika rock, came suddenly on a rollicking party of Juángs dancing naked, and ordering them to adopt leaves on the moment as a covering, laid on them the curse that they must adhere to that costume for ever or die.*

Legends.

This story is told for the Juángs rather than by them. Their own idea simply is the converse of the rule of civilized nations. They deem that the fashion of dress should never change, and that for females especially it should be simple and cheap. The notion must tend to conserve the Juángs in their present habits of hill and forest life. They must be where there is a plentiful supply of the material of nature's providing. I have not heard of any of the tribe having settled in places where it would be difficult to follow their inclination in dress.

The old men tell me that they, the males, used to wear kopins† made from the bark of a tree called Tumba. This is a tradition that takes them back to the days when they had the woods to themselves and knew nothing of piece-goods.

* I am informed by Captain J. Johnstone that he has at length induced the Juáng females to clothe themselves, he supplying the first robes. If no misfortune follow the innovation, it will probably be permanent; so when the Juáng girls posed themselves for the photographs from which the illustrations given with this work were taken, it was almost their last appearance in *leaves*.

† 'Kopin,' a narrow strip of cloth worn round the loins and between the legs.

The Reverend S. Hislop has informed us that in the remote parts of the Chanda district some of the Madian division of the Gonds are attired like the Juángs. He says, "the women wear no clothes at all, instead of which they fasten with a string passing round their waists a branch of leafy twigs to cover them before and behind." He says a similar custom is said to obtain amongst the Chenchwás that inhabit the jungles between the Madians and Masulipatam. It did exist till about 30 years ago among the Holiers in the vicinity of Mangalor.

The Singbhúm Kols have a tradition that they were once similarly attired, and during the American war, when cotton was so dear, they told the cloth merchants that they would revert to their leaves if cloth was not sold cheaper! Manchester beware!

Physical traits.

The predominating physical characteristics of the Juángs, as I saw them massed in their village, appeared to me to be great lateral projection of the cheek bones or zygomatic arches and general flatness of feature; forehead upright but narrow and low and projecting over a very depressed nasal bone; nose of the pug species, alae spreading; mouths large and lips very thick, but upper jaw rarely prognathous, though the lower jaw and chin are receding. Hair coarse and frizzly; prevailing color a reddish brown, from 27 to 29 inclusive, of the color table.

I observe that some of them had oblique eyes of the Indo-Chinese type, but in this feature there was considerable variety.

Tattooing.

It is noticeable that the Juáng women tattoo their faces with the same marks that are used by the Múndas and Kharriás, and (probably adopted from the Múndas) by the Oráons. Three strokes on the forehead just over the nose, and three on each of the temples. They attach no meaning to the marks, have no ceremony in adopting them, and are ignorant of their origin.

Stature.

They are a small race like the Oráons, the males averaging less than five feet in height. The women not more than four feet eight inches. The Ho girls of Singbhúm look like giantesses beside them, and the males in stature and carriage are equally inferior to the Ho men. The Juáng males have round shoulders, and walk with a slouching pace. The Hos are upright in carriage, and have a stately manly stride, nor is it necessary to go to Singbhúm to find Hos to compare with them. Many of the latter tribe have emigrated from Singbhúm and taken up their abodes with the Juángs and Bhúiyas in the Keonjhur hills, and, though in an inferior position working as farm laborers, the Hos retain their superiority of physique. The Juángs appear to bend under their burden-bearing lot. The Hos never, if they can help it, carry burdens, the use amongst them of the block wheeled carts being almost universal.

Religion.

The Juángs appear to be free from the belief in witchcraft, which is the bane of the Kols and perniciously influences nearly all other classes in the Jungle and Tributary Mahals. They have not, like the Kharriás, the reputation of being deeply skilled in sorcery. They have in their own language no terms for 'God,' for 'heaven' or 'hell,' and, so far as I can learn, no idea of a future state. They offer fowls to the sun when in distress, and to the earth to give them its fruits in due season. On these occasions an old man officiates as priest, he is called Nágam. The even tenor of their lives is unbroken by any obligatory religious ceremonies.

2 P

Marriages.

Marriage is recognized, but is brought about in the simplest manner. If a young man fancies a girl, he sends a party of his friends to propose for her, and if the offer is accepted, a day is fixed, and a load of rice in husk is presented on his behalf. The bridegroom does not go himself to the bride's house, his friends go for her and return with her and her friends, and they make merry, eating and dancing, and all stay and make a night of it. In the morning the bridegroom dismisses the bride's friends with a present of three measures of husked and three of unhusked rice, and this is a full and sufficient solemnization. A man may have more wives than one, if he can afford it, but no Juáng has ever ventured on more than two at a time. They are divided into tribes and are exogamous.

Disposal of the dead.

They burn their dead, and throw the ashes into any running stream, and their mourning is an abstinence for three days from flesh and salt. They erect no monuments, and have no notion of the worship of ancestors. The dead are burned with their heads to the south; in this they agree with the Hos and their cognates, and differ from the Hindus. If cremation is found to be the custom of many of the aboriginal tribes, may it not have been the practice of the earliest of mankind and account in some measure for the rarity of human bones in alluvium containing flint implements. If the Juángs had borrowed the custom from the Hindus, they would have followed the practice of the latter in placing the corpse on the pyre. All the ribes that I have fallen in with speaking dialects of the Kolarian languageb urntheir dead.

Oaths.

The Juángs swear on earth from an ant hill and on a tiger skin. The ant hill is a sacred object in the eyes of the Kharriá tribe, and the tiger skin is introduced, when Hos and Santáls are sworn.

SECTION 2.—THE KHARRIÁS.

The tribes that are linguistically most closely allied to the Juángs are the Kharriás. They are found in Singbhúm in a very wild state, living much in backwoods and on the tops of hills apart from the Hos and Bhúmij, who are somewhat in dread of them, as these isolated Kharriás have the reputation of being great wizards. They are found in the Mánbhúm hills bearing the same name, and I apprehend that the people called 'Bírhor' in the Hazáríbágh District are of the same tribe. The Bírhors call themselves Hindus, live in the jungles, and subsist on wild animals, honey, and what they can obtain by the exchange of jungle produce with people of the plains. They are great adepts at ensnaring monkeys and other small animals, and sell them alive or eat them. They have no cultivation whatever, but they are apparently Kolarian, as among themselves they converse in Kol. They sell chob, a strong fibre of which ropes and string for various purposes are made, honey, wax, and sikas, the sticks like bows for carrying loads banghy fashion, and banghy ropes; and with the proceeds and the spontaneous edible productions of the forest they manage to exist and clothe themselves. There are people called Bírhors in Chútiá Nágpúr proper and Jashpúr, who live in an equally wild state, but communicate with each other in a dialect of Hindí. They are a small, dirty, miserable looking race, who have the credit of devouring their parents, and when I taxed them with it, they did not deny that such a custom had once obtained among them.*

* A further notice of the Bírhors is given below.

The Kharriás are also seen in villages with other tribes as farm laborers, but in the Chútiá Nágpúr estate they are found in large communities, and the Kharriás belonging to these communities are far more civilized than those who live apart.

Distribution.

The best settlements lie near the southern Koel river, one of the streams that rise on the Chútiá Nágpúr plateau, the principal source of the Bráhmani.

This river the Kharriás venerate as the Santáls the Damúdar, and into it they throw the ashes of their dead. At the village of Aghurma not far from it, I collected about me a number of the tribe, and they gave the following account of themselves.

Their ancestors were formerly settled between Rohtás and Patna. They quarrelled with their relations and fled into the jungles, and wandered till they came to the Koel river, where finding unoccupied lands to suit them, they settled first at a place they called Pora on that river, from whence they spread in different directions; but their settlements have much diminished in consequence of the interference of interlopers who obtained from the Raja the farms of their villages, and many have gone to settle in the estate called Bírú Kasalpúr,* the landlord of which gives them lands to clear on very fair terms.

Traditions.

But there was also a tradition that they had come from the south, and that, driven from the country they had originally occupied, they had ascended the valley of the Koel till they found themselves in their present location. Their veneration for the Koel, and the fact that in some customs where they differ from the Kols, they approach the practices of Dravidian tribes supports this account, but both may be true. They may have fallen back south from the Gangetic provinces, passed through the Vindhyan range, and come gradually round to the south-eastern watershed of Chútiá Nágpúr.

They worship the sun under the name of Bero. Every head of a family should, during his life time, make not less than five sacrifices to this divinity; the first of fowls, the second of a pig, third of a white goat, fourth of a ram, and fifth of a buffalo. He is then considered sufficiently propitiated for that generation and regarded as an ungrateful God, if he does not behave handsomely to his votary. In praying to Bero, they address him as 'Parmeswar,' the Hindí word for God. The Ho term 'Sing bonga,' they do not know. The sacrifices are always made in front of an ant hill, which is used as an altar.

Religion.

This peculiar mode of sacrificing has fallen into desuetude among the Hos and Múndas, but on my making some enquiries on the subject from old men of those tribes, I was informed that it was orthodox, though not now generally practiced.

Their religious festivals are almost identical with those of the Múndas, and will be described in the account of that tribe. In worshipping Bero, the head of the family, with the Kharriás as with the Hos, acts as priest, but at the Sarhúl and other 'Pújás' or sacrifices offered in behalf of the community, a person is employed as village priest, whose office and name—Páhn—appear to me to have been introduced into Chútiá Nágpúr by the Oráons. The Hos have no priests.

From the Hindus they have adopted the custom of solemnizing the boring of the ears of the children, and the occasion when the hair is for the first time tied up. They have further ceremonial observances similarly derived; but this probably will only be found

* The south-western corner of Lohardagga district.

among the Kharriás on the Koel, who are much mixed up with Hindus and are under Hindu headmen. I have no doubt their village communities were at one period organized like those of the Múndas, and that they had headmen and village officers of their own tribe, but every trace of this is swept away, and it is strange that whilst the Múndas and Hos struggled for, and maintained, their old institutions, the Kharriás should have submitted to so degrading a change.

Marriage.

The primitive idea of marriage with the Kharriás was a dance and a feast when the bride was first taken to the abode of her lord; they have no word for marriage in their own language, but after certain festivities the bride and bridegroom are left to the mselves, and next morning are carriedto the river, and they and all the party bathe and wash their garments; but under the Hindu term 'bibah' certain ceremonies are superadded, borrowed from their neighbours, or to give the ceremony more importance in the eyes of the Hindus. On reaching the house of her father-in-law, the bride and bridegroom are bathed and anointed; and the bridegroom marks his bride with red lead on her forehead. It will be observed that as with the Juángs the girl is brought by her own friends to the bridegroom's house, and the ceremonies such as they are take place there.

The nuptial dances of the Kharriás are very wild, and the gestures of the dancers and the songs all bear more directly than delicately on what is evidently considered the main object of the festivities, the public recognition of the consummation of the marriage. The bride and bridegroom are carried through the dances seated on the hips of two of their companions.

Dancing is an amusement to which the Kharriás, like all Kolarians, are passionately devoted. The only noticeable difference in their style is that in the energy, vivacity and warmth of their movements they excel all their brethren.

Disposal of the dead.

I have already noticed that the Kharriás I am describing burn their dead, and putting the ashes in an earthen vessel, throw it into the river. They afterwards set up in the immediate vicinity of their houses tall rough slabs of stone, and to these as representing the departed they make daily oblations.

On the whole, their customs sufficiently conform to those of the Múndas to confirm the relationship suggested by the affinity of the tongues; but at the same time there is dissimilarity enough to indicate that, though they were originally one people, it must have been after a very long separation that they again met on the banks of the Koel.

These Kharriás are respectably dressed and comfortably housed, and as they are fair cultivators, they are well supplied with wholesome food. They, therefore, have very little resemblance to the Kharriás of the backwoods,* who live as precariously as beasts of prey, and it is difficult to imagine their being of the same race.†

* *Vide.*—Proceedings Asiatic Society, Bengal, for August 1868, p. 120, Mr. Ball's paper on the Kherriahs.

† It is a singular circumstance that some tribes of Kharriás profess to be intensely exclusive in regard to cooking and eating. This characteristic I found most developed in villages of Chútiá Nágpúr where Kharriás were associated with Oráons under Bráhman proprietors; and it is a common saying in that part of the country that every Kharriá must have his 'hariah,' *i. e.* cooking pot. He may not allow even his wife to cook for him, and if a stranger enters a house in which he keeps his earthen drinking, and cooking vessels, and water pots, evety vessel is polluted and the whole are destroyed or thrown away. This class of Kharriás are especially filthy in their habits, and it is not improbable that Hindus may have been more than ordinarily harsh in excluding them from their kitchens and inner apartments, and that the Kharriás retaliate by out-casting every body.

There is a tradition that Kharriás with another tribe called Puráns were the aborigines of Mohurbhanj, one of the Katak Tributary Mahále. They aver that they and the family of the chief, (Bhanj,) were all produced from a Pea-fowl's egg, the Bhanj from the yoke, the Puráns from the white, the Kharriás from the shell.

The Koel Kharriás are in point of physique much on a par with the Múndas, rather coarser perhaps in feature and figure, but where they differ approximating more to the appearance of a north-eastern tribe.

Tattooing.

The women are all tattooed with the marks on the forehead and temples common to so many of these tribes. Three parallel lines on the forehead, the outer lines terminating at the upper end in a crook and two on each temple. The Juáng marks of this nature take up a larger space on the forehead and temples than those of the Múndas, the lines being longer and further apart. The Kharriás in regard to the space over which the marks extend, occupy a middle place between the Juángs and Múndas.

I have had no opportunity of ascertaining if the peculiarity noticed by Mr. Ball in treating of the Mánbhúm Kharriás,—their abstaining from the flesh of sheep and the use of its wool—is common to the Kharriás of Chútiá Nágpúr; but I think, I should have heard of it, if it had been so. It is possible that the Kharriás Mr. Ball fell in with may call themselves the sheep tribe; if so, they would according to the custom of other Kolárians be debarred from making any use of the animal.

SECTION 3.—THE MÚNDAS, HOS, BHÚMIJ.

Though the old Hindu bards are generally vindictively strong in the epithets of abuse they hurl at the aboriginal tribes, some of them, in their ambition to explain all things sacred and profane, deemed it necessary to assign to the Dasyus a genealogy which affiliates them with the best blood of the Aryans. The ugliest and blackest of the people of the Vindhyan Mountains were preternaturally the offspring of King Vena, and even for the Kols a noble ancestor has been found.

The following legend is quoted from Colonel Wilford's essays.* Yayáti divided his empire among his five sons. To Puru, the youngest, he gave India, or the middle part; to Yadu, the ancestor of Krishna, the South or Deccan; the North, to Anu; and the West, to Turvasu. The offspring of Turvasu, according to the Harivansa, settled in the south, and the tenth generation from him inclusive, consisting of four brothers, Pándya, Kerala, Chola, and Kola, divided the empire they had inherited. Kola lived in the northern part of the Peninsula and his descendants are called Kols or Kolers to this day, and from them India was called *Kolaria*.

This places the chief seat of the Kols in Talingána, but it does not appear there are any of the race now there, or that the language spoken has in it any traces of Kol.†

I have already in my account of the Cheros and Kharwárs noticed that Bihár, the ancient Magadha, has numerous antiquities attributed to the Cheros and Kols, and from the traditions handed down it appears that the sovereigns of the country were at one time Cheros, the people being for the most part Kols. Doctor Buchanan Hamilton, the topographer, points to Kábar, the most important of the ruins in Bihár, attributed to the Cheros or Kols, as evidently the work of a powerful ruler and probably the strong-hold of the princes of the race. These legends of the Cheros and Kols are still preserved in

---

* Asiatic Researches, vol. IX, pages 91 and 92.

† Buchanan Hamilton, Topography of Behar.

2 Q

Bihár. The antiquities, forts and ruins in all parts of the district are by the present inhabitants universally ascribed to that ancient dynasty and primitive race.

In the account of Sháhábád the same author states that "by far the most numerous monuments of antiquity in that district are attributed to the Cheros, to whom, it is universally admitted, the whole country belonged in sovereignty; the ancient name of the country was 'Kekata' (Kíkata), and all the tract west of the Son retained that name, whilst the name of the country to the east formerly a part of Kekata was changed to Magadha."*

The Cheros of Kíkata, like the Rajas of Chútiá Nágpúr, claim the honor of being descended from the great serpent who is King of Hell, that is to say, the Devil "which is considered a very ancient and honorable connection."

The Sháhábád tradition regarding the expulsion of the Cheros is that they were conquered by the Savaras. That would be by a Dravidian tribe, and it may be that they were driven out by the irruption of the people from whom the Oráons and Rájmaháli Pahárias are descended, or by the Bhúiyas whom I also class as Dravidian and regard as identical with the tribe in Katak that are still called Suars or Savaras.

The Savaras ruled in Kíkata after the expulsion of the Cheros, it is said, from 421 to 911 of the Sáliváhana, or A. D. 500 to 990, when their Raja Phudi Chandra was expelled by Jayadeva, a descendant of Bhoja Raja, or some say by Bhoja Raja himself, who founded Bhojpúr and was the ancestor of the Bhojpúr Rajas.†

The following passages from the Rigveda, quoted in Dr. Muir's Sanskrit texts (vol. II, page 362), show that the Aryans had at a very early period come in contact with the people of Kíkata.

"What are thy cows doing among the Kíkatas.‡ They yield no milk for oblations and they heat no fire." In the commentary it is explained that Kíkata was a country inhabited by a people who were not Aryans, and the following lines are quoted from the Bhágavata Purána (1, 3, 24). Then when the Kali age has begun, a person named Buddha, son of Anjana, will be born among the Kíkatas, in order to delude the Asuras. The commentator explains "that is in the District of Gayá."§ The Kíkatas therefore were people who lived in Magadha or Bihár. The Dravidian people who are said to have expelled them from a portion of the country, are always called Siviras in the Puránas, and it is probable that the snake race, Cheros and Kols, to whom the antiquities are ascribed, were Kíkatas.

The Kíkatas according to the commentator Sáyana being destitute of faith say "what fruit will result from sacrifices, claims or oblations? rather eat and drink, for there is no other world but this"— a doctrine modern Kols decidedly subscribe to.

In his account of Gorakhpúr, Buchanan Hamilton says, there are many Nágbangsis in that district now considered Rájpúts and acknowledging the Raja of Chútiá Nágpúr as the head of the family. If this be so, these Nágbangsis are almost probably, as he is, of Kol extraction, *i. e.*, they are Múndári.

---

* According to Colonel Wilford this change was made about the time of Jarásandhu, who, he says, was the first king of Magadha before denominated Kikata.—*Asiatic Researches, vol. IX, page* 91.

† Buchanan.

‡ The Kols do not use the milk of their cows.

§ Muir's Sanskrit texts, vol. II, page 363.

It appears therefore that the Múndas, of whom I am now going to treat, were once located in Magadha, and were still there when Gautama was born, and it has been noticed that the Buddha Gayá sculptures pourtray not Aryan but Turanian or Kol features. The priests of Ceylon have a tradition, noticed by Captain Malony, that in Magadha where Gautama* was born, the art of writing was unknown. Buchanan says that the chief people, the Cheros, probably accepted his doctrine, whilst the lower orders, the Kols, rejected them, and whilst the Cheros became Aryanised, the Kols adhered to the life of freedom and impurity in which they are still found.

The Kols are according to these legends the earliest settlers in the Gangetic valley that we hear of; and they had been long established there and had attained some advance in civilization, when they were dislodged, partly by the Savaras of the bards who carried their conquests beyond the Ganges and have left us the Kocch tribe that conquered Kámrúp and are still lords of Kocch Bihár, the Rájmahál Highlanders, the Oráons, and the Bhúiyas, as the scattered remnants of the nation they founded.

Of the great Kol empire we have now no such remnants in the Bihár Division. The Chero chiefs, on being expelled from it, fell back into Palámau, whilst the chief seat of the Múnda race is now the plateau of Chútiá Nágpúr.

The people I am now about to describe comprise the Múndáris or Múndas of Chútiá Nágpúr proper, the Bhúmij of Mánbhúm, and the Larka Kols or Hos of Singbhúm. These three divisions of the race would give us about 850,000 souls, thus—

Múndáris	400,000
Hos or Larkas	150,000
Bhúmij	300,000
TOTAL ...	850,000

The Chútiá Nágpúr plateau is so connected with the great Vindhyan range, that it may be almost considered a part of it. It is, I believe, a portion of the country formerly known as the great Dandaka forest, and it was also called Jhárkhand,† the forest tract, and when the Múndáris first appeared in it, was doubtless all covered with such grand sâl timber as we still find in unreclaimed parts. It forms the heart of a territory in which the Múndáris have been settled for ages, and in which other tribes of the aborigines of India have found a secure ayslum, retreating from all sides up the courses of the rivers that have their sources on the plateau. The conquered races ascended and found refuge from the common enemy in an elevated and beautiful region that is itself a gignatic natural fortress.

The mean elevation of the plateau thus occupied is upwards of two thousand feet above the sea level. In the West, it rises to three thousand six hundred, and to the East and South, its lower steppe, from eight hundred to a thousand feet in elevation, comprises a great portion of the Mánbhúm and Singbhúm Districts. Rivers flow from it in all directions forming grand water-falls as they bound from the upper plateau to the lower levels. The whole is about fourteen thousand square miles in extent.

* Asiatic Researches, Buchanan Hamilton.

† In the fifth Report of the Select Committee it is called Jharknund, Chutea Nagpur, and Kukera. The latter is still the name of one of the Parganas. In the report it is said that it is called Nágpúr from its diamond mines. The Raja has in his possession a diamond worth about Rs. 40,000, the product of these now fabulous mines.

The central table land, on which the tribes rallied, is admirably adapted for defence. The approaches to it from the North, North-West, East, and South, are exceedingly precipitous, the paths winding up defiles which a handful of resolute men could hold against hosts of invaders. The highlands in the Western and South-Western direction stretch into Sirgúja and Jashpúr, uniting with the Vindhyan mountains in a Western direction and the Sátpúra range to the South-West. They divide the waters of the Narbadá andMahánadí, forming a covered way by which fresh accessions of cognates strengthened the growing colonies of Kols on the 'Jhárkhanda,' and thus were founded the "strongholds of the ten chiefs" referred to in the Puránas, and in Colonel Wilford's essays, as the Dasarna, or ten forest forts east of the Son.*

These Jhárkhand or Chútiá Nágpúr chiefs appear to have maintained those isolated and elevated defensive positions throughout the long series of Hindu dynasties, and came with an indifferent reputation under the Muhammadan Government, as in the report of the 'Select Committee' it is stated that the Bírbhúm District was conferred by "Jafar Khán on Asad-ulla Pathán, to guard against the incursions of the barbarous Hindus of Jhárkhand." It is curious that they should be called Hindus, but the Muhammadans probably regarded as such all who were not of their own faith. Mr. J. Grant, 'Chief Serishtadar,' writing of them in A. D. 1787, thus speaks of the country and its people. "This highland district, including Palamaw, Ramghur and Chutea Nagpur hath since the days of Ptolemy been geographically termed the three 'Bellads' or cantons in Arabic, and from which its modern appellation of Velayt may be a corruption if not derived from another root of the same language, modified to express a foreign dependent Government."†

"It is also generally described under the name of Kokera, more commonly called *Nagpore*, from the diamond mines of that place, as giving most importance to the whole country, making part of the same mountainous tract of land barren of every thing, except the most precious jewels in the world. Yet, perhaps, this portion of unfruitful country might be still more interestingly distinguished by delineating the character of its inhabitants who are undoubtedly an original savage race, differing extremely in appearance, religion, language, and manners, from the Hindu Lowlanders of Hindustan." (Vth Report, vol. 1, page 503).

From this it would certainly appear that Jhárkhand has, to a comparatively recent period, been regarded by Hindus as out of the pale of Hindustan, occupied by a people who differed from them in religion, in customs, appearance and language.

I have never found much in Múnda or Bhúmij folklore that threw light on the early history of the race. The families that rank highest among them have lost such traditions in the hazy fables which Hindus have invented for them. The lower classes, as a rule, declare themselves to be autochthones, and even the chiefs found their claims to be of noble birth on miracles that took place in the country which they call their fatherland; but in a manuscript account of the family of the Rajas of Chútiá Nágpúr I possess, it is stated that the Múndáris came to Jhárkhand, afterwards called Chútiá Nágpúr, from Pipra and Pálígarh, names that occur in the Santál traditions. It is also stated that the Múndas as well as the Oráons fought with the Lowrik Sumwara, no doubt the Lowrik

* Asiatic Researches, vol. XIV, page 384. The Son or Soane River.

† But the three Viláyats refer to Bihár, Bengal, and Orissa; not to Palámau, Chútiá Nágpúr, and Rámgarh.

Sowrik of the Oráons, whom I suppose to have been '*Saráwaks*' or Jains, and were worsted, and having to fly from their own country, they successively occupied Jaipúr, Chítor, Simaliya, Ruhidás, and at last found themselves in Jhárkhand. It is noticeable that the Ruhidás hills are said to have afforded a refuge, or temporary resting place, to the Kharwárs, the Kharriás, the Múndáris and the Oráons, but whilst the Múndáris seldom speak of Ruhidás as a place they are interested in, I have often heard them speak of it as the place that the Oráons came from. It is not, however, improbable that several tribes of aborigines may have made a stand in the Ruhidás and Kaimúr Hills at different times, before they were finally forced back into Palámau, Jhárkhand, and the Vindhyan Hills.

The Múndáris say they had no Raja when they first took up the country, now called Chútiá Nágpúr. They formed a congeries of small confederate states. Each village had its chief also called a Múnda, literally 'a head' in Sanskrit; and as a village often consisted of one family, the inhabitants were all of Múnda dignity, and hence it became a name for the whole tribe. What the original name for the tribe in their own language may have been, I do not know, but as the Múndáris on the plateau call themselves Konk Pát Múnda, Konk or Konkpát may have been a national denomination. They appear to have only one word for ruler, the term 'Gúmki,' and they apply it to every one in authority. In the Mánbhúm District, the word Múnda becomes 'Múra,' which is also Sanskrit, and has the same meaning. As these Kols have taken up the word Múnda, the Santáls have appropriated the term 'Mánjhi,' and the Bhúmij 'Sirdár.' The Múndári villages had each its staff of officers, and from the customs that still prevail in most old villages, the organization that has descended from very primitive times, appears to have been very complete.

I must now proceed to give the fable of the origin of the family of the Raja of Chútiá Nágpúr, as it is told in the family annals. We have already heard some thing of the snake race in connection with the 'Kíkatas,' but the branch of the family established in Chútiá Nágpúr, whether it came from Kíkata, or was produced in the country to which it gave that name, had its own version of the snake story.

Mythical origin of the Chútiá Nágpúr Rajas.

It is well known that Raja Janamejaya, in revenge for the death of his father, compassed the destruction of the whole of the Nág or serpent race, and prepared a 'yajñya', or great incantation service for the purpose; the total annihilation of the race was, however, prevented on the eve of its accomplishment by the interference of Astíka Muni, and amongst those that were saved was the great Nág Pundaríka.

In the 3044th year of the Kaliyug, Pundaríka Nág assumed the form of a Bráhman, and repaired to the house of a certain Bráhman of Benares, to perfect himself in a knowledge of the sacred books. The learned instructor became so pleased with his pupil, that he gave him to wife his only child, the beautiful Párvatí; but though Pundaríka had the power to assume at pleasure any form, in the same way that our vulgar devil cannot get rid of his cloven foot and some say his tail, the Nág could not divest himself of his double tongue or his foul breath, and as it was of vital importance that his wife should not discover his real character, he always slept with his back to her. However one day, or night I should say, she managed to get round him, and found out his unpleasant peculiarities, and she interrogated him sharply as to the meaning of his being

2 R

thus different from the mortals of her acquaintance, and to divert her attention, he proposed they should make together a pilgrimage to Púrí (Jagannáth). To this she gave her assent, and delighted at the prospect of visiting that fashionable watering place, she forgot the unpleasant peculiarities of her husband, and cheerfully accomplished the pilgrimage. They returned through Jhárkhand in which the Múndas and Oráons were both then established, but on reaching the hill of Sútiámba, the time arrived for her being delivered of her first child, and when the pains seized her, she remembered the forked tongue and again eagerly sought for explanation.

There is even at the present day a current belief that a woman's curiosity at such moments must at all risks be gratified, and though the result of the announcement would be the immediate separation of the immortal Pundaríka and his mortal wife, he felt himself bound to indulge her wishes, and after disclosing to her wondering ears his marvellous history, he plunged into a pool and disappeared from her sight.

Párvatí was now inconsolable at the catastrophe she had brought about by her insatiable curiosity. In the midst of her grief and remorse her child was born, but instead of rejoicing at its birth, she prepared for herself a funeral pyre and became a 'Sati.'

At this juncture a Sákadwípa Bráhman appears on the scene bearing an image the idol of the sun. He slaked his thirst at the pool, and when about to proceed on his journey, found he could not lift the idol that he had hitherto carried without difficulty, and whilst pondering on this, his eyes fell on a child lying sheltered and guarded by a great hooded snake. This was Pundaríka in his proper form protecting his child. Addressing the Bráhman, he narrated his own history and foretold that the child would become the Raja of the country to be called Nágpúr, that the Bráhman was to be his Purohit and the idol his tutelary deity. The boy, he said, was to be called Phaní-Mukuta Ráya, that is, 'the snake crowned,' and promising on his own part to return when his presence was necessary, he confided the child to the Bráhman, and again plunged into the pool and disappeared.* It is in commemoration of this event that the Raja and chief members of the Nágbangsi family always wear turbans, so arranged as to make the head dress resemble a serpent coiled round the head with its head protruding over the wearer's brow. The seal of the Maharaja and arms of the family show as a crest a cobra with a human face under its expanded hood, surrounded by all the insignia of royalty.

Near Sútiámba dwelt Madura who was Raja, or Mánki, of one of the Parhás.† To his house the Bráhman repaired with the infant, and the Mánki was easily induced to take charge of the foundling and bring it up as his own child. He had a son of the same age, and when both the boys were twelve years old, Madura convened the Parhá chiefs, and, it is said, the neighbouring Rajas, the Raja of Sirgúja and the Ditya Raja, that is, the Raja of Pátkúm who claims descent from Vikra Maditya, and it was then agreed that Phaní-Mukuta Ráya should be proclaimed Raja of Chútiá Nágpúr.

The Oráons had at this time established themselves in the North-Western part of the plateau and were present at Phaní-Mukuta Ráya's inauguration as Raja. The next

* According to the family annals, this occurred A. D. 104.

† And was also a chief of influence in the confederacy.

event recorded is the marriage of the Snake Raja with a daughter of the Sikharbhúm Raja, that is of the ancestor of the present Raja of Pachet. There was an awkward hitch when the Pachet Bráhmans asked for Phaní-Mukuta's pedigree, horoscope, and record of his birth, and the match would not have taken place, if Pundaríka had not appeared and proved to the satisfaction of the ambassadors from Sikharbhúm that the marriage proposed would be no misalliance. It is especially mentioned that the Múndas and Oráons all got drunk at the wedding and had a fight.

The "snake crowned" was acknowledged by all the Parhá chiefs on the central plateau of Chútiá Nágpúr proper, but the inhabitants of the lower steppe would have nothing to do with him. They, however, followed the lead of the highland chiefs and elected Rajas of their own, all miraculously nurtured foundlings, and all through their representatives now claiming to be Rájpúts. Thus have originated the Chiefs of what are called the five parganas of the Lohardagga District and most of the Mánbhúm zamíndárs. I only know one of them who has the sense to acknowledge his Múndárí descent, but the conclusion that they are all of that race, is forced on us by their position, their fables of origin, and the fact that they all intermarry. Some have indeed made other alliances with good Hindu families, and owe to this an improved personal appearance in the present generation. I do not, however, suppose that all the Mánbhúm zamíndárs are Kols. Some few are Súdras, some are Bágdis, and the zamíndárs of the Northern Jungle maháls are all Bhúiyas.

The place pointed out as the scene of the birth of the first Nág Raja is Pithauria, a considerable market town on the Northern face of the plateau overlooking the valley of the Damúdar in Pargana Sútiámba. Many Múndáris regard this part of the country as the cradle of the race, but it is not at present most densely populated by people of that tribe. The representatives of the Madura of the tradition are still to be found tenaciously clinging to the ancestral site and the graves of their forefathers, and, though simple peasants, enjoying considerable influence which they sustain by performing at the proper seasons the festivals that commemorate their former power. At all places in the Province of Chútiá Nágpúr that are, or have been, the head quarters of the sovereign or chief, a festival is annually solemnized in his honour called the 'Ind-parab.' Amidst great rejoicings an enormous umbrella, attached to the end of a mast some forty feet in length, is raised like a maypole by the united force of all the people that can be collected. At Sútiámba to the present day, two of these poles are annually set up, one in honour of Madura, the other to the Nágbangsi Raja, and the latter must not be moved from the ground till Madura's umbrella is well aloft.

In support of the antiquity of the Nágbangsis of Chútiá Nágpúr there is collateral evidence in the annals* of the Kharonda dependencies of the Central Provinces: Jaggannáth Deo, the last member of the Gangabangsi families who reigned there, finding himself without heirs, sent to Chútiá Nágpúr for a Nágbangsi who founded the present dynasty of Kharonda, 860 years ago.

The boy selected was a brother of the Satranjigarh chief. This was a collateral branch holding a maintenançe grant, and it can be shown that many generations of Nágbangsi Rajas had passed away before this branch of the family took root.

* Selections, Records, Government of India, No. 30, Report by Colonel Elliot.

Unfortunately as those Rajas became great potentates among Hindus, they grew to despise the impure Kols, their subjects, and as the latter were not inclined to submit quietly to degradation and were not unmindful of what the Nágbangsis owed them, they revolted against such ingratitude, and the Rajas found it necessary to seek extraneous aid to control them. Foreigners were gradually introduced to whom lands were assigned for military services, who assisted or supported the Raja in the innovations he wished to introduce, and Bràhmans were encouraged by grants of villages to settle in the country and to aid in civilizing it after their fashion. Their attempts at proselytising were not unsuccessful amongst the Múndáris. The chief men of that tribe were by degrees induced to see something very honorific and desirable in the distinction conferred by the 'poita,' the thread indicating that the wearer is a Bráhman or a Rájpút, and without altogether jilting their ancient sylvan deities, they commenced paying their addresses to the new order of gods and goddesses that the Bráhmans and their now Bráhman-ridden Rajas were endeavoring to bring into fashion, but the change did not extend to the masses generally. They saw the encroachments on their rights and liberties that were threatened, and preferred the freedom of action and license they had hitherto enjoyed. The whole body of Oráons held steadily to this view, and thus while most of the chiefs in Nágpúr and Mánbhúm adopted Bráhmanical ideas, the Oráons and bulk of the Múndáris remained in their pristine state, and though intermarriage between the two peoples was not allowed, they otherwise harmoniously amalgamated as one nation.

The system of government that obtained among the Múndas and Oráons of Chútiá Nágpúr before their policy was disturbed by the conversion of their chief may still be discerned in their existing organization. This country was divided into groups of twelve or more villages, called 'Parhás,' each under a headman, who was generally called the 'Múnda,' and though not recognized by the authorities in the political divisions of the present time, the people still acknowledge the 'Parhá' jurisdiction, and questions affecting their social relations are still adjusted in 'Parhá' conclave.* Each village had besides its establishment of hereditary public servants, and these still exist. The principal of these are the representatives of the most influential of the patriarchs. They originally formed the colony, and each is literally a pillar of the little state called 'Khúnt.' The head of one of these Khúnts or families is the chief or Múnda, of another the Páhn, or priest, and there is sometimes a third called 'Máhato,' the Múnda's deputy.

The headmen had no superior rights in the lands cultivated by other villagers, they were not landlords but chiefs, and they and the people acknowledging them held the soil they cultivated in virtue of their being the heirs of those who first utilized it, and when it became necessary to distinguish such men from cultivators of inferior title, the former were called 'Bhúinhárs,' breakers of the soil.

This is not, perhaps, the only country where we find in the cultivators the actual descendants of a primitive people who first brought the land under cultivation, but I do not know where else to look for a people who having lived under different forms of government yet link themselves with a remote antiquity by the continuous and not unsuccessful struggle they have maintained to preserve in their integrity their prescrip-

* In the Kolhán of Singbhúm, the Parhá, or as it is there called the Pirhi, system is now fully maintained; but there and in some parts of Chútiá Nágpúr proper the head of a Parhá is called a Mánki.

tive rights. Against infringement of these the Kols have in all ages protested and sometimes fought, and though in numerous instances the force of circumstances has hopelessly transferred the proprietary right from the aborigines to the zamíndár or his assign, many thousands have succeeded in retaining what has come down through their family from pre-historic times to a period when, under a law recently passed by the Bengal Government, these rights are being defined and registered, and they may look forward to their being transmitted in their integrity to their remotest posterity.

When the Múndáris and Oráons submitted to a Raja, and all were required to contribute to his maintenance, the people in each village were divided into two classes. The more privileged who retained the designation 'Bhúinhár,' had to give honorary attendance and constituted the militia of the state. The remainder supplied food and raiment, and these obligations were eventually commuted to money payment or rent, and the lands cultivated by this class were called 'Rajhas,' or rent-paying, in contradistinction to the 'Bhúinhári' which was no doubt originally rent-free. At a later period, the Raja was allowed to hold in each village a proportion of land called Manjihas, which was cultivated for his sole benefit; and the persons who cultivated this land for him or his assigns had lands allotted to them, subject to no other service and no rent, called 'béth kheta.' Besides the above, there were lands set apart for the expenses periodically incurred in the propitiation of the national and local deities, and the Kols thus provided against the dangers that threatened their gods from the impending changes of belief. The produce of the lands has never, that I am aware of, been appropriated to the service of the Hindu divinities, though the people contribute something yearly towards the public worship of 'Káli' inaugurated by the zamíndárs; if, however, the villages were all to adopt a new religion, they would doubtless assert their right to devote the assets of what may be called their church lands to the service of the newly adopted faith.

The circumstances under which the Raja's ancestor rose to power precludes his making any division of the 'Ráj.' It remains to this day an undivided estate, and the succession to it is regulated by local custom of primogeniture acknowledged under Regulation X of 1800; but as the families increased, the younger members or collateral branches were supported by maintenance grants, which lapse to the parent estate on failure of heirs male to grantee. These were among the earliest of the alienations which changed so greatly the relations between the chief and his people; the latter had agreed to serve and support him, but they were now compelled to serve and support his assigns, and soon the assigns included not only relations but the Bráhmans and mercenaries who received grants for religious or military services, and lastly foreign (all people not belonging to the province were so considered) farmers to whom leases of villages were given in supercession of the Kol headman.

Chútiá Nágpúr, as part of Bihár, was ceded to the British Government in A. D. 1765;* but the earliest arrangement with the Raja of which I find any record occurred in

* It is recorded in the *Akbarnámah* that about the year 993 A. H. (1585 A. D.), Mádhú Singh, Zamíndár of Kokrah, *i. e.*, Chútiá Nágpúr, was forced to submit to Shahbáz Khán, one of Akbar's Generals, and a few years afterwards or in 1591, Mádhú Singh and Lakhmí Rái of Kokrah served with the Emperor's army under Mán Singh in effecting the conquest of Orissa. According to the local chronicle Mádhú Singh, or as he is there called Madhúkar Sháh was the 43rd of the Nágbangsí line of Rajas; but it is recorded in the same history that the 41st Raja Bairí Sál first submitted to Delhi, and his successor Durjun Sál failing to pay the tribute agreed upon, was attacked by Ibráhím Khán, taken prisoner, and carried to Delhi. This event is noted in the Memoirs of Jahángír, and took place in 1615 A. D.

A. D. 1772, when it is stated that the chief appeared before Captain Camac commanding a force in Palámau, and after exchange of turbans* with the Company's representative, duly acknowledged himself a vassal of that great power, gave as tribute Rs. 3,000 and agreed to do service against the Mahrattas. The oldest settlement deed is dated 1179 Fasli, by which Raja Dripnáth Sahi of Khúkhra, *alias* Nágpúr, agreed to pay 12,000 rupees, *viz.*, *mál* or rent 6,000 rupees, *nazránah* or tribute, 6,000. For some years after this, the Raja was allowed to administer the territory as the chief of a tributary mahál, but in 1816 or 1817, it was found necessary to deprive him of magisterial powers; the estate was placed under the Magistrate of Rámgarh, who held Court alternately at Sherghátí and Chatra. Natives of Bihár who were considered foreigners in Chútiá Nágpúr were sent into the country as Police officers, and occasionally the Názir of the Rámgarh Magistrate's Court was deputed with extraordinary powers to inspect and report on the administration.

Arrangments for Government made by the English.

Up to A. D. 1831, when the most serious revolt of the Kols of Chútiá Nágpúr occurred, there can be no doubt that the changes of government which had taken place were not beneficial to them. They were neglected by their new masters, oppressed by aliens and deprived of the means they had formerly possessed of obtaining redress through their own chief. The Raja, by no means satisfied at his own loss of dignity and authority, gave but surly answers to complainants who came before him. The Darogahs (Native Police officers), the highest resident officials under the British Government, declared it was not competent to them to decide on the grievances that then most harassed the Kols; these were complaints, that they had been dispossessed by foreigners, Muhammadans, Sikhs, and others, who had obtained from the sub-proprietors farms of the Kol villages over the heads of the Kol headman; but it often happened that the unfortunate Kol who with difficulty made his way to the far off station found the tables turned on him when he got there. A host of witnesses in the pay of the opposite party were already there prepared to prove "that he had not only no rights in the land, but was a turbulent rebel besides."

Major Roughsedge, the first Political Agent for the South-Western Frontier, notices a case of this kind that occurred in A. D. 1811. Some disturbances had broken out in Tamárh, and troops were sent there, but the officer in command reported that they arose entirely from the oppression practised by the Tamárh Raja on one of his vassals named Raghunáth Singh, and on this the officer was allowed to enter into negotiation with the malcontents, who hoping for redress returned to their allegiance. In this hope Raghunáth Singh went to the court then sitting at Chatra.† "The evidence kept in readiness against him by the Tamárh zamíndár caused his committal to the Court of Circuit, and the result was his condemnation to transportation or imprisonment for life."

For years after this event, Tamárh continued in a disorganized state, and in 1820, serious disturbances broke out, and two Kols, Rudu and Kantu, at the head of three hundred followers for a long time defied the

Disturbances.

* In regard to this exchange of turbans, the family annals tell a strange tale. In the Raja's turban were some very valuable diamonds, which it is insinuated had excited the cupidity of Captain Camac. The proposal for the exchange emanated, it is said, from him. He declared it was the English method of swearing eternal friendship, but the Captain had no diamonds in his head dress, and the Raja evidently concluded that he had been rather 'done' by the Company's Officer.

† Letter from Major Roughsedge to the Magistrate of Rámgarh.

authorities, and were not reduced till military operations on an extensive scale were undertaken against them.

Insurrection, 1831-32.

The Kol insurrection of 1831, though no doubt only the bursting forth of a fire that had long been smouldering, was fanned into flame by the following little episode:—

The brother of the Mahárája and holder of one of the maintenance grants which comprised Sonpúr, a pargana in the Southern portion of the estate, gave farms of some of the villages over the heads of the Mánkis and Múndas to certain Muhammadans, Sikhs, and others who had sought and obtained his favor. Twelve villages that had belonged to Singrai Mánki were thus given to the Sikhs, and not only was the Mánki dispossessed, but two of his sisters were seduced or ravished by these hated foreigners. A similar complaint was made against the Muhammadan farmers. One of them had acted very oppressively towards a Múnda of Bandgáon in Singbhúm and, it was said, had abducted and dishonored the Múnda's wife. These men and some other Mánkis of Sonpúr who were equally dissatisfied invited all the Kols of Sonpúr, Tamárh, and Bandgáon, to assemble at the village of Lankah in Tamárh. The meeting took place and the conveners addressed the assemblage. "The Patháns and the Singhs (Sikhs)," they said, "have dishonored us; the Kunwar Harnáth Singh has forcibly deprived us of our villages, which he has given to the Singhs. Our lives are no longer of value. We are all brethren, let us act together."

It was agreed that the wrongs inflicted on them could no longer be tolerated. They would at once "commence* to burn, plunder, murder, and eat."

This was no vain threat. A few days after the meeting, on the 11th December, 1831, a raid was made on the village of Kamrang held in farm by a Muhammad Alí Náik, and two hundred head of cattle carried off. On the 20th December, a number of villages bordering on Singbhúm held in farm by Hari Singh and Diyál Singh, Sikhs, were plundered and burned by a body of 700 Kols under Súrga, the aggrieved Múnda of Singbhúm, Singrai Mánki, and others, and one of the Sikhs was wounded. These villages formed part of the estate from which Singrai had been ejected. On the 25th December, several villages held in farm by Káli Khán and Saifullah Khán were plundered and burned, and one of the Khán's men was thrown into the fire. On the 2nd January, 1832, Kamrang was again attacked, and next day they sacked Jafar Alí's village and murdered him and ten of his people including the unfortunate Kol female whom he had seduced. The Názir of the Sherghátí court now appeared on the scene, and sent to the Kols to say that if they would desist from disturbing the peace of the country, their lands would be restored to them. They replied, they would attend to no orders but those that emanated from the Mahárája of Chútiá Nágpúr; that they would not leave a single foreign farmer alive; they would destroy every village in Sonpúr Pargana, even Govindpúr where Harnáth Sáhi resided, and then they would wash their weapons in the river Káro that flows by his house!

In the meantime the arrows† of war were being circulated through the country like the fiery cross, and by the middle of January the Múndáris and Oráons had all entered

---

* Deposition of Singrai Mánki.

† An arrow passed from village to village is the summons to arm, and sent to any one in authority it is an open declaration of war. The Hos of the Bhor Pír in Singbhúm thus avowed their intention to espouse the cause of the dethroned Raja of Porahát in 1857, and summoned their brethren.

with zeal into the spirit of the insurrection. The country appears to have been entirely unprepared for such an event, troops there were none, the police stations were generally abandoned, and even the hereditary zamíndárs, connections of the Raja's, sought safety in flight. In every pargana the villages in which 'Sads' (Hindus) resided were destroyed, and all 'Dikos' (foreigners) who fell into the hands of the insurgents were murdered. The subordinate* Rajas of Rahe, Búndú, Tamárh, Barwa, though neither Sads nor Dikos, narrowly escaped with their lives, when those places were all sacked and destroyed.

With the exception of the force from Singbhúm that came to the aid of the insurgents and were the most formidable division of the rebel army, it does not appear that the Kols in their work of destruction moved far from their own homesteads, as the 'Sad' portion of each village was plundered and burned by the Kols of that or neighbouring villages. The murders were most numerous in the Doísa and Korámbe Parganas, as the 'Sads' there were unprepared for the attack, and none were spared that fell into the hands of the insurgents.

Troops to put down the insurrection were of course being collected from different points and were gradually being concentrated in the disturbed district; but before military operations could be undertaken, the insurgents had done all that they had threatened to do and might, though it is not again mentioned, have washed their weapons in the Káro and retired. Captain (the late Sir Thomas) Wilkinson reached Pithauria, which as I have already stated is on the brink of the northern face of the plateau, about the middle of January, and the work of incendiarism was then in full blaze.

Captain Wilkinson was without sufficient force to penetrate far into the disturbed districts, but he lost no time in compelling the villages near Pithauria to submit. This was not done without fighting, and, indeed, the insurgents on more than one occasion threatened his position, advancing against it with a force estimated at about 3,000 fighting men, but they appear to have been easily repulsed. The inhabitants of the large village of Nagrí between Ránchi and Pithauria had been particularly active in the work of destruction, and had avowed their determination to fight to the last; but an expedition was sent specially against them with the unequivocal instructions "attack, slay and destroy," and to such orders energetically carried out, the Nagrí heroes speedily succumbed. This is a very primitive Oráon village which up to the present time retains all the old institutions; the bachelors hall with the banners, yak's tails, trumpets, and drums, &c., and the dancing arena in front where often songs are sung that remind the young men how their fathers 'went out' in 1832. The subjugation of Nagrí was followed by the submission of most of the northern villages, but the Oráons of the west and Múndáris of the centre and the south showed no inclination to lay down their arms, and the insurrection now spread into Palámau where it was taken up by the Kharwárs, merely it would seem for the love of the thing. It grew serious, however, and a squadron of cavalry making its way to Chútiá Nágpúr through that pargana found itself so hotly opposed in one of the hill passes, that the officer in command deemed it necessary to make a retrogade movement and await reinforcements.

---

* Lál Jitnáth Sáhi of Ginjo and Kapilnáth of Salgi are prominently noticed as honorable exceptions. They held to their respective villages, and repulsed several attacks made on them.

Not till the middle of February were the troops in a position to operate on a scale adequate to the occasion. Then three columns were formed to start simultaneously from three points* in the northern part of the plateau, and sweep the country in parallel lines as they moved from north to south.

The right and centre columns met with little opposition, the heads of villages submitting as they advanced, but the left column when they reached Sonpúr found that the Kols had abandoned their villages, and with their flocks and herds and families had taken refuge in the hills. In attempting to dislodge them, the troops, especially a detachment of the 3rd Light Cavalry, suffered some loss. The columns, however, were now concentrated in the south. Bindrai Mánki, Singrai's brother, and Súrga, the heroes of the episode, held out to the last, but on the 19th March, 1832, these leaders came into camp and surrendered to the Commissioner, the remaining sirdárs all then tendered their submission, and the insurrection was at an end.

Great changes in the administration followed this insurrection. The disturbed districts and jungle mahāls with the dependent tributary mahāls were organized as a non-regulation province under the name of the South-Western Frontier Agency; the system of zamíndárí police, under which authority was restored to the chiefs to whom the people had been accustomed to look for its exercise, was established in Chútiá Nágpúr; the border Mánkis whose dispossession from their tenures was the main cause of the insurrection, were reinstated, and the zamíndárs were deprived of the power of ousting them without the orders of the European officer now placed at the head of the district. They obtained title deeds constituting them ghátwáls, or guardians of the passes, and officers of police, and that position they still hold.

The Bhúmij.

The insurrection of Chútiá Nágpúr and Palámau was speedily followed by disturbances in the southern portion of the Mánbhúm District in which the Bhúmij Kols were the chief actors.

Near the boundary of Chútiá Nágpúr, the term Bhúmij as applied to this class is seldom used. The Kols who form the bulk of the population call themselves Múndas or, as the name is usually pronounced in Mánbhúm, Múras. The title Bhúmij, 'the children of the soil,' is given to the members of the tribe settled further east; but, generally, if asked to what class or caste they belong, they say 'Sirdár.' In Dhalbhúm the Bhúmij call themselves, and are called by the Singbhúm Kols, 'Matkúm.'

Geographical distribution.

The Bhúmij are, no doubt, the original inhabitants of Dhalbhúm, Baráhbhúm, Pátkúm, Bágmúndí, and still form the bulk of the population in those and adjoining estates. They may be described roughly as being chiefly located in the country between the Kasai and Subarnarekhá rivers. They had formerly large settlements to the north of the former river, but they were dislodged by Aryans, who as Hindus of the Kúrmí caste now occupy their old village sites. The Bhúmij have no traditions of their own origin, generally asserting that they were produced where they are found; but some who dwell in the vicinity of old Jain temples declare that the founders of the temples preceded them; though they can tell us nothing of those founders, nor of the architects of the ruined and deserted Hindu temples existing as additional marks of a prior occupation of the country by a more civilized people.

* Tiko, Churia, Pithauria.

I have elsewhere* noted that these Bhúmij were probably the 'Vajra Bhúmi' (the terrible indigénes) who are described as abusing, beating, shooting arrows at, and baiting with dogs, the great Saint Vira, the twenty-fourth Jina or Tirthankara of the Jains, an account of whom will be found in Volume IX of the Asiatic Researches.

Chuárs.

The Bhúmij of the Jungle Mahâls were once, under the nick-name 'Chuár,' the terror of the surrounding districts, and their various outbreaks were called 'Chuárís.' On several occasions since they came under the British rule, they have shown how readily a Chuárí may be improvised on very slight provocation. I do not know that on any occasion they rose like the Múndáris simply to redress their own wrongs. It was sometimes in support of a turbulent chief ambitious of obtaining power to which according to the courts of law he was not entitled, and it was sometimes to oppose the Government in a policy that they did not approve, though they may have had very little personal interest in the matter.

Recent disturbances.

Thus in the year A. D. 1798, when the Pachet estate was sold for arrears of revenue they rose and violently disturbed the peace of the country till the sale was cancelled. After hostilities had continued for some time, in reply to a very pacific message sent to them by the officer commanding the force, they asked if the Government were going to sell any more estates? I do not think that the settlement of any one of the Bhúmij Jungle Mahâls was effected without a fight. In Dhalbhúm the Raja resisted the interference of the British power, and the Government set up a rival, but after various failures to establish his authority, they set him aside and made terms with the rebel. In Baráhbhúm, there was at one time a disputed succession. The courts decided that the eldest born of Raja Viviká Naráin, though the son of the second wife, should succeed in preference to the son of the first wife, the Pát Rání. The Bhúmij did not approve of the decision, and it was found necessary to send a military force to carry it out. This was the origin of the last disturbance known as Gangá Naráin's rebellion, which broke out in 1832.†

Lakhman, the son of the Pát Rání alluded to above, continuing to oppose his brother, was arrested, and died in jail leaving a son Gangá Naráin.

On the death of Raja Raghunáth Singh, he also was succeeded by the son of his second Rání, who was declared by the Sudder Court to be heir in opposition to a claim again set up by Mádhab Singh, the younger son, but the son of the Pát Rání; but failing in his suit, Mádhab Singh resigned himself to his fate and was consoled by being appointed díwán, or prime minister, to his brother. In this capacity he made himself thoroughly unpopular, more especially by becoming an usurious money-lender and extortionate grain-dealer, and soon Gangá Naráin found that in opposing a man so detested, a majority of the people would side with him. Accordingly in the month of April 1832, he, at the head of a large force of ghátwáls, made an attack on Mádhab Singh and slew him. This foul crime was committed with great deliberation, cunning, and cruelty. Mádhab was seized and carried off to the hills to be sacrificed. Gangá Naráin himself first smote him with his battle axe, then each Sirdár Ghátwál was compelled

* Journal, Asiatic Society, Bengal, for 1866, p. 186, Note on Mánbhúm.

† Decisions of the law courts in succession cases have on other occasions been the cause of disturbances in the Jungle and Tributary Mahâls. The last affair of the kind was in 1868, when the Hill Bhúiyas of Keonjhur revolted against their present chief on the ground that he was not of pure blood or born in lawful wedlock. In determining what the local custom is in such cases, the views of the people should always be ascertained.

to discharge an arrow at him, and thus all the leading Ghátwáls became implicated in the plot. A system of plundering was then commenced, which soon drew to his standard all the 'chuárs,' that is all the Bhúmij of Baráhbhúm and adjoining estates. He attacked Baráhbazár where the Raja lived, burned the Munsiff's (Native Civil Judge) cutcherry and the police station from which the police had fled, but three unfortunate peons (runners) of the Munsiff's Court were caught and killed.

The officials and police fell back on Bardwán, and for some time Gangá Naráin had the country at his mercy; and he sacked every place worth plundering; but in November following a force was collected, consisting of three regiments of Native Infantry and eight guns, and military operations against the insurgents commenced. They were soon driven to take refuge in the hills, but being pressed there also, Gangá Naráin fled into Singbhúm and endeavoured to enlist in his favor the reputed invincible and irrepressible Larkás; they were just then at issue with one of the chiefs who claimed supremacy over a portion of them, the Thákur of Kharsáwán, and though they were not unwilling to join in the row, they wished before they committed themselves to Gangá Naráin's leadership to test his capacity to lead. They, therefore, demanded that he should, in the first place, make an attack on the fort of the Thákur of Kharsáwán. In complying with this request he was killed, and the Thákur had the pleasure of sending his head to Captain Wilkinson, with a letter quite in the style of Falstaff when after the battle near Shrewsbury, he said, "there is Percy. If your father will do me any honor so; if not, let him kill the next Percy himself. I look to be either Earl or Duke, I can assure you."

Traditions.

I have not been able to discover that the Bhúmij possess any independent traditions of migrations. Those who live in proximity to Chútiá Nágpúr recognise no distinction between themselves and the Múndas. They intermarry and associate and coalesce in all matters indicating identity of race, for, though it may be said that they are not much troubled with caste prejudices, there is no portion of the old Indian population which is quite free from it. The Bhúmij further east have become too Hinduized to acknowledge the relationship. The Dhalbhúm Bhúmij consider themselves autochthones, and will not admit that they are in any way connected with the Múndas, Hos, or Santáls. It is pretty certain that the zamíndárs of all these estates are of the same race as their people, though the only man among them whom I found sensible enough to acknowledge this, was the Raja of Bágmúndí; the others all call themselves Kshatryas or Rájpúts, but they are not acknowledged as such by any true scion of the illustrious stock. In claiming to be Rájpúts they do not attempt to connect themselves with any of the recognized families of the tribe, but each family has its own special legend of miraculous production.

The family legend of the Raja of Baráhbhúm may be given as a specimen of their skill in making pedigrees.

Legend of the Baráhbhúm family.

"Nath Varaha and Késvaraha, two brothers, quarrelled with their father, the Raja of Virat, and settled in the court of Vikramaditya. (This has some connection with the tradition of the adjoining estate Pátkúm, the Raja of which claims descent from Vikramaditya.) Kés the younger was sawn into two pieces, and with his blood Vikram gave a 'tíká'* to the eldest and a pair of

* Mark on the forehead.

umbrellas, and told him that all the country he could ride round in a day and night should be his. Nath mounted his steed and accomplished a circuit of eight 'yojanas,' whatever that may be, within the time specified, and a precious stiff line of country he took in riding round what is now Baráhbhúm, but it must be all true as the print of his horse's hoofs are still visible on the southern slopes of the hills.

With one or two exceptions all the Ghátwáls (captains of the border and their men) of the Bhúmij part of the Mánbhúm and Singbhúm Districts are Bhúmij, this is a sure indication of their being the earliest settlers. They were the people (like the Múndári Bhúinhárs in Chútiá Nágpúr, the Bhúiyas in Bonai, Gángpúr, Keonjhur, &c., Gonds in Sirgúja and Udaipúr) to whom the defence of the country was entrusted The Bhúmij Ghátwáls in Mánbhúm have now after all their escapades settled down steadily to work as guardians of the peace.

Dhalbhúm.

The Raja of the extensive zamíndárí of Dhalbhúm is no doubt of Bhúmij extraction, but for him the Herald's college of the period failed to manipulate a Rájpút descent. His ancestor was a washerman, who afforded refuge to the Goddess Kálí when, as Rankini, she fled from a demon in Pachet. The Goddess, in gratitude, gave the washerman a young Bráhmaní, a ward of her own, to wife, and the Rajas of Dhalbhúm are the descendants of this union. The origin of the story appears to be that a Bhúmij chief of Dhalbhúm, probably, at the instigation of a Bráhman stole from its shrine in Pachet an image of Rankini and set it up as his own tutelary deity. The shrine from which the image was abstracted is shown at the village of Para near Parúlia in Mánbhúm, and it became the popular object of worship in Dhalbhúm by all classes of the people there. Rankini especially rejoiced in human sacrifices. It is freely admitted that in former years children were frequently kidnapped and sacrificed at her shrine, and it cannot be very positively asserted that the practice of offering such victims has long been discontinued.

At the shrine of this goddess a very cruel scene was enacted every year till 1865, when with the concurrence of the zamíndár it was put a stop to. It was called the 'Bindaparab', and Ganganárain probably had it in his mind when he so cruelly disposed of Mádhab Singh.

Binda parab.

At this parab two male buffaloes are driven into a small enclosure, and on a raised stage adjoining and overlooking it, the Raja and suite take up their position. After some ceremonies the Raja and his Purohit'* discharge arrows at the buffaloes, others follow their example, and the tormented and enraged beasts fall to and gore each other whilst arrow after arrow is discharged. When the animals are past doing very much mischief, the people rush in and hack at them with battle axes till they are dead. The Santáls and wild Kharriás, it is said, took great delight in this festival, but I have not heard a murmur at its discontinuance, and this shows it had no great hold on the minds of the people.

Tenures.

Many of the Bhúmij tribe are well off. Some of them who are Sirdár Ghátwáls are in virtue of their office proprietors of estates comprising each from one to twenty manors, but as the most substantial tenants under them are also hereditary Ghátwáls, rendering service and paying besides but a

* Family priest.

very low fixed rent, these Ghátwálí estates are not so valuable to the proprietor as villages on the ordinary tenure would be.

The Bhúmij live in commodious, well-built houses, and have about them all the comforts to which the better class of cultivators in Bengal are accustomed. Those who live quite amongst the Bengalis have retained very few of their ancient customs; none perhaps, except the great national amusement, the gay meetings for dance and song both at their villages and at 'yátras', which are characteristic of all Kols.

Physical traits.

In appearance they are inferior to the Hos of Singbhúm and to the best of the Múndas of Chútiá Nágpúr. They are short of stature but strongly built, and like the Santáls rather inclined to fleshiness. In complexion they are variable, like the Múndas ranging from a dark chocolate to a light brown color; they observe many of the Hindu festivals but retain their sacred groves in which they still sacrifice to the old Gods. They have generally left off eating cow's flesh in which their unreformed brethren in Singbhúm and Chútiá Nágpúr indulge, but eat fowls.

The Bhúmij have, in a great degree, lost the simplicity and truthfulness of character for which their cognates are generally distinguished. They have acquired from the Bengali Hindus the propensity to lie, but they have not the same assurance or powers of invention, and their lies are so transparent, that they are easily detected.

Mr. Ball of the Geological Survey informs me that he found in the Bhúmij country of Dhalbhúm some remains of an ancient settlement which was said to have been the abode of a Raja who had two tongues. This is the only tradition I have heard directly connecting the Bhúmij with the snake race, the Nágbangsí,* but it is an independent testimony to the wide-spread influence of that mysterious people.

In the religion of the Kols there are no traces of snake worship, if it be not hidden in their name for the rainbow 'Lúrbeng,' which means 'a serpent.' I have noticed, however, the occurrence in Chútiá Nágpúr of people apparently allied to the Kols who call themselves Nágbangsís, though not allied to the Nágbangsí family of Chútiá Nágpúr, and the Nágesars, also called Kisáns, and among the old sculptures that are found in the country are images of serpents or snakes which must have been intended for altar pieces.

SECTION 4.—THE HO OR LARKA KOLS.

Geographical distribution.

The district of Singbhúm in which the Ho or Larka Kols are located lies to the south-east of Chútiá Nágpúr proper, or between 22° and 23° of north latitude, and 86°53′ and 85°-2′ of east longitude. It measures 124 miles in extreme length from east to west, and 64 miles in its greatest breadth from north to south. The total area is by survey 4503 square miles; of this 1905 square miles constitute the exclusively Ho territory known as the Kolhán. The most fertile and highly cultivated portion of this tract surrounds the station of Chaibása at a general level of seven hundred and fifty feet above the sea, and here are massed about two-thirds of the Kolhán population. To the south of this extending to the Baitarní river, the general level rises to upwards of 1000 feet, and the Kols of this plateau are less civilized and more turbulent than those of the lower

* Who, till they became mortals, had forked tongues like serpents.

steppe. The whole district is undulating, traversed by dykes of trap which rise in rugged masses of broken up rock, and the views are on all sides bounded by ranges of hills rising to 2900 feet. To the south-west bordering on Chútiá Nágpúr is a mountainous tract of vast extent sparsely inhabited by the wildest of the Kols, this, however, appears to be the region from which they first descended into the Singbhúm plains. Saranda bordering on Gángpúr at the extreme south-west of the district is called 'Saranda of the seven hundred hills.' It is a mass of mountains which rise to the height of 3500 feet, and contains but a few poor hamlets nestled in deep valleys belonging for the most part to a very unreclaimed tribe of Kols. The inhabitants of the western hills bordering on Chútiá Nágpúr generally retain the name of Múndas, and connect themselves rather with the people of Chútiá Nágpúr than with the Hos of Singbhúm.

Traditions.

The Hos appear to have no traditions of origin or migrations that throw much light on their history. They generally admit that they are of the same family as the Múndas, and that they came from Chútiá Nágpúr. The Oráons sometimes say that the exodus of the Hos was caused by *their* invasion, but I cannot believe that the Hos could ever have given way to so inferior a race, and the tradition usually received is that the Oráons made friends with the Múndas and were allowed to occupy peaceably the north-western corner of the plateau where the former apparently had never taken root. The Hos are the only branch of the Kols that have preserved a national appellation. The Múndas of Chútiá Nágpúr are sometimes called Kokpát*, or Konkpát, Múndas, and that may be a national word, but 'Ho' 'Hore' or 'Horo' means in their own language 'man', and they are not the only people that apply to themselves exclusively the word used in their language to distinguish human beings from brutes. They probably left Chútiá Nágpúr before their brethren there had assumed the Sanskrit word Múndá as their distinctive name, taking with them their old constitution of confederate village communities under hereditary head men, which system they have retained to the present day; but they did not find in Singbhúm an unoccupied country. It is admitted on all sides that one part of it was in possession of the Bhúiyas and another held by the people who have left many monuments of their ingenuity and piety in the adjoining district of Mánbhúm, and who were certainly the earliest Aryan settlers in this part of India, the 'Saráwaks' or 'Jains.' The former were driven from their possessions in what is now the Kolhán, and fell back into Porahát. What became of the Jains we know not, they have left their marks in Dhalbhúm and the eastern and north-eastern quarters of the district; and it is not improbable that the Sudras, Goálas and Kúrmís now settled in Porahát, Kharsáwán, Saráikela and Dhalbhúm may be remnants of the colonies they founded, but it is also probable that many were absorbed into the family that conquered them, and this may account for the greater beauty of the Hos as compared with other Kols, and for their having in use a number of common vocables of Sanskrit origin, though they insulated themselves as much as possible, despised the Hindus, and for a long time had little or no intercourse with them. A very intelligent observer, Mr. Ball of the Geological Survey,

Mines.

informs me that local tradition ascribes to the Jains all the copper mining works, the traces of which are seen in Saráikela and Dhalbhúm. The present population know nothing of the art, but the Jains appear

* Perhaps the name sometimes given to the country 'Kokera' may have some connection with Kokpát.

to have fully understood it, and English speculators have found to their cost that the operations of the old miners were thoroughly exhaustive.

It is probable that the chief who was called Raja of Singbhúm and his brethren were originally more intimately connected with the Dravidian Bhúiya tribe than with the other races that make up the score of the population. The military force on which the Raja chiefly depended were Bhúiyas; his tutelary deity, the Pawri Devi,* was a Bhúiya divinity, corresponding with the Thákuráni Mái of the Keonjhur Bhúiyas; and the tradition regarding the founder of this family is that he was as a boy discovered in a hollow tree which a Bhúiya forester was cutting down. But the Singh family legend is somewhat different. They claim to be, and are by noble families now admitted to be, Kshatryas of true blood. Their ancestor came as a knight-errant from Márwár, a very Jain country now, whatever it may have been in those days, and was adopted by the Bhúiyas; but a dispute subsequently arose between the Singhs and the Bhúiyas, the former coalesced with the Kols; and when with their assistance they had put down the Bhúiya revolt, they claimed supremacy over both tribes.

Family legends.

According to the annals fabricated by Bráhmans in glorification of the Singh family, the Hos first appeared in Singbhúm as part of a marriage procession '*barát*' with a bride from Nágpúr for the Singh Raja, but however they came, they obtained possession of the best part of the country and have never yielded an inch of the territory they then appropriated. Ethnologically their position is singular and interesting; speaking themselves the Kol language only, they occupy a basin whose barrier of hills restrains the flow and blending together of the three great Sanskrit derivatives Hindí, Bengali, and Uriya, which but for this obstacle of an insulated language would have found a trijunction boundary point in the centre of Singbhúm. It is generally supposed that that name was given to the country from the patronymic of the chiefs, but without propounding anything very extravagant, it is just as likely that it is derived from their name for God, the Creator, Singbonga.

The Singbhúm Rájpút chiefs have been known to the officers of the British Government since A. D. 1803. In that year, the Marquis Wellesley, Governor-General, caused friendly communications to be addressed to Kunwar Abhirám Singh, ancestor of the present Raja of Saráikelá, in regard to the assistance he was invited to render and which he promised to render in the prosecution of the war against Maharaja Rághojí Bhonsla. The Kunwar is assured that the British Government will always respect his rights to hold his territory free of rent. In no treaty that I have ever seen is there any mention of a cession of Singbhúm. The Saráikelá chief was communicated with, because his territory adjoined the Jungle Mahals then under the Company; but between British officials and the people of the Kolhán there does not appear to have been any intercourse previous to the year 1819. Of the interior of their country, for years after the acquisition of all the surrounding districts, nothing whatever was known. The Hos would allow no strangers to settle in or even to pass through the Kolhán, and pilgrims to Jagannáth had to make a circuit of several days journey to avoid it. In March 1819, the Political

Intercourse with the British Government.

* A corruption of Pahárí Deví, 'the Hill Goddess.'

Agent, Major Roughsedge, directed his Assistant to proceed to Porahát to negociate a settlement with its chief, who as the head of this family of chiefs was called Raja of Singbhúm. The officer was instructed to collect all possible information regarding the country, and "*especially of the extraordinary race called Larkas.*" The Assistant, however, did not succeed in penetrating so far into the interior as to come in contact with them. Writing of them in the following year, Major Roughsedge says, "The Raja and Zamíndárs of Singbhúm who are in attendance on me have so formidable an opinion of the power and ferocity of these savages that, notwithstanding the considerable force under my command, they are evidently much alarmed, and have made a formal protest against the danger of the march.

Attempts to subjugate them.

The chiefs who thus trembled at the thought of penetrating into the country of the Larkas were at that time pressing on the Agent their claims to supremacy in the Kolhán, and asserting that the Kols were their subjects in rebellion, urging our Government to attack them and force them to return to their allegiance; but they admitted that for more than fifty years they had been unable to exercise any control over them, and it really appears quite an open question whether the Kols were ever really subject to them or not. Old Kols have told me that they honored and respected the Singh chiefs, but regarded them till they quarrelled rather as friends and *allies* than as rulers; but if they ever were subjects, they had achieved their liberty in various hard fought fields, and their autonomy might have been respected. Three formidable but abortive attempts to subjugate them are noted in Major Rougsedge's dispatches, one made by Dripnáth Sáhi, the grandfather of the present Raja of Chútiá Nágpúr at the head of more than 20,000 men assisted by the troops of the Raja of Singbhúm; the second by Raja Jagannáth Sáhi of Chútiá Nágpúr with almost an equal force in A. D. 1770, and a third in 1800, an invasion from the Mohurbhanj (Mayurbhanj) side headed by a Gond chief called the Mahápáter of Bámanghátí. On the first of these occasions the Larkas drove the Nágpúr men out of Singbhúm with immense slaughter. The scene of the second battle, the centre of an extensive and elevated plain, was pointed out to Major Roughsedge by an eye witness, who told him that the action was fought at noon-day in the month of May, when the heat must have been frightful. The Raja's troops succumbed to the first onslaught of the Larkas, many hundreds were slaughtered on the battle field, and many more were killed or died from thirst in the retreat, the Larkas pursuing them for ten miles till the fugitives had surmounted the steep ascent into their own country.

It appears that after these attacks on their independence, the Larkas retaliated on all the border villages of neighbouring states. Sonpúr, Belsia, and Basia, in Chútiá Nágpúr, were ravaged by them for several years and whole villages depopulated. They also laid waste the adjoining portion of Gángpúr, Bonai, Keonjhur, and Mohurbhanj, but some of the raids on the Southern districts, were undoubtedly instigated by the Singbhúm Raja. It was usual indeed for these chiefs, when they wished to annoy a neighbour, to incite the Kols to make a raid on him, and these were, I think, the only invitations of the Singbhúm chiefs that they ever attended to. Whenever there was a row, they eagerly entered into it, and all malcontents invariably sought their assistance.

Major Roughsedge was particularly struck with the fine physique and manly independent bearing of the men of the first deputation that waited on him. They entered his tent, and after admiring it a little, it suddenly occurred to them that it was a convenient place for a siesta, so stretching themselves at full length on the carpets, they coolly composed themselves to sleep! Of their appearance he says they were as much superior in size and form to their brethren of Chútiá Nágpúr "as wild buffaloes to the village herds."

Major Roughsedge at the head of his battalion of Artillery, Cavalry, and Infantry entered their country with the avowed object of compelling them to submit to the Rajas who claimed their allegiance, but he did his best to conciliate them and was at first in hopes he had succeeded, but apparently they had made up their minds to employ against him the tactics which had been so successful in their encounters with the Nágpúr armies. He was allowed to advance unmolested into the heart of their territory and to take up a position among their finest villages, at Chaibása on the Roro River, near the present station of that name. Here some camp followers were, in sight of the camp, attacked by a body of armed Larkas, one killed and others wounded, and the Larkas, after this feat, were seen moving away in the direction of the hills, but the pickets and a troop of cavalry under command of Lieutenant Maitland, were sent out to intercept them. The result I will give, nearly in Major Roughsedge's own words. Lieutenant Maitland making a sweep so as to cut off the retreat of the Larka party, they at once assailed him with a flight of arrows, but finding they made no impression with these weapons, "these savages, with a degree of rashness and hardihood scarcely credible, met the charge of the troop half way in an open plain, battle axe in hand." The result was of course a terrible slaughter of the unfortunate Kols, not more than half the party effecting their escape to the hills.

"Lieutenant Maitland now moved rapidly towards the village where the grass cutter had been killed and found standing near the corpse and prepared for action, a second party of 60 men who behaved with still greater desperation, rushing at the troop and striking like furies at both horses and men until the whole were sabred. They directed their attack chiefly at the horses killing two and wounding several; only two suwárs were wounded".

That evening Major Roughsedge found his rear threatened and mails intercepted, and sent a strong party out next day to attack a body of Larkas assembled in arms at the village of Gutiálor. Lieutenant Maitland, the officer in command, found a host in arms ready to oppose him, and on approaching the village was received with repeated discharges of arrows, which caused him considerable loss. To drive them from the shelter afforded by the enclosures he set fire to the village, but still there was an obstinate resistance and numbers were slaughtered before they could be induced to lay down their arms and accept quarter. The officer himself narrowly escaped death in a personal conflict with a Larka.

In the above and other encounters the Larkas suffered greatly; the conclusion dawned on them that they were no longer invincible, and to avoid further devastation of their villages, the whole of the Northern Pírs submitted and entered into engagements to acknowledge and pay tribute to the Raja of Singbhúm. But Major Roughsedge had yet to meet the still fiercer Kols of the Southern Pírs, and in his progress towards Sambhalpúr he had to fight every inch of his way out of Singbhúm leaving them unsubdued. On his quitting the district, a war broke out between the Larkas who had

2 W

submitted and those who had not. One hundred well-armed Hindustani irregulars under a Native Officer were sent by the Agent to the support of the Raja and his allies of the Northern Pírs, and this for a time gave them the advantage, but the Súbadár, having been unfortunately induced to enter the Kolhán to assist in levying a contribution, was attacked and he and most of his party cut up. The Kols then advanced on a small fort, in which the remainder of the Hindustanis sought shelter; they were driven out of the enclosure and in their retreat twelve were killed and ten wounded.

After this the Kols ravaged the best part of the Singbhúm Raja's estate and threatened Saráikelá and the chiefs; who all again implored the assistance of the Agent against their Kol subjects!

In 1821, a large force was employed to reduce the Larkas, and after a month's hostilities the leaders, encouraged by a proclamation, surrendered. They earnestly prayed at this time to be taken under the direct management of the British Officers, but unfortunately their wishes were not complied with. They were compelled to enter into agreements to pay tribute to the chiefs at the rate of eight annas for each plough; but after a year or two of peace, they again became restive and resumed their old practices of pillage and plunder, committing raids and laying waste neighbouring villages, not unfrequently, however, at the instigation of the chiefs. Other matters then engaged the attention of the authorities, and for many years no attempt was made to restore order to Singbhúm, or seriously to check the predatory predilections of its turbulent inhabitants. This encouraged them to extend the circle of their depredations; they ravaged Dhalbhúm, devastated Bámanghátí and penetrated far into Chútiá Nágpúr, but the assistance rendered by them to the Nágpúr Kols in 1831-32, was too gross a defiance of the Government to escape the serious notice of the authorities.

The judicious officer who was now Agent to the Governor-General for the newly formed non-regulation Province the South-Western Frontier, the late Sir Thomas Wilkinson, at once recognised the necessity of a thorough subjugation of the Kols and the impolicy and futility of forcing them to submit to the chiefs. He, therefore, proposed an occupation of Singbhúm by an adequate force, and when the people were thoroughly subdued, to place them under the direct management of a British officer to be stationed at Chaibása in the heart of their country. These views were accepted by Government, and in furtherance of them two regiments of Native Infantry, a brigade of guns and the Rámgarh battalion, the whole force commanded by Colonel Richards, entered Singbhúm in November, 1836. Operations were immediately commenced against the refractory Pírs, and by the end of February following all the Mánkis and Múndas had submitted. There appears to have been very little actual fighting during this campaign. All the most important parts of the Kolhán were visited by the Agent and his troops, the men whom it appeared desirable to make examples of in consequence of their having been leaders in the previous lawless proceedings were given up or captured, and the others readily acquiesced in the arrangements proposed.

Their submission.

Engagements were now taken from them to bear true allegiance to the British Government, and it was deemed necessary to stipulate that they should no longer obey the orders of the chiefs to whom they had previously been required to submit. Six hundred and twenty villages, with a population estimated at the time at 90,000, of whom two-thirds were Larkas or Hos, were thus brought, and have since remained, under the immediate control of the British Government, and simple rules for the administration of this new acquisition, which in all their salient and peculiar features are still in force, were drawn up and promulgated.

The system of Government through heads of Pírs and heads of villages found to exist was maintained. The former officers had under them from three to a dozen villages. They were recognised as the head police officers of their circle and the collectors of the Government dues, and were empowered to dispose of petty disputes of a civil or criminal nature, but were not authorized to inflict any punishment. The Múnda exercised authority in his village as Police officer subordinate to the Mánki, the Pír officer, and assisted in collecting the revenue. The assessment at eight annas for each plough, imposed by Major Roughsedge, was continued, and under it the rental was about Rs. 5,000. In 1854, an assessment on the same principle but double the former rates was introduced; this gave Rs. 17,700 which was fixed for twelve years.

During this period the revenue was paid with the utmost punctuality. The area of cultivation rapidly increased, and there was every reason to suppose that the people were contented and making fair progress in civilization and prosperity; but in 1857 the disturbances that supervened on the mutinies caused a serious but brief check.

In that year the detachment of the Rámgarh light infantry, stationed at Chaibása, following the lead of the native officers and men with the head quarters of the battalion, mutinied, and were marching to join their comrades at Ránchí with the contents of the Chaibása treasure chest, when the Kols of the Pírs round the station armed, collected in thousands and denying the right of the *Sipáhís* to remove the money that had been collected as revenue from them, they intercepted the detachment on the banks of a river and held them most completely in check, till a mandate arrived from the Porahát Raja to send the whole party to him.

After some delay, the Porahát Raja determined to deliver these mutineers into the hands of the British officers who had in the meantime returned to Ránchí, and three or four thousand Larka Kols of the southern Pírs volunteered to act as escort, and this duty they faithfully performed.

But unfortunately, after discharging this essential service, the Porahát Raja went into rebellion, and a considerable section of the Kols considered it their duty to support him. The campaign that ensued was tedious and difficult, as driven from the plains the rebels took refuge in the mountain fastnesses in which Singbhúm abounds, and for months during the rains, our troops could do no more than blockade their positions and protect the peaceable villages from their onslaughts. In December, 1859, detachments moved to the rear of the Raja's hill retreat, whilst a cordon of posts was established in his front. At last an attack was made in which many important captures were effected, and though the Raja with his wives escaped for the moment, they found every avenue of retreat barred, and they surrendered to the Commissioner on the 15th February, 1859.

The Kols had early in the struggle, considering the inequality of weapons, shewn themselves not unworthy of their former fame as savage warriors, but they were cowed by the 'enfields' of a Naval Brigade which formed part of our force; and after a few casualties at long ranges they avoided open attack, and their warfare latterly was confined to cutting off stragglers and burning the villages of the well-disposed.

The capture of the Raja at once put an end to the disturbances; those who had been in arms returned to their houses and ordinary pursuits, like lambs to a fold, and the Mánkis, resuming with zeal their police functions, readily arrested and sent up for trial all heinous offenders that could not be amnestied.

On the whole there has been great progress since the Kols became directly subject to the Government. Under the judicious management of a succession of officers whose names will always be household words in the Kolhán, Tickell, Haughton, Davies, Birch, Hayes, these savages have been gradually tamed, softened, and civilised rather than subjugated. Not a dozen years ago, they steadily opposed the opening of roads through their territory, removing from the villages to the hills, (their usual custom when dissatisfied and excited), till the obnoxious posts set up to mark the alignment were taken down and the project abandoned. Now their country is in all directions traversed by good roads made by themselves under the superintendence of their officers. New sources of industrial wealth have been opened out, new crops requiring more careful cultivation introduced, new wants created and supplied, even a desire for education has been engendered and fostered, and already well educated Kols are to be found among the ministerial officers of the Chaibása courts.

In 1867, the twelve years' settlement of the plough tax expired, and so great an advance had been made, that it was considered time to introduce a regular assessment on the lands and remove the reproach that a district so prosperous did not defray the ordinary expenses of its Government.

Settlement of 1867.

For some two or three years previous to the settlement of 1867, every means were taken to prepare the Kols for the impending change. In 1866, a great meeting was held and the consent of the headmen obtained to all that was contemplated. They admitted that it was incumbent on them to pay their share of the burdens of the state, agreed that their lands should be measured and assessment made on the lands instead of on the ploughs; and this was completed next year by Dr. Hayes. In fixing the rates, an estimate was made of the quantity of land that a man ordinarily cultivated with one plough, for which he paid Rs. 2. This was taken as the basis of the new assessment and it might, therefore, be assumed that there was no great enhancement; but the result gave a gross rental of Rs. 64,808, nearly treble the amount of the plough tax. The Kols were somewhat startled at first, but it has been cheerfully accepted. They made no attempt to shirk the measurements or to conceal their lands; on the contrary, their great desire was to have all the land they could call their own entered in the register that they might have a full record of rights.

The total net revenue from the Kolhán now fully defrays all expenses of its administration, and if the present admirable self-governing system be maintained, it will no doubt, ere many years elapse, give a large surplus.

SECTION 5.—THE MÚNDAS, HOS, BHÚMIJ.

The Hos.

Having thus indicated the geographical position of the people that we have to consider under the name of Múndári or Múnda and given a sketch of their history, I now proceed to describe their more prominent ethnic peculiarities, and in doing so I propose to select the Hos as the branch of the people, who, from their jealous isolation for so many years, their independence, their long occupation of one territory, and their contempt for all other classes that came in contact with them, especially the Hindus, probably furnish the best illustration, not of the Múndáris in their wildest state, but of what, if left to themselves and permanently located, they were likely to become. Even at the present day, the exclusiveness of the old Hos is remarkable. They will not allow aliens to hold lands near their villages, and, indeed, if it were left to them, no strangers would be permitted to settle in the Kolhán. Now there are settlements of Goálás, Kúrmís and others, but though such settlements are under the authority of the Kol Mánki of the Pír, the Kols hold little communication with them and jealously watch and circumscribe the spread of their cultivation; for they argue that they are themselves rapidly increasing and the waste lands should all be reserved for their progeny. The only persons of alien race they tolerate, and so far as suits their own convenience associate with, are the few 'Tántis' (weavers), 'Goálás,' (herdsmen), potters, and blacksmiths, who ply their respective trades for the benefit of the community; but these people, who are in all probability remnants of the Aryan colonies that the Hos subjugated, must learn their language and generally conform to their customs. The old Hos will not conform to theirs. It is only the rising generation that takes kindly to the acquisition of another language.

The Hos have a tradition concerning the creation of the world and the origin of the human race which is given in Colonel Tickell's account of the tribe published in Volume IX of the Journal of the Asiatic Society of Bengal, page 797.

Kol Genesis.

* Ote Borám and Sing Bonga were self-created, and they made the earth with rocks and water, and they clothed it with grass and trees, and then created animals, first, those that man domesticates, and, afterwards, wild beasts. When all was thus prepared for the abode of man, a boy and a girl were created, and Sing Bonga placed them in a cave at the bottom of a great ravine and finding them to be too innocent to give hope of progeny, he instructed them in the art of making 'Illi,' rice beer, which excites the passions and thus the world became peopled.

This little story the old Mánkis are fond of telling with all sorts of indecent details.

Legend regarding the origin of different nations.

When the first parents had produced twelve boys and twelve girls, Sing Bonga prepared a feast of the flesh of buffaloes, bullocks, goats, sheep, pigs, fowls, and vegetables, and making the brothers and sisters pair off, told each pair to take what they most relished and depart. Then the first and second pair took bullocks and buffaloe's flesh, and they originated the Kols (Hos) and the Bhúmij (Matkum); the next took of the vegetables only, and are the progenitors of the Bráhmans and Chatris; others took goats and fish, and from them are the Sudras. One pair took the shellfish and became Bhúiyas; two pairs took pigs and became Santáls. One pair got nothing, seeing which, the first pairs gave them of their superfluity, and from the pair thus provided spring the Ghásís who toil not, but live by preying on others. The Hos have now assigned to the English the honor of descent from one of the first two pairs, the elder. The only incident in the above tradition that reminds one of the more highly elaborated Santál account is the divine authority for the use of strong drinks.

Groves.

The religion of the Múndári possesses a Shamanistic rather than a Fetish character. They make no images of their gods, nor do they worship symbols, but they believe that though invisible to mortal eyes, the gods

* Ote Borám is but another name for Sing Bonga.

2 x

may, when propitiated by sacrifice, take up for a time their abode in places especially dedicated to them. Thus they have their "high places" and "their groves"—the former, some mighty mass of rock to which man has added nothing and from which he takes nothing, the latter, a fragment of the original forest, the trees in which have been for ages carefully protected, left when the clearance was first made, lest the sylvan gods of the places disquieted at the wholesale felling of the trees that sheltered them should abandon the locality. Even now if a tree is destroyed in the sacred grove (the **Jáhirá** or **Sarna**), the gods evince their displeasure by withholding seasonable rain.

Divinities.

Sing Bonga, the creator and preserver, is adored as the sun. Prayer and sacrifice are made to him as to a beneficent deity who has no pleasure in the destruction of any of his creatures, though, as a father, he chastises his erring children, and to him our gratitude is due for all the benefits we enjoy.

He is said to have married **Chando Omol**, or the moon, but she deceived him on one occasion and he cut her in two, but repenting of his anger, he allows her at times to shine forth in full beauty. The stars are her daughters.

The worship of the sun as the supreme deity is the foundation of the religion of the Kols in Chútiá Nágpúr and also of the Oráons who address him as Dharmí, the Holy one. He is not regarded as the author of sickness or calamity, but he may be invoked to avert it, and this appeal is often made when the sacrifices to the minor deities have been unproductive.

The Kharriás consider that each head of a family is bound to make a certain number of offerings to Sing Bonga during his life time, and he may complete the complement and clear the account as soon as he pleases. This is not now practised by the Hos or Múndas, but I have been informed that they regard it as a very orthodox custom.

The other deities are all considered subordinate to Sing Bonga, and though they possess supernatural powers, there are cases beyond their authority, and when they are invoked in such cases, it is their duty to intercede with Sing Bonga and so obtain for their votaries the solicited relief. This notion of the intercessional power of the minor spirits is remarkable.

Chanala Desum Bonga and his wife Pángora have been included among the minor deities of the Hos, but these are the styles under which Sing Bonga and his wife Chando Omol desire to be worshipped by female votaries. Chanala is to women what Sing Bonga is to men.

The following singular story has recently been recounted to me by a Múndári Páhn, or priest, of a village in the southern quarter of the Chútiá Nágpúr District. It makes out that the minor deities are really fallen angels, like Satan and his host.

There were formerly people in heaven who served Sing Bonga. They absented themselves from work (deponent says from cutcherry) because after seeing their faces in a mirror, they found they were in God's image and, therefore, his equals. Thereupon God kicked them out of heaven, and they fell in a place that goes by the name of 'Terasi Pirhi Ekasibadi.' They found here quantities of iron ore, and they immediately made seven furnaces and commenced smelting it, and the fire from them burnt the trees and the grass, and the smoke and the sparks ascended to heaven. This went on night and day. It disturbed Sing Bonga, and he gave orders that if they worked all day, they must stop all night; and if they worked all night, they must stop all day, but they would not obey. Sing Bonga then sent two king crows and an owl to warn them, but they did not attend, and they tried to catch the birds with their furnace tongs and spoil their long tails. Then he sent a crow and a 'Lipi' (lark); the crows were formerly white but the Vulcans caught the crow sent by Sing Bonga and smoked it black, and they made the Lipi red and flattened its head, but the orders of Sing Bonga were not carried out. Other messengers were sent with no better success; then Sing Bonga resolved to go himself, and he stopped at the house of Lútkum Háram and Lútkum Búrhi, an old couple who made charcoal, and he served them incognito for some time and amused himself by playing with the smelter's children. They played with balls of iron, he with eggs, but the eggs smashed the iron balls. When the old man and his wife went to the woods to make charcoal, they left Sing Bonga in charge of the hut and told him to watch the dhán laid out to dry, but he played all the time and the fowls ate up the dhán except a few grains, and when the old couple returned, they mourned for the loss of their dinner; but Sing Bonga consoled them, and taking the few grains that were left, he filled all the pots with them, and when the old people accused him of having stolen rice to make good what was lost by his carelessness, he answered mildly, "no, God gives it."

The furnaces of the smelters were now continually falling in, and the smelters sought an 'Ojha'* to ascertain the cause, but as they could not find one, they placed rice on a winnowing fan, and it led them to Sing Bonga, and they asked him what they should do. He replied, you must offer a human sacrifice; but they could not find a man, and returned to Sing Bonga who said that he himself would be the sacrifice. Then under his direction they made a new furnace and instead of iron ore, they put Sing Bonga into it, and blew the bellows and when there was sufficient heat, as they had been instructed, they sprinkled water on the fire, and Sing Bonga appeared uninjured, but from the furnace flowed streams of gold and silver, and precious stones shining like the sun. Then Sing Bonga said, "See what one person has done; if you all pass through the furnace, what a heap of wealth you will have!" They agreed to be smelted, and they entered the furnace, and were shut up, and Sing Bonga made their wives blow the bellows. When the people inside began to howl, the women were alarmed, and would have stopped, but Sing Bonga said, "Blow away! they are only quarrelling over the division of the spoil." Thus they were all destroyed, because they had not obeyed the word of Sing Bonga. Then the women said, "You have killed our husbands, what are we to do?" Sing Bonga then assigned to each of these women a locality, and they became the minor deities or bhúts, male and female; some had rocks, some groves, some pools, some rivers, as their abodes, and thus originated the Naiads and Dryads, the Marang-Búrú or Búrá-Bonga of the hills, the Desa-ulis of the groves, and the Naga Eras of the streams.

The next in order among the gods is Marang-Búrú† or Búrá Bonga, the mountain god. The highest or most remarkable hill or rock in the neighburhood is the shrine

* Diviner. The word 'ojha' means 'entrails,' and the person alluded to is so called, because he looks into futurity by examining the entrails of birds.

When a vacancy occurs in the office of priest of a village, a 'Súp' or winnowing fan with some rice is used, and it takes the person who holds it to the individual on whom the mantle has fallen.

† The great mountain. The 'Tay-an Song,' great mountain, is the name of one of the gods worshipped by the Chinese and Mandu Tartars. See "*Social Life of the Chinese*," by Rev. J. Doolittle, vol. i. p. 259.

of this deity or spirit. The Kols evidently recognise the importance of wooded hills in securing the needful supply of rain, and trusting entirely to rain for irrigation, and regarding Búrú Bonga as the head of the heavenly water department, they naturally pay him special attention. Every third year, in most places, buffaloes are sacrificed in his honor, and fowls and goats every year. He is also invoked in sickness. In Chútiá Nágpúr a remarkable bluff, near the village of Lodhma, is the Marang-Búrú or Mahá-Búrú for a wide expanse of country. Here people of all castes assemble and sacrifice—Hindus, even Muhammadans, as well as Kols. There is no visible object of worship; the sacrifices are offered on the top of the hill, a bare semi-globular mass of rock. If animals are killed, the heads are left there, and afterwards appropriated by the Páhn, or village priest. Hindus say that the Marang-Búrú, as a deity, is the same as Mahádeo, but under what name the Muhammadans pay devotions to him I know not. They aver, however, that they cannot exist in Chútiá Nágpúr without propitiating the local deities.

Every village has in its vicinity a grove reputed to be a remnant of the primeval forest left intact for the local gods when the clearing was originally made. Here Desauli, the tutelary deity of the village, and his wife, Jhár-Era or Mabúrú, are supposed to sojourn when attending to the wants of their votaries. There is a Desauli for every village, and his authority does not extend beyond the boundary of the village to which his grove belongs; if a man of that village cultivates land in another village, he must pay his devotions to the Desauli of both. The grove deities are held responsible for the crops, and are especially honored at all the great agricultural festivals. They are also appealed to in sickness.

The next in order are Naiads, 'Nága-Era,' who presides over tanks, wells, and any bodies of stagnant water (called Ekhir-Bonga by the Múndáris), and Garhá-Era, the river goddess. They, too, are frequently, and no doubt very truly, denounced as the cause of sickness, and propitiated by sacrifices to spare their victims.

The remaining spirits are the ancestral shades, who are supposed to hover about, doing good or evil to their descendants. They are often denounced as the cause of calamitous visitation, and propitiatory offerings are made to them; but besides this, a small portion of the food prepared in every house is daily set apart for them. The ancestors are the Penates, and are called 'Ham-ho.'

The ancestors of the wife have also to be considered; they are called 'Horatan-ho', because sacrifices to them are always offered on the path 'Hora,' by which the old woman came as a bride to the house.

The name of the deity to be invoked in cases of sickness is ascertained by divination. This is done in various ways. One of the most usual is by dropping oil into a vessel of water; the name of a deity is pronounced as the oil is dropped; if it forms one globule in the water, it is considered that the right name has been selected; if it splutters and forms several globules, another is tried. The person who applies this test is considered a professional, but he has no priestly office. There is nothing like a hereditary priesthood among the Hos. In every village there are one or more influential elders to whom the duty of performing the general sacrifices is assigned, but on other occasions the head of the family is according to the patriarchal model its priest.

It has been said that the Hos and Múndas, like the Karens, have a tradition of the destruction of the human race, all but two persons, by deluge, but of this I have not been able to discover a trace, and it appears incompatible with their tradition of the origin of different races. '**Lúrbeng**' is in their language a serpent, properly a water-snake, and the same name is poetically given by them to the rain-bow, and by a simple reasoning on cause and effect, they say "the serpent stops the rain," but it requires stronger imaginative powers than I possess to eliminate from this a tradition of the deluge.

The Múndas consult auguries in selecting the site of a house or village with prayer to Sing Bonga. A small quantity of rice is placed in holes made at the four corners of the selected site where it is left all night, and if found undisturbed in the morning, the site is good. Prayer is offered twice—*first*, that the test applied may truly indicate, if the site be good or bad; *secondly*, for a blessing on the chosen site.

Ho Tribes.

The Hos and Múndas are divided into tribes called **Kílis**, and a man must not marry a girl of his own Kíli. The Múndáris, like the Oráons, adopt, as their tribal distinction, the name of some animal, and the flesh of that animal is tabooed to them as food, as the Eels, the Tortoise. With one exception I do not find among the Kílis of the Larkas or Hos the names of any animal. The 'Murmu', or Nilgai, is common as a tribal name to Hos and Santál.

The following are Ho Kílis—the list is not exhaustive:—

1. Būriūli.	7. Murmu.	13. Tibu.
2. Pūrthi.	8. Marli.	14. Hembarun.
3. Sincoi.	9. Kisku.	15. Podoro.
4. Baipoi.	10. Hansda.	16. Munduia.
5. Sundi.	11. Tudi.	17. Lagori.
6. Bandi.	12. Chorai.	18. Kalundia.

Those in the second column, *i. e.,* seven to twelve inclusive, are common to Hos and Santáls.

Ho Villages.

The Ho villages of the old settlements in the best cultivated portion of the Kolhán are often prettily situated on hills overlooking their flat terraced rice fields and undulating uplands. The sites are well marked by very ancient and noble tamarind trees, with mangoe and jack trees and bamboos, and they form very pleasing features in otherwise very pleasing landscapes. The houses, constructed by the better class of cultivators, nestling among the trees, are roomy with substantial mud or wattled walls and thatched roofs, a neat verandah and well-raised plinth. The out-houses are so placed as to form, with the family residence, three or four sides of a square, having a large pigeon house in the centre. The place where the ashes of the dead are deposited is generally near the Múndá's house, and the great slabs, used as grave-stones under the shade of the grand solemn tamarind trees, are the favorite seats of the elders when they meet after their work to gossip, smoke, or talk over parish affairs.

Though pigs are bred in the villages, they are accommodated with well-constructed styes, and the farm premises are kept tolerably clean. These remarks do not, however, apply to the houses of the laborers, which are small and miserable. The Hos take great interest in poultry, and fully appreciate the excellencies of a good fat capon. Capons are generally found in Ho villages, but the owners are not always willing to dispose of them, and the Hos have been subjected to much obloquy, because they prefer to keep such delicacies for their own use.

2 Y

Another incentive to the breeding of fowls is their great love of cock fighting; at all market-places on market days, and at other places on regular fixed days, they have great meetings for this amusement. The cocks are armed with cruel steel spurs, and the combat is always *à l'outrance*, the winning cock gaining for his master the corpse of his foe. I have noticed with some pleasure that women frequenting the markets kept aloof from the cock-fights, and there was feminine delicacy and tenderness in this abstinence from which the fair sex of some civilized nations might take a lesson.

Cock fights.

The Kols also breed ducks and geese, and they keep sheep and goats for food, but it is generally for the purpose of propitiatory sacrifice that they are slaughtered and eaten. Bullocks and buffaloes are also so used. The village cattle are during the day under charge, not of their owners, but of the village herdsmen of the Gor or Goálá caste, who are paid in grain for their services. The Kols, like most of the Indo-Chinese hill races, make no use of the milk, but the herdsmen are not absolutely prohibited from doing so.

In the villages of the Southern Pírs, which have more the appearance of recent settlements, the houses are so much scattered, that families may almost be said to live apart, or a village consists of a number of separate hamlets; but in the older villages, though each house stands within its own plot of ground, they are pretty close together, and the community appear very socially inclined.

The Hos of Singbhúm and the Múndáris of the Southern Parganas of the Lohardagga District are physically a much finer people than the Bhúmij, the Santáls, or any other of the Kolarians previously described. The males average five feet five or six inches in height, the women five feet two. The average height of a number of the Juáng tribe I found to be for males less than five feet, and women four feet eight. In features the Hos exhibit much variety, and I think in a great many families there is considerable admixture of Aryan blood. Many have high noses and oval faces, and young girls are some times met with who have delicate and regular features, finely chiselled straight noses, and perfectly formed mouths and chins. The eyes, however, are seldom so large, so bright and gazelle-like as those of pure Hindu maidens, but I have met strongly marked Mongolian features, and some are dark and coarse like the Santáls. In colour they vary greatly, 28-29 and 30 of Brossac's table are about the commonest tints, the copper tints, I may say. Eyes dark brown (about two of Brossac), hair black, straight or wavy, and rather fine, worn long by males and females, but the former shave the forehead. Both men and women are noticeable for their fine erect carriage and long free stride. The hands and feet are large but well formed. The men care little about their personal appearance. It requires a great deal of education to reconcile them to the encumbrance of clothing, and even those who are wealthy move about all but naked, as proudly as if they were clad in purple and fine linen.

Physical traits.

The women in an unsophisticated state are equally averse to superfluity of clothing. In remote villages they may still be seen with only a rag between the legs fastened before and behind to a string round the waist. This is called a 'botoi;' the national dress is however a long strip of cloth worn as a girdle round the loins, knotted behind and the ends brought between the

Dress.

legs and fastened to the girdle in front, but in the principal group of villages about Chaibása the young women dress themselves decently and gracefully. The style of wearing the hair is peculiar, collected in a knot artificially enlarged, not in the centre of the back of the head, but touching the back of the right ear. Flowers are much used in the 'coiffure.' The neck ornaments most in vogue a year or two ago, were very small black beads, but in this one small item of their simple toilette, fashion changes, and the beads most prized one year are looked on with repugnance the next.* As with the Santáls very massive bracelets and armlets are worn, and anklets of bell-metal. It is a singular sight to see the young women at the markets subjecting themselves to the torture of being fitted with a pair of these anklets. They are made so that they can just, with great violence, be forced on. The operation is performed by the manufacturers, who put moistened leather on the heel and instep to prevent excoriation. The girl clinging to and resting on one of her companions cries bitterly at the violence inflicted on her. and the operation is a long one but when it is over she admires her decorated foot and instep and smiles through her tears.

The Ho women have adopted as their distinctive mark by 'Godna,' an arrow which they regard as their national emblem. A Ho unable to write, if asked to attach his mark or sign manual to a document, does so by making a rude representative of an arrow. The Múnda women use the same godna marks as the Juángs, and the Kharriás previously described.

The Larkas are lightly assessed, and cultivating their own lands, never join any of the numerous bands of laborers emigrating to the tea districts. They refuse to hear the voice of the recruiter, charm he never so enticingly. They care not to work for hire, and never, if they can avoid it, carry loads. The use of the block wheeled dray is universal among them, and all the carrying necessary in their agricultural operations is done by it.

Social and domestic customs. Child-birth.

After the birth of a child† both mother and father are considered unclean, 'bisi,' for eight days, during which period the other members of the family are sent out of the house, and the husband has to cook for his wife. If it be a difficult case of parturition, the malignancy of some spirit of evil is supposed to be at work, and after divination to ascertain his name, a sacrifice is made to appease him. At the expiration of the eight days, the banished members of the family return, friends are invited to a feast, and the child is ceremoniously named. The

Naming the child.

name of the grand-father is usually given to the first born son, but not without an ordeal to ascertain if it will prove fortunate. As the name is mentioned, a grain of 'úrid' (pulse) is thrown into a vessel with water, the name is adopted if it floats, rejected if it sinks.

The Hos have a pleasing custom of introducing into their families the names or titles of persons they like, irrespective of creed or race. Thus Major, Captain, Tickell, Doctor, have become common names in the Kolhán. The names thus introduced will, probably, remain in the Kolhán for ages. The writer of an article that appeared not long ago in the *Calcutta Quarterly Review* appears to be under the impression that this custom of naming Kol children after officers had been introduced by the missionaries.

---

* Necklaces of real coral and silver coins are now all the rage.

† Settlement Report by Doctor Hayes.

The missionaries have had nothing to do with it. It is a spontaneous act of good will on the part of unconverted Hos.

There are no religious ceremonies between childhood and marriage.

Marriages, &c.

Owing to the high price placed on daughters by their fathers, the large number of adult unmarried girls seen in every considerable village in the Kolhán, is a very peculiar feature in the social state of the community.

In no other country in India are spinsters found so advanced in years, and in many of the best families grey headed old maids may be seen, whose charms were insufficient to warrant the large addition to the usual price called 'pan,' imposed in consideration of the high connection that the union would confer. The 'pan' is calculated, and for the most part paid, in cattle, indicating that the custom dates from a time when there was no current coin, and fathers of Mánki dignity demand from forty to fifty head of cattle for each of their girls. Dr. Hayes finding that in consequence of this practice, the number of marriages was annually diminishing, and immoral intimacy between the sexes increasing, convened in 1868 a meeting of representative men for the express purpose of discussing this question, and after a long debate it was unanimously agreed that a reduction should be made.

It was resolved that in future a 'pan' was not to exceed ten head of cattle, and that if one pair of oxen, one cow, and seven rupees were given, it should be received as an equivalent for the ten head. For the poorer classes it was fixed at seven rupees. Even thus modified the 'pan' in Singbhúm is higher than it is in Chútiá Nágpúr for the multitude. The Mánkis and head men of the latter country conforming to the Hindu customs, have given up exacting it.

In olden times young men counteracted the machinations of avaricious parents against the course of true love by forcibly carrying off the girl, and still at times evade extortion by running away with her. Then the parents have to submit to such terms as arbitrators think fair; the abduction it was necessary to put a stop to, and elopements are not considered respectable, so until the conference, prices had a tendency to rise rather than fall. The old generation of Mánkis vehemently opposed any reduction. The second generation, since the accession of the British, are now in the ascendant, and they entertain more enlightened views, but, notwithstanding the compact, I have not yet heard of a marriage in high life in which the reduced 'pan' has been accepted.

Ho girls of the period.

It is certainly not from any yearning for celibacy that the marriage of Singbhúm maidens is so long postponed. The girls will tell you frankly that they do all they can to please the young men, and I have often heard them pathetically bewailing their want of success. They make themselves as attractive as they can, flirt in the most demonstrative manner, and are not too coy to receive in public attentions from those they admire. They may be often seen in well assorted pairs returning from market with arms interlaced, and looking at each other as lovingly as if they were so many groups of Cupids and Psyches, but with all this the "*men will not propose*."

Tell a maiden you think her nice looking, she is sure to reply, "Oh yes,! I am, but what is the use of it, the young men of my acquaintance don't see it." Even when a youth has fully made up his mind to marry, it may happen that fate is against the happiness of the young couple; bad omens are seen that cause the match to be postponed or broken off, or papa cannot, or will not, pay the price demanded. When a young man has made his choice, he communicates the fact to his parents, and a deputation of the friends of the family, is sent to the girls' house to ascertain all that should be known regarding her family, age, appearance, and means. If the information obtained and the result of the inspection be satisfactory, and the omens observed on the road have been propitious, an offering is made on the part of the young man, and if it be received, the deputation are invited to stay and are feasted.

The report of the deputation being favorable, a day is fixed for a meeting between the parents and the terrible question of the 'pan' discussed. At this point, many matches are broken off, in consequence of greediness on one side or stinginess on the other. The amount agreed on has to be paid before the day can be fixed for the marriage, and when delivery of the cattle is made, a pot of beer has to be given from the bride's side for each animal.

At last if all this is got over, the appointed day arrives, and the bride is escorted to the village of her intended by all her own young female friends with music and dancing. The young men and girls of the village, and those invited from neighbouring villages, form a cortège for the bridegroom. They go out and meet the bride's party, and after a dance in the grove, in which the bride and bridegroom take part, mounted on the hips of two of their female friends, they enter the village together, where there is a great feast, a great consumption of the rice beer, and much more dancing and singing. Ceremony there is none, but the turning point in the rite is when the bride and groom pledge each other. A cup of beer is given to each; the groom pours some of the contents of his cup into the bride's cup, and she returns the compliment. Drinking the liquor thus blended, they become of one 'Kíli' that is, the bride is admitted into her husband's tribe, and they become one.* This has, I believe, succeeded an older custom of drinking from the same cup.

"The bride touched the goblet, the knight took it up,
He drank off the wine, and he threw down the cup."

After remaining with her husband for three days only, it is the correct thing for the wife to run away from him, and tell all her friends that she loves him not, and will see him no more. This is, perhaps, reparation to the dignity of the sex injured by the bride's going to the bridegroom's house to be married, instead of being sought for and taken as a wife from her own. So it is correct for the husband to show great anxiety for the loss of his wife and diligently to seek her, and when he finds her, he carries her off by main force. I have seen a young wife thus found and claimed and borne away, screeching and struggling in the arms of her husband, from the midst of a crowded bazaar. No one interferes on these occasions, and no one assists. If the husband cannot manage the business himself, he must leave her alone.

---

* It is worthy of notice that in the marriages of the Chinese a precisely similar custom obtains. "After the worship of the tablets they (bride, and bridegroom) rise to their feet and remain standing in silence, while they are helped to their wedding wine. One of the female attendants takes the two goblets from the table, and having partially filled them with a mixture of wine and honey, she pours some of the contents from one to the other several times, she then holds one to the mouth of the groom and the other, to the mouth of the bride, who continue to face each other and who then sip a little wine. She then changes the goblets and the bride sips out of the one just used by the groom, and the groom sips out of the one just used by the bride. Sometimes only one goblet is used." *Social Life of the Chinese*, by Revd. J. Doolittle, vol. I, page 87.

After this little escapade, the wife at once settles down, assumes her place as the well contented mistress of the household, and, as a rule, in no country in the world are wives better treated. Dr. Hayes says "a Kol or Ho makes a regular companion of his wife. She is consulted in all difficulties, and receives the fullest consideration due to her sex." Indeed it is not uncommon to see in the Kolhán, husbands so subject to the influence of their wives, that they may be regarded as henpecked. Instances of infidelity in wives are very rare. I never heard of one, but I suppose such things occur as there is a regulated penalty. The unfaithful wife is discarded, and the seducer must pay to the husband the entire value of the 'pan.'

Kind treatment of their wives.

The Múndári marriages, as solemnized in most parts of Chútiá Nágpúr, have more ceremonies, some of which appear to have been taken from the Hindus, at all events the ceremonies I allude to are common to Hindus and aborigines; but it is not always easy to predicate by whom they were originated. We may, however, safely assert that practices common to both, which are not in accordance with the ritual prescribed in the Vedas, are derived from the aborigines.

Múndári marriages.

Among Múndas having any pretensions to respectability, the young people are not allowed to arrange these affairs for themselves. Their parents settle it all for them, French fashion, and after the liberty they have enjoyed, and the liaisons they are sure to have made, this interference on the part of the old folk must be very aggravating to the young ones. The 'pan' varies from Rs. 4 to Rs. 20, but the marriage feast is very liberally provided, and as it takes place at the bride's house, the expense chiefly falls on her father. When the day for the wedding is fixed, the bridegroom goes in some state to the bride's house, the young men who accompany him "a gallant band with sword and brand" fantastically dressed, and as they approach the village of the bride, her friends come out to meet them in similar guise, and a mimic fight takes place which ends in the simultaneous rush of the whole party into the village, making a terrible row. The bride and bridegroom are now well anointed with turmeric, and then taken and wedded not to each other but to two trees, the bride to a mahwá (bassia latifolia) the groom to a mangoe, or both to mangoes. They are made to touch the tree with 'sindúr' (red lead), and then to clasp it, and they are tied to it. On returning they are placed standing face to face, the girl on a curry stone over a plough share, supported on sheaves of grass or corn. The bridegroom stands ungallantly treading on his wife's toes, and in this position touches her forehead with the red lead, she touches his forehead in a similar manner. The bridesmaids then, after some preliminary splashing and sprinkling, pour a jar of water over the head of each, this necessitates a change of raiment, and apparently concludes the ceremony as the young people going inside to change, do not appear again till the cock crowing announces the dawn or its approach. At the first crow the bridesmaids, who with the young men have been merrily keeping it up all night with the song and the dance, burst into the nuptial chamber and bring forth the blushing bride and her bashful lord and *their clothes.* They all go to the river or to a tank to wash the clothes and bathe, and parties of boys and girls form sides under the leadership of the bride and bridegroom, and pelt each other with clods of earth. The bridegroom next takes a water vessel and conceals it in the stream or water for the bride to find. She then conceals it from him, and when he has found it, she takes it up, filled with water, and places it on her head. She lifts her arm to support the pitcher, and the bridegroom standing behind her with his bow strung, and the hand that holds it lightly resting on her shoulder, discharges an arrow through the pretty loop-hole thus formed into the path before her. The girl walks on to where the arrow falls, and with head erect, still bearing the pitcher of water picks it up with her foot, takes it into her hand, and restores it to her husband with a graceful obeisance. She thus shews she can adroitly perform her domestic duties, and knows her duty to her lord and master, whilst he, on his part, in discharging an arrow to clear her path of an imaginary foe, indicates that he is prepared to do his duty as her guide and protector for life.

The Hos are fair marksmen with the bow and arrow, and great sportsmen. From childhood they practise archery; every lad herding cattle or watching crops makes this his sole pastime, and skill is attained even in knocking over small birds with blunt arrows. They also keep hawks, and the country in the vicinity of their villages is generally destitute of game. In the months intervening between the harvest home and the rains, they frequently go in large parties to distant jungles; and with them, as with the Santáls, there is every year in May a great meet for sport, in which people of all classes of the neighbourhood and surrounding villages take part. From the setting-in of the rains to the harvest, the time of the people is fairly employed in cultivation, to which they pay great attention. The women have their full share of labor in the fields, indeed, the only agricultural work they are exempted from is ploughing. They work from early morn till noon, then comes the mid-day meal, after which their time is pretty much at their own disposal. The young people then make themselves tidy, stroll about the village, or visit neighbouring villages, and the old people sitting on the grave stones, indulge in deep potations of rice beer, and smoke, and gossip, or sleep.

Amongst the amusements of the Hos, I must not omit to mention *pegtops*. They are roughly made of blocks of hard wood, but their mode of spinning and playing them, one on another, is the same as with us. Peg topping has been noticed as a Kásia amusement, see page 58.

Agriculture.

Their agricultural implements consist in the ordinary wooden plough tipped with iron, a harrow, the **kodálí**, or large hoe, a sickle and the **tangí**, or battle-axe, for it is used for all purposes; the block-wheeled dray, and an implement to remove earth with, in altering the levels of land to prepare it for irrigation and rice cultivation. The latter consists of a broad piece of board, firmly attached to a pole and yoke, so that its edge touches the ground at an angle as it is drawn by oxen or buffaloes attached to it. The Hos make these agricultural implements themselves; every man is to some extent a carpenter, handy with his adze, and clever in simple contrivances.

The Kols plough with cows as well as oxen, but it is to be recollected that they make no other use of the animal as they never touch milk. Buffaloes are preferred to bullocks as plough cattle. They have a rude kind of oil-press in every village.

The Múndáris and Larkas raise three crops of rice, the early or **Gora**, the autumnal or **Bád**, and the late or **Bera** crop. Indian corn and the millets Murwa and Gondali, are also cultivated as early crops. Wheat, gram, mustard seed (sesamum), they have recently taken to as cold-weather and spring crops. Tobacco and cotton they have long cultivated, but not in sufficient quantities even for their own consumption.

They have no notion of weaving, and if left to their own resources for clothing, would probably resume their leaves, but every village has one or two families of 'Tántis' or weavers, who are now almost undistinguishable from the Hos. The villagers make over their cotton to the weavers, and pay for the loom labour in cotton or grain.

Arts.

The Kols generally understand the smelting of iron. Their country is pretty rich in that mineral, but it is the wilder clans, the mountain Kharriás, the Bírhors, and in Lohardagga or Palámau, the Asúrs and Agariahs, that chiefly utilize it, the people who devote themselves to it regularly paying no attention to the cultivation of the soil. The Múndas have also acquired the art of washing for gold in the streams and rivers that drain the plateau of Chútiá Nágpúr, or rise in the bordering hills which are all auriferous, but the average quantity obtained is not more than suffices to give a bare subsistence to the persons employed in it, though this includes men, women, and children. The richest field, Sonapet, is the valley of the Sonai river below the plateau opening on Kharsáwán. The population are all Múndáris, enjoying a rich soil, a most romantic and sequestered situation, and to complete it as a terrestrial paradise, low fixed rents. This was secured to them after the insurrection of 1831, in which they lustily joined.

Ho Feasts and Dances.

The Hos are a purely agricultural people, and their festivals are all connected with that pursuit. In describing these festivals I avail myself of information on the subject kindly collated for me by W. Ritchie Esq., District Superintendent, Singbhúm. The chief requisite for festivities of all kinds is the preparation of an ample quantity of the home-made beer, called Illi. It is made from rice which is boiled and allowed to ferment till it is sufficiently intoxicating, and its proper preparation is considered one of the most useful accomplishments that a young damsel can possess.

The Hos keep seven festivals in the year. The first or principal is called the Mágh Parab, or Desauli Bonga. This is held in the month of Mágh, or January, when the granaries are full of grain, and the people, to use their own expression, full of devilry. They have a strange notion that at this period, men and women are so over-charged with vicious propensities, that it is absolutely necessary for the safety of the person to let off steam by allowing for a time full vent to the passions.

The festival, therefore, becomes a saturnale, during which servants forget their duty to their masters, children their reverence for parents, men their respect for women, and women all notions of modesty, delicacy, and gentleness; they become raging bacchantes.

It opens with a sacrifice to Desauli of three fowls—a cock and two hens, one of which must be black, and offered with some flowers of the Palás tree *(Butea frondosa)*, bread made from rice-flour, and sesamum seeds. The sacrifice and offerings are made by the village priest, if there be one, or if not, by any elder of the village who possesses the necessary legendary lore, and he prays that during the year they are about to enter on, they and their children may be preserved from all misfortune and sickness, and that they may have seasonable rain and good crops. Prayer is also made in some places for the souls of the departed. At this period an evil spirit is supposed to infest the locality, and to get rid of it, the men, women, and children go in procession round and through every part of the village, with sticks in their hands as if beating for game, singing a wild chant and vociferating violently till they feel assured that the bad spirit must have fled; and they make noise enough to frighten a legion. These religious ceremonies over, the people give themselves up to feasting, drinking immoderately of rice-beer till they are in the state of wild ebriety most suitable for the process of letting off steam.

The Ho population of the villages forming the environs of Chaibása are at other seasons quiet and reserved in manner, and in their demeanour towards women gentle and decorous; even in the flirtations I have spoken of, they never transcend the bounds of decency. The girls, though full of spirits and somewhat saucy, have innate notions of propriety that make them modest in demeanour, though devoid of all prudery; and of the obscene abuse so frequently heard from the lips of common women in Bengal, they appear to have no knowledge. They are delicately sensitive under harsh language of any kind, and never use it to others; and since their adoption of clothing, they are careful to drape themselves decently as well as gracefully, but they throw all this aside during the Mágh feast. Their natures appear to undergo a temporary change. Sons and daughters revile their parents in gross language, and parents their children; men and women become almost like animals in the indulgence of their amorous propensities. They enact all that was ever pourtrayed by prurient artists in a bacchanalian festival or pandean orgie; and as the light of the sun they adore and the presence of numerous spectators seem to be no restraint on their indulgence, it cannot be expected that chastity is preserved when the shades of night fall on such a scene of licentiousness and debauchery.

This festival is not kept at one period in all the villages. The time during which it is held in different villages of a circle extends over a period of a month or six weeks, and under a preconcerted arrangement, the festival commences at each village on a different date, and lasts three or four days; so the inhabitants of each may take part in a long succession of these orgies, and as the utmost liberty is given to girls, the parents never attempting to exercise any restraint, the girls of one village sometimes pair off with the young men of another and absent themselves for days. Liaisons thus prolonged generally end in marriages.

The ordinary Ho dance is similar to that which I have described as the Rasa dance of the Santáls, an amorous but not a very rapid or lively movement; but the Mágh dance is like a *grande galope*, a very joyous, frisky, harum-scarum scamper of boys and girls through the village, and from one village to another.

The Múndáris keep this festival in much the same manner as the Hos, but one day is fixed for its commencement everywhere, the full of the moon in Mágh, and there is less commingling of the boys and girls from different villages. The resemblance to a Saturnale is very complete, as at this festival the farm laborers are feasted by their masters and allowed the utmost freedom of speech in addressing them. It is the festival of the harvest home; the termination of one year's toil and a slight respite from it before they commence again. At this feast the Múndáris dance the Jádúra, remarkable for the very pretty and peculiar manner in which the lines of performers interlace their arms behind their backs.

The next in the order of festivals is what is called 'Bah Bonga' by the Hos, corresponding to the Sarhúl of the Múndáris. 'Bah' means flower, and the festival takes place when the sál* tree is in full bloom in March or April, a favorite season with many

* Called in Múndári 'Sárjum.'

3 A

tribes; for it is then that the death of Gautamá is commemorated. With the Hos and Múndáris it is held in honor of the founders of the village and the tutelary deity or spirit, called Darhá by the Oráons. The boys and girls collect basketfuls of the flowers, make garlands of them, weave them in their hair, and decorate their houses with them. Each house makes an offering of these flowers and sacrifices a cock. The people dance for a couple of days and nights incessantly and refresh themselves meanwhile with beer, but in the Kolhán it is the quiet style of dance, and there are no open breaches of decorum. The dance on this occasion of the Múndáris is called the Bahni, the boys and girls poussette to each other, clapping their hands and pirouetting, so as to cause *dos-à-dos* concussions, which are the source of much mirth.

The selection of the sál flowers as the offering to the founders of the village is appropriate, as there are few villages that do not occupy ground once covered by sál forest, and at this period new ground, if there be any, is cleared for cultivation.

The third festival is the 'Damurai' which comes off in May, or at the time of the sowing for the first rice crop. It is held in honor of the ancestral shades and other spirits, who if unpropitiated, would prevent the seed from germinating. A he-goat and a cock are sacrificed.

The fourth festival is the 'Hero Bonga' in June, the Múndáris call it 'Harihar. It is to propitiate Desáúli and Jáhir Búrhi for a blessing on the crops. In the Múndári villages every house-holder plants a branch of the Bhelwa in his field, and contributes to the general offering which is made by the priest in the sacred grove, a fowl, a pitcher of beer, and a handful of rice. In Singbhúm a he-goat is offered.

This is followed by the Bah-Towli Bonga, which takes place in July. Each cultivator sacrifices a fowl, and after some mysterious rites, a wing is stripped off and inserted in the cleft of a bamboo and stuck up in the rice-field and dung-heap. If this is omitted, it is supposed that the rice will not come to maturity. It appears more like a charm than a sacrifice.

This corresponds with the 'Karam' in the Kol villages of Chútiá Nágpúr, where the 'hoja' is danced; the women in this dance follow the men and change their positions and attitudes in obedience to signals from them. When the movement called 'hoja' is asked for, the women all kneel and pat the ground with their hands in time to the music, as if coaxing the earth to be fruitful. On the day appointed, a branch of the Karam tree is cut and planted in the Akhrá, or dancing place. This festival is kept by Hindus in Chútiá Nágpúr as well as by Kols.

The sixth festival is the offering of the first fruits of the harvest to Sing Bonga; it is solemnised in August when the Gora rice ripens, and till the sacrifice is complete, the new rice must not be eaten. The offering in addition to the rice is a white cock; this is a thanks-offering to the Creator and Preserver. It is called Jum-nama and considered of great importance. To eat new rice without thus thanking God is regarded as impious.

The seventh festival is the Kalam Bonga, when an offering of a fowl is made to Desáúli on the removal of the rice straw from the threshing floor, 'kalam', to be stacked.

The Páhns, or priests, of the Kol villages in Chútiá Nágpúr have another festival for the performance of which they are in possession of some rent-free land called 'dálikatári.' The sacrifices are every second year a fowl, every third year a ram, every fourth year a buffaloe, to 'Marang Búru,' and the main object is to induce him to send seasonable rain.

The above are all general festivals, but the Hos on their individual account make many sacrifices to the gods. In cases of sickness and calamity, they commence by sacrificing what is small and of little value ; but if the desired change is retarded, they go on until the patient dies, or their live stock is entirely exhausted.

Superstitions, witchcraft.

All disease in men or animals is attributed to one of two causes, the wrath of some evil spirit who has to be appeased, or to the spell of some witch or sorcerer, who should be destroyed or driven out of the land. In the latter case a 'Sokha', or witch-finder, is employed to divine who has cast the spell, and various modes of divination are resorted to. One of the most common is the test by the stone and 'paila.' The latter is a large wooden cup shaped like a half cocoa-nut used as a measure for grain. It is placed under a flat stone as a pivot for the stone to turn on. A boy is then seated on the stone, supporting himself by his hands, and the names of all the people in the neighbourhood are slowly pronounced, and as each name is uttered, a few grains of rice are thrown at the boy. When they come to the name of the witch or wizard, the stone turns and the boy rolls off; this, no doubt, is the effect of the boy's falling into a state of coma and losing the power of supporting himself with his hands. In former times, the person denounced and all his family were put to death in the belief that witches breed witches and sorcerers. The taint is in the blood. When during the mutinies the Singbhúm District was left for a short time without officers, a terrible raid was made against all, who for years had been suspected of dealings with the evil one, and the most atrocious murders were committed. Young men were told off for the duty by the elders; neither sex nor age were spared. When order was restored, these crimes were brought to light, and the actual perpetrators condignly punished, and since then we have not only had no recurrence of witch murderers, but the superstition itself is dying out in the Kolhán. In other districts, accusations of witchcraft are still frequently made, and the persons denounced are subjected to much ill-usage, if they escape with their lives. Some of the Sokhas, instead of divining the name of the person who has cast the evil eye on the suffering patient, profess to summon their own familiar spirits who impart to them the needed information. The Sokha throws some rice on a winnowing sieve and places a light in front of it. He then mutters incantations and rubs the rice, watching the flame, and when this flickers, it is owing to the presence of the familiar, and the Sokha to whom alone the spirit is visible pretends to receive from it the revelation which he communicates to the enquirer to the effect that the sufferer is afflicted by the familiar of some rival Sokha or sorcerer or witch whom he names. The villagers then cause the attendance of the person denounced, who is brought into the presence of the sufferer and ordered to haul out his evil spirit. It is useless for him to plead that he has no such spirit, this only leads to his being unmercifully beaten, his best line of defence is to admit what is laid to his charge and to act as if he really were master of the situation; some change for the better in the patient may take place, this is ascribed to his delivery from the familiar, and the sorcerer is allowed to depart; but if there is no amelioration in the condition of the sick person, the chastisement of the sorcerer is continued till he can bear no more, and not unfrequently he dies under the ill-treatment he is subjected to or from its effects.

A milder method is, when the person denounced is required to offer sacrifices of animals to appease or drive away the possessing devil; this he dare not refuse to do, and if the sickness thereupon ceases, it is of course concluded that the devil has departed; but if it continue, the sorcerer is turned out of his home and driven from the village, if nothing worse is done to him.

It must not be supposed that these superstitions are confined to the Kols, they are common to all classes of the population of this province. I have noticed in my account of the Agarias their prevalence in the Southern Tributary Mahâls, and the alleged existence of secret witch schools, where damsels of true Aryan blood are instructed in the black art, and perfected in it by practice on forest trees. Even Bráhmans are sometimes accused. I find in a report by Major Roughsedge, written in 1818, an account of a Bráhman lady who was denounced as a witch and tried, and having escaped in the ordeal by water, she was found to be a witch, and deprived of her nose.

The Sokha does not always denounce a fellow-being; he sometimes gives out that the family bhút is displeased and has caused the sickness; and in such cases a most extensive propitiatory offering is demanded, which the master of the house provides, and of which the Sokha gets the lion's share; and I find an instance of the oracle giving out that Desáúli, the village bhút, had caused the trouble; but on further enquiry, it was averred that a spiteful old woman had on this occasion demoralised the honorable and respectable guardian of the village, and though he was propitiated, the hag was made to suffer very severely for her malignancy.

It will be seen that it is not only women that are accused of having dealings with the imps of darkness. Persons of the opposite sex are as frequently denounced; nor are the female victims invariably of the orthodox old hag type. In a recent case, eight women were denounced by a Sokha as witches, who had introduced epidemic cholera into the village, and caused a terrible mortality, and among these were some very young girls. They were ill-treated until they admitted all that was imputed to them, and agreed to point out and remove the spells they had prepared. They pretended to search for dead birds which, it was said, they had deposited as charms, but nothing was produced, and one of the poor creatures, fearing further-ill usage, destroyed herself by jumping into a well.

In Singbhúm the wild Kharriás are looked upon as the most expert sorcerers, and the people, though they not unfrequently seek their aid, hold them in great awe.

The Hos and other tribes have a firm belief that there are magicians who have the power to assume at will the form of a beast of prey, and the person who gains this unenviable notoriety, is naturally one against whom every man's hand is raised. A Kol, tried for the murder of one of these wizards, stated in his defence (and he spoke as if he believed implicitly what he was narrating), that his wife having been killed by a tiger in his presence, he stealthily followed the animal as it glided away after gratifying its appetite, and saw that it entered the house of one Pusa, a Kol, whom he knew. He called out Pusa's relatives, and when they heard his story, they not only credited it, but declared they had long suspected Pusa of such power and acts; and entering his house, where they found him and not the tiger, they delivered him bound into the hands of his accuser, who at once slew him. In explanation of their having so acted, they deposed that Pusa had one night devoured an entire goat, and roared like a tiger whilst he was eating it; and on another occasion, he informed his friends that he had a longing for a particular bullock, and that night that very bullock was killed by a tiger!

Omens.

I have alluded to their belief in omens, which are always studied before any important step in life is taken, but from the attention paid to them, when the preliminaries of a marriage are being arranged, it is clear that the parties I am describing regard the choice of a wife as the most important step that they have to take. A very full list of these omens will be found in Volume IX of the Journal of the Asiatic Society of Bengal. A few as specimens will suffice here.

If the cry of a flying-squirrel is heard by the deputation on their route to view the bride, it is so bad an omen that no further steps are taken.

If on the road the branch of a tree falls without apparent cause, the death of the parents of both parties may be soon looked for if the marriage take place.

If the dung-beetle is seen on the path rolling his disproportionately large ball of dung, it portends poverty. It might have suggested industry and perseverance!

If certain birds light on the Ásan tree,* or if snakes cross the path, it portends wealth.

A troop of Hanumán monkeys gives promise of larger herds of cattle.

If a bird lights on a *keond*, or ebony tree, the bride sought is sure to be a vixen.

Meeting women carrying full water-pots is auspicious, with empty water-pots the reverse.

Food.

The Hinduised Múnda abstains from most meats which Hindus consider impure, but it is not safe to place a fat capon in his way. Other Múndas and all the Hos eat beef, mutton, goat's flesh, fowls, fish, hares, and deer. Pigs are not much relished except by the poorest classes, and the flesh of bears, monkeys, snakes, field mice, and other small game that the Oráons and Santáls affect, the Múndas and Hos do not approve of. They will take from our hands cakes, bread, and the like, but not cooked rice.

In regard to cooked rice these tribes are exceedingly particular. They will leave off eating if a man's shadow passes across their food. Very few of this people have been known to take to trade as a pursuit, but the Kols of one small section of Chútiá Nágpúr, Tamárh, known as Tamárias, are an exception. They are employed chiefly as brokers for the purchase of the produce of the wilder parts of the Kolhán; but owing to extension of the market system, and a growing predilection on the part of the Kols for more direct dealings with the traders, the Tamárias' occupation as brokers is on the wane. The Singbhúm Kols have of late years very generally taken to rearing the tusser silk-worm, and the money that they obtain by the sale of the cocoons goes a long way towards paying their revenue.

Law of inheritance.

An equal division of property amongst the sons appears to be the prevailing custom of inheritance, but they live together as an undivided family until the youngest boy attains his majority, when the division is made. The sisters are regarded as live-stock and allotted to the brothers just as are the cattle. Thus, if a man dies, leaving three sons and three daughters and thirty head of

* Terminalia tomentosa.

cattle, on a division each son would get ten head of cattle and one sister, but if there be only one sister they wait till she marries, and divide the 'pan.'

Funeral ceremonies.

The funeral ceremonies of the Hos are deserving of special notice, as they show great reverence for the dead; and the variety and singularity of the rites performed may materially aid us in tracing the connection of the people we are describing. In my account of the Kásias, I have already drawn attention to the similarity between their funeral ceremonies and those of the Hos. The funeral rites of the Hos and Gáros have also many points of resemblance.

On the death of a respectable Ho or Múnda, a very substantial coffin is constructed and placed on faggots of firewood. The body, carefully washed and anointed with oil and turmeric, is reverently laid in the coffin, and all the clothes, ornaments, and agricultural implements that the deceased was in the habit of using are placed with it, and also any money that he had about him when he died. Then the lid of the coffin is put on, and faggots placed around and above it, and the whole is burned.

The cremation takes place in front of the deceased's house. Next morning water is thrown on the ashes, search made for bones, and a few of the larger fragments are carefully preserved, whilst the remainder with the ashes are buried. The selected bones are placed in a vessel of earthen-ware, we may call it an urn, and hung up in the apartment of the chief mourner, generally the mother or widow, that she may have them continually in view, and occasionally weep over them. Thus they remain till the very extensive arrangements necessary for their final disposal are effected. A large tombstone has to be procured, and it is sometimes so ponderous that the men of several villages are employed to move it, and some wealthy men, knowing that their successors may not have the same influence that they possess, select, during their life-time, a suitable monument to commemorate their worth, and have it moved to a handy position to be used when they die. When required for use, it is brought to the family burial-place, which, with the Hos, is close to the houses, and near it a deep round hole is dug for the reception of the cinerary urn. When all is ready, a funeral party collect in front of the deceased's house, three or four men with very deep-toned drums, and a group of about eight young girls. The chief mourner comes forth carrying the bones exposed on a decorated tray, and a procession is formed. The chief mourner with the tray leads, the girls form in two rows, those in front carry empty and partly broken pitchers and battered brass vessels, and the men with drums bring up the rear. The procession advances with a very ghostly dancing movement, slow and solemn as a minuet, in time to the beat of the deep-toned drums, not directly, but mysteriously gliding now right now left, now marking time, all in the same mournful cadence, a sad dead march.

The chief mourner carries the tray generally on her head, but at regular intervals she slowly lowers it, and as she does so the girls also gently lower and mournfully reverse the pitchers and brass vessels, and looking up for the moment with eyes full of tears, they seem to say, "Ah! see! they are empty."

In this manner the remains are taken to the house of every friend and relative of the deceased within a circle of a few miles and to every house in the village, and as the procession approaches each habitation in the weird-like manner described, the inmates all come out, and the tray having been placed on the ground at their door, they kneel over it and mourn, shedding tears on the remains as their last tribute of affection to their deceased friend. The bones are thus also conveyed to all his favorite haunts, to the fields he cultivated, to the grove he planted, to the tank he excavated, to the threshing floor where he worked with his people, to the 'Akhrá,' or dancing arena, where he made merry with them, and each spot which is hallowed with reminiscences of the deceased draws forth fresh tears from the mourners. In truth, there is a reality in their sadness that would put to shame the efforts of our undertakers and the purchased gravity of the best mutes, and it is far less noisy and more sincere than the Irish 'keening.' When this part of the ceremony is completed, the procession returns to the village and slowly gyrating round the great slab, gradually approaches its goal. At last it stops, a quantity of rice, cooked and uncooked, and other food, is now cast into the grave, and the charred fragments of bone transferred from the tray to a new earthen vessel placed over it. The hole is then filled up and covered with the large slab which effectually closes it against desecration. The slab, however, does not rest on the ground, but on smaller stones which raise it a little.

With the Múndas as among the Kásias these slabs may cover the graves of several members of a family, but the ghost of a Ho likes to have his grave all to himself.

A collection of these massive grave stones indelibly mark the site of every Ho or Múndári village, and they may now be found so marking sites in parts of the country where there have been no Kols for ages; but in addition to the slab on the tomb, a megalithic monument is set up to the memory of the deceased in some conspicuous spot outside the village. The pillars vary in height from five or six to fifteen feet, and apparently fragments of rock of the most fantastic shape are most favored. Close to the station of Chaibása on the road to Keonjhur may be seen a group of cenotaphs of unusual size, one eleven feet two inches, another thirteen feet, and a third fourteen feet above the earth; and many others of smaller dimensions. The groups of such stones that have come under my observation in the Múnda and Ho country are always in line. The circular arrangement so common elsewhere I have not seen.

The subjoined sketch with which I have been kindly favored by Mr. Ball of the Geological Survey of India will give the reader a clear conception of the appearance

Memorial stones, at Pokuria, 4 miles south of Chaibasa. The highest stone is eight feet four inches above ground.

of these cenotaphs. It will be seen that some are almost grotesque in form. The stone No. 1 in the sketch is to the memory of Khundapáter, the father of Paseng, the present Mánki of Pokuria, Nos. 2 and 3 are in memory of Kanchi and Samári, young daughters of the Mánki, and No. 4 in memory of his son.

Among the horizontal slabs under the tamarind trees in the village of Pokuria, Mr. Ball noticed one over the grave of Seni, a former wife of Paseng. It measured 17 feet 2 inches in length. Its greatest width was 9 feet 2 inches and thickness from 10 inches to a foot. Its weight was estimated at about six tons. This slate was procured in the bed of a river about three miles off. It was brought on a wagon constructed for the purpose, from three to four hundred men having been engaged in its transit.

When cenotaphs are first set up, they appear rising from an earthen platform on which it is supposed the ghost of the departed may rest. This is gradually washed away, and the older monoliths have no trace of it.

When stones are not procurable, wooden posts are put up supporting carved wooden images of birds or beasts.

I think that Múndas who embrace Christianity might be allowed to retain as much of the above beautiful funeral ceremonial as they wish to preserve. There is nothing in it repugnant to our own religious sentiments. In truth, I think it evinces a greater reverence and affection for the deceased than the hurried burial out of our sight that we ourselves adopt, and in all probability it is the oldest method. Sanitary requirements compel us to forego the old revered custom of burying our dead in graveyards round the church where our aspirations to meet them again are expressed, but if we took example from the Kols we might revert without danger to this time-honored custom of our forefathers, and Christian Kols conserving the ancient practice would retain their picturesque burial grounds under the tamarind trees in the village, or set up memorial stones round their village churches.

Hades.

I do not find that the present generation of Kols have any conception of a heaven or a hell that may not be traced to Bráhmanical or Christian teaching. They have some vague idea that the ghosts of the dead hover about, and they make offerings to them, and some have like the Chinese an altar in the house on which a portion of the 'daily bread' is offered to them; but unless under a system of prompting often inadvertently adopted, they will not tell you that this after-existence is one of reward or punishment.

Oaths.

When a Ho swears, the oath has no reference whatever to a future state. He prays that if he speak not the truth, he may be afflicted with as many calamities as befel Job, that he may suffer the loss of all his worldly wealth, his health, his wife, his children, that he may sow without reaping or reap without gathering, and finally, that he may be devoured by a tiger. It is a tremendous oath, and it is a shame to impose the obligation of making it on so generally truthful a people; but they swear not by any hope of happiness beyond the grave; and the miserable wandering life they assign to the shades can only be looked forward to with dread. They fear the ghosts and propitiate them as spirits of a somewhat malignant nature, but can have no possible desire to pass into such a state of existence themselves.

The funeral ceremonies I have described are what I myself witnessed. Colonel Tickell tells us that on the evening of the burning of the corpse certain preparations are made in the house in anticipation of a visit from the ghost. A portion of the boiled rice is set apart for it,—the commencement, we may presume, of the daily act of family devotion above noticed,—and ashes are sprinkled on the floor, in order that should it come its footprints may be detected. The inmates then leave the house and, circumambulating the pyre, invoke the spirit. Returning, they carefully scrutinise the ashes and rice, and if there is the faintest indication of these having been disturbed, it is at once attributed to the return of the spirit, and they sit down apart shivering with horror and crying bitterly as if they were by no means pleased with the visit, though made at their earnest solicitation.

I have often asked the Kols if their custom of casting money, food, and raiment on the funeral pyre, is at all connected with ideas of the resurrection of the body, or if they thought the dead would benefit by the gifts bestowed. They have always answered in the negative, and gave me the same explanation of the origin and object of the custom that I received from the Chulikata Mishmis of Upper Asám.* They are unwilling to derive any immediate benefit from the death of a member of their family; they wish for no such consolation in their grief. So they commit to the flames all his personal effects, the clothes and vessels he had used, the weapons he carried, and the money he had about him; but new things that have not been used are not treated as things that he appropriated, and they are not destroyed; and it often happens that respectable old Hos abstain from wearing new garments that they become possessed of, to save them from being wasted at the funeral.

When the interment of the bones is accomplished, the event is made known far and wide by explosions that sound like discharges from heavy guns. This is sometimes done through the agency of gunpowder, but more frequently by the application of heat and cold to fragments of schistose rock, causing them to split with loud noises.

In summing up the character of the people I have been describing, it is necessary to separate the Hos from their cognates; the circumstances under which the character of the former has been developed are different, and they are, in my opinion, physically and morally superior to the Múndas, Bhúmij, and Santáls.

They appear to me to possess a susceptibility of improvement not found in the other tribes. They have been directly under our government for about thirty-seven years, and coming to us as unsophisticated savages, we have endeavoured to civilize without allowing them to be contaminated, and whilst they still retain those traits which favorably distinguish the aborigines of India from Asiatics of higher civilization, a manner free from servility, but never rude, a love, or at least the practice, of truth, a feeling of self-respect rendering them keenly sensitive under rebuke, they have become less suspicious, less revengeful, less blood-thirsty, less contumacious, and in all respects more amenable to the laws of the realm and the advice of their officers.

They are still very impulsive, easily excited to rash, headstrong action, and apt to resent imposition or oppression without reflection, but the retaliation which often extends to a death-blow is done on the spur of the moment and openly, secret assassination being a crime almost unthought of by them. As a fair illustration of their mode of action when violently incensed I give the following:—

A Bengali trader accustomed to carry matters with a very high hand among his compatriots in the Jungle Mahâls, demanded payment of a sum of money due to him by

* *Vide* page 21.

a Ho, and not receiving it, proceeded to sequestrate and drive off a pair of bullocks, the property of his debtor. The Ho on this took to his arms, let fly an arrow which brought down the money-lender, whose head he then cut off, went with it in his hand straight to the Deputy Commissioner, and explaining to that officer exactly what had occurred, requested that he might be condemned for the crime without more ado! Murders are not now more frequent in the Kolhán than in other districts, latterly less so; but when one does take place, the perpetrator is seldom at any trouble to conceal himself or his crime.

The pluck of the Hos displayed in their first encounter with our troops and former wars, I have often seen exemplified on minor occasions. In competitive games they go to work with a will, and a strenuous exertion of their full force, unusual in natives of India. Once at the Ránchí Fair there was a race of carriages often used by travellers in Chútiá Nágpúr drawn and propelled by men. One of these came from Singbhúm and had a team of Hos; a collision took place early in the race, and the arm of one of the Ho team was badly fractured. It fell broken by his side, but he still held on to the shaft of the carriage, and cheering and yelling like the rest went round the course.

The extreme sensitiveness of both men and women is sometimes very painfully exhibited in the analysis of the numerous cases of suicide that every year occur. A harsh word to a woman never provokes a retort, but it causes in the person offensively addressed, a sudden depression of spirits or vehement outbreak of grief, which few persons would a second time care to provoke. If a girl appears mortified by anything that has been said, it is not safe to let her go away till she is soothed. A reflection on a man's honesty or veracity may be sufficient to send him to self-destruction. In a recent case, a young woman attempted to poison herself, because her uncle would not partake of the food she had cooked for him. The police returns of Singbhúm show that in nine years, from 1860 to 1869, both inclusive, 186 men and women committed suicide in that district.

I have already spoken of them as good husbands and wives, but in all the relations of life their manner to each other is gentle and kind. I never saw girls quarrelling, and never heard them abuse or say unkind things of each other, and they never coarsely abuse and seldom speak harshly to women. The only exception I know is when they believe a woman to be a witch; for such a one they have no consideration. They have no terms in their own language to express the higher emotions, but they feel them all the same.

The Múndáris are not so truthful and open as the Hos, nor do I consider them, as a rule, so manly and honest; but then the Múndas have lived for ages under conditions ill-calculated to develope the good qualities for which I have given the Hos credit. There has been a continued struggle to maintain what they consider their right in the land against the adverse interest of the landlord or his assigns. The very conditions under which most of them hold their lands place them in a position of dependence and inferiority, as they have to labour for their landlord as well as pay rent to him. Moreover, they live among a people who look down on them as a degraded race, and one of whose favorite theories is, that the Kols were created to serve them. This, no doubt, must be as demoralising as it is aggravating, and in many places the

Múndáris and Oráons have listened to it so long that they begin to accept the doctrine, and calmly subside into the position of serfdom allotted to them.

The licentiousness indulged in by Múndáris and Hos at their great festival is of course incompatible with purity and chastity, and there is no doubt that the majority of the elders are terrible sots; but in Singbhúm the rising generation show a disposition to abandon sottish and licentious habits, and it is satisfactory to know that they can be entirely weaned from them. About seven thousand Múndas have now embraced Christianity, and recently the movement has extended to the Hos of Singbhúm. One of the Mánkis with all his family and a considerable number of his villagers have been baptized, and, generally speaking, all those who have embraced our religion have entirely withdrawn from participation in the wild revelry of their pagan brethren. Their pastors have made this a test of their sincerity, and it is no doubt a very severe one. The women must lay aside all their trinkets, and should not be seen, even as spectators, at dances. The last condition is too hard, and is, I know, frequently evaded; but the first is readily acquiesced in, and native female converts look with astonishment at the jewelry displayed on the persons of European ladies even in church, and wondering ask—"Have they been baptized?"

In regard to breaches of chastity and sins against modesty which I have noticed, it is to be observed that whatever is done on these convivial occasions is confined to their own people. The instances of Múnda or Ho girls committing themselves to acts of impropriety with males of another tribe are exceedingly rare, and such a thing as prostitution or its baneful effects is entirely unknown among them. It is, I think, true that the race generally are duller of comprehension and more difficult to teach than Hindus or Muhammadans, and with the exception of those who embrace Christianity, the Múndas are usually unwilling to learn; but the Hos have of late years evinced considerable interest in education, and the progress they make is satisfactory, their anxiety to learn and wonderful diligence making up for sluggishness in intellect.

SECTION 6.—THE SANTÁLS.

Geographical Distribution.

The Santáls are found at intervals, sometimes in considerable masses, but more generally much scattered, in a strip of Bengal, extending for about 350 miles from the Ganges to the Baitarní, bisected by the meridian of Bhágalpúr or 87° east longitude, and comprising the following districts:—Bhágalpúr, the Santál Parganas, Bírbhúm, Bancúra, Hazáríbágh, Mánbhúm, Mednípúr, Singbhúm, Mayurbhanj, and Balasore. The Santál Parganas, or Santalia, said to contain upwards of two hundred thousand Santáls, may now be regarded as the nucleus of the tribe, but it does not appear to have been one of their original seats. Buchanan Hamilton, in describing the Hill tribes of Bhágalpúr and its vicinity, makes no mention of Santáls. The aboriginal tribes he fell in with are called 'Malers,' the Rájmahál Hill men proper and their kindred, a Dravidian people. It is singular that no old colonies of Santáls or other Kolarian tribes are found between the Himalayas and the Ganges. The Santál settlements that now border on that river or skirt the Rájmahál Hills are readily traced back to more southern districts, and their own traditions hardly support the theory of their northern origin. Indeed, when we find that the Kolarian races have left their trail in Asám, that it may be followed throughout the Siam States and Burma to the Pegu district, and is faintly discerned in the adjoining islands, that it may be taken up at Point Palmyras and clearly traced along both banks of the Damúdar river till it reaches the hills and table-land of Chútiá Nágpúr, it is scarcely reasonable to assume that they have all come direct from the Himalayas. The Damúdar, rising in Palámau, divides the Hazáríbágh and Chútiá Nágpúr plateaux, and draining the northern face of the one and the southern face of the other, discharges itself into the Húghlí, near the mouth of the latter river. It is the terrestrial object most venerated by the Santáls; and the country that is most closely associated with their name, which they apparently regard as their fatherland, is between that river and the Kasai.

There is no doubt, however, that Santáls colonised parts of the Hazáríbágh district and parts of Bírbhúm at a very remote period, and it is chiefly by migrations from those colonies that the modern Santalia has been formed.

The Dáman-i-koh.

In 1832* a considerable impetus was given to the northward movement in the action taken by Government to secure to the Rájmahál Highlanders their possessions in the hills that form the turning point of the Ganges at Sáhibganj. To prevent the encroachments of the lowland zamíndárs of the Bhágalpúr district, which were constantly exciting reprisals from the Highlanders, a tract of country measuring nearly three hundred miles in circumference was separated and marked off by large masonry pillars, and of all the land within those pillars the Government was declared to be head proprietor, and the Hill people were informed that their rights in it would be respected so long as they conducted themselves peaceably. But the Hillmen only cared for the highlands and the tract included within the pillars called the Dáman-i-koh, or skirts of the hills, and the valleys running into the hills were available for other settlers, and were speedily taken up by Santáls. In a few years the Santál population in the Dáman had increased from three thousand to eighty-three thousand souls, when the colony received a check by the Santál insurrection of 1854.

For a history of this rebellion and the causes that led to it the reader may be referred to Mr. Hunter's interesting volume, called 'Rural Bengal.' The Santáls, starting with the desire to revenge themselves on the money-lenders who had taken advantage of their simplicity and improvidence, found themselves arrayed in arms against the British Government, and it was not without bloodshed that the insurrection was suppressed; but it led to their being re-established under a more genial administration in what are called the Santál Parganas. In the Dáman-i-koh their own form of self-government is to some extent restored to them. The villages are farmed to the head-men, called Mánjhis, who are also the sole guardians of the peace, a system that had been already introduced with success into the Kolhán of Singbhúm.

Nomadic habits.

In marked contrast to the Kolarians of the Múnda and Ho divisions, the Santáls, as a rule, care little for permanently locating themselves. A country denuded of the primeval forest which affords them the hunting grounds they delight in and the virgin soil they prefer, does not attract them; and when, through their own labor, the spread of cultivation has effected this denudation, they select a new site, however prosperous they may have been on the old, and retire into the

* See "Notes on a Tour through the Rájmahál Hills," by Colonel Walter Sherwill, Journal, Asiatic Society of Bengal, No. VII of 1851.

backwoods, where their harmonious flutes sound sweeter, their drums find deeper echoes, and their bows and arrows may once more be utilized. The traditions of their ancient migrations are rendered obscure by the succession of dissolving views to which this nomadic habit introduces us, but they nevertheless tenaciously cling to a wild and remote tradition of their origin; and though much scattered and intermingled with other races whose creeds and customs they have partially adopted, they are characterised by many old practices that they lovingly cling to, and they are one of the tribes which has preserved the form of speech that in all probability predominated in the Gangetic provinces before the Áryan conquest.

Houses.

But though prone to change, the Santáls are not indifferent to their personal comfort, and are more careful in the construction of their homesteads and villages than their cognates. Their huts, with carefully formed mud walls and well raised plinths and snug verandahs, have a neat, and, owing to their love of colour, even a gay appearance. They paint their walls in alternate broad stripes of red, white, and black—native clays and charcoal furnishing the pigments; moreover, the houses are kept perfectly clean, and by partitions decent accommodation for the family is provided.

In the situation of their villages they generally seek insulation, and would gladly, if they could, exclude all foreigners, especially Bráhmans; but as they clear lands that they do not care to retain and render habitable, regions that wild beasts would without them be sole lords of, they are soon followed into their retreat by the more crafty and enterprising Hindu, and the result often is they have to submit to, or give way to, the intruders. It frequently happens that the Hindu intruder improving on the Santál cultivation and making more money by it, obtains from the landlord a lease of the village at a rent the Santál would not think of paying or demanding, and so the pioneers of civilization are prematurely forced to move on.

The Santáls have of late been the most honored of the aboriginal races in Bengal in the attention that enquirers have directed towards them. In Mr. Mann's monograph we have an interesting account of their social state, and in the work by Mr. Hunter, above alluded to, an elaborate and admirably written essay on their religion, customs, and language, that have made them, no doubt, the best generally known of our Bengal non-Áryans; but instead of following these accounts, I will give the information I have myself collected about the Santáls in this province.

Vast numbers of the Santáls now settled in Santalia emigrated within the last century from the Hazáríbágh district, but there are still large settlements of the tribe in Kharakdia to the north of Parisnáth, and in the hill country between Gola and the Damúdar; and some intelligent and influential head men, called Parganaits. One of these, Bágh Rái Parganait, from a Damúdar settlement, gives me orally the following version of the mythical origin and progress of the tribe.

Legends.

BÁGH RÁI'S NARRATIVE.—"A wild goose coming from the great ocean a lighted at Ahirí Piprí, and there laid two eggs. From these two eggs a male and female were produced, who were the parents of the Santál race. From Ahirí Piprí our progenitors migrated to Hara Duttie, and there they greatly increased and multiplied, and were called *Kharwárs*. Thence they removed to Khairagarh and Hurredgarhí, and eventually settled in Chai Champá in the Hazáríbágh district, where they remained for several generations.

3 D

"There were many Bírhors in that country (they are still to be found there), and one of them seduced a Santál girl; she bore a child and cast it on a dung-heap, where it was found by the Paramánik and Jag Mánjhi; they brought it home and fostered it, and the child grew up and became a very powerful man, whom no one could withstand, and he demanded a wife. They said that no Santál girl should ever marry the son of a Bírhor. Then the strong man, to whom they had given the Hindu name of Mádhú Singh, declared he would violate all the Santál virgins, if one were not bestowed on him in marriage. The Santáls above all things regard the honor of their maidens, and greatly alarmed at this threat, they resolved to abandon Chai Champá to be rid of Mádhú Singh. In one night they all left with their women and children, cattle and moveables, and proceeding to Chútiá Nágpúr, the country of the Múndas, they came to 'Marang Búrú' (the great mountain), the god of that people, and prayed to him that Mádhú Singh and the Bírhors might not be permitted to overtake them, and he, interposing his great mass between them and their pursuers (the path wound up a steep ghát and round from the north to the south side of the mountain), effectually protected them. Thus our fathers became votaries of Marang Búrú, the god of the Múndas, offering sacrifices of goats to him, and we continue to worship him to this day, assigning to him a place in the sacred grove with Jáhir Era and Monika. Our ancestors made no sojourn in Nágpúr, but went on to Jhalda, then in possession of the Múndas, though now the Hindu Kúrmis hold it." [This is confirmed by the fact that all the old village sites in Jhalda are marked by the indelible monolithic monuments of the Múndas.] "They next tried Pátkúm, but found no resting place among the Bhúmij, and pushed on to Saont, and finding much forest there, settled and built good houses and began to enjoy themselves, according to our custom, and to dance, play, and sing. But the Saont Raja, seeing our maidens dancing, took a fancy to them, and demanded that one should be given to him. This was refused, and the people dreading the consequence of refusal, left the Saont country and went to Sikhar. It was from our long sojourn in Saont that we took the name of Santál; we were previously called Kharwárs. We formed numerous villages in what is now the eastern part of the Mánbhúm district; but as we increased and the jungle disappeared, colonies of our people went west and took up Sonábádí and Guttiárí in the Gola Pargana (Hazáríbágh district) and Sikhar, through which the Damúdar flows. My ancestor was the leader of the colony that took up Sonábádí. There were many Kharwár Rajas in those days, and one was established at Gola, to whom my ancestor paid tribute. In the time of my grandfather, Kangál Parganait, the Ghátwálí system was introduced (that is, they were required to protect the roads and passes), and it was in his time that the English were first seen in our country. One of them carrying a red stick, and thence called Lál-láthí, came to Sonábádí. He had followers with brass-engraved plates on their breasts and two strange looking dogs, and he asked for the head man, and when my grandfather appeared, they tied him up and ordered him to point out land on which a bungalow could be built, and on my grandfather giving the land he was released. There was much iron ore lying about. Lál-láthí immediately set the smelters at work, made quantities of iron and sent it all out of the country."

Thus briefly and quaintly Bágh Rái tells, according to his light, the history of his race from the creation to the establishment of British rule. The delineation of the first bold Briton that appeared amongst them, energetic and practical, is evidently a life picture. The explanation regarding Lál-láthí is probably nothing more than a Santál gloss on the word 'Wiláyatí,' foreigner. The tradition that Bágh Rái gives of the origin of his race will be found at length, though somewhat differently told, in Mr. Hunter's 'Rural Bengal' and Mr. Mann's work. If, as is not impossible, the Santáls crossed the Bay of Bengal in coming to India, the wild goose may be the white sailed vessel that bore them. The more detailed versions of the legend have been obviously filled in from Bráhmanical sources. The Santáls now speak of the Damúdar as their sea, and the ceremonies in honor of their dead are always considered incomplete till some charred fragment of the burnt body is committed to the stream to be borne away to the ocean.

I am unable to identify the Ahirí Piprí, but Khairágarh and Chai Champá are in the Hazáríbágh or Rámgarh district, and to Chai Champá remote Santáls, as well as those in this district, frequently allude.

At Chai there is an old fort, the walls of which, of earth and stones, enclose a space of about five acres of land. The tradition about it is, that it was the abode of Jangra, a Santál Raja, who destroyed himself and his family on hearing of the approach of a Muhammadan army under General Sayyid Ibráhím Alí,* *alias* Malik Bayá. A Muhammadan officer named Hazrat Fath Khán Duála was placed in charge of the fort, and on his dying there, a place of worship or 'Dargá' was erected near his grave. There is another fort at Mángarh, four miles from Chai, which is also assigned by tradition to a Santál chief called Mán Singh. He abandoned his fort on the approach of the Muhammadans. At and about Chai it is said that there were formerly six Santál chiefs, three in Bihár and three in the Hazáríbágh district.

Saont, supposed to have given the Santáls their present name, is Silda in Mednípúr.

Saont.

About the time that I was transcribing Bágh Rái's narrative, my friend Bábú Rakháldás Haldhar, Assistant Commissioner, Chútiá Nágpúr, was, at my request, making some enquiries regarding Santáls in the eastern district, and without having heard what Bágh Rái had stated, he wrote to ask me if this might not be the place where the Santáls first settled. He tells me that Pargana Silda, in which the Santáls still predominate, is properly called Samanta Bhúmi, and that Chatna, adjoining it, but in the Mánbhúm district, is admittedly a corruption of the same name. Whether this name was first given to that part of the country in consequence of its being inhabited by 'Saontals,' or that the people took the name from the country as stated by Bágh Rái, I cannot tell; but putting together all the facts and legends that we possess, it is probable that the Santáls were originally located in Eastern Bengal from the sea-coast inwards, and that colonies were gradually pushed on to the Hazáríbágh district, or to Chai Champá and Kharakdia, and from thence northward, and that Bágh Rái's account of their movement eastward from Chai Champá to Saont through Chútiá Nágpúr is the reverse of what took place.

Relationship with the Kharwárs.

Another very remarkable circumstance touched on by Bágh Rái is the implied relationship between the Santáls and Kharwárs. In writing about the latter long before I had seen Bágh Rái (*vide* page 130), I gave some reasons for suspecting such a relationship, and Mr. Mann and Mr. Hunter

* He is also called Malik Bayú, and was a General of Muhammad Tughluk. He died in the second year of Fírúzsháh's reign, on the 13th Zil Hajjah, 753 A. H., or 20th January, 1353 A. D. His tomb is in the town of Bihár. The legends of the district frequently mention his name.

both note that Kharwár, or a name like it, is an old name of the Santáls. In the traditions of Bihár and Sháhábád, as given in Buchanan Hamilton's work, the Cheros, Kols, and Kharwárs are blended together, and it is probable that the Santáls are not wrong in claiming relationship with the Kharwárs, but by their own account the Santáls have never played a prominent rôle in history; always clinging to the skirts of hills and forests and constantly shifting, they appear never to have advanced beyond the polity of a village community. Ignoring all relationship with other Kolarians, they yet have no tradition that they ever formed a nation or had a Raja or ruler of their own; and though great vocalists and melodists, they have no song commemorative of ancient glory. When they rose in 1855 A.D., it is probable that they contemplated no more than the extermination of their tormentors, the money-lenders. It is at all events the first time we hear of them in revolt, though so constantly migrating to avoid oppression. I cannot but think that the Múndas and Hos, who tenaciously cling to their holdings and have always shown themselves ready to fight for them if necessary, must have the prestige of superior birth. There are many reasons for supposing that the Cheros, who were a ruling race, and the Múndas and Hos, are of the same stock, but the Santáls and Kharwárs may have become one people with them after having been subjugated.

The Santáls, like the Kharwárs, belong to, or have mixed much with, the dark races of India. The Cheros, Hos, and Múndas are, on the whole, fairer and preserve more distinctly traits of the Tartar type.

Physical traits.

The Santáls are noticeable for a great vagueness in the chiselling of the features, a general tendency to roundness of outline where sharpness is more conducive to beauty, a blubbery style of face, and both in male and female a greater tendency to corpulency than we meet in their cognates. Their faces are almost round; cheekbones moderately prominent; eyes full and straight, not obliquely set in the head; nose, if at all prominent, of somewhat a retroussée style, but generally broad and depressed; mouth large, and lips very full and projecting; hair straight and coarse and black. Mr. Mann notes of them, and I concur in the remark, that their cast of countenance almost approaches the Negro type. The females, he says, have small hands and feet, and are ox-eyed, and these are characteristics which the tribes linguistically allied to them do not possess. Mr. Hunter describes them as about the same height as the ordinary Hindu, but I should feel inclined to consider them as rather below that standard; he further well characterises* them, as "created to labour rather than to think, better fitted to serve the manual exigencies of the present than to speculate on the future or venerate the past."

Tribal divisions.

The Santáls, like the Israelites, are divided into twelve tribes: 1, Sáran; 2, Murmu; 3, Marli; 4, Kisku; 5, Bésera; 6, Hansda; 7, Túdi; 8, Baski; 9, Hemrow; 10, Karwar; 11, Chorai; 12, * * Except No. 11, the above agree with the nomenclature of tribal divisions of Santál tribes given in Mr. Mann's work; numbers 1, 2, 3, 4, 6, 7, and 11 with the names of the seven sons of the first parents in Mr. Hunter's essay. Numbers 2, 3, 6, 9 and 11 are found in the list of the tribes of the Singbhúm Larka Kols, or Hos. This is remarkable, as the legends of origin handed down among the Larkas have little in

* 'Rural Bengal,' page 146.

common with the traditions of the Santáls; and though the former also assign twelve sons to the first parents, they were the primogenitors, not of the various tribes, or kílis, of Hos, but of different families of mankind, including Hindus and Santáls, the latter being the offspring of the youngest pair, who, when told to separate from the family, selected pig as their staple food. The names given above include only one to which a meaning is attached, 'Múrmu,' which signifies the Nílgáo, *Portax (Antelope) pictus*, and the Múrmus may not kill the animal whose name they adopt, nor touch its flesh.

Polity.

The polity of the Santáls is very patriarchal. In each village there is, 1st, a Jag-mánjhi, whose most important duty is apparently to look after the morals of the boys and girls, and if he is at all straightlaced, they must often lead him a hard life of it; 2nd, a Parámánik, whose business it is to attend to the farming arrangements and to apportion the lands. He disallows any monopoly of peculiarly fertile rice lands; all must take their share of good and bad. He has to look after the interests of new settlers and to provide for guests, levying contributions for the purpose on the villagers. All the offices are hereditary; when a new settlement is formed the office bearers are elected, after that the next of kin succeeds. There is a village priest who is called Naia (Náyaka, *vulgo* Láyá). This is a word of Sanskrit derivation, and as they have no name in their own language for such a functionary, it is probably not an original institution. He has lands assigned to him, but out of the profits of his estate he has to feast the people twice in the year—at the festival of the Sarhúl, held towards the end of March, when the Sál tree blossoms, and at the Moi Muri festival, held in the month of Ásin (September—October), for a blessing on the crops. At the Sohrai feast, the harvest home, in December, the Jag-mánjhi entertains the people, and the cattle are anointed with oil and daubed with vermilion, and a share of the hándia, rice beer, is given to each animal. Every third year in most houses, but in some every fourth or fifth year, the head of the family offers a goat to the sun god 'Sing Bonga' for the prosperity of the family, especially of the children, "that they may not be cut off by disease, or fall into sin." The sacrifice is offered at sunrise on any open space cleaned and purified for the occasion. A very important distinction is observed by all the Kolarians in the motive of the sacrifices to the supreme deity and those by which the minor gods are propitiated. To Sing Bonga the sacrifice is to secure a continuance of his mercies and for preservation. The other deities are resorted to when disease or misfortune visit the family, the sacrifice being to propitiate the spirit who is supposed to be afflicting or punishing them.

Festivals.

The supreme deity.

Worship of ancestral manes.

Ancestors are worshipped, or rather their memory is honored, at the time of the Sohrai festival, and offerings made at home by each head of a family. In the meantime the Naia propitiates the local devils, 'bhúts.' In many villages the Santáls join with the Hindus in celebrating the Dúrgá Púja, the great festival in honor of Devi, and the Holi in honor of Krishna. Their own priests take no part in the ceremonial observances at those Hindu feasts; they are left to the Bráhmans.

Priestly functions.

The person or persons who have to offer sacrifices at the Santál feasts have to prepare themselves for the duty by fasting and prayer and by placing themselves for some time in a position of apparent mental absorption. The beating of drums appears at last to arouse them, and they

3 E

commence violently shaking their heads and long hair till they work themselves into a real or apparent state of involuntary or spasmodic action, which is the indication of their being possessed. They may then give oracular answers to interrogatories regarding the future, or declare the will of the spirit invoked or about to be propitiated. When the demoniacal possession appears to have reached its culminating point, the possessed men seize and decapitate the victims and pour the blood into vessels ready placed for its reception.

Among the Santáls in Chútiá Nágpúr, Sing Bonga, the sun, is the supreme god, the creator and preserver. The other deities are 'Jáhir Era,' Monika, and Marang Búrú, and they are all malignant and destructive. In the eastern districts the tiger is worshipped, but in Rámgarh only those who have suffered loss through that animal's ferocity condescend to adore him. If a Santál is carried off by a tiger, the head of the family deems it necessary to propitiate the 'Bágh Bhút' (tiger devil). Occasionally the villagers all join in sacrificing a bullock or buffalo to Marang Búrú. They have no very clear conception to what Búrú, or mountain, their devotions should be especially paid, but he is honored as Lord of the Jungles. The Santáls further east adore deities and Chando Bonga, the moon god, and Bágh Bhút, the tiger; and to be sworn on a tiger-skin is the most solemn of oaths.

Minor deities.

Santáls who, under the example and precept of Bengali Hindus, have abjured some practices considered impure by the latter, are called Sat Santáls, that is, pure Santáls; but there is a national antagonism between them and the Hindus that prevents any close fraternization or communion between the races. They are not over-particular about food, but nothing will induce them to eat rice cooked by a Hindu, even by a Bráhman. Unfortunately during the famine of 1866 this was not known to us. The cooks who prepared the food distributed at the relief centres were all Bráhmans, and it was supposed that this would suit all classes, but the Sántals kept aloof, and died rather than eat from hands so hateful to them. They have no tradition to account for this bitter feeling. The animosity remains, though its cause is forgotten.

Food.

The Santál parents have to undergo purification five days after childbirth; a kind of gruel is prepared, and after a libation to Sing Bonga or Marang Búrú, it is served out to the mother and the other members of the family. An eldest son is always named after his grandfather, other children after other relations. The Santáls have adopted as a rite the tonsure of children and do not appear to recognise the necessity for any other ceremonial observance till their marriage when adult. Child marriage is not practised.

Social customs.

There is no separate dormitory for the boys and girls in a Santál village. Accommodation is decorously provided for them in the house of the parents, but the utmost liberty is given to the youth of both sexes. The old people, though affecting great regard for the honor of the girls, display great confidence in their virtue. Unrestrained they resort to markets, to festivals and village dances in groups; and if late in the evening, they return under escort of the young men who have been their partners in the dances or have played to them; no harm is thought of it.

The peculiar emblem of the Santáls should be the flute; they are distinguished from all people in contact with them by their proficiency on that instrument. Made of bamboo not less than one inch in diameter, and about two feet in length, they are equal in size to the largest of our concert flutes

Music.

and have deep rich tones. This faculty of playing the flute and a general knowledge of singing and dancing were, they say, imparted to them by their first parents, and it was also by their first parents that they were taught the mysteries of the home brew, and they, therefore, consider there can be no great harm in freely indulging in it.

Dances.

There is always reserved an open space in front of the Jag-mánjhí's house as a dancing place. To this the young men frequently resort after the evening meal, and the sound of their flutes and drums soon attract the maidens, who smooth and adjust their long hair, and adding to it a flower or two, blithely join them.

It is singular that in this national amusement of the Santáls we have handed down to us a most vivid living representation of one prominent scene in the sports of Krishna in Vraja and Vrindávana. There is nothing in modern Hindu life that at all illustrates the animated scenes so graphically delineated in the Puráns; but the description of the 'Rasa' dance in chapter XIII, book V, of the Vishnu Purán, might be taken literally as an account of the Santál 'Júmhir.' We have in both the maidens decked with flowers and ornamented with tinkling bracelets, the young men with garlands of flowers and peacocks' feathers, holding their hands and closely compressed, so that the breast of the girl touches the back of the man next to her, going round in a great circle, limbs all moving as if they belonged to one creature, feet falling in perfect cadence; the dancers in the ring singing responsive to the musicians in the centre, who fluting, drumming, and dancing too are the motive power of the whole, and form an axis of the circulár movement.

Thus, as the pivot for the dances, sometimes sported Krishna and his favorite companions, "making sweet melody with voices and flutes," but more frequently they took their places in the ring, "each feeling the soft pressure of two maidens in the great circling dance."

We are told that Krishna when he thought the lovely light of autumn propitious for the Rása dance, with Ráma commenced singing sweet low strains in various measures such as the Gopís (milkmaids) loved, and they as soon as they heard the melody quitted their homes and joined him; just so, on a moonlight night, the Santál youth invite the Santál maidens. Professor Wilson, in his note on the passages of the Vishnu Purán referred to above, observes that the 'Rás Yátra' is celebrated in various parts of India in the month of Kartika (October), but that a circular dance of men and women does not form any prominent feature at these entertainments, and he doubts if it ever is performed. In the late autumn months the Kols and Oráons have numerous yátras or játras, at which these circular dances are performed by thousands. I will revert to these yátras in describing the Oráons of Chútiá Nágpúr.*

Marriages.

With such freedom of intercourse, it follows that marriages are generally love matches, and, on the whole, happy ones; but it is considered more respectable if the arrangements are made by the parents or guardians without any acknowledged reference to the young people. The price to be paid for the girl, averaging five rupees, with presents of cloths to her parents, having been determined on, a day is fixed for a preliminary feast, and afterwards for the marriage itself, and a knotted string; which shows the number of days that intervene, is kept as a memo-

* See also description of the dance of the Hayas, page 106.

randum. Each morning one of these knots is removed by the impatient lover, and when the last is loosened, the bridegroom and his friends with noisy music set out for the abode of the bride. As they approach the village, the Jag-mánjhi comes out to meet them, attended by women with water to wash the feet of the guests, who are then escorted to the house of the bride, and the two mingling together merrily sing, dance, and feast in front of the bride's chamber. At the last quarter of the night, the bridegroom makes his appearance riding on the hip of one of his comrades, and soon after the bride is brought out by a brother or brother-in-law in a basket. Then comes the inevitable 'sindra dán.' The groom daubs his lady-love on the crown and brow very copiously with vermilion (sindúr), and the assembled guests applaud with cries of 'hari bol.' The bride and groom who have fasted all the day now eat together, and this is supposed to be the first time that the girl has sat with a man at her food. It is creditable to the Kolarians that this custom has been retained through ages, notwithstanding the derision with which it is viewed by all Hindus. On the following day before the party breaks up, the young people are thus admonished by one of the sages—"Oh boy! oh girl! you are from this day forth to comfort each other in sickness or sorrow. Hitherto you have only played and worked (as directed), now the responsibility of the household duties is upon you; practise hospitality, and when a kinsman arrives wash his feet, and respectfully salute him." No priest officiates during a Santál marriage. The social meal that the boy and girl eat together is the most important part of the ceremony, as by the act the girl ceases to belong to her father's tribe, and becomes a member of her husband's family.

Santáls seldom have more than one wife, and she is treated with most exemplary kindness and consideration. Should the husband be for any reason, as her barrenness, induced to seek a second partner during her lifetime, the first wife is never deposed from her position as head of the household; the second wife must obey her and serve her.

Daily life.

A Santál in prosperous seasons leads a pleasant life. He is either busy with his cultivation or playing his flute, or dancing with the girls, or engaged in the chase. He throws himself with ardour into the latter pursuit, and in hunting down beasts of prey he evinces great skill and powers of endurance and indomitable pluck. They have every year a great hunting festival in which thousands take part. These expeditions are organized with as much care and forethought, as if the hosts engaged in them were about to undertake a military campaign, and take place in the hot season, when the beasts have least cover to conceal themselves in. When the array of hunters reaches the ground on which operations against the wild beasts are to commence, they form a line of beaters several miles in length, every man armed with a bow and arrows and a battle-axe, and accompanied by dogs, who, though ugly creatures to look at, appear, like their masters, to be endowed with a true hunting instinct. When they emerge from the woods on open spaces, the game of all kinds that are driven before them suddenly appear. Birds take wing and are beaten down with sticks or shot with arrows; quadrupeds, great and small, are similarly treated, and in this way deer, pig, jungle fowl, peafowl, hare, &c., are bagged; but tigers and bears on these occasions of open warfare are generally avoided.

Hunting expeditions.

These hunting excursions last for four or five days, and at the end of each day the Santáls feast merrily on the contents of their bags and thoroughly enjoy themselves.

Their rule in regard to possession of an animal killed is that it belongs to him who first wounded it, no matter by whom the *coup de grace* may have been inflicted.

The Santáls employed in the police force are very highly spoken of by an officer who long commanded them. They may not be expert detectives in tortuous cases, but in following up dacoits and attacking them when caught, they are far superior to the ordinary Bengali constables, and many instances of their activity and pluck have been related to me. Living as they generally do on the edges of forests, their constitutions are proof against malaria, and they may be employed on outpost duty in localities that are deadly to most people. They have been thus utilized on the grand trunk road in places where the jungle comes down to the road.

Character as police constables.

It often happens that the virtues of Santáls employed in the police "are sanctified and holy traitors to them," their truthfulness and honesty cause them to be mistrusted by the more corrupt members of the force, and if their officer is not careful in protecting them, they are often worried into resigning it; besides, their peccadilloes are watched and reported by men who are hostile to them, and this often bars their promotion or leads to their dismissal. It is said that they are losing their character for truthfulness; I have not myself found this. The Santáls in Singbhúm, who live much to themselves, are a very simple-minded people, almost incapable of deception.

The Santáls dress better than most of their cognates. This also, it appears, is derived from the instruction of their first parents, who appointed the size of the garments that were to be worn respectively by male and female, but omitted to teach their offspring how they were to be made. They have no weavers among their own people. According to the tradition, the progenitors of the race gave their children an ornamental rather than a useful education; they taught them to sing and dance and play on the flute and drum, but failed to instruct them in any useful art.

Costume.

The women wear ample 'sárís,' a large thick cloth not less than six yards in length with a gay red border. One-half of this forms the lower garment secured at the waist, but not so as to impede the free action of the limbs; the other half is passed over the left shoulder, leaving the right shoulder, arm, and part of the breast free, and allowed to hang down in front. It is not, as with Hindu maidens, used also as a veil. The heads of young girls are generally uncovered, displaying a mass of black, rather coarse, but sometimes wavy hair, gathered into a large knob at one side of the back of the head, ornamented with flowers or with tufts of colored silk.

'Their arms, ankles, and throats* are each laden with heavy brass or bell-metal ornaments. I had a quantity of these ornaments weighed and found that the bracelets fluctuated from two to four pounds,' and the entire weight sustained by one of these belles was found to be no less than thirty-four pounds of brass or bell-metal. The average may be estimated at about twelve pounds.

The Santál women are represented by all who have written about them as exceedingly chaste, yet the young people of the different sexes are greatly devoted to each other's society and pass much time together. No one has observed of them that they have customs of an immoral tendency such as obtain among the Múndas and Oráons; but I do not suppose there is in this respect much difference between the three tribes. In all

* From Colonel Walter Sherwill's notes.

these the results of the nocturnal dances and freedom of intercourse must be pretty much the same, and Jag-mánjhis have admitted to me that they have plenty of such love affairs to arrange.

Funeral ceremonies.

In funeral ceremonies the Santál varies from the practice of the Ho and Múnda tribes. The body is borne away on a chárpái (cot) by kinsmen, and when it reaches a cross-road, some parched rice and cotton seed are scattered about as a charm against the malignant spirits that might throw obstacles in the way of the ceremony; it is then taken to a funeral pile near some reservoir or stream and placed on it. The son or brother is the first to apply fire to the body by placing a piece of burning wood on the face of the corpse, and soon all that is left are ashes and a few charred fragments of bones of the skull which are carefully preserved. Towards evening, it is customary for a man to take his seat near the ashes with a winnowing fan, in which he tosses rice till a phrensy appears to seize him, and he becomes inspired and says wonderful things. After the incremation, the immediate relatives of the deceased have to undergo a quarantine, as impure, for five days. On the sixth, they shave themselves and bathe, and after the sacrifice of a cock repair for consolation to the nearest liquor shop.

In due course the bones that have been saved are taken by the nearest of kin to the Damúdar. He enters the stream bearing the sacred relics on his head in a basket, and selecting a place where the current is strong, he dips and commits the contents of his basket to the water, to be borne away to the great ocean as the resting place of the race.

All inquirers on the subject appear to have arrived at the conclusion that the Santáls have no belief in a future state. The pilgrimage to the Damúdar with the remains is simply an act of reverence and affection unconnected with any idea that there is a place where those who have left this world may again meet.

It is to be observed that when the Santáls in disposing of their dead differ from the Múndas, the former approximate to the Bráhmanical custom. It is in fact a rough outline of the Bráhman ritual, and only wants filling in. The halting at cross-roads and the scattering of rice, the application of fire first to the head by a relation, the collecting of the charred bones, especially those of the head, are all included in the ceremonies enjoined on Bráhmans and orthodox Hindus.

The Bráhman, like the Santál, carefully preserves the bones in an earthen vessel; he is ordered to bury them in a safe place till a convenient season arrives for his journey to the sacred river—in his case the Ganges—where he consigns the vessel with its contents to the waters.

SECTION 7.—THE BÍRHORS.

Bírhors and Mádhú Singh.

The reference to Mádhú Singh and the Bírhors in the foregoing pages caused me to make further inquiry regarding that tribe in the Hazáríbágh district, and I have been favored by Bábú Kálidás Pálit, Assistant Commissioner, now in charge of the Rámgarh Estate, with some particulars about them, which I subjoin.

I have already noticed the Bírhors in the paper on the Kharriás, supposing them to be a kindred tribe. Among themselves they speak the Kol language, but can also converse freely in such Hindí as is spoken in this province.

The Bábú visited some of their settlements; he found that the tradition about Mádhú Singh was evidently known to them, but they were disinclined to give any information about him. An old Bírhor of 85 years was communicative on other subjects, and commenced on that of Mádhú Singh, but the moment he mentioned the name, his wife shut him up, and the old man would say no more.

Houses.

The Bírhors were found living in the jungles on the sides of hills in huts constructed only of branches of trees and leaves, but so made as to be quite watertight; their huts are as small as those of the Juángs, previously described. The entrance door faces the east, and is about two feet from the ground. A man and his wife and young children sleep together in this small hut six feet square, but grown up children are provided with separate huts; they lie on date tree leaf mats spread on the ground. They have hardly any cultivation, and never touch a plough. A man with his family who not long ago left their community and took to cultivating in the plains, are now considered outcasts. The men spend their time in snaring hares and monkeys, collecting edible roots and jungle fruits and the chob *(Bauhinia scandens)* bark, of which they make strings for various purposes. They are seldom seen in the villages, but the women frequent the markets to sell their ropes and jungle produce.

Legends.

The Bírhors affirm that they and the Kharwárs are of the same race descended from the sun. They came, seven brothers, to this country from Khairágarh (in the Kaimúr hills); four went to the east, and three brothers remained in the Rámgarh district. One day when the three brothers were going out to fight against the chiefs of the country, the head dress of one of them got entangled in a tree. He deemed it a bad omen, and remained behind in the jungle. His two brothers went without him and gained a victory over the chiefs, and returning found their brother employed in cutting the bark of the chob. They derided him, calling him the Bírhor,* or chob cutter; he replied that he would rather remain a Bírhor and reign in the jungles than associate with such haughty brothers. Thus originated the Bírhors, lords of the jungles. The other two brothers became Rajas of the country called Rámgarh.

Numerical strength.

The number of the Bírhors is limited, estimated at not more than 700 for the whole Hazáríbágh district. They are quite a nomadic race, wandering about from jungle to jungle, as the sources of their subsistence become exhausted. There are about ten families in the jungles near the village of Rámgarh, forty in the vicinity of Gola, ten in the jungles of Jagesar, and forty families about Chatra and Datar. Major Thompson, in his report on Palámau, speaks of them as the aborigines of that district. They are found in Chútiá Nágpúr proper, in Jashpúr, and in Mánbhúm.

The women dress decently; they have marks of tattooing on their chest, arms, and ankles; they have no such marks on the face.

Women.

After childbirth a woman remains in her hut for six days, and has no food, except medicinal herbs. Then the infant is taken out, not by the ordinary door, but by an opening made in the opposite wall; this, it is believed, protects it from being devoured by a tiger or bitten by a snake.

---

* *Bírhor* is Múnda for a woodman or forester.

Marriages.

Parents arrange the marriage of their children. The father of the bridegroom pays three rupees to the father of the bride. They have no priests, and the only ceremony is drawing blood from the little fingers of the bridegroom and bride, and with this the tilak is given to each by marks made above the clavicle. This, as I have elsewhere noted, I believe to be the origin of the practice now so universal of marking with red-lead. The convivialities of feasting and dancing conclude the day.

The ceremony takes place in the bride's house, and next morning she is taken to her husband's; but after remaining there two days she returns to her father's to complete her education and growth at home.

Disposal of the dead.

Their ceremonial in regard to the dead is quite Hindu. They burn the body and convey the remainder of the bones afterwards to the Ganges, they say; but probably any stream answers. They do not shave for ten days as a sign of mourning; at the end of that time all shave and they have a feast.

Deities.

The Bírhors worship female deities and devils. They have assigned to Devi the chief place among the former, and the others are supposed to be her daughters and grand-daughters; she is worshipped as the creator and destroyer. The devils are Bíru Bhút, who is worshipped in the form of a raised semi-globe of earth—Bíru is also the Kharriá god—and Darhá, represented by a piece of split bamboo three feet high, placed in the ground in an inclined position, called also the 'Sipáhí,' sentinel. This is the immediate guardian of the site, as a god or devil of a similar name is with the Múndas and Oráons. A small round piece of wood, nearly a foot in length, the top painted red, is called 'Banhi,' goddess of the jungles. Another similar is Lugu, the protectress of the earth. Lugu is the largest hill in Rámgarh, so this is their Marang Búrú.

An oblong piece of wood, painted red, stands for 'Mahá Máya,' Devi's daughter. A small piece of white stone daubed with red for her grand-daughter, Buria Mái; an arrow head stands for Dudha Mái, Buria's daughter. They have also a trident painted red for Hanumán, who executes all Devi's orders.

Sets of these symbols are placed one on the east and one on the west of their huts, to protect them from evil spirits, snakes, tigers, and all kinds of misfortune.

It is not easy to place the Bírhors from what is above disclosed, but the fact that, though a wandering and exclusive people, they commune in the Múnda language, is, I think, sufficient to establish that they belong to the Kol race; and then they have the Múndárí-Oráon deity Darhá and adore the Bíru of the Kharriás.

The people with whom they exchange commodities are all Hindus or Hinduised, so it is not surprising that they should take up Hindu notions.

Alleged cannibalism.

In notes of a tour in the Tributary Mahals, published in the Journal of the Asiatic Society of Bengal, I described the revolting cannibalism of which the Bírhors are accused, and I will repeat it here, though I have no faith in the story. "With much trouble some Bírhors were caught and brought to me. They were wretched-looking objects, but had more the appearance of the most abject of one of those degraded castes of Hindus, the Domes or Pariahs, to whom most flesh is food, than of hill people. Assuring me that they had themselves given up the practice, they admitted that their fathers were in the habit of disposing of the dead in the manner indicated, *viz.*, by feasting on the bodies; but they declared they never shortened life to provide such feasts, and shrank with horror at the idea of any bodies but those of their own blood relations being served up to them! The Raja of Jashpúr said, he had heard that when a Bírhor thought his end was approaching, he himself invited his kindred to come and eat him. The Bírhors brought to me did not acknowledge this.

We are reminded of Herodotus' description* of the Padœi, who killed and feasted on all who fell sick, and of the Kalatii, who ate their parents.

SECTION 8.—THE KORWÁS.

The country jointly occupied by the Múndas proper and the Oráons extends in a westerly direction to longitude 84° 30′ east, and on reaching that meridian at about latitude 23° 15′ north, we find ourselves in the centre of a dependency of Chútiá Nágpúr, called Barwah, connected and bounded by the plateau of Chútiá Nágpúr, Sirgúja, and Jashpúr, a combination of hill and dale, well-cultivated plains and forest-clad mountains, just suited to the mixed population that dwell in it.

The Asúras.

The tract is rich in iron ore, and in the hills we find a branch of the family living almost entirely by iron smelting, who, strange to say, like the fallen angels of the tradition given at page 186, are commonly designated Asúras, infidels, and have taken quite kindly to the name. It must, however, have been originally given to them as a term of reproach, and we may observe that it is an epithet frequently applied to the Nág or serpent race in the sacred writings.

The Asúras of Barwah do not, however, acknowledge the tradition of the rise of the Nágbangsí family, nor honor the memory of Madura. Singbonga they just recognise, and the worship of the supreme deity by that name does not appear to have extended beyond this point; they know nothing of Marang Búrú as a god, but they worship the great hills near them by other names. Nevertheless, from their name, their vocation and position, we must infer their connection with the vulcans kicked out of heaven by Singbonga, for I find in Barwah the very place Ekásí where they alighted on earth. They are also called Agorias.

The Korwás.

Mixed up with the Asúras and not greatly differing from them, except that they are more cultivators of the soil than smelters, we first meet the Korwás, a few stragglers of the tribe which under that name take up the dropped links of the Kolarian chain, and carry it on west, over the Sirgúja, Jashpúr, and Palámau highlands till it reaches another cognate tribe, the Kúrs or Muásis of Réwá and the Central Provinces, and passes from the Vindhyan to the Sátpúra range.

In the fertile valleys that skirt and wind among the plateaux, other tribes are now found intermixed with the Korwás, but all admit that the latter were first in the field and were at one time masters of the whole; and we have good confirmatory proof of their being the first settlers, in the fact that for the propitiation of the local spirits Korwá baigas are always selected.

Whether the Korwás always cling to the highlands from choice or were forcibly expelled from the more productive lowlands, it is difficult to determine. As lords of the whole, they could no doubt have chosen the soil and situation that best suited

* Quoted in Latham's Desc. Ethnology, Vol. II, p. 304.

them; but I am inclined to think that the genuine unreclaimed Korwás, glorying rather in the wild life of the hunter than in the tame pursuits of the agriculturist, have from the remotest antiquity lived by choice as highlanders, thoroughly despising the lowlanders, who indeed appear to have been too much in dread of them ever to have disturbed them.

The savage and almost nomadic life that they lead is not favorable to increase of population, and I do not think the tribe now numbers more than fourteen thousand souls; but they assert themselves, and their neighbours support the statement, that they were at one time more numerous and powerful, and it is possible that many of the broken tribes now found scattered throughout this part of India once formed with the Korwás a people united under some rude form of government.

We find in Sirgúja as in other nooks and corners of Hindustan temples and other ruins exhibiting considerable architectural skill, lying forlorn and deserted amidst a population who live themselves in huts of the rudest construction which they are incapable of improving. Each little state has its history which carries you back to some mythic period, but no history or even tradition that touches the ruins. Some are Buddhist, some Hindu, but beyond the symbols that determine to which of those religions they appertained, there is nothing to indicate when or by whom they were constructed.

Ruins at Dípadhí.

A group of such ruins may be seen on the main road from Ránchí through Sirgúja in a valley on the banks of the Kanhar river at a place called Dípadhí. To the north is the Jamira, to the south the Khúria, plateau, both occupied by hill Korwás, and the villages in the valley are all inhabited by people of the aboriginal stock, Kolarian and Dravidian, with a sprinkling of Hindus of the lowest caste, the descendants probably of Áryan helots.

The lowlanders have a tradition that these ruins belong to a period when the dominant people in the country were Saonts, and they connect the Korwás with the Saonts. On one side of the road are the remains of a fort and stone building where the Saont Raja lived; on the other side may be traced the remains of three temples dedicated to Shiva and Durgá, and amongst the sculptures is a colossal figure, too much mutilated to be properly identified, supposed to be the Saont Raja himself.

No one could imagine that the wild Korwás ever possessed the skill to construct such buildings, or that they are descended from a people who worshipped in them. In their rough paganism there is not now a trace of Hindu teaching, and though highly superstitious and impressionable, they have not the smallest reverence for the mysterious-looking gods of the unknown architects of the temples. But these and other similarly isolated ruins in Sirgúja and Barwah support the hypothesis that at a remote period prior to its subjugation by Gonds, this country contained colonies of Áryans, whose first attempts were to proselytize rather than subjugate, but who were not successful, as their very name is lost, and the works of art they left behind are attributed to the savages who withstood them. It is probably under similar circumstances that ruins in Bihár, Tirhut, and other places are attributed to the 'Chero-Kol-Ráj.'

The name Saont or Saonta directs us to the Santál branch of the Kols, and as I have already noticed, there is in Sirgúja a small tribe so called. I had not seen much of them when I penned the brief account that is given of them in the chapters devoted to Hinduized aborigines, but I have since met many of the tribe. They are the sole inhabitants of the magnificent tableland forming the southern barrier of Sirgúja, called the Mainpát, or more correctly perhaps the Manipát. They are a small tribe living scattered over the vast area of the plateau in about a dozen hamlets, and they are strong in the belief that they were especially created to dwell there, or that they and the plateau somehow sprung into existence together, and cannot be separated. I saw a number of them when I was last* in Sirgúja, and from their features I should be inclined to class them as Kols, but they have some customs and notions which they must have derived from the Dravidian Gonds. They acknowledge Dúlhadeo as a household god, and follow the customs of the Gonds and other southerners in their marriage ceremonies; but there is one point, a very striking one, in which their funeral rites are quite in accord with those of the Saonts. They told me without my having in the least led them to the point that after burning their dead they throw the ashes into a rapid stream with the view to their being borne away to the great ocean, which they called 'Samudra.' The Santáls also use a term of Sanskrit derivation, but they say 'Ságar'. It is singular that the Saonts, believing themselves to be autochthonous on the Mainpát, which is 250 miles from the nearest seaboard, and isolated as they are, should have so fully realized the idea that the discharge of rivers is into a great ocean, and still more so that they should have preserved the custom of consigning their dead to it,—a custom which in speaking of the Santáls, Dr. Hunter poetically styles "the reunion of the dead with the fathers."

Deities.

They worship the sun as Bhagawán, and like the Kharriás offer sacrifices to that luminary in an open place with an ant-hill for an altar. The Mainpát is their Marang Búrú, and as it is 16 miles long, 12 miles broad, and rises 3,850 feet above the sea level, it is not unworthy of the name; but they do not use that or any other Kol term. The great Mainpát is their fatherland and their god. They have it all to themselves except during the summer months, when it becomes a vast grazing field for the cattle of Mírzápúr and Bihár. They have heard that there are Saonts elsewhere (I have met with some from the eastern borders of Sohágpúr who told me they lived in caves), but they are not Mainpát Saonts, and the Mainpátias do not seek alliances with aliens. Their marriages are among themselves, though they number not more than one hundred and twenty families. This interbreeding is not prolific, and they diminish in numbers as years roll on.

The Saonts are armed like the Korwás with bows and arrows, and the peculiar battle-axe of the country, but it is against the beasts of the forest that these weapons are used. Formerly the Mainpát was a magnificent hunting field, especially noted for its herds of antelope and gaur. The late Maharaja of Sirgúja strictly preserved it, but on his death it fell into the hands of his widow, a very money-loving old lady, who allowed it to become one of the great grazing tracts, and the pasturage alone gives her an income of £250 a year; but the wild animals have in consequence withdrawn from it.

The position of the Saonts is altogether very curious, and though they now speak no language but a rude Hindí, the evidence is, on the whole, favorable to their being a remnant of the ancient Kol aborigines of Sirgúja, cut off from connection with those people by successive inroads of other races or tribes. Their substitution of a Hindí

---

* 1869-70.

dialect for their own language seems to indicate that they were first subjugated by Áryans. The Gond chiefs only count about twenty-four generations in Sirgúja, and they have all adopted the Hindí language.

Korwá Chiefs.

There were in existence within the last twenty years as highland chiefs and holders of manors four Korwá notables, two in Sirgúja and two in Jashpúr; all four estates were valuable, as they comprised substantial villages in the fertile plains held by industrious cultivators, and great tracts of hill country on which were scattered the hamlets of their more savage followers. The Sirgúja Korwá chiefs were, however, continually at strife with the Sirgúja Raja, and for various acts of rebellion against the Lord Paramount, lost manor after manor, till to each but one or two villages remained.

This was their position when the mutiny of 1857 broke out, and like many others they thought that the disturbances and anarchy that supervened afforded them an opportunity of recovering what they had lost. Placing themselves at the head of their clansmen, they committed a series of raids on the lowland villages. Wholesale plundering and murdering were resorted to for a time, but ere long the insurrection was cut short by the capture of the two chiefs; one* of them who was convicted of murder was hanged, the other† was amnestied, but died.

The two Jashpúr thanes conducted themselves right loyally at this crucial period, and they are now prosperous gentlemen in the full enjoyment of their estates, the only Korwá families left that keep up any appearance of respectability. One‡ of them is the hereditary Díwán of Jashpúr, lord of the whole mountain tract of Khúria and Maini, and chief of perhaps two-thirds of the whole tribe of Korwás. The other holds an estate called Kakia, comprising twenty-two villages in the lowlands and some hill country. Both these families abjure the impure practices of their tribe, and, spurning alliances with the ordinary Korwás, have continued interbreeding for several generations. They hope in time that their intimate connection with the Korwás will be forgotten, and in the next century they will probably come forth full-fledged Rájpúts. Indeed, I was surprised to find that the Bráhmanical heralds college had not yet given either of them a legend of miraculous birth or independent lineage. But though affecting Hinduism, they dare not altogether disown the spirits of the hills and forests that their ancestors adored, and they have each at their head-quarters a Korwá Baiga, or pagan priest, to propitiate the gods of the race. I could not find a member of either family, male or female, who would condescend to speak one word of Korwá. In this, however, they are not singular, as I observed that even the poorer Korwás when once settled in the plains, were unwilling to converse in their own tongue. The Laird of Kakia has recently assumed the imposing name of Mánjhí Mahendra Náráin Sáhi; but notwithstanding this ebullition of vanity, he is an intelligent man, a kind landlord, an excellent farmer, and as portly and jovial a host as a traveller could wish to meet. His farm, premises, and dwelling house are spacious, well arranged, and kept scrupulously clean. The family residence contains under one roof numerous apartments and occupies one whole side of a large quadrangle; two comfortable houses forming the north side afford accommodation to other married members of the family; opposite are the cow-sheds, and filling up the front side of the quadrangle there is

* Dharm Singh. † Jagmohun Singh. ‡ Mandraj Singh.

a long substantial building for strangers, pilgrims and attendants, through which is the principal entrance. In the centre of the quadrangle there is a pavilion open on all sides, and here I was invited to seat myself, whilst the young ladies of the house brought vessels and water to wash my feet. I have been particular in giving this description in order to show that a Korwá, however unpromising the material, is susceptible of culture, and can become a useful member of society.

The Díwán is no doubt the representative of the family which gave chiefs to the Korwás when the tribe was dominant in this Jashpúr hill tract. The aboriginal inhabitants were all either Korwás or *Nagesars,* who are commonly called 'Kisáns,' that is, cultivators. It is probable that Kisáns and Korwás are of common origin; the former are noticed in my chapter on Hinduized aborigines, but their origin is uncertain; there is a Dravidian as well as Kolarian element in the Jashpúr population, and it is doubtful to which they are nearest of kin, but, on the whole, the preponderance of evidence is in favor of their Kol extraction. They cannot speak the Kol language, but it is found that Korwás, deserting the hills and joining the Kisáns in permanent rice cultivation in the valleys, lose their language and most of their tribal peculiarities, and become so like the Kisáns that it is difficult to discriminate between the two.

History.

The present Raja of Jashpúr fully admits that the Díwán's ancestors were the original rulers of the country. His own family counts only seventeen generations since assuming the sceptre, and were first established in the lowlands, where the remains of their ancient stronghold may still be seen. They were Kharwárs, whom I suppose to have been an offshoot of the same race, and their tradition, that they were driven out of Belonja in Bihár, may refer to the break up of the Chero-Kol-Kharwár nation, formerly located in Kíkata or Khinkat, afterward Magadha. The family having established themselves in the lowlands gradually brought the highlands under subjection, but the great highland chief only yielded on condition that he was to be acknowledged and maintained as the second person in the realm, the Lieutenant or Díwán. This was conceded, and from generation to generation there was no breach of the contract till the grandfather of the present Raja, disregarding the ancient policy of his family, confided the affairs of the ráj to his foster brother, a Kahár named Anand Rám. The hereditary Korwá Díwán, Munáwar Singh, resenting this, a small civil war ensued which lasted for many years, and was still in active operation when Jashpúr with Sirgúja and other territory was ceded to the British Government by Appá Sáhib in A. D. 1818. Some of the Company's troops were sent to co-operate with the Raja against his refractory vassal, but they made very little impression on the Korwás, and Munáwar Singh fought till he died in A. D. 1821.

His son Maniar Singh, who had been captured during the hostilities and detained in custody, was now released, and under the guarantee of the British Government reinstated in all the hereditary honors and possessions of the family, since when the Jashpúr Korwás have always conducted themselves peaceably and loyally.

Hill Korwás.

The Hill Korwás are the most savage-looking of all the Kolarian tribes. They are frightfully wild and uncouth in their appearance, and have good-humouredly accepted the following singular tradition to account for it. The story was communicated to Captain Samuells, Assistant Commissioner, by a Korwá of Sirgúja, but the Jashpúr section of the clan never heard of it.

3 H

Their legends.

The first human beings that settled in Sirgúja being very much troubled by the depredations of wild beasts on their crops, put up scarecrows in their fields, figures made of bamboos dangling in the air, the most hideous caricatures of humanity that they could devise to frighten the animals.

When the great spirit saw the scarecrows, he hit on an expedient to save his votaries the trouble of reconstructing them. He animated the dangling figures, thus bringing into existence creatures ugly enough to frighten all the birds and beasts in creation, and they were the ancestors of the wild Korwás.

Stature, &c.

They are short of stature and dark brown in complexion, strongly built and active, with good muscular development, but, as appeared to me, disproportionately short-legged. The average height of twenty Sirgúja Korwás whom I measured was five feet three inches, and of their women four feet nine only. In feature, the characteristic types are not very prominent; a breadth of face from the lateral projection of the zygomatic arches and narrowness of forehead are the most remarkable traits; the nose, chin, and mouth are better formed than we generally find them among the rude tribes of the Dravidian stock; and notwithstanding the scarecrow tradition, the Korwás are, as a rule, better-looking than the Gonds and Oráons. The males, I noticed, were more hirsute than the generality of their cognates, many of them cultivating beards or rather not interfering with their spontaneous growth, for in truth in their toilettes there is nothing like cultivation. They are as utterly ungroomed as the wildest animals. The neglected back hair grows in matted tails which fall behind like badly frayed ropes, or is massed in a 'chignon' of gigantic proportions, as preposterous as any that the present tasteless period has produced; sticking out behind sometimes a foot from the back of the head.

Women.

The women appear ground down by the hard work imposed on them, stunted in growth, black, ugly, and wretchedly clad, some having only a few dirty rags tied round their persons, and in other respects untidy and unclean. On them falls the double task of labour in the fields and of providing the daily bread for the miserable household. They have all the burdens, but none of the privileges, of women. The man may follow his instincts as a hunting animal, and bow and arrow in hand search the hills for the meat that his soul loveth; but he, day after day, returns unsuccessful, and in the meantime the woman has been hunting for and digging up wild esculent roots, or culling wild vegetables, hewing wood and drawing water, and woe betide her if she has not been more successful than her lord.

The most savage of the Korwás answer well the description given in the Puránas of the inhabitants of the Vindhyan mountains—black skins with flat faces, projecting chins, and tawny hair. The tuft by way of beard at the end of their chins, without whiskers, gives that feature its apparent prominence, and the rusty tint that their long matted hair acquires by their neglect of it, would appear tawny in comparison with the well lubricated locks of the Bráhmans.

The Korwás of Khúria.

The Korwás occupying the Khúria plateau are equally wild and savage-looking, and few of them can converse in any language but their own, but they are some degrees fairer, and have better features than the coal black savages of the Vindhyan.

They live in small detached hamlets, consisting each of three or four miserable huts, or sometimes in single huts far apart. It is said by their neighbours, and admitted by themselves, that they live thus to avoid the bloody brawls which generally follow their attempts to form communities.

Sometimes they build their huts like eagles' eyries on the ledges of mountain precipices in the most inaccessible places. From below you may see such huts hanging as it were to a steep cliff, and wonder how the owners, if without wings, approach them.

The Korwá population of Khúria does not exceed 2,000 souls. They have that great table-land all to themselves, except when a few Ahírs with their cattle seek its fresh pastures after the first fall of the regular rains; but from its remote situation, Khúria is not so frequented for grazing purposes as the table-lands of Sirgúja, Palámau, and other places.

Cultivation.

The Khúria plateau averages 3,400 feet above the sea level, and rises to 4,000 feet. It is the cradle of many waters; affluents of the Son, the Damúdar, and the Mahánadí radiate from it, so it is no unimportant watershed. Seamed by these streams, there is no want of variety in the scenery which alternately presents to view miniature prairies covered with long grass and swelling uplands forest-clad. The Korwá cultivation is chiefly in the latter. So the prairies are left to the wild beasts and the cattle. What is called in the Eastern Districts the jhúm system of cultivation and in the common Chútiá Nágpúr dialect daho, is here widely resorted to. Ploughs are not used in this elevated region. In the cold weather the hoar frost is almost every morning thick on the ground, and on this account there is no winter crop of rice. Their principal crop is the pulse, called Arhar *(Cajanus Indicus)*, and they have their harvest joy when it is gathered in December; then for three or four days they are social and abandon themselves to savage revelry, dancing, feasting, drinking, and giving themselves up to unbridled debauchery. At other times, utterly indifferent to culinary art, they now make cakes of millet flour, split peas, and honey, and this is their special luxury, their plum-pudding for the festive season. Little else is known of the nature of their orgies, but dancing with them, as with all their cognates, is a passion, and if they perform when in a seasonable state of wild ebriety, armed to the teeth as I saw them dancing when sober, the incidents of the ball must be often more sensational than amusing. In civilized society, young men lose their hearts in this pleasant and exciting amusement, but Korwá gallants have been known in the most literal sense to lose their heads.

Dances.

One morning, when encamped in a valley of Khúria, my slumbers were broken at a very early hour by a chorus of Oráon youths and maidens who were dancing and singing not 100 yards from the tent, their song strangely mingling with or suggesting my dreams. I must have been long listening before I could collect my thoughts sufficiently to comprehend the object and cause of the loud, but not unmelodious, morning carol. On my emerging at length to acknowledge the compliment, upwards of one hundred naked savage-looking Korwás, all armed, sprang up from the grass, as if they had been lying there in ambush, and were on slaughter bent, but instead of attacking me and chopping me up with battle-axes, they too burst forth into rude song, utterly extinguishing the gentler strains of the Oráons, and forming a huge circle or rather coil they hooked on to each other by the arms and wildly danced. In their hands they sternly grasped their weapons, the long stiff bow and arrows with bright broad barbed heads and spirally feathered reed shafts in the left hand, and the gleaming battle-axe in the right, some of the men accompanies the singing on deep-toned drums and all sang, but I was surprised to find that the songs were in a Hindí dialect like the songs of the Boyars, and the melody was the same. A few scantily clad females formed the inner curl of the coil, but in the centre was the Choroœgus, who played on a stringed instrument, promoting by his grotesque motions unbounded hilarity, and keeping up the spirit of the dancers by his unflagging energy.

The instrument was of curious construction. The bar subtending the wires was connected with two hollow dried gourds acting as sounding boards; on one of them was a very fair miniature representation of a tiger, and as the performer moved his hand to strike the lute, he worked a string which caused this latter animal to bob up and down and twist round and dance in time to the music like a veritable Jim Crow. This was the most elaborate specimen of Korwá art that I had seen.

Stature, &c.

The average height of the men who formed this dancing group was five feet four inches, the tallest five feet eight; their sole garment was a rag passing between the legs and attached before and behind to a string round the waist. Their matted back hair was either massed into a chignon, sticking out from the back of the head like a handle from which spare arrows depended hanging by the barbs, or was divided into clusters of long matted tails, each supporting a spare arrow, which, flinging about as they sprang to the lively movements of the dance, added greatly to the dramatic effect and the wildness of their appearance. The women were very diminutive creatures, on the average a foot shorter than their lords, clothed in scanty rags, and with no ornaments except a few tufts of cotton, dyed red, taking the place of flowers in the hair, a common practice also with the Santál girls. Both tribes are fond of the flower of the coxcomb for this purpose, and when that is not procurable, use the red cotton.

The dancing was, on the whole, very spirited, and resembled pretty closely a Múnda Jádura.

Weapons.

The Korwás are considered formidable as bowmen, but I was not struck with the accuracy of their aim. I think that an average corps of our fair archers would make more golds, but they pull an enormously stiff bow and drive their arrows with a force that I have never seen equalled by amateurs. The barbed arrow heads are nine inches long and one and a half in breadth. These they make themselves of the iron they smelt in their own hills; they use the battle-axe very adroitly.

Food.

The Korwás cultivate newly cleared ground, changing their homesteads every two or three years to have command of a virgin soil. They sow rice that ripens in the summer, vetches, millets, pumpkins, cucumbers, some of gigantic size, sweet potatoes, yams, and chillis. They also grow and prepare arrowroot, and have a wild kind which they use and sell. They have as keen a knowledge of what is edible amongst the spontaneous produce of the jungles as have monkeys, and have often to use this knowledge for self-preservation, as they are frequently subjected to failure of crops, while even in favorable seasons some of them do not raise sufficient for the year's consumption, but the best of this description of food is neither palatable nor wholesome. They brought to me nine different kinds of edible roots, and descanted so earnestly on the delicate flavor and nutritive qualities of some of them that I was induced to have two or three varieties cooked under their instructions and served up, but the result was far from pleasant; my civilized stomach indignantly repelled the savage food, and was not pacified till it had made me suffer for some hours from cold sweat, sickness, and giddiness.

Storing grain.

They pack their grain in small parcels done up lightly in leaves. These they bury, and they told me that grain so packed remained unimpaired for years. They have no prejudices whatever in regard to animal food.

Trade.

The Korwás trade in honey, beeswax, arrowroot, resins, gums, stick lac, and iron from their own hills and of their own smelting. This is considered the best metal for battle-axes, and is in great request wherever they are used.

Religion.

The Korwás are unacquainted with the legends of their Múnda cognates. Those in Sirgúja told me that they knew nothing whatever of Bongas, and worshipped no gods. They sacrifice only to the manes of their ancestors, and as this ceremony must necessarily be performed by the head of each family, they have no priests. In Jashpúr they have Baigas, and the Khúria Korwás have at least one shrine to which all occasionally resort for worship, the shrine of the Khúria Rání. I was unable to visit it, but made minute enquiries, and I understand it to be a small cave in a rock which rises abruptly from a stream, with a nook in front of it, about half-way up the Khúria plateau. It is supposed to be the abode of a sanguinary deity, of course a female, more like the blood-thirsty goddess of the Gonds, the prototype of the Hindu Kálí, than any of the Kol objects of worship. All the Korwás adore her, but she is more especially the tutelary deity of the Díwán. This family have to make a great sacrifice to her every third generation. The last was made by the father of the present Díwán, and the Korwá laird of Kakia who was present gave me a humorous account of it.

Thirty to forty buffaloes were with difficulty driven to the place and immolated together with an incalculable number of goats, but the ceremony was brought to an abrupt close by a mysterious rumbling noise in the cave and a tremulous motion of the rock, probably an earthquake, which caused the whole party to fly at the imminent risk of their lives. One can well imagine the terror of the awe-stricken votaries, worked into a high pitch of excitement by the bloody rites,—wading in the gore of the victims—as brute after brute was decapitated. The goddess is a mystery even to her priests, for into the cave no mortal has ever penetrated. No doubt when the rumbling was heard, and the rocks shook, a dreadful appearance was expected, but notwithstanding the cost incurred in invoking her, no one was bold enough to await the result.

Marriages.

I could obtain no information regarding Korwá marriages. The Díhí Korwás adopt the Gondí ceremonies; their hill brethren have, I believe, none at all, nor could I find that they had, like their cognates, any tribal distinctions by which restrictions on intermarriages were imposed.

3 I

The Korwás on the highlands of Sirgúja are occasionally exceedingly lawless. They were at one time organized in bands of marauders and appeared to subsist altogether by pillage, which was not seldom accompanied by murder, but for some years they have been well conducted, the leaders having for the most part been induced to take up lands in the plains.

Marauding habits.

They have shown great cruelty in committing robberies, putting to death the whole of the party attacked, even when unresisting, but they have what one might call the savage virtue of truthfulness to an extraordinary degree, and, rightly accused, will at once confess and give you every required detail of the crime. When several are implicated in one offence, I have found them most anxious that to each should be ascribed his fair share of it, and no more, the oldest of the party invariably taking on himself the chief responsibility as leader or instigator, and doing his utmost to exculpate as unaccountable agents the young members of the gang.

Cruelty. Truthfulness.

SECTION 9.—THE KÚRS, KURKUS, OR MUÁSÍS.

Very few Korwás are met with beyond the western confines of Sirgúja ; but when on passing into the next state, *Korea*, we lose them, we at once pick up links to carry on the chain of congeners to the far West.

The family now in possession of the Korea Estate call themselves Chauhán Rájpúts. In their annals it is stated that the Balands were originally rulers in Korea as in Western Sirgúja, where there exist the ruins of many great works traditionally ascribed to them. They were driven out by a combined attack of Gonds and Kols. The latter are called Kronch Kols, and their chiefs, it is said, held Korea for eleven generations. They were subjugated by the Chauhán Chief Dhaurel Singh, the ancestor of the present Raja of Korea, about 600 years ago. If this be true, Korea must have been one of the last countries held by a Kol dynasty, and this may account for its retention of the name Korea, or Kolia, as the country of the Korwás or Kols.

Whilst still in Sirgúja amongst the Korwás, I fell in with a colony of people speaking the same language who called themselves Koraků, but they appeared to be far in advance of the Korwás in civilization, and acknowledged no kindred with them. About a dozen young men and six comely and neatly dressed girls came to my camp, and danced and sang, and made themselves very agreeable.

The movement and melody were Bhúiya rather than Kol, but the flower-decked hair of the maidens was uncovered, and in their frank address, freedom from prudery, and in the palpably joyous manner with which they received and returned the attention of their partners, they reminded me of the Ho or Singbhúm Kol girls.

The Korakús knew nothing of the Múnda system of religion; they have dipped into Gondí and Hindí mythology, and evolved from both sufficient to fill their minds with fear of malevolent spirits, if not with reverence for good ones. They worship the cloud-capped table-lands which surround them, giving to them Gondí and Hindí names.

The Palámau Brijias evidently belong to the same family. In a short vocabulary of their language kindly sent to me by Mr. L. R. Forbes, Assistant Commissioner, Palámau,

I find that their common word for man is 'Kúrako,' which is simply the plural of Kúr or Kúra (in Múnda a boy), and we have thus a term equally near the Koraku and Korwá of Sirgúja, and the Kúr* of Gáwílgarh.

Koraku and Korwá.

In the appendix to the essay on the tribes of the Central Provinces by the late Rev. S. Hislop, published since his death by Sir Richard Temple, the latter tribe is spoken of as Kúrkus, in another place they are called Kúrs, but it is noted that those who live on the Mahádeva Hills prefer to be called Muásí. Now, leaving Sirgúja and passing into Korea and Chánd Bhakhár, we at once find ourselves among the Muásis who are there usually called Mawásí Kols, and thus we trace a well-defined thin line of the race all through Gondwáná and right across the continent till we come among the Bhíls. There is a pargana in Réwá called Marwasi, from which, perhaps, the name is derived, but Mr. Hislop suggests its derivation from the Mahwá tree *(bassia latifolia)*, and this their own legend confirms.

Captain W. S. Samuells, Assistant Commissioner, Chútiá Nágpúr, has favored me with some interesting information regarding the Muásí, picked up by him whilst recently employed in laying down the boundary between Réwá and Bengal. Their tradition of origin takes us again to the serpent race. Some time after the creation of the world, there issued from the earth a male and female, Nága Bhúiya and Nága Bhúiáin, that is, evidently the earth serpent and his wife. They had power over and worshipped nine demons whose names as pronounced by the Muásís are given below. They are apparently all taken from the Hindu mythology. The 1st, called *Barhona*, is no doubt Varana, the spirit of the waters; the 2nd, *Andhiar*, the spirit of darkness; the 3rd, *Rakas* (Rakshásas), the demons of the forest; the 4th, *Chitáwur*, which I do not recognise; the 5th, *Pát*, the spirit of the mountain; 6th, *Danu*, are Dánawas, the sons of Dánu, described in the Puránas as Asúras, enemies of the gods and subordinates of the great serpent king Kásuki; 7th, *Bhainsásur*, the buffalo demon; 8th, *Agin*, probably for Agni, the fire demon, and 9th, *Kolara*, not found in the sacred books, perhaps a special Kol demon. The Nága and his wife, after living many years on the earth's surface, had a son which was apparently what they had been waiting for, as on the birth of the child they wrapped it in a sheet, left it under a Mahwá tree and disappeared. The child was found and taken to the Raja of Kanauj, who gave it the name Mahwásí and adopted it. The boy grew up and marrying became the father of two sons, and the Raja gave them the country called Ganjar. This they held for many years, paying tribute to the Kanauj ruler, but they increased and multiplied and grew proud, and refusing to pay the accustomed tribute, the Raja gave their country to two warriors from Kálinjar, named Apla and Adal. They made war on the Muásís, subjugated them, and brought the leaders bound before the king, who caused a loaded banghy to be laid across the shoulders of each, and pronounced sentence that they and their descendants were thenceforth for ever to bear burdens.

Nága legends.

It is evident that this is another version of the legend previously narrated from the annals of the Chútiá Nágpúr Nágbangsí family†. In both we find the snake father, the deserted child and the doom

Religion.

* In the Central Provinces Gazetteer, Kúrs are noticed as occupying hill tracts in Betúl (Baitool), in Chhindwárá, in Hoshangábád, in Nimár, and as the only inhabitants of Mánjrod on the Taptí.

† *Vide* page 165.

to burden-bearing, showing the alien origin of the tradition and the devices adopted by the foreigners to reduce the aboriginal races to a perpetual condition of servitude. We learn from the essay of the Rev. S. Hislop that the chief objects of adoration to the Muásís of the Central Provinces are the sun and the moon. They also worship at the shrine of Sultán Sakada, whom they suppose to have been a king among them in former times. The Muásís of Barár and in the western tributary estates of Chútiá Nágpúr worship Bhavaní, a name of Durgá, and Gansám or *Ghanasyáma.* The latter is a name of Krishna, but the *Gansám* of the Muásís and Gonds is said to have been formerly a Gond chief who was devoured by a tiger at an early age just after his marriage. Cut off at such a moment, it was unreasonable to suppose that his spirit would rest. One year after his death, he visited his wife, and she conceived by him, and the descendants of the ghostly embrace are, it is said, living to this day at Amodah* in the Central Provinces. He about the same time appeared to many of his old friends, and persuaded them that he could save them from the maws of tigers and other calamities, if his worship were duly inaugurated and regularly performed; and in consequence of this, two festivals in the year were established in his honor; but he may be invoked at any time, and in all sicknesses and misfortunes his votaries confidently appeal to him.

Priests. Invocations.

The Baiga is always the medium of communication, but he assembles the people to aid him in the invocation. Musical instruments are produced, dancing commences, and the invocation to the spirit is chanted until one or more of the performers manifest possession by wild rolling of the eyes and involuntary spasmodic action of the muscles. The affection appears contagious, and old women and others who have not been dancing become influenced by it in a manner that is horrible to contemplate. Captain Samuells, who frequently witnessed the incantation, is confident that no deception whatever is practised. As at revivals where similar scenes are produced by professing Christians, each person seized or exalted loses for a time all self-control, and the body, limbs, and neck are worked in the most exhaustive manner, till the Baiga interposes and relieves the victim.

The affection, says Captain Samuells, comes on like a fit of ague, lasting sometimes for a quarter of an hour, the patient or possessed person writhing and trembling with intense violence, especially at the commencement of the paroxysm. Then he is seen to spring from the ground into the air, and a succession of leaps follow, all executed as though he were shot at by unseen agency. During this stage of the seizure he is supposed to be quite unconscious, and rolls into the fire, if there be one, or under the feet of the dancers without sustaining injury from the heat or the pressure. This lasts for a few minutes only, and is followed by the spasmodic stage. With hands and knees on the ground and hair loosened, the body is convulsed, and the head shakes violently, whilst from the mouth issues a hissing or gurgling noise. The patient next evincing an inclination to stand on his legs, the bystanders assist him and place a stick in his hand, with the aid of which he hops about, the spasmodic action of the body still continuing and the head performing by jerks a violently fatiguing circular movement. This may go on for hours, though Captain Samuells says that no one in his senses could continue such exertion for many minutes. When the Baiga is appealed to, to cast out the spirit, he must first ascertain whether it is Gansám himself or one of his familiars

* I do not find this name in the Central Provinces Gazetteer. It may be Almod "in and round the Mahádeo group of hills."

that has possessed the victim. If it be the great Gansám, the Baiga implores him to desist, meanwhile gently anointing the victim with butter; and if the treatment is successful, the patient gradually and naturally subsides into a state of repose from which he rises into consciousness, and restored to his normal state, feels no fatigue or other ill-effects from the attack.

This is certainly the most thorough form of demon worship with which we have met, and one that must appear to its votaries to testify to its own reality each time it is resorted to.

Hinduized practices.

In many of their social customs, the Muásís of the western Tributary Mahâls and Réwá conform to Hinduism; in some they have adopted Gondí practices. Amongst other notions which they have taken from the Hindu model, is that of the wife not eating with the husband, but satisfying herself with what he leaves; it is singular how readily this Hindu fashion so degrading to the woman is followed. Some of the Hindu customs after childbirth, as ceremoniously giving first food to the child, shaving its head, &c., they profess to have adopted, but without the assistance of Bráhmans, who have not yet intruded on the functions of the Baiga.

Marriage customs.

With the view of ascertaining correctly what are the marriage customs of the Muásí, Captain Samuells handsomely offered to dower a young lady, if a wedding could be improvised; and a well-matched pair, whose course of true love had been hitherto baffled by their poverty, joyfully availed themselves of the opportunity. Captain Samuells has kindly favored me with a note of the result, from which I take the following:—

The proposal must emanate from the father of the girl, whose duty it is to spot a bridegroom as soon as his daughter becomes marriageable. We may presume that he consults his child before he makes any overtures in her behalf, and knows well the house to which her inclination would guide her. If the offer is favorably received, the father of the selected swain visits the proposer, sees the girl, and leaves his first offering at the shrine of her beauty in gallons of rice beer. The contracting parties then agree as to the guerdon that is to be paid to the father of the girl; this is not paid in cattle, as in Singbhúm, or in cash, but in rice, and four *mans* of grain are deemed a very fair equivalent, so cheap are women held. The girl's father then invites his friends to a feast, and announces the engagement, and the next stage is the solemn delivery of the stipulated bonus in rice. This is brought and measured out by the groom's best man, and it is the privilege of the bridesmaids to thwart the proceeding by pilfering from the heap, and the best man and his friends have to make occasional raids after the girls, who, if caught, pay penalty as bridesmaids should.

The marriage ceremony takes place eight days after the delivery of the rice. In the evening, the bridegroom's cavalcade proceed to the bride's residence, his gallant comrades all mounted and careering on hobby horses! made of bamboos, except one warrior, who bestrides a representation of an elephant! The groom, however, is borne on the shoulders of his best man, clad all in white, and crowned with a chaplet of reeds. They halt at a short distance from the bride's house, and there await her party. Presently emerges a troop of girls all singing, headed by the mother of the bride, bearing on her head a vessel of water surmounted by a lighted chirágh (lamp). When they get near enough to the cavaliers, they pelt them with balls of boiled rice, then coyly retreat, followed of course by the young men; but the girls make a stand at the door of the bride's house, and suffer none to enter till they have paid toll in presents to the bridesmaids. The party is now received by the bride's brother, who appears with offerings of water and food; the bridegroom dismounts and seats himself on the ground, and the bride's mother coming forward stuffs between his jaws five mouthfuls of cooked food. She then washes his mouth, gives him a kiss, and invites him to go inside; but here the best man interposes demanding guerdon, and till this has been paid refuses to allow the bridegroom to advance a step.

In the inner court-yard a bower is constructed of leafy branches of the sál tree supported on a frame-work of bamboos. In the centre is the 'Bhanwar,' here represented by a bamboo post passing through the canopy, round which the bride and bridegroom have to make a certain number of revolutions. It rises from a platform on which mats made of fresh green leaves are spread for the young couple and their chief supporters.

The bridegroom on entering the court-yard is conducted by the women to the inner apartments, and presented to the bride; then with their garments tied together they are both led out and seated in their places in the bower. At this time some of the young men are invited to go inside to partake of a repast prepared for them, and whilst they are so engaged, the two fathers wash the feet of the young couple. There is then a pause in the ceremonies, of which the lively bridesmaids avail themselves to pour on the unfortunate bridegroom a torrent of not very delicate chaff.

Further preparations are now made for the Bhanwar ceremony. A vessel full of water and a lighted lamp are placed near the pole, and a curry-stone on which is arranged seven little heaps of rice and turmeric. When all is ready the chief bridesmaid and best man lead the young couple once round the post, then leave them to perform the remainder of the revolutions themselves, and each time as they approach the curry-stone, the bridegroom causes his bride to kick away one of the heaps of rice and turmeric. When the seventh is knocked off, the best man seizes the pole and violently shakes it, and on this the people all exclaim, "It is done." The wedded pair are then taken inside, and after spending some time together, come out to receive the congratulations of their friends, and retire again to the chamber prepared for them. Next morning all adjourn to the camp of the 'barát,'* where a breakfast is provided by the father of the bride.

Captain Samuells was unable to induce a Muási to die, in order that he might, as an eye-witness, describe what then takes place; but I have said enough of the funeral ceremonies and cenotaphs of the cognate tribes, and here close my account of the Kolarians.

* The bridegroom's party.

Tables showing the different dialects of the Múnda or Kol language spoken in Chútiá Nágpúr, Katak, and the Central Provinces, compiled for* COLONEL DALTON'S *'Ethnology of Bengal' by* BABU RAKHAL DAS HALDAR, *Assistant Commissioner, Chútiá Nágpúr.—With Vocabularies of the Khási and Talain languages added for purposes of comparison.

[N. B.—Babu Rakhal Das Huldar has added specimens of declensions, conjugations, and short sentences to show the grammatical construction of the Múnda language.]

ENGLISH.	MUNDARI.	SANTAL.	KORWA.	KHARRIA.	JUANGA.	HO.	KURI OR MUASI.	TALAIN OR MON.	KHASI.
One	miád	mi'	miátáng	moiñ	moin	miád	nekor	mway	uwei.
Two	báriá	báreá	bátáng	ubátháng	umbar	bariá	bár-ku	pa	arh.
Three	ápiá	peá	peitang	uphethang	i-gota	ápia	akor or apkor.	pe	lai.
Four	upuniá	poneá	chár-gotáng	iphan tháng	gandá-mi,	upuniá	upanko.	pon	sau.
Five	moneá	mone	pánchgotáng	molegothang	...	moñyá	moneiku	pa-tson	san.
Six	turiá	turui	chhaugotáng	tibhurthang	...	turuiá	tureiku.	ka-roung	hinrew.
Seven	eá	eáe	sátgotáng	thámgotháng	...	áyá	yeiká	kha-pau	hin-ieu.
Eight	iraliá	irál	áthgotáng	iralgothang	...	iriliá	ilarku or ilariá.	khasan	phrá.
Nine	àreá	áre	nau-gotáng	áregothang	...	areá	areiku	khasi	khyndai.
Ten	gelná	gel	das-gotáng	ghol	...	gel	gelku	t'sau	shi-pheu.
Twenty	hisi	isi	...	moiñ kudi	...	hisi	bis (s.)	pa-sau	arh-pheu.
Fifty	bàrhisigelná	bárisigel	...	ubákudighol	...	barhisigel	...	patsu-tson	san-pheu.
Hundred	mone hisi, or say (s)	mone isi, or say.	sao	moiñsay	...	sau	chovi	kalun	shi-spah.
I	ing or áing	ing	angoá, ingyuñ	ing	ain	ing, aing	in	awai	nga.
Of me, or mine.	iñgyäñ	ting, tingyan	engal	ingyáñ	ainyá	ingá	ing [yá?]	kharu-awái	jong-ngá.
We two	áling	áláng, aling	...	...	...	áling	...	...	...
Of us two	aláñgyañ	táling, táliñagya.	...	...	...	alingyá	...	...	...
We	ále, or ábu	ále, or ában	angá	ele	áindera	ále, ábu	ale	pwá	ngi.
Of us / Our	áleá or ábuá.	tale, tában	ála-a	elá	...	alea, ábuá	nan	kharu-awai-tau.	jong-ngi.
Thou	ám	ám	amo	ám	ámde	ám	ám	bai	pha.
Of thee / Thine	ámáñ	tám,	ama	ámá	ámá	ámá	ámá	kharu-hpá	jong-me.
You two	áben	áben	...	...	...	áben	...	...	...
Of you two	ábenañ	táben,	...	...	...	ábená	...	...	...
You	ápe	ápe	ápa saban	ámpá	ámderá.	ápe	ápe	bin-tau	phi.
Of you	ápeá	tápe,	apaádo	ámpáá	...	ápeá	...	kharu-hpay-tau.	jong-phi.
Your	ápeá	tápe	apaádo	...	...	ápeá	...	kharu-hpay-tau.	jong-phi.
He	ini'	huni	mormika	uki, hoje	árá, nái	áy, áyo	han	nyá	u.
Of him	ini'já	tái	eniá	...	...	ayá	...	kharu-nyung	jong-u.
His	ini'já	tái	eniá	hokorá	...	ayá	...	kharu-nyung	jong-u.
They two	inkin	hunkin	...	...	...	áking	...	...	...
Of them two	inkiná	tákin	...	...	...	ákingiá.	...	...	...
They	inku	hunko	mormikano	ukiár	...	áko	arko	nyi-tau	ki.
Of them	inkuá	táko	inkuá	...	...	akoá	...	kharum-yin-tau.	jong-ki.
Their	inkuá	táko	inkuá	ukijháriá	...	ákoá	...	kharum-yin-tau.	jong-ki.
Hand	ti'	ti'	timu	ti'	itihi	ti'	...	tway	ka kti.

English.	Mundari.	Santal.	Korwa.	Kharria.	Juanga.	Ho.	Kusi or Muasi.	Talain or Mon.	Khasi.
Foot ...	katá ...	kátá, jángá	katam ...	katá ...	ijing ...	kata ...	jang ...	htsihn ...	ka slajat.
Nose ...	muhuñ ...	mu ...	mumu ...	mu ...	muttái...	muá, mutá	mu ...	...	ka kby mút.
Eye ...	me'd ...	me ...	medmi ...	mod ...	emmor...	met ...	met, med	mot ...	ka kby mat.
Mouth ...	mochá ...	mochá ...	ahamu ...	tamod ...	tamoni	á ...	mache, musan.	khamoupan	ka shintur.
Tooth ...	ḍáṭá* ...	ḍáṭá ...	tiringmi ...	gone ...	gone ...	dántá ...	tiding ...	nget ...	ka bainiat.
Ear ...	lutur ...	lutur ...	luturmi ...	lutur ...	lutur ...	lutur ...	lutur ...	khato ...	ka shkor.
Hair ...	u'b ...	u'p ...	u'bmi ...	ului ...	jhuntá...	u'p ...	katha, up	swet ...	ka shniuh.
Head ...	bo' ...	baha' ...	bohmi ...	boko ...	boká ...	bo' ...	dui ...	katau ...	ka khleh.
Tongue ...	áláng ...	áláng ...	alangmi ...	lang ...	eláng ...	aláng ...	...	...	ka thylliit.
Belly ...	lái' ...	lái' ...	lajmi ...	laij ...	itib ...	lái ...	lái ...	...	...
Back ...	doyá ...	deá ...	dehimu ...	kundab ...	kenapá	deá ...	bhawadi	...	...
Iron ...	mereñd ...	menthe ...	lohá (s.) ...	lu'ang ...	lohá (s.)	med ...	lohá (s.)	kasway ...	u-nár.
Gold ...	sámrom ...	sámánom ...	soná (s.) ...	soná ...	soná (s.)	sámrom	sunná ...	...	ka ksier.
Silver ...	rupá (s) ...	rupá (s.) ...	rupá (s.) ...	rupá (s.) ...	rupá (s.)	rupá ...	chándi (h.)	...	ka rupa (s.)
Father ...	appu ...	bábá, ápu ..	ápu ...	appá ...	bábá ...	ápu ...	bá, abba	má ...	ukypa.
Mother ...	engá ...	áyo, engá...	ingá ...	madam ...	boy-i ...	engá ...	aya, má	yá ...	kakyme.
Brother ...	hágá ...	dádá, baihá	dadá ...	dáda ...	boka or ká.	báo, undite.	dádá ...	...	u para.
Sister ...	misi ...	dái, ...	áji ...	kulamdai...	áji ...	misi ...	jiji ...	...	ka para.
Man ...	horo ...	har ...	horku ...	lebu ...	juáng, mánush (s.) kamaholo	ho, horo	koro ...	karu ...	u briu.
Woman ...	erá kori ...	kuri ...	koriku ...	konsel ...	juangde	erá ...	japai ...	...	ka briu, ka kynthei.
Wife ...	erá ...	erá, máiju	erá ...	konday ...	kutomge (P.)	erá ...	...	...	ka tyn-ga.
Child ...	hon ...	gidirá, hopon	hopon ...	adhro(P.) ...	wáriki(P.)	hon ...	tádei ...	...	u or ka khynnah.
Son ...	korá, bábu	korá-gidirá	korá hopon.	betá (h.) ...	kano, kanda ...	koá-hon	kon ...	...	u kun.
Daughter ...	kori ...	kurí-gidirá	kuri hopon, erá hopon.	beti (h.) ...	kándi ...	kui-hon	konjái...	...	ka kun.
Slave ...	dási ...	guti ...	dhángar ...	kongher ...	...	dási ...	...	...	mrau.
Cultivator ...	kisán (s.) ...	chasá, chási	kisan (s.) ...	kísuo ...	...	hertanai (P).	...	...	...
Shepherd ...	merom-gupinig.	gupi ...	rut ...	meromgupá	...	gupinig	...	...	...
God ...	singbongá	singbongá	ber ...	singbongá...	bhagwán (s.) ...	singbongá.	...	...	u blei.
Devil ...	eigkan bongá	bongá ...	bhut (s.) ...	bhut (s.) ...	bhuto (s.)	bongá ...	...	...	u ksuid.
Sun ...	singi ...	singchándo	beru ...	bero ...	belá ...	singi ...	gomoi...	tangway ...	ka sngi.
Moon ...	chándu ...	chando ...	bango ...	lerang ...	lerang...	chandu	gumong, chando.	khatu ...	u bainai.
Star ...	ipil ...	ipil ...	pilu ...	musing ...	kujimdá	ipil ...	epal, idin	noung ...	u khlur.
Fire ...	sengel ...	sengel ...	sengel ...	timsong ...	lálái ...	sengel...	singal...	ka-mol ...	kading.
Water ...	dá ...	da' ...	dáu ...	dá ...	dág ...	dá' ...	da ...	dhihk ...	ka um.
House ...	orá ...	orá' ...	oráo ...	o ...	in-yá ...	oá ...	urá ...	hnyi ...	ka iing.
Horse ...	sádom ...	sádom ...	ghorá (s.)...	ghorá (s.) ...	ghorá (s.)	sádom...	ghodgi	chway ...	u kulai.
Cow ...	urig, gái ...	gái ...	gái ...	orèig ...	orai ...	uri ...	gai (s.)...	karuu ...	ka massi.
Dog ...	setá ...	setá ...	kuttu ...	solo' ...	setag, sello	setá ...	chitá, setá	kalá ...	u kseu.
Cat ...	pusi ...	pusi ...	pusi ...	billi, pusi ...	billi ...	pusi, bilai	minnu...	pakway ...	ka miaw.
Cock ...	sím ...	sim ...	sím ...	sing koi ...	sángoi.	sim ...	...	...	u sim.
Duck ...	gere ...	gere ...	...	kononhásá	hans (s.)	gere ...	...	...	ka hán.
Ass ...	gadhá (s.)...	gádhá (s.)...	gadhá (s.)...	gadhá ...	godo ...	ga dhá...	...	...	gaddá (s.)

English.	Mundari.	Santal.	Korwa.	Kharria.	Juanga.	Ho.	Kuri or Muasi.	Talain or Mon.	Khasi.
Camel	unt (s.)	unt (s.)	ut (s.)	unth (s.)	...	unt	...	...	ut (s.)
Bird	ore	chenre	titiju, ore	konter	kontere	oe	titit	kha-ten	ka sim.
Go	sen	sen	duo seno	dai seno	onde	seno	...	aara	leit, khie.
Come	hiju	hiju	dubu	áij	dende	huju, setre	...	kalonra	wan.
Eat	jom	jom	jome	ioñge	...	jome	...	tsi	bam.
Beat	ru	dál	nagada	gille	...	ru	...	...	dat.
Sit	du'b	durap	durup	dokona	dokona	du'b	...	khagyo	shong.
Stand	tingu	tingu	chanran	berona	...	tingun	...	monlet, kha-tau.	ieng.
Die	goij	guja'	ganjjá	goig	goju	goij	...	...	...
Give	em	em	emjá	tergore	ánádi	eme	...	ka	ai.
Run	nir	nir	nirjam	dhaen	dadobore	nir	...	garitaa	phet.
Up	chetan	chetan	ubh	tubhlung	ulingá	sermáre	...	atotá	ha-nong, ha-jerong.
Down	latar	latar	...	tuta	loká	subare	...	kha-ta-ta	sha-ram, ha-ram.
Near	nárej	thenre	bat	mojhi	hassen-yá?	náite	merá	tsouk	ha-jan.
Far	sánging	sánging	sanin	disá	lanká	sánging	atár	nu-ma-way	jing-ngai.
Before	'ayar	sámáng, má-náng.	arang	sengná	onáku?	'ayarte	...	...	shiwa.
Behind	doyá	táyom	hortoma	lorho	kinomitá?	danangre	...	...	diin.
Who	okoi	okoe	eá	átá lebu	...	okoi	tune, eiye	nyay-gau-rau	u-ba, ka-ba, ki-ba.
What	chiá	chetko	chilá	iki	...	chiá	tune, yo	mu-gau-rau	ka-ei, kamno.
Why	chiá-lágin	cháh, chedá	karalajá	iná	mándu?	chikan mente.	...	mu-parau	na ka ba lei.
And	'ado	'ado', ár	aorá	edo	...	'ando	...	young	ruh, de.
But	batkamá	menkhan	...	...	...	batkamá	...	...	hin-rei.
If	idu (s.)	khán	...	...	...	idu	...	...	la da.
Yes	he	hun, ho	hán	hán	hán	eyá	...	tot-kwai	ho oid.
No	ká	'ah, báng,	erensena	ombo	...	báno	...	ha-teen	ah, wau, em.
Alas	eh	ehe, oho	...	háy	...	háy!	...	...	waw.
A father	'appu	'apu	...	ápá	...	ápu	...	...	u kypá.
Two fathers	'appukin	'apukin	...	ubárápá	...	apukin	...	...	ki ar kypá.
Fathers	'appuko	'apuko	...	jugháy ápa	...	apuko	...	...	ki kypá.
Of a father	'appuá	'apureá	...	ápáiñá	...	apuá	...	...	jong kypá.
Of fathers	appukoá	'apukoreá	...	jugháyápá-iñá.	...	apukoá	...	...	jong ki kypá.
To a father	'appuke	'aputhe	...	ápáte	...	apu	...	...	ia kypá.
To fathers	áppukoke	ápukothe	...	jugháyápáte	...	á pu ko	...	...	ia ki kypá.
From a father	áppute	ápukhon	...	ápálo'	...	a pu te	...	...	na da kypá.
From fathers	áppukote	ápu ko khon	...	jugháyápálo'	...	ápu kote	...	...	na da ki ky-pá.
A daughter	kori-hon	kuri gidirá	...		...	ku i hon	...	...	ka kun.
Two daughters.	kori-hon kin	kurigidirákin	...		...	kui hon kin.	...	...	ki ar ka kun.
Daughters	kori-honko	kurigidiráko	...		...	kui hon ko	...	...	ki ka kun.
Of a daughter	kori-hon ra	kurigidiráreá	...	same as the noun "father" is declined.	...	kui hon'á.	...	...	jong ka kuu.
Of daughters	korihonkoá	kurigidiráko-reá.	...		...	kui hon koá.	...	...	jong kika kun.
To a daughter	korihonke	kurigidirá-the'	...		...	kui hon	...	...	ia ka kun.
To daughters	korihokoke	kurigidiráko the'.	...		...	kui hon ko	...	...	ia ki ka kun.

English.	Mundari.	Santal.	Korwa.	Kharria.	Juanga.	Ho.	Kuri or Muasi.	Talain or Mon.	Khasi.
From a daughter	korihonte ...	kurigidirákhon.	...	...	...	kuihonte	...	...	na ka kun.
From daughters	korihonkote ...	kurigidirá kokhon.	...	...	...	kuihonkote.	...	...	na ki ka kun.
A good man ...	bugin horo ...	bugi har ...	...	bes lebu	...	bugi ho...	...	...	bha briw.
Two good men	bugin horokin	bugi harkin ...	...	ubár bes lebu.	...	bugi hokin	...	...	ar bha briw.
Good men ...	bugin horoko...	bugi harko ...	...	jugháy bes lebu.	...	bugi hoko	...	...	ki bha briw.
Of a good man	bugin horora ...	bugi har reá ...	...	...	...	bugi hoá	...	...	jong bha briw
Of good men ...	bugin horokoá	bugi harkoeá	...	...	...	bugi hokoá.	...	...	jong kibha briw.
To a good man	bugin horoke...	bugi harthe' ...	...	...	...	bugi ho	...	...	ia bha briw.
To good men ..	bugin horokoke	bugi harkothe'	...	...	...	bugi hoko	...	...	ia ki bha briw.
From a good man	bugin horote...	bugi harkhon	...	..	...	bugi hote	...	...	na bha briw.
From good men	bugin horokote	bugi har kokhon.	...	...	...	bugi hokote.	...	...	na ki bha briw.
A good woman	bugin kori ...	bugi kuri ...	...	bes konsel	...	bugi erá	...	...	bha ka briw.
Good women ...	bugin koriko...	bugi kuri ko ...	...	jugháy bes konsel.	...	bugi eráko	...	...	kibha kabriw.
A bad boy ...	eigkan korá ...	bári' korá ...	...	ombáru betá.	...	etká koá	...	...	sniw kynna.
A bad girl ...	eigkan kori ...	bári' kuri ...	...	ombáru beti.	...	etká kui	..	...	sniw ka kynna.
Good ...	bugin ...	bugi ...	...	bes ...	diaraw...	bugi ...	awal (p.)	kha ...	ba bha.
Better ...	batri bugin ...	uri bugi ...	...	...	...	...	...	...	ba kham bha.
Best ...	isu bugin ...	uri utár bugi...	...	...	...	...	...	...	ba bha kham tam.
High ...	salángi ...	usul ...	...	tubhlung	jáling ...	...	...	...	bajerong.
Higher ...	batri salángi...	uri usul ...	...	...	...	...	...	...	kham jerong.
Highest ...	isu salángi ...	uri utár usul...	...	...	...	...	...	...	bajerong khamtam.
A horse ...	sándi sádom ...	ándiá sádom ...	...	ghorá ...	...	sándi sádom.	...	...	u kulai.
A mare ...	engá sádom ...	engá sádom ...	...	ghori ...	...	engá sádom.	...	...	ka kulai.
Horses ...	sándi sádomko	ándia sádomko	...	jugháy ghorá.	...	sándi sádomko.	...	...	ki kulai.
Mares ...	engá sádomko	engá sádomko	...	jugháy ghori.	...	enga sadomko.	...	...	ki ka kulai.
A bull ...	hádá ...	ándiá ...	...	ándiá oreig.	...	hárá ...	...	...	u massi.
A cow ...	gái ...	gái ...	...	gái ...	...	gái ...	...	...	ka massi.
Bulls ...	hádáko ...	ándiáko ...	...	...	...	hárako	...	...	ki massi.
Cows ...	gáiko ...	gáiko ...	...	...	...	gáiko ...	...	...	ki ka massi.
A dog ...	kotá, setá ...	setá ...	...	solo' ...	...	setá ...	...	...	u kseu.
A bitch ...	koti ...	engá setá ...	...	koti solo'	...	engá seta	...	...	ka kseu.
Dogs ...	kotáko ...	setáko ...	...	...	...	setáko	...	...	ki kseu.
Bitches ...	kotiko ...	enga setáko ...	...	...	...	engá setáko.	...	...	ki ka kseu.
A he-goat ...	sándi merom...	ándia merom...	...	botá merom.	merom...	bodá merom.	bongara, siri.	khapa ...	u blang.
A she-goat ...	engá merom ...	engá merom ...	...	pathiá merom.	...	engá merom.	...	...	ka blang.
Goats ...	meromko ...	meromko ...	...	jugháy merom.	merom...	meromko	...	...	ki blang.
A male deer ...	sándi jilu ...	ándiá jel ...	...	ándiá khajár.	...	sandi jilu	...	...	...

English.	Mundari.	Santal.	Korwa.	Kharria.	Juanga.	Ho.	Kuri or Muasi.	Talain or Mon.	Khasi.
A female deer	engá jilu	engá jel	...	mái khajár.	...	engá jilu	...	...	...
Deer	jilu	jel	...	khajár	harin (s.)	jilu	...	...	...
I am	ing menángyán	menángyan	...	...	ayasime	ing mená	...	...	...
Thou art	ám menámeán	menámá	...	...	...	ám mená	...	...	...
He is	ini' menájá	menáiá	...	...	...	áyo mená	...	...	...
We are	ále menáleá	menáleá	...	...	...	ábu mená	...	...	...
You are	ape menápeá	menápeá	...	...	...	ápe mená	...	...	...
They are	inku menákoá	menakoá	...	...	...	áko mená	...	...	...
I was	ing táikiná	táheñ kánáing	...	...	...	ing tain kedá.	...	...	...
Thou wast	am táikiná	táheñ kánám	...	...	...	am tain kedá.	...	...	...
He was	ini'taikináy	táheñ kánáy	...	...	...	áy tain kedá.	...	...	...
We were	'ale taikinále	táheñ kánále	...	...	...	ábu tain kedá.	...	...	...
You were	'ape táikinápe	táheñ kánápe	...	...	...	ápe tain kedá.	...	...	...
They were	inku táikináko	táheñ kánáko	...	...	...	áko tain kedá.	...	...	...
Be	hobáome	táheume	...	...	...	tainme	...	...	...
To be	hobá (s.)	táhente,	...	...	...	tainteá	...	...	don.
Being	hobátan	táhenkáte	...	...	...	tainiente	...	...	...
Having been	hobálenete, hobájánete.	táhenente	...	...	...	tainkedte	...	...	...
I may be	ing hobá dhá rioteá.	táhen choing	...	...	...	ing hobá dhái otea.	...	...	...
I shall be	ing hobáwá	táhen áing	...	...	...	ing hobáwá.	...	...	...
I should be	hobáwáing honáng.	táhenko' áing	...	...	...	hobáwá inghonáug.	...	...	...
Beat	ruime	dáleng me	...	...	...	rui me	...	...	...
To beat	ru	dálte	...	...	...	ruteá	...	...	...
Beating	rutan	dálkáte	...	...	...	rutan	...	...	...
Having beaten	rulijáte, rukijáte.	dálkete	...	...	...	rukedte	...	...	...
I beat	ing ruiá	dáláing (?)	...	...	...	ing ruiá or rutaná	...	...	...
Thou beatest	'am ruiá	dálám (?)	...	...	...	ám rutaná	...	...	...
He beats	ini' ruiá	dáláy (?)	...	...	...	áyo rutaná.	...	...	...
We beat	'ale ruia	dálále (?)	...	...	...	ále rutaná	...	...	...
You beat	'ape ruiá	dálápe (?)	...	...	...	ápe rutaná	...	...	...
They beat	inku ruiá	dáláko (?)	...	...	...	áko rutaná.	...	...	...
I am beating	ing ruiajaing	dálkáteáing	...	...	...	ing rutaná	...	...	...
I was beating	ing ruiajátaikináing.	...	...	...	...	...	...	...	...
I had beaten	ing rukijaing	...	...	...	...	ing ruikeda.	...	...	...
I may beat	ing rudháriáiteá	...	...	...	...	ing ruidháiá.	...	...	...
I shall beat	ing ruiáing	...	...	...	...	ing ruia	...	...	...
I should beat	ruiáing honáng	...	...	...	...	ing ruia honáng.	...	...	...

English.	Mundari.	Santal.	Korwa.	Kharria.	Juanga.	Ho.	Kuri or Muasi.	Talain or Mon.	Khasi.
I am beaten ...	ing ruing jomeádá.	dál boyu' kán tingyáñ	...	...	...	...	...	...	...
I was beaten ...	ing ruing jomkedá.	dálhoi enting yán.	...	...	...	...	...	...	...
I shall be beaten	ing ruing jomea	dál boyu' tingyán.	...	...	...	...	...	...	...
I go ...	ing senoá ...	...	...	...	ain onde	ing senoá	...	...	...
Thou goest ...	ám senoá ...	...	...	...	...	ám senoá	...	...	...
He goes ...	ini' senoá ...	...	...	...	...	áyo senoa	...	...	...
I went ...	ing senoená ...	...	...	...	unde ...	ing senkedá.	...	...	...
Thou wentest...	am senoená ...	...	...	...	...	ám senkedá.	...	...	...
He went ...	ini' senoená ...	...	...	...	...	áyo senkedá.	...	...	...
Go ...	senome ...	...	...	...	...	senome	...	...	...
Going ...	senotan ...	...	...	...	...	senotán	...	...	...
Gone ...	senlenáte ...	...	...	...	...	senokedte	...	...	...
What is your name?	ámá chikan nutum?	...	...	ámá í imi? ...	...	ámá chikan numu?	...	...	...
How old is this horse?	ne sádom chimin sermá hobákaná.	...	...	í ghorá kitte umer áij?	...	ne sádom chimin sermáy hobiena.	...	...	...
How far is it from here to Ranchi?	netáyte Ránchi chimuang sánginyán?	...	...	utitáy Ránchi kitte disá?	...	...	...	...	...
How many sons are there in your father's house?	ámá áppum oráre chimin horo koráhonko mená koá?	...	...	ámá áponmá o'te kittegothang betá kiáing?	...	...	...	...	...
I have walked a long way today.	ing tising isu sángingaing senkedá.	...	...	ing jugháy disá cho'lai'king.	...	...	...	...	...
The son of my uncle is married to her sister.	kákáingyán hon ini'já misi te ke doá kajáy	...	...	kákaingyañ betá hokorá kulamdáyá betidom bihái oki.	...	...	...	...	...
In the house is the saddle of the white horse.	oráre pundi sádomra jin mená.	...	...	o'te osel ghorá á jin áij.	...	...	...	...	...
Put the saddle upon his back.	ini'já doyáre jin ládime.	...	...	hokorá kandabte jin lá'degore.	...	...	...	...	
I have beaten his son with many stripes.	ing ini'já hon teke khub chábukteing hanrsá kija.	...	...	hokorá betáte ing khub chábuk lo' gile.	...	...	...	...	...
He is grazing cattle on the top of the hill.	ini'buru chetan re urijay gupi taná.	...	...	hoje oreig birutobhlung gupá ná lá si.	...	...	...	...	...
He is sitting on a horse under that tree.	endáru subáre ini'sádom che tau re du'bakanay.	...	...	ho dáru tutá te boje ghorá tobhlung te dokosi.	...	...	...	...	...
His brother is taller than his sister.	ini'já hágá ini'já misi te te salángiá.	...	...	hokorá kulam dái lo' hokorá bhái jelhomáij.	...	...	...	...	...
The price of that is two rupees and a half.	enára gonong bár taká ádli mená.	...	...	hokorá gining ubár rupea áth áná.	...	...	...	...	...

English.	Mundari.	Santal.	Korwa.	Kharria.	Juanga.	Ho.	Kuri or Muasi.	Talain or Mon.	Khasi.
My father lives in that small house.	ingyán áppuing en huding orá re taintanay.	...	...	ingyañ ápáing o' konon o'te áij.	...	...	...	...	...
Give this rupee to him.	neá taká ini'ke emai me.	...	...	f rupeá hokárte tergore.	...	...	...	...	...
Take those rupees from him.	ini'tayte en soben taká áuime.	...	...	hokorá tai jhári rupeá ole.	...	...	...	...	...
Beat him well and bind him with ropes.	ini'ke besleká rukid pagáte ini'ke toli me.	...	...	hokár te bes bo gile edo keke-te tolgore.	...	...	...	...	...
Draw water from the well.	kuánte dá' odonge me.	...	...	kuáñ tay dá' bibe ro ole.	...	...	...	...	...
Walk before me.	ingyán áyarte senome.	...	...	...	...	...	...	...	...
Whose boy comes behind you?	amá táyomte okoyá korá hijutanay? ...	...	...	á má kundabte ber betá de'ltá.	...	...	...	...	...
From whom did you buy that?	okoy tá' te ám enákem kring lá?	...	...	berá táy hoje songob.	...	...	...	...	...
From a shop-keeper of the village.	háturem miur dokándár táy te.	...	...	po'dá dokandar tay songoiñ.	...	...	...	...	...

Separate list of Vocables of the Juáng language.

English.	Juanga.
Numerals.	
One ...	moiñ.
Two ...	ambár.
Three ...	igota.
Four ...	ganda mi.
Five ...	panchugota.
Six ...	choogota.
Seven ...	satgota.
Eight ...	atgota.
Nine ...	naugota.
Ten ...	dasgota.
Twenty ...	kuri.
Pronouns.	
I ...	aing.
Of me, mine ...	aingiah.
We ...	aing loko.
Thou, those...	aru, am.
You, of you, your ...	apáre.
He, of him, his ...	ai, aráh
They, of them, their ...	ereki.

English.	Juanga.
Miscellaneous Words.	
Wife ...	kutomo.
Son ...	landa.
Daughter ...	kunchelan.
Cultivator ...	tasi.
God and sun ...	bero.
Devil ...	bhuto.
Moon ...	lerang.
Star ...	kujimda.
Water ...	dah.
House ...	jáhngniá.
Horse ...	ghora.
Hare ...	ne.
Cow ...	orai.
Dog ...	selo.
Cat ...	bilai.
Cock ...	senkoi.
Hen ...	senkoi.
Duck ...	honso.
Ass ...	godo.
Camel ...	uto.
Bird ...	konter.

ENGLISH.	JUANGA.
Hand	iti.
Foot	ijing.
Nose	muthe.
Eye	emor, emet.
Mouth	tomor.
Tooth	gone.
Ear	lútúr.
Hair	junta.
Head	boká.
Tongue	elang.
Belly	itib.
Back	kinop.
Iron	loa.
Gold	suna.
Silver	rupa.
Father	bá.
Mother	boin.
Brother	ká.
Elder sister	ajini.
Younger sister ...	bukai.
Young woman ...	selan kongher.
Man	munoso.
Young man	parla munoso.
Old man	komdor munoso.
To-day	ekono-mising.
To-morrow	tera.
Day-after-to-morrow ...	miang.
Fourth day	moreng.
Yesterday	tera domong.
Good	dio.
Bad	kánáh, bagi.
Goat	merom.
Deer	silip.
Sambur	seram.
Forehead	emong.
Cheek	galo
Chin	putom.
Moustache	
Beard	niso.
Whiskers	
Quick	begi.
Slow	batin.
Till	sumosing.
Firewood	songon.
Paddy	bua.

The plural is denoted by adding *loko* to the word as—

Brother	ka.
Brothers	ka loko.

ENGLISH.	JUANGA.
Fish	karom.
Go, *v.*	dai, domong domrai.
Come, *v.*	oa.
Bring, *v.*	oro.
Die, *v.*	goje.
Eat, *v.*	nu.
Beat, *v.*	nubujiko.
Give, *v.*	diana.
Dance, *v.*	nikijiko.
Sit, *v.*	dakno.
Plough, *v.*	sie.
Stand, *v.*	tongua.
Run, *v.*	dhour.
Up	alingta.
Down	tariloka.
Before	sengna.
Near	dena.
Far	lanka.
Behind	kinom.
Who	apre.
What	biri.
Why	kotha-biri.
Yes	hoi.
No	haklah.
Alas	ere-biri.
Thigh	bulu.
Skull	antu.
Leg	emojing.
Black	kaliah.
White	hándrá.
Red	sundru.
Shoulder	taran.
Arm, Forearm ..	bati.
Elbow	antukoro.
Fingers	anguti.
Toes	konoujing.
Cloth	kotoe.
Tall	jaling.
Short	huari.
Bow	kakah.
Arrows	kakom.
Quiver	katkom.
Axe	harsiah.
Sword	turuli.
Matchlock	nori.
Salt	bulung.

Sex is shown by adding *andeah* and *petah* respectively—

Male Goat	andeah merom.
She Goat	petah merom.

GROUP VIII.

DRAVIDIAN.

Introductory Remarks.

The Dravidian element enters more largely into the composition of the population of Bengal than is generally supposed. I believe that a large majority of the tribes described in the foregoing pages as Hinduised aborigines, might with propriety have been included in this group. The people called Bhúiyas diffused through most of the Bengal districts and massed in the jungle and tributary estates of Chútiá Nágpúr and Orissa, certainly belong to it, and if I am right in my conjecture regarding the Kocch nation, they are of the same stock. I roughly estimate the Bhúiyas at two and a half millions, and the Kocch at a million and a half, so that we have in these two peoples about one-tenth of the Bengal population, who in all probability should be classed as Dravidian.

But my design in the present division of the subject is to treat only of tribes who have preserved the rudiments of an original language having more or less connection with the Támil or Dravidian tongues. They comprise four great divisions of the aborigines, numbering in all about one million and one hundred thousand souls, as follows:—

Oráons of Chútiá Nágpúr and other places	600,000
Rájmahál Hillmen	400,000
Gonds in Bengal	50,000
Kandhs in Bengal	50,000

The bulk of the Gond population is in the Central Provinces, where they have been numbered at a million and a half. The Oráons and Rájmahálís are for the most part located in Bengal, but the form of speech which they have both retained, connects them closely with the Támil and Telugu-speaking people. The languages of the more civilized of the southern nations have been largely enriched by drafts from the Sanskrit source, but the rudiments of the primitive speech have been singularly preserved notwithstanding the submission of the upper and civilized classes to Bráhmanical institutions and their adoption of the Hindu religion. Dr. Muir observes of the Bráhmans that "though by their superior civilization and energy they placed themselves at the head of the Dravidian communities, they must have been so inferior in numbers to the Dravidian inhabitants as to render it impracticable to dislodge the primitive speech of the country and to replace it by their own language. They would, therefore, be compelled to acquire the Dravidian dialect." Thus, though breaking up into different nations, there is a marked uniformity between the Támil, Telugu, Canarese, and Malayalim languages and sufficient accord between them and the dialects of the Gonds and other hill tribes to substantiate their affinity. The Kandhs are of Madras rather than of Bengal, and they too extend into dependencies of the Central Provinces. The vocabularies appended to this chapter show less resemblance between the Dravidian languages and the Kandh and Savara, of which specimens are given; but in respect to the last-mentioned tribes, the information I possess is very inadequate for the purposes of comparison. I do not venture to enter on any disquisition regarding the origin of the Dravidian people, but quote the following passage from the appendix to the second volume of Dr. Muir's Sanskrit Texts,* as comprising the theories or surmises on the subject now commonly received.

"Regarding the question whether the non-Aryan tribes of the north and south are themselves of the same stock, Dr. Caldwell remarks that the Dravidians may be confidently regarded as the earliest inhabitants of India; or at least the earliest that extend from the north-west, but it is not so easy to determine whether they are the people whom the Aryans found in possession or whether they had already been expelled from the north by the irruption of another Scythian nation." Without deciding this point positively, Dr. Caldwell is led by the apparent differences between the Dravidian languages and the aboriginal element in the northern vernaculars to incline to the supposition that the Dravidian idiom must belong to an older stage of Scythian speech; and if this view be correct, it seems to follow that the ancestors of the Scythian or non-Aryan portion of the North Indian population must have immigrated into India at a later period than the Dravidians; and must have expelled the Dravidians from the greater portion of Northern India before they were themselves subjugated by a new race of Aryan invaders from the north-west. In any case Dr. Caldwell is persuaded that it was not by the Aryans that the Dravidians were expelled from Northern India, and that as no reference occurs either in Sanskrit or Dravidian to any hostilities between these two races, their primitive relations could never have been otherwise than amicable. The pre-Aryan Scythians by whom Dr. Caldwell supposes that the Dravidians may have been expelled from the northern provinces are not, he considers, to be confounded with the Kolas, Santáls, Bhíls,† Doms, and other original tribes of the north, who, he supposes, may have retired into the forests before the Dravidians, or like the Bhután tribes have entered into India from the north-east. The language of the forest tribes Dr. Caldwell conceives to exhibit no affinity with the aboriginal element in the North Indian vernaculars. We have, therefore, according to the views thus summarily expounded, four separate strata, so to speak, of Indian population :—

'*First* and earliest, the forest tribes such as the Kolas, Santáls, Bhíls, &c., who may have entered India from the north-east.

Second—The Dravidians, who entered India from the north-west and either advanced voluntarily towards their ultimate seats in the south of the peninsula, or were driven by the pressure of subsequent hordes following them in the same direction.

---

* Dr. Muir's Sanskrit Texts, Volume II, pp. 485 to 487.

† I do not think that in the above extract the Bhíls are correctly associated with the Kolas and Santáls. From such fragments of their language as I have seen, I incline to the opinion that they are Dravidian, not Kolarian; but it is difficult to determine as they apparently retain very few words of their primitive speech.

Third—We have the race (alluded to at the end of the preceding head No. 2) of Scythian or non-Aryan immigrants from the north-west, whose language afterwards united with the Sanskrit to form the Prakrit dialect of Northern India.

Fourth—The Aryan invaders.'

Section 1.—The Oráons.

Geographical distribution.

The Khurũkh or Oráons of Chútiá Nágpúr are the people best known in many parts of India as '**Dhángars**,' a word that from its apparent derivation (*dang* or *dhang*, a hill) may mean any hillmen, but amongst several tribes of the southern Tributary Mahάls, the terms Dhángar and Dhángarin mean the youth of the two sexes both in highland and lowland villages, and it cannot be considered as the national designation of any particular tribe. The Oráons are found massed in the northern and western parts of Chútiá Nágpúr proper, in the eastern parts of Sirgúja and Jashpúr, and scattered in Singbhúm, Gángpúr, Bonai, and Hazáríbágh, all in the Chútiá Nágpúr province, and in Sambalpúr of the Central Provinces; but all the scattered colonies are offshoots from the nucleus of the race in the districts first mentioned.

Numerical strength.

The Oráons in the Lohardagga District, which includes the whole of Chútiá Nágpúr proper, number 362,480, in Sirgúja about 20,000, Jashpúr 25,000, and diffused through the other districts mentioned above, employed in the tea districts, in the Mauritius, Demarara, and other places, there are as many more as would, I think, make up a total of 600,000.

Migrations.

According to the traditions I have received from the most venerable and learned of my Oráon acquaintances, the tribe has gradually migrated from the western coast of India. Some of the elders point to Gujrát as the starting point, by others the Konkan is given as the cradle of the race (the latter derivation is adopted by the Rev. William Luther of the Chútiá Nágpúr Mission, who has kindly favored me with an account of the tribe written by himself), and thence, it is supposed, is derived the name Khurũkh, by which they invariably call themselves. Oráon appears to have been assigned to them as a nickname, possibly with reference to their many migrations and proneness to roam. The people of the Konkan are called Kaunkanas in the topographical list from the Mahábhárata in the Vishnu Purán, but the affection of the Oráons for gutturals is marvellous.

The Oráons all agree in this, that they were for many generations settled on the Rohtás and adjoining hills and in the Patna District, and they say that they were driven from that part of the country by the Muhammadans, but as they declare they were in Chútiá Nágpúr before the birth of Phaní Mukuta Rái, the first Nágbangsi Raja, and the present Raja of that illustrious race claims to be the 52nd in descent from Phaní Mukuta, they must have been under the sway of the Nágbangsis before Muhammad was born.

The Oráons have a tradition that when driven from Rohtás, they divided into two parties. One under the chief went north towards the Ganges and eventually occupied the Rájmahál hills, the other under the chief's younger brother went south-east. This tradition of a separation is borne out by the evident affinity in language, and similarity

3 N

in customs of the Oráons and Rájmahálís, and, though the latter do not acknowledge the relationship, their common origin may be considered as established; and as the Rájmahálís are Málas or Málavas, it may be assumed that the Oráons are Málavas too.

Leaving Rohtás they proceeded up the Son into Palámau, and pursuing their course eastward along the Koel found themselves eventually on the highlands of Chútiá Nágpúr.

They emerged on the north-western and western portions of the plateau, where they found but a few scattered colonies of the Múnda race, and, according to the tradition which I have received, were permitted to settle without opposition from that people. The Rev. William Luther records that they attacked and dislodged the Múndas who retreated into the hills bordering on Singbhúm, but it is difficult to believe that the Oráons ever vanquished the progenitors of the Larka Kols, and after minute enquiries I do not find any such tradition in the part of the country alluded to. There are still a few Múndas in the specially Oráon quarter of Chútiá Nágpúr, who are acknowledged and looked up to as the descendants of the founders of the villages in which they live. This is hardly compatible with the supposition that they were subjugated and driven out by the new arrivals. The Oráons, indeed, maintain that they were then a more advanced people than the Múndas, and that they introduced cultivation by ploughs into Chútiá Nágpúr. This may be true, for the Múndas are still partial to the dáhó or *Jhúm* system of tillage so prevalent among the Indo-Chinese families.

Geographical features of the district.

The country thus colonized is the most gently undulating portion of the Chútiá Nágpúr plateau, lying between the sources of the Koel, the Damúdar, and the Subarnarekha, and comprising the well cultivated tract more than forty miles in breadth between the towns of Lohardagga and Ránchí. In these days it presents to view vast areas of terraced rice-fields, divided by swelling uplands, some well wooded with groves of mango, tamarind, and other useful and ornamental trees, some bearing remnants of the ancient forests preserved from the days when the axe was first heard in them, as a refuge for the startled Sylvan sprites. Still more remarkable as landmarks are the protuberant rocks which on all sides meet the eyes, either in great fragments of granite and gneiss fantastically piled up so as to appear in the distance like heaps of ruins hundreds of feet in height, or majestically rising to the same altitude in huge semiglobular masses, like domes of sunken temples. In many places acres of rock just show above ground, as if the crust of the earth had been there stripped bare, and such spots the Oráons especially affect as sites for villages: the flat or gently undulating rock affording them threshing floors, that only require to be swept, hard surfaces on which to spread out their grain and cowdung fuel to dry, holes which they can use as mortars for the pounding of their rice, and very convenient dancing places.

Besides these features the landscape is generally bounded on one or more sides by ranges of hills rising to fourteen hundred feet above the average altitude of the plateau, or three thousand four hundred feet above the level of the sea.

Houses.

The domiciles of the humble men who claim to be the original lords of the soil assort but ill with such grandeur of scenery. The Oráons are wanting in the organ of constructiveness, and their huts, badly built, and incapable of affording decent accommodation to a family, are huddled together in a manner little conducive to convenience, health, or decorum. Groups of houses are built in rows of three or four facing each other, and forming a small enclosed court, seldom properly drained or cleaned. In these huts the human beings and cattle have common tenancy. The pigs alone have buildings appropriated to their own use.

The walls of the huts are of mud, but, when constructed of the red laterite soil of which the uplands are generally composed, they are as durable as if built of brick and mortar, though but a foot in breadth; there is no limit to the permanency of such walls when protected by roofs; and, even when exposed, all that is necessary to render them durable is to prevent the direct action of the rains by some slight covering of leaves or straw by way of coping. The worst of this method of building is that holes are dug to supply the material, which are ever afterward receptacles of filth and hot-beds of fever.

Very few villages are now found tenanted only by Oráons. The majority have been assigned to middlemen, whose more pretentious tiled dwellings with their upper stories look down patronisingly or contemptuously on the low thatched gable-ended huts of the aborigines, and it may be surely predicated that the grander the manor house the poorer and more squalid are the huts that surround it.

Tenures.

The constitution of an Oráon village is the same as that of the Múndári. In each the hereditary Múnda, or headman, and the hereditary Páhn have their lands on privileged terms as the descendants of the founders of the village. The hereditary estates of the two families are called 'Khúnts;' there is sometimes a third Khúnt called 'the Máhato,' on all of which a very low rent is fixed, but there are also conditions of service attached. These may now be commuted to cash payments at the instance of either party.

Priests.

There is also in charge of the Páhn the land dedicated to the service of the village gods. The priestly office does not always go from father to son. The latter may be ignorant and disqualified, he may be a Christian, therefore when vacated it is filled by divination. The magic 'súp,' or winnowing sieve, properly spelled like a divining rod, conducts the person holding it to the door of the man most fitted to hold the office. A priest there must be; an Oráon community cannot get on without one. The fate of the village is in his hands; in their own phraseology it is said that 'he makes its affairs.' He is also master of the revels which are for the most part connected with religious rites. The doctrine of the Oráons is, that man best pleases the gods when he makes merry himself, so that acts of worship and propitiatory sacrifices are always associated with feasting, drinking, dancing, and love-making.

The Múnda or Máhato is the functionary to whom the proprietor of the village looks for its secular administration. In contradistinction to the Páhn who *makes* ('banátá') the affairs, the Máhato *administers* ('chalátá') them, and he may be removed if he fail to give satisfaction.

The Bachelor hall.

In all the older Oráon villages, when there is any conservation of ancient customs, there is a house called the Dhúmkúria, in which all the bachelors in the village must, when not absent from it, sleep under penalty of a fine. Precisely similar institutions are met with amongst the Hill Bhúiyas of Keonjhur and Bonai, and, from the notes left by the late Rev. S. Hislop, I find, they are common to other Dravidian tribes. I have already observed that the domiciles of the Oráons have insufficient accommodation for a family, so that separate quarters for the young men are a necessity. The same remark applies to the young unmarried women, and it is a fact that they do not sleep in the house with their parents. Where they do sleep is somewhat of a mystery. They are generally frank enough when questioned about their habits, but on this subject there is always a certain amount of reticence, and I have seen girls quietly withdraw when it was mooted. I am told that in some villages a separate building is provided for them like the Dhúmkúria, in which they consort under the guardianship of an elderly duenna, but I believe the more common practice is to distribute them amongst the houses of the widows, and this is what the girls themselves assert if they answer at all when the question is asked; but however billeted, it is well known that they often find their way to the bachelor's hall, and in some villages actually sleep there. I not long ago saw a Dhúmkúria in a Sirgúja village in which the boys and girls all slept every night. They themselves admitted the fact, the elders of the village confirmed it, and appeared to think that there was no impropriety in the arrangement. That it leads to promiscuous intercourse is most indignantly denied, and it may be there is safety in the multitude; but it must sadly blunt all innate feelings of delicacy. Yet the young Oráon girls are modest in demeanour, their manner gentle, language entirely free from obscenity, and whilst hardly ever failing to present their husbands with a pledge of love in due course *after* marriage, instances of illegitimate births are rare, though they often remain unmarried for some years after reaching maturity. Long and strong attachments between young couples are common. Dhúmkúria lads are no doubt great flirts, but each has a special favorite amongst the young girls of his acquaintance, and the girls well know to whose touch or pressure in the dance each maiden's heart is especially responsive. Liaisons between boys and girls of the same village seldom end in marriage. It is considered more respectable to bring home a bride from a distance,* but it does not follow from this that there is no preliminary love-making. Maidens of one village go frequently on visits to their friends in another and stay several days, and sisters can always arrange to have for visitors the girls whom their brothers are best pleased to see. It is singular that in matters of the affections, the feelings of these semisavages should be more in unison with the sentiments and customs of the highly organised western nations than with the methodical and unromantic heart schooling of their Aryan fellow countrymen.

The Dhúmkúria fraternity are under the severest penalties bound down to secrecy in regard to all that takes place in their dormitory; and even girls are punished if they dare to tell tales. They are not allowed to join in the dances till the offence is condoned. They have a regular system of fagging in this curious institution. The small boys serve those of larger growth, shampoo their limbs, and comb their hair, &c., and they are sometimes subjected to severe discipline to *make men* of them.

The Ákhra.

Immediately in front of the Dhúmkúria is the dancing arena, called 'Ákhra,' an open circus about forty feet in diameter with a stone or a post marking its centre. It is surrounded by seats for tired dancers

* It is singular how universal this feeling is. Even amongst ourselves there is always a fiction that the bridegroom comes from afar for his bride, it would be indecorous for him to appear in church as if he came from the same quarter, and he bears her away to some distant land after her marriage.

or non-dancing spectators, and shaded by fine old tamarind trees that give a picturesque effect to the animated scene, and afford in their gigantic stems convenient screens for moonlight or starlight flirtations. During the festive seasons of the year, dancing at the Ákhra commences shortly after dark every night, and, if the supply of the home brew holds out, is often kept up till sunrise. Very rakish do the dancers appear in the early morning after a night so spent. On some occasions the circus is laid down with red earth which pulverises under the many twinkling feet and rises in a lurid cloud about the dancers, till the garments, the dusky skins, and the black hair of the performers become all of brick-dust hue; ordinarily on the party breaking up at dawn, they proceed from the Ákhra to their usual avocations and work as cheerfully and vigourously as if their night had been passed in sound sleep. This says much for the wholesomeness of the beverage that supplies them with the *staying* power.

Physical traits.

The Oráon youths, though with features very far from being in accordance with the statutes of beauty, are of a singularly pleasing class, their faces beaming with animation and good humour. Their costume is peculiar, and shows off to great advantage their supple, pliant, light figures, which are often models of symmetry. They are a small race averaging 2′ 5″, but there is perfect proportion in all parts of their form, they have not the squat appearance or muscular development of the short Himálayan tribes; but though lightly framed like the Hindu, they are better limbed. There is about the young Oráon a jaunty air and mirthful expression that distinguishes him from the Múnda or Ho, who has more of the dignified gravity that is said to characterise the North American Indian. The Oráon is particular about his personal appearance only so long as he is unmarried, but he is in no hurry to withdraw from the Dhúmkúria community, and generally his first youth is passed before he resigns his decorative propensities.

Coiffure of the men.

He wears his hair long, gathered in a knot behind, supporting, when he is in gala costume, a red or white turban. In the knot are wooden combs and other implements useful and ornamental with numerous ornaments of brass and looking glass. At the very extremity of the roll of hair gleams a small circular mirror set in brass, from which and also from his ears, bright brass chains with spiky pendants dangle, and as he moves with the springy elastic step of youth and tosses his head like a high mettled steed in the buoyancy of his animal spirits, he sets all his glittering ornaments in motion and displays as he laughs a row of teeth, sound, white, and regular, that give light and animation to his dusky features.

Dress of the men.

His middle garment consists of a long narrow strip of cloth carefully adjusted, but in such a manner as to leave him most perfect freedom of limb, and allow the full play of the muscles of the thigh and hip to be seen. He wears nothing in the form of a coat; his decorated neck and chest are undraped, displaying how the latter tapers to the waist, which the young dandies compress within the smallest compass. In addition to the cloth, there is always round the waist a girdle of cords made of tusser-silk, or of cane. This is now a superfluity, but it is no doubt the remnant of a more primitive costume, perhaps the support of the antique fig leaves.

Out of the age of ornamentation nothing can be more untidy or unprepossessing than the appearance of the Oráon. The ornaments are nearly all discarded, hair utterly

3 o

neglected, and for raiment any rags are used. This applies both to males and females of middle age.

Dress of the women.

The ordinary dress of the women depends somewhat on the degree of civilization of the part of the country in which you make your observations. In the villages about Lohardagga, a cloth from the waist to a little below the knee is the common working dress; but where there is more association with other races, the persons of young females are decently clad in the coarse cotton cloth of the country, white with red border. Made up garments are not worn except by the converts to Christianity. The one cloth six yards long is gracefully adjusted so as to form a shawl and a petticoat. The Oráons do not, as a rule, bring the upper end of the garment over the head and so give it the functions also of a veil, as it is worn by the Bengali women; they simply throw the end of the dress over the left shoulder, and it falls with its fringe and ornamented border prettily over the back of the figure. Vast quantities of red beads and a large heavy brass ornament shaped like a torque are worn round the neck. On the left hand are rings of copper, as many as can be indued on each finger up to the first joint, on the right hand a smaller quantity; rings on the second toe only, of brass or bell metal, and anklets and bracelets of the same material are also worn.

Coiffure of the women.

The hair is, as a rule, coarse and rather inclined to be frizzy, but by dint of lubrication they can make it tolerably smooth and amenable, and false hair or some other substance is used to give size to the mass (the chignon) into which it is gathered, not immediately behind, but more or less on one side, so that it lies on the neck just behind, and touching, the right ear, and flowers are arranged in a receptacle made for them between the roll of hair and the head. The ears are, as usual with such people, terribly mutilated for decorative purposes; spikes and rings are inserted into holes made in the upper cartilage, and the lobe is widely distended.

When in dancing costume on grand occasions they add to their head-dress plumes of heron feathers, and a gay bordered scarf is tightly bound round the upper part of the body.

Features.

Although the Oráons, when young, both male and female, have countenances which are pleasant to look upon from their good humoured and guileless expression, they must, on the whole, be regarded as a dark complexioned and by no means well favored race. When we see numbers of them massed together as in a market, the features that we find to predominate are excess of jaws and mouth, thick lips pushed out by the projection of the jaws and teeth, a defect which age increases, the teeth becoming more and more porrect till they appear to radiate outwards from the upper jaw. The forehead is low and narrow, but not, as a rule, receding, and the eyes have nothing very peculiar about them, often bright and full with long lashes and straight set, sometimes small and dim but not oblique. These upper features give them a human and intelligent expression notwithstanding the Simian characteristics of the lower. There is the indentation usual in the Turanian races between the frontal and nasal bones, but the latter are more pronounced than we find them in the Lohitic tribes. The color of the majority is of the darkest brown, almost black, but the observer may not only pick out individuals in the crowd who are of complexion as light as the average Hindu, but may find villages in which all the Oráon inhabitants are light brown to tawny. The fact is, they have to a surprising degree the faculty of assimilating their own color and features to those of the people amongst whom they dwell, and it may be generally remarked that when there are good looking Aryans in the same village with Oráons, the complexions of the latter become brighter, and the features more in accordance with a classical standard of beauty. Not long ago a man came to me whom I took to be a follower of the prophet from the west country, but I ascertained that he was a scion of a respectable Oráon family. I went to his village and found it to be a small place inhabited by Oráons and Patháns; the latter had been settled there for many generations, and were living on terms of perfect amity with the primitive inhabitants notwithstanding the intervention of pigs. I could not help noticing aloud the singular resemblance between the two families; the remark was received with some indignation, but more laughter, and the indignation was quite subdued when I told those concerned that women were in the habit of bringing forth children in the image of the people they *saw* daily, as well as with the lineaments of their ancestors. The old wives all acquiesced in this view.

Tattooing.

The Oráon women are all tattooed in childhood with the three marks on the brow and two on each temple that distinguish a majority of the Múnda females. One must have taken it from the other, and as we find the isolated Juángs and scattered Kharriás have the same marks, I consider it established that the Kols originated the fashion. The young men burn marks on their forearm; this is part of the discipline of the Dhúmkúria, one of the ordeals that the boys have to go through to make them hardy and manly. Girls when adult, or nearly so, have themselves further tattooed on the arms and back.

Food.

The Oráons live generously, more frequently partaking of flesh than their neighbours, but their cooking is wretched, and they have themselves a proverb* expressive of the low state of their culinary skill. Their chief food is rice and the pulse called úrid or kalai. They seldom cultivate vegetables, but many wild plants and the tender leaves of the pipul *(ficus religiosa)* and other trees are used by them as pot herbs. Besides esteeming field mice and such small game as great delicacies, they eat the flesh of bullocks, goats, buffaloes, sheep, tigers, bears, jackals, foxes, snakes, lizards, most birds, all fish, tortoises, and large frogs, but prefer pork to everything, and their villages swarm with pigs. They indulge to an immoderate degree in rice beer, which is made in every house, and it is not an uncommon event for a traveller to arrive at an Oráon village and find every soul in it drunk. I recently noted the following entry in the journal of an officer out on duty: "Arrived at the village of ——— at 10 A. M., but unable to proceed to business, as the people are all drunk." They will drink spirits when they have the opportunity, but indulge in no narcotics except tobacco, which the males chew and smoke; of gánja, bháng, and opium they have a wholesome dread.

Births.

Women think little of the perils of childbirth, and perform the office of midwife for each other; yet during labor, and for fifteen days afterwards, the mother is liable to the influence of a spirit called Chordewan, who, appearing in the form of a cat, causes injury to the womb; to avoid which

* Khurñkhar nunna akhnai ona caluar. 'The Oráons are good laborers, but bad cooks.' Revd. W. Luther's MS.

the husband must all the time indicated keep a fire burning, and the woman must live on gruel. When the woman is considered fit to appear in public, the child is named. A number of old crones meet for the purpose, and sit like witches round a vessel filled with water into which a grain of rice is thrown as the name just thought of for the child is announced. If the grain sinks the name is adopted, if it floats, it is rejected and another chosen. The name of the day of the week is often given, as Etwár to a boy, Etwári to a girl born on Sunday, Sumár and Sumári for Monday, but these are Hindu terms; they have no such names for the week in their own language. Most of the common names are, by a change of termination, adapted to male or female, as Birsa, Birsi, Dúlká, Dúlki, Chamrá, Chamri. The Oráons attach no importance to the operation of tonsure, but the heads of young children are kept shorn till they are six or seven years of age, after which the hair is allowed to grow till the girl approaches maturity; then it is incumbent on her to gather it in a knot behind, and this process enforces a considerable change in her habits. As a girl with cropped head, or locks flowing, she may eat whatever food is given to her, no matter by whom it has been prepared, but when she obeys her mother's injunction to 'bind her hair,' she is restricted to what is cooked by her own people. Young men retain this freedom of appetite till their marriage.

Marriages.

From what has already been stated relative to courtship, it will be understood that the marriage of children is not in favor amongst the Oráons. When a young man makes up his mind to marry, his parents or guardians go through a form of selection for him; but it is always a girl that he has already selected for himself, and between whom and him there is a perfect understanding. The parents, however, have to arrange all preliminaries, including the price of the damsel, which is sometimes as low as Rs. 4. In the visits that are interchanged by the negociators, omens are carefully observed by the Oráons, as by the Múndas, and there are, consequently, similar difficulties to be overcome; but when all is settled, the bridegroom proceeds with a large party of his friends, male and female, to the bride's house. Most of the males have warlike weapons, real or sham, and as they approach the village of the bride's family, the young men from thence emerge, also armed, as if to repel the invasion, and a mimic fight ensues, which, like a dissolving view, blends pleasantly into a dance. In this the bride and bridegroom join, riding each on the hips of one of their friends.

A bower is constructed, in front of the residence of the bride's father, into which the bride and bridegroom are carried by women, and made to stand on a curry-stone, under which is placed a sheaf of corn, resting on a plough yoke. Here the mystery of the *Sindúr dán* is performed, but the operation is carefully screened from view, first by cloths thrown over the young couple, secondly by a circle of their male friends, some of whom hold up a screen cloth, while others keep guard with weapons upraised, and look very fierce, as if they had been told off to cut down intruders, and were quite prepared to do so. In Oráon marriages, the bridegroom stands on the curry-stone behind the bride, but, in order that this may not be deemed a concession to the female, his toes are so placed as to tread on her heels. The old women under the cloth are very particular about this, as if they were especially interested in providing that the heel of the woman should be properly bruised. Thus posed, the man stretches over the girl's head, and daubs her forehead and crown with the red powder, '*sindúr*,' and 'f the girl is allowed to return the compliment (it is a controverted point whether she should do so or not), she performs the ceremony without turning her head, reaching back over her own shoulder and just touching his brow. When this is accomplished, a gun is fired, and then, by some arrangement, vessels full of water, placed over the bower, are capsized, and the young couple, and those who stand near them, receive a drenching shower-bath. They now retire into an apartment prepared for them, ostensibly to change their clothes, but they do not emerge for some time, and when they appear they are saluted as man and wife. Dancing is kept up during their retirement, one of the performers executing a '*pàs seul*' with a basket on her head, which is said to contain the trousseau.

The Oráons have no prescribed wedding garments. They do not follow the Hindu custom of using saffron colored robes on such occasions. The bride is attired in ordinary habiliments. No special pains are taken to make her lovely for the occasion. The bridegroom is more dressed than usual. He wears a long coat and a turban. Nor have the Oráons any special days or seasons for marriages. The ceremony may take place in any month of the year, but, with all natives, the hot, dry months are generally selected, if possible; there is not then much work on hand. Granaries are full, and they prefer those months for marching and camping out.

When the bride reaches her husband's house, food is offered to her, but she scornfully or sulkily refuses to touch it, and continues in this temper till something is presented to her that she considers worthy of her acceptance, then she unbends, and, smiling on her new friends, eats.

Friendship.

The young Oráon girls always appear on friendly terms with each other, but a custom obtains amongst them by which the ties of friendship are made almost as binding as those of marriage. It is not exclusively an Oráon practice, but it is more generally resorted to by the girls of that tribe than by other maidens.

Two girls feel a growing attachment for each other. They work together, sing together, and strive to be always together, till they grow so fond, that a sudden thought strikes one or other of them to say "let us swear eternal friendship." The formula being in Chútiá Nágpúr Hindi—"Toi uor main *gui jurabi* amren phúl lagábi." Then each plucks flowers and neatly arranges them in the other's hair. They exchange necklaces and embrace, and afterwards jointly, from their own means, prepare a little feast, to which they invite their friends of their own sex, who are made witnesses to the compact, and this ceremony is considered complete.

From that hour they must never address, or speak of each other, by name. The sworn friend is "my *gui*," or my flower, or something of the kind. They are as particular on this point as are Hindu women, not to mention the names of their husbands.

A young man makes a demonstration of his affection for a girl in a similar fashion. He sticks flowers in the mass of her back hair, and if she subsequently return the compliment, it is concluded that she desires a continuance of his attention. The next step may be an offering to his lady love of some nicely grilled field mice, which the Oráons declare to be the most delicate of food. Tender looks and squeezes whilst both are engaged in the dance are not much thought of. They are regarded merely

3 P

as the result of emotions naturally arising from pleasant contiguity and exciting strains; but when it comes to flowers and field mice, matters look serious.

Tribal divisions.

The Oráons are divided into tribes, and are what a recent author on the subject of primitive marriage calls exogamous, as are also the Múndas. I have shown above that the Oráons preserve very remarkably the symbol of the marriage by capture. The family or tribal names are usually those of animals or plants, and when this is the case, the flesh of some part of the animal or fruit of the tree is tabooed to the tribe called after it.

The following are names of tribes :—

Tirki ...	... must not eat '*Tirki*,' young mice.	
Ekhar ...	... must not eat head of tortoise.	
Kirpotas ...	... do not eat the stomach of the pig.	
Lakrar ...	... must not eat tiger's flesh.	
Kujrar ...	... must not eat oil from this tree or sit in its shade.	
Gedhiar ...	... must not eat ...	... Kite.
Khakhar ...	... must not eat ...	... Crow.
Minjar ...	... must not eat ...	... Eel.
Kerketar ...	... must not eat ...	... The bird so called.
Barar ...	.. must not eat from the leaves of the *Ficus Indicus*. (These are used as plates).	

There is no such thing as slavery among the Oráons, many are in a position to employ farm laborers, and those are generally engaged for the year. They receive their food daily, and two or three rupees for the year's work, the last instalment of which is always paid at the Saturnalia called the Mágh festival.

Dances and music.

The Oráons have adopted all the Múnda dances, and improved on them. They have one called the Oráon's **jádura**, which is quite a refinement on the ordinary jádura, most complicated in step and figure, but the movements in it are executed with wonderful precision by girls accustomed to dance it together. They commence at a very early age to learn this accomplishment. Children may be seen practising their steps whose powers of toddling are but rudimentary. They positively dance as soon as they can walk, and sing as soon as they can talk. Their voices are more musical than those of the generality of native children. They are naturally accurate timists, and have good ears; and the choir singing *in parts* of the Oráon and Múnda converts is most remarkable. They acquire with facility, and sing correctly, pieces of sacred music, that very few English parish church choirs would attempt.

The tribe I am treating of are seen to best advantage at the great national dance meetings called **Játras**. They are attended by all classes of the people, but the most conspicuous groups are those that come from the Oráon, or from the Oráon-Múnda villages.

The Játras are held on appointed days, once a year, at different places chosen as convenient centres. They are generally large mango groves in the vicinity of old villages, formerly the head quarters of the Parhá, and on the evening preceding the gathering, there is a sacrifice to the tutelary spirit, followed by a carousal in the village, and the elders of that village are sure to be all very drunk on the following morning.

As a signal to the country round, the flags of each village are brought out and set up on the road that leads to the place of meeting. This incites the young men and maidens to hurry through their morning work and look up their Játra dresses which are by no means ordinary attire. Those who have some miles to go put up their finery in a bundle to keep it fresh and clean, and proceed to some tank or stream in the vicinity of the tryst grove, and about two o'clock in the afternoon may be seen all around groups of girls laughingly making their toilettes in the open air, and young men in separate parties similarly employed. When they are ready, the drums are beaten, huge horns are blown, and thus summoned, the group from each village forms its procession. In front are young men with swords and shields or other weapons, the village standard bearers with their flags and boys waving yaks' tails, or bearing poles with fantastic arrangements of garlands and wreaths intended to represent umbrellas of dignity. Sometimes a man riding on a wooden horse is carried horse and all by his friends as the Raja, and others assume the form of, or paint themselves up to represent, certain beasts of prey. Behind this motley group the main body form compactly together as a close column of dancers in alternate ranks of boys and girls, and thus they enter the grove where the meeting is held in a cheery, dashing style, wheeling and countermarching, and forming lines, circles, and columns with grace and precision. The dance with these movements is called Khariah, and it is considered to be an Oráon rather than a Múnda dance, though Múnda girls join in it. When they enter the grove, the different groups join and dance the Khariah together, forming one vast procession and then a monstrous circle. The drums and musical instruments are laid aside, and it is by the voices alone that the time is given; but as many hundreds, nay, thousands join, the effect is grand. In serried ranks so closed up that they appear jammed, they circle round in file, all keeping perfect step, but at regular intervals the strain is terminated by a 'húrúrú,' which reminds one of Paddy's 'huroosh' as he "welts the floor," and at the same moment they all face inwards and simultaneously jumping up come down on the ground with a resounding stamp that marks the finale of the movement, but only for a momentary pause. One voice with a startling yell takes up the strain again, a fresh start is made, and after gyrating thus till they tire of it, the ring breaks up, and separating into village groups they perform other dances independently till near sunset, then all go dancing home.

I have seen Játras that were attended by not less than five thousand villagers, all in the happiest frame of mind, as if nothing could occur to ruffle the perfect good humour of each individual of the multitude. The elders are often muddled with beer, but never cross in their cups, and the young people are merry from excitement. The shopkeepers from the neighbouring towns attend and set up stalls, so that it becomes a kind of fair at which business in sweets and trinkets is brisk.

Banners.

The banners exhibited at the Játras are relics of the old Parhá system. Properly it is not every village, but every Parhá that may bear a distinctive flag, and it is a *casus belli*, if the ancient device of one village is improperly assumed by another. The banners are triangular in shape and of unusual size. They fly them plain white, plain red, and striped red and white. I have never seen any form of cross.

It is not an unfrequent occurrence in Oráon dances for the free joyous movements of one or more of the girls to be suddenly transformed into involuntarily spasmodic action, somewhat akin to the demoniacal possession by Ganshám, described in a previous chapter, and probably not far removed from what are known in some Christian countries as 'exaltations' in so-called revivals. Young girls of nervous temperament are most liable to these attacks. After dancing for some time, the motions of head, body, and legs appear to become intensified and cease to be voluntary, and though the girl seized usually drops, the violent rolling and nodding of the head and movements of the limbs continue. The bystanders in the belief that they are dealing with the spirit by whom the girl is possessed unmercifully pummel her till she ceases to struggle, then after a few minutes of utter prostration, she revives, and resumes her place amongst the dancers as if nothing had happened. It is said, there is one particular strain which girls cannot long sing without being thus affected. I believe, it is the song which usually accompanies the patting of the ground movement described in the account of the Múnda dances.

Religion.

The religion of the Oráons is of a composite order. They have no doubt retained some portion of the belief that they brought with them to Chútiá Nágpúr, but coalescing with the Múndas and joining in their festivals and acts of public worship, they to a certain extent took up their ideas on religion and blended them with their own. There is, however, a material distinction between the religious systems of the two people. The Múndas have no symbols and make no representations of their gods; the Oráons and all the cognates whom I have met with have always some visible object of worship, though it may be but a stone or a wooden post, or a lump of earth. Like the Múndas, they acknowledge a Supreme God, adored as Dharmi or Dharmesh, the Holy One, who is manifest in the sun, and they regard Dharmesh as a perfectly pure, beneficent being, who created us and would in his goodness and mercy preserve us, but that his benevolent designs are thwarted by malignant spirits whom mortals must propitiate, as Dharmesh cannot or does not interfere, if the spirit of evil once fastens upon us. It is, therefore, of no use to pray to Dharmesh or to offer sacrifices to him; so though acknowledged, recognised, and reverenced, he is neglected, whilst the malignant spirits are adored. Here we have a savage's solution of the antagonistic principles of good and evil, happiness and misery, and not a bad illustration of what untutored man, with no aspirations beyond this life, may imagine. How, they reason, could a benevolent and omniscient Creator subject his creatures to suffering? yet suffer they do, often without fault of their own, and to cause this there must be other powers at work, who act independently of and in opposition to the Creator. These malignant spirits afflict us, because (as children learn that dogs bark and bite) 'it is their nature to do so.' I do not think that Oráons have an idea that their sins are visited on them either in this world or in a world to come. It is not because they are wicked that their children or their cattle die, or their crops fail, or they suffer in body, it is only because some malignant demon has a spite against them, or is desirous of fleecing them. Their ideas of sin are limited. Thou shalt not commit adultery, thou shalt not steal, thou shalt not bear false witness against thy neighbour, is about as much of the decalogue as they would subscribe to. It is doubtful if they see any moral guilt in murder, though hundreds of them have suffered the extreme penalty of the law for this crime. They are ready to take life on very slight provocation, and in the gratification of their revenge an innocent child is as likely to suffer as the actual offender. There is one canon of the Mosaical law that they in former years rigorously enforced,—"Thou shalt not suffer a witch to live." I have dwelt on this subject in treating of the Múndas, and need only say that the Oráons are quite as inveterate against reputed witches as the Múndas, and if left to themselves, the life of elderly females would be very insecure. As it is, a suspected old woman (and sometimes a young one, especially if she be the daughter of a suspected old one) is occasionally condemned, well drubbed, and turned out of the village, and she does not always survive the treatment she is subjected to. If we analyse the views of most of the Oráon converts to Christianity, we shall, I think, be able to discern the influence of their pagan doctrines and superstitions in the motives that first led them to become catechumens. The Supreme Being who does not protect them from the spite of malevolent spirits has, they are assured, the Christians under His special care. They consider that, in consequence of this guardianship, the witches and bhúts have no power over Christians, and it is, therefore, good for them to join that body. They are taught that for the salvation of Christians one great sacrifice has been made, and they see that those who are baptized do not in fact reduce their live-stock to propitiate the evil spirits. They grasp at this notion, and long afterwards when they understand it better, the atonement, the mystical washing away of sin by the blood of Christ, is the doctrine on which their simple minds most dwell.

Converts.

I have not found amongst the pagan Oráons a trace of the high moral code that their cousins of the Rájmahál hills are said to have accepted. I consider that they have no belief whatever in a future state, whilst to the Rájmahális is attributed a profound system of metempsychosis. The Oráons carry that doctrine no further than to suppose that men who are killed by tigers become tigers, but for other people death is an annihilation. As the sole object of their religious ceremonies is the propitiation of the demons who are ever thwarting the benevolent intentions of Dharmesh, they have no notion of a service of thanksgiving; and so far, we may regard the religion of the Múndas as of a higher order than theirs. When suffering or misfortune befall a man, he consults an augur 'Ojha' as to the instrument of his affliction, and acts according to the advice given. The Ojha has it in his power to denounce a mortal or a particular devil. The method employed has been described in the account of the Múndas, and the result is the same. If a fellow-being is denounced, it is said that he has caused his familiar to possess and afflict the sufferer, and the denounced is seized and tortured, or beaten, to force him to effect the expulsion of the evil spirit. But the family or village Bhút may be accused; the Ojha, under inspiration, of course, decides what is to be sacrificed, and frequently ruins, if he does not cure, the patient consulting him. In the process of propitiation, the fetish nature of the Oráon system is shown. The sorcerer produces a small image of mud, and on it sprinkles a few grains of rice. If fowls are to be the victims, they are placed in front of this image, and if they peck at the rice it indicates that the particular devil is satisfied with the intention of his votaries, and the sacrifice proceeds. The flesh of the animals killed is appropriated by the sorcerer, so it is his interest to have a hecatomb, if possible.

Casting out devils.

In regard to the names and attributes of the devils, the Oráons who live with Múndas sacrifice to Marang Búrú and all the Múnda Bongas. The Oráons on the western portion of the plateau, where there are few Múndas, ignore the Bongas, and pay their devotion to Darhá, the Sarna Burhi

Minor deities.

(lady of the grove), and the village *Bhúts,* who have various names. Chanda, or Chandi, is the god or goddess of the chase and is always invoked preparatory to starting on great hunting expeditions. Any bit of rock, or stone, or excrescence on a rock, serves to represent this deity. The hill near Lodhma, known to the Múndas as Marang Búrú, is held in great reverence by the Oráons. To the spirit of the hill, whom they call Baranda, they give bullocks and buffaloes, especially propitiating him as the *Bhút,* who when malignantly inclined frustrates God's designs of sending rain in due season to fertilize the earth.

In some parts of the country Darhá is almost the only spirit they propitiate. If fowls are offered to him, they must be of divers colors, but once in three years he should have a sheep from his votaries; and once in the same period a buffalo, of which the Ojha or Páhn gets a quarter. The Oráon must always have something material to worship, and for Darhá a representation of a ploughshare is set up on an altar dedicated to him, and renewed every three years.

Ghosts.

Besides this superstitious dread of the spirits above named, the Oráon's imagination tremblingly wanders in a world of ghosts. Every rock, road, river, and grove is haunted. They believe that women who die in childbirth become ghosts, called Chorail,* and such ghosts are frequently met hovering about the tombstones, always clad in robes of white, their faces fair and lovely, but with backs black as charcoal, and inverted feet; that is, they walk with their heels in front: they lay hold of passers-by and wrestle with them, and tickle them, and he is lucky, indeed, who, thus caught, escapes without permanent injuries. If, however, the man be brave and resolute, he may always overcome the ghost, but if the person caught is some luckless wight returning from a fair or dance, who, like Tam O'Shanter, had been "drinking divinely," woe betide him! He is found next morning senseless, with a twisted neck, and the services of a sorcerer, or medicine-man are necessary to set him right again.

The Bhagats.

Towards Lohardagga many Oráons take the name of Bhagat, the corruption of Bhakt, and attach themselves to some Bráhman or Gosáin who gives them 'Mantras.' The Bhagats, without absolutely abandoning the religious observances of their ancestors, adopt the worship of Síva or Mahádeo; have in their houses, or on their premises, the usual monolithic emblem of that deity, and keep brazen images of Ganesh and other Hindu gods. The Bhagats rather discourage the unrestricted intercourse between the youth of the two sexes that their ancestors smiled upon, and do their best to keep their girls from joining in the dances, but the young men heed not the injunctions of the elders on this point, and the girls evade them as much as possible. The Bhagats conform to Hindu notions regarding what should be considered clean and unclean for food, and they will not eat or drink with the people of their own tribe who are not Bhagats. I have been informed by a Christian convert, who formerly belonged to the Bhagat fraternity, that in some villages near Lohardagga, they annually make an image of a man in wood, put clothes and ornaments on it, and present it before the altar of a Mahádeo. The person who officiates as priest on the occasion says:—"O, Mahádeo, we sacrifice this man to you according to ancient customs. Give us rain in due season, and a plentiful harvest." Then, with one

* From Rev. Mr. Luther's M.S.

stroke of the axe, the head of the image is cut off, and the body is removed and buried. The Gonds make a similar offering to their Baradeo, and it is not always in effigy that the human sacrifice is made. There are grounds for concluding that the practice was observed by all the peoples of Dravidian origin.

Festivals.

The Oráons and Múndas keep the same festivals, but, according to Mr. Luther, the Karm is, with the former, the most important. It is celebrated when the time arrives for planting out the rice grown in seed beds, and is observed by Hindus, as well as by Kols, and other tribes. On the first day of the feast, the villagers must not break their fast till certain ceremonies have been performed. In the evening, a party of young people, of both sexes, proceed to the forest, and cut a young Karma tree, or the branch of one, bearing which they return in trumph,—dancing, and singing, and beating drums,—and plant it in the middle of the 'Ákhra.' After the performance of a sacrifice to the Karma Deota by the Páhn, the villagers feast, and the night is passed in dancing and revelry. Next morning all may be seen at an early hour in holiday array; the elders in groups, under the fine old tamarind trees that surround the Ákhra; and the youth of both sexes, arm-linked in a huge circle, dancing round the Karma tree, which, festooned with garlands, decorated with strips of colored cloth and sham bracelets and necklets of plaited straw, and with the bright faces and merry laughter of the young people encircling it, reminds one of the gift-bearing tree so often introduced at our own great festival, and suggests the probability of some remote connection between the two. Preparatory to the festival, the daughters of the head men of the village cultivate blades of barley in a peculiar manner. The seed is sown in moist, sandy soil, mixed with a quantity of turmeric, and the blades sprout and unfold of a pale yellow, or primrose color. On the Karma day, these blades are taken up by the roots, as if for transplanting, and carried in baskets by the fair cultivators to the Ákhra. They approach the Karma tree, and, prostrating themselves reverentially, place before it some of the plants. They then go round the company, and, like bridesmaids distributing wedding favors, present to each person a few of the yellow barley blades, and all soon appear, wearing, generally in their hair, this distinctive decoration of the festival. Then all join merrily in the Karma dances, and malignant, indeed, must be the *Bhút* who is not propitiated by so attractive an ovation. The morning revel closes with the removal of the Karma; it is taken away by the merry throng and thrown into a stream or a tank, but after another feast, dancing and drinking are resumed; and on the following morning, the effects of the two nights dissipation are often, I fear, very palpable.

The Karm festival.

At the Karma feast, the children are all presented with new garments, but, lightly clad as they are, the expense of this to paterfamilias is not ruinous.

I have noticed that this festival is celebrated by Hindus as well as by the tribes I am describing, and the authority for observing it is a passage in the Bhavishya Purána, of which Babu Kálídás Pálit has kindly favored me with a translation.

Narod having asked by what actions and 'vratas' (religious observances), virtue, wealth, desire, and final emancipation, are to be attained, Náráin replies:—

"There was a beautiful city named Báránashi, where a highly respectable Bráhman, named Dev Surma, resided. He had two sons, the elder named Karma, and the younger

Dharma. One day Dev Surma informed his sons that he wished to make over to them his property, and devote the remainder of his life to meditation on a future state, and he accordingly divided between them all that he possessed. In a short time after receiving his share, Karma, by his extravagance, was reduced to such indigence, that he was obliged to resort to begging for his subsistence. One day, the wife of Karma Surma said to her husband, "Oh, my lord! please go to-day to your brother who is rich and wealthy". Her husband, according to her words, went to his brother's house. On that day Dharma Surma was employed in the field with his laborers in transplanting the rice plants. Karma engaged himself in the work with them. When the sun set and fearful night approached, Dharma, after taking his meal in the field, went home. Karma Surma waited as a servant with the laborers at his door, but his rich brother gave him neither rice nor paddy. Much depressed, he was returning home, when, on his way, he saw some males and females of the village worshipping the Karma tree, by adorning it with flags and flowers, and presenting it with *naivedya,* (oblation) incense and other articles. He asked them what was the object of this 'vrata.' They told him that it would avert all kinds of misfortune, and that whoever, after fasting, properly performed it, seldom suffered from distress. Hearing this, he returned home, and told all to his wife, who joyfully received this account of the vrata, and made a vow to perform it. Accordingly, on the eleventh lunar day of the increasing moon of Bhadra, just at night-fall, Karma Surma and his wife planted the Karma tree and rice plants together in the yard of the house and worshipped it, keeping a lamp burning, and offering sandal, flowers, naivedya, and incense, and giving money to the Bráhmans. By performing this chief of vratas, he obtained enormous wealth. Thus, those who with their *wives* perform this ceremony, become rich and happy in this world; and their sons and grandsons become rich and happy too; and all ultimately go to the heaven of the Gods!"

My simple Oráons are only intent on obtaining a good harvest, and that is, doubtless, the original motive for the feast. It is noticeable in the above passage, that it does not profess to explain the origin of the ceremony, but shows how a Bráhman was first induced to imitate what he had seen the people of the country performing; and considering how the territory in which the custom most prevails is inhabited, and the deep interest taken in the feast by the non-Aryan tribes, we may infer that the narrative of the Purána is to explain how a festival of the aboriginal people was adopted by Hindus. The necessity of the females of the family joining in the ceremony is against its Hindu origin, and all the observances have a geniality about them, and, at the same time, a decorum which are not usually characteristic of Hindu, Puranic, or Tantric rites.

The 'Karma' or 'Kelikadamba' is the *Nauclea parvifolia.* I do not know what attributes the tree possesses to render it so sacred, but it is singular to find it prominently noticed in botanical works, as a native of the Konkans, from whence the Oráons are said to be derived. One of the Puránas, explaining why this tree is to be worshipped, tells us that Krishna delighted in climbing it, and concealing himself in its dense foliage. From a Kadamba tree he leaped into the serpents' pool, and subdued the snake king Kaliya.*

* Vishnu Purána, Wilson's translation, Chapter VII.

The Sarhúl festival.

The Oráons have some observances during the Sarhúl festival that differ a little from those of the Múndas. Their idea is that, at this season, the marriage of 'Dhartí,' the earth, is celebrated, and this cannot be done till the Sál trees give the flowers for the ceremony. It takes place, then, towards the end of March, or beginning of April, but any day whilst the Sál trees are in blossom will answer. On the day fixed, the villagers accompany their Páhn to the Sarna, the sacred grove, a remnant of the old Sál forest in which the Oráons locate a popular deity called the Sarna Búrhi, or woman of the grove, corresponding with the 'Jáhir Era' and Desauli of the Múndas. To this dryad, who is supposed to have great influence on the rain, (a superstition not unlikely to have been founded on the importance of trees as cloud compellers,) the Páhn, arriving with his party at the grove, offers five fowls. These are afterwards cooked with rice, and a small quantity of the food is given to each person present. They then collect a quantity of Sál flowers, and return laden with them to the village. Next day the Páhn, with some of the males of the village, pays a visit to every house, carrying the flowers in a wide open basket. The females of each house take out water to wash his feet as he approaches, and, kneeling before him, make a most respectful obeisance. He then dances with them, and places over the door of the house, and in the hair of the women, some of the Sál flowers. The moment that this is accomplished, they throw the contents of their water vessels over his venerable person, heartily dousing the man whom, a moment before, they were treating with such profound respect. But to prevent his catching cold they ply him with as much of the home brew as he can drink, consequently, his reverence is generally gloriously drunk before he completes his round. The feasting and beer drinking now become general, and after the meal, the youth of both sexes, decked with Sál flowers (they make an exceedingly becoming head-dress), flock to the Ákhra, and dance all night and best part of next day.

Funeral ceremonies.

Where a death occurs in an Oráon family it is made known to the village by the loud lamentations of the women, who loosen their hair, a demonstration of grief which appears to prevail in all countries, and cry vigorously. They lay out the body on the common cot, called 'chárpái,' and after washing it carefully, convey it to the appointed burning place, covered with a new cloth, and escorted by all the villagers, male and female, who are not, for some reason, unable to attend. In some families the funeral procession proceeds with music, but others dislike this custom, and nothing is heard but the cries of the women. Arrived at the place where the funeral pile has been prepared, the body is again washed, and the nearest relations of the deceased make offerings of rice, and put rice into the mouth of the corpse, and some put pice or other coin. The body is then placed on the pile and anointed, and further offerings of rice are made, and the pile is ignited by a father or mother, a wife or a husband. When the body has been consumed, notice is given in the village, and there is another collection of friends and relatives to collect the charred bones which remain. These are placed in a new earthen vessel, and ceremoniously taken to the village, and as the procession returns, parched rice is dropped on the road to mark the route selected. The cinerary urn is suspended to a post erected in front of the deceased's late residence, the guests are feasted, and the party then breaks up.

In the month of December or January next ensuing, the friends and relations are all again collected to witness the disposal of the bones, in the place that, from the first establishment of the community, has been appropriated to the purpose. This is a point on which the Oráons are exceedingly tenacious, and even when one of them dies far from his home, his relations will, if possible, sooner or later, recover the fragments of his bones, and bear them back to the village, to be deposited with the ashes of his ancestors. The burial ground is always near a river, stream, or tank. As the procession proceeds with music to this place, offerings of rice are continually thrown over the cinerary urn till it is deposited in the grave prepared for it, and a large, flat stone placed over it. Then all must bathe, and after paying the musicians, the party returns to the village. The money that was placed in the mouth of the corpse, and afterwards saved from the ashes, is the fee of the musicians. The person who carried the bones to the grave has to undergo purification by incense, and the sprinkling of water. It is to be observed that this ceremony occurs in each village but once in the year, and on the appointed day the ashes of all who have died during the year are simultaneously relegated to their final resting place. No marriage can take place in a village whilst the bones of the dead are retained there. The most ardent lovers must patiently await the day of sepulture.* The marriage season commences shortly after it.

Conclusion.

The Oráons, if not the most virtuous, are about the most cheerful of the human race. Their lot is not a particularly happy one. Not one of their own people now occupies a position which would give him the power to protect, or influence to elevate them from the state of degradation into which a majority of the tribe have long ago fallen. They submit to be told that they were especially created as a laboring class. They have had this so often dinned into their ears, that they believe and admit it; and I have known instances of their abstaining from claiming, as authorised by law, commutation for the forced labor exacted by their landlords, because they considered that they were born to it. There are indeed some amongst them, stern yeomen, who cling with tenacity to the freeholds they have inherited, and will spend all they possess, even their life's blood (and peradventure shed blood) in defending them, but the bulk of the people seldom rise in their own country, above the position of cottiers and laborers. There the value of labor has not risen in proportion to the advance that has taken place in other parts of India, and Oráons are easily induced to migrate for a time to other climes, even to regions beyond the great 'black water,' where their work is better remunerated. But those who return with wealth thus accumulated, regard it not. They spend in a month what would have made them comfortable for life, and relapse into their lot of labor and penury, as if they had never had experience of independence and plenty. I believe they relish work, if the task-master be not over-exacting. Oráons sentenced to imprisonment without labor, as sometimes happens, for offences against the excise laws, insist on joining the laboring gangs, and wherever employed, if kindly treated, they labor as if they felt an interest in the work. In cold weather or hot, rain or sun, they go cheerfully about it, and after some nine or ten hours of toil, (seasoned with a little play and chaff amongst themselves,) they return blithely home, in flower decked groups

* Which is called 'Hadbári.'

holding each other by the hand or round the waist, and singing. When I first saw them, this struck me as a very noteworthy characteristic; for, as a rule, the working classes of all countries, especially in India, move unsociably in Indian file. It is only people of fine organization, and gentle nurture, and the aborigines of Chútiá Nágpúr, who voluntarily walk abreast and linked together in line. The Oráons have acquired this habit from their naturally genial dispositions, and their dancing drills and parades.

SECTION 2.—THE MÁLERS—PAHÁRIAS OR HILLMEN OF RÁJMAHÁL.

Geographical extent.

The Rájmahál hill country extends from the banks of the Ganges at Segrígallí, in Latitude 25° 15′ north, and Longitude 87° 3′ east, to the Bráhmani river, and the boundary of the Bírbhúm district, a distance of seventy miles. To the south of the Bráhmani the hills continue to the river Dwarká as the Rámgarh hills of the Bírbhúm district.

It has been often asserted that the Rájmahál hills are a continuation of, and that they form the northern and eastern limit of, the Vindhyan range; but this has not been confirmed by more recent and detailed examination, for particulars of which I am indebted to Mr. V. Ball, of the Geological Survey of India.

Mr. Ball observes that "physically, both the Rájmahál and Rámgarh hills may be regarded as forming an isolated group, the north-eastern extremity of which constitutes the turning point of the Ganges.

Physically, these hills are quite detached from the Vindhyan range.

Geologically, there is nothing in common between them. The Vindhyan being composed of quartzite sandstone, limestones, and shales of great age, and the Rájmahál hills of overflowing basaltic trap of comparatively recent age, which rests upon coal measures, and metamorphic (gneissose) rocks."

The measures taken to separate the Rájmahál hills from the circumadjacent country with the view of terminating the disputes and collisions which were constantly occurring between the proprietors of estates in the plains and the hillmen or Pahárias, have already been detailed in my account of the Santáls. By this measure, which was carried out in A. D. 1832, the chief proprietary right in this interesting country has centred in the Government, and the authorities were empowered to deal with the claims on the soil, preferred by the hill people, in an equitable and liberal spirit.

The Dáman-i-koh.

Round the skirts of the hills a cordon was drawn embracing a tract called, from that circumstance, the Dáman-i-koh; and on the hills within this line reside the Málers, or Malairs, who may be allowed to designate themselves as the 'asal,' or true, Pahárias. The skirts and valleys of the Dáman are occupied by Santáls, whose settlement in this part of the country is comparatively recent. So long as the new colonists confine themselves to the Lowlands, the Pahárias, from their lofty eyries, look down on their rapidly increasing cultivation with indifference, but the slightest attempt on the part of the Santáls to encroach on the hills, arouses their jealousy, and ensures the expulsion of the intruder. Sometimes, indeed, they watch, with chuckling complacency, the labors of a Santál, who, presuming that silence means consent, has been beguiled into clearing for a short distance the slopes of the hills, but the moment he commences to cultivate, he finds from very significant threats that he must withdraw, and leave the hillmen to profit by his toil.

Dr. Buchanan estimated the Málers at 35,340 souls; but the Sajáwal, or Native Superintendent, told him that there were, in all, 80,000 houses, which would give a population of not less than 400,000.

The Rájmahális describe themselves as divided into clans, but from all the information I have been able to procure on this subject, I am inclined to define the divisions as sectarian rather than tribal, arising from some having been indoctrinated with Hindu notions of purity in the matter of food, whilst others retain their liberty of conscience and appetite.

The Málers call themselves the Asal Pahárias, because they have not subjected themselves to any restrictions in regard to what they eat. The people of the southern, or Rámgarh, hills, called Mál, have another division called Kúmhárs, who abstain from cow's flesh, from flesh of animals which die a natural death, and will not partake of food that has not been cooked by themselves; repudiate all notions of consanguinity with the impure feeding Northerners, to whom they apply the term *Chit*, which is probably the reverse of complimentary. I have no doubt that they have, besides the above, the usual family or tribal distinctions, but they have not been noticed.

The Málas of the Purána topographical lists have been variously placed by commentators. Professor Wilson referring to the position assigned to the *Mála* of Kálidása's poem, the Meghu Dàta, places it in Chattísgarh; Colonel Wilford assigns as the position of the country or people Málabhúm in Midnapore. We have no reason for supposing that the Rájmahál Málers came from that eastern district, but with reference to the Oráon tradition of the western origin of the tribe, we might assume that the *Málavas* of the Vishnu Purána, supposed to be the people of Málwá, the country to the north of the Vindhyan range, between Bundelkhand and Gujrát, were the prototypes of our Rájmahál Pahárias. We have a tribe called Mál or Már, scattered over Sirgúja, Palámau, Belounja, &c., who are now a thoroughly Hinduised people, and resemble Hindus in appearance. *They* declare, they came originally from Málwá; it is said by them, and of them, that they at one time formed the bulk of the population in Palámau, but there are very few there now. Málwá is the chief seat of the Bhíl race, who are considered aborigines of that district. Málavas and Bhíls may be identical, and our Pahárias and Bhíls cognates.

Although the Málers were the first of the aboriginal tribes of Bengal that were prominently noticed by the officers of the East India Company, our information regarding their customs and ethnic peculiarities are derived almost entirely from a monograph by Lieutenant T. Shaw, published in 1795, A. D., in vol. IV of the Asiatic Researches. The accurate investigator and topographer, Dr. Buchanan, refers us to that paper, instead of giving us his own observation; and another more modern enquirer, the late Colonel Walter Sherwill, who surveyed the hills, acknowledges that, for most of the information regarding the customs and religion of the tribe given by him, he is indebted to Lieutenant Shaw.

I have never had an opportunity of personal intercourse with them, and am, therefore, entirely dependent on the writers above mentioned, and some manuscript notes which have been kindly drawn up at my request by Mr. William Atkinson of Rájmahál.

From all I can learn the Málers have no traditions throwing any real light on their history. They do not endorse the story of their common origin with the Oráons and migration with them from the west, preserved by the latter people; on the contrary, they aver that the human race was first produced on the hills to which they cling. This is their tradition, as related by Lieutenant Shaw:—

Traditions of origin.

"Seven brothers were sent from Heaven to people the earth, the eldest fell sick whilst the remainder were preparing a great feast. It was arranged that each was to take of the food that he preferred and go to the place he had chosen to live in. One took goat's flesh and went to a distant country, and his progeny are Hindus; another, from whom the Musalmáns are descended, took flesh of all kinds, except pork. It is not stated what the third took, but he originated the Kharwárs. The fourth took hog's flesh, went north, and from him sprang the Kiratís; a fifth became the ancestor of the Kawdir (? Koda, Kora, Kola, tank-digging Kols). The sixth took food of all kinds and went far away, and it was not known what had become of him till the English appeared, when it was at once concluded that they were the descendants of the omnivorous brother. The seventh brother was named Málair; he was the eldest who was sick; they gave him all kinds of food in an old dish, thus he became an outcast, and was left in the hills, where, finding neither clothes nor means of subsistence, he and his people necessarily became thieves, and continued in that vocation till taught better by Mr. Cleveland"!

This wild legend is only useful as indicating the people with whom the Málers have successively come into contact. They recognise, and attempt to account for, the existence of Kiratís, Kharwárs, Kols, Hindus, Muhammadans, and the English, but apparently none of their own cognates were known to them. The story gives us no clue to migrations, but the Oráon tradition brings the whole nation gradually from the Western Gháts to Rohtás, where it is said they were established for a long period, till attacked and driven out by Aryans. They divided into two parties, one selecting the Rájmahál hills, the other, the highlands of *Jhárkhand* or Chútiá Nágpúr, as their place of refuge. They assign to this flight from Rohtás a comparatively recent period, making out that their conquerors were Muhammadans, but this is inconsistent with the more reliable accounts we have of the long sojourn of the Oráons in Chútiá Nágpúr.

Before they had been weaned from lawless pursuits by the judicious treatment of Mr. Cleveland and other British Officers, the Pahárias appear to have been left to their own notions of Government, and though, according to Lieutenant Shaw, they possessed a code of ethics of singularly elevated tone, their practices are represented as utterly savage and cruel. We are told that if a man of one village had a claim on a person subject to a different Mánjhí, and settlement was evaded, he made application to his own chief, who assembled his vassals and seized the offender after plundering the village in which he resided. The plunder was appropriated by the chief and his followers. The accused was detained until his relations paid what had been originally claimed with costs; the costs including full compensation to the persons who in the raid on the village had been pillaged.

Under the Muhammadan Government, the inhabitants of the Rájmahál hills were the terror of the surrounding country; but they were encouraged in predatory habits by the zamíndárs at the foot of the hills, who invited the chiefs to plunder neighbouring estates, giving them a passage through their territory for the purpose, on condition of getting the lion's share of the spoil. Thus tempted and encouraged, they grew (as they themselves admit) to live on plunder, and not only were the roads near the hills unsafe, but boats on the Ganges hugged the northern bank of the river to avoid them. Under the British Government a corps of Light Infantry was specially organised to keep these mountaineers in order, the two successive commandants of which were the first to impress the hillmen with a new sense of their obligations to the rulers of the country and to pave the way for their submission to Mr. Augustus Cleveland,* who to this day is revered by them as their great benefactor and reclaimer.

Mr. Cleveland's plan appears to have been to preserve, as far as possible, their system of self-government, and to utilize the rude administrative machinery that he found in existence. On condition of their becoming responsible for the good behaviour of their adherents, the chiefs were salaried according to their rank. The head of a 'Tappah'† received ten rupees a month, his deputy three rupees, and the Mánjhí, or head, of each village two rupees.

Further to secure their co-operation, Mr. Cleveland formed from their young men a regiment of archers, 1,000 strong; and within two years from their first formation, they had so gained his confidence, that he gave them fire-arms, and they became the Bhágalpúr hill-rangers; which were in existence till disbanded on the reorganization of the Native Army after the mutiny in 1857.

Origin of the Non-Regulation system.

The difficulties experienced by the Government of the East India Company in dealing with the Rájmahál hillmen, and the exceptional measures they found it necessary to resort to, first opened their eyes to the fact that their laws, however wise, were not applicable to all their subjects. Thus originated the *Non-Regulation system*. We have this enunciated in the preamble to Regulation 1 of 1796, which is worth quoting for the brief and reliable account it gives of the condition of the tribe.

Preamble to Reg. 1 of 1796.

"The hills situated to the south and west of Rájmahál, and other parts of the district of Bhágalpúr, are inhabited by a distinct race of people, entirely differing in manners, customs, and religion, from the inhabitants of the circumjacent country, and who, as far as can be traced, never acknowledged the authority of the Native Government."

"Being destitute of manufactures, and but little acquainted with agriculture, they subsisted principally by plunder; and their incursions into the low country, which were attended by every species of cruelty, had almost desolated the districts to which they had extended."

In consideration of their uncivilized state, and entire ignorance of the language,‡ laws, and customs of the Hindus and Muhammadans, it was determined, on the 14th of June 1782, that the inhabitants of the hills should not be subject to the ordinary tribunals; but that all crimes and misdemeanours should be tried by an assembly of their chiefs, under the superintendence of the Magistrate, who was ordered, in particular cases, to report the sentence passed by the assembly for the revision of the Governor-General in Council.

* Collector of Bhágalpúr, died A. D. 1784.

† A local division comprising several villages.

‡ In Mr. Cleveland's time.

The Regulation provided that the Magistrate should commit all important cases to be tried before an assembly of hill chiefs. He was to attend the trial as Superintending Officer, and confirm or modify the sentence, if not exceeding fourteen years' imprisonment. Higher sentences were referred to the Nizámat Adáwlat, as the Supreme Criminal Court was then called. This unusual procedure was followed till 1827, when the law was repealed by Regulation 1 of that year; the mountaineers were then declared amenable to the ordinary courts, but some of the hill Mánjhís were to sit with the Magistrate as Assessors, when he tried cases in which the hillmen were concerned, and he was also authorised to adjudicate summarily in disputes about land, succession, and claims to money, when the value of the suit did not exceed one hundred rupees. These were most salutary provisions, as there is nothing so unsatisfactory and bewildering to an unsophisticated hillman, as to be bandied about from one court to another in search of a Judge with the jurisdiction that suits his case.

Regulation 1 of 1827.

Although the accounts hitherto published do not show as much similitude between the social customs of the Oráons and Rájmahális as the Oráon legend of their consanguinity and the similarity of their language might lead us to expect, I believe that if one who was familiar with the Oráon peculiarities were to visit the Rájmahális, he would find that where they differed, it was owing to the influence on each of the foreigners they had during a long separation severally come in contact with, and a close analysis would prove that where Oráons and Múndas most differ, the former are generally in accord with the Rájmahális, and when the Rájmahális are at variance with the Oráons, it is owing to the former having been indoctrinated by Hindus.

We learn from Lieutenant Shaw's paper, that the Pahárias have a firm belief in the transmigration of souls. Their high-toned, moral code is, in respect to rewards and punishments after death, entirely based on that doctrine which, with the code, was, it is said, revealed to their first parents by the Creator. It will be sufficiently understood by a perusal of the following little homily.*

Religion. Metempsychosis.

Whoever obeys God's commandments will behave well in all respects. He will neither injure, abuse, beat, nor kill any one; nor rob, nor steal, nor waste food or clothes, nor quarrel; but he will praise God morning and evening: and the *women must do this too.* When a good man has lived this life as long as God pleases, God sends for him and says, "you have behaved well, and have kept my commandments, and I will exalt you, but for a season you must remain with me." The object of this sojourn is not stated, but when it is completed, the spirit of the good man is remitted to earth, to be born again of a woman as a Raja or Chief, or in some higher position than that he previously held. If he show shimself unmindful or ungrateful in his exaltation, his days are cut short, and he is born again as an inferior animal.

Pahárí ethics.

The abuse of riches or other good gifts is often punished in this world. The riches disappear, or calamity befalls the offender. Concealment of crime, as murder, or adultery, is looked on as a great aggravation of the offence. It becomes still more heinous, if

* Asiatic Researches, vol. IV., page 48.

the object of the concealment is to throw blame on another. God sees all that is done, and though mortals may be deceived, and punishment fall on the innocent, the really guilty is sure in the end to suffer a greater calamity than he inflicts. Suicide is a crime in God's eyes, and the soul of one who so offends shall not be admitted into heaven, but must hover eternally as a ghost between heaven and earth, and a like fate awaits the soul of the murderer.

Retribution.

The above is a brief abstract of the Pahárí doctrines and ethics communicated to Lieutenant Shaw by an intelligent mountaineer, a Súbadár of the hill-rangers, who had been a protege of Mr. Cleveland's, and had received some education from him. I suspect the Súbadár was himself the 'Menu' of his tribe, and that many of his precepts were inspired by his patron. The notices given of the minor deities that the Pahárias revere, and of the propitiatory rites practised, are more in accordance with the ordinary customs and notions of the aboriginal tribes, than the passages above quoted.

Divinities.

The Málers call God Bedo, and the title affixed to the name of all their deities is Gosái or Gosáin, a corruption, apparently, of the Sanskrit Goswámi. The word Nad is sometimes used. The minor deities are as follow :—

1st.—Raxie. When a man-eating tiger infests a village, or a bad epidemic breaks out, Raxie has to be sought, and with the aid of the priest or diviner, a black stone, which represents the God, is found and set up under a large tree, and hedged round by plants of the 'Sij,' *Euphorbia.*

2nd.—Chal or Chalnad is similarly sought when any calamity befalls a village, and he also is found as a black stone and set up under a Mukmum tree. In his house the Chitarin festival is held every three years, at which a cow is sacrificed.

3rd.—Pow Gosáin, the God of highways, invoked by all persons going on a journey. His altar is under a Bel tree *Œgle marmelos* and the offering is a cock. One such sacrifice may serve many journeys. It is not repeated unless the votary meets with an accident.

4th.—The tutelary deity of each village community is called Dwára Gosáin. This may be the same as the Oráon *Dárá* or Darhá. Whenever, from some calamity falling on the household, it is considered necessary to propitiate this deity, the head of the family clears a place in front of his house, and sets up a branch of the tree called Mukmum, which appears to be held very sacred, like the 'Karm' in Chútiá Nágpúr; an egg is placed near the branch, then a hog is killed, and friends feasted; and when the ceremony is over, the egg is broken and the branch placed over the suppliant's house.

5th.—Kul Gosáin, the Ceres of the mountaineers,* is annually worshipped, when the sowing season approaches, with the sacrifice of a wether goat or hog by those who can afford it, or of a fowl by persons in indigent circumstances. The offering is made by the head of each family under a tree near which the Mukmum branch is set up, but the village priest assists, and drinks some of the blood of the victim or pretends to do so; a fore-quarter of the animal killed is presented to this Mánjhí.

* Shaw, Asiatic Res., vol. IV, page 62.

6th.—The god of hunting is called Autga, and at the close of every successful expedition a thank offering is made to him. This is the favorite pastime, and one of the chief occupations of the Málers, and they have their game laws which are strictly enforced. If a man losing an animal he has killed or wounded seeks for assistance to find it, those who aid are entitled to one-half of the animal when found. Another person accidentally coming on dead or wounded game and appropriating it, is subjected to a severe fine. The Mánjhí, or head of the village, is entitled to a share of all game killed by any of his people. Any one killing a hunting dog is fined twelve rupees; certain parts of an animal are tabooed to females as food. If they infringe this law, Autga is offended and game becomes scarce. When the hunters are unsuccessful, it is often assumed that this is the cause, and the augur never fails to point out the transgressing female who must provide a propitiatory offering. The Málers use poisoned arrows, and when they kill game, the flesh round the wound is cut off and thrown away as unfit for food. Cats are under the protection of the game laws, and a person found guilty of killing one is made to give a small quantity of salt to every child in the village.

Game laws.

7th.—Gumu Gosáin is sometimes associated with Kul, but he is specially invoked as a deity of no small influence, and a person desirous of propitiating him must abstain from all food prepared in his own house, and must not partake of the meat offered in the sacrifice; the obligation of abstinence extends to five days after the ceremony.

The last of the gods on Lieutenant Shaw's list is

8th.—Chamda Gosáin, evidently one of the most important, as it requires so extensive an offering to appease him, that only chiefs and men of wealth can afford to make the attempt. The supplicants have to ascertain from the priests or augurs what they have to provide and act implicitly according to their orders. They may have to supply one dozen of hogs, as many goats, with rice and oil in proportion, and a quantity of red lead. Three bamboos are procured and a number of strips of bark prepared and attached to the bamboos as tricolored streamers, the ends being painted black and red and the centre left the natural color. To one of the bamboos ninety of these streamers are attached, to another sixty, to the third twenty, and the poles are further decorated with peacock's feathers; they are then set up as the Chamda Gosáin in front of the house of the person who organises the sacrifice, and offerings are made to them. After feasting, the guests spend the night in dancing, three of them, relieved at intervals, supporting the bamboo effigies of Chamda. In the morning special sacrifices are offered in the house of the master of the ceremony and in his fields for a blessing on what is produced in each, progeny and crops. The *Mukmum* branch sprinkled with blood marks the spot where the altars have been raised. At the close of the ceremony, the bamboos are taken inside and suspended from the roof of the votary's house in token of his having performed the full sacrifices required of him.

According to Buchanan the Málers had formerly priests called Naiyas or Laiyas, but these men do not now exercise priestly functions, which have devolved on the Demanos who were previously only diviners, and the office was separate from that of the priesthood. The Demanos are elected by inspiration like the Pope, and after their call they spend a certain number of days in the wilderness in (as they make their flock believe) intimate communication with Bedo Gosáin. From the time that any one devotes himself to the profession of priest and augur, his hair is allowed to grow like a Nazarite; his powers of divination entirely disappear if he cuts it. Before he is admitted to full orders, his ability to foretell events correctly must be verified, and he must prove by the performance of some stupendous work beyond the strength of one man, that he is supernaturally aided by the supreme being. The priest may be a married man, but after entering into holy orders he must refrain from associating with or touching any woman except his wife. Having undergone all the tests, his nomination is finally confirmed by the Mánjhí of the village, who ties a red silk thread to which cowries are attached round his neck, and binds a turban on his head. He is then allowed to appear at the periodical sacrifice of buffaloes celebrated by the Mánjhí in the month of January, and must drink some of the blood of the victim.

Priests.

At this festival a branch of the Mukmum tree is planted in front of the Mánjhí's house, and under its shade the great man sits on a chair or stool which is reserved for such ceremonies. Taking rice from the priest he scatters it about, and all who are supposed to be possessed with devils scramble for it. The demoniacs are then bound till a buffalo is slaughtered, when they are released, in order that they may taste of the blood which cures them! The skulls of the animals killed on these occasions are preserved on stages erected in front of the Mánjhí's house, on which are also deposited trophies of the chase, heads of spotted deer, wild hog, porcupine, nilgái, barking deer, hare, &c.

The heads of animals sacrificed on other occasions are the perquisites of the priests, the remainder is eaten by males only who are invited to the feast. Women are not permitted to touch the sacrificial meat or the flesh of any animal that has not been killed in a particular way, by a blow on the side!

There are two processes of divination; Lieutenant Shaw calls one Satani, the other Cherin. The former is a test by blood sprinkled on Bel leaves. In the latter the knowledge is obtained by watching the direction of the oscillations of a pendulum.

Divination.

As so many years have elapsed since Lieutenant Shaw drew up his account of the Pahárias, we might expect at the present time to find many and important changes in their customs, but the following précis of notes on the tribe with which I have been kindly favored by Mr. W. Atkinson of Rájmahál shows that they are very conservative in their sociology.

The Pahárias are divided into three tribes, the Málers, the Mál, and the Kumár; the first retain more of the habits of their ancestors than the other two, and are rather proud of their unbounded liberty in the matter of food. They say, they eat anything that Christians eat, and a little more, for they turn not away from the carcasses of animals which have died a natural death.

They have priests, Daimonos (Demanos), and priestesses, Khiendri, who when officiating become wildly excited, as if demoniacally affected. The priest rolls on the ground in his phrenzy, but the priestess must maintain an erect position. The Pahárias all adore the sun as Bedo or Bero Gosáin. They have no special seasons for worshipping him, but when offerings are made to the minor deities, prayers are addressed also to the great God Bedo. This is quite in unison with the Oráon theology.

They have material representations of all their gods. They make wooden images which are honored for a season as idols, but they are renewed every year, and the old ones are discarded and thrown away as rubbish, when the festival for which they are made is over. This may be derived from the Hindu custom at the Durgá and other festivals, but if properly analysed it might be found to be identical with the Oráon practise of breaking up and throwing away with rubbish the altars of earth they construct for invocation purposes when they have no longer use for them.

Colonel Sherwill in his paper on the Rájmahál hills* gives a sketch of some Pahárí idols called elephant gods, which are probably of a more permanent character. They have a very fetish appearance. In each village a shed is put up for the tutelary Gosáin in which stones are placed to represent him and his attendants. This practice is found to prevail in most Hindu villages, and was in all probability derived from the aborigines. The single stone that is seen in some may be the origin of the *ling* worship. The minor deities now invoked by the Pahárias for good harvests are Chal, Singpat, and Raxi.† The priests are still under the obligation to drink some of the blood of the animals sacrificed, but the priestesses are exempted from this part of the ceremony.

The Pahárias appear to be singularly timid or shy and averse to strangers. This has been noticed by every European who has visited them; and Mr. Atkinson tells me that they have not to this day got over their diffidence and reserve, but apparently they are rarely visited by officers, and I have observed equal timidity and seeming inhospitality in Oráon villages when first visited; but with frequent intercourse the feeling wears off and they become very sociable.

The Pahárias have great reverence for the noble forest trees of their native hills, and from Colonel Sherwill's descriptions it‡ appears that their principal villages are built on sites which are richly adorned by them. The village of Simuria is described as buried in a fine forest of magnificent *Nauclea* and *Noaria*, and the old chief pointed out with sorrow the denuded appearance of an adjacent hill, all the old timber on which had been felled by some Missionary who had made preparations for building there but had abandoned the design.

Villages.

The villages are described as having rather a civilized appearance. Gaupára, one of the largest, containing eighty houses, with four hundred inhabitants, is built on the summit of a high range of hills. It is surrounded by gardens enclosed with neat hurdle fences containing vegetables, mustard, tobacco, plantains, date, and other palms; and in the centre of the villages and shading the houses are luxuriantly growing tamarind, pípal, mango, and jack trees, clumps of bamboos, palms, and plantains. The houses are built with care, all of wattled bamboo, no mud whatever being used in their construction, and numerous out-

* See Journal, Asiatic Society, Bengal, for 1851, page 552.

† Singpat is apparently new.

‡ Sherwill, Journal, Asiatic Society, Bengal, 1851, page 586.

houses, pig-sties and well-stored granaries bespeak plenty and comfort. A long bamboo is fixed in the ground in front of each house to ward off evil spirits.

Besides the dwelling houses, there are a number of well thatched round and rectangular granaries supported on posts in which the harvest of Indian corn and millet is carefully stowed away. The 'machâns' often give a peculiarly Malayan aspect to the villages. The Rájmahális do not as a rule use rice; they aver that it does not agree with them.

Colonel Sherwill noticed in the thickest part of the jungle on the hills several places where mystic ceremonies had been performed. These were marked by two upright posts supporting a beam from which depended old baskets, calibashes, earthen pots, old wooden mortars, winnowing fans, and other articles of domestic use; at other places the collections were of old arms; and at a short distance from the posts small earthen vessels were observed full of blood and spirits. We are not told the object of this curious collection, but the first is no doubt the Rájmaháli version of the Oráon ceremony called the 'rog-pelowa,' expulsion of an evil spirit that has been afflicting the village with disease amongst cattle or men.

I nowhere find any description of the dances or of the songs of the Pahárias.

Dances

Mr. Atkinson found the Málers exceedingly reticent on the subject, and with difficulty elicited that they had a dancing place in every village, but it is only when under the influence of God Bacchus that they indulge in the amusement. All accounts agree in ascribing to the Pahárias an immoderate devotion to strong drink, and Buchanan* tells us that when they are dancing, a person goes round with a pitcher of the home brew and without disarranging the performers who are probably linked together by circling or entwining arms pours into mouth of each, male and females, a refreshing and invigorating draught. Buchanan considers the origin of this custom to be the feeling that in no other way would they drink fair.

Their national drink.

The beverage is the universal pachwai, that is fermented grain. The grain, either maize, rice or janera (*Holcus sorghum*) is boiled and spread out on a mat to cool. It is then mixed with a ferment of vegetables called bakar and kept in a large earthen vessel for some days; warm water may at any time be mixed with it, and in a few hours it ferments and is ready for use.

Bachelors' clubs.

I have been informed by the Revd. Mr. Droese, Missionary at Bhágalpúr, that the Oráon custom of excluding the unmarried adults of both sexes from the family residence is followed by the Pahárias, and that the Bachelors' hall and maidens' dormitories are institutions of the Rájmahál hills as well as of the Chútiá Nágpúr highlands (See section on Oráons, page 248).

Costume and physical traits.

Buchanan says that the Málers are fully as well dressed and as cleanly in their persons as the ordinary peasantry of the plains, and their women possess more valuable ornaments than the lowland females of the cultivating class.

The Máler is represented as short of stature and slight of make. He is particular about his hair which he wears well oiled and combed in a knot on the top of his head.

* Buchanan—Topography of Bhágálpúr, page 125.

The features are of a mild Tamulian type. The nose indeed is not prominent, but it is broad below, having circular rather than elliptical nares; their faces are rather oval than lozenge shaped; their lips are, as a rule, full, but their mouths and chins are pretty well formed, and the facial angle is good;* their eyes are of the Aryan or Circassian form, not buried in fat and obliquely set like Chinese, but full and straight in the head. This would answer very well for a description of the better looking Oráons, especially where there is a reason for suspecting some slight intermixture of blood, and it is said that the Pahárias were in former days much given to the capture of wives from the plains, but with or without such admixture the Dravidian eye is always, I think, more Circassian than Mongolian.

Mr. V. Ball, of the Geological Survey, has favored me with the following description of the Asal Pahárias. Their mode of dressing the hair is peculiar; most of it is collected in a knot behind the head, but two long locks are generally left free and hang over the ears. The men have an erect carriage and generally active figure; there is nothing singular in their costume, but they are fond of red turbans, and being for the most part well to do are able to gratify their fancy.

The women are often endowed with good figures and sometimes pretty faces. Their dress is extremely graceful and effective. It consists of an ordinary white skirt, with a square of gay colored striped, or banded, tusser silk, one end of which is passed over the right and under the left shoulder, and the opposite corners tied; the other end is tucked in under the skirt at the waist. Red coral necklaces are worn in great profusion, but metal ornaments, such as the Santáls delight in, are scarcely used at all.

Love.

The Hill lads and lasses are represented as forming very romantic attachments exhibiting the spectacle of real lovers "sighing like furnaces," and the cockney expression of "keeping company" is peculiarly applicable to their courtship. If separated only for an hour, they are miserable, but there are apparently few obstacles to their enjoyment of each other's society, as they work together, go to market together, eat together, and sleep together! But if it be found that they have overstepped the prescribed limits of billing and cooing, the elders declare them to be out of the pale, and the blood of animals must be shed at their expense to wash away the indiscretion and obtain their re-admission into society.

Marriage ceremony.

On the day fixed for a marriage, the bridegroom with his relations proceeds to the bride's father's house, where they are seated on cots and mats,† and after a repast the bride's father takes his daughter's hand and places it in that of the bridegroom, and exhorts him to be loving and kind to the girl that he thus makes over to him. The groom then with the little finger of his right hand marks the girl on the forehead with 'sindúr,' vermilion, and then linking the same finger with the little finger of her right hand he leads her away to his own house.

Polygamy.

Polygamy is allowed and practised, and if a man dies leaving several widows, they can become the wives of his brothers or cousins, but only one to each. In regard to tribal or other restrictions on marriage, I find no information except that a man may not marry a near relation.

---

* Buchanan, Topography of Bhagulpore, page 123.

† *Vide* Asiatic Researches, Vol. IV., page 70.

3 U

Burial ceremonies.

The Pahárias bury their dead, unless it be a priest's body that they have to dispose of. In that case it is carried on a cot into the forest and placed under the shade of a tree, where it is covered with leaves and branches and left. The reason assigned by them for treating Demános exceptionally is, that their ghosts are exceedingly troublesome if the bodies are laid in the village cemetery. The bodies of people who die of contagious diseases are similarly disposed of.

In other cases the corpse is taken on its cot to the burial-ground and buried with the cot. When the grave is filled up, stones are put up round and above it. Over the grave of a chief a hut is constructed, which is surrounded by a fence, and for five days after the funeral the retainers and vassals are all feasted. At the end of a year, there is a second season of feasting, and if within that period a man should have lost his wife, he must not marry again, and there can be no division or distribution of the deceased's property till the second feast is given. The eldest son, if there be one, takes half, and the other half is equally divided amongst the agnates. Nephews by sisters get no share.

Veracity.

In concluding his report on the mountaineers, Lieutenant Shaw gives them a high character for veracity; he says they would sooner die than lie.

Mál Pahárias.

In the Rámgarh Hills of the Bírbhúm District and at the foot of the Rájmahál hills there are villages and detached houses occupied by a tribe who call themselves Mál Pahárias, but who appear to be altogether unconnected with the Rájmahál hillmen. Mr. Ball informs me that these people reminded him of the Kharriás and Pahárias met with in Mánbhúm, who belong to the Kolárian group, but their language does not lead me to infer any very close affinity between them and the Kols. I am indebted to Dr. Coates for a specimen of their language, which I have added to the vocabulary appended to this chapter, though I cannot say I have found in it analogues sufficient to justify its association with the Dravidian dialects, but it is equally unlike Kol. The vocables were obtained from a prisoner in the Hazáríbágh Central Jail, who came from Naia Dumka, and he gave also the following account of some customs of his brethren:—In calling themselves Mál, they are of opinion that they declare themselves free from most of the impurities practised by the Rájmahális, whom, the prisoner says, they call Savaras. They dance like the Kols and are fond of the amusement, and have one great festival in the year in the month of January or Mágh, corresponding with the great harvest joy of the Hos and Múndas. It is called 'Bhúindeb,' which is evidently Hindi, the earth god. The Máls plant in their dancing place two branches of the sál tree, and for three days they dance round these branches, after which they are removed and thrown into a river, which reminds one of the Karma festivals as solemnised by the Oráons and Kols in Chútiá Nágpúr. On this occasion the men and women dance *vis-à-vis* to each other, the musicians keeping between. The men dance holding each other above their elbows, the left hand of one holding the right elbow of the other, whose right hand again holds the left elbow of the arm that has seized him. The fore-arms touching are held stiffly out and swayed up and down. They move sideways, advance, and retire, sometimes bending low, sometimes erect. The women hold each other by the plams, interlacing the fingers, left plam upon righ plam and left and right fore-arms touching. They move like the men

They dance at births (galwari) and at weddings (behar), and have a dance called 'jhumar' for any time or season. This sounds very like the Santál or Múnda name for the same, and may be borrowed from the Santáls, their neighbours.

I have no information regarding the religion of this tribe, except that they worship the earth and sun.

SECTION 3.—THE GONDS.

In most old maps of India, the territorial name Gondwána is printed across the greater portion of the territory now known as the Central Provinces. Gondwána extended from the Vindhyan mountains to the Godávarí, and embraced the Sátpurá range. Of the districts now under the Lieutenant Governor of Bengal, it included Korea, Sirgúja, and Udaipúr, but Gond colonies are found as far east as the Katak Tributary Maháls, where they blend with the Kandhs and the Sauras, or Savaras, and they extend to Khandesh and Málwá in the west, where they touch the Bhíls.

Numerical strength.

A considerable proportion of the population of this tract—the core of India—are Gonds, and they are by far the most numerous of the aboriginal people still found there. According to the census of 1867, there are a million and a half of Gonds in the Central Provinces, of Bhíls 25,454, and of Kúrkús or Kols 39,114.

Historical notices.

Under what system or form of government the primitive inhabitants of Gondwána lived, when they were the sole possessors of the country, we have nothing to show. It was no doubt in a rude state, with scanty settlements separated by vast intervals of virgin forest and uninhabited hills, under numerous petty chiefs—sometimes confederates, but oftener at war with each other—till in course of time Aryan sages or warriors penetrated into the fastnesses, astonishing the savages by their knowledge and prowess: and Bráhmanical doctrines, permeating the country, tinged the primitive paganism without obliterating it. The Gond chiefs and all who wished to appear respectable in the eyes of their civilized visitors accepted what they could comprehend of the new faith, but the Bráhman policy was ever to leave the hewers of wood and drawers of water in their ignorance, so that whilst the 'upper ten thousand' were gradually Hinduised and partially civilized, the lower classes were left in the unreclaimed state in which we find some of them to this day.

The Hindu subjugators of the Gonds are traditionally styled Rájpúts. They formed alliances with the people of the land, especially with the families of the chiefs, and hence sprung up a superior class of Gonds who assumed the title of Rájpúts or Ráj Gonds, and by them several kingdoms were formed. The most northern of these *"had its capital at Mandla and at Garhá (near the modern city of Jabalpúr) and dominated the greater part of the Narbadá valley. Of the two midland kingdoms one had its capital at Deogarh on the southern face or slope of the Sátpurá range, overlooking and commanding the plains which now belong to Nágpúr. Deogarh is now ruined and utterly desolate, but it was a city before Nágpúr was even a village. The other midland kingdom had its capital at Kherlá, a hill commanding the rich valley of Baitúl in the heart of the Sátpurá range. To this also belonged the celebrated forts of Gávílgarh and Narnálá, both in the same hills."

* Administration Report by Sir R. Temple for the year 1862.

"The southern kingdom had its capital at Chándá on the Wardhá, and comprised a vast but wild territory: it stretched far up to the north-east and again, commanding the Godávarí, stretched far down to the south. These four dynasties existed at least some time before the formation of the Mughul Empire. They were brave and independent, but they could never have been rich or powerful."

It is said that the Hindu dynasties first established in Gondwána or Central India lost ground during the sectarian war between Budhists and Bráhmans;* the Gond chiefs availed themselves of the opportunity to re-assert their independence, which they apparently maintained till the decline of the Hindu power. Subsequently, though the northern and southern Gond kingdoms succeeded in preserving their autonomy, the remainder were gradually subjugated or made tributary by the Muhammadans. The midland kingdom was thoroughly reduced, and its princes forced or induced to embrace the Muhammadan faith.

Bakht Buland.

Bakht Buland, the Gond Raja of Deogarh, was the first to apostatize. He went to Delhi and embraced the Court religion, hoping thus to obtain favor and protection in his contests with his neighbours. He is described by Sir Richard Jenkins as an able administrator. He encouraged the resort to his Court of Hindus and Muhammadans of ability, and it is said that much of the success of the Mahratta Government, subsequently established, was owing to their adoption of the institutions formed by Bakht Buland. His descendants, availing themselves of the assistance of the Mahrattas in their intestine wars, suffered the wily leaders of that restless people to obtain a footing in Gondwána, which in the end led to its subjugation by Raghojí Bhonsla, who died in 1755, A. D. His descendant Madhují Bhonsla, after the celebrated fight at Sítábaldhí, had to succumb to the British power, and died in exile at Jaudhpúr in 1818.

Classification.

The above brief sketch will explain how at the present time we find Gonds who have retained their primitive customs and ancient faith; Gonds who, adopting Hinduism as a more fashionable and civilized religion than their own, hold to its tenets without altogether abandoning their old gods; Gonds who wear the Bráhmanical cord as members of the twice-born class and conform strictly to Hinduism; and Muhammadan Gonds.

In taking the census, it is probable that many of the two latter classes are returned as Hindus or Muhammadans, and that, therefore, the one and a half million is not their full tale in the Central Provinces. If we add the Gonds of Bengal and Madras, we shall certainly have upwards of two millions of souls, perhaps nearly three. My business is chiefly with the Gonds of Bengal, but I find I must make excursions into the Central Provinces to obtain glimpses of the raw material of the race. Of Bengal territory, one half of Sirgúja, the whole of Korea, and Udaipúr, appear to have been dominated by Gond dynasties. But although they were included in the Gondwána of the old geographers, I am in doubt as to their having been first occupied by Gonds. The chiefs of these estates have for many generations taken up positions in the peerage of India as Rájpúts or Kshatriyas, but their claim to the distinction rests on no very firm footing. According to their traditions, they were either specially raised on the spot to rule over the wild countries they are found in, or they came as knights-errant in the Indian

* Settlement Report of the Bhandára District, by A. J. Lawrence, Esq., B.C. S., p. 56.

days of chivalry, and forced or induced the savages to accept them as rulers. Can it be really true that people, zealous of their independence, thus chose rulers? I was told in Bámra, one of the dependencies of the Central Provinces, that this had happened there within the last 300 years. The country was originally divided into distinct nationalities, Gonds, Kandhs, and Bhúiyas, each under an independent chief of their own race or tribe, till they chose as their ruler the ancestor of their present Raja, who, being a Hindu and a Rájpút, introduced a fourth nationality of his co-religionists, to avoid the indignity of receiving the 'tilak' of investiture from impure hands. We find in all the tributary estates that the tribe, or tribes, who originally predominated, form still under the so-called Kshatriya or Rájpút Rajas the landed aristocracy of the country. Thus, in Sirgúja, Korea, and Udaipúr, the principal subproprietors are Gonds; in Gángpúr, Bonai, Keonjhar, &c., Bhúiyas; in Chútiá Nágpúr and many of the Jungle Mahâls, Kols. In Bámra, where, as I have said, three nationalities meet, representatives of each tribe are in possession of fiefs. The Gonds joined the Bhúiyas as colonists in Bonai, and we find in the south of that small state two fiefs held on terms of military service by Gonds, whilst the Northern tenures of the same kind are held by Bhúiyas.

In the Singbhúm District there are many colonies of Gonds, but they are there styled Dorowas. They are also called Náiks, and are probably brethren of the clan thus noticed in the Central Provinces Gazetteer, page 138.—"The Náik or Dhurwe Gonds are found in the south of the district (Chándá), but their numbers are very small. They appear under the Gond kings to have been employed as soldiers, and at the present day to prefer such service to agricultural work. They are divided into seventeen families or houses." The majority of this tribe were formerly settled in Bámanghátí, a part of Mayurbhanj. They were the military retainers and clansmen of the Mahápáter, who held all Bámanghátí in virtue of his office, but after many years of opposition to his feudal Lord, the Raja of Mayurbhanj, he broke out into open insurrection, forced the Government to interfere, and the result was, that he and all his people were banished from Bámanghátí and permitted to settle in Singbhúm.

All the Gonds above noticed, as located in Bengal, have adopted Hinduism, wholly or partially, and I have not met with one individual in the entire tract who would own to a knowledge of the Gondi language, or who had retained habits and customs characteristic of his race.

The Rautias.

There is a powerful tribe,* numbering about 15,000, in Chútía Nágpúr called Rautia, who are probably of the Gond family; they were at an early period introduced by the Nágbangsí Raja to aid him against his irrepressible Kol subjects, and they obtained grants of land as military colonists, which their descendants still hold. They resemble the Gonds in feature and in disposition; but as they aspire to be of Aryan descent, have lost all trace of their original language, and follow the customs of Hindu Súdras, it is impossible to be certain of their affinities.

They made their first appearance in a place called Panári, and though now scattered, they still maintain there a Rautia Páhn, or Baiga, *i. e.*, priest, who performs for the tribe the worship of their tutelary deity called Mahadán, whom I take to be the same as the

* Essay on Gonds, by Revd. S. Hislop, pp. 4 and 6.

3 w

Bura Deo of the Sirgúja and Singbhúm Gonds, and Bada Deo and Badial Pen of the Southerners.

Tribal divisions.

The Gond landed gentry in Korea and Sirgúja do not claim to be indigenous. They say that their ancestors came into Sirgúja from Mandla and Dángargarh on the disruption of the Gond kingdoms in Central India by the Muhammadans. They all call themselves Ráj Gonds; the following are given as tribes of the smaller fry:—1, Badiya; 2, Koram; 3, Paoli; 4, Múrpási or Múrpáchi; 5, Siamb; 6, Merkand. Amongst the Singbhúm Gonds, or Dorowas, I found—1, Bursa; 2, Nága; 3, Múrpáchi; 4, Merkam; 5, Ko siamb; 6, Kariamb; and 7, Suriam.

The Gonds of the Central Provinces are divided into twelve and a half tribes,* *viz.*, Ráj Gond, Raghawál, Dadave, Katulya, Pádál, Dholi, Ojhyál, Thotyal, Koilábhutál, Koikopál, Kolám, Mádyál, and an inferior sort of Pádál as the half class. The first four, with the addition according to some of the fifth, are classed as pure Gonds styled 'Koitor', which Mr. Hislop considers to have reference to their love for hills, but other denominations have been given.

The Dholis are so called from their being employed to beat the dhola, a drum.† The Ojhyál are augurs, from *ojh*. Thotyal means 'maimed,' and signifies a low tribe who are employed as bards. The Koilábhutál bring up their daughters as dancing girls and prostitutes. The Koikopál are herdsmen, the word being a Gondi corruption of the Hindi 'Gopál.'

The other tribes are all more or less Hinduised, and to no small extent apparently demoralised in consequence. Amongst the non-reformed aborigines, prostitution and professional dancing and singing are unknown, as is also any division of the tribe or people according to occupation, but in the Kolam and Máriá we have apparently the primitive type not found in Bengal, and it is to them we must look for typical peculiarities of the race.

The Kolams.

"The Kolams† extend all along the Kandi-Konda, or Pindi, Hills on the south of the Wardhá River, and along the table-land stretching east and north of Mánikgad and thence south to Dautanpali, running parallel to the western bank of the Pránhítá." They do not intermarry with other Gonds, and there is considerable difference between their language and what is given to us as ordinary Gondi in Mr. Hislop's vocabulary, but it appears to be pretty closely allied to Telugu. Of their sociology, all that is noticed is, that amongst them the marriage by capture is fashionable. All may be agreed between the parties beforehand, nevertheless the bride must be abducted for the fun of the thing, but the bridegroom has only to overcome the opposition of the young lady's female friends,—it is not etiquette for the men of her village to take any notice of the affair.

The Máriás.

The Máriás appear in Bastar, Chándá, and other southern dependencies as **Máriás**. The name is apparently derived from the Gondi term for a tree, 'Mara,' but they are also called **Jhoriás**, from 'jhodi,' a brook. This is the name given to the gold-washers in Chútiá Nágpúr, who are in all probability Gonds likewise. The more civilised Gonds in the southern dependencies are called **Máriás, Hulbás,** and **Badiyas.**

---

* Essay on Gonds, by Revd. S. Hislop, pp. 6 & 7.

† Hislop's paper, p. 10.

The Máriás are described as an intensely shy people; so much so that those who are most accustomed to deal with them are not admitted to an interview. The officer who collects their annual rent, approaches a Máriá village, beats a drum, and retires. The customary dues are then deposited for him at a spot previously agreed upon and left for him to appropriate.

Their shyness.

The uncivilized Máriás have very little clothing, either for warmth or purposes of decency,* and as their bodies are generally begrimed with ashes and dirt, they do not present an attractive appearance.

Appearance.

They shave the head, leaving only a top knot, but as the process is a very painful one, they rarely have recourse to it, and the neglected hair grows in a matted and most untidy form. They wear as many as fifteen small ear-rings in one ear, and round the waist a girdle of cowries, or a girdle of ten to fifteen cords, attached to which is a tobacco pouch and a naked knife. A hatchet hanging from the shoulders, or a bow and arrows, completes the costume of a Máriá in his native wilds.

It has been reported that the women of some of the Hill Máriás of Bastar are clad only in leaves like the Juángas of Keonjhar, but as I do not find that any leaf-clad tribes have actually been identified as Gond by competent persons, I think it probable that the people alluded to may be a section of the Juángas, who are linguistically and otherwise connected with the Kols. The dress of the Mádiá, or Máriá, Gonds of Bastar described by an observer† is for the women a cotton cloth round the waist, which is often the sole garment, but for full dress a wrapper is added. They are tattooed on the face and on the thighs, but the particular marks are not described. They wear small brass ear-rings and a profusion of white bead necklaces, and sometimes an iron loop encircles the neck, on which brass and iron rings are strung to make, I suppose, a pleasing jingle.

Dress.

Captain Glasford sought in vain for the leaf-clad Mádiá ladies; but he notices a tribe called Gadbás or Gudwas, and gives a specimen of their language, from which it appears that they speak a Kol rather than a Gondi dialect, and dress in cloth made from the fibre of the Kuring tree.

The Gadbás.

A Máriá woman, after giving birth to a child, has to remain in retirement for a whole month,‡ and unless she has a daughter old enough to serve her, she must cook for herself the whole time.

Social peculiarities. Births.

The bachelors are excluded at night from the family residence; and like the Oráons and other tribes described have a common dormitory, in which they are compelled to sleep.

Betrothals take place about two years before marriage. The father, making all arrangements for his son, settles with the father of the bride; but a method of divination is employed to ascertain if the proposed union is likely to prove a happy one. Two grains of rice are separately dropped into water contained in a brass plate: these are supposed to represent the boy and the girl. If the grains come together, it is auspicious. It forebodes ill, if they separate. Fourteen rupees is the average price of a bride, with the addition of Rs. 2 to her father,

Betrothals and marriages.

---

* Colonel C. Glasford. Selections from Records 'Government of India,' No. XXXIX, page 39. The Máriás and Jhorias in Bastar form, it is said, 45 per cent. of the total population.

† *Ibid.*, p. 41.

‡ Reverend S. Hislop, p. 9.

to pay for the pig he has to furnish for the feast. A large quantity of liquor has also to be provided. When the payment has been made, the bride-elect makes a round of farewell visits to her friends, and receives from each presents according to their means. In Bastar, when the bridegroom goes with his friends to fetch his bride, the shrinking maiden seeks refuge in a neighbour's house, and hides herself amongst the rafters, from whence, when found, she is ruthlessly dragged down, and borne away to her fate.

In Nágpúr the marriage ceremonies of the Gonds resemble those of the Oráons already described.

In Group VII, section 8, on the Muásís or Kúrs, I gave a description of a marriage ceremony performed in the presence and at the expense of Captain W. L. Samuells, of which the hero and heroine were Muásís. Visiting the same neighbourhood in the following year, Captain Samuells found that several couples had postponed their marriages on hearing that he was coming, and were eagerly expecting him, and he selected a pair of Gond lovers to be made happy under his patronage. The ceremony was apparently the same as that observed on the former occasion, and, in truth, I believe that the previous wedding was solemnized rather according to the Gond than the Muásí or Kol rituals; but in lieu of Ghansám, there was a frightful apparition of two demoniacs, possessed by a spirit called 'Bágheswar', the tiger-god, who fell ravenously on a bleating kid and gnawed it with their teeth till it expired. The possessed men otherwise conducted themselves in a frantic manner, the wedding guests beholding them in awe-stricken silence, and it was not till the spirit had been duly exorcised that the demoniacs subsided into a tranquil state. This was effected by the father of the bride, who poured down the throat of each, first a liberal allowance of rice-beer, and then a quantity of ghee (clarified butter), which apparently lubricated a passage for the demons' departure, and they were left in peace. Captain Samuells writes:—"The manner in which the two men seized the kid with their teeth and by that means killed it, was a sight which could only be equalled on a feeding day in a Zoological Garden or Menagerie."

The tiger-god.

This tiger-god is held in awe by numerous tribes who dwell in the vicinity of that animal's haunts, but the apparition on the present occasion was of a spirit specially attached to and connected with certain tribes of Gonds occupying the hill country between Sirgúja and Rewá. The master of the feast was of one of these tribes; it was in his family ages ago that the tiger-spirit was born, and for some years so faithfully served his father in the flesh, that the latter was inconsolable when the creature died; but it was subsequently found that whenever a marriage took place, the spirit, like an Irish Banshi, re-appeared and conducted himself in the violent manner described.

Religion.

It appears from the interesting* notes left by the late Reverend L. Hislop, that the wild Gonds of Chhindwárá and other places are distributed into sects known by the number of gods they each pay devotion to. Some are worshippers of two, some of three, some of more, up to seven gods, and there are restrictions on the intermarriage of different classes of worshippers, which, however, are not very clearly defined.

The names of the gods are different in different places, a five-god worshipper of Chhindwárá gave them as—1, Pharsi Pen, or Dula Deva; 2, Nurma; 3, Gangara; 4, Rayetal; 5, Badiatal. Here Dula Deo has the first place and is made one with Pharsi,

* In his Appendix 1.

a warlike deity, but he is reverenced as a household god throughout a very extensive area. He is the chief object of worship to the Boyars of Sirgúja, Rewá, and other places; and I was told in Jashpúr that his worship there had become so popular, or was deemed so essential, that every family of every caste or tribe, even Bráhmans, had altars dedicated to him in their houses. Gangara is sometimes called Budha, and placed at the head of the list. This was probably in the days of Budhist ascendancy. Each divinity has his particular symbol; Dula Deo or Pharsi, a battle-axe fastened to a tree; Nurma, a round piece of wood; Gangara, four links of an iron chain; Rayetal and Badiatal, a rude image of a tiger in iron; but round stones may be set up as the representative of any or all the gods, the number of stones indicating the number of gods worshipped. This is common to all tribes of the Dravidian group; and we frequently see, in villages where there are Gonds, two curved posts, one much shorter than the other, which are said to represent the tutelary deities, male and female, of the locality. The names Salei, Mal, Palo, Chawar, and Kham, or Kank, are also given, but we have no information regarding their different attributes.

The Gonds are, however, found to have one common object of worship, called according to the linguistic peculiarities of the locality, Búra Deo, Báda Deo, or Badiál Pen. Pen and Deo mean the same, but the signification of Búra or Báda I am not sure of. Major Macpherson tells us that Búra Pen, the Kandh god, means 'the god of light.' Mr. Hislop no doubt rightly conjectures that Badiál Pen, whom he also calls Badhal Pen, and the Kandh god is the same; but he translates Badhal in one place (page 14) as 'the old god,' though in a note to the same page he quotes as if affirming the Calcutta Review in translating the words 'Sun-god.' If Búra deo means 'old god,' it should, I suppose, be written 'Búrhá,' but in the way the word is pronounced, I do not detect the aspirate.

Feasts.

The Singbhúm Gonds, though in most matters completely Hinduised, have a grand festival once every year in honor of Búra Deo. At the appointed time all the adult males of the tribe proceed to the forest, and clear a space round an ásan tree (*Terminalia tomentosa*), and then offer a sacrifice in front of an altar on which the symbol of Búra Deo is set up. After which they enjoy a 'ban bhojun,' or pic-nic in the woods, every man contributing to the feast. The mahwá tree (*Bassia latifolia*) is also held sacred by the Gonds, and truly no product of nature has greater claims on their gratitude. I was credibly informed that the Gonds in Sirgúja formerly offered human sacrifices to Búra Deo, and they go through the form of doing so still—a form prescribed, I believe, in the Jogini Tantra. Not long after the cession of Sirgúja by Appá Sáhib to the British Government, one of the Gond zamíndárs was arrested and imprisoned for having seized the 'Ráj Guru,' the head priest of the Sirgúja family, and sacrificed him before the altar of Búra Deo. There is no doubt that this was done, though the Gond died in jail before he could be tried for the crime; but his estate was confiscated. The Gonds now make up an image of a man with straw or other material, and find that it answers the purpose just as well.

Human sacrifices.

In regard to the faith or religious belief of this people, I find very little on record, and the Gonds with whom I have conversed, have no ideas on the subject, except such as they have been indoctrinated with by the Bráhmans or Gosáins, at whose feet they now sit.

3 x

Sir Richard Temple, in editing Mr. Hislop's essays, has given us a translation of a very long Gondi poem, which it is said is recited by their bards; but it is so obviously derived from Hindu teachers, of wild imagination, that it cannot be regarded as embodying any true Gondi traditional lore.

Story of Lingo and the legend of the origin of the Gonds.

The 'argument' is, that the twelve families of Gonds are sprung from a boil which rose on the hand of Kalia Adao, who was similarly produced from the hand of Mahádeva. These Gonds filled the hills and valleys, and were distinguished by their promiscuous appetites and high odour. They stank in the nostrils of Mahádeva, and he shut them up in a cave, all except four brothers, who escaped. But Parbati loved the Gonds and *their smell*, and missing the latter, she engaged herself in devotional exercises to ascertain what had become of them. 'Bhagován,' God, listening to her prayer caused Lingo to be produced from a flower. He was fed on honey that dropped from the flowers of a fig tree. At nine years of age, he started on his travels and came on the four Gond brothers above mentioned. He remained with them, and helped to clear and prepare lands for cultivation, and in all he did he displayed miraculous power. One day they killed some deer, but had no fire wherewith to roast the venison. Then Lingo directed them to the abode of a giant Rikad, who had an old wife and seven lovely daughters. The youngest of the brothers was deputed, and he tried to steal the fire, but was detected by the giant who gave chase to the thief; but Lingo made a lute and going to Rikad's house played and sang so charmingly, that the old giant delighted danced, and the old wife delighted danced, and so pleased were the seven daughters, that they left the paternal roof and followed Lingo home. He gave the seven girls to the four Gonds; to the three eldest each two, and one to the youngest, and having prepared the bower and garlands, instituted and performed the marriage ceremonies proper for Gonds. "Lingo, the holy Saint," would not himself take a wife, and when the girls, fired by his insensibility to their charms, made love to him, he sternly rebuked them, but when they proceeded to take liberties with him, he flogged them. In revenge they reported to their husbands that Lingo had dishonored them, and the husbands put their benefactor to death in a very cruel manner.

Bhagován, however, restored Lingo to life, and he then undertakes the delivery of the Gonds whom Mahádeva had shut up in a cave, and after accomplishing a series of tasks set him by that god, he obtains their release, and they form a settlement in the forest under his guidance. Lingo is next found calling before him all the Gond gods or devils and giving them names, and he then causes himself to be possessed by each in turn, and dances and prophesies, and a ritual of offerings and sacrifice is established. Next, by the selection of a venerable man of the assembly to be Pardhán, an order of priests is established. The Pardhán was instructed to negotiate marriages, and a ritual of marriage was given out which embraces all the ceremonies, of probable Hindu origin, observed among the Gonds of the present day. Lingo further enjoined his Gonds to practise hospitality, and gave them permission to sing, dance, laugh, and drink, as much as they liked.

Of the personages mentioned in the above disjointed legend, the Gonds whom I have met with know nothing. I have frequently questioned them on the subject, but they never apparently had heard of Lingo and his feats. Some Murpachi, or four God Gonds, in Bamra told me they had heard of Lingo, but he belonged to the Western Gonds.

Disposal of the dead.

The half-Hinduised Gonds we meet in Bengal have no peculiar funeral ceremonies, and, so far as I have been able to judge, evince but little reverence for their dead; but *amongst the Máriás, who are probably the best type that we possess of the primitive Gond, the dead are '*waked*' in the Irish fashion. Summoned by a peculiar beat of a drum, all the Máriás within hearing attend. A cow is killed, ample provision of the intoxicating beverage called Lundi is made, and the guests are feasted. If the deceased was an adult male, the body is next secured by cords to a Mahwá tree in an erect posture and then burned. This is a very singular variation from the ordinary method, and has in all probability some special and local origin. The funeral rites are performed by the nephew of the deceased. After cremation, the ashes are collected and buried by the side of a road; a large slab of gneiss is erected over the grave; and the tail of the slaughtered cow is attached to it as a token that the obsequies of the deceased have been decently performed. Children and women are always buried, and perhaps further enquiry by Captain Glasford, to whom I am indebted for the above account, would have shown that amongst the Máriás as amongst the Káurs, all males who die unmarried are similarly disposed of.

The Máriás, like the Kols and Oráons, are deeply imbued with a dread of witchcraft and of the power of the evil eye, and when there is the slightest suspicion that a death has ensued from such a cause, the burning of the body is postponed till it is made to point out the delinquent. The relations solemnly call on the corpse to do this, and the theory is, that if there has been foul play of the nature indicated, the body on being taken up will force the bearers to convey it to the house of the person by whom the spell was cast. If this be three times repeated the owner of the house is condemned, his place is destroyed, and he is expelled from the district.

Characteristics.

Socially I consider the Hinduised or semi-Hinduised Gonds to be the least interesting of the great families of the aborigines of India. They have none of the lively disposition of the Oráons, or of the free dignified demeanour which characterises many of the Singbhúm Kols. They are in character reserved, sullen, and suspicious. They are indifferent cultivators and careless about the appearance of their homesteads, and they are withal singularly ill-favored, and though some of the wealthier families have formed series of alliances with other races which have improved their looks, I can point to many who have tried this in vain, and who show to this day features more closely resembling the lower Negro type than any I have met with amongst the tribes of Bengal. They often have short crisp curly hair, and though it is said, and no doubt truly, that this is far removed from the regular woolly covering of a Negro's head, I have generally found such hair in conjunction with features very noticeably Negro in type, and accompanying a very dark skin. They are larger and heavier in build than the Oráons or Kols, and with none of the graceful physique to be found in both these tribes.

It is probable that a more accurate knowledge of the wild hill Gonds would have enabled me to have shown that they are not devoid of those pleasant traits which render us generally partial to the primitive hill races. The description given by an officer† of the Dhúr Gonds in Narsinghpúr proves that they have much in common with other tribes of Central India. They are represented as a wild race, supported by a blind

* Captain Glasford's Report, Selection, No. XXXIX, quoted above.

† Mr. C. Grant, C. S., Selections, Government of India, No. LIII, page 10.

fatalism through lives of privation, disease, and danger. "A true Gond will commit a murder, but he will not tell a lie. Though skilled in medicinal herbs, in illness he prefers trusting to fate. He will not turn from a tiger, but will fly from cholera. Like a dog he sets fidelity above all other virtues, and will without hesitation take life at the bidding of his master. These qualities adapt the Gonds for services of danger, and they are said to make admirable miners in the coal mines of Mohpání."

They have been tried as soldiers and were not found wanting in pluck, but they cannot be made to submit to discipline.

These Gonds are described as flat nosed, thick lipped, straight haired, with frames short and thick set. The few who pass unscathed the constant risks and hardships of their forest life, are remarkable for longevity, and do not readily show signs of old age.

A Gond ordinarily retains sound teeth and black hair to the day of his death. In this particular they have the advantage over many kindred tribes. The happy disposition of the Oráon does not avert the decay to which most people have to submit as they approach the close of life.

Artizans.

The hill Gonds appear to be very backward in arts. An artizan of their own race is rarely met with, but like other tribes they have availed themselves of the services of low Aryan craftsmen who live with them, accommodate themselves to Gond habits of impurity, and in return for a scanty means of subsistence do all the weaving and pottery required.

Amongst the social customs that are described, it is strange to find no mention of the pastime which the Oráons and Kols are so passionately fond of—dancing,—but I believe this may arise from their reticence before strangers. I have expressed my belief that the *Boyars of Sirgúja, &c., are a tribe of Gonds, and *they* dance and sing merrily enough. A description of a Boyar dance that I witnessed may help the solution of the question of their consanguinity. Half a dozen young women holding hands as low down by their sides as possible, and bending their bodies forward till the clasped hands are within a foot of the ground. The men, in front of them, and detached, with drums and girdles of bells, singing, playing, and capering sometimes in an erect position, sometimes squatting on their hams. The girls' step is very simple and quiet. The left foot is advanced a short step, the right foot brought up to its heel, then right retires and left assumes its former position, but as they move they sidle round so as to make a half circle. The girls were all neatly clothed and clean and in good condition, but not beauties, both sexes had broad snub noses, large mouths, thick projecting lips, faces round from fulness of cheek, brown skins. Girls very plump figures: and this was the burden of their song.

No one sings with me, who will be my spouse?
The tiger seizes the Asúr (iron smelter) and eats him, who will be my spouse?
Go father and mother, who will be my spouse?
Why do I want a pitcher?
Why need I a support for it?
There is no one to ask for water,
Who will be my spouse?

* I have written 'Boyars', because I find the word so spelt in maps, and it appeared to me to be in accord with the pronunciation; but I find that the Jashpúr and Sirgúja chiefs write it Bhúinhárs. Some of the tribe whom I recently conversed with, declared that they and the 'Parheyas' were of one family. This is quite possible. See page 131 for Parheyas, and 134 for Boyars. The Boyars may be a connecting link between the Gonds and Oráons.

SECTION 4.—THE KANDHS.

Geographical distribution.

In the most southern region of Bengal, from the eastern limit of Gondwána to the sea coast, are situated the feudal dependencies or Tributary Mahâls, in which alone the Kandh race are found. The meridional limit of their western extension passes through Bámra, and, except as wanderers from their fatherland, they are not found further north than the 22nd degree of latitude. They extend south as far as Bastar, whence their position as the aboriginal people is taken up by the Savaras or Sauras.

There appears to be a difference of opinion amongst authorities as to the origin or derivation of the name. Some consider it to be a kindred word with Gond, and that it should be written Kand, both being derived from the Tamul 'Kandas,' a hill. Others say that it is derived from 'Kandra,' an arrow; but however derived, unlike most names of the kind, it is accepted by the people as their national designation, and as I am informed that in Orissa it is usually written Kandh, I will retain that spelling.

My personal acquaintance with the Kandhs is very limited. I have seen a few in attendance on tributary chiefs, and have fallen in with some families of the tribe in the Bonai dependency; but they had been too long dwelling in a servile position amongst aliens to have retained any distinctive or typical characteristics of their race, and could converse only in Uriya. I noticed, however, that physically they were finer men than the people about them, who were Gonds, Bhúiyas, and Páns (Pánvas). They were as tall as the average Hindu, and not much darker in complexion; while in features, many of them might have been taken for Hindus of the laboring classes.

Their carriage and bearing reminded me of the Larkas of Singbhúm. It struck me at the time that they were a mixed race; that in them the Kol, the Gond, and the Aryan, were probably blended, and if there be no error in the accounts we receive of them, one of their peculiarities is an utter disregard of the precautions practised by neighbouring tribes for the preservation of the purity of the blood. It was a custom with some of them to destroy their own female children and buy as wives daughters of aliens. Very little appears to have been known of the Kandhs till British officers were brought face to face with these mountaineers whilst engaged in operations for the reduction of the great Gúmsur estate in the Ganjám District, the chief of which had rebelled and taken refuge amongst them. Mr. Stirling, in his account of Orissa or Katak, notices them as forming the principal part of the population of "Killah Rámpúr, which was thence called the 'Kandrah Dandpát,' and adds that "the natives have the idea of a district situate between Daspalla, Boad, and Gúmsur, inhabited entirely by this tribe, which they call Kandra. This then was the extent of our knowledge of the people when British troops entered Gúmsur in 1835.*

Human sacrifices.

The astounding discovery was then made that we included amongst our fellow subjects a whole people who practised human sacrifice and female infanticide on a scale and with a cruelty which had never been surpassed by the most savage of nations, and from that period to the close of the year

* In a report by Major Roughsedge, dated 25th March 1821, he notices that two Kandhs had been introduced to him by the Raja of Boad. One of them named Ghási Malik was soon after implicated in the attack on a village that was plundered by the Kandhs, when twenty of the villagers were murdered. This is the first mention I have found of the Bengal Kandhs in official documents.

3 Y

1861, the strenuous efforts of very able officers were directed to the repression of these most appalling crimes.

Hitherto the Government had exercised little or no interference with the inhabitants of what are called the Máliahs or hill districts, between the Mahánadí and Ganjám, and this added greatly to the difficulty of carrying out the policy adopted, which was an attempt to eradicate the deeply rooted superstitions of a whole nation with the least possible display of force. It was hoped that something might be effected through the chiefs; but it was found that they exercised but a nominal control over the Kandh Máliahs.

The Meriah sacrifices, as they were called, and Kandh female infanticide, may now be regarded as amongst the plague spots of the land which have been effectually cured and obliterated by the enlightened treatment and strong hand of the British Government. It seems to be admitted, not only that the practices have ceased, but that the people have been actually weaned from the fears and superstitions which gave rise to them. Nevertheless, no account of the Kandhs would be complete without a description of the mysterious and awe-inspiring rites of a Meriah sacrifice, and a detail of the circumstances under which female infants were so unmercifully massacred.

The Kandhs are strictly an agricultural people, and the salient points of their religious belief all have reference to the fertilization of the earth. They are divided into two sects. One called Búra, worship the supreme God under that name, and hold human sacrifice in abhorrence. The other sect devote themselves to Tári, the earth-goddess, who, by shedding her own blood on sterile soil, manifested to her votaries its marvellously beneficial effects, and persuaded them that this process of fertilization must be continued by periodical human sacrifices in her honor.

It was incumbent on the Kandhs to purchase their victims.* Unless bought with a price, they were not deemed acceptable to the goddess, and, as a rule, victims from their own tribe were not thus procurable; but it sometimes happened that in bad seasons, Kandhs were reduced to selling their children, and they might then be purchased as Meriahs.

The agents employed were usually people of the Pán or Pánwa class, a low tribe of bastard Hindus, who are found diffused amongst the population of all the Tributary Maháls, under different denominations, as Páns or Pánwas, Chiks, Gandas, Pankas.

These agents sometimes purchased, but more frequently kidnapped, the children, whom they sold to the Kandhs, and they were so debased that they occasionally sold their own offspring, though they knew of course the fate that awaited them.

The word Meriah † is Uriya, not Kandh. The Kandhs call the victims Toki or Keddi. Persons of any race or age and of either sex were acceptable, if purchased, or the children of purchased Meriahs. Numbers were bought and held in readiness, and, during their period of probation or preparation, were well treated and fed. Male and female Meriahs were encouraged to cohabit, and other persons might have intercourse with female Meriahs, and in this manner numbers of children were produced, who were all treated as dedicated to destruction. If a male Meriah had intercourse with the daughter of a Kandh, it was considered a distinction.

* Account of Religion of the Kandhs, by Major Macpherson, Journal, Royal Asiatic Society, Vol. XIII, part ii.

† *Loc. cit.*, page 244.

Ten or twelve days before the time appointed for a sacrifice, the hair of the victim selected, till then unshaved, is cut off, and the villagers, having bathed, go to the sacred grove with the priest, who there invokes the goddess, and proclaims to her that they are preparing for her the repast she loves best, and implores her favor in return. The festival itself lasts three days, and it is a time of unbridled license, drunken feasting and mad dances "under excitement which the goddess is believed to inspire, and which it would be impious to resist."* On the second morning, the victim who has been kept fasting from the preceding evening, is carefully washed, dressed in a new garment, and led forth from the village in solemn procession, with music and dancing, to the Meriah grove. This, as with the Oráons and other tribes, is a remnant of the old forest, kept sacred from the axe and haunted by ghosts and spirits. In the centre of the grove a post is set up sometimes between two plants of the '*Sankissar*' shrub, to which the victim is bound in a sitting posture by the priest. He is then anointed with oil, ghee, and turmeric, adorned with flowers and worshipped, and there is now great contention amongst the bystanders to obtain some relic of his sacred person, even a portion of the unguent with which he has been anointed. He is thus left all night, during which the licentious feasting of the previous night is resumed, and the air resounds with horrid revelry. At noon on the third morning these orgies terminate, and "the assemblage proceeds with stunning shouts and pealing music to consummate the sacrifice."

The victim must not die in bonds, and to prevent escape, of which there have been instances, the arms and legs are broken, or stupefaction by opium is produced.

The priest now offers up prayers to the earth-goddess for full granaries, increase of children, cattle, pigs, and poultry, and for the decrease or disappearance of tigers and snakes; besides which, each individual of the assembled multitude gives expression to the wish that is at the moment uppermost in his thoughts. The priest then recites the tradition of the origin of the sacrifice and the necessity they were under of continuing it, and this, according to the author I am now chiefly quoting, is followed by a very long and somewhat sentimental, but at the same time argumentative, conversation between the priest and Meriah, the object of the one being to show that the victim must calmly submit to suffering in a cause so greatly to the benefit of mankind, and that he had nothing to complain of, as the Kandhs had purchased him for that especial purpose; and of the other, to prove that he had been cruelly deceived, that he had not been a party to his own sale, but believing that he had been purchased as a laborer, he had honestly worked for his employer.

The actual sacrifice to the earth goddess was performed in different ways, all brutal enough—brutality is indeed too mild a term to apply to it. Major Macpherson's account proceeds as follows:—

"The priest, assisted by the chief and one or two of the elders of the village, now takes the branch of a green tree, cleft several feet down the centre. They force the victim to place himself within the reft, fitting it, in some districts, to his throat. Cords are then twisted round the open extremity of the stake, which the priest, aided by his assistants, strives with his whole force to close. He then wounds the victim slightly with his axe, and on this, the crowd throws itself on the sacrifice and strips the flesh from the bones, leaving untouched the head and intestines." The remains are next day burned

* *Loc. cit.*, page 246. The whole of the above account is taken from the same work.

on a funeral pile, with a further sacrifice of a sheep; and the ashes are scattered over the field, or are made into a paste with which the floors of the houses and granaries are smeared. Subsequently a bullock is given to the father or procurer of the victim, and another is sacrificed and eaten at the feast which terminates the rite; but one year after the human sacrifice, the blood thirsty Tári Penna is reminded of it by an offering of a pig.

Major Macpherson further notes that the Meriah in some districts is put to death slowly by fire, the great object being to draw from the victim as many tears as possible, in the belief that the cruel Tári will proportionately increase the supply of rain!

Colonel Campbell* thus describes the *modus operandi* in Chinna Kimedy. "The miserable Meriah is dragged along the fields, surrounded by a crowd of half intoxicated Kandhs, who, shouting and screaming, rush upon him, and with their knives cut the flesh piece-meal from his bones, avoiding the head and bowels, till the living skeleton, dying from loss of blood, is relieved from torture, when its remains are burnt and the ashes mixed with the new grain to preserve it from insects."

Captain MacVicar,† in a report dated the 6th April 1851, thus describes the mode of performing the sacrifice in Máji Déso, midway between Boad and Patna. "On the day of sacrifice, after the appointed ceremonies, the Meriah is surrounded by the Kandhs, who beat him violently on the head with the heavy metal bangles, which they purchase at the fair, and wear on these occasions. If this does not destroy life, an end is put to his sufferings by strangulation by means of a slit bamboo. Strips of flesh are then cut off the back, and each recipient carries his portion to the stream which waters his fields, and there suspends it on a pole. The remains of the mangled carcass are then buried, and funeral obsequies are performed and repeated a year afterwards." This is apparently in imitation of the Hindu *shradh*.

But it was more usual for the fragments of flesh to be buried in the fields. When a sacrifice took place, a deputation from all villages of Tári Kandhs within a certain radius attended it, and returned the same day, or as rapidly as possible, with the flesh, a little of which was given to each head of a family. To secure its arrival in time, it was sometimes sent by relays of men and conveyed with postal fleetness fifty or sixty miles.‡

Female infanticide.

Hideous and extraordinary as were the bloody rites above described, it appears to me more wonderful and shocking that female infanticide should have prevailed to such an exterminating extent amongst the Kandhs. The neighbouring races all treat their female children with exemplary tenderness, most of them indeed regard the girls as marketable and valuable property, to be carefully nurtured, in order that they may grow in beauty and appear to the best advantage when called for.

The Kandhs had to pay high prices for wives of their own tribe—a fact which they assigned as one of their reasons for wishing to get rid of their maidens. Mr. Russel, of the Madras Civil service, in a report§ dated August 1836, first brought the subject to notice. The expenses attending the marriage rites were then said

* Report, dated 17th March 1849, Selections, Home Department, No. V, page 108.

† *Loc. cit.*, page 116, Captain MacVicar's Report.

‡ Colonel Campbell.

§ Selections from the Records of Government of India, Home Department, No. V, page 2.

to be the motive. They killed their own girls and purchased wives from other parts of the country. The custom was not universal. It was practised in what was called the middle Kandh region, but even there some tracts were honorably excepted, as Digi and Bodo Ghoro. Major Macpherson* reported in April 1842, that in many villages he did not find a single female child. Amongst the causes assigned are, 1*st*, that male births are increased by the destruction of female infants; 2*nd*, that it is better to destroy girls in their infancy than to allow them to grow up and become causes of strife afterwards; but the most probable solution of the question was brought to light by Captain McNeile after visiting the districts of Putiadeso, Sorobisi, Korkapatah, Jhúmka, and Ryaghada, where infanticide, both male and female, prevailed to an appalling extent.†

When a child is born, ‡an astrologer called a Jani or Desauri is summoned and consulted by the parents. He constructs a horoscope or pretends to do so, and consults a palm-leaf manuscript called a '*punji*', in which are written sentences interspersed with rude pictures of gods and devils. After certain ceremonies the 'stylus' of bone or ivory, used to write on the palm-leaf, is thrust into the book, and the fate of the child is decided according to the image or sentence which it strikes. If from this test it be predicted that the child is not likely to prove a blessing to its parents, but rather that misfortune may befall them if they attempt to rear it, the living infant is placed in a new earthen pot and removed in the direction of the point of the compass from which, if the child were spared, evil might be expected, and buried. A fowl is sacrificed over the grave.

The Desauris are generally Uriyas, who practise on the credulity of the Kandhs, but in Korkapatah and Jhúmka the Desauris are Kandhs, who do not use a '*punji*,' but do the astrology and vaticination themselves.

Of the numerous Meriahs recovered from the Kandhs, a large proportion were young girls, who, becoming wards of Government, were brought up with some care, and were more or less educated. It was deemed good policy to give some of these damsels in marriage to Kandh bachelors of respectability, and it was expected that they at least would not outrage their own feeling as mothers by consenting to the destruction of their offspring. Subsequently, however, Colonel Campbell ascertained that these ladies had no female children, and on being closely questioned, they admitted that at their husbands' bidding they had destroyed them.

I now proceed to detail briefly the measures which were undertaken to repress these barbarous customs.

Measures to suppress the barbarous customs.

The first action taken by the officers of Government towards reclaiming the Kandhs was an effort to release the Meriahs. It was found that the Kandhs were inclined to yield to mild coercion in the matter, and Mr. Russel, in a despatch, dated 11th May 1837, reported that 29 Meriahs had been surrendered. Some had been kidnapped, who were restored to their friends; 18 were children from three to ten years of age, who had been sold to the Kandhs by their

* *Loc. cit.*, page 47. Report of April 1842.

† Another reason comes from Ganjám, "that deceased female ancestors are re-born in the same families." MS. Report by Captain Smith, Assistant Agent.

‡ Selections, Madras Government, No. LXXXI, Captain A. C. McNeile's Report, dated 12th May 1867.

3 Z

parents; they were retained as Government wards. In the following year, Captain Campbell, then Assistant Collector in charge of Gúmsur, effected the release of 100 Meriah children, and it was found that they comprised people of all races, religion or caste, even Kandh children were amongst them.

In a despatch, dated July 1838, Lieutenant Hill, of the Survey Department, described the practice of human sacrifice as existing in the Kandh Máliahs of Gúmsur in Daspala, Boad, and Sohnpur, just south of the Mahánadí, and in Chinna Kimedy, Pedda Kimedy, Jaipúr, and Bastar. The Bastar Raja had the credit of having himself organised the most extensive sacrifice that had ever been heard of, on which occasion twenty-seven adult males had been immolated; in fact it was not supposed that any Kandh Máliah was free from the stain.

The proceedings on the Madras side led to enquiries being made on the Bengal side, and there also some Meriahs were given up to the demand or at the request of Messrs. Ricketts and Mills, but it was found that in the feelings of the people, or in their determination to carry on a custom which they believed necessary to their existence, no real change had been effected. They indeed gave up some Meriahs, but reserved many and bought more; and the sacrifices continued. The Agent to the Governor General, South-Western Frontier, in 1844, finding that the Kandhs in the Tributary Mahâls under his jurisdiction were no better than their neighbours, entered on the field and succeeded in obtaining the release of a few Meriahs, but all officers employed were now convinced that far more stringent measures than those hitherto adopted were necessary, and a special agency under one Head, armed with full authority to use force, was advised.

On the Madras side, from the time of the Gúmsur war, several officers had been engaged in measures, mostly of a conciliatory nature, to wean the Kandhs from their dark superstitions. In 1844, Lieutenant Hicks was appointed Assistant Superintendent, Tributary Mahâls, for the repression of human sacrifices. Moral pressure was, however, all that was attempted, and though Meriahs were recovered, and some were snatched from the very altars, the sacrifices did not cease. The number, however, had, it was said, diminished from hundreds to ten or a dozen per annum; but this improvement was not general. It is noticed* that the Kandhs of Boad had promised acquiescence in the wishes of Government, but they deemed it right to offer Tári enough to last her a long time before they gave it up, and the valedictory sacrifice is said to have comprised one hundred and twenty-five victims.

In 1845, the Government of India determined on bringing all the Kandh Máliahs under one system of management, and Act XXI of that year was passed, separating them from the ordinary jurisdiction of the Courts with a view to their being placed under special rules. And, in November 1845, Captain William Macpherson, who had been long employed in the Kandh districts, and to whom we are indebted for so much valuable information about the people, arrived in Ganjám with the title of "Agent, Governor General, for the suppression of human sacrifices and female infanticide in the hill tracts of Orissa." But still the orders were to abstain from violence, and the first season's operations were not encouraging.

The Kandhs of Boad had become impressed with the notion that further yielding on their part would lead to their taxation and subjection to forced labor: and early in 1846,

* Macpherson's Memorials of Service, page 246.

we find them threatening or making an attack on the Agent's camp and demanding and obtaining the restoration of rescued Meriahs. This led to reprisals, which of course greatly impeded the proposed policy of conciliation, and affairs were further complicated by the rebellion of the Raja of Angúl, one of the tributaries on the Mahánadí, who appears to have fomented to the utmost the resistance of the Kandh tribes. Serious disturbances followed; troops were employed on a large scale and all authority temporarily transferred from the Agent to the Officer in Command, Brigadier General Dyer.

I have no details of the military operations which followed. On the 21st of April 1847, Lieutenant-Colonel Campbell was appointed Agent, and coming on the scene with powers to coerce, which were perhaps all that was wanting to ensure success to the measures of the previous agency, he was soon in a position to report* the submission of the Bisai Chiefs of the Kandh hill tracts visited by him, and the restoration of peace to the disturbed districts. The operations against Angúl were successful. The Raja was deposed and subsequently captured, and as his estate was confiscated there was no difficulty in bringing into subjection all the Kandhs whom he had influenced. With Boad there had been at first some difficulty, but on the 1st April 1848, Colonel Campbell reported that with one or two exceptions all the influential men had pledged themselves by the most solemn oaths, (sworn on a tiger skin and on some earth) thenceforth to abandon human sacrifices, and in earnest of their sincerity 235 Meriahs were given up. During the following season, the Saurada Máliahs and the more remote hill region of Chinna Kimedy were visited by the Agency.

Chinna Kimedy was found to be divided into seven districts each under a Hindu chief or Páter, subdivided into Matahs, (groups of villages or parganas), and villages each under a Kandh headman called Máji (so this title is found thus far south). There was little intercourse between the districts owing to feuds. The country is described as in steppes. In the second range of hills the villages are far apart, and with few exceptions poor, and the country has a neglected unreclaimed appearance, a succession of hills covered with sál and bamboos. The districts on the upper ranges are more picturesque, and the cultivated valleys appear fertile; but throughout this hilly region, whether bountifully or sparingly dealt with by nature, human sacrifice and female infanticide generally prevailed, the only exceptions being in the districts of Sarangad, Chandraghari and Degi of Kosadah.

The annual season for the sacrifice was about to commence when the Agent marched into this country; but though not previously visited for the repression of human sacrifice, the design of holding it was at once abandoned, and eventually the whole people agreed to submit to the conditions proposed, and engaged to try if Tári would not, after all, be as well pleased with the blood of beasts as with human sacrifices. In this year, 1859, two hundred and six Meriahs were given up.

It was satisfactory to find that in the Boad highlands no blood had been shed since the last visit, and the Gúmsur Máliahs were reported equally free from the stain.† It had providentially happened that an unusually productive and healthy season had distinguished the first year's dreaded intermission of the rite. We can well

* Kandh Agency, and Calcutta Review, page 138. Colonel Campbell's Report to Government, 1st April 1848.

† Colonel Campbell's Report, 18th March 1859.

conceive the anxiety that must have been felt by the whole tribe as they watched the sprouting seed and ripening grain and their joy when in the full promise of a bountiful harvest they felt assured that the earth goddess did not resent their abandonment of the ancient custom.

The total number of Meriahs given up in the two seasons was 547.

It is useless to follow the operations of the Agent through the remainder of the Kandh districts. In Jaipúr it was found that human sacrifices had been annually offered to Maniksoro, the god of wár, as well as to the earth goddess, and the ceremony was performed in the following manner:—

A stout wooden post about six feet long is firmly fixed in the ground. Close to it a narrow grave is dug. The victim is tied to the post by his long hair; assistants to the officiating priest hold out his arms and legs so that the body is supported over the grave with the face downwards. The priest standing on the right side then recites an invocation to the god, praying for success in battle and preservation "from the tyranny of kings and their officers," and as he prays he at intervals hacks at the neck of the unfortunate victim avoiding the infliction of a mortal wound. Then the priest addresses him in consolatory words, assuring him that he would soon have the honor of being devoured by the great god Maniksoro for their benefit, and that his obsequies would be performed decorously, and reminding him, if still unreconciled to his fate, that they had bought him for this special purpose from his parents. He is then decapitated, the body falls into the grave, and the bleeding head remains suspended from the post till the birds devour it.

Colonel Campbell had some difficulty in Jaipúr, but eventually succeeded there, as elsewhere, rescuing or causing to be given up 77 Meriah males, and 117 females. The following extract from Colonel Campbell's last published report sums up the work:—

"It affords me heartfelt satisfaction to be able to report thus of the suppression (I will not presume to say of the complete suppression,—for that will depend on our future supervision and watchfulness) of the Meriah rite in Gúmsur, Boad, Chinna-Kimedy, Jaipúr, Kalahándy, and Patna."

Strange to say after the suppression of human sacrifices in the Máliahs of Jaipúr it was found that the practice existed in the low country, and the agent, Captain A. C. McNeile, wrote* that in suppressing it there, he had to deal with relatively civilized and educated men and not with semi-barbarous tribes. It does not appear that Kandhs were implicated; the victims were generally of the 'Túra class' purchased from their parents. At the town of 'Mulcagherry,' 100 of these children reserved for sacrifice were found and were surrendered.

On the 18th December 1861, in consequence of the arrangements which had been made for the organization of Police in the Ganjám and Vizagapatam agencies, the special agency for the hill tracts of Orissa was abolished.

With regard to the existing feeling of the Kandhs on the subject which led to the formation of the hill tract agency, I append an extract from MS. notes written by Mr. T. E. Ravenshaw, now Superintendent, Katak Tributary Estates, on the Kandh Máls, in his jurisdiction:—

---

* Madras Selections. Captain A. C. McNeile's Report, dated 1st May, 1855.

"Human sacrifice is, I believe, completely forgotten. The people have no objection to talk about it and point out the spots where the rite was performed, but they speak of their former superstitions on the subject as a delusion. They thought, they say, that human blood improved the quality of the turmeric, their most profitable crop; but they now find that the earth yields its increase as before and the turmeric is as good as ever it was." Mr. Ravenshaw does not find that animal sacrifice has been substituted, or that flesh of any kind is now buried to fertilize the earth. The superstition has entirely died out. He adds that infanticide where it was practised is also entirely suppressed.

Tribal divisions.

There is nothing on record which gives us any clue to the early history of the Kandhs. We find them occupying the highlands of the southern hill districts of old Orissa, following the ramification of ranges into various petty states, and claimed as subjects by the chiefs of those states whom Mr. Stirling and the historians of the Meriah operations recognise as Hindus, and who like the hill chiefs further north style themselves Rájpúts. It appears probable that in the Kandhs we have all that remains of the aboriginal inhabitants of this region, and that they were masters of the entire country, the lowlands as well as highlands, till they were forced back into the hills by the extension of the Hindu kingdom of Orissa; but the Hindu chiefs, if such they be, exercised very little authority over them, at least over those who lived in the Máliahs or highlands. Major Macpherson divides the Kandhs into three classes, Betiah, a servile class, who worked for hire or held lands on conditions of labor; Beniah who occupied the skirts of the hills and paid rent for their lands or held them on a more honorable description of service; and Máliah or highlanders who were virtually independent, though they performed homage to the chief on his accession, and, if well disposed to his service, occasionally took the field at his bidding.

The social organization and government of the Máliah Kandhs very closely resemble the ancient polity of the Múndas, which we still to a great extent preserve in the Singbhúm Kolhán.

Polity of the Kandhs.

Over each village an elder presides* called an Abbaye corresponding with the Singbhúm Múnda; and a number of adjacent villages form a district under a district Abbaye like a Singbhúm Pír under its Mánki. The district Abbaye is, or ought to be, the lineal descendant or representative of the leader of the colony when the settlement was first made.

In addition to the above, Major Macpherson gives us a tribal Abbaye or Patriarch, the representative of the common ancestor of the tribe; but as the division into tribes is not now geographically defined, people of various tribes living in one village, the duties of the tribal patriarch are chiefly to take notice of breaches of tribal rules. It is probable enough that formerly each tribe had its own locality, and as they took wives on the exogamous principle, they had to win their brides from a quarter more or less remote; but this system is now broken up: people belonging to various tribes inhabit the same village, and there is nothing to prevent a man marrying a girl of the same street if he likes, except that it is more dignified to go to a distance for a wife.

In addition to the above, there is a federal Abbaye, the representative of a superior chief formerly selected to superintend the affairs of as extensive a tract of country as

* Calcutta Review, vol. 5, page 35.

could be conveniently placed under him. The offices are all hereditary; but in regard to the federal Abbaye, though the succession never goes out of the family, the next-of-kin is sometimes set aside for a more competent relative.

National Assembly.

The federal Abbaye may when he pleases convene a council of the heads of the people. They sit in the open air in concentric circles, the inner circle composed of the district and the tribal Abbayes, outside are the village Abbayes, and outside them the general public. Women may attend, but they take no part in the discussion. Major Macpherson highly commends the loyalty of the Kandhs to their head men. It is said that their devotion to the federal Abbaye "is equal to any that the annals of humanity record."*

Procedure.

Oaths.

At the great councils disputes regarding property and offences of all kinds are enquired into, and witnesses are examined on oath. The litigants are forced to put into their mouths rice moistened with the blood of a sheep which had been sacrificed to the earth goddess, and this, it is supposed, will inevitably cause the death of the person so sworn who swerves from the truth. If the dispute is about land, a morsel of the soil similarly placed has the same effect. They are also sworn on the skin of a tiger, like the Kols; on the skin of a lizard (invoking scaliness of skin on the false witness); on the earth of an ant-hill; and on a peacock's feather.

Penal code.

Serious offences against the person, homicide, and severe wounding, are regarded as private wrongs, and compensations may be adjudged. In murder-cases all the property of the murderer may be made over to the family of the deceased. In cases of wounding any portion of the offender's goods may be awarded to the injured party, and he is further bound liberally to provide for all the wants of the wounded man till his recovery. The code on the subject of unfaithfulness of wives is contradictory. In one place we are told that the husband may put the adulterer to death, in another that the latter has only got to make good the amount paid for the girl when she was asked in marriage.

Succession.

Succession to real property is always through males. Shares of personal property may be given to daughters. The rule of primogeniture is not acknowledged. The real property is divided amongst the sons. By one author† it is asserted that no division of property can take place during the lifetime of the father, by another,‡ it is said that a son on his marriage quits the paternal roof and becomes a householder, receiving a share of the land from the hands of the father. Girls are not allotted to the shareholders as is the case in Singbhúm, but the brothers are jointly responsible for their care till they marry.

Proprietorship in lands.

The Máliah Kandhs§ consider themselves absolute proprietors of the soil they cultivate, and in this view of their right, which was no doubt at one time common to all the primitive tribes, they are supported by the fact that even by the British Government they have not yet been required to pay rent. Mr. Ravenshaw informs me that if a Kandh of the Kandh tracts in modern Orissa be asked to specify his position or calling, he answers boldly, "I am a zamíndár."

* Calcutta Review, Vol. V, page 42. † Major Macpherson.

‡ Lieutenant Frye, on the Kandh population of Orissa, Journal, Royal Asiatic Society, Vol. XVII.

§ Lieutenant Frye.

The chiefs have no pretensions to any right over the soil which is adverse to this claim of their people, and this is a point which has unfortunately in many instances been lost sight of in dealing with the aboriginal tribes. An Abbaye can have no right to alienate his title and interest in a village or district, yet such alienations have taken place in cases precisely analogous, and have been upheld by Courts acting in blind ignorance of the true position of the parties, thereby creating endless complications and intense dissatisfaction.

Sites of villages.

The Kandhs love to build their houses on the slopes of the valley overlooking their cultivation which winds like a river amongst the hills.

Houses.

The houses are small and low, but substantially constructed of plank inserted horizontally in grooves cut in the corner posts. The whole surface is plastered with mud. Each hut contains usually three apartments, in the centre the family dwells, one is used exclusively for cooking, and the third is a store-room. There is but one door which in the cold season is firmly closed, while the family sleep round a wood fire burning on a central hearth. The roof, as well as the sides, is sometimes of plank. The houses have no plinths.

Separate accommodation for bachelors and spinsters.

In each village there is a house assigned to the bachelors as their dormitory and club, and another for the maidens, and as it is said that chastity is not one of their virtues, and that free intercourse between the sexes is not discouraged, it may be assumed that the separation contemplated in this arrangement is not very rigidly enforced. I learn, however, from Mr. Ravenshaw's notes that in Boad the girls' dormitories are under charge of an elderly matron, who sleeps inside and locks the door. She sleeps very sound, I dare say.

Customs at child birth.

Births are celebrated on the seventh day after the event by a feast given to the priest and to the whole village. The name is determined as with the Kols. The names of ancestors are called over as grains of rice are thrown into water, but Major Macpherson* adds that the oracle is required to show which of the ancestors is regenerated in the person of the child. The Kols have not the faintest idea of anything of the kind as the name of persons still living are frequently selected.

Priests.

According to the same author every Kandh village has its priest, but they have no official privileges or endowments, their only emoluments consisting of the fees paid by those who employ them, or in gifts from the community, when the religious ceremonies they conduct have a favorable issue. There appears to be no Levite class. The priestly office may be assumed by any one, who fancies or boldly asserts that he has been called thereto by a mandate of the deity duly communicated in a vision or dream. At the human sacrifices and mystic rites in honor of the earth goddess, the Jani, a recognized priest, always officiated; but every head of a family could on ordinary occasions assume priestly functions, and the whole spirit of the Kandh policy renders it probable that originally all sacerdotal offices were combined in the patriarchs of families, villages, or circles, and that the mysterious Meriah rites and an order of priests came in together. I do not find any mention of priests in Mr. Ravenshaw's notes—their occupation is gone. Major Macpherson records

* Major Macpherson, Calcutta Review, Vol. V, page 31.

the singular circumstance, that a class of Hindus are employed by the Kandhs as priestly co-adjutors in the service of the minor divinities. This alone would indicate that there has been a great change in their religion; but it is probable that the low Hindus alluded to are but the Ojhas or Sorcerers whom the witchcraft superstition has called into existence. The belief of the Kandhs regarding sickness and physical afflictions of every description is the same as that of the Kols and Oráons.

Religion.

Our knowledge of the religion of the Kandhs is derived from a very elaborate essay on the subject by the late Major J. C. Macpherson, C. B., which was read before the Royal Asiatic Society in 1852. The paper has been reproduced in the memorials of that officer published in 1865. It propounds a system of theocracy and ethics more profound than one would expect to find amongst so ignorant a people, but it appears to me to be a melange of Genesis, the several Hindu systems and primitive paganisim. Colonel Campbell, who was for so many years employed amongst the Kandhs, is somewhat sceptical as to the purely Kandh origin of the scheme of religion thus ventilated; but under the peculiar circumstances of the race, it is quite possible that such a system may have been gradually built up for them by Bráhmans, Gosáins, and other Hindus, who not only lived amongst them, but joined in their sacrifices, supplemented with notions gleaned from Missionary teaching or books.

The fundamental doctrines appear to be a belief in a Supreme Being, the source of good, and Creator of the universe, called Búra Penu, the god of light, or Bela Penu, the sun god, the same as the Dharmi of the Oráons and the Bedo Gosáin of the Rájmahálí highlanders who injured no one, and whom it was not therefore necessary to propitiate, and his wife Tári, who in antagonism to her husband, became the originator of all the ills that befall mankind. We are told that Búra Penu found his wife "wanting in affectionate compliance," which in a note is explained to mean that she declined to scratch his back; but this simple domestic difference put it into Búra Penu's mind to clothe the world with vegetation, fill it with animal life and finally to create human beings to pay him the adoration and veneration which he expected and could not obtain from his wife. Mankind was created exempt from moral and physical evil, and thus enjoyed free intercourse with God. They lived without labor on the spontaneous abundance of the earth in perfect harmony, peace and innocence, and knew not that they were naked till Tári, like the old serpent, filled with envy at their happiness, sowed the seed of sin in their hearts, and like Pandora introduced all the ills that flesh is heir to. A few who withstood temptation and bore up against the powers of darkness, were elevated to the position of secondary gods, to whom the regulation of the affairs of the fallen brethren was consigned; but the consequences to the latter were terrible. The earth no longer yielded her abundance. Animals previously innocuous became vicious and destructive to life. Snakes became venomous and some plants poisonous. Man found out that he was naked and encumbering himself with clothing, lost the power of soaring through the air and skimming through the water, which in innocence he had possessed, and fierce strife raged between Búra and Tári, each contending for mastery.

Out of this contest two great sects arose, one holding that Búra, the other that Tári, had come off triumphant.

The sect of Burá believed that Búra punished Tári by the curse on her sex, tantamount to the "in sorrow thou shalt bring forth children," and that Tári, however malevolent and destructive she may be, can only strike when Búra permits. The sect of Tári believe that their goddess cannot be frustrated by Búra in her evil designs, but if she can be persuaded by adoration to abstain from injuring, man will be free from misfortune. She alone therefore should be propitiated.

Notwithstanding the tiff between Búra and Tári, their union was fruitful, and six godlings were produced to meet the primary wants of fallen man.

First, Pidzu Pennu, the rain god; second, Burbhi Pennu, the goddess of spring, who gives new vegetation and first fruits; third, Pitteri Pennu, the god of increase and gain; fourth, Klambo Pennu, the god of the chase; fifth, Lohá Pennu, the iron god or god of war; sixth, Sundi Pennu, the god of boundaries.

The above clearly indicate the most important requirements of such a people, and I do not doubt that the gods on this list may have been very generally recognised. They are styled inferior deities of the first class.

The addition of a seventh deity to the above also included amongst the children of Búra Pennu was clearly an after-thought. Dinga Pennu, the judge of the dead, is probably the Hindu Yama.*

The third class of gods are the descendants of the human beings who resisted evil. They are now the presiding spirits over villages, hills, streams, tanks, fountains, houses, forests, ravines, and orchards. Each of these gods is worshipped when his turn comes, that is, when a requisition is made on the department over which he presides. Offerings are presented, and for each a special form of address is to be found in Major Macpherson's essay, which is poetical enough to be introduced in an epic, but in the aggregate they are too long for my purpose. In one of these invocations the priest is made to say, truly enough, "Were we, O god of streams, constantly to expend our means upon your rites as well as those of the other gods, we should lose our lands, and then where would be your worship?"

The Kandh Yama has no sinecure, for the Kandhs are represented by Major Macpherson as possessing each four souls. Colonel Campbell and other writers who are well acquainted with their habits, did not discover that, in their own estimation, they had any souls at all, and this is certainly more in unison with the creed of their neighbours, but it appears that many Abbayes were men of education fond of studying the mysteries of the Hindu religion, and as it was from them that Major Macpherson chiefly derived his information, I am not surprised that the religious views of these authorities embraced the Hindu doctrines of metempsychosis and 'nirvana', or final absorption into the deity, which I think must be what is meant by †"restoration to communion with Búra." The notion of four souls apparently resolves itself into this, that the more enlightened Kandhs had adopted the Hindu doctrine of the immortality of the soul, and its liability to an immense variety of probations by successive re-births in an improved state or lower condition, according to the views taken by the divine judge of the life just quitted; until,

---

* In Major Macpherson's first essay on the religion of the Kandhs, read before the Royal Asiatic Society on the 20th November 1841, there is no reference to Dinga Pennu. The name first appears in the second essay, which was published in part II, Vol. XIII, of the Journal, Royal Asiatic Society.

† See 'Memorials of Service', page 92.

purged of all taint, it is finally absorbed into the divine essence. This theory disposes of three of the souls described by Major Macpherson, *viz.*, first the soul that is beatified, secondly, the soul that has to bear punishment for an ill-spent life; and thirdly, the soul that is re-born in the tribe, which must all be regarded as the one soul of the Hindus in different conditions. The fourth soul Major Macpherson describes as a soul which dies on the dissolution of the body, or in other words there is a belief in no soul at all, which is probably the creed of most untutored Kandhs.

Of the Kandh gods, Búra and Tári alone dwell in heaven*, Dinga resides on a rock or mountain in the region beyond the sea, from which the sun rises, so the souls have to cross the water (query, the Baitarani or Styx) to get to him. It is called Gripavali,† the leaping rock. This idea is also apparently borrowed from the Bráhmans.

The other Gods of the Kandhs live exclusively upon the earth. But when they move, they skim along at a short distance above its surface invisible to human eyes, but seen by the lower animals. They feed on the sacrifices offered to them, but also help themselves, as the farmer knows to his cost when he finds blind ears in his corn.

The rites observed at the Meriah sacrifices to the blood-thirsty Tári have been described. Her gentler husband, the supreme god Búra, receives the adoration of all his votaries at the same period of the year,‡ and though it is supposed that Búra demands no blood, a pig is at this season sacrificed in his honor, and the blood scattered widely about. At the festival there is much dancing, feasting, and drinking, and every kind of licentious indulgence. Many of the Búra-ites practised female infanticide and justified the act as one which was permitted and even enjoined by Búra, who by the conduct of his wife was unfairly prejudiced against all the sex.

I proceed now to avail myself of the information kindly furnished by my friend Mr. T. E. Ravenshaw, C. S., Commissioner of Katak, regarding the Kandh country in his province.

The Boad Kandhs.

At the close of the operations for the suppression of Meriah sacrifices in Boad, the chief of that dependency doubting his capability of controlling the Kandhs on that question, and dreading the consequence to himself of any relapse on their part, ceded to Government all that portion of his territory which comprised the Kandh Máliahs or as they are now styled Máls. This portion of Boad rises abruptly about 1,500 feet, and the approaches to it are all very steep and difficult ascents. They lead you to an undulating plateau portioned off by numerous ranges of low hills in the valleys between which wind the principal sheets of cultivation. The villages are prettily situated on the borders of the cultivation, and the hills rising from behind them are densely covered with sál.

The size of the villages varies in proportion to the water supply. In a few places the clearings are extensive, and the settlements have a thriving and comparatively civilized appearance.

The area of this tract known as the Katak Khand Máls is 480 square miles, and the population, numbering 45,000 souls, live in 677 villages.

* Journal, Royal Asiatic Society, Vol. X, page 228.—'Memorials of Service', page 92.

† The residence of the Hindu Yama is at the extremity of the earth *floating* on the waters.

‡ Memorials of Service, page 107.

Present government.

No revenue whatever is derived from the Kandhs. The Superintendent (Mr. Ravenshaw) has a native assistant called a Tahsíldár (tax collector), which appears rather a misnomer, who resides in the Máls and has the powers of a Subordinate Judge and Assistant Magistrate. A Police force is maintained consisting of one inspector, one sub-inspector, eight head constables, and forty-nine constables, but there is little crime. The only heinous cases are homicides committed in drunken broils or in disputes about land. I have already adverted to the tenacity with which they cling to their right in the soil. They consider it inextinguishable. They utterly scorn the notion of being barred from re-entry by a statute of limitation. No amount of adverse possession, however undisturbed, could, according to their code, transfer to another their title to the land.

The large divisions of the Kandh hill country are called Máliahs, Málos, or Máls. These are sub-divided into groups of villages called Mutahs. They recognise the authority of one chief over all the Máls, called Mahá Mullik (málik?) His position is that of the federal Abbaye previously described. The village headmen are called simply máliks. There is no mention of a Tribal málik or Abbaye.

Besides the indigenous Kandh headmen, each Mutah, and sometimes each large village, has an officer called Bisoi, who is always an Uriya. They were originally established as 'go-betweens' and interpreters between the Raja and the Kandhs; they speak both languages and being well versed in Kandh customs, often obtain great influence. Of late years they have acquired lands by intrigue or purchase from the Kandhs who were better advised when they would not part with an inch of the soil to an alien.

The Páns.

The low bastard Hindu people called Páns, already noticed as procurers for the Meriah sacrifices, are numerous in Boad. In the Chútiá Nágpúr tributary states this class are found, but are regarded both by Hindus and aborigines as vile. The Kandhs associate with them on a more equal footing, allowing them to hold lands and to share in the village festivals. They also ply their trade as weavers, and the poorest of them work as farm laborers, cultivating land belonging to Kandhs and making over to their landlords half the produce as rent.

Drinking.

The Kandhs also tolerate Hindus of the Sundi (Sandika), or spirit distilling, caste, as, though inveterate drunkards, they cannot distill for themselves. Sundis are traders as well as distillers;—a good deal of the trade of the country is in their hands, and some of them have accumulated considerable wealth.

The Kandh huts are built for the accommodation of the father, mother, and younger children only. At 8 to 11 years of age, boys and girls are ejected from the nest, and have to take up their abodes in their respective clubs till they marry and build nests for themselves.

Marriage customs.

Female infanticide was not one of the sins of Boad, and the evil consequences of the system are not found there. The Boad Kandhs repudiate the notion of intermarriage with other races, and sexual selection is carried on in a rational manner. A man is not encouraged to indulge in matrimony till he has the means of supporting a wife in a house of his own; when thus eligible he joins confidently in the village dances and makes his choice, and if fathers and mothers after this make themselves disagreeable, they may look out for an elopement. The young couple disappear and keep out of the way till the parents relent, and the price of the girl is accepted.

It would appear that most hill tribes have found it necessary to promote marriage by stimulating intercourse between the sexes at particular seasons of the year. Mr. Darwin would, perhaps, call this a reversion to the Balyen or love seasons of feathered ancestors. At one of the Kandh festivals held in November all the lads and lasses assemble for a spree, and a bachelor has then the privilege of making off with any unmarried girl whom he can induce to go with him, subject to a subsequent arrangement with the parents of the maiden.

The Kandhs are as fond of dancing as the Oráons, and like them have a dancing place in every village, surrounded by stones or wooden seats and shaded by venerable trees.

The instruments are drums, tambourines and a reed instrument with a sound like that of an indifferent bag-pipe.

The performers of both sexes pay particular attention to their dress and to the arrangement of their hair. The ball dress when complete is apparently similar to that of the Oráons when similarly engaged.

Dances.

In commencing the dance the girls form themselves into semi-circles of two rows. They stand close together, keeping their position by the touch only, as the hands are employed in holding the dress, which they occasionally extend by opening out their arms and as they do so waving the draperies and at the same time forming a long line instead of a semi-circle. As the excitement increases, the girls sing, the young men respond, and the movement becomes brisker until the whole breaks into a romp in which the girls pinch the boys and peck at them with their hands like the Juáng girls when performing as vultures. In other respects the dance appears to be of the Bhúiya class.

The men have a separate war dance, armed to the teeth and decorated with red cloth and feathers. They divide into two parties, and a mimic fight takes place. One side gives way, the other pursues, a man falls; he is set on by the opposite party and carried off in triumph as a fallen foe.

Another dance represents a bison hunt; one man with the horns and skin of the animal takes to his heels followed by the remainder, who capture him after a brief chase, and bear him back as a trophy.

The cessation of internecine struggles, abolition of demoralising rites, and settlement to peaceful pursuits, has had a most salutary effect on the condition of the Kandhs. I quote descriptions of them before and after the cure.

Lieutenant J. P. Frye, writing of them in 1857, says*—

Dress.

"Cloth being an article of very limited import, the use of dress is confined amongst all to the narrowest bounds admitted by decency. The Pátro himself is distinguished by a species of robe of office, consisting of a red blanket with variously colored fringe, but the ordinary Kandh is more scantily clad than the Uriya, and his mode of dress more repulsive to decency, the only scrap of cloth worn being old and foul. The festival dress consists of a long

* Journal, Royal Asiatic Society, Part I., Vol. XVII, page 13.

narrow slip of cloth with fringed ends worn so that the end hangs down like a tail. But the head-dress is the characteristic feature of a Kandh's vanity. The hair, which is worn very long, is drawn forward and rolled up till it looks like a horn projecting from between the eyes. Around this it is his delight to wear a piece of red cloth and insert the feathers of favorite birds, as also his pipe, comb, &c. On the western frontier cloth was unknown and strips of paper sufficed to procure fowls and rice. The clothing of the women is nearly as limited as that of the males. The bosom is invariably exposed, and a single cloth round the loins, scarcely reaching to the middle of the thigh, the sole garment."

Mr. Ravenshaw, writing in 1871, says:—"The Kandhs formerly possessed little property of any sort. A red cloth or a brass plate was rare. Now-a-days in most of the more respectable houses you see brass vessels in tolerable profusion. They have acquired considerable wealth in silver and brass ornaments, and where they formerly went half-starved and half-naked, they have now abundance of food and a liberal supply of raiment. Cultivation has extended, and they grow large quantities of cotton, oil seeds, and turmeric for export."

I learn further from Mr. Ravenshaw's notes that the Kandhs now manifest a desire for education and moral improvement. They propose to establish schools at their own expense, and agree to submit to any well-concerted measures for the suppression of drunkenness; and they couple with this a petition for a recognised system of administration of justice through their own elders—a proposal which, in my opinion, should meet with every encouragement.

Disposal of the dead.

The burial service of the Kandhs is not very impressive. The bodies are ordinarily burnt without ritual or ceremony,* but ten days after the death the friends of the deceased meet for a feast and console themselves with a bout of drinking. An Abbaye, however, is not so easily disposed of. When a man of this dignity dies, the event is proclaimed by the beating of drums and gongs, and thus summoned the heads of villages attend the funeral. The body is laid out in state on a funeral pyre, and near it a flag denotes where a large bag of grain and the personal effects are deposited. It is then fired, and the family and people of the village perform the funeral dance round the flag whilst the faggots are burning. The effects are then made over to the tribal Abbaye. The village priest, though present, takes no part in the ceremony. The dancing round the flag is continued at intervals till the tenth day, when there is a gathering of the tribe, and the succession of the heir is proclaimed.

* Macpherson, Memorials of Service, page 73.

English.	Tamul.	Telugu.	Canarese.	Tulu.	Oraon.	Rajmahali Paharia.	Ramgarha or Naia Dumka Paharia.	Gond.	Kandh.	Savara or Saura.
One ...	wondru	okati ...	vondu ...	vonji ...	unta ...			undi ...	randí, ra ...	aboy*
Two ...	irendu	randu ...	yeradu	raddá ...	eur ...			rand ...	rí ...	bagu*
Three ...	múndru	mudu ...	múru ...	muji ...	mund ...			mund ...		yági*
Four ...	nangu ...	nalugu	nalku ...	nal ...	nach ...			nalung ...		vonji*
Five ...	anjei ...	aidu ...	aidu ...	ainá ...				seiung ...		mollayi*
Six ...	áru ...	áru ...	aru ...	aji ...				sarug ...		kudru
Seven ...	yezsu ..	yedu ...	yelu ...	yel ...				yedung		gulji
Eight ...	yettu ...	yenimidi	yentu ...	yenmo ...				yermud		tamuji*
Nine ...	onbadu	tommidi	vombattu	vorambo ...						tinji*
Ten ...	pattu	padi ...	hattu ...	pattá ..	Hindi terms used.	Ditto.	Ditto.	Ditto.	Ditto.	galiji*
Twenty ...	irupadu	iruwei ...	ippattu	irvo ...						vokoḍi*
Fifty ...	ainbudu	yabai ...	aivattu	aivo ...					galiji ...	bágu koḍi galiji*
Hundred	núru ...	núru ...	nuru ...	nudu ...				nur ...	kodi ...	mollovi koḍi*
I ...	nan ...	nenu ...	nánu ...	yan ...	en ...	en ...	mni ...	anna ...	anu ...	gná*
We ...	nangul	manamu	naum ...	yenkul ...	em ...	en ...	ambi ...	amot ...	amu ...	móni*
Thou ...	ni ...	nivou ...	nínu ...	yi ...	nin ...	nina ...	tui ...	imme ...	inu ...	aman*
You ...	ningul	miru ...	nium ...	nikul ...	ním ...	nina ...	tumhi ...	immet ...	ninga ...	aman*
He ...	avan ...	wadu ...	avanu ...	aye ...	ás ...	áth ...	gai ...	hore ...	ivanju, a ...	ani*
They ...	ávargal	wáru ...	avaru ...	akul ...	ár ...	owar ...	hohoya	hurk ...	avi ...	ani*
Mine ...	yennudaya	nayokka	nannadu	yennau ...	enghai ...	...	muhar ...	nawa ...	nae ..	gránate*
Our ...	yengalu-daya	mana-yokka	namma	yenkulna ...	...	...	...	mawa ...	nai ...	moni, nate
Thine ...	unnudaya	niyokka	ninnadu	ninnau ...	emghae	...	...	niwá ...	...	amonanate
Your ...	ungalu-daya	niyokka	nimma	nikulna ...	..	...	...	niwa ...	ni ...	...
His ...	avanú-daya.	vadiokka	avana ...	ayana ...	asoai ..	...	...	hona ...	ovani tana	aninate
Their ...	avarga-ludaya	wariyok-ka	avara ...	akulna ...	asgai ...	...	wuhor (B)	hon. wora	...	aninate*
Hand ...	...	...	kai ...	kai ...	he*kh*a ke *kh*a.	rátu, tettu	thébona	kyk ...	kájju ...	ase
Foot ...	pádam	pádamu kulu.	páda ...	pado ...	*kh*ed ...	khed, tekua	chapta ...	kal ...	mada, kádu	ajal
Nose ...	mukku	múku ...	mugu ...	munku ...	*moy* ...	muna ...	...	masor ...	mungeli ...	amu
Eye ...	kangul	kanlu ...	kannu ...	kánna ...	*kh*án ...	...	dhenda ...	kan ...	kánká ...	amét
Mouth ...	...	...	bái ...	bai ...	vai ...	toro ...	thonthono	...	láá ...	...
Tooth ...	palgal ...	panlu ...	hallu ...	kuli ...	pála ...	pála ...	bóthí ...	palapalk	pátká ...	ajágna
Ears ...	kádugul	chevvalu	kivi ...	kebi ...	kévudá ...	kedu ...	kanwé ...	kavi ...	kõriu lao, kríu	alu
Hair ...	meir ...	ventru-kalu	kudlu ...	romo ...	chuti ...	tale ...	chw ...	chuti ...	talow meri tlamberi	un
Head ...	talai ...	tala ...	tale ...	tare ...	kuku, ku-*kh*á.	koku ...	mundri (H).	talá ...	talo, tláu.	abúb
Tongue ...	nak ...	nálika ...	nálige ...	nalai ...	tat*kh*a ...	turthe ...	...	wanja ...	vangosi ...	...
Belly ...	walrú ...	pottá ...	hotte ...	banji ...	kul ...	kochu ...	...	pir ...	lútu ...	...
Back ...	muduvú	vipu ...	bennu ...	beri ...	ko*kh*a, med.	koku ...	...	morchul, parki.	...	...
Iron ...	irumbu	inumu ...	kabina ...	karbo ...	pan'ha ...	lohar ...	mású ...	kachchi	loha ...	...
Gold ...	pon ...	bánga ramu	chinna ..	bangar ...	sona (H)	sonai (H)	sona (H)	sono ...	sona ...	...
Silver ...	vellie ...	vendi ...	belli ...	bolli ...	rupa (H)	chandi (H)	rupa ...	kuro ...	táká ...	...
Go ...	po ...	poutam	hogu ...	po ...	kalai ...	eken (to go)	ekore (to go).	handana	salba ...	ma
Eat ...	tinu ...	tinu ...	...	...	ona ...	tophen (to eat)	tindiana (to eat)	tindana (to eat)	jinba ...	...

English.	Tamul.	Telugu.	Canarese.	Tulu.	Oraon.	Rajmahali Paharia.	Ramgarh or Naia Dumka Paharia.	Gond.	Kandh.	Savara or Saura.
Sit ...	ulkara...	kurchun-data.	kútuko..	kullu ...	oka ...	oken ...	...	uddana (to sit)	kapka ...	...
Father...	appa ...	abba ...	tandé ...	amme ...	baba ...	abu ...	búba ...	baba ...	abu ábá ...	...
Mother ..	tai ..	amma, tali	tayi (tai)	appe ...	ayo ...	aya ...	mainy...	ya, ma, bau	iya, tálli, ájá	...
Brother ..	anná tamlie...	anná tammudu	sahodari	{ palaye (elder). megge (younger). }	annako	nuna ...	...	dádá, tamúr	dádá, támbesá	...
Sister ...	ukka ...	ukka ...	sahodari	pali, megdi	ankoi ...	nuni ...	dídí, núní	taka bai	vai ...	...
Man ...	manidan	manúshí	manushu	naramani...	al alla ...	male ...	maler ...	mánwál	mandra, lok-ka mdehe, gáttánju	robal
Woman ..	pendu...	ádadi ...	hengsu, stri ...	ponjo ...	múkha...	pile ...	bátker...	ad ...	asa mai gat-tári	amihelonjeo
Wife ...	...	...	hendati...	budeddi ...	mukha...	dani ...	pacho ...	maiju ...	kduá ...	...
Child ...	pullei ...	bálá ...	magu ...	bale ...	hadha ...	mokalh ...	...	chawá...	mira ...	...
Son ...	magan	koduku	maga ...	mage ...	tangdas	engadhi ...	rochwa...	marri, tudal.	mríenju ...	robal pasi (boy)
Daughter	magal...	kutru ...	magalu	magal ...	tangda ...	moki ...	batker...	miár ...	budi, mráu	amchelon (girl)
Slave ...	(caret)	(caret)...	(caret)...	(caret) ...	(caret) ...	...	...	...	áliá (servant)	...
Cultivator	...	...	besáya-gára.	besáyagára	...	...	..	...	...	...
Shepherd	...	...	kuruba ..	mepunaye...	...	...	...	...	odámáháriá	...
God ...	...	...	devaru ..	dever ...	dharmi, nad.	gothiéne...	gosain mosán.	penu deva	penu ...	sonám
Devil ...	bhuta ...	bhut ...	bhuta ...	bhuto ...	bhút ...	nad ...	dakin ...	...	pedari, pida-rani	bota
Come ...	va ...	ra ...	ba ...	bala ...	bárai ...	barén (to come).	...	wara ...	vamu ...	ya
Beat ...	...	...	hodiyu...	hák ...	la'wai ...	badjen (to beat).	...	Jiana ...	vemu ...	tide
Stand ...	nila ...	niluvutá	nillu ...	untu ..	chowai...	chien (to stand ..	thiai (to stand).	nittana	níte ...	...
Sun ...	suryam	suryadu	suria ...	suria ...	bírí ...	báre ...	béla ...	surial ...	bélá ...	oyum (also sky)
Moon ...	nela, chandran.	yennala	chandra	chandre singol	chanda...	belpo ...	chandra (H)	nalej ...	dhanju, dá anju	angai
Star ...	tárakei	chukka	nakshatra	darai ...	binko ...	binki ...	tarai ...	sukum	sukhanga, suká	tútúe
Fire ...	nerupu	nippu ...	...	...	chitzechitz	chíchú ...	chíchú...	kis ...	nari, náni...	togo
Water ...	tunnir...	nilu ...	niru ...	nır ...	am ...	ámú ...	ámma ...	yer ...	sidrú, kakeri	ada
House ...	vidu ...	illu ...	mane ...	illá ...	vipa ...	ada ...	dhako ...	ron ...	yeda, iddu...	asin
Horse ...	kudurai	guram	kudre ...	kudre ...	eph ...	...	ghoda ...	kodá ...	...	kúrta
Cow ...	pasumadu	au ...	dhana...	petta ...	gúnrí ...	ou ...	bárdi ...	tali muda	kodi ...	tangli
Dog ...	nai ...	kukka...	nai ...	nai ...	alla ...	ole ...	...	nei ...	nahuri na-huni	kinchoi
Cat ...	punai ...	pilli ...	bekku...	puche ...	berkha...	...	birao ...	bilal ...	mea ...	drúmi
Cock ...	cháwal	punju ...	hunha, hunja.	punje ...	khair ...	kono, kair	kúkrá ...	ghoghoti	kaská ...	...
Duck ...	...	...	battu ...	battá ...	ghéri ...	bataki ...	kátó ...	...	...	...
Ass ...	...	...	katte ...	katta ...	gadhá ...	...	...	...	...	...
Camel ...	...	...	vonte ...	vonte ..	unth ...	úndi ...	...	...	...	...
Bird ...	kuruvi...	pitta ...	pakshi...	pakhi ...	ora ...	pagu ...	gugri ...	pitte ...	pota ...	ontí*
Die ...	savu ...	chau ...	sayu ...	saipuni ...	...	...	...	sayana...	sáná, sá ...	...
Give ...	kudu ...	ivu ...	koduvadu	korpuni ...	ch ia ...	chiyen ...	chíore ...	siana ...	sisdu, sidu	...
Run ...	woda ...	urkota	vadu ...	par ...	bunga ...	venghen ..	jhingai	vittana...	geddu ...	...

ENGLISH.	TAMUL.	TELUGU.	CANARESE.	TULU.	ORAON.	RAJMAHALI PAHARIA.	RAMGARH OR NAIA DUMKA PAHARIA.	GOND.	KANDH.	SAVARA OR SAURA.
Up ...	..	...	mele ...	mitta ...	merka ...	mekthi ...	...	...	kniti ...	...
Near ...	kitta ...	daggira	hatra ...	kaital ...	hidhé, hirj	banano ...	ántre ...	karum...	...	...
And ...	um ...	nunnú...	mattu ...	nana ...	dara ...	...	aw ...	úndyy...	...	...
Yes ...	am ...	avunu...	havadu, handu.	andá ...	...	mula ...	ron (hon)	hingi ...	á á ...	jadité*
Down ...	...	...	kelage...	tirtá ..	*khekh*el	bere, argi .	...	...	nére ...	...
Far ...	dúram...	dúramu	dura ...	duro ...	gétéhá...	géche ...	dighuo...	lak ...	...	sangayi*
What ...	yènna ...	yimi ...	yenu ..	dane ...	endar ...	edh ...	kisga ...	bang ...	anna, yiana	...
But ...	...	...	adaru ...	andala ...	pahe ...	...	...	...	...	...
No ...	ille ...	ledu ..	illa ...	ijji ...	mala ...	mala ...	malaga	halli ...	...	yajo*
Before ...	munne...	yedatta	mundé	dumbu ...	mandbar	agdu ...	godri ...	munnai..	...	...
Behind...	pinne ...	yenaka	hindé ...	piran ..	*khokh*a...	koakwaje	...	paja ...	vea ...	...
Why ...	yen ..	yenduku	...	...	endhar ...	endher ...	...	bassáti...	...	...

NOTE.—Támul and Telugú from Revd. S. Hislop's works edited by Sir R. Temple, K. C. S. I.; Canarese and Tulu, furnished by Alexander MacCallum Webster, Esq., C. S., Collector of Canara; Oráon, from local sources; Rájmaháli Pahária, from a MS. belonging to the Asiatic Society of Bengal; Naia Dúmka Pahária by Dr. Coates, Superintendent of Jail, Hazáríbágh; Gond, from Revd. S. Hislop; Kandh, from Captain Frye's publications, and a MS. by V. Ball, Esq., Geological Survey, to whom I am also indebted for some Savara vocables; Kandh and Savara words marked with an asterisk, from Dr. Hunter's work.

GROUP IX.

THE ARYANS.

INTRODUCTORY REMARKS.

In many works on India, especially in Marshman's History, we are told that the original settlers, whose characteristics we have been describing in the foregoing pages, were driven from the plains by fresh colonies of immigrants, and these were in their turn conquered by the Hindus, who brought their religion and language with them from regions beyond the Indus, and having reduced the inhabitants to a servile condition *branded* them with the name of Súdra. I do not know on what authority the Súdras are thus treated as a distinct people, nor do we find that they ever were in fact reduced to a servile condition. Bráhmans, in the pride of their self-exaltation, certainly flung hard words at them, and writing on stilts treated them as prostrate; but it is reasonable to suppose that they were, from the very first, as they now are, the working bees of the hive, the bone and sinew of the nation, the real supporters of the whole fabric.

Professor H. H. Wilson, in his essay, No. 2, on the religious practices of the Hindus, thus briefly describes the four castes,—*first*, the Bráhmans whose duties were to study and teach the Veds and to conduct the domestic worship of the next two classes; *second*, the Kshatriya, the warrior and prince, whose duties were to fight and govern; *third*, the Vaisya, the merchant and farmer; *fourth*, the Súdras, who supplied artificers, laborers and servants to the other three. The Súdras were subjected to much indignity and injustice, but their condition was never so bad as that of the helot, the bondsman or the serf. They were free masters of their own property and at liberty to settle where they pleased. Intermarriage between all four castes took place, and the only check upon them was the degradation of the children. *They* were not even Súdras. They, therefore, formed new castes, distinguished according to their mixed descent and the occupations which came to be peculiarly their own.

A very large proportion of the Hindu population is, if the Purāns are to be believed, the offspring of these mixed alliances. According to different authorities, the number of inferior castes so originated ranges from 30 to upwards of 40, and includes some of the most useful of the people, as carpenters, smiths, weavers, potters, fishermen, braziers. Strange to say, the caste called Chandala, vilest of all, whose chief duty is the removal of dead bodies, is sprung from the union of a Súdra male with a female of the Bráhman caste. It was only in the event of their not obtaining service in the house of one of the

4 D

twice-born that a Súdra was permitted to practise a trade or profession, but there was no interdict against his engaging himself in agricultural pursuits either as proprietor, farmer, or mere cultivator.

The above mode of accounting for the varieties of classes is fanciful and nonsensical, but the object of the propounders of the idea was doubtless to preserve the purity of the upper classes by degrading the offspring of those who married beneath them, and it pre-supposes the point I argue for, that the upper and lower castes of the Hindu population do not spring from different stocks.

An intelligent native friend of mine gives me the following as an old tradition preserved in the Mahábhárat:—

"There is no virtual distinction of castes; all were Bráhmans, so men were created, but different trades and professions produced the different classes."

In the Váyu Purána there is a somewhat similar passage.* In speaking of the Tretá age the author says there were then no castes, orders, varieties of condition or mixture of castes; they were alike in form and age without distinction of lower and higher.

It appears to me necessary, to a proper understanding of the ancient Hindu population or constitution of the Aryan people established in India, to treat all four castes as originally homogeneous, but divided into two great classes, the pastoral and agricultural, and we have in the present day the type of these two classes in the two most numerous of the Hindu castes, the Gopas or Goálas, and the Kúrmis.

They formed the raw material on which Bráhman and Budhist priests and reformers successively worked; the horizon from which the other classes arose or fell. It is obvious that Bráhmans, Kshatriyas and Vaisyas, each strictly following the position assigned to them, could not from their very constitution have had separate or distinct national existence. Isolated they would have been as *disjecta membra,* wanting a stomach and digestive organs.

It was on the other hand necessary to the existence and progress of the pastoral and agricultural tribes that they should have their warriors, a section of the population devoted to the profession of arms, who fought the aborigines, and defended the new colonies, and it is probable that having this duty exclusively assigned to them they were exempted from the labour of tillage or care of the flocks and herds, and thus was formed the military class or Kshatriyas; and it appears very natural that this class, thus privileged, should become dominant and monopolize the ruling power, and gradually arrogate to themselves a separate and nobler descent than that of the tillers of the soil.

Great numbers of the agricultural tribes have traditions that they too were once Kshatriyas, or might have been, but preferring the plough to the sword, were obliged to give up the distinction of wearing the thread, the emblem of the twice-born.

In regard to the Bráhmans, there is nothing that I know of to militate against the theory that they were eliminated in a similar way; but it is highly probable that the Rishis or Munis, the magi or sages, from whom they claim descent, were of different origin, probably Egyptian, and that the doctrines eventually enunciated and adopted by the

* Quoted in Muir's Sanscrit Texts, Vol. I, page 29.

Aryans were derived from two or more distinct sources. Some of the Rishis* appear to have been established in India as missionaries to the primitive inhabitants long before its conquest by the Aryans. These holy sages are frequently spoken of as occupying hermitages far in advance of the Aryan settlements in the midst of the wild Rakashas or Dasyus. Some they succeeded in converting, others resisted and reviled them, but the sages, miraculously supported or aided, held their ground. The connection of the old Rishis with the aborigines may be referred to in the following passage from the story of Nahusha,† as told in the Mahábhárat,—"This energetic prince slew the hosts of the Dasyus and compelled the Rishis to pay tribute." But the old Rishis, whatever may have been their origin, formed alliances with Aryan girls without regard to caste. The sage Vyása, compiler of the Veds, was the son of a Kaibartini, that is, a fisherman's daughter, whom his father, a Rishi, had married, and the offspring of such alliances might be priests, warriors, princes, or anything else. Tod, in his 'Annals of Rájásthán,' tells us that in the early ages of the Solar and Lunar dynasties, from which the Bráhmans and Kshatriyas spring, the priestly office was not hereditary in families; it was a profession, and the genealogies exhibit frequent instances of branches of these races terminating their martial career, abandoning the world, and starting a religious sect, and their descendants sometimes continued in the priestly office, and sometimes reverted to the profession of arms; but after the conclusion of the struggles between the two lines described in the Rámáyan, the military class appears to have withdrawn from all desire to enter the priesthood. Thus in those days there was no hereditary priesthood. The priestly offices were held by men told off or called to the work who were required or inspired to live for years a life of meditation or seclusion as a preparation for the avocation.

Like the priests of the Roman Church in the middle ages, they were the repositories of all the lore of the age, and having the power, they freely used it to twist and distort the annals of the people and the records of their faith into instruments of glorification of their own class, till they gradually obtained for themselves recognition as a separately and divinely begotten, heavenly inspired race entitled to adoration.

For the production of the professional castes, it is not necessary to have recourse to interdicted alliances. Amongst primitive people, the children naturally take to the trade of their father, and we need go no further to account for such tribes or castes as oil-pressers, potters, boatmen, gold-washers, fishermen, &c.

Thus we may expect to find, and do find, a certain uniformity of feature pervading all the Natives of Hindustan who may be classed amongst the four great divisions into which the Hindus are divided and their off-shoots, with physical and moral characteristics of one prevailing mould. There is, on the whole, in Hindus of pure blood a very marked conservation of beauty of feature of the Aryan type. We certainly see great variety, sometimes startling variety, of complexion, not unfrequently unmistakeable evidence of mixture of race, and in some classes, as a whole, less delicacy of feature and form than in others. This is to be expected. The out-door, rough employment of some renders them dark and coarse, when compared with others who are subjected to no

* The sage Gautama (Muir's Sanskrit Texts, Vol. II, page 382) is described in the Mahábhárat as having become like the Dasyus from living amongst them.

† Muir's Sanskrit Texts, Vol. I, page 67.

exposure or severe manual labour; but amongst the hard-worked Kúrmis may be seen occasionally maidens and youths with all the delicacy of feature, beauty of form, and fairness of complexion, that are more especially the attributes of the twice-born, and I have seen amongst Goálá girls worthy representatives of the pretty milkmaids, amongst whom the amorous Krishna passed so much of his time.

I do not doubt that the Aryans had their helots, and I consider that we have in the really servile castes 'the Chandalas, lowest of men,' Pariahs, Doms, and others, the people to whom, from time immemorial, the vilest offices have been assigned, and who so seldom rise from their abject condition, the descendants of those very helots; but I find no reason for the assertion that the progenitors of the modern Súdras were helots. Manu, the great propounder of Bráhman supremacy, indeed, proclaimed that the Súdras were to serve the other three classes, but no degrading offices were imposed on them, and the service was optional. It was the mass of the people they thus attempted to depress; morally they succeeded in the influence they obtained. The Súdras became priest-ridden, and were domineered over by Kshatriyas, but though bullied, they were never enslaved.

Neither do I find any evidence of their being a conquered race. The terms applied to the Súdras, though purposely humiliating, are very different from the epithets of bitter resentment that are launched by the bards and hymn writers against the Dasyus, who, from the description* given, are obviously the dark-skinned aborigines who had the audacity to defend themselves against the Aryans. In one of the oldest Vedic accounts of the origin of castes, it is stated that the Súdras were created by Brahma as "*the nourishers,*" a good name for those to whose labor the earth yielded her riches for the benefit of all classes.

The condition of the *four* castes, when created by Bráhma, is thus described in the first book of the Vishnu Purán (*Wilson's translation*).—'They abode wherever they pleased. They were free from every impediment, pure hearted, and blameless in every observance.'

The province of Chútiá Nágpúr protected from invasion by its elevation, and the natural barriers that surround it, afforded an asylum to the ancient races, in which they long existed as a dominant people, maintaining their independence for ages after the subjugation or expulsion of their congeners from the Gangetic provinces. It was one of the last countries in which the Aryans obtained a footing: their intrusion is indeed so recent that the struggle for supremacy between the two races is even now going on. The Aryans are still regarded as foreigners, and in some parts of the country, as in the Kolhán of Singbhúm, never allowed to forget that they are intruders, but in other parts the aborigines show a tendency to give way to them.

Here then we have a glimpse of the process long since worked out elsewhere. We see the two races in juxtaposition yet opposed. The moral and physical distinctions between them are, as a rule, most marked, and they naturally divide themselves into only two nationalities. For the Hindus there is only one general term—Sud, or Sudh, or Sudhán, which includes all castes, Bráhmans, Rájpúts, Goálás, Kúrmis, Kahárs, &c., and they distinguish themselves by that term, which means pure, when differencing themselves from the aborigines, whom they call Kol, vile or impure, or Chuár, robber.

---

* See quotation from the Vrihad Aranyaka Upanishad of the Yajur Ved, in Muir's Sanskrit Texts, Vol. I, page 13.

The Kols quietly accepted the distinctive denomination. Uniting in themselves a Dravidian and Kolarian element (the Oráons and Múndas), they were in want of a generic term to distinguish them from the Sudhs, but to the latter they also apply the epithet 'Diku,' a word of uncertain meaning, but not intended to be complimentary.

The word Súdra is, I doubt not, from the same Sanskrit root as Sud, meaning 'to purify.' If the Súdras had always been regarded as a helot race born to a servile condition, why should this honourable epithet have been applied to them? I think it was of old, what it is now in Chútiá Nágpúr, the term by which the Aryans *en masse* chose to distinguish themselves from the Dasyus or Kols or Mlechchas. They were all "the pure people," but the twice-born, the first three classes, were the lords, spiritual and temporal, and the knights and burgesses. The fourth class were the ordinary people.

The three upper classes were under very strict obligations to qualify themselves for the maintenance of the superiority assigned to them by birth. It was incumbent on every male of those classes to pass the first stage of his life as a religious student, and it is declared that a twice-born, whether Bráhman, Kshatriya, or Vaisya, who has not studied the Veds, falls, even whilst living, into the condition of a Súdra, and his descendants after him; but a Vaisya of the present day studies only his ledgers, and the representatives of the military classes are, as a rule, as innocent of literature as were the knights of the middle ages.

SECTION 1.—BRÁHMANS.

The mysterious Rishis or Munis above alluded to appear to be the first persons to whom the name of Bráhman was applied. They were the light of their age, and are supposed still to shine on us, as the seven great stars of the Great Bear. They were anchorites of great reputed sanctity, but judging from the highly-coloured anecdotes of their private life that are handed down to us, of very questionable moral character. Many of them were of the royal blood of the solar line; but though they lived as ascetics, they did not consider continency or celibacy as essential to their condition. Their *liaisons* included maidens of high and low degree, goddesses and nymphs, princesses, and fishermen's daughters, and the greatest monarchs were glad to bestow their daughters upon them. They became thus the most noble ancestry that an Indian family could claim descent from, and from their reputed progeny the Bráhmans were started as a hereditary priesthood.

The creation of three privileged classes instead of one was no doubt a device to reconcile the 'upper ten thousand' generally to the innovation.

The ceremonial ritual, subsequently promulgated as Bráhmanical, lays down rules of daily routine for the guidance of the twice-born, which are only adapted to a people who had settled permanently in a tropical climate. They inculcate constant ablutions involving a protracted immersion of a part of the body in cold water, whilst long recitations are made that would be intolerable in a cold climate; in some cases very light clothing is enjoined, and in all temperance in food and abstinence from strong drink.

It must be allowed that if Bráhmans elevated their caste by writing down the lower classes, they did not assign to themselves very easy duties. A Bráhman should

4 E

study hard in his youth, and practise austerity and devotion during the remainder of his existence. His life is passed, if he acts up to the ritual enjoined, in the performance of prescribed ceremonies and religious duties of a singularly monotonous and uninteresting character. From the moment of his awaking at earliest dawn, till he retires at night, there is a rule not only for every action of his life, but even for his thoughts and meditations. These will be found detailed in the pages of Wilson and Colebrooke,* and in the Puráns. They are too prolix and numerous to be treated of here.

The Bráhmans of Bengal are descended† from five priests invited from Kányakubja by Ádísura, King of Gaura, who is said to have reigned A. D. 1077. They are therefore of comparatively recent importation, and the priestly duties were previously in the hands of Súdras. In the eastern province of Asám, the ancient Kámarúpa, there are still large and very ancient religious establishments presided over by Súdra priests, and there are others the head priests of which were of the same order till within the last century, but into which Bráhmans have now insinuated themselves. The names of the five imported priests were, Bhatta Náráyana, of the family of Sándilya; Daxa, of the family of Kásyapa; Chhándara, of the family of Vatsa; Sríharsha, of the family of Bharadwája; and Vedagarbha, of the family of Sávarni.

At the period when these priests were invited by the King of Gaura, some seven hundred inferior Brahmans, called from their number Saptasati, and a few Vaidicas resided in Bengal. Of the former, none are now found in that country; five families of the Vaidicas are extant, but are not permitted to intermarry with the Bráhmans of Rárná.‡

Many of the Bráhmans of Lower Bengal have assiduously cultivated the decidedly superior ability that their class may lay claim to, and, well educated and enlightened, fill with credit important offices under Government, or attain high positions as merchants or traders. The Bráhmans also include a numerous body of industrious and energetic farmers and cultivators. They engage in all the operations of agriculture except that of holding the plough, and support themselves creditably by honest labor.

The Bráhmans of the present day, who devote themselves exclusively to priestly duties, are far out-numbered by those who have taken to secular pursuits. The most ignorant amongst the former are usually the most bigoted and assuming, and I think there are no more intolerant and offensive members of the class than may be found in Bihár and Chútiá Nágpúr. There we find men who with but little or no knowledge of their books or duties arrogate adoration of their miserable persons by all classes. These men will enter into familiar conversation with an acquaintance in a public place, and continue to talk and smile as if they were entirely regardless of the necessity they were under of having at the same time frequently to withdraw the foot from the slipper in order that the passers-by might have the opportunity of kissing it!

I do not wish to disparage Bráhmans; they are unquestionably physically and mentally a fine race of men, and considering the false position their pretensions place

* See Vishnu Puran, Book III, Chapter 11, &c. Colebrooke, page 77.

† Colebrooke, p. 277.

‡ Country east of the Bhagírathí.

them in, and the natural repugnance they must feel to descend to the level of ordinary mortals, it is all the more creditable to the class that so many amongst them have given up this masquerading as gods, and appear before the world as enlightened and useful members of society.

SECTION 2.—RÁJPÚTS, OR KSHATRYAS.

The pretensions of the Rájpúts of the day to represent the Kshatryas of days gone by are not generally allowed by Bráhmanical writers, many of whom maintain that the Kshatryas were destroyed by Parasuráma; but this fable of the total annihilation of the race is contradicted by the very writers that assert it, and I doubt not that many noble families of Rájpúts scattered throughout India have as much right to consider themselves truly scions of the great lunar race as the Bráhmans have to claim descent from the saints of the solar line, but there are many noble and respectable families now admitted into the fraternity of the Rájpúts, and calling themselves Kshatryas, who have very little Aryan blood in their veins. It is a fact that many rajas and chiefs, who are invested by Bráhmans in due form at the proper age with the sacred string, and who may show you a pedigree proclaiming their descent through fifty generations from a Rishi, or a cow, or a snake, or some other animal or thing, are Kols, or Bhúiyas, or Gonds.

The Rájpúts, under the Bengal Government, are chiefly to be found in Bihár. Buchanan, in his account of that district,* estimates them at 14,000 families, and enumerates 34 tribes; this nearly equals the number given by Tod in his account of the tribes of Rájásthán, and amongst the names that may be found in both lists are Chauháns, Ráhtors, Chandel, Bághel, Báyis, &c. To these Chútiá Nágpúr adds Nágbangsis, Sikhar, Raksel, and others, who are acknowledged as good Rájpút families and intermarry with the best; though, with the exception of the Raksel, I do not think that any of them trace their descent out of the province.

Very good specimens of country gentlemen may be found amongst the Rájpút landlords of Western Bengal. Where, as is sometimes the case, primogeniture is the local custom or family usage, and estates have been long in the family, the best relations generally exist between the landlord and the peasantry; indeed it will be found that a very indifferent landlord is, in such estates, more respected and beloved than the most indulgent new man. Good or bad, they live amongst their people 'like a fine old English gentleman, all of the olden time.' They may fleece the tenants sometimes when they levy contributions for marriages, or to reimburse themselves for some act of needless extravagance, but in whatever tends to the dignity of the family, the people deem themselves personally concerned and give without demur, and it is a satisfaction to them when the duties of hospitality are religiously observed by their chiefs. The objects of their charity are often the reverse of worthy, but still 'the poor seldom pass unrelieved from their gates.'

The class of Native gentlemen that I speak of are not the inert sensualists that wealthy Bengalis so often become; they are fully capable of enjoying field sports; they generally ride well, are good shots and keen sportsmen. They are sure to have a

* Buchanan, Vol. I., p. 159.

good battery of guns by the best English makers, good horses, dogs, elephants, and hawks, and even fishing tackle. As already remarked, a Rájpút claiming to be one of the twice-born is bound to study the Veds, and to perform most of the religious duties that are enjoined on Bráhmans. I know some Rájpút gentlemen who, acting up to the Bráhmanas or sacred precepts, spend a great part of the day in devotion, such as it is, but the Bráhmans are after all the most indulgent and accommodating of religious guides. Any Rájpút gentleman who finds the observances prescribed tedious or irksome *may hire a Bráhman to do it all for him.* The Rájpút may be shooting or hawking whilst it goes on,—the result is the same so far as his spiritual welfare is concerned.

I have said the rites of hospitality are considered a sacred duty. The guest, of all others, who is received with most distinction in the house of a noble Hindu is a bridegroom. He is treated with divine honors. Any visitor that the raja wishes very particularly to distinguish is received in somewhat similar fashion. He is met at some distance on the road by the host and escorted to the castle or house preceded by musicians, attended by a well-dressed suite bearing silver sticks and other insignia of the host's rank, and flanked and followed by armed men, horse and foot; the latter with long matchlocks, which they discharge *ad libitum*. As the cavalcade reaches the castle, there issues from a side gate a procession of females in saffron-coloured garments bearing lights, water, and unguents. They precede the guest into the castle, and tender their services to wash his feet.

This truly oriental attention may often be met with in the south-west frontier districts of Bengal. It is practised by all classes of the people. Once, in passing by the house of a wealthy Goálá, I was invited by the owner to enter. A chair was placed for me in a veranda of the inner court, and the females of the family summoned. They came with water in a flat brass vessel and turmeric. They looked aghast at my boots, and were proceeding to operate on the leather, when I told them to remove the obstacle; they did so, and having fairly accomplished their devoir, they tried to restore the hose to its place, but failing in this, they got frightened and fled.

VAISYAS.

Whatever may have been originally the occupation of the third class, the Vaisyas, those who now claim to belong to it, are nearly all merchants and traders. The Agarwálás, Oswáls and some Bañias are of this class, but they are for the most part foreigners in Bengal. They leave their homes in Western India early in life, and return to them when they have made their fortunes. In Bengal Proper it is doubtful if there be any true Vaisyas domiciled. The mercantile class are either Bráhmans, who enter largely into it, Chatris or Rájpúts, and numerous Sahús, Modis and Banias who are of various inferior castes.

SECTION 3.—THE KÁYASTHS.

I believe that in the present day the Káyasths arrogate to themselves the position of first amongst commoners, or first of the Súdras, but their origin is involved in some mystery. No one appears to know much about them, the sacred writers and bards make no mention of such a class, and they have not, that I can hear of, any annals of their own. They say they came into Bengal in the train of the Bráhmans from Kanauj introduced by Adisura, but this does not account for their origin. The fact seems to be that as organized systems of Government were established, a demand for a new class of scriveners arose with duties that neither Bráhmans nor Vaisyas had time, or thought it consistent with their dignity, to attend to, and a fresh dive was made into the great Súdra element and a new order eliminated. Intelligent Káyasths make no pretensions to be other than Súdras. From their appearance we might say that the first selection was made of people with weak bodies and strong intellect, of small courage, but great cunning, and that physical beauty was of less consequence than sharpness of wit. However they worked their way out of obscurity, and are now boldly in the foreground as a well defined and very influential class. They are largely employed as clerks in Government offices, and attain to much higher official positions; they supply accountants to the landed gentry, and the Native bar opens a wide field for their peculiar talents. The potent pen which has thus elevated them is their favorite object of worship. The festival of Srípanchami observed by most learned Hindus in honor of Saraswati, the goddess of learning, is especially celebrated by Káyasths. Pens and ink-stands are collected cleaned and arranged, strewn with flowers and barley blades, and there must be no writing on that day except with chalk. A puny Káyasth will shake the pen, thus honored, in the face of a club-bearing athlete or staff-bearing police man, and declare, often with truth, that he is armed with a more effective weapon than either of them.

Having established themselves as a distinct class, the Káyasths looked about for a new pedigree and found one that was vacant at the time, and suited them exactly.

When Yáma sits in judgment on the dead, Lálá Chitragupta turns over the pages of the register in which the good and bad deeds of men are recorded by him. This worthy the Káyasths selected as their ancestor. He had several sons from whom the different tribes of Káyasths derived their origin.

1. Sribástab.	7. Mathur.
2. Ambashtha.	8. Saksená.
3. Karan.	9. Aithaná.
4. Bhattanagar.	10. Kulasreshtha.
5. Gaura.	11. Nijam.
6. Válmika.	12. Suradhwaja.

Some interested authorities wishing to extricate the caste from the degradation of belonging to the fourth class, declare that Chitragupta or Chitra Sen was created from the dust that covered the body of Brahmá. Others maintain that Chitra was the son of Bhuttidatta, created especially as chief of the Súdras. The book called the Rudrayamal states that the Ambashthas, who in Bihár are the most numerous class are not pure Súdras, but were born of a Vaisya mother by a Bráhman father. The Ambashthas first appeared in Magadha. Next to them, in numbers, are the Sribastab, who are said to have first appeared in Tirhut.

The Maitis or Mahantis of Singbhúm and Orissa are Karanas.

The Káyasths wish to be considered orthodox Hindus, and in their mode of life and observance of rites and ceremonies follow pretty closely the injunctions of the Puráns. In marriages, in funeral ceremonies and the adoration paid to the dead, they are strict observers of Bráhmanical doctrines, and perhaps there is no class more antagonistic to widow marriage than they are, but they are much addicted to ardent spirits. I know of no caste of Hindu which more openly and freely indulges in intoxicating beverages.

4 F

SECTION 4.—PASTORAL TRIBES. THE GOPAS.

I believe all the authorities are agreed in assigning to the Gopas a high place amongst Súdras, though there may be a difference of opinion as to whether all the tribes of the pastoral family are entitled to so honorable a position.

In ranking the Gopas, their intimate connection with their Hero and God Krishna is allowed to have its weight. Originally a cow-herd himself, he rose to be chief of the pastoral race and his history is theirs. Wheeler, in his delightful analysis of the Mahábhárat, thus epitomizes it; "He, Krishna, appears to have belonged to a tribe well known in Hindu History as the Yádavas, or descendants of Yadu. These Yádavas were a nomadic race who grazed cattle and made butter, and occasionally migrated to different places accompanied by their cows and waggons. The time and circumstances under which they first entered Hindústán are alike unknown. At the birth of Krishna they appear to have settled in the neighbourhood of the city of Mathurá, the modern Muttra, about 120 miles to the south of Hastinápúr."

Of the Ahírs or Gopas who were the companions of the youth of Krishna at Mathurá we have various accounts.

It is contended by some authorities that they were Vaisyas, who were degraded in consequence of having introduced castration amongst their herds,* but the Brahma Vaivarta Purán makes out the whole group that sported in Brindában to have been gods and goddesses out masquerading.

According to this authority the immortal Rádhá had, by a curse, been condemned to a sojourn on earth as a maid of Brindában, and Krishna to console her came into the world in mortal form as her lover.

This was the main object of his incarnation, but the other gods implored him not to lose the opportunity of laboring in his divine capacity for the moral elevation of mankind, so he divided his time between preaching and love-making.

Immense numbers of Ahírs or Gopas still cling to the nomadic life of their ancestors. Seeking the high grazing grounds of Central India and Western Bengal they form encampments on the pasture lands where they reside with their wives, families, and herds till the grass in the neighbourhood is exhausted, subsisting entirely on the proceeds of their milk and butter. The houses they use are constructed of large bamboo mats; they can be taken to pieces and removed like tents.

But a still larger section of the tribe have quite given up this wandering life, and forming permanent villages have settled down as good farmers and cultivators, only distinguishable from other agriculturists by a possession of larger herds of cattle, by the greater care bestowed on them and in profiting more by the sale of butter and milk.

The religious festivals observed by the Gopas are chiefly those in honor of their god and hero Krishna.† Professor H. H. Wilson describing the Doljátrá which begins in the fourteenth day of the light half of Phalgún, or about the middle of March, when the image of Krishna is put into a swing at dawn, noonday and sunset, says, "the caste of Gopas or cowherds is everywhere prominently conspicuous in this ceremony, especially so amongst the Uriyas, and at the Doljátrá or Holi they not only renew their own

* Buchanan, Vol. I. p. 169.

† Essays on Religion of the Hindus, Vol. II, page 226.

garments but all the harness and equipments of their cattle. They also bathe them and paint their foreheads with sandal and turmeric."

"They themselves collect in parties each under a leader or chorœgus whom they follow through the streets singing and dancing and leaping, as if wild with joy. A curious part of their proceedings suggesting analogies, possibly accidental, with some obsolete usages amongst ourselves, is their being armed with slender wands, and as they go along the leader every now and then halts, and turns round to his followers, and the whole clatter their wands together for an instant or two, when they resume their route repeating their vociferations and songs chiefly in praise of Krishna, or in commemoration of his juvenile pastimes." The Holi is not always exclusively connected with Krishna. There are different legends concerning a witch so called, who is burned in effigy during the festival; but one of them is, that she presented herself as a nurse to Krishna with poisoned nipples to destroy him, but he knowing her malignant intenton nevertheless applied his lips to the venom, and sucked till the whole substance and the vitality of the witch was absorbed to her utter destruction and the infant's benefit.

We have a very large Goálá population in parts of Singbhúm and the adjoining Tributary Mahåls of Katak and Chútiá Nágpúr, especially in Keonjhar. They do not appear to have any particular legend to account for their being where they now hold rather a subordinate position, the Bhúiyas or Kols being the dominant races; but they are, on the whole, the most flourishing of the peasantry in that part of the country.

They are not all of one family, and do not profess to be all of one race. Those that call themselves Mathurábásis claim to be pure Gopas, and are fond of making pilgrimages to Brindában. They are the handsomest and most truly Aryan looking of the lot. The Magadha Goálás have a much commoner appearance. The latter are suspiciously like Kols.

The features of the Mathurábásis are high, sharp and delicate, and they are of light-brown complexion. The Magadha features are undefined and coarse, and they are dark complexioned, and have large hands and feet. Seeing the latter standing in a group with some Singbhúm Kols, there is no distinguishing one from the other. There has, doubtless, been much mixture of blood.

In every Kol village there are a few of these Goálás who look after the Kol cattle and are paid for doing it. They thus hold a very subordinate position, but the Mathurábásis never stoop to this. They are found as extensive farmers, employing a number of aborigines as 'Kámias' or farm laborers, and it is astonishing how easily they succeed in seducing Kols from their independent position as peasant proprietors to become their servants. They do not however forsake their hereditary calling; they keep large herds of buffaloes and cows, and freely sell the milk and butter, the latter in the form of ghee. They live very generally in village communities and have their hereditary village headman, who with a council of village elders decides all questions of caste. They claim amongst other things the right of disposing of widows, but are now seldom permitted to exercise it.

I am indebted to Bábú Rakhál Dás Háldar, Assistant Commissioner, for the following account of the Sadgops who may be regarded as at the head of the Gopas of Bengal.

The Sadgops, literally superior Goálás, are now more an agricultural than a pastoral caste; but whatever predilection other agricultural castes may have for the worship of Ráma, the Sadgops are not peculiarly attached to that divinity. They devote themselves more particularly to Krishna like other Goálás, but this is a common case with all the castes now known as Súdras. Krishna's religion is the most actively proselytizing form of Hinduism now existing, and it is absorbing gradually all the castes, aboriginal, Aryan, and mixed. If, therefore, it be a fact that the agricultural tribes are found to be peculiarly devoted to Ráma and the pastoral tribes to Krishna, that distinction will soon cease to exist, as evidently Ráma's religion and all other forms of Hinduism are on the decline.

The Sadgops, like every other Súdra caste, are impure on account of child birth for one month, not ten days as is the case with the Bráhmans. They are impure for the same period after a death in the family. They do not perform the three important rites which constitute the second birth of the Bráhman, Kshatrya and Vaisya, *viz.*, the (1) *karna bedha*, or piercing of the ear, (2) *chúrá karana*, or tonsure, (3) *upanayana*, or investiture with the thread.

In weddings the following ceremonies are gone through :—

1. Gáyehalud—anointing the 'var' or bridegroom, with turmeric, two or three days previous to the wedding.
2. Jalsawá—ceremonious drawing of water by village girls for the 'var's' bath.
3. Adhibás,—a tray in which samples of 22 articles in common use are placed is presented to the 'var' by being made to touch his forehead, and the same time a bunch of dúb grass is tied to his wrist.
4. Nándimukh,—sacrifice to deceased ancestors.
5. Snan,—ceremonious bathing of the 'var,' in a space 'ch'háonitála', enclosed by four plaintain trees with the water obtained by 'jalsawá.'
6. Baran,—the forehead of the var is touched with betel leaves, a winnowing fan, &c.
7. Kanakánjali,—address of his mother to him at parting, when she asks, "Where are you going, my son," and he replies "to bring you a maid servant (or slave), mother!"

The bride in her own house has to go through the ceremonies 1 to 6.

When the var enters the bride's house, he is received by the village barber, who throws on him sugar and rice, and the var then takes his seat for a time in the assembly room, and converses with the young men, whilst the pandits in loud tones wrangle on questions concerning their laws or ritual.

The var is then taken inside and stands within the ch'háonitála, whilst five or six married women walk round him seven times bearing the 'adhibás' tray, a pitcher of of water, &c. The bride is brought in on a tray and carried round the var seven times, after which the 'subhadrishti,' auspicious interview, is permitted, that is the bride and var look at each other, often for the first time.

They are then both taken to the place where the guests and the pandits are assembled, and the ceremony proceeds. The bride's father performs adoration of the var, whilst he says "I give away my daughter to you." The var and bride are made to say to each other, "What is my body is thine, what is thy body is mine", and they exchange flower garlands. The var then touches the bride's forehead with the sindúr, or red lead, which apparently completes the ceremony.

The var must now re-enter the female apartment, where he is subjected to much banter by the female friends of the bride, which he must bear as best he can. Great liberty of speech is allowed on this occasion, and the jokes that are made and the songs that are sung, are not always very delicate. The bride is now taken to her future home, where other ceremonies await the couple, which are of little interest and need not be detailed.

Gareris or Shepherds.

The Gareris, or shepherd tribe, are in dignity of caste in much the same position as the Gops. In the west of India, they founded a dynasty, that of Holkar, which still flourishes. They tend sheep and make blankets from their wool—a bad conjunction of trades, as the poor sheep are invariably shorn when blankets are in most request.

SECTION 5.—AGRICULTURAL TRIBES.—THE KÚRMIS, KOLÍTAS, AND ÁGAREAHS.

The Kúrmis.

It is probable that in the Kúrmis we have the descendants of some of the earliest of the Aryan colonists of Bengal. Tradition, at all events, assigns to them a very ancient place in the country, and many antiquities, now concealed in dense jungle or rising as monuments of the civilization of bygone days amidst the huts of half-savage races now occupying the sites, are ascribed to them and attest the advance they had made in civilization at a very early period.

In his account* of Gorákhpúr, Buchanan gives the Kúrmis a high position amongst Hindus of the Sudra caste. A Kúrmi zamíndár is spoken of, the proprietor of Paráona, who had obtained the title of Raja from Ásaf-ud-Daulah, but was obliged to resign it, as it gave offence to the older Barons, the proud Rájpúts of the district. The family are nevertheless deemed noble, and it would be considered a breach of their privilege, if any of them were seen at the tail of a plough. There are tribes called Saithawar and Patanawar, who having attained or aspiring to a similar position, dislike being called Kúrmis. In Southern India this tribe is most commonly called Kumni or Kunbi.

Mr. Campbell in his Ethnology of India† says, the Kúrmis are numerous in the central and eastern parts of the North-Western Provinces, where they are well known as a very industrious class of cultivators, and he traces them from the Lower Duáb to the Jabalpúr and Ságar territories along both sides of the Narbadá and in Málwá. Farther west in Gujrát they form the main body of the best cultivating population, and throughout the whole of the Mahratta country. In short, if they were all told, they would be found to be the most numerous of all the castes in India.

Kúrmis in Chútiá Nágpúr.

In the province of Chútiá Nágpúr the ancestors of the people now called Kúrmis appear to have obtained a footing among the aboriginal tribes at a very remote period, and in more than one part of Mánbhúm have supplanted them. There are traditions of struggles between them and the Kolarian aborigines of these regions, and though the latter generally managed to hold their own, we find in some places Kúrmi villages established on sites which we know from the groups

* Page 468.

† Journal, Asiatic Society of Bengal, Special Number, 1866, page 92.

of rude stone pillars or cenotaphs still conspicuous were once occupied by Bhúmij or Mundas, and in others vestiges of ruined temples appertaining to Hindú and Jain settlements, both most likely belonging to successive generations of Kúrmis, amidst villages that have for ages been occupied by Bhúmij.

Origin of the family of the Raja of Pachet.

The Kúrmis settled in the western part of Mánbhúm told me they had been there for fifty-two generations. The Pachet Raja claims just so many descents from the deserted child that is said to have founded his race. A babe was discovered in the woods by the Kúrmis drawing its nourishment from a cow. This they took and brought up, and afterwards adopted as their Raja. As the family cannot trace back its origin rationally out of the district, and there is no particular reason for supposing them to be Bhúmij or Múnda, I think that they are more likely to be of Kúrmi extraction than descended from the cow nurtured foundling, but they prefer the latter origin and are welcome to it. There are other high families of Kúrmi origin. Sindiah is the descendant of a Kúrmi Patel of Satara, and the celebrated Bhonsla family were originally Patels of Deori, and also, I believe, Kúrmis.

In Gorákhpúr, Sháhábád, and Bihár, Buchanan reckoned 66,333 families of Kúrmis, but they are numerous in most of the districts of Bengal. In the Central Provinces * they have Jhárí Kunbís, or Kunbís of the woods, who were probably the persons who first cleared those woods, and Mahratta Kúnbís, descendants of the followers of Rághuji I., who came with him from Berar and the Deccan.

Though the Kúrmis include so many noble families, their social position in Bengal Proper is not high. They are not even 'Jala-charaniya,' or a tribe from whose hands a Hindu of the higher castes would drink water, but in Bihár this honor is accorded to them.†

The social customs and religious observances of Kúrmis vary much in different districts.

When they are found in common tenancy with non-Aryan tribes, they conform to many usages which they must have acquired from the latter, and, following their example, swerve considerably from orthodox Hindu practices.

The Kúrmis employ Bráhmans as priests in all ceremonies except marriages. A Kúrmi can marry at any age and have as many wives as he fancies, and can also divorce a wife at pleasure.

The brides may be infants or adult girls. Widows may marry again. A married woman wears an iron ring on her wrist, the removal of which by the husband proclaims her divorced and free to take another.

Marriage customs.

In the marriage arrangements and ceremonies of the Kúrmis and other Súdra castes, there are several practices which are not found in the ritual enjoined by the Purános, but may be traced in the ceremonies followed by the aboriginal tribes, and there is besides a certain amount of fiction introduced, much of which appears to point to some period when the circumstances of the people were very different from what they are at present.

* Settlement report published by Government.

† I am indebted to Babu Rakhal Dás Háldar, Assistant Commissioner, for most of this information regarding Kúrmis of Bengal.

The bridal parties amongst the aboriginal tribes often meet in hostile array at the entrance of the village of the bride, and a mimic fight takes place before the bridegroom's party is permitted to enter, and this custom is followed by some Kúrmis and other Hindu castes.

After proposals have been made and accepted a ceremony called 'Duar Khanda' is performed, which appears to be then rather superfluous. Seven or eight of the bridegroom's friends and relations go to the bride's house, and appear there and are received there as strangers come from afar. They are asked who they are and where they come from and for what purpose. They in reply describe themselves as travellers overtaken in a storm, giving fictitious names. They are hospitably treated, and in the more primitive parts the women bring water and turmeric and wash their feet. Before they take leave they ask to see the young daughter of the house of whose beauty they have heard so much. The bride is thus inspected and the party return with their report to the 'var' or bridegroom. Then on behalf of the bride, or to gratify her curiosity, a similar visit is paid to the 'var' by a party of her friends.

The wedding day is now fixed, and till it takes place, the bride and bridegroom are in their respective abodes subjected to daily ablutions in a somewhat public and ceremonious manner. On the wedding morning, the 'var' is first married to a mango tree. He embraces the tree, is for a time tied to it in a particular manner with a thread, and he daubs it with red lead. Then the thread is removed from the tree, and is used to attach some of the leaves to the 'var's' wrist. The 'var' now takes an affectionate leave of his mother. The form of speech that passes between them is used on like occasions by all Hindus. She says, "Where art thou going, my son?" "To bring thee a maid servant," is the dutiful and often over-true reply.

However short the distance may be from the 'var's' to the bride's house, if they live next door to each other, there is always a fiction of a long journey having to be undertaken to reach it, and it is usual for the 'var' to be carried to his destination seated on a covered platform borne on men's shoulders, which is called the *jaház, i. e.*, ship.

Although a bridegroom is amongst Hindus always treated with great respect, it is customary with the Kúrmis for the brethren of the bride to treat the 'var' somewhat roughly, teasing and chaffing him, probably to try his temper. This continues till he presents his tormentors with new clothes. The bride is now introduced into the assembly, and the gifts prepared for her by her father-in-law, and the 'var' presented. She is then taken by her friends to a Mahwa tree, which she must wed as the 'var' wedded the mango, and she is brought back to the bower of Hymen in a basket. The 'var' then applies the sindúr to her forehead, making a red mark between the eyes, and the guests all shout "haribol, sindradán."

In some places, as in Singbhúm, they touch and mark each other with blood as a sign that they have become one flesh, and this is probably the true origin of the singular but very universal custom of 'sindradán.' They are now man and wife, and receive the congratulations of their friends, and next morning go home together on the 'jaház,' the bride sitting submissively at her husband's feet.

The presence of a Bráhman is not necessary to give validity to a Kúrmi marriage. They consult a Bráhman astrologer as to whether the marriage is likely to prove happy and fruitful, or otherwise, and he is sometimes asked to name a fortunate day, but his aid is not otherwise sought.

The Kúrmis do not appear to have any anti-Hindu religious ceremonies, but one of their festivals, the Akhan Játra, or cake festival, is noticeable. On the last day of the month of Pús (in the middle of January) when the granaries are full, the people make cakes in the shape of a double cone called 'gargaria pitha,' put on their best attire and assemble on a green outside their village, and the young men and women form circles and dance and sing. This is followed by a joust of archery: a cock is thrown up in the air, and this is continued till one of the young men manages to shoot the bird with an arrow. The successful archer is then treated as the hero of the day.

The Akhan Játra.

The Kúrmis are a brown to tawny colored people, of average height, well proportioned, rather lightly framed, and with a fair amount of good looks. They show well shaped heads and high features, less refined than Bráhmans, less martial than Rájpúts, of humbler mien even than the Goáiás; but except when they have obviously intermixed with aborigines, they are unquestionably Aryan in looks. Grey eyes and brownish hair are sometimes met with amongst them. The women have usually small and well-formed hands and feet.

Physical traits.

In some districts the Koiris appear to be more numerous than the Kúrmis. The distinction between them is, that the former are generally market gardeners as well as agriculturists. They rear vegetables, tobacco, opium, and other produce that requires more careful cultivation than the staple crops, but they are also good agriculturists as well as gardeners.

The Koiris.

Buchanan estimated that there were 30,000 families of Koiris in the Sháhábád District, and 45,000 families in Bihár. I have no means of estimating their number elsewhere. In Chútiá Nágpúr they bear no comparison to the Kúrmis in numbers, and I imagine that this is the case in most districts of Bengal. It is perhaps the opium cultivation that has attracted so many of them to Bihár.

The Koiris are generally allowed to be 'Satsudras,' pure Súdras. Their own tradition is, that they were produced specially by Mahadeo and Parbatí for the gardens of the holy city of Benares.

The Sakiars are, I am told, a tribe of Koiris, not a distinct caste.

A learned pandit informs me that the derivation of the name is 'Ku,' earth, and 'Ari,' enemy. They are so called from their constant attacks on the soil. Koiris, men and women, are always troubling it.

They observe the Bráhmanas more strictly than most Sudras and inferior castes. Six months after birth the first food is given to a child by a Bráhman from rice, 'mahápraschád,' that has been offered to idols. At the age of five or six, boys and girls have their ears pierced by the guru, or priest, who is a Sanyási Gosáin, not a Bráhman, and the 'mantra' is at the same time given; but as the child does not always recollect the mysterious words imparted to him, they are repeated to him when he grows older. No other ceremony occurs till marriage, which takes place when the boy is ten to twelve and the girl seven to ten.

The preliminaries are first arranged by mutual friends, who meet at the house of the bride. If they come to an agreement, small sums of money are interchanged. The boy's friends give four annas and a half, and the girl's friends one and a half, and this is an engagement.

But as a betrothal it is incomplete till the ceremony called 'sugan bándhná' is performed. Ten or more of the boy's friends with music and a Bráhman go to the girl's house; her friends are also invited and the ceremony commences by the father of the girl and the father of the boy, each spreading a new cloth on the ground. The Bráhman then takes some dhán from the store of the bride's father, and places it in the hands of the maiden who throws it on the cloth spread by her father-in-law that is to be. The Bráhman next takes some grain that has been brought from the bridegroom's house, and this is thrown on the cloth spread by the father of the maiden. The cloths are then rolled up with the grain in them, the bride retains that which was brought from her betrothed's house. The friends of the latter take away the cloth produced by the bride's father.

Eight days after the above ceremony the marriage takes place. A Bráhman priest presides, and the service is strictly Bráhmanical. At the conclusion of the orthodox ritual the bride and 'var', their scarfs tied together, are made to perform seven times a circuit round a collection of vessels containing water, grain, oil, and a light. This is called the 'Bhanwar.' The girl goes first, she carries one of the cloths with grain and the boy the other, and allowing the grain to drop they thus mark the circuits they make.

When all is over, the boy is taken into the women's apartments and invited to eat, but he will not touch food till a present is made to him. In the same manner when the bride first appears amongst the females of her husband's house, she obstinately declines all refreshments till bribed to eat. The 'jaház' is used by the Koiris as well as by the Kúrmis.

Widows may marry again, but for such a union the full marriage ceremony is not needed; an interchange of gifts and the presentation of the sindúr is all that is requisite. This is called Sagoi. The offspring of such a marriage are considered legitimate. It is usual for a younger brother to take his elder brother's widow unless she objects.

The 'Grám Deotás,' village gods, of the Koiris, at least of those that I have met with, are 'Sukha,' 'Parameswari' and 'Mahávíra, Hanumán.' Altars to these three are in each house, one altar to all three and a plant of 'tulsí' in the court yard.

They keep the Hindu festivals of 'Janmoshtomi' and the 'Sívarát,' and like many other Hindus settled in Chútiá Nágpúr, the Pagan festival of 'Karma', and every three years they make offerings on a hill known as the Marang Búru of the Kols, the god that is invoked by the aborigines, especially when rain does not fall in due season.

The Kolitas.

In my account of the people of the valley of the Bráhmaputra, I have noticed the Kolítas as the remnant of the earliest Aryan colonists of Asám. They were an important section of the population of the ancient Kámarúpa, including Rangpúr in older times, and are now looked on as the purest of the old Hindu people in Asám. I had met with them in no other place till I visited the Tributary Mahals of the South-Western Frontier, and from what I saw of them there, I am inclined to class them as a purely agricultural tribe connected with the Kúrmis.

4 H

They form a considerable portion of the agricultural population of Sambalpúr, and appear in Bonai as the best cultivators and most substantial people there.

I found them occupying villages together with Gonds, and Kandhs; but these, the probable representatives of the aborigines of the place, had nearly all fallen into the position of farm servants to the Kolítas who had large substantial well stocked farm yards and very comfortable houses. I was freely admitted into their domiciles, and the women and children all presented to me. They afterwards came to my tent and sat there. The 'pardah'* system was entirely unknown to them.

The old men told me that the Kolítas came originally from Mithila in the days of Ráma, and it is to that deified hero that they chiefly pay their devotions. There was a temple to Rádha Krishna in the middle of one of the villages, but this had been put up for them by the Raja, and though they worshipped there also at his request, they did not neglect their favorite Ráma.

Physical traits.

Though doubtless best part Aryan in blood, there is, I think, a slight deterioration arising from admixture with the less comely aborigines. Their color varies from coffee to tawny yellow, or from 43 to 45 of the table published in the *Memoires de la Société d'anthropologie*. The mouths are well formed, though large; eyes generally large, full and clear, many hazel. I especially observed that many of the fair sex were distinguished by well-marked eyebrows and long eyelashes. The noses are not aquiline or prominent, but there is no remarkable deficiency of nasal bone, though the feature is often inclined towards the pug species. They have straight foreheads, but a want of breadth across the temples which takes from the oval of the face. The men show moustache and beard, but little whisker. They are well proportioned and about the average height of Hindus of the lower provinces.

The Kolítas generally allow their girls to grow to maturity before they give them away in marriage. I saw many full grown spinsters in the villages that I visited.

A very large proportion of the agricultural class of the Katak Tributary Estates are Kolítas. They are generally called there 'Ṭása', for 'Chása', but if you ask them to define their *caste* less vaguely, they will tell you they are 'Kolíta Tása', or 'Or Tása,' and the 'Kolíta Tása' are, I understand, most numerous. The Or Tása are a different caste, but there appears to be very little real difference between them and the Kolítas; they are all considered to be Sat Sudra.

The Ágareahs.

The Ágareahs, a small but very thriving tribe of Hindu cultivators in the Tributary Mahâls, may be noticed amongst the agricultural classes. According to their tradition they are called Ágareahs from having come from Ágra. They were there, they say, Kshatryas, but having been subjected to some persecution by the ruler of the State they left it, and taking up new lands in a new country cast aside their sacred thread, the badge of the twice-born, with all its privileges and obligations, and took to the plough.

Their appearance favors their pretensions to be of good blood. Tall, well made, with high Aryan features and tawny complexions, they look like Rájpúts, but are more industrious and intelligent than the generality of the fighting tribe.

* Practice of secluding females.

The women are spared from all out-door labour, but are not secluded, and have their own share of industrial avocations as well as household duties. They spin their own cotton and give the yarn to the weavers, who return it to them in piece goods. They are all decently, and even handsomely clothed, and have a good store of silver ornaments. The girls are betrothed at a very early age, but remain in their fathers' houses till they grow up into women, so one of the evils of early marriage is avoided. I made enquiries amongst a number of young girls, and found that all above seven years old were betrothed and wore the silver ornaments which had been given to them when they became engaged.

At the marriage a Bráhman priest officiates, but it must be a Bráhman from the North-Western Provinces. They do not employ the Utkala Bráhmans. They have only one for a large tract of country, he goes his rounds and marries them all off periodically. They are orthodox Hindus in most customs, but they allow widows to remarry, and they bury the dead, but at any time when the bones are dry, the principal joints and part of the skull are taken up and conveyed by the representative of the deceased to the Ganges. This service is often neglected. My informant told me that his father, grandfather, and great-grandfather's bones were all in the ground and on his conscience. The bones taken are called 'Ashta,' 'Ashtáng,' as representing the eight parts of man. The young girls, though betrothed, appear to enjoy great liberty. Some of them are very pretty, bright-looking creatures of reddish light-brown complexion; fine glossy long black hair; very bright eyes, remarkable for the clearness of the conjunctive membrane; slight flexible graceful figures; teeth white and regular; faces not disfigured by paint, and no *godna*, or marks of tattooing, except on hands and legs. The hair is very neatly and elaborately dressed, secured by a large silver ornament. I have seen among them many pairs of grey eyes, and long eye-lashes are a prevailing feature.

It is reported in Gangpúr, where there are some three or four thousand Ágareahs, that the beauties I have been describing and all Ágareah females are witches. There is among all classes in Gangpúr a wide-spread and deep-rooted belief in witchcraft. It is equally dreaded by the wildest and by the most civilized of the people, and I have had before me proceedings in several cases in which it appeared that Ágareah women had been badly treated to drive the spirit out of them or make them give up the black art. I have been told that in Gangpúr there are old women, professors of witchcraft, who stealthily instruct the young girls. The latter are all eager to be taught and are not considered proficient till a fine forest tree selected to be experimented on is destroyed by the potency of their 'mantras,' or charms, so that the wife a man takes to his bosom has probably done her tree and is confident in the belief that she can, if she pleases, dispose of her husband in the same manner, if he makes himself obnoxious.

TRADING CLASSES, ARTIZANS, MIXED AND IMPURE TRIBES.

I am reminded that I have already exceeded the allotted space, and I must bring this work to a close with a very brief notice of some remaining sections of the population of Bengal.

Trades.—Amongst the Hindus, all trades are hereditary, and each forms a caste, the persons belonging to which must not marry out of it. These guilds are not included amongst the four classes by the ancient exponents of the Hindu system. They are absurdly declared to be the issue of marriages between a male of one or other of the recognised castes with a female of another, and are thence called the Mixed Classes, of whom from thirty to forty are enumerated, including the tribes to whom the vilest offices are assigned.

Some trades are deemed honorable, and those who follow them are placed at least on a footing of equality with members of the fourth or Sudra class; others are dishonorable, and cause the degradation of the fraternity who practise them. Dr. Buchanan tells us that the following members of the trading classes rank as Sudras in the Patna division :—

Sang tarásh	Stone-cutters and masons.
Thathéra	Workers in bell-metal.
Kansára	Ditto and braziers.
Tambúlí	Sellers of betel (piper).
Málís	Gardeners.
Baraí	Cultivators of betel.
Kandú	House-builders. (Women parch grain).

The blacksmiths, are pure in Bengal, but not in Bíhár. The Nai or Napits, barbers, are pure in Bengal, impure in Bihár. In some places they have certain priestly functions assigned to them (originating probably in the importance attached to the operation of shaving on some occasions), and are respected accordingly.

It is not in all instances easy to explain why certain trades are regarded as degrading. The Barhaís, carpenters, are considered impure—I know not why—and so are the indispensable Kumbhárs, potters, because, it is said, they cut the throats of the vessels which they make when they remove them from the wheel. The Lakheri, or workers in lákh, are in the same class.

The following are included amonst the lowest class of Hindus; none of the other castes would touch water drawn by them :—Binds, Chaing or Chain, fishermen, boatmen, and general labourers; Kewots and Malers, fishermen only. A man may fish for sport without loss of dignity, and people of good caste may catch fish for their meals in baskets, traps, &c., but the man who makes it his profession, is a degraded creature. Jogis and Patwas, rearers of the silk-worm and weavers of silk, are impure, though many of this class acquire wealth, and they are, on the whole, a well-favored people.

The weavers of cotton piece-goods are deemed vile, and in consequence I believe of the low position assigned to them by their co-religionists, great numbers embraced Islám and are now called Joláhas. The oil-pressers, Kúlhús or Télis, though pushing a most lucrative trade and living well, are in the class I am describing; so are the Pásis, whose chief duty is to express the juice of palm trees. Dabgárs, who make the leathern vessels for holding ghee, and all other workers in leather, the Mochís in Bengal, the Chamárs in Bihár, are *ex-officio* impure; and truly the skinning of deceased cattle and seething the skins is not a sweet employment, but some years ago a reformer arose amongst this "worshipful company," who established a sect called Satiámas, led by a reformer who professed deism and inculcated cleanly habits and purity of life. Many thousands of Chamárs were converted, and they are now described in the Gazetteer of the Central Provinces as "a regenerate people, frugal and temperate."

We must discard as altogether absurd the Hindu notion of the trade and low menial classes having been deduced from an illicit commingling of the recognised castes; but the absolute exclusion of persons so essentially necessary to society is an additional proof of the fallibility of the theory that the twice-born, meaning Bráhmans, Kshatryás and Vaisyas, were in themselves a complete nation. I have already shown that they could have had no ploughmen, and they surely could not have existed without manufactures of any kind or menials for the low offices; for it must be remembered that they could not employ their own sanctified hands on works declared derogatory to their caste. It is clear that a large proportion of the existing trading classes always belonged to the Hindu Aryan nation; but as some of them have the honor of being regarded as people from whose hands the twice-born condescend to take water, and others are so degraded that their touch is pollution, it appears to me probable that certain offices and trades were exclusively performed by slaves, and the Aryans introduced a very numerous body of these helot artificers and low menials into India.

Weavers.

I have observed that weavers are conspicuous amongst the craftsmen thus degraded and still despised, and that many of them in consequence became Muhammadans. I think this also explains why we now find so many thousands of them in the special preserves of the aboriginal races. I have noticed in my account of the Hos of Singbhúm, the Tantís, weavers of apparently Hindu origin, whom we find domesticated as essential constituents of every Ho village community. We have besides thousands of weavers in the Páns or Pánwas, Gándas, Chiks of the Southern Tributary Estates, and the Pábs and Pánikas of the western districts. In feature these people are Aryan or Hindu rather than Kolarian or Dravidian. Their habits are all much alike, repudiating the Hindu restrictions on food, but worshipping Hindu gods and goddesses, and having no peculiar customs which stamp them as of the other races. This helot weaver caste, if I am right in thus characterising them, cannot number less than 50,000 in the province of Chútiá Nágpúr.

Ghásís.

But far viler than the weavers are the extraordinary tribe called Ghásís, foul parasites of the Central Indian hill tribes, and submitting to be degraded even by them. If the Chandalas of the Puráns, though descended from the union of a Bráhmani and a Sudra, are the "lowest of the low," the Ghásís are Chandalas, and the people, who further south are called Pariahs, are no doubt of the same distinguished lineage. If, as I surmise, they were Aryan helots, their offices in the household or communities must have been of the lowest and most degrading kinds. It is to be observed that the institution of caste necessitated the organisation of a class to whom such offices could be assigned, and when formed, stringent measures would be requisite to keep the servitors in their position. We might thence expect that they would avail themselves of every opportunity to escape, and no safer asylums could be found than the retreats of the forest tribes. Wherever there are Kols, there are Ghásís, and though evidently of an entirely different origin, they have been so long associated that they are a recognised class in the Kol tradition of creation, which appropriately assigns to them a thriftless career, and describes them as living on the leavings or charity of the more industrious members of society. There are not fewer than 50,000 Ghásís in the Kol countries. Their favorite employment is no doubt that of musicians; no ceremony can take place or great man move without the accompani-

4 I

ment of their discordant instruments, drums, kettle-drums, half-drums, and huge horns, to proclaim the event in a manner most horrifying to civilised ears.

Doms.

The habits of the widely-spread Dom class are as impure as those of the Ghásís, and they get their living much in the same fashion; they are to be found in all parts of Bengal and Northern India, living on the outskirts of villages. They are seldom seen working in the fields; they are employed to kill dogs and remove dead bodies, and sometimes as executioners, and when they have none of these congenial tasks to perform, they make baskets.

Dosáds.

The Dosáds or Doshâds are another type of a low-caste tribe, living freely and according to Hindu notions, impurely, but apparently rather of Aryan than Turanian origin. The men, who are of strong build and as tall as the average Hindu, have coarse features, but with nothing of the Chinese or Negro about them. They have adopted the worship of the demon Ráhú, who is supposed to cause eclipses by his periodical attacks on the sun and moon in revenge for having had his head cut off by Vishnu. The Dosáds not only adore him, but claim to be his descendants, their upper class from Ráhú and his wife, and their second class from Ráhú and his wife's *femme de chambre.* Their mode of worshipping their founder is as demoniacal as he could wish. The faithful ascend ladders formed of sword blades, so placed as to bring the sharp edge in contact with the sole of each foot, pressing as it ascends, and they afterwards walk through a ditch filled with blazing faggots on which oil or ghee is poured to intensify the heat, with no more injury than was sustained by Shadrach, Meshach, and Abednego in the fiery furnace. The Dosáds aspire to higher employment than the Ghásís and Doms, They serve as village watchmen and sometimes as Police and as Court runners. They too started a reformer some three or four years ago; but after a year's trial of abstinence, they came to the conclusion that it did not suit them and relapsed.

Bedyas.

The wandering gipsy-like tribe of Bedyas are found in most Bengal Districts, and so indifferent is their character that they are usually placed under the special surveillance of the Police. They are a branch of the Bázígar or Nat family, a good account of whom is to be found in vol. VII of the Asiatic Society's Researches, page 458. They are jugglers, fortune-tellers, rope-dancers, beggars, wanderers, and bird-killers, and their pursuits are further indicated by their having a slang, or rogue's language, only understood by themselves. They submit to circumcision and call themselves Muhammadans, but they have many Hindu customs and idolatrous practices, and consult bráhmans on particular occasions. Though scattered and nomadic, they are organised as communities and have "head centres" in different localities. They sometimes call themselves Mánjhí and Mahalí.

Rájwárs.

Having no space left, I must spare my readers a long account of the mongrel tribes. I think we may reckon amongst them the Rájwárs, a tribe well known in the Gya and adjoining districts as troublesome characters, especially addicted to highway robbery. Dr. Buchanan was disposed to class them amongst the aboriginal races, chiefly in consequence of their impure practices. Traditionally they appear to connect themselves with the Bhúiyas, but this is only in Bihár. The Rájwárs in Sirgúja and the adjoining estates are peaceably-disposed cultivators, who declare themselves to be fallen Kshatryas; they do not, however, conform to Hindu customs, and they are skilled in a dance called *chailo*, which I believe to be of Dravidian origin. The Rájwárs of Bengal admit they are derived from the misce-genation of Kúrmis and Kols. They are looked upon as very impure by Hindus, who will not take water from their hands.

Báoris and Bágdis.

The Báoris and Bágdis are, I conceive, the remnant of an aboriginal race who by intermarriage with low-caste Hindus have nearly effaced their primitive lineaments. The Bágdis are now employed as fishermen, palki-bearers, and general laborers, but some holders of large estates in Eastern Bengal are of this family. I consider that the fact of Báoris being still in possession of Ghátwálí tenures as ancestral, shows that they had once a proprietary interest in the soil. Babu Rakhal Dás Háldar suggests that the name is derived from the Sanskrit *vávár*, barbarian, the root of the Asám Abor; but in Asám the word opposed to Abor, which is applied only to independent tribes, is Bori, which means dependent or subjugated, and that seems in every way more appropriate to the condition of the Báori, who appear to have meekly accepted their burden-bearing lot, both men and women hiring themselves out as day-laborers or accompanying travellers on journeys. The men carry palkís.

The Báoris have some singular customs. They are excluded from caste if they kill a heron or a dog. In regard to the heron, it is the emblem of the tribe, and its flesh they must not eat; but in regard to dogs, I was gravely informed by some of their elders that as they killed and ate cows and most other animals, they deemed it right to fix on some beast which should be as sacred to them as the cow to the Bráhman, and they selected the dog because it was a useful animal while alive and not very nice to eat when dead,—a neat reconciliation of the twinges of conscience and cravings of appetite.

INDEX.

4 K

4 L

4 M

FRONTISPIECE.

"THE REST AT NOON."

Group of Oráons taken at Ránchí by T. F. PEPPÉ, *Esq.*

Fig. 1.—BÚDUWÁ, an Oráon youth, age 22 years.

Height	5 ft. 2 in.
Measurements of head:—	
Short diameter, in front	5 inches.
Ditto ditto, behind	6 ,,
Long ditto	7½ ,,
Length of arm from acromion process to end of middle finger	29½ ,,
Color 28.	

Fig. 2.—ET'THO, an Oráon girl, age 15 years.

Height	5 ft. ½ in.
Measurements of head:—	
Short diameter, front	4⅛ inches.
Ditto ditto behind	5⅛ ,,
Long ditto	7⅛ ,,
Circumference	20¼ ,,
Arm, acromion to olecranon	11¾ ,,
Olecranon to end of middle finger	16 ,,
Acromion to ditto	26 ,,
Color between 29 and 30. Iris 2.	

Fig. 3.—SÁONI, Oráon girl, age 16.

Height	4 ft. 8 in.
Circumference of head	20½ inches.
Arm, acromion to end of middle finger	25½ ,,
Color 27. Iris 2.	

Fig. 4.—SÚKÚ, an Oráon girl, age 12.

Height	4 ft. 8½ inches.
Circumference of head	20½ ,,
Short diameter, front	4½ ,,
Ditto ditto behind	5½ ,,
Long ditto	7 ,,
Length of arm, acromion to end of middle finger	26 ,,
Color 28. Iris 1.	

Fig. 5.—SAUNDÍ, an Oráon girl, age 14 years.

Height	4 ft. 7½ in.
Measurements of head:—	
Short diameter, front	4½ inches.
Ditto ditto behind	5½ ,,
Long ditto	6⅞ ,,
Length of arm, acromion to end of middle finger	23 ,,
Color 28.	

For account of the Oráons, see Section 1, Group VII, page 245.

PLATE I.

From a Photograph by DR. SIMPSON.

KHAMTI.

The chief seat of the Khamtis, who are a branch of the Shán or Tai race, is in Bor Khamti, a Province of Burmah, on the Upper Irrawaddy. Several colonies from thence have settled in Upper Asám, on both banks of the Brahmáputra River, east of Sadiya. They are Budhists in religion, and by far the most intelligent of the tribes of the North-Eastern Frontier.

For account of the Khamtis, see pp. 5 to 9.

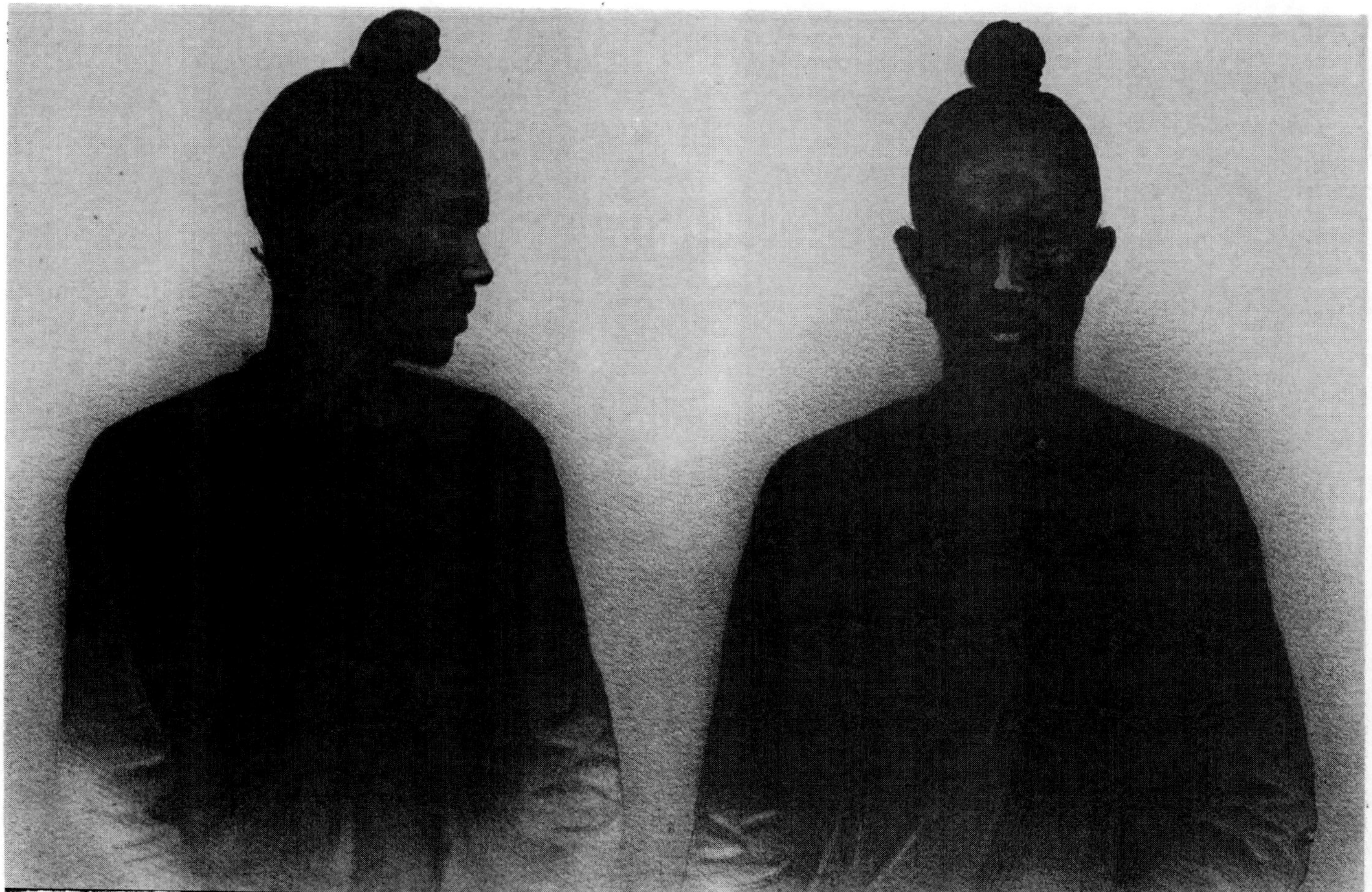

PROFILE. FULL FACE. HANHART, LITH.

KAMTI.

PLATE II.

From a Photograph by DR. SIMPSON.

Fig. 1.—KHAMTI FEMALE.

This is a very typical representation of a young Khamti woman. The elevation of the hair on the crown of the head indicates that she is married, and the style is recommended as dignified and becoming. Unmarried girls wear it in a roll low down on the occiput. They are exceedingly industrious, spin, weave, dye, and embroider, and can themselves make up all that they wear. The jacket is ordinarily of cotton, dyed blue; the petticoat of the same material, and round the waist a colored silk-scarf as a sash. But the dress of the lady in the illustration is of richer material—black velvet boddice and silk skirt. The ear ornaments are of amber.

Fig. 2.—CHÚLIKÁTÁ WOMAN.

A typical, but not a favorable specimen of a Chúlikátá, or crop-haired, Mishmí woman.

See note to Plate VII, and pp. 18 to 21.

RANHART, LITH

KHAMTI WOMAN   CHULIKATA MISHMI

PLATE III.

From a Photograph by DR. SIMPSON.

Fig. 1.—A capital specimen of a SINGPHO CHIEF.

The father-land of the Singphos, or Kákús, the Kakhyens of the Burmese, is the valley of the Sgin Mae-khá, or great eastern branch of the Irrawaddy. Their settlements in Asám sweep round the extreme Eastern Frontier from the Dápha Bhúm, the loftiest of the hills south of the Brahmáputra in Asám, to the Patkye (Patkoi) Range, which separates Asám and Burma, and banks of the Bori Dihing River. The word 'Singpho,' adopted by the members of the tribe settled in Asám, merely means 'man' in their own language. See pp. 9 to 13.

Fig. 2.—ABELO, CHÚLIKÁTÁ MISHMÍ CHIEF.

Measurements.

Height	66 inches.
Of head with callipers :—	
Short diameter of skull, in front	$4\frac{3}{8}$ inches.
Do. do. do., behind	$5\frac{3}{8}$,,
Long diameter	$7\frac{1}{8}$,,
Circumference	$22\frac{1}{4}$,,
Arm, from acromion to olecranon	$13\frac{1}{2}$,,
Forearm, from olecranon to end of middle finger	18 ,,
Arm from acromion process to end of middle finger	$28\frac{1}{2}$,,

This is a very favorable specimen of a Chúlikátá, who are generally much coarser in feature and fierce in expression. This tribe are found in the hills to the north of Sadiya in Upper Asám, between the Digáro and Dibong Rivers. See also Plate IX.

Vide note to Plate VII, and pp. 18 to 21.

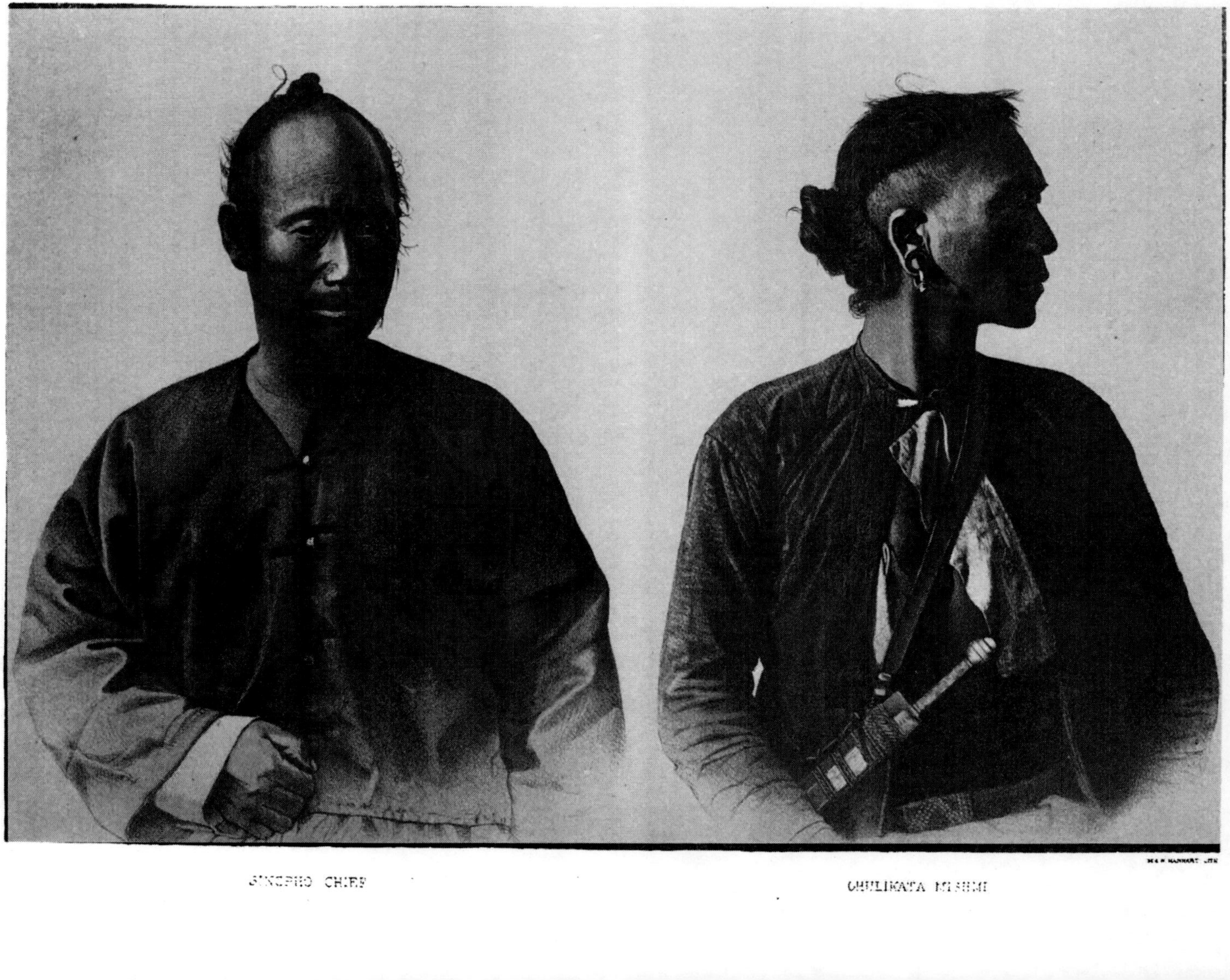

SINGPHO CHIEF CHULIKATA MISHMI

PLATE IV.

From a Photograph by Dr. Simpson.

Male and Female of the Tain or Digáru Mishmí Tribe.

These are both good average specimens of the tribe. They are, as a rule, fairer and with softer features than the Abors, acquiring from their journeys across the snow a becoming ruddiness of complexion. The young women have generally pretty figures, which their costume shows to advantage. The frontlet, a thin plate of bright silver, is a picturesque and becoming ornament, worn on the forehead by all women who can afford it. They are a quiet, inoffensive people, occupying the hills and skirts of the hills between the Digáru and Dillí Rivers, two of the north hill-affluents of the Brahmáputra, and devoting themselves chiefly to trade.

See pp. 13 to 18 for an account of the Mishmís.

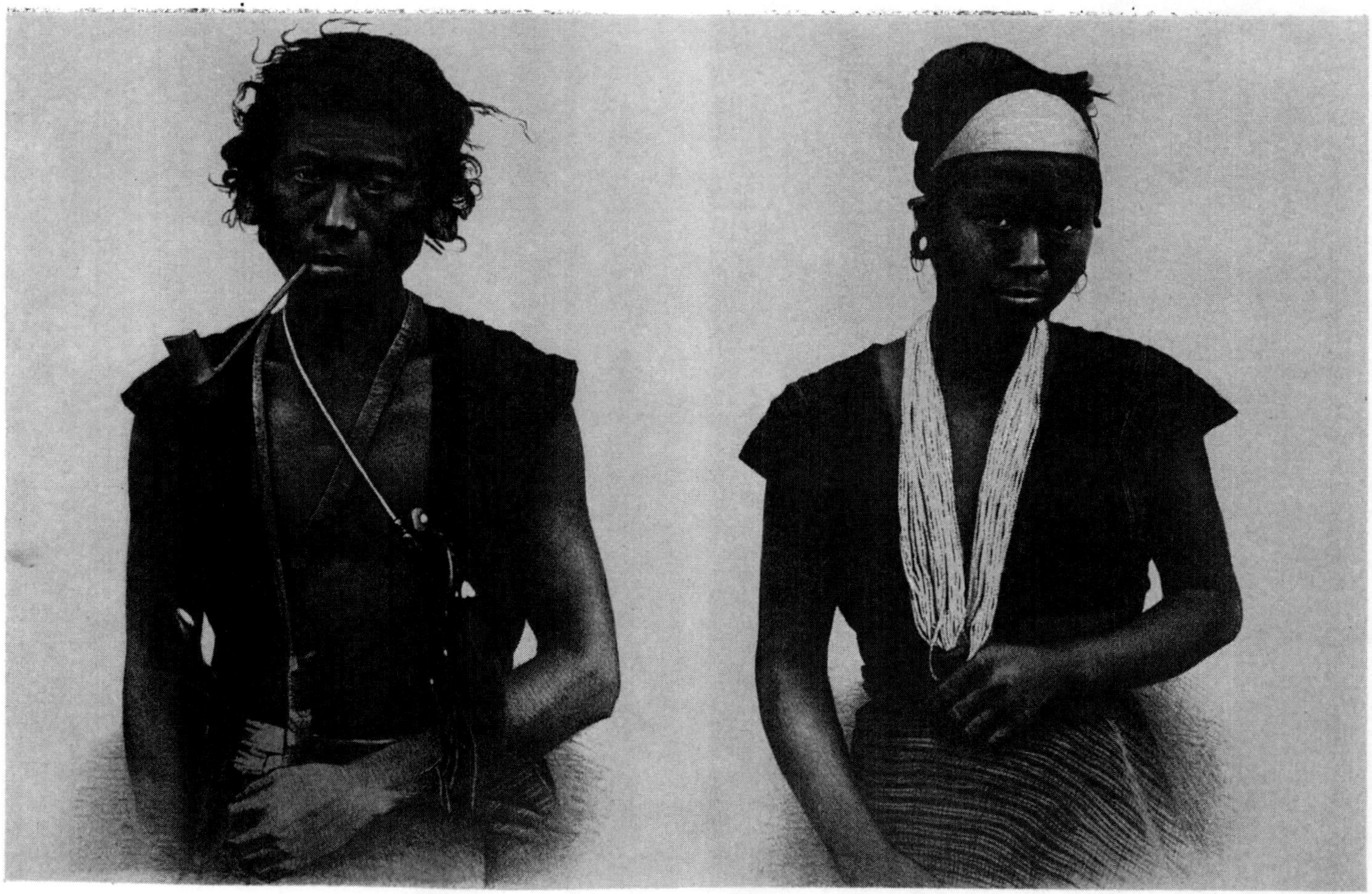

MANSART LITH

MAN DIGARU MISHMI WOMAN.

PLATE V.

Group of Digáru Mishmís.

HANHART LITH.

GROUP OF DIGARU MISHMIS

PLATE VI.

From a Photograph by DR. SIMPSON.

Group of MIZHU or MIZU MISHMÍS.

Of the Mishmí tribe who are in habits of intercourse with Asám, the Miju or Mizhu live in the farthest East. In their commercial journeys between Asám and Tibet, they cross the snowy range, and so appear in warmer vestments than are in use by the tribes who seldom quit the valley. The long coats of the male figures are of woollen fabrics, or mixed wool and nettle fibre. The white frontlet on the forehead of the girl is a thin plate of silver; the coil round her neck of thick brass wire. The weapons shown are long spears, dirks and straight swords, the latter and their pipes of brass are of Tibetan manufacture.

See pp. 13 to 18 for account of the Mishmís.

HANHART LITH.

GROUP OF MIJU MISHMIS.

PLATE VII.

From a Photograph by Dr. Simpson.

Group of Midhi or Chúlikátá Mishmís.

This tribe occupies the hills north of Sadiya, but their country is so difficult of access, that very little is known about it. They trade between Tibet and Asám, when at peace; but they are considered the most treacherous and aggressive of all the North-Eastern tribes, though more skilled in arts and manufactures than their neighbours, the Abors to the East, and the Mishmís to the West. They are called Chúlikátá, or crop-haired, from their having originated the modern fashion of cutting the hair straight across the forehead. The men cut theirs to the level of the rims of their wicker helmets as far as the back of the ear; both sexes wear it long behind.

For account of the Chúlikátás, see pp. 18 to 21.

HANHART LITH

GROUP OF CHULIKATA MISHMIS.

PLATE VIII.

From a Photograph by DR. SIMPSON.

Fig. 1.—An admirable and thoroughly typical representation of a Tain Mishmí girl.—*Vide* Plate VII, and page 17.

Fig. 2.—A Bor Abor girl, belonging probably to some village near the great Dihong River in the Sub-Himálayan range. These ladies crop their hair all round as the least troublesome method of disposing of it. The illustration gives a capital representation of their strongly marked Mongolian features, and their coarse, good-tempered faces. This young girl's costume and the ornaments are all apparently from the North: the blue vitreous turquoise-like beads, which our glass manufacturers cannot imitate, and cornelian and agate pebbles.

MANHART LITH

MISHMI WOMAN. BOR ABOR WOMAN

PLATE VIIIA.

From a Photograph by DR. SIMPSON.

A MIJU or MIZHU MISHMÍ in undress.

MIJU MISHMI.

PLATE IX.

From a Photograph by DR. SIMPSON.

A CHÚLIKÁTÁ MISHMÍ Chief in full dress.

N. B.—This plate has been erroneously lettered as a Miju Mishmí. The portrait represents the same individual, taken in full face, as is shown in profile in the right hand figure of Plate III, which see.

HANHART LITH

MIJU MISHMI

PLATE X.

From a Photograph by Dr. Simpson.

Group of Bor Abors.

If a traveller were to cross the Himálayas in about Longitude 95°E., he would soon, after entering the hills from Asám, find himself amongst the clans who are thus designated by the Asamese. They are a rough rude race, but are not without some good qualities.

The word Abor is Asamese, and means 'independent,' and it is applied to the northern hill clans nearest the plains between the Dibong and the Dirjmo Rivers, because they never were subjugated or interfered with by the old Asám Government, and seldom appeared at all amongst the Asamese. The Abors, as a matter of policy, have always asserted that the clans of the same people further North are very numerous and powerful, and from these reports the name Bor (great) Abor was assigned to them; but I have no faith in such accounts of their power. The Abors obtain goods from both sides. They export some commodities from Asám to Tibet, but chiefly buy in the North with the money of the South, and accumulate wealth. The Bor Abors, on the other hand, always appear poor and mainly dependent on the resources of their own impracticable country.

For account of the Abors, see pp. 21 to 28.

GROUP OF BOR ABORS.

PLATE XI.

From a Photograph by DR. SIMPSON.

Figs. 1 and 2.—ABOR CHIEF.

This is a thoroughly good specimen of the Dihong Abor, of whom a tolerably full account will be found in Section 5, Group I, but I avail myself of this opportunity to supply an important omission in the description. The rugged rocky soil, on which their villages are built, has probably originated a unique custom of sepulture, by which very small graves are required. The dead are trussed up so that the chin rests on the knees, and are placed in the small chamber prepared for them in a sitting posture.

The goitre with which the original of the illustration was evidently afflicted, is a common disease amongst the Abors.

FULL FACE. PROFILE.

HANHART LITH.

BOR ABOR.

PLATE XII.

From a Photograph by Dr. Simpson.

A Dhoba Abor.

This tribe of Abors have their settlements in the hills between the Dirjmo and Sísí Rivers, which discharge their waters into a northern channel of the Brahmáputra called the Búri-Súti, opposite the Debrogarh.

A colony of Dhoba Abors were located by the Revd. E. Higgs on his farm near Debrogarh. Attended by the young men of this party, he visited their hills in 1855, and was hospitably received by them. The account given of the Hill Míris in Section 5, page 31, applies in most points to this tribe also.

HANHART LITH.

DHOBA ABOR

PLATE XIII.

From a Photograph by DR. SIMPSON.

A DHOBA ABOR, an admirable typical specimen of the clan.

The helmet of this chief is decorated with boar's tusks, so as to give an effective protection to the head; for no ordinary blow would cut through them. The ornament hanging just over the clavicle is the palate and the upper jaw of some feline, studded with cowrie shells. The large necklaces are formed of beads of a vitrified substance exactly resembling turquoise. He has a 'Lama' sword, a weapon of Tibetan manufacture.

Section 5, Group I, page 21.

DHOBA ABOR

PLATE XIV.

From a Photograph by Dr. Simpson.

Fig. 1.—A Phakiál.

The Phakiáls or Phákís are incidentally referred to in the foregoing pages as one of the Shán tribes established in Asám; their principal settlement is on the Dihing River near Jaipúr, and it is believed that they have been there since the time of the first Ahom kings, and were placed where we find them on the high road to Hukong and Mogoung of Upper Burmah to keep up the intercourse between the Ahoms and their Shán brethren of Mogoung.

They follow generally the customs of the Khamtis (see Section 1, Group I), but the Phákí women have adopted the fashion of the Burmese ladies in the cut of their petticoat, wheih is open down one side, so as to give a classical freedom to the limbs.

Fig. 2.—An admirable specimen of an old Miri Woman from one of the villages on the banks of one of the Upper Asám rivers. These Míris have all emigrated from the Abor Settlements, and, according the Abors, are run-away slaves.

For account of the Miris, see Section 5 (2), Group I, pp. 28 to 35.

FAKIAL. MIRI

PLATE XV.

From a Photograph by DR. SIMPSON.

Míris, Male and Female.

These are also Míris of the valley, emigrants or refugees from the hills, but not of the same clan as the woman represented in Plate XIV. They appear to me to be members of the *Chútiá-Mírí* tribe, who claim connection with the *Chútiás,* or Kacháris, once the dominant race in the Upper and Central portions of the Asám Valley. Though for centuries settled in the plains, the Míris mix little with the other races, and have preserved their northern ethnic peculiarities in a remarkable degree. They are well portrayed in this Plate.

See page 29.

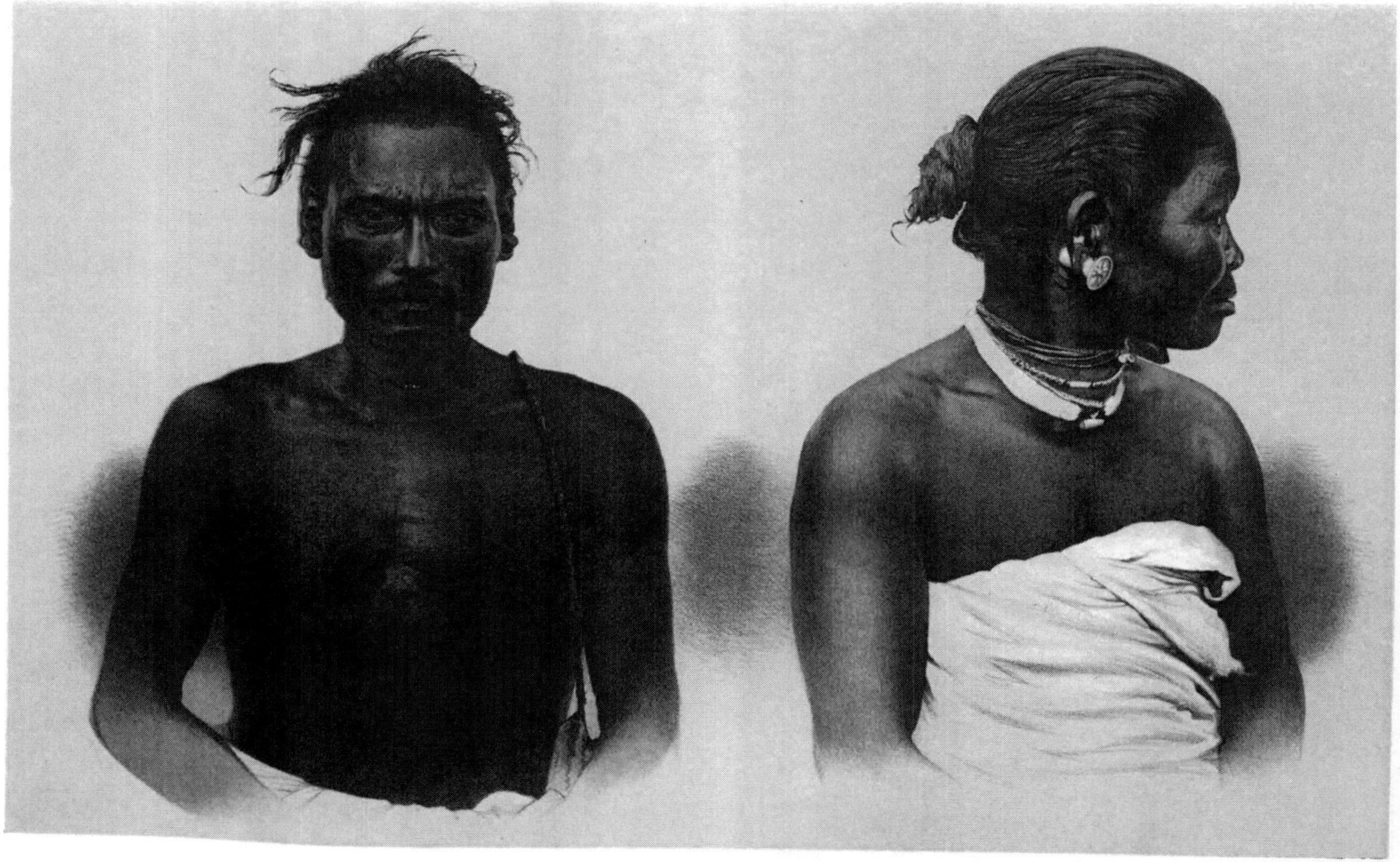

HANHART LITH

MAN. MIRI. WOMAN

PLATE XVI.

From a Photograph by Dr. Simpson.

Nágá Chief.

The wild inhabitants of the southern barrier of the Asám Valley, from the Dihing River in Upper Asám to the Kopilí in the lower part of the Valley, are all called Nágás; but the Doyang River divides the clans into two groups, and we find little affinity between the tribes on the right and left banks of that stream.

The warrior represented in Plate XVI is a chief of one of the clans of the Eastern or Upper Nágá Group. In fantastic eccentricity of costume, the Nágás take the lead of all the tribes described in this work. Their love of decoration is only equalled by their antipathy to clothing. They study ornamentation and manage to produce a very picturesque effect. The materials chiefly used are shell, ivory, boar's tusks, beads of agate and other pebbles, goat's-hair dyed scarlet and other colors, brass and glass. Their arms are adorned like their persons. The plate is a good illustration both of the decorative propensity and the physical traits of the people. As usual amongst animals when the male takes great pride in his personal appearance, the female withdraws from the contest, the Nágá women appear to care little for dress.

See Section 6, Group I.

BANHART LITH.

NAGA CHIEFTAIN.

PLATE XVII.

From a Photograph by Dr. Simpson.

Male and Female of the Námsáng Nágá Tribe.

The Namsángya Nágás are found in the hills south of Jaipúr in Upper Asám, near Hukunjuri tea garden, and from constant intercourse with the plains are more civilized and better clad than the clans of the interior. They have possession of salt springs, the produce of which enables them to obtain, without much labor, the raiment, ornaments, and addition to food which they require.

See Section 6 of Group I, page 38.

Pl XVII.

KANHART LITH.

NAMSANG NAGA MUTTUCK.

PLATE XVIIA.

From a Photograph by DR. SIMPSON.

Male and Female from MUTTUCK, ASÁM.

The term Muttuck (Matak) is generally applied to a sect of the Hindú Asamese properly called Moamáriah, who, under a very warlike priest, rose in rebellion, and all but subverted the Asám Government in A. D. 1784. The Ahom Rájah applied for assistance to the British Government, and troops under a British Officer were sent, by whom the insurrection was quelled, and the Moamáriahs were permitted to settle in the tract called Muttuck (Matak). Moamáriahs are not all of the same caste or race; but the majority are, I believe, Ahoms. The male figure may serve as a good type of an Asamese Hindú. The woman is a fair specimen of the Hindu-Ahom hybrid, of which I believe a considerable proportion of the population of Asám is composed. The costume is that of a well-to-do Asamese girl. She wears no jacket or bodice, but a scarf of fine silk with embroidered border is lightly wreathed round her bosom, leaving one arm and shoulder bare, as shown in the picture. The lower garment is usually of the drab thicker silk called 'múga.'

See page 79.

MAN. MUTTUCK. WOMAN.

PLATE XVIII.

Male and Female of the LOWER NÁGÁ GROUP.

This is an admirable illustration of one of the Nágá tribes, who are found in the hills south of the Nowgong District, between the Doyang and Kopilí Rivers, in the Asám Province. There is nothing that I know of except the name to connect these clans with the tribes east of the Doyang. Their features are harsher, more decidedly Mongolian; and their language, which is quite different, associates them with the Manipúri and Kúki tribes and their cognates.

See page 44.

FEMALE. HILL NAGA. MALE.

FARRANT LITH.

PLATE XIX.

From Photographs by Dr. Brown, *late Political Agent, Manipúr.*

Figs. 1, 2, & 3 are natives of the Manipúr Valley, where a more civilized type of the people of the surrounding hills have formed a little nation under a monarchical form of government. The features of the Manipúris, male and female, and the peculiarities of their costume, are fairly represented in the illustration, but the young girl should have had a spencer.

See page 48.

Fig. 4.—Angami Nágá.

This was one of the most warlike and troublesome of the Nágá tribes, till, after years of raids on villages of the British pale and retaliatory or conciliatory expeditions into their country, the Nágá hill district was established, and a station for a Deputy Commissioner with an armed Police force formed at Sámúgúting on the right bank of the Dhansiri River. The Angámi Hills lie between that river and the Doyang and northern boundary of Manipúr. The illustration represents an Angámi from the Manipúr side of the valley.

See Section 7, Group I, page 48.

MUNIPURI
(Hindu.)

ANGAMI-NAGA.

MUNIPURI
(Married Woman)

MUNIPURI
(Young girl.)

HANHART LITH

PLATE XX.

From Photographs by DR. SIMPSON.

KACHÁRI, Male and Female.

The Kacháris, called by Mr. Hodgson Bodo, are diffused throughout a very wide extent of country. It appears certain that they were at one time the dominant race in the upper valley of the Brahmáputra, but though they overran a country pre-occupied by Aryans, and many of them adopted the religion and language of the more civilized race with whom they thus came in contact, their physiognomy to this day shows that they have, as a rule, managed to retain their purity of blood, and their northern physical traits have not, like those of the Ahoms, been obliterated or modified by intermixture with the Aryan people.

For account of the Kacháris, see Section 2, Group II, page 83.

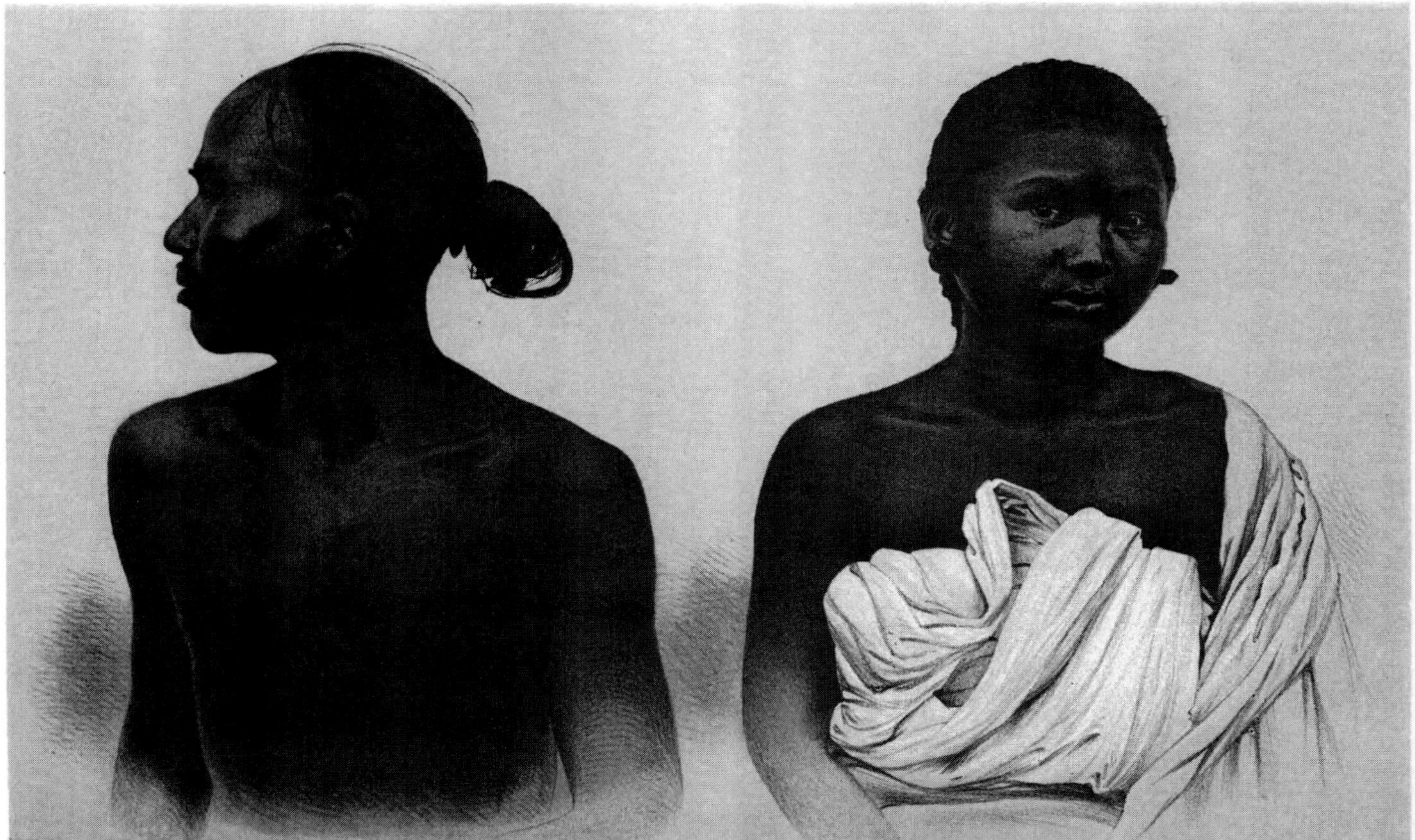

HANHART LITH.

KACHARI.

PLATE XXI.

From Photographs by Dr. Simpson.

Kúkis, Male and Female.

Although the Kúkis are, doubtless, connected with some of the North-Eastern tribes, it is only within the present century that they have made their appearance on the Asám frontier as emigrants from southern regions, propelled in a northern direction by the pressure of the kindred Lusháí tribes. They appear very well clad in the illustration, but it is alleged that they were in a very nude state when first seen in Kachár. They are known to extend from the neighbourhood of the Mugs of Arakan to Kachár and the confines of the Asám Nágá tribes, a distance of 300 miles.

See Section 7, Group II, page 44.

Pl. XXI.

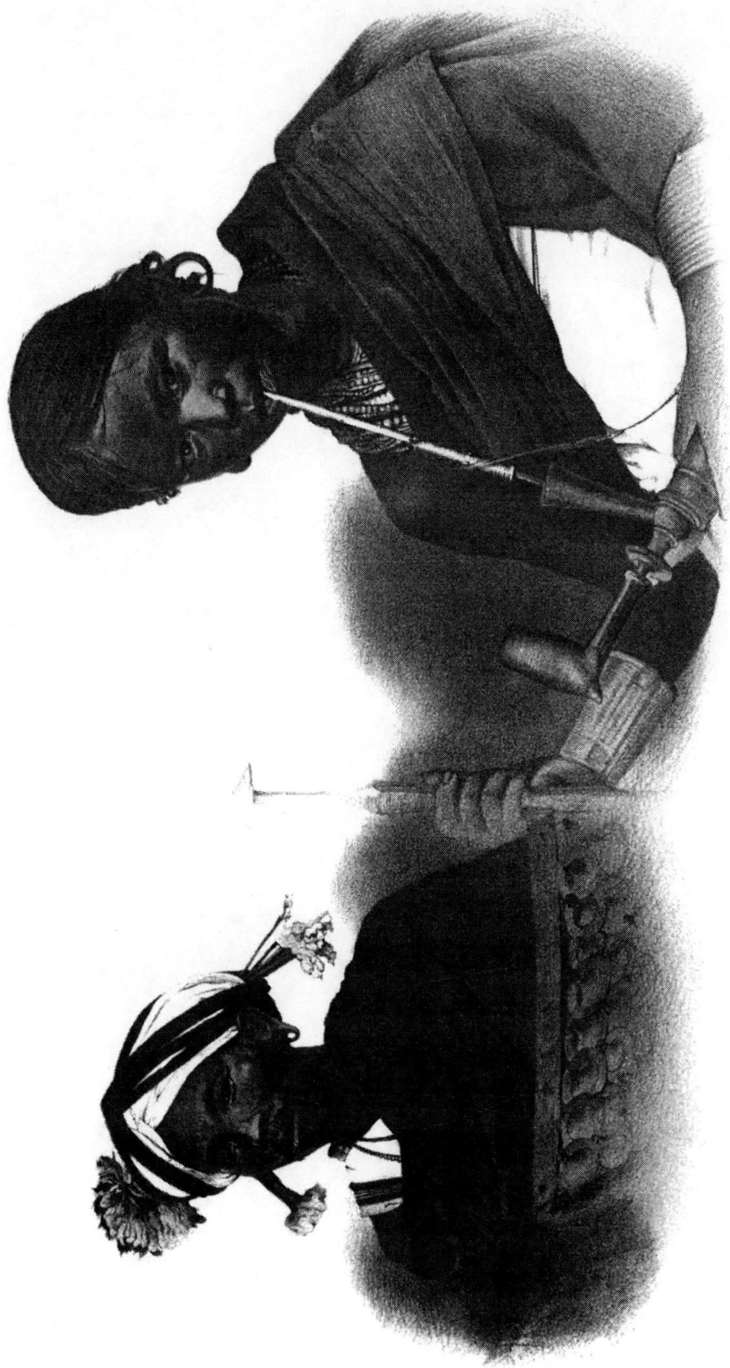

PLATE XXII.

GÁRO WOMEN and HEAD OF A GÁRO BOY.

The old lady, figure 1, I take to be an Abéngya Gáro female from the portentous size of her ear ornaments. The female without these decorations and the fillet of cloth round her head is not, I think, a Hill Gáro, but belonging to a family settled in the plains. Unless the fashions have changed since the days of my acquaintance with them, neither of the women are in the national costume; the cloth wrapped round the bosom is the effect of contact with the serpent, or people of the plains.

Figure 3 is a capital typical portrait of a Gáro lad, with retroussé nose, small oblique eyes, mouth well formed, but large and full, neither forehead nor chin receding, the facial angle being ordinarily good.

See Section 10, Group I, pages 58 to 68.

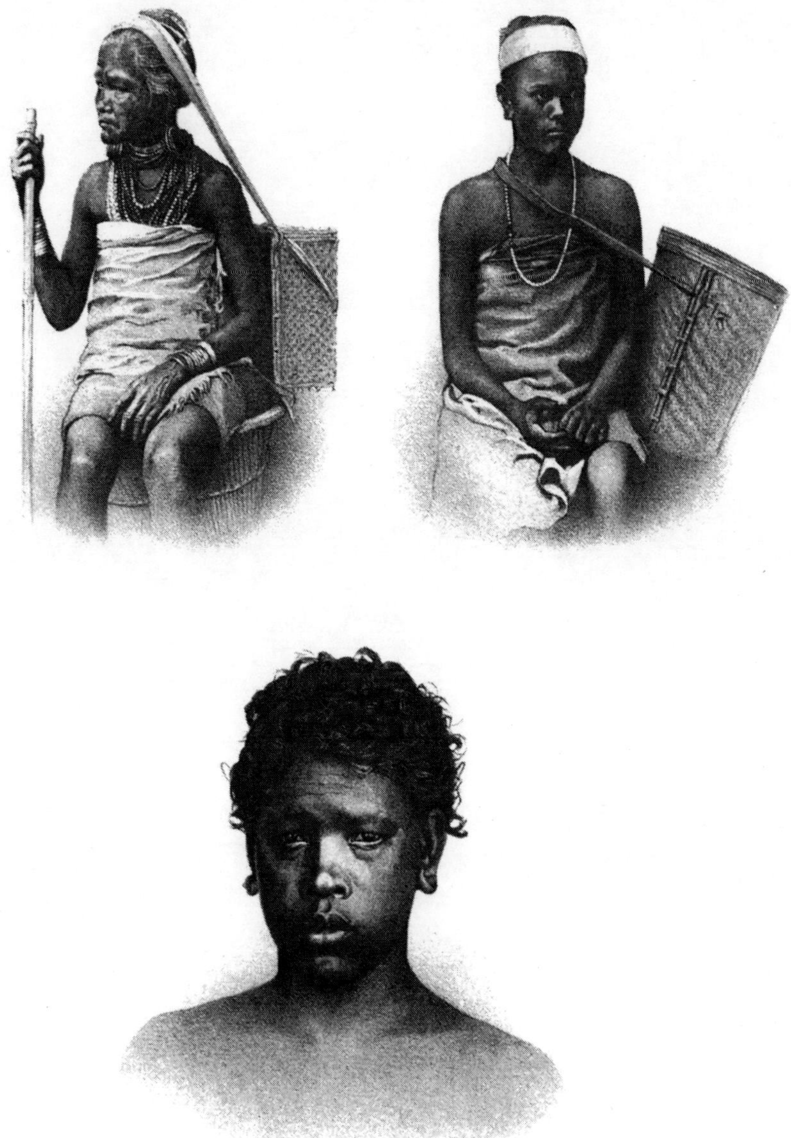

GAROS.

PLATE XXIII.

From Photographs by Dr. Simpson.

Bhútias or Búts, Male and Female.

These are very favorable specimens of the inhabitants of Bútan. They are evidently portraits of well-to-do people wearing gems and gold and silver ornaments, not ordinary beads. Such high aquiline noses are rarely seen on the faces of Búts, but are occasionally met with amongst all the Northern tribes.

See Section 1, Group III, pages 95 to 100.

MAN BHOTIA WOMAN.

PLATE XXIV.

From Photographs by DR. SIMPSON.

LEPCHAS (SIKKIM).

This beautiful specimen of a Sikkim Lepcha woman should have had a page to herself. It presents us with the finest type of the Mongolian physiognomy: a well formed head, features somewhat flat, but with a good mouth, forehead and chin, and luxuriant hair. The Sikkim Lepchas differ materially from the Dhurma Lepchas.

The Lepchas are found in Western Bútan, Eastern Nepál, and in the small state between both, called Sikkim. They are well known at Dárjiling.

See Section 2, Group III.

MAN

WOMAN.

LEPCHA.

PLATE XXV.

Photographed by Dr. Simpson.

Limbú Male and Female.

The very respectable-looking gentleman here represented and the richly bedizened old lady belong, I presume, to the upper class of Limbú society. The Limbús, or Kerantis, are represented by Mr. Hodgson and others as approximating in appearance to the darker Turanian race in color and feature, but the old lady is apparently of light complexion, and has a very Mongolian type of face.

See Section 3, Group III, page 102.

PLATE XXVI.

Fig. 1.—A Mug.

I know nothing of this miserable-looking creature. He does not at all correspond with the description of a Mug given at page 112. He is probably one of the hybrids from Chittagong so called, who serve us as cooks, and very good cooks they make.

Fig. 2.—A 'Ho' or Kol of Singhbúm.

From a Photograph by Dr. Simpson.

Boyi. Age 22 years.

Measurements.

Height	5 ft. $5\frac{1}{2}$ in.
Callipers:—	
Short diameter of head in front	$5\frac{1}{10}$ in.
Ditto ditto at back	5 „
Long diameter of head in front to back.	$7\frac{1}{2}$ „
Circumference of head	$21\frac{2}{5}$ „
Length of arm from acromion to olecranon	$13\frac{2}{5}$ „
Ditto from olecranon to tip of middle finger	18 „

This is a good typical representation of a young Singhbúm Ho or Kol of the clan, os' Kili, *Koada-dah*. In his right hand he grasps the national weapon called 'tánghir. This division of the Kols, called also the Larka, or warlike, Kols, are found only in Singhbúm.

See Section 4, Group VII.

Pl XXVI.

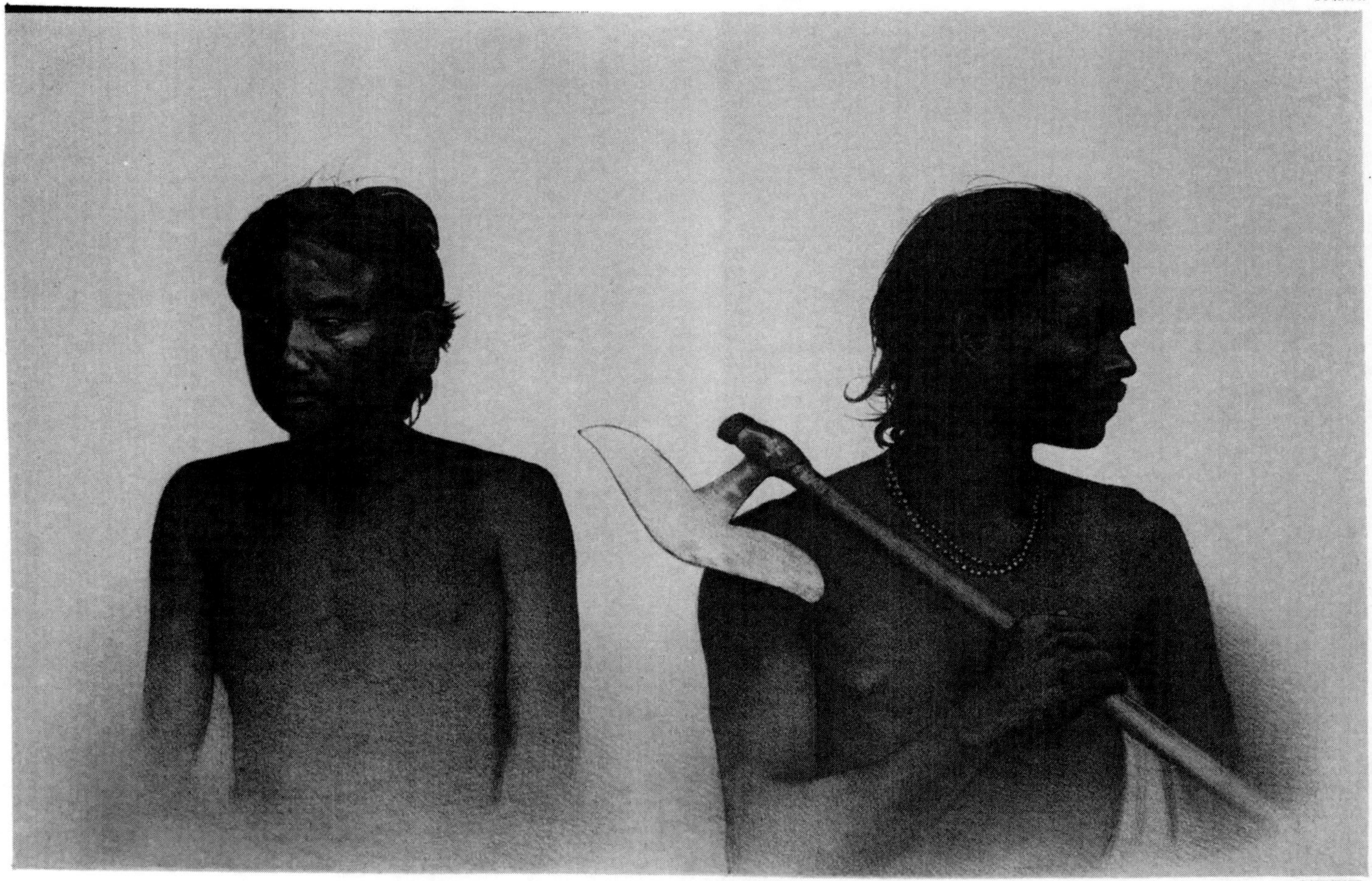

HARHART, LITH.

MUG. HO.

PLATE XXVII.

From a Photograph by DR. SIMPSON.

MUNDAS OF CHÚTIÁ NAGPÚR, male and female.

SANICHERIA, bachelor, aged 25; Spinster, aged 15.

The above are Mundas of villages close to Ránchí, the capital of the Province of Chútiá Nagpúr, who living with Oráons have adopted their style of decoration. They are good typical representatives of the race, though not handsome specimens. They show the breadth of face and obliquity of eye, which affirm the north-eastern origin ascribed to them. This pair were working for me as garden coolies, when their photographs were taken by Doctor Simpson, but I have lost sight of them for some years. They were both of a bright copper color, 29 of Brossai's Table.

See Section 3, Group VII, for account of the Mundas.

DAWSON, LITH.

MUNDAS.

PLATE XXVIII.

This is a representation of a dancing group composed of Oráons and Mundas of Chútiá Nagpúr, from a photograph by Doctor Simpson, taken in Colonel Dalton's garden at Ránchí.

The young men on the right hold the village flags, drums, chaunrs and regalia; and the girls are placed so as to indicate how their arms are interlaced in the dance, called 'jádúr.' It was found impossible to make them pose in a dancing attitude. The flags were furled to keep them quiet as it was a windy day.

See page 254.

HANHART LITH

KOL.
DANCING GROUP

PLATE XXIX.

From a Photograph in the Album of the Asiatic Society.

Santáls.

The large head in this plate is not a handsome specimen of a Santál, but he represents a large division of the family, fairly, and affirms what I have said, page 212, that they have a "blubbery style of face."

The Santáls of this type are, as a rule, of dark complexion, and it is probable that they have mixed much with the dark races; but I have seen Santál communities with finer features and light brown complexion, and am sorry I have not a more pleasing illustration of this tribe.

See Group VII, Section 6.

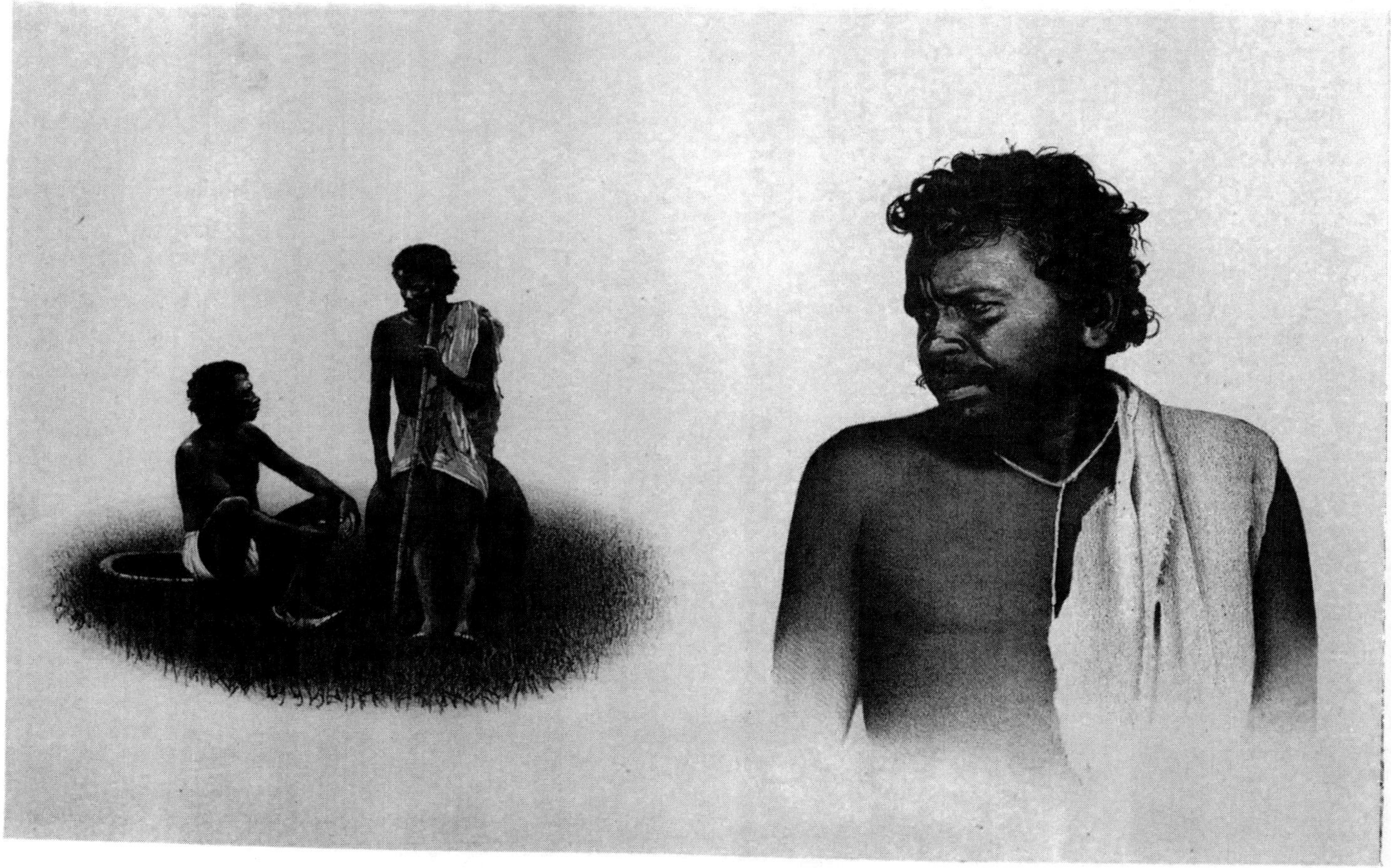

SANTALS.

PLATE XXX.

From a Photograph by Dr. Simpson.

\ Group of Korwas.

This is one of the wildest of the Kolarian tribes. They are found in the hills of the Sirgúja and Jashpúr Estates in the Province of Chútiá Nagpúr.

See Section 8, Group VII, page 228.

HANHART IMP.

KORWALI.

PLATE XXXI.

From a Photograph by Dr. Simpson.

Fig. 1.—An Oráon of Chútiá Nagpúr, aged, when picture was taken, about 23.

Fig. 2.—Rómia, an Oráon girl of Chútiá Nagpúr; age, when the picture was taken, 15.

These are very fair specimens of the great Oráon tribe who have been sometimes called the 'navvies' of India. The nucleus of the tribe is in Chútiá Nagpúr proper, from whence they have spread as settlers to all the surrounding districts, and as laborers to Asám, Kachár, Mauritius, the West Indies, and other British and French Colonies.

For a full account of the Oráons as they exist in their father-land, see Section 1, Group VIII.

PL. XXXI

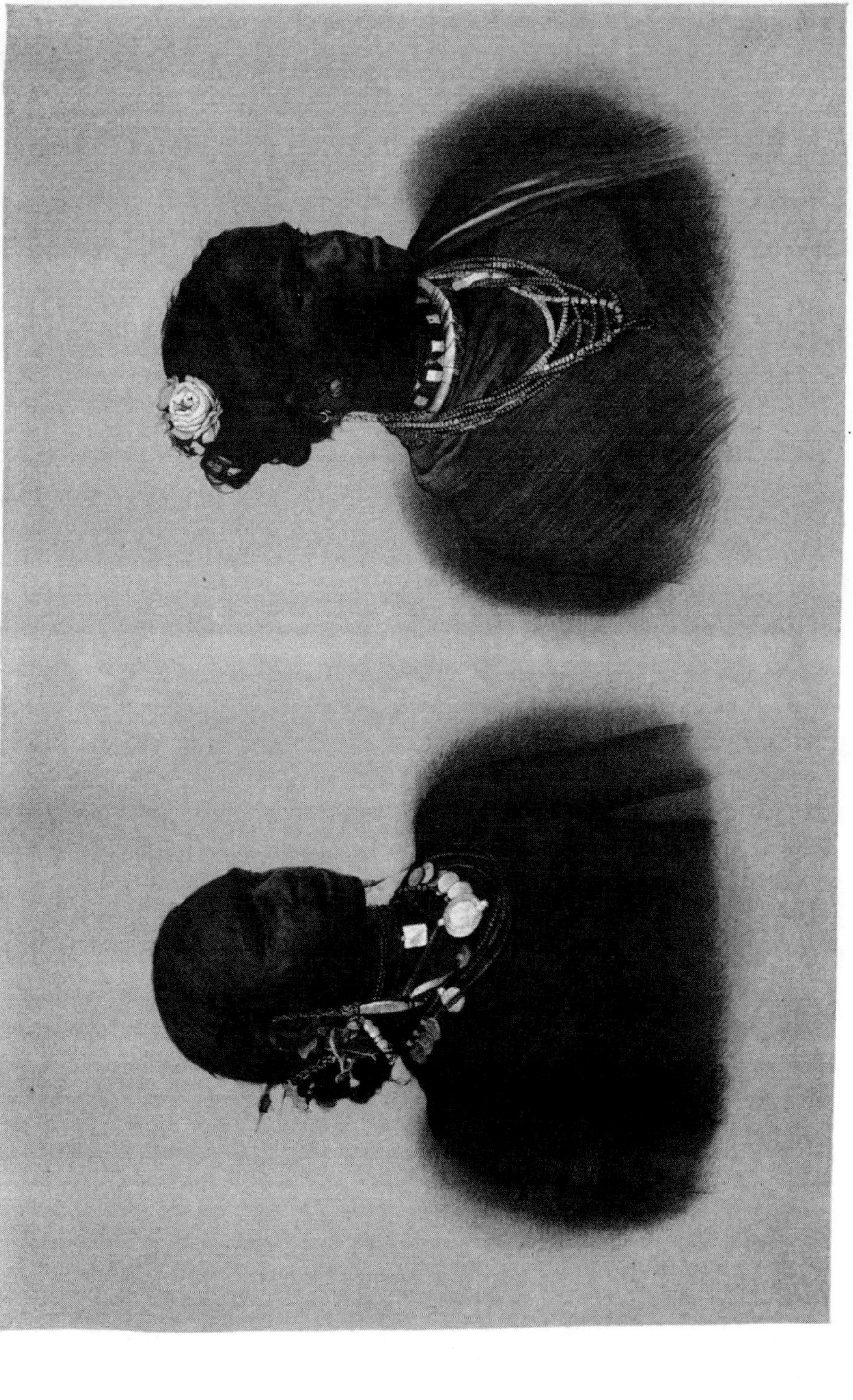

DALTON

PLATE XXXII.

KOCCH, Male and Female.

Two upper figures are representatives of the Kocch Nation, a very ancient people who were once numerous and powerful in Matsya-désh, and Kámarúpá, and still retain their dominancy in Kocch Behar. In my account of this people I disconnect them from the North-Eastern tribes with whom they have often been affiliated, and suggest that they may be allied with the Dravidian races. I have no description of the plate, but they are evidently very dark and in features resembling some of the Central Indian tribes as the Gonds.

For an account of the Kocch, see Section 4, Group II, page 89.

KÚKIS.

For particulars of Kúkis, see explanation to Plate XXI.

KUKI.

PLATE XXXIII.

From a Photograph by Mr. Tosco Peppé.

Juang Girls.

This illustration of the most primitive of the Kolarian race was obtained at Gonásíka in Keonjhar, noticed in the account of this tribe as the legendary cradle of the race. The beads or bugles forming the girdles are of fine earthen-ware made by themselves. The bracelets are of brass and the necklaces of glass beads or flowers. The rest of the attire is of leaves. Mr. Peppé had immense difficulty in inducing these wild timid creatures to pose before him, and it was not without many a tear, that they resigned themselves to the ordeal. It is right to mention that they were brought in from the forest where they had been searching for their daily bread which chiefly consists of forest produce, and their leaves were not as neatly arranged as they would have been if the girls had had time to make a fresh toilette.

See Section 1, Group VII, page 153.

JUANG GIRLS

PLATE XXXIV.

Very typical specimens of the Juang Tribe.

This is from another of Mr. Tosco Peppé's photographs taken at Gonásíka in Keonjhar, one of the Katak Tributary Estates. The young man keeps his spare arrows hanging by the barbs from his matted black hair, as is also the custom of the Korwás.

See Plate XXX.

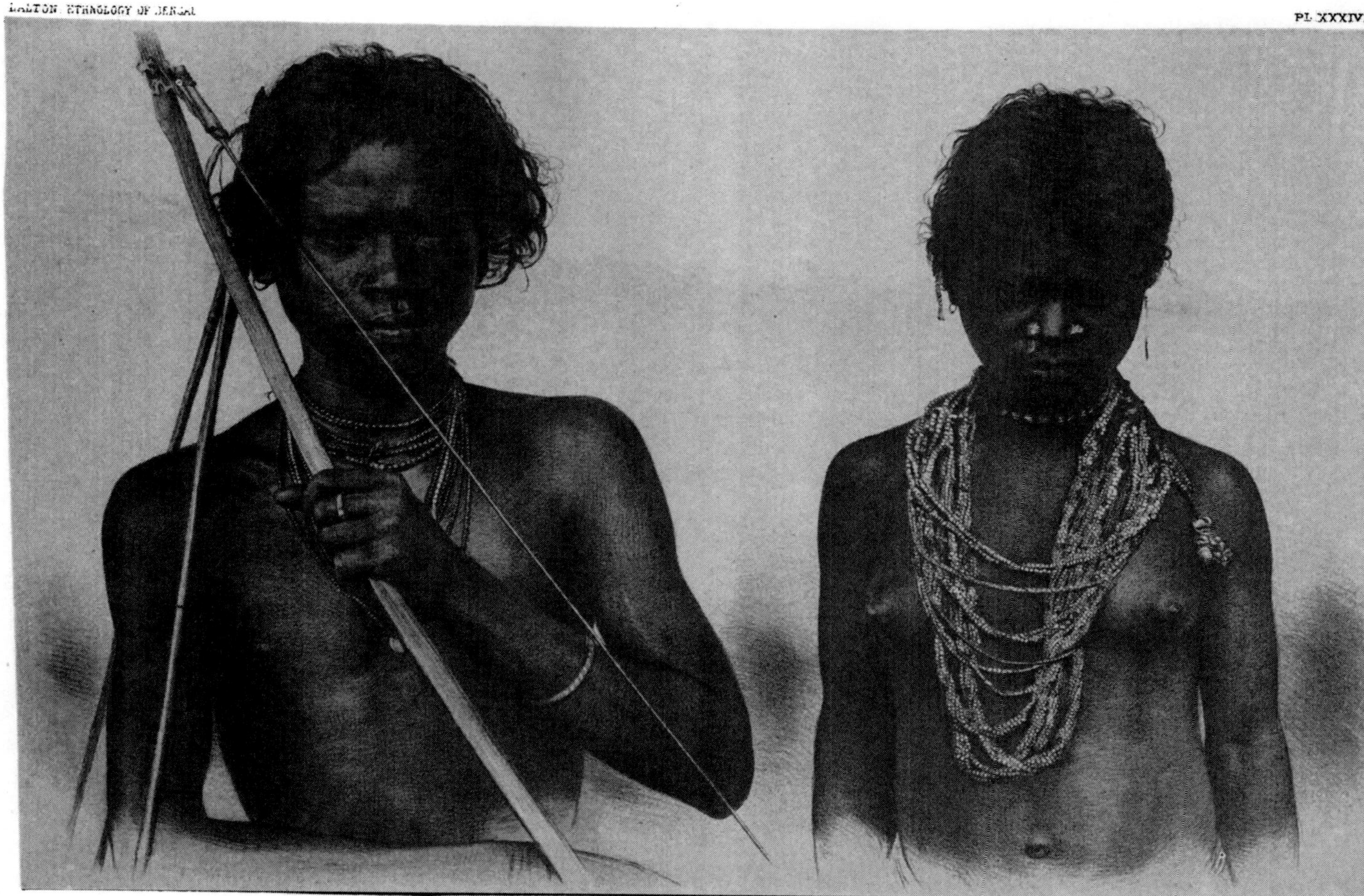

HANHART. LITH

MALE JUANG. FEMALE

PLATE XXXV.

From Photographs by MR. TOSCO PEPPÉ.

Male and Female of the BENDKAR TRIBE.

I have assigned to the Bendkárs of Keonjhar a relationship with the Sauras or Savaras. They have only been met with in Keonjhar, and they are found there in small communities widely separated. The man holds the only implement that they use in tillage. It is the origin of the plough! The handle with the crook is all one piece of wood, in the illustration the crook is made to appear as if it was fitted on to the handle, but this is incorrect, there is no joint, and there should have been no shade at the junction. The only use they ever make of cattle is to offer them as sacrifices to the Gods. Thus we have in the Bendkárs a people who in their agriculture use neither iron nor cattle.

See Section 3, Group VI, page 149.

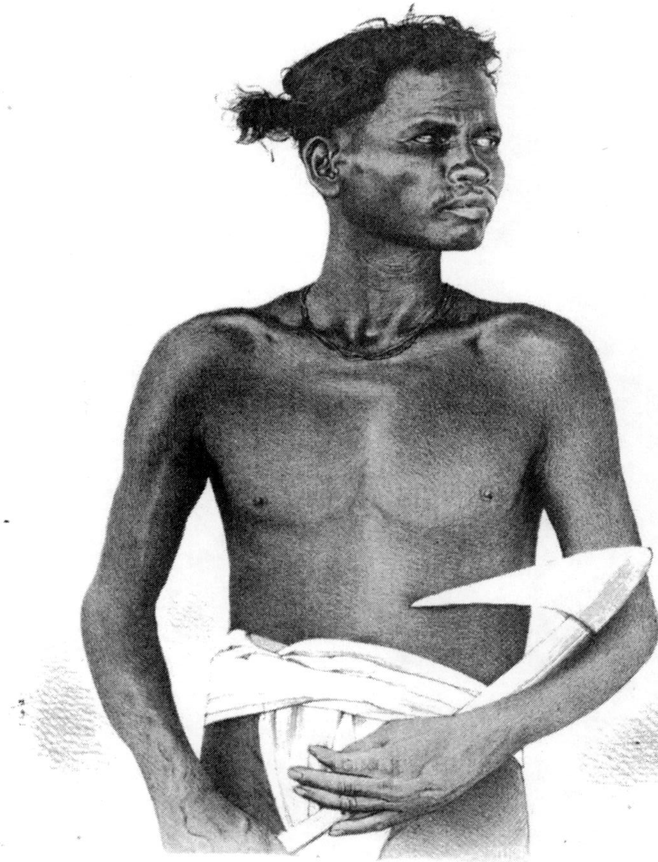

MALE

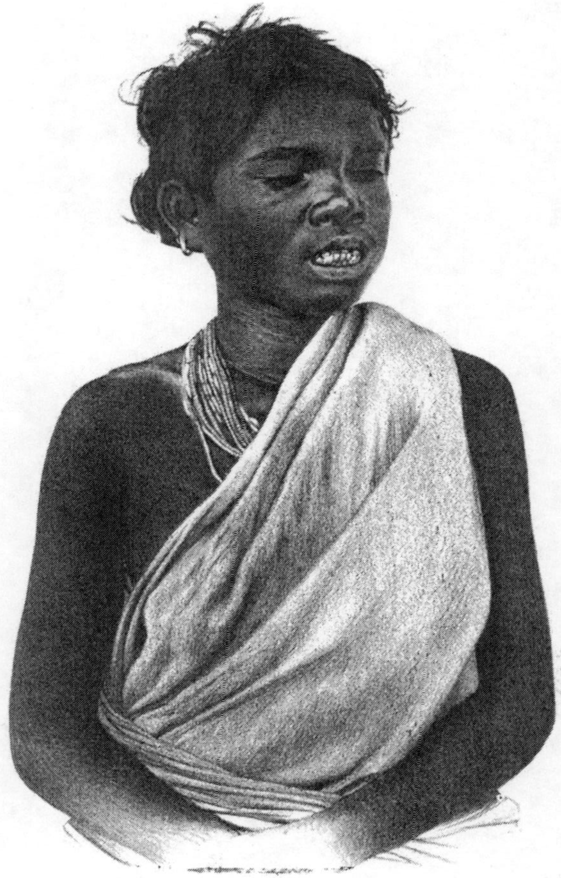

FEMALE

BENDKAR

PLATE XXXVI.

From a Photograph by MR. TOSCO PEPPÉ.

HO OR LARKA KOL FEMALES.

Fig. 1.—' JAMA', a girl of the Saondi Kili (tribe) of the village of Narsánda, near Chaibása in Singhbhúm, age about 16 years,—height . . . . . . 58 inches.

Measurement of head by callipers—

Short diameter in front	$4\frac{5}{12}$	inches.
Ditto ditto behind	$5\frac{1}{2}$	,,
Long ditto	$7\frac{1}{10}$	,,
Circumference	20	,,
Of arm,—From acromion to olecranon	10	,,
From olecranon to tip of middle finger	$15\frac{3}{20}$	,,
From acromion to ditto ditto	24	,,

Color 30.

This is a fair average specimen of the 'Ho girl of the period,' in the modern style of dress, one long thick cotton cloth with a deep red border. See page 192.

Fig. 2.—Group, young girl and old woman of the same tribe.

The old lady appears in the national costume, which she finds very convenient as a working dress and cool withal. See page 190.

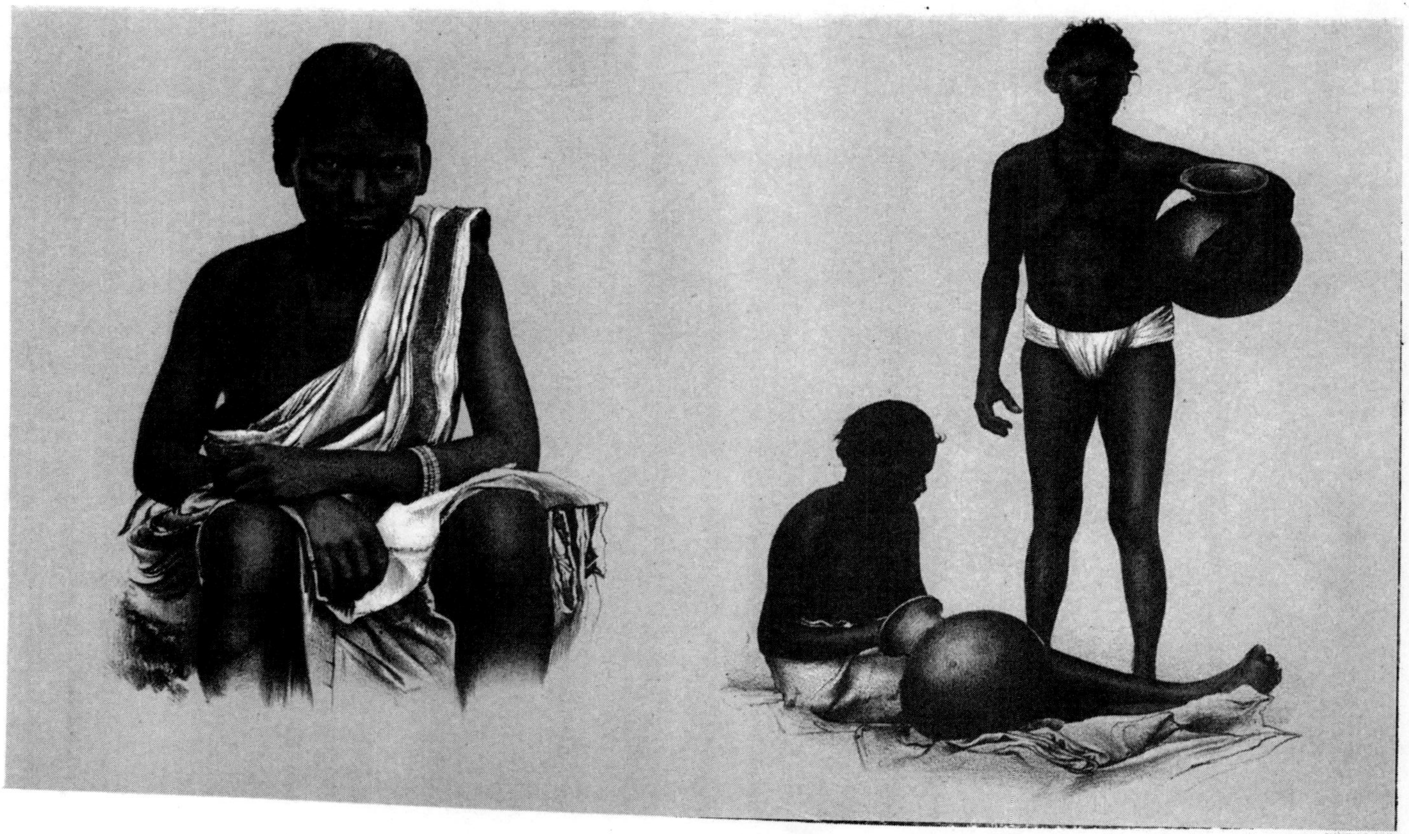

HANHART LITH.

GIRL

HO.

WOMAN

PLATE XXXVII.

From a Photograph by Mr. Tosco Peppé.

Paòri (or Pahari) Bhúiyas of Keonjhar, Male and Female.

The Bhúiyas are a widely spread people, holding a very low position as laborers and carriers in Bihár and Western Bengal, but appearing as lords of the soil in the Southern Tributary Estates.

The illustration represents a male and female of the Keonjhar Hill Bhúiya tribe, who in manners, customs, and features retain more of the idiosyncracies of the race than the sophisticated members of the family further north.

The following measurements of Bhúiyas are taken from a paper by Doctor Coates:—

Height	5 ft. $2\frac{6}{8}$ in.
Short diameter of head	$5\frac{4}{8}$ inches.
Long ditto ditto	$7\frac{2}{8}$ "
Circumference	21 "
Length of arms	5 ft. $2\frac{6}{8}$ in.

Color 42.

This however must have been a short specimen. The Gangpúr Bhúiyas average about 5 feet 5 inches in height.

See pages 139 to 150.

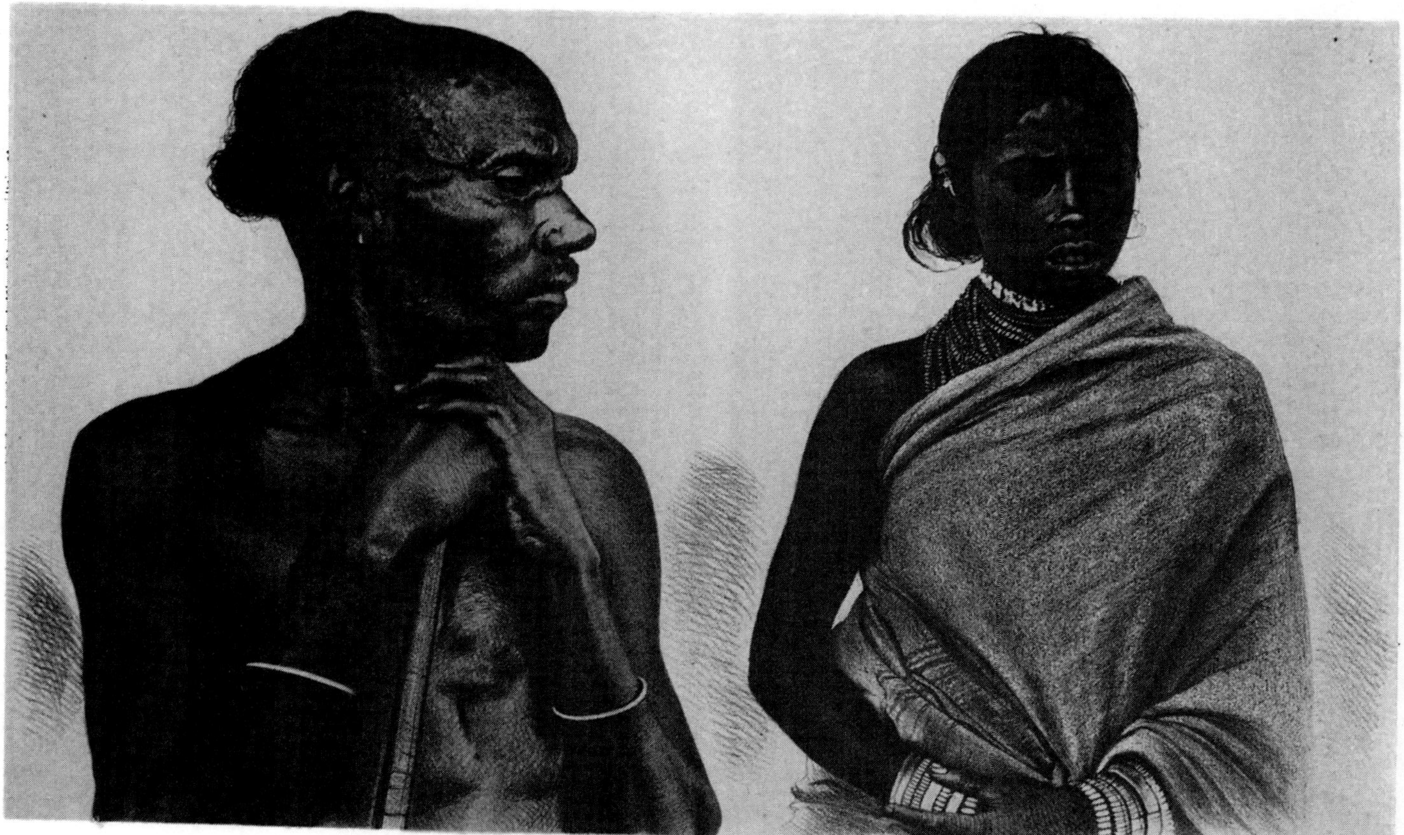

HANHART LITH.

MALE

BHUIYA
OF KEONJHAR

FEMALE